Advertising
Principles

Advertising
Principles

Choice
Challenge
Change

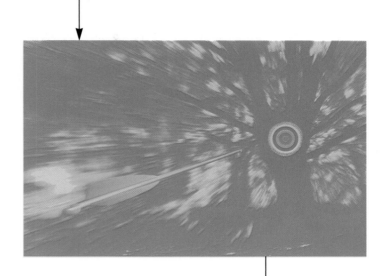

Bruce G. Vanden Bergh
Michigan State University

Helen Katz
DDB Needham Worldwide

NTC Business Books
a division of NTC/CONTEMPORARY PUBLISHING COMPANY
Lincolnwood, Illinois USA

Acquisitions Editor: Lynn Mooney
Product Manager: Judy Rudnick
Design Manager: Ophelia M. Chambliss
Interior design: Preface, Inc.
Cover design: Annette Spadoni
Cover photo: Superstock
Production Manager: Margo Goia
Production Coordinator: Denise Duffy

ISBN: 0-8442-2990-3

Acknowledgments begin on page 551, which is to be considered an extension of this copyright page.

To Jo-Ann, Schuyler, Evelyn, Steve, and Gary—
A small but strong family.

Bruce G. Vanden Bergh

To my parents, Peter and Joan Katz, who have always made the right choices, taken on and overcome many of life's challenges, and adapted to changes over the years.

Helen Katz

Brief Contents

Contents

Part Two   **The Challenge of Strategy in Marketing and Advertising**   142

CHAPTER FIVE   INTEGRATED MARKETING COMMUNICATIONS STRATEGY   144

Part Four   The Challenge of Advertising Creativity   404

Preface

Our Challenges

The field of advertising is currently undergoing some of the most sweeping changes in its short history. Everything from strategic thinking to new technology to expanding international markets has converged on practitioners, academics, and students, causing us to rethink the field of advertising. These changes are creating new choices and challenges for students and professionals alike. One of our primary challenges as authors of this text was to articulate these choices, challenges, and changes, and to help students develop the necessary tools to understand and tackle the transformations currently taking place. This focus is, in fact, reflected in the title of the book: *Advertising Principles: Choice, Challenge, and Change.*

We recognized, however, that equipping students with the necessary tools and information was not enough. Our second, and no less important, challenge in writing this text was to foster the natural energies and enthusiasm of the introductory advertising student. These students possess a youthful excitement about the opportunities and challenges that they face, and it was our goal to communicate our own passion for advertising—a passion that has been developed through years as practitioners and teachers—and, in so doing, to fuel these energies. This effort is evident throughout the text, in the content, writing style, pedagogy, and organization.

Our Choices

Many current introductory advertising texts attempt to include information on every conceivable topic—plus the kitchen sink. This breadth of coverage dilutes the focus on key issues and topics, and as a result, these books are successful only in dampening the enthusiasm of the students using them. For this reason, we felt that it was important to identify and focus our energies on a handful of areas that we con-

sidered most important. These key areas of focus are as follows:

- A real-world perspective.
- Brand building.
- Integrated marketing communications.
- Global perspective.
- Changing technology.
- The increasing diversity of markets.
- Creativity in media.
- Breadth of creative ideas.
- Strategic foundations of advertising and marketing planning.

By directing our energies to these areas, we were able not only to provide a more clear and solid base of information but also to create a springboard for students' interest and enthusiasm.

Our Changes

Reflecting our goals both to inform and educate and to inspire, our text differs from other texts in a number of important ways.

Presentation Style

In order to instill in students the passion for advertising that we ourselves have, we have endeavored throughout the book to make it as "user friendly" as possible. First and foremost, the text is written in a conversational style and tone designed to talk directly to the student. Also, we have included a large number of visual aids, including exhibits that highlight and exemplify the text coverage, boldfaced terms that identify new terms and key concepts, and many special boxed features that focus on specific areas of the industry and on critical changes that are occurring in advertising today. The goal of all of these efforts is to involve students in the learning process. Rather than simply lecturing to them in an abstract and theoretical fashion, we have instead chosen to pose questions, discuss options, and challenge them to think about the issues we raise, not simply in the chapter reviews but throughout the entire text.

Organization

This text is organized into four sections, each of which contains four chapters. This symmetrical arrangement was not forced on the content but evolved from the orderly way in which advertising planning and execution takes place. In addition to naturally supporting our key areas of focus, this format allows instructors and students to more easily measure the bites they want to take from the text's content.

Part One of the text, "The Challenging Business of Advertising," first offers a case history of Saturn's brand-building campaign, a quintessential illustration of state-of-the-art strategic thinking. We share our colleagues' and students' desire to "get to the heart of the matter" as quickly as possible, so we have started with this model campaign in order to stimulate interest and to set the stage for the rest of the text. From this fast start, we develop in the remainder of Part One the industry, economic, societal, regulatory, and global environments in which advertising operates.

Part Two of the book, "The Challenge of Strategic Marketing and Advertising," consists of four chapters that, together, cover the basic elements involved in building the marketing and advertising foundations for an advertising campaign or marketing communications program. We have streamlined this foundation to include the current thinking on brand building and the role of integrated marketing communications strategy in the advertising development process. Our consumer behavior chapter is presented within the context of how consumer insight can lead to a successful advertising strategy. Next, we discuss the basics of strategic and evaluative research with an eye to how advertising planning is improved by research. Finally, we conclude this foundation-building section with a nuts-and-bolts discussion of segmenting and selecting target markets and audiences, setting objectives, and allocating budgets.

Based on the real-world of advertising media planning as it takes place in a major advertising agency, Part Three, "Media Strategy: Challenges and Choices," presents the changing and challenging world of media with a focus on strategic thinking and integration with marketing communications elements such as sales promotion, direct marketing, and public relations. Chapters 10 and 11 provide a contemporary picture of all major advertising media plus new media forms such as the Internet.

Part Four of the book, "The Challenge of Advertising Creativity," takes the student through the imaginative yet exacting world of advertising creativity. In Chapter 13, we show how creativity applies specifically to the development of advertising, while emphasizing the importance of creative strategy. Chapter 14 expands on these topics by illustrating the essentials of advertising copywriting. Chapter 15 takes the reader through art direction and its substantial impact on the creation of effective and outstanding advertising. Appropriately, the text ends with the details of producing the ads that are the products of the context and process we have laid out in the preceding chapters.

Pedagogical Features

As with the other aspects of this text, the book's pedagogical features were designed to facilitate students' comprehension of the principles of advertising and to increase their involvement in and enthusiasm for their own learning.

LOOK BEFORE YOU LEAP   This chapter-opening element presents the key chapter concepts. These concepts, which are structured in the form of questions that might be posed by students, function as a snapshot of the chapter contents and serve to pique student interest and curiosity.

RESET QUESTIONS   Placed at the end of each major section of text, these short questions provide students with a quick check of their comprehension. Difficulty in answering these questions is a signal that the student should review the related concepts.

AROUND THE GLOBE   As the name suggests, Around the Globe essays present topics related to the international aspects of advertising; these topics include the pitfalls of translating domestic advertising messages for international campaigns, cultural differences in advertising, conducting market research in international markets, and overcoming communication hurdles.

ADSCAPE   These vignettes provide more in-depth coverage of eclectic topics in the field of advertising, including identification of the changing roles and responsibilities of advertising professionals, discussions on the success or failure of specific campaigns, and coverage of specific notable individuals in the field of advertising.

TECHNOLOGY WATCH   Technology Watch boxes serve as a platform for the identification of new technological advances and for a discussion of the impact that technology has on various aspects of advertising.

CONSUMER INSIGHTS   Consumer Insights boxes present interesting perspectives on consumer trends and issues. These boxes give the reader insights beyond the text material into what makes people tick as consumers.

KEY TERMS   This list, provided at the end of each chapter, recaps all of the important terms and concepts presented in the chapter. Page references are provided to allow the student to easily review the relevant text material.

REVIEW QUESTIONS   The Review Questions provided at the end of each chapter are designed to provide students with a quick check of their retention and understanding of key concepts.

DISCUSSION QUESTIONS   Extending the students' use of the key chapter concepts, Discussion Questions involve the application and the extrapolation of those ideas to new situations or problems.

INTERACTIVE DISCOVERY LAB   Interactive Discovery Lab activities challenge students to take their newly acquired knowledge outside of the classroom and into the real world. These questions and projects encourage students to use the resources available on campus and in their communities to extend their understanding and application of the advertising principles being discussed.

ADVERTISING HISTORY   These vignettes, which appear at the end of each of the four text parts, provide short discussions of the history of advertising from the beginning of the twentieth century to the present. This material is designed to provide the student with a historical perspective on the forces behind the growth of advertising and the development of specific advertising approaches and techniques.

Teaching Resources

INSTRUCTOR'S MANUAL   The Instructor's Manual contains an overview, a detailed lecture outline, activities and projects suitable for individuals or small groups, and a list of additional published resources for every chapter. Each chapter's lecture outline includes unique in-class examples, discussion questions, in-class activities, definitions of key terms, and notes for incorporating exhibits from the text into your presentation.

PRINTED TEST BANK   The test bank consists of 2000 original test questions, written specifically for this text. Each chapter includes multiple-choice, fill-in, short answer, and essay type questions. Each question also has a text page reference, difficulty rating, and rationale, if applicable.

COMPUTERIZED TEST BANK   (Windows) All of the test bank questions are available on MicroTest III test-generating software for Windows. You can create tests by selecting test questions found in the test bank or by writing your own.

VIDEO PROGRAM   A video collection has been assembled specifically for classroom use with this text. This collection was designed to allow professors to more fully explain key concepts, as well as to make available many additional, highly current examples.

FULL-COLOR TRANSPARENCIES   The acetate package contains over 100 full-color acetates, including key ads, tables, and graphs from the book, plus a wealth of ads that do not appear in the text.

POWERPOINT® This disk contains nearly 300 PowerPoint® slides, including both material from the book and original material. The slides present topics in a variety of formats—tables, graphs, lists, and outlines. You do not need PowerPoint® software to make classroom presentations using this package.

Acknowledgments

Writing a textbook requires the collaboration and understanding of a lot of people over a substantial amount of time. As we look back on the development of our book, we would like to thank all of the talented and creative souls who contributed to the final product.

Reviewers

First and foremost, we would like to acknowledge all of our colleagues who contributed their time and expertise to the shaping and fine-tuning of this book. Their input—both their manuscript reviews and the insight they provided regarding their students and courses — was invaluable to our efforts.

We would especially like to thank the following reviewers, who submitted reviews commissioned by our publisher, NTC/Contemporary Publishing:

Tim Bengston, University of Kansas
Roy K. Busby, University of North Texas
Carol Calder, Mount St. Mary's College
Michael J. Dotson, Appalachian State
    University
Norman D. Leebron, Drexel University
Douglas R. Robideaux, Central Missouri
    State University
Lynne Masel Walters, Texas A&M
    University
Kurt Wildermuth, University of Missouri

Special Collaborators

We would like to thank Keith Adler of Michigan State University and Gary Wilcox of The University of Texas at Austin for their work on the early stages of the manuscript. Keith, in particular, contributed substantially to the research, art direction, and production chapters. Gary worked on the art direction and production chapters, and he provided important content on advertising regulation.

Our Professional Support Groups

Our colleagues at DDB Needham in Chicago and Michigan State University deserve thanks not only for simply putting up with us but also for providing information and expert advice when we asked for it. Our colleagues in the academic world were always forthcoming with help. In particular, we would like to thank Steven Helle at the University of Illinois, Wei-Na Lee at The University of Texas at Austin, Bettina Cornwell at the University of Memphis, and Bonnie Reece and Janice Bukovac at Michigan State University. Steve helped us to hone our legal analyses. Wei-Na and Bettina helped in the area of global advertising and marketing and cultural issues. Bonnie provided her expertise in the management and strategy areas. Janice, who teaches Michigan State's introductory advertising course, provided insights from her experience teaching hundreds of students each semester.

Our NTC Team

We worked with numerous people at NTC/Contemporary Books in completing this project. Among those, Andy Winston was responsible for taking on the book when it was in its infancy and shepherding it through the review and revision process that is so agonizing and yet necessary to the writing process. Andy had that rare combination of foresight, courage, and patience that the project required to get it on its way and keep it going.

The following group of collaborators had the unenviable task of doing all of the late-night detail work without which you cannot bring a book to the final production stage. Liz McDonell did an outstanding job of editing and fine-tuning our chapters so that they became the cohesive whole you see here. Amy Winston served as final copyeditor, photo and art coordinator, and hand-holder as the chapters came back from Liz and were submitted for typesetting. Lynn Mooney joined NTC/Contemporary as an acquisitions editor, and she quickly adopted our project as her own. She was indispensable in the final stages of seeing the project through to publication.

There are many talented people at NTC/Contemporary who worked on the production of our book. We thank them not only for the quality of their work in designing and producing our text but also for their patience as we submitted our manuscript as fast as we could but never fast enough to allow them to do their jobs worry free.

These special team members include Product Development Manager Tana McDonald, Executive Editor Marisa L'Heureux, Product Manager Judy Rudnick, Production Manager Margo Goia, Production Coordinator Denise Duffy, and Design Manager Ophelia Chambliss.

Our Personal Support Groups

Finally, we would like to thank our families for their encouragement and support. Bruce's family had to endure that roll of the eyes every time they asked him how the book was going. Bruce's wife Jo-Ann and son Schuyler never let go of their faith that he would successfully complete the project. For Helen, the encouragement and understanding of her husband Eric, and the smiles and laughter of her children—Stephanie, Caroline, and Vanessa—have made all of the long hours and hard work worthwhile. We have faced many choices, challenges, and changes in creating this book, and we hope that you, in turn, will think carefully about the choices you make as you enter the endlessly challenging and changing world of advertising.

Bruce G. Vanden Bergh
Helen Katz

Advertising
Principles

Part One

The Challenging Business of Advertising

Part Four
The Challenge
of Advertising
Creativity

Part Two
The Challenge of **Strategy**
in Marketing and Advertising

Part Three
Media Strategy:
Challenges and Choices

Chapter One

The Advertising Campaign

SATURN CORPORATION SCORES A PERFECT 10 WITH CONSUMERS

Consumer expectations regarding quality, reliability, and service in the automotive marketplace are always on the rise. Saturn Corporation's goal when it started was not to meet these expectations but to exceed them. This was an enormous challenge.

One area on which Saturn focused was customer service, an area that typically generates the most complaints from consumers, but also an area where the most gains could be made. As one Saturn employee said, "We wanted to give owners the kind of treatment they'd expect when purchasing a luxury car."

Saturn dealers started their relationship-building with new owners right away with their now legendary new-vehicle-delivery ceremony. New owners receive their cars filled with a tank of gas, they are given flowers, Saturn dealer employees applaud, and pictures are taken. In short, the customer is made to feel important.

Once the customer leaves the dealer lot the real relationship-building starts, as the company uses a series of communication ve-hicles to keep in touch. Owners receive the magazine, *Vision,* twice a year. They are sent service reminders, an anniversary card after the first year of ownership, and invitations to events at the dealership. Dealers also hold barbecues, holiday events, and car-care clinics to encourage owners to maintain their cars at Saturn dealers.

Saturn makes good use of database marketing to target its various consumer segments and maintain its hard-earned relationships with owners and prospects. Some of these databases are maintained at the dealership level

a d i f f e r e n t k i n d o f

COMPANY

What's so different about Saturn? It's no big deal, if you ask
us. We just try to build and sell the best cars we know how.
Then back them up with the kind of service we'd like to get
ourselves.

It's no secret that plenty of people thought we'd be out of
business by now. But, it seems that developing a more
democratic way of managing our business, building a more
sophisticated manufacturing complex in Tennessee and
finding a more responsible way of treating our customers
wasn't such a crazy idea after all. Different, maybe. But,
crazy? Nah.

If you'd like to find out more about Saturn and some of

A Different Kind of Company ⟶ **Welcome** • Saturn in the Community • **CarClub**
Let's Talk • **Saturn Stuff** • **General FAQs**

Document: Done

---

so that Saturn can follow up with owners as well as those who did not buy a Saturn. Saturn has database information on its almost 2 million owners, 10,000 members of the Saturn club, and those who enter information into the "extended family" database at its Web site.

Saturn's success in exceeding expectations can be measured in a number of ways. Saturn garnered over 10 percent of the small-car market in 1995. This percentage reflects Saturn's ability to attract women to the Saturn brand through its no-haggle pricing strategy and superior treatment at the dealership, and the company's appeal to young, first-time buyers. In addition, Saturn has drawn a substantial number of import buyers back to an American company. Also, Saturn gets high marks in annual consumer satisfaction surveys, indicating that it not only can make the sale but it can keep it as well. However, perhaps the biggest sign of success is how other automotive manufacturers and dealers have "Saturnized" their approaches to car buyers. Clearly, Saturn has established itself as a unique company that is worthy of being patronized by consumers and copied by competitors.

Source: Beth Negus, "Saturn Orbits Loyalty," *Direct,* 1 September 1996, 27.

1

We would like to introduce you to the topic of advertising by presenting an entire advertising and marketing communications plan before we show you how it is put together. The following case example provided by the Saturn Corporation demonstrates how to build a corporation and brand from scratch. It is a model case. Saturn Corporation and its advertising agency, Hal Riney & Partners, had the opportunity to work as a team from the very beginning—from the inception of the Saturn Corporation in 1985. And we believe that, together, they achieved unparalleled success in the planning and implementation of an advertising and marketing communications campaign.

The Saturn case also helps to illustrate how change in the marketplace—generated both by pressure from competitors and by the changing desires of consumers—creates problems that demand new solutions. Change always presents new challenges and choices for advertisers. How they respond can ultimately determine their fate in the marketplace. Saturn's marketing communications program is a quintessential example of what a company can achieve when it responds proactively to those challenges.

The Saturn Orbit

Every so often a company comes along that is an advertising or marketing student's dream because its success demonstrates in dramatic fashion how sticking to the basic principles of advertising and marketing communications pays off. The Saturn Corporation's experience, from its inception through to its current success, is just such a dream. Before we get into the plan, let's look first at a brief history of the Saturn Corporation, and then at the principles behind the company's success.

Saturn's Launching Pad

The Saturn project to build a new car company from scratch was conceived by former General Motors (GM) Chairman Roger B. Smith "as a laboratory in which to reinvent his company."[1] Smith announced GM's intent to push ahead with the development of the Saturn Corporation on 7 January 1985, at a time when Japanese automotive manufacturers were winning large chunks of market share in the U.S. auto market—principally at the expense of GM. Sales of imported cars in the United States had achieved an all-time high in terms of market share, and the Japanese carmakers were the big winners with over 22 percent of the market.

The first Saturn cars reached the market in 1992. By 1994 it was apparent that Saturn had joined rare company—the 1950s Ford Thunderbird, the VW Beetle and Ford Mustang of the 1960s, and the Ford Taurus of the 1980s—as a widely known and respected brand.[2] The Saturn Corporation achieved its quick success by developing and executing a brand-building plan that integrated seven key areas of corporate, marketing, and communications strategy. The company's overall mission provided the direction for everything from how employees would be treated, to how the company would be marketed, how the distribution system would be set up to sell cars, how Saturn would relate to its customers, and how marketing communications would be executed and integrated.

Saturn's Mission

All business and marketing programs should start with a clearly stated corporate mission. Because the Saturn Corporation was a new company, it had the opportunity to establish a clear mission apart from anything General Motors had done in the past. The Saturn Corporation's mission from the outset was to market compact cars "developed and manufactured in the United States that are world leaders in quality, cost, and consumer satisfaction."[3] This idea is formally embodied in Saturn's corporate mission and philosophy, which are shown in Exhibit 1–1.

The competitive market had an enormous influence on Saturn's mission. Saturn had to set its sights high. Exhibit 1–1 illustrates that Saturn wanted to create, build, and sell a world-class car that could entice American car buyers away from the top-selling Japanese nameplates, such as the Acura Integra, Honda Civic, Toyota Corolla, and Nissan SR2. To those who created Saturn, "world class" meant quality, a principle that was deemed to be a fundamental element of everything for which Saturn stood.

To achieve this kind of quality, it was essential that it be reflected in the entire Saturn culture. It was decided early on that the type of culture needed to deliver on this promise would have to be built separate from the existing GM culture, which was extremely large and somewhat bureaucratic. (It is important to emphasize that although Saturn was planned as a division of General Motors, it was designed from the outset to be completely separate and distinct, and not simply an additional marquee standing alongside Buick, Cadillac, Chevrolet, Oldsmobile, and Pontiac.) GM started the process by selecting a group of 99 employees from labor and management to decide on the type of organizational structure required to create the car and brand that would fulfill Saturn's mission. The group visited 60 successful companies to see how they were run. This experience resulted in the creation of a team/partnering approach to everything Saturn had to do, from designing and making the car to determining the role of an advertising agency in promoting Saturn.[4]

EXHIBIT 1–1

SATURN MISSION

Market vehicles developed and manufactured in the United States that are world leaders in quality, cost and customer satisfaction through the integration of people, technology and business systems and to transfer knowledge, technology and experience throughout General Motors.

©1990 Saturn Corporation

S01 00016
0591

SATURN PHILOSOPHY

We, the Saturn Team, in concert with the UAW and General Motors, believe that meeting the needs of Customers, Saturn Members, Suppliers, Dealers and Neighbors is fundamental to fulfilling our mission.

To meet our customers' needs:
- Our products and services must be world leaders in value and satisfaction.

To meet our members' needs:
- We will create a sense of belonging in an environment of mutual trust, respect and dignity.
- We believe that all people want to be involved in decisions that affect them, care about their jobs and each other, take pride in themselves and in their contributions and want to share in the success of their efforts.
- We will develop the tools, training and education for each member, recognizing individual skills and knowledge.
- We believe that creative, motivated, responsible team members who understand that change is critical to success are Saturn's most important asset.

To meet our suppliers' and dealers' needs:
- We will strive to create real partnerships with them.
- We will be open and fair in our dealings, reflecting trust, respect and their importance to Saturn.
- We want dealers and suppliers to feel ownership in Saturn's mission and philosophy as their own.

To meet the needs of our neighbors, the communities in which we live and operate:
- We will be good citizens, protect the environment and conserve natural resources.
- We will seek to cooperate with government at all levels and strive to be sensitive, open and candid in all our public statements.

By continuously operating according to this philosophy, we will fulfill our mission.

Saturn—The Car And The Company

Let's assume for right now that by 1992 the Saturn Corporation would be able to deliver on the company's mission to build a world-class car. Many a company had tried that before, only to fail to convince consumers that the product would indeed live up to promises made in advertising and other forms of marketing communications. Here, once again, Saturn had a challenge and a choice. In response to this challenge, Saturn diverged from convention and decided to sell the values, culture, and philosophy of the company rather than the features of the car.

Saturn could not communicate the complexities of its new approach without the help of an advertising agency with which it also could partner to effectively position both its car and the company effectively in consumers' minds. The search for an agency began in 1987. At that time, Saturn's advertising and marketing communications budget was projected to be in the neighborhood of $100 million. More than 50 advertising agencies pitched the account, but the agency that eventually would win the account was not among them. Instead, with the help of GM's Philip Guarascio, Saturn went after Hal Riney & Partners. Riney's shop is a San Francisco-based agency known for folksy campaigns like the one they created for Bartles & Jaymes wine coolers. Saturn selected Hal Riney & Partners as its communications partner in May 1988, almost two and one-half years before Saturn sold even one car.[5]

Hal Riney was a key partner in the early decisions that would eventually impact how consumers viewed the car and company. Some of these decisions appear simple and obvious in hindsight. But these strategic and tactical choices were much more difficult to make at the time, because Saturn and Hal Riney were trying to fashion future success by taking a very different approach to selling cars in the U.S. For example, Saturn decided that each dealership would be called "Saturn of (location)," as the newspaper ad in Exhibit 1–2 illustrates. In this way, the focus was placed on the Saturn name and not the dealership owner's name, such as "Joe Smith's Saturn." This strategy to put the Saturn name first was extended to the names of the different car models as well. The Saturn coupe was the Saturn SC, and two versions of the sedan were the SL1 and SL2.[6] Unlike most car lines, there was no double naming at Saturn—no Accords, Luminas, or Sables to remember along with the manufacturer's name.

Another major decision that Saturn and Riney made was to focus the early advertising and marketing communications efforts on the people who worked for Saturn in an effort to get consumers rooting for the company. Saturn started this marketing communications strategy with a documentary film entitled "Spring in Spring Hill" that covered the start-up of the company. The film is very emotional and talks about the commitment of Saturn employees to the success of the company. The documentary was initially used internally for training and to explain the Saturn philosophy to suppliers and the press. Dealers also used it to secure loans, and the film even aired on the cable network VH-1.

Keeping with this concept, Saturn's first television spot, "Going Home," focused on GM employees' decision to move from Michigan to Saturn's factory in Spring Hill, Tennessee. This plant was not only physically distant from GM headquarters but also, and perhaps more importantly, even farther away in terms of its culture. The GM employees joining the Saturn experiment had to leave a lot behind in order to participate in this new venture, and this spot illustrated the emotional attachment of Saturn employees to the new company and to the new ideas it embodied.

To some extent, Saturn's subsequent advertising campaign was based on this same strategy of focusing on people and their relationships to the car and company.[7] For example, the television spot "Launch Day" expresses the pride of an employee in being part of the process that designed and built the Saturn car. In this spot, the employee expresses his feelings of being a valued member of a team that is working toward a significant end, and he anticipates the joy of seeing the final fruits of his labor—the first Saturn to roll off of the assembly line.

Saturn of Okemos
4th Annual
Customer Appreciation Day

HOLIDAY PARTY

Saturday, December 14th, 1996
10:00 a.m. to 3:00 p.m.
Magic • Santa • Clown • Prizes

SCHEDULE OF EVENTS

Magic Show • Karl Karl Magician
11:00 a.m. and 2:00 p.m.

Fun-EBone Clown • Car Care Clinic • 12:00 noon
Door Prizes • Food & Beverages
Have your child's picture taken with Santa
We will be accepting donations for the
Haslett Food Bank and Toys For Tots

347-7890

*Don't miss this party for all of
our loyal Saturn of Okemos
customers & their families!*

EXHIBIT 1–2

Getting The Brand Message Out To The Media

In developing its strategy for launching a new vehicle, Saturn could not afford to ignore what its competitors were doing in the advertising marketplace. As we noted earlier, Saturn had identified its key competitors as cars such as the Acura Integra, Honda Civic, Toyota Corolla, and Nissan SR2. An analysis of how much these companies were spending in the mass media and which media they were using illustrates the level of spending to which Saturn had to commit in order to get its

---

EXHIBIT 1–3   Media Expenditures for Saturn and Its Competitors, 1989–1996

	ACURA	HONDA	NISSAN	SATURN	TOYOTA	TOTAL
1989						
Ad spending	$92,188	$98,467	$174,753	$0	$169,637	**$535,045**
Share of spending	17%	18%	33%	0%	32%	
1990						
Ad spending	$106,307	$116,912	$198,541	$31,591	$216,062	**$669,413**
Share of spending	16%	17%	30%	5%	32%	
1991						
Ad spending	$101,563	$130,616	$137,469	$88,637	$238,451	**$696,736**
Share of spending	15%	19%	20%	13%	34%	
1992						
Ad spending	$96,299	$144,590	$151,222	$76,691	$237,688	**$706,490**
Share of spending	14%	20%	21%	11%	34%	
1993						
Ad spending	$114,213	$132,617	$178,734	$87,499	$258,198	**$771,261**
Share of spending	15%	17%	23%	11%	34%	
1994						
Ad spending	$126,115	$195,828	$218,653	$140,752	$276,853	**$958,201**
Share of spending	13%	20%	23%	15%	29%	
1995						
Ad spending	$101,762	$219,160	$224,774	$169,812	$243,192	**$958,700**
Share of spending	11%	23%	23%	18%	25%	
1996						
Ad spending	$98,201	$213,649	$207,957	$179,731	$235,724	**$935,262**
Share of spending	11%	23%	22%	19%	25%	

Note: Figures presented are in thousands of U.S. dollars.
Source: Competitive Media Reporting, 1997.

---

company and brand message out to its target consumers.

As Exhibit 1–3 illustrates, Saturn's four key competitors spent a total of about half a billion dollars on advertising for the 1989 calendar year. This was Saturn's first pre-launch year, and it did not advertise while Hal Riney & Partners was developing Saturn's advertising strategy. From 1990 to the year of Saturn's full launch in 1992, the five auto companies (now including Saturn) increased total media spending by one-third, to $706 million. Part of this increase could be attributed to Saturn's entry into the advertising marketplace; it spent a total of $120 million in the two years prior to its launch.

Another way to look at Saturn's media spending is to see how large its "voice" was against its competitors. That is, of all the spending by its competition, what proportion did Saturn have? In 1990, Saturn's share of the total expenditures was just five percent. The next year, Saturn's share approached that of Acura's. By 1995 and 1996, Saturn's share of expenditures grew to 18 and 19 percent, re-

spectively. Notice that while the four competitors maintained their spending levels in dollars, their share of category spending fell because of Saturn's success and its ability to increase its spending.

Saturn's Relationship With Its Customers

Saturn established from the beginning that people were the most important part of the Saturn philosophy. We have seen how this choice was executed in Saturn's early ads, which focused on building pride and commitment among employees. In the second year of advertising, the focus shifted from the employee to the customer, although employee ads continue to run as an ongoing part of Saturn's strategy even today. The storytelling style of all of the Saturn ads sets a tone for the entire marketing communications campaign, which personifies the company without screaming mom and apple pie at Saturn's educated target audience. The magazine ad in Exhibit 1–4, the copy of which deserves a close read, presents a story about a Saturn owner and her new car

EXHIBIT 1–4

that helps to humanize the company. In a slight twist on the customer-focused approach, the advertisement in Exhibit 1–5 tells the story of a small-town security guard who uses a stock Saturn SL1 as a patrol car.

The print ad shown in Exhibit 1–6 sends a more direct message to consumers, addressing the fear that a lot of people have of even going into a dealership. This ad emphasizes another important building block in Saturn's strategy to change the way cars were built and sold: the no-haggle pricing and sales strategy.

Saturn's Relationship With Its Dealers

Saturn's approach to selling cars at the dealer level was another innovative choice that appears to be quite logical in hindsight. Saturn recognized that consumers simply do not like the high-pressure tactics of most car salespeople, who are typically working for a sales commission on each car sold. In response, Saturn decided to eliminate the sales commission in favor of a salary, thereby removing the need for dealers to use high-pressure tactics.

EXHIBIT 1–5

EXHIBIT 1–6

Instead, Saturn salespeople are called consultants and have been carefully trained to assist potential buyers, not pressure them.

Saturn also changed the way dealers' market areas of operation were established and organized. Traditionally, auto dealers for the same manufacturer are allowed to operate in the same geographic area or market. This sets up the likelihood of head-to-head price competition among dealers selling the same brand or nameplate. Rather than bowing to tradition, Saturn heeded the recommendation of potential dealers, who urged Saturn not to let this happen because it would lead to the very situation that the company wanted to avoid: price haggling. This approach required that Saturn attract dealers who would take the responsibility for as many as six Saturn dealerships in a market area.[8]

The strategic brilliance of Saturn's approach to its dealer network and sales system has been identified as the most difficult part of its marketing and advertising program for competitors to duplicate. This is because the old way of selling cars is an ingrained culture that is hard to change. While car styles or car advertising can be copied, the Saturn culture would be very hard to imitate unless a company started from scratch the way Saturn did.[9]

Saturn Targets Its Brand Character

Saturn knew from the outset that its consumer market was different from typical GM consumers, as well as car buyers in general. Exhibit 1–7 provides a demographic profile of Saturn owners and how they differ from the general population. In short, Saturn owners are more upscale than the general population. This means that they are better educated, earn more money, and have more prestigious jobs than the average person.

Saturn also knew that it had to communicate a brand character that provided this market with an image that would allow them to express their car-buying attitudes. The attitudinal differences that Saturn thought had to be addressed in its marketing communications strategy included the following:

EXHIBIT 1–7   A Demographic Profile of Saturn Owners

	PERCENT OF SATURN OWNERS WHO ARE IN THIS DEMOGRAPHIC GROUP	COMPARED TO THE GENERAL PUBLIC, SATURN OWNERS ARE MORE OR LESS LIKELY TO BE IN THIS DEMOGRAPHIC GROUP
Men	44.5	less
Women	55.5	more
Parents	32.2	less
Education		
College graduates	36.7	more
High school graduates	28.0	less
Age		
Age 18–24	15.8	more
Age 25–34	34.1	more
Age 35–44	23.0	more
Age 45–54	17.7	more
Age 55–64	5.6	less
Age 18–34	49.9	more
Age 25–54	74.9	more
Employment Status		
Working full time	73.6	more
Working part time	8.7	less
Occupation		
Professional	16.0	more
Executive/administrative	16.8	more
Clerical/technical/sales	23.5	more
Annual Household Income		
$60,000+	39.3	more
$50,000+	50.9	more
$40,000+	67.3	more
Under $10,000	3.9	less
Region		
Northeast	24.4	more
North Central	26.2	more
West	18.1	less
South	31.3	less
Marital Status		
Single	28.7	more
Married	63.5	more
Ethnic Group		
White	96.2	more
Black	1.1	less
Spanish-speaking	7.1	less

Source: Mediamark Research, Inc., *Doublebase 1996 Study.*

1. Quality, reliability, and durability of the products as the primary reason for purchase.
2. Import-oriented but willing to take a chance on a new American corporation and product—more leading edge.
3. Motivated by value (not necessarily the lowest price/best deal).
4. Intelligent, well educated, well informed.
5. Searching for something "better" (regardless of whether they currently own an import or domestic product).
6. Young at heart, but spread across many life stages.[10]

Saturn's brand-building marketing communications were developed to reflect the corporate philosophy of treating people, whether they are employees or customers, with respect and like a friend. Advertising and other marketing communications had to present the company and cars as friendly, creative, precise, and international. Saturn's storytelling ads not only conveyed a friendly feeling but also demonstrated a responsiveness to the environmental, emotional, and physical needs of all of its customers. Saturn ads are known for reflecting a diversity of people, as the magazine ad in Exhibit 1–8 illustrates.

EXHIBIT 1–8

EXHIBIT 1–9

Saturn set out to establish itself as an innovative company. This had to be supported with cars that were perceived to be the standard for styling, spirit, intelligence, and value. The ad in Exhibit 1–9 integrates the real-person-as-owner approach with the high standards, spirit, and value demanded by someone who races his Saturn car. Notice how the ad promotes improvements in the Saturn Coupe in an interesting manner. More recently Saturn was selected by GM to build and distribute its first electric car, the EV1, further establishing the company as a leader in automotive innovation. The electric car has been introduced in California where customers can lease the EV1 for close to $500 a month.

Saturn's ability to execute its overall strategy and deliver on its promises has set it apart from many other companies. The precision with which Saturn strives to provide its customers with the best overall buying and driving experience has led to high levels of consumer satisfaction for its cars. Saturn has developed an owner loyalty program that builds a sense of fellowship among Saturn owners. It is not unusual for people who buy their first Saturn to be welcomed to the Saturn family by those who already own one.

Some of the activities that Saturn uses to create this sense of belonging are done at the dealer level. Look back at Exhibit 1–2, which illustrates a dealer event for Saturn owners that is designed to show the dealer's appreciation to those who purchased cars at the dealership. This type of event is a local version of Saturn's 1994 homecoming event, in which 44,000 owners were invited to Spring Hill, Tennessee. The event was done on a grand scale, with entertainment by Wynonna Judd, dancing, barbecues, a plant tour, and mingling with celebrities part of the overall experience.[11] "Homecoming," a television spot based on the 1994 event, was then used to extend the feelings and imagery of the festivities to owners who couldn't attend and to attract potential buyers to the brand.

Saturn's Web site (shown in Exhibit 1–10) amplifies this sense of belonging and allows Saturn owners and prospects to interact and get involved with the entire Saturn family. Among the many pages that make up the Web site is an "extended family database," which is shown in Exhibit 1–11. Here owners can list their profiles to share with other Saturn owners. There is also an interactive pricing Web site page, which is illustrated in Exhibit 1–12.

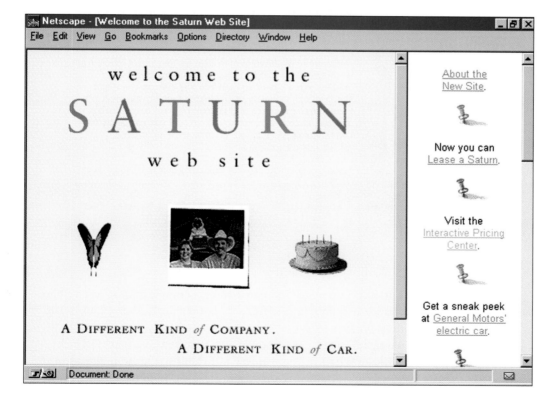

EXHIBIT 1–10

EXHIBIT 1–11

EXHIBIT 1–12

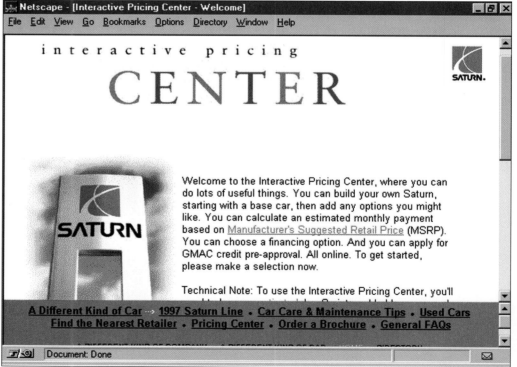

In perhaps a somewhat ironic move, Saturn is now selling its cars in the country where most of its competitors originate, Japan. The company has hired the eighth largest Japanese agency, Dai-Ichi Kikaku (DIK), to help with strategy and marketing in this new venture. Saturn's goal is to reach a sales figure of 100,000 in Japan by 2000.[12] The company's overall expansion plans are reflected in the link to its Saturn of Japan Web site, shown in Exhibit 1–13, and in the print advertisement shown in Exhibit 1–14 that

EXHIBIT 1–13

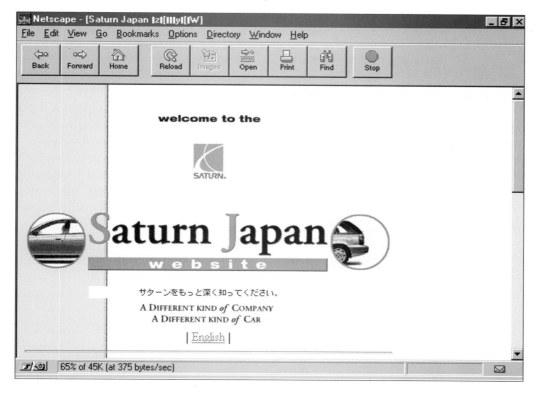

EXHIBIT 1–14

announces the opening of Saturn of Yokohama.

Saturn wants to maintain the same approach it has used in the U.S., transferring its carefully created corporate and consumer culture to Japan. It does have several barriers to overcome, however. The Japanese have a fairly low opinion of most American-made cars, although a third of Japanese car dealers now carry at least one imported make. If Saturn decides to establish its own dealership network, as it did in the U.S., it may face problems because of the high cost of land in Japan. On the positive side, trade barriers between the U.S. and Japan are being reduced, making it easier for U.S. companies to sell there; and at the same time, the Japanese are becoming more value-conscious and open to the idea of buying foreign brands.[13]

The international element of Saturn's marketing strategy is evident elsewhere, too. Saturn has set up dealerships in Canada and Taiwan, reflecting the company's intent from the beginning to be an international company and to build brand loyalty across cultural and geographic boundaries.

Has Saturn been able to build brand loyalty and maintain its brand character? Has its strategy to forge a lasting relationship with Saturn buyers worked? R. L. Polk's 1995 study of car owner loyalty, relationship with dealer, and vehicle reliability had Saturn in the top spot among small-size car brands.

EXHIBIT 1–15   Saturn's Brand Creation System

PRIMARY DRIVERS OF BRAND EQUITY	BRAND EQUITY DIMENSIONS	CHALLENGES TO MAINTAIN EQUITY
Advertising Retail presence Publicity Word of mouth	**Awareness**	Maintain awareness in the face of reduced news value and competitive clutter
Advertising Slogan/position Spring Hill plant Retail experience Integrated communication Relationship based on brand identity	**Brand Associations** Committed employees Enthused customers Spring Hill plant Different company/car Retail experience Liking/friend U.S. car in Honda Civic class Treat customers with respect	Need to communicate the Saturn message to those new to the brand in the face of pressures to talk product, not company
Product design Manufacturing commitment New organization/culture Empathy with employees Empathy with customers Slogan/position Money-back guarantee	**Perceived Quality**	Maintaining actual quality after the initial excitement is over and in the face of competitors' efforts to improve their position
Friendship relationship Retail experience Pride in U.S. company	**Loyalty**	Keep relationship strong over time
Market area concept Corporate culture	**Retail System**	Keep the retail culture in place in the face of slow sales and imitation

Source: David Aaker, *Building Strong Brands* (New York: The Free Press, 1996).

David Aaker, in his book *Building Strong Brands,* has summarized how Saturn created its brand.[14] This summary is shown in Exhibit 1–15. This table presents five dimensions of the brand: awareness, brand associations, perceived quality, loyalty, and retail system. The first column lists the primary drivers, or choices, about programs that Saturn made to achieve its brand goals. Many of these strategic drivers have been discussed in this chapter. The third column describes the challenges Saturn faces to maintain its brand image and the loyalty it has created.

Challenges Ahead

Saturn has set the bar very high. It has created a culture that could be more difficult to maintain than it was to create. Its competitors are starting to copy some of Saturn's innovations in the way it treats its employees and customers. Inevitably, over time, Saturn's competitive ad-

vantage will wear off. It will have to continue to be innovative to stay ahead of the curve. In fact, "Innovate" is the name of a mid-size car it is planning for the 1999 model year. Saturn is not standing still with its advertising and marketing, either. For its 1998 models, the focus of national TV commercials will shift from car owners to employees and product benefits. Meanwhile, in print, Saturn has developed a series called "continuum," showing simple photos on a timeline, with words or questions to attract the curiosity and attention both of loyal customers and people unfamiliar with the car. An example appears in Exhibit 1–16. The target consumers remain younger, educated, fairly affluent adults in their 30s.[15]

The past, present, and future challenges for Saturn are reflective of the realities of the advertising and marketing communications business in that success always leads to new choices and challenges in a marketplace that is in a constant state of change.

EXHIBIT 1–16

Chapter Two

The Advertising Industry

THE CHANGING NATURE OF AGENCY-CLIENT RELATIONSHIPS

It isn't often that agencies and their clients, the advertisers, get to celebrate significant milestones in their relationship.

Given that the average tenure of the advertiser-agency relationship has fallen from 7.2 years in 1984 to just 5.3 years in 1997, a relationship that lasts beyond that might be considered a bonus. So in 1995 when the Leo Burnett Company celebrated its 50th year working with the Pillsbury Company, it was truly a special occasion. Burnett's relationship with what was then called the Minnesota Valley Canning Company in fact began even earlier, in 1935, the year the Leo Burnett agency opened its doors for business. (Minnesota Valley Canning Company was one of the agency's original three accounts.) The success of Burnett's creation of the Jolly Green Giant mascot inspired Minnesota Valley to change its name to the Green Giant Company; that company was, in turn, bought by Pillsbury in 1979. Grand Metropolitan Company purchased Pillsbury in 1988. Burnett is now one of the three major ad agencies working

for the Pillsbury division of the Grand Metropolitan company that spends more than $130 million a year on advertising its products.

More often than not, the headlines are made when agencies and clients split after having been together for a long time. Anheuser-Busch Company left its agency of 79 years, D'Arcy Masius Benton and Bowles; Kodak and J. Walter Thompson parted ways after 66 years; and Delta Airlines moved its account from BBDO after 60 years. What causes advertisers and agencies to remain together or to split after so many years?

There is no simple answer. But as advertisers are faced with more challenges in their businesses (globalization, increased competition, tighter cost structures), they sometimes choose to try to resolve their problems by switching advertising agencies. It may also be an outcome of the more short-term thinking that characterizes U.S. businesses today, focusing on

There's no "Fee-fi-fo-fum" about this Green Giant. His song is a kindly song about his products, and it goes like this—

"Packed at the fleeting moment of perfect flavor"

His gold isn't laid by a goose; it is grown in tall, juicy kernels of golden corn.

His peas don't grow to the sky, but grow large while very young and tender.

His seeds are not magic beans, but exclusive breeds of peas and corn.*

If you believe in honest, tried-and-true American labels, you can still believe in giants—*Green Giants.*

Packed only by Minnesota Valley Canning Company, headquarters, Le Sueur, Minnesota, and Fine Foods of Canada, Ltd., Tecumseh, Ont. Also packers of the following brands: Niblets Mexicorn, Del Maiz Cream Style Corn and Niblets Asparagus.

Green Giant Peas · **Niblets Whole Kernel Corn**
Our exclusive breed—S-537   *Our exclusive breed—D-138*

producing results for the next fiscal quarter rather than looking ahead to generating sales over the next two to three years.

But for many, the current state of the advertiser-agency relationship exemplifies the fact that, despite all of the technology and changes going on in the advertising industry, it remains what it has always been—a people business. From the beginning, the advertising industry has always been

based on relationships between people. If those turn sour, no amount of creativity can compensate for the changes taking place.

Whatever the reason, and no doubt there are several, the nature of the advertising business is changing. Even as some brands or companies celebrate 40 or 50 years with a single agency, others move their accounts after only a few months or a few years. Some advertisers are abandoning longstanding relationships with one or more agencies in order to consolidate their global business at another. Others are adding agencies to their roster to encourage some creative competition and to search for the best possible ideas to help them be successful.

Advertisers and agencies are all coming to terms with an industry, and an environment, where choices, challenges, and changes are par for the course. Expect to see more of this in the years ahead!

Sources: Mark Gleason, "MIA on Madison Ave.: Agency, Client Loyalty," *Advertising Age*, 27 January 1997, 3, 42–43; and Mark Gleason and Laura Petrecca, "Split Decisions Grow As Advertisers Seek Edge," *Advertising Age*, 11 November 1996, 1, 20.

LOOK BEFORE YOU LEAP

- Who are the key players in the advertising industry, and what are their roles?

- How are advertisers structured, and what do they do?

- What are the roles of the various people who work in an advertising agency?

- What different kinds of agencies are out there?

- Why are the media becoming increasingly global?

- What kinds of jobs are there in the media field?

2

The Advertising Industry

When you turn on the television to watch "Monday Night Football" and catch a Bud Light commercial right before the program begins, or open your new issue of *Rolling Stone* magazine and see an ad for Gap clothes facing the table of contents, you probably don't stop to think about how many people were involved in getting those messages in front of you. Whether or not you like the ads and find them effective, the industry that has been built to put them together is vital to the marketplace in which we live.

Indeed, the creation of an advertising campaign is not something that happens just by intuition or inspiration alone. It also requires the hard work and diligence of many individuals and, in most cases, many different companies. In this chapter, we will examine the roles of the various players in the development of an advertising campaign to see how each contributes to the final "production"—the advertisement you see on television or in a magazine. First, we will take a look at the advertisers, followed by the agencies, and then the media. We will end the chapter with an overview of these same entities on a global scale.

First, it is important to realize just how small the advertising industry is. According to U.S. government statistics, about 395,200 people are classified as being employed in this industry (227,200 working in advertising and 168,000 in agencies).[1] That compares with 750,000 lawyers and 550,000 computer programmers, or 2.7 million truck drivers and 252,000 mail carriers, for example. Slightly more than half of the total employed in advertising are female.[2] Within the advertising industry overall, jobs are divided between agencies, advertisers, media, and suppliers. Globally, about $300 billion is spent on advertising, with the U.S. being the largest single contributor to that amount. Exhibit 2–1 shows the number of people employed in the advertising industry by U.S.–based agencies, while Exhibit 2–2 offers an overview of the industry's structure.

The advertising industry consists of four principal entities: advertisers, agencies, the media, and suppliers. As shown in Exhibit 2–2, advertising can be produced directly by the advertisers, or it can be produced with the assistance of an agency. In either case, suppliers often work alongside to help create the finished product. Commercial production houses, for example, put ads onto film. Research suppliers that conduct measurement on consumer behavior or audience response also play an important role in campaign development. Many individuals and businesses are involved in bringing an ad campaign to life. Suffice it to say, the advertising industry is extremely diverse in its functions and roles.

As illustrated in Exhibit 2–3, the advertising industry relies on two sources of income to function successfully. The first, which directly supports advertisers, is income from consumers, who buy advertisers' products and services. That income is then used by advertisers to hire agencies. The second major source is from the media. This income comes from consumer payments for media such as newspapers, magazines, or cable television. Both types of income are tied closely to the overall economic health of the country. In times of recession, consumers spend less on goods and services as well as on media. As a result, spending on advertising generally declines during these tough economic times, even though there is considerable research evidence to indicate that those firms that continue to advertise during a recession come out of it in a far stronger position than their competitors who may have cut back on ad expenditures.[3]

Advertisers: Who They Are, What They Do

The term **advertiser** encompasses a wide range of companies and individuals. It is defined as a company or individual that spends money to convey a persuasive advertising message to the public.[4] When an advertiser solicits the help of an agency, it is often referred to as the **client.** An advertiser can be a huge corporation such as Procter & Gamble, which spends more than $2.4 billion per year on advertising, or it can be Joe's Copy Shop on Main Street, which might spend $300 a year putting flyers on the windshields of cars in the town parking lot. In 1995, some of the 100 leading advertisers in the U.S. included retailers such as Sears, Roebuck, and car makers such as Ford Motor Company. Other top advertisers included restaurants such as McDonald's Corporation, entertainment conglomerates such as Walt Disney Company, services such as AT&T, and pharmaceutical giants such as SmithKline Beecham.

The brands that these companies promote are even more numerous. Companies such as Procter & Gamble or Philip Morris produce literally hundreds of different brands for consumers. Philip Morris Companies, for example, makes everything from its well-known tobacco brands to food products such as Velveeta Cheese in its Kraft subsidiary and Miller Beer in its Miller Brewing Company segment. Many of the best-known brand names have been around for a long time. As Exhibit 2–4 shows, families were enjoying Crayola crayons and Kellogg's Rice Krispies as far back as the 1920s.

Advertisers also can be classified by whether they are trying primarily to reach consumers, other businesses, or the agricultural industry. Although the main focus of this book is consumer advertising, you should recognize that business-to-business and farm advertising each represent distinct and important segments of the overall advertising industry.

EXHIBIT 2–1   Advertising Industry Employment by U.S.-Based Agencies

REGION	EMPLOYEE TOTALS	OFFICE TOTALS
Top 500 Agencies		
Worldwide	126,342	2,408
U.S.	70,476	1,135
Non–U.S.	55,866	1,273
Top 100 Agencies		
Worldwide	104,273	1,769
U.S.	48,411	497
Non–U.S.	55,862	1,272

Note: Data presented is for calendar year 1993.
Source: "50th Annual Agency Report," *Advertising Age,* 13 April 1994, 50.

EXHIBIT 2–2   The Structure of the Advertising Industry

EXHIBIT 2–3   Consumer Support for the Advertising Industry

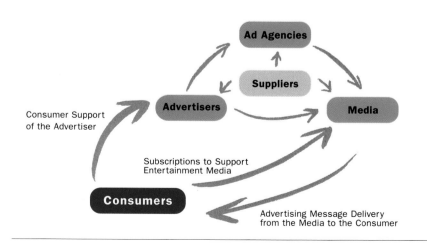

The methods used by different advertisers to reach their target audiences are as varied as the industries themselves. For a company that aims its messages at young adults, as consumer products giant PepsiCo might, it makes sense to spend the bulk of its money in major media such as television and radio. On the other hand, Pharmacia & Upjohn, a leading pharmaceutical products company, places more than half of its advertising dollars in highly specialized communications programs to reach health professionals. Exhibit 2–5 compares the PepsiCo and Pharmacia & Upjohn media spending patterns for 1995. Notice that PepsiCo puts the largest amount of its media money into media that reach the most consumers—national and local television. For Pharmacia & Upjohn, which has a far more specialized focus, the largest proportion of its media spending goes into media that can target the exact groups it wishes to reach, such as doctors or people with specific medical conditions. It, therefore, primarily uses magazines, which can also be quite narrowly targeted.

The Traditional Advertiser Hierachy

The organizational structure of an advertiser varies considerably, in part because of the great variety of advertisers' sizes and functions. One consistent feature is that advertising is almost always found within the marketing department. That means advertising operates along-

---

EXHIBIT 2–4 Well-Known Long-Lasting Brands Aimed at Families

DECADE	BRAND	DECADE	BRAND
1920s	Crayola Crayon Good Humor Ice Cream Kellogg's Rice Krispies Lincoln Logs Wheatena Yo-Yo	**1950s**	Clairol Color Rinse Frisbee Hula Hoops Jell-O Pudding Kool-Aid Minute Rice Play-Doh Swanson TV Dinner
1930s	Bisquick Campbell's Chicken Noodle Soup Dreft Detergent Fritos Monopoly Nescafe Instant Coffee Ritz Crackers Snickers Bars Viewmaster Windex	**1960s**	BacOs Barbie Coffeemate G.I. Joe Lucky Charms Pampers
		1970s	Bounce Stove Top Stuffing
1940s	Cheerios Lego M&Ms Scrabble Slinky Tide	**1980s**	Cabbage Patch Kids Perrier Water Transformers Scrabble Trivial Pursuit

Source: Lorraine Glennon, "1926–1996: Celebrating the American Family," *Parents Magazine*, August 1996, 49–113.

EXHIBIT 2–5 U.S. Media Spending by Two Different Kinds of Advertisers: PepsiCo and Pharmacia & Upjohn

MEDIA	PEPSICO	PHARMACIA & UPJOHN
Magazine	$7,427	$37,631
Sunday magazine	1,073	5,999
Newspaper	1,779	176
National newspaper	323	151
Outdoor	4,991	1
Network TV	362,107	31,911
Spot TV	285,138	8,477
Syndicated TV	13,072	5,180
Cable TV networks	43,736	26,853
Network radio	517	1,118
National spot radio	10,033	657
Yellow Pages	6,000	0
Measured media	736,196	118,155
Unmeasured	460,847	85,633
Total	**1,197,043**	**203,788**

Notes: Data presented are for calendar year 1995. Figures are in thousands of U.S. dollars.
Source: "100 Leading National Advertisers," *Advertising Age,* 30 September 1996, 545.

side units focusing on related functions such as sales promotion, research, creative services, and distribution. A typical structure for many companies that have advertising specialists among their staff is shown in Exhibit 2–6. Product managers are said to have *line responsibility* because they are held accountable for the success of the brand, or line. Product managers typically report to the director of marketing, or division director. Other positions, such as the research director, the director of advertising, and their direct reports, are said to be *staff positions* because while they work for the company, they do not have direct responsibility for the profit or loss of a brand. Notice too that the advertising agency may report to either the product manager or the director of advertising.

CENTRALIZED ORGANIZATIONAL STRUCTURE

The organizational structure of advertising companies can be divided broadly into one of two forms: centralized or decentralized. In a *centralized organization structure,* such as the one shown in Exhibit 2–7, decisions about advertising are made from one central location, usually the company's headquarters. Nestlé, for example, has all of its marketing decisions approved by its international headquarters in Vevey, Switzerland, and McDonald's Corporation centralizes its national marketing in Oak Brook, Illinois. The key benefit to such a structure is that efficiencies can be found in terms of both personnel and ad budgets. For smaller companies in particular, a centralized structure works well. It ensures that all of the brands are working towards the company's overall marketing goals, and it is easier to look for synergies between them. Under a centralized structure, the advertising agency will work primarily with the corporate marketing staff, rather than with regional or local personnel.

DECENTRALIZED ORGANIZATIONAL STRUCTURE

Many companies are moving to a *decentralized organizational structure,* recognizing the complexities of having numerous brands and, frequently, numerous locations. In such a setup, such as the one shown in Exhibit 2–8, some marketing and advertising decisions are made at the corporate level—either by a corporate marketing staff or by management at the corporate level—while the day-to-day activities are handled by staffs that are

EXHIBIT 2–6   The Typical Product Management Structure

EXHIBIT 2–7   A Centralized Organizational Structure

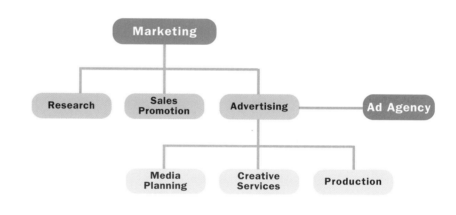

EXHIBIT 2–8   A Decentralized Organizational Structure

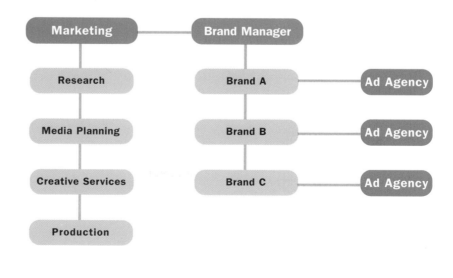

GENERAL MOTORS CORP.

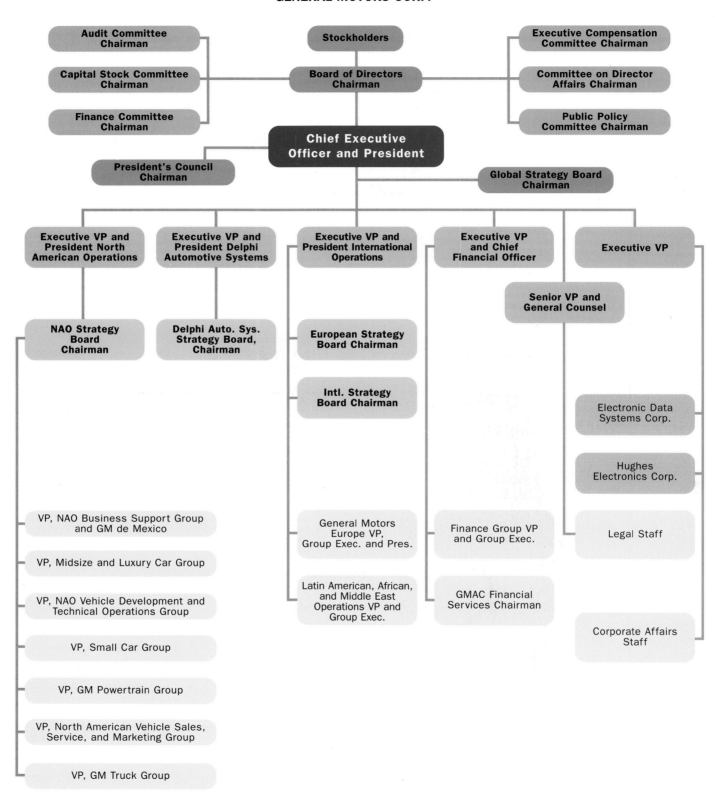

EXHIBIT 2–9 *(continued)*

SATURN CORPORATION

```
                        ┌─────────────────┐
                        │    President    │
                        └─────────────────┘
                                 │
                        ┌─────────────────────────┐
                        │ Administrative Assistant │
                        └─────────────────────────┘
```

| EDS | Vice President Purchasing | Vice President Manufacturing | Vice President General Counsel | Vice President People Systems |
| Vice President Corporate Communications | Vice President Sales, Service, & Marketing | Vice President Finance | Vice President Engineering | Consulting Services |

Source: John L. Maurer, Judith M. Nixon, and Terrance W. Peck, eds., *Organization Charts,* 2nd ed. (New York: Gale Publishing, 1996), 82–83, 179.

responsible for individual brands. This system, also called **brand management,** was established by Procter & Gamble (P&G) as early as 1931. The company realized that its soap brand, Camay, was competing not only with Lever Brothers' Lux soap but also internally against its own Ivory Soap. So P&G set up a system under which each of its brands operated semi-independently, competing with each other within the company for corporate support and resources. This change resulted in advertising with an emphasis on the brand name rather than the company's name.

In 1984, Procter & Gamble led the way again by shifting from brand management to **category management.** In this structure, people who work on individual brands report to more senior staff who are responsible for a particular category. These people are known as **category managers.** At Procter & Gamble, for instance, there might be one person in charge of all laundry detergents (of which P&G has 18 different brands). The brand manager for, say, Tide, would report to this category manager who, in turn, reports to top management. General Mills has category managers for its cereals, yogurt, baking goods, and restaurant categories. Ameritech Corporation, one of the seven regional Bell operating companies, has category managers overseeing its local phone service, small business services, cellular phones, and Yellow Pages operations. Usually, one man-

ager is responsible for a particular brand or category. The manager's job is to handle all of the elements of marketing, including production, distribution, pricing, and promotion. Advertising comes into play under this last element, promotion, along with sales promotion, public relations, and direct response activities.

This type of decentralized structure offers the benefit of brand and category managers being able to respond more rapidly to changing conditions in the marketplace. Rather than having to wait for a corporate decision on how to respond, a brand can act almost immediately when it faces a new situation. For example, when Hewlett-Packard (H-P) realized that sales of its DeskJet printers for home use were rising, the brand manager was able to develop a new strategy to pursue home computer users and small businesses rather than the larger companies at which H-P had previously aimed. The use of consumer-oriented media and a move into mass retailers such as Wal-Mart and Office Depot helped the computer printer manufacturer increase its share of the market from 54 percent to 60 percent in one year.[5]

In a decentralized organizational structure the advertising agency works directly with the product manager, rather than with a corporate marketing staff. For managers who handle several different brands, this may mean they end up working with more than one agency at a time. Other functions within the decentralized structure are similar to those in the centralized organization. Research, media, creative services, and production may all report to the head of marketing, who is working on all of the company's brands.

The way that companies are organized depends on many factors, including size and type of business. For example, while General Motors, one of the biggest car makers in the world, has an extremely complicated and extensive organization, its spin-off division, Saturn, is far simpler in the way it is structured. A comparison of the corporate structures of these two companies is shown in Exhibit 2–9.

SMALLER ADVERTISERS   Of course, the organizational structures we have discussed thus far tend to occur in larger companies. If you added up every company that advertises in the Yellow Pages, the number of advertisers in the U.S. would be huge. Most of these smaller companies have no need for an advertising or marketing "department," however, let alone a category or brand manager.

In smaller companies, it may be the part-time job of one individual in the company to determine where and when to advertise, place the ads (and possibly even write them), and monitor the response. For example, Sharp Printing, an independent copyshop in Peoria, Illinois, with billings of $450,000, has no set advertising budget or formal marketing plan. In 1994, it spent $40,000 on advertising. Half of the money went to ads on outdoor billboards, with the remainder split between local radio and local television. And as with many small businesses' advertising expenditures, much of the advertising was in the form of barter, where the company offers its products or services in exchange for free space or airtime.

R E S E T

1. How is the advertising industry supported? What sources of revenue does it enjoy?
2. What are the two main types of organizational structures among advertisers? How do they differ?

Advertising Agencies: Who They Are, What They Do

An **advertising agency** is a business that assists advertisers in all stages of the advertising process, from account management and planning to message creation, media planning, and research. Advertising agencies are a fairly new entity. Prior to about 150 years ago, it was the media (first newspapers, then magazines) that created the advertisements that appeared in their pages. They acted as *brokers* of their space. Several agencies in the U.S. lay claim to being the "first." Depending on how first is defined, J. Walter Thompson, Grey Advertising, and NW Ayer have all declared themselves the earliest U.S. agency. Many believe, however, that the first real advertising "agent" was Volney Palmer, who began in 1843 to solicit newspaper ads from companies in his hometown of Philadelphia. Palmer actually represented the newspapers rather than the advertiser, but he was nevertheless responsible for collecting the advertising copy and payment from the advertiser and seeing that it appeared in the newspaper.

By the beginning of the twentieth century, the main function of an ad agency was still the selling, or brokering, of advertising space in newspapers. The agent would buy the space, re-sell it to advertisers, and take a commission on the space sold. The system was generally disliked because only the agent knew the difference in value between the initial purchase price and the final selling price. With the publication of Rowell's *American Newspaper Directory* in 1869, the situation changed. This guide to 5,000 newspapers offered "a description of all the newspapers and periodicals published in the United States, Dominion of Canada and Newfoundland, and of the towns and cities in which they are published." By providing circulation figures and estimates on the accuracy of those numbers, Rowell's *Directory* was the first attempt to quantify the size of an ad's potential audience.

One agency, NW Ayer, then began using an **open contract rate**, whereby both advertiser and agency agreed on the financial terms of the space purchased. The agency received a 15 percent commission on the cost of the space, which soon became the standard method of

EXHIBIT 2–10   The Top 10 U.S. Agencies

RANK	AGENCY	HEADQUARTERS	WORLDWIDE GROSS INCOME
1	McCann-Erickson Worldwide	New York	$1,386.1
2	BBDO Worldwide	New York	1,280.2
3	Young & Rubicam	New York	1,271.2
4	DDB Needham Worldwide	New York	1,266.1
5	J. Walter Thompson Co.	New York	1,119.1
6	Ogilvy & Mather Worldwide	New York	986.5
7	Grey Advertising	New York	935.5
8	Leo Burnett Co.	Chicago	866.3
9	Foote, Cone & Belding	Chicago	798.9
10	Ammirati Puris Lintas	New York	775.4

Notes: Data presented are for calendar year 1996. Figures are in millions of U.S. dollars.
Source: "53rd Annual Agency Report," *Advertising Age,* 21 April 1997, 52.

payment in the advertising industry. Agencies offered additional services, such as help on writing the ads themselves and counseling their clients on which newspapers to use. Gradually, they started to include research as well.

By the early twentieth century, agencies that offered advertisers all of these elements—message creation, media placement, research, and the like—came to be known as **full-service agencies.** The handling of client relations, or account management, became the fourth key department in the agency. The top 10 agencies, ranked by worldwide gross income, are shown in Exhibit 2–10. Full-service agencies organize their accounts in this manner, putting together creative, media, research, and account management personnel to work on a specific brand. Smaller agencies may combine the jobs of several areas into one, such as having one person handle both media and research, or have account executives also undertake media duties.

The invisible lines between functions can sometimes get in the way of proper teamwork, with creatives unhappy if a media person comes up with a copy idea, or account executives not allowing the researchers to deal directly with the client. Efforts to break down such barriers have intensified in recent years,

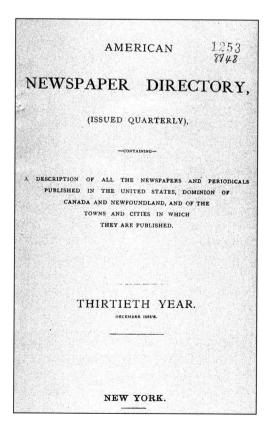

AMERICAN

1253
8748

NEWSPAPER DIRECTORY,

(ISSUED QUARTERLY),

—CONTAINING—

A DESCRIPTION OF ALL THE NEWSPAPERS AND PERIODICALS PUBLISHED IN THE UNITED STATES, DOMINION OF CANADA AND NEWFOUNDLAND, AND OF THE TOWNS AND CITIES IN WHICH THEY ARE PUBLISHED.

THIRTIETH YEAR.

DECEMBER ISSUE.

NEW YORK.

Rowell's *American Newspaper Directory,* published in 1869, provided the circulation figures of over 5,000 newspapers. This publication was the first tool available to advertisers for quantifying the size of the potential audience for their advertising messages.

with concerted efforts to develop truly *interdisciplinary groups* that cross all functions. These interdisciplinary groups may be called by various names, including account circles, team architecture, or business service teams, and this team approach may even be reflected in the floor plan of the company, so that all of the people who work on a given brand assignment are physically located next to each other, rather than, as in times past, working in the "creative" area or the "media" area.

As described in "Adscape: Virtual World," TBWA Chiat/Day has gone even further with its restructuring, replacing employees' physical office space with a "virtual" office, that is, one that is not permanent. You must realize, however, that TBWA Chiat/Day's arrangement remains an anomaly in the industry and has itself

been criticized for removing the all-important human factor in the idea-creation process. People enjoy coming to work in part for the social interaction. Indeed, one might argue that because advertising is a communications business, that type of mixing should be inherent in the process.

The Traditional Agency Hierarchy

Traditionally, advertising agencies are divided into four functional areas: creative, account management, research, and media. They usually are organized as *brand teams*, with representatives from each functional area working together to solve a client's problem. An example of one agency's organizational structure is shown in Exhibit 2–11, with each of the four

AdScape

. . . .

Virtual World

Jay Chiat, former chairman and CEO of TBWA Chiat/Day, Inc., is reputed to have originated the notion of turning his agency into a "virtual" office. In a world where many people work on computers, communicate by telephone, electronic mail, and fax, and attend meetings by videoconference, Chiat thought there was little need for employees to sit in individual offices all day; the work could be done from any location.

The switch from standard office to virtual was not as simple as Chiat had hoped, however. In addition to people's natural resistance to change, there were many other issues to consider. Would people still work in departments? Who would be in control of the clients' business? Where would the still-necessary meetings

occur, in cyberspace or face-to-face? In an industry that relies so heavily on communications and personal contacts, what would be the impact on both client and employee relations of working in a virtual environment?

The physical changes were easier to handle than the emotional and psychological ones. The interior of TBWA Chiat/Day's Venice, California, office was torn out and replaced with "project rooms," one for each client. Now, everything to do with that client takes place there: research, media, creative, and client services. The group working on that piece of business shares everything as a team. Each room also is electronically linked to a central library for easy access to research and other information. In addition, the agency's em-

ployees can access this library from any offsite location equipped with a phone jack, making it possible to work from just about anywhere.

As for the meeting rooms, there are several types to choose from: living rooms for casual conversations; creative rooms with equipment to display and discuss campaigns; and larger, more formal rooms full of the latest multimedia equipment designed for client meetings or big presentations. There is also a clubhouse where people meet to talk, eat, shoot pool, or relieve their stress by hitting a punching bag.

The move to virtuality also required a change in the organizational structure. Rather than having the typical hierarchy, titles have been simplified to two levels of partnership: managing partners and part-key areas reporting to the chief operating officer, then up to the president and chairman/chief executive officer. Here, we will look briefly at the responsibilities of each functional area.

CREATIVE DEPARTMENT   An advertising agency's main purpose is, of course, to create ideas—how to sell a product or service, how to advertise it, where to advertise it, and how to give consumers a valid reason for purchasing it. The creative department is responsible for bringing an ad campaign to life. It is here that the ideas are turned into actual advertising messages designed to speak to relevant audiences to inform them of the benefits that a particular product or service can offer them.

Most creative personnel (or **creatives**) work in pairs, combining the talents of a writer (**copywriter**) with those of an art director. The writer in the team comes up with the idea—what to say and how to say it; then, the art director gives the words life by depicting the people (or objects or creatures) who will express those words. In smaller agencies, these dual roles often are combined into a single individual who is responsible for both artwork and scriptwriting.

Creatives may spend hours trying to come up with new, original ways to convey the ideas they have for a brand, but they do not work in a vacuum. Instead, they work according to the strategic plans put together by other members of the ad agency team. They have to know whether the objective of the campaign is to increase sales, market share, or product usage; whether the target is young

ners. Employees are organized into client teams that focus on specific pieces of business, sharing responsibility for whether that business succeeds or not, and being rewarded when it does.

Since TBWA Chiat/Day implemented this virtual concept in both its Venice, Calfornia, and New York offices, modifications have been made. In a dynamic and changing environment like advertising, it is vital to keep on the forefront of innovation. "It's like white water rafting," explains Laurie Coots, TBWA Chiat/Day's director of marketing, North America. "You have to go faster than the river or you'll drown." The virtual office continues to evolve, with the goal being to provide the most efficient work environment that fosters creativity.

QUESTIONS
What was TBWA Chiat/Day's rationale for moving toward a "virtual agency"? Do you think this is really the agency of the future? Why or why not?

Source: Adapted from the Chiat/Day Web site (http://www.chiatday.com), November 1993; and Jack Feuer, "'Trading' Places," *Interactive Media*, 20 March 1996, 19.

The project rooms, group meeting areas, and lack of individual spaces in the "virtual" offices of TBWA Chiat/Day, Inc., underscore this agency's movement toward a team-oriented approach to advertising.

mothers, middle-aged adults, or teenagers; whether the messages are designed for radio, newspapers, or outdoor billboards; and whether the basic brand benefit is increased cleaning power, greater value for money, or financial rewards for using it. These objectives are determined by account management along with the client.

That does not mean that creatives are mere "order takers," coming up with ideas based solely on what they are given. They typically will find out more on their own about the product or service, trying it out for themselves so that they can understand the consumer's point of view. It also is up to the copywriter and art director to convince other agency team members to accept their ideas, requiring them to become salespeople for their work. In addition, it is the creatives' responsibility to oversee work done by outside creative suppliers, such as print or broadcast production houses or free-lance workers. The key functions of creatives are summarized in Exhibit 2–12.

ACCOUNT MANAGEMENT The primary role of an **account manager,** or *account executive,* is to represent the agency to the client and vice versa. This involves more than simply answering the client's questions and responding to his or her concerns (although both of those are critical parts of the job); it also necessitates knowing as much about the client and the brand as possible.

The job of account manager also requires a comprehensive understanding of the industry (category) in which the brand operates and, even more importantly, keeping up with changes that take place either with the brand or its competitors in the brand's environment. For example, when Duncan Hines introduced a new baking mix into the marketplace, it was the job of the account executives working on the rival Betty Crocker brand to find out as much as possible—and as fast as possible—about what the impact of the new product might be on their client's brand. Account managers deliver and convey the strategic plan for

EXHIBIT 2–11   Sample Organization Chart for an Agency

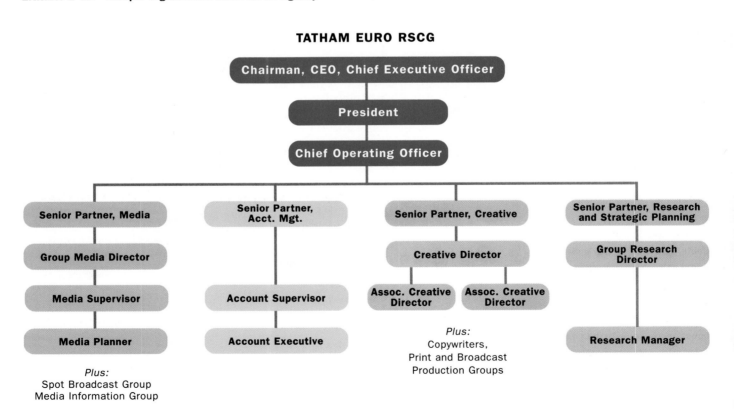

Source: John. L. Maurer, Judith M. Nixon, and Terrance W. Peck, eds., *Organization Charts,* 2nd ed. (New York: Gale Publishing, 1996), 209.

the brand to the creative team. The strategy, based on research among consumers, is designed to explain the marketing objectives (e.g., increase sales or market share) and the role advertising will play in achieving those objectives (e.g., increase brand awareness, encourage additional product use).

Another key role of account management personnel is coordination. They are responsible for ensuring that all plans are produced accurately and on time, that all client questions are answered, and that they represent the client's concerns within the agency in order to produce an effective ad campaign. After the client has approved the plans, it is then up to the account executive to ensure that the campaign is executed appropriately. This might involve lining up the "talent" to produce and appear in the commercial, getting legal approval for all copy used, attending the shoot when a TV commercial is filmed to ensure that it meets the client's desires, or coordinating with other agencies involved in the client's business. Exhibit 2–13 lists all of the responsibilities of the account manager.

RESEARCH It is in the research department, sometimes known as *strategic planning,* that consumers are scrutinized. The primary role of the **researcher** is to learn as much as possible about how consumers interact with the client's brand, and how it fits into their lifestyle. Researchers ask such questions as, What do consumers think of Samsonite luggage? How often have they shopped at Sears in the past month? What do they think of the idea of putting McDonald's restaurants into Wal-Mart stores? Once ads have been developed, researchers usually test them among a small group of consumers to gather their reactions before deploying the ads on a large-scale basis. They ask questions such as, What do consumers like and dislike about the ads? How effective are the ads in motivating consumers to purchase the product or use the service? How do the ads compare to competitive messages?

The research department also is responsible for assessing how effectively a message is communicated. After the campaign begins, the researchers find out what consumers think about it. After several months, the message may be tested again to see if it is still working or whether people are tired of it. How have consumers' attitudes towards the product changed?

EXHIBIT 2–12   Key Functions of Creatives

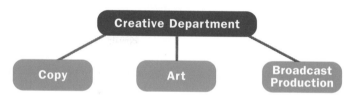

- Creates the ideas, images, and words that make up commercials and ads.
- Learns about the product or service to be advertised, the marketing strategy, the consumer or potential consumer, the media to be used, the production budget, and the competitors' advertising.
- Engages in first-hand activities that provide opportunities to experience a product or service from a consumer's point of view.

- Shares common and guided goals that match the advertising and marketing strategy.
- Pitches ideas to other agency departments.
- Contracts and oversees any outside print or broadcast production assistance.

EXHIBIT 2–13   Key Account Management Functions

- Represents the agency to the client and the client to the agency.
- Maintains a good relationship with the client.
- Responsible for quality of service to the client.
- Has thorough knowledge of the client's business from product development through marketing operations, marketplace conditions, and advertising practices.
- Helps the client set goals and a budget.
- Articulates the client's needs to agency research, creative, and media departments.

- Coordinates the day-to-day work of all branches of the agency for the account.
- Moves and promotes ideas both inside the agency and to the client.
- Oversees the advertising business assigned to the agency.
- Analyzes competitive activity and consumer trends.
- Reports clients' billings and forecasts agency's income.
- Determines that the final product is profitable and effective for the client and the agency.

Can they remember the main points of the message? These kinds of questions are answered by various types of research, from consumer surveys to small discussion groups to observations of what people actually do with the brand when they have it. Exhibit 2–14 summarizes the main responsibilities of those who work in research.

Within the research department, you often will find the agency's information center, or in-house library. Any data, reports, or other information that might be relevant to any specific brands the agency works on, together with general information of importance to all departments within the company, are housed in the information center. This includes research journals on consumer behavior; government statistics on employment, income, and expenditures; or reference files with articles culled from trade magazines on issues such as shorter-length commercials, Hispanic advertising, or telemarketing. In addition, the information center may subscribe to many advertising-related reports, magazines, or newsletters. The information center is not just a research-oriented haven. It also can provide invaluable assistance in the creative process. Collections of pictures help art directors correctly reproduce a particular animal or location, while dictionaries and other books may help writers find the exact phrase or word they need.

Account Planning. Especially in the United Kingdom, the role of the account executive is frequently merged with that of the research person into a function known as the **account planner.** The account planner "is essentially the account team's primary contact with the outside world; the person who, through personal background, knowledge of all pertinent information, and overall experience, is able to bring a strong consumer focus to all advertising decisions."[6] In other words, the account planner must bring the consumer's voice to all of the advertising development. For Goodby, Silverstein & Partners in San Francisco, to find the consumer's voice for the Polaroid Corporation meant sending cameras and film to a selected group of participants and finding out what kinds of pictures they took, which lead them to develop the notion that the advertising should be designed to give people ideas about how to use their cameras.[7]

The difference between an account planner and an agency researcher lies mainly in their use of data. Whereas the researcher gathers data and perhaps provides some initial interpretation, the planner's role is to analyze the information and determine how best to incorporate it into the creative product. As Jane Newman, director of strategic planning at Merkley Newman Harty, puts it, "The core concept of account planning is to bring consumer insight into the development of advertising." Damien O'Malley, head of account planning at DDB Needham in New York, notes that the function brings in "new ideas and an interest in the communication process by spending time with consumers to learn what they think."[8]

One of the first U.S. agencies to adopt this function was Chiat/Day, in the early 1980s. For the 1995 introduction of the Nissan Altima car, TBWA Chiat/Day in Los Angeles found that consumers perceived such a midsize car to be a family model, even though the car was designed to appeal to young singles or older empty-nesters. That led the agency to create a campaign that positioned the Altima as a luxury car at a midsize price, acting as a bridge between what these people would ideally like to have and what they could afford.[9]

About 40 agencies now use account planners, including large shops such as FCB. One of the attractions of this new position is that it

EXHIBIT 2–14   Key Functions of Research

Research Department

- **Understands the wants, desires, thoughts, concerns, motivating forces, and ideals of the consumer.**

- **Becomes an expert on consumer behavior.**

- **Researches secondary data and conducts focus groups and one-on-one interviews.**

- **Tests consumer reactions to new advertising copy, tracks sales volume, and studies buying trends.**

- **Acts as an advisor to the account, creative, and media departments for specific accounts.**

- **Helps develop, refine, and evaluate potential strategies, and assists in the creative process by providing insight on the consumer.**

- **Oversees "out-of-house" research firms who handle specialized survey situations such as shopping mall sampling.**

can replace more expensive research departments, combining the roles of the consumer researcher with the account executive. In addition, those who advocate account planning claim that it brings research closer to the creative product. Although a few large agencies have adopted this approach, it is far more prevalent among small or medium-size shops. These include Mullen Advertising in Massachusetts; Weiss, Whitten, Stagliano in New York; and Goodby Silverstein in San Francisco. "Consumer Insight: Getting Mileage from Milk" (page 39) offers a terrific example of the added assistance an account planner can offer.

MEDIA   As ads are being developed or concepts are tested with consumers, the people working in the media department determine where and when those messages should be placed. In the past, with relatively few media options available (radio, TV, magazines, and newspapers), media's role was fairly straightforward: Find the most appropriate medium in which to deliver the message, and then choose from the limited number of programs or titles within that medium to find the one(s) most appropriate for the target audience.

Today, the world has changed. Instead of three major broadcast television networks from which to choose, there are now at least 50 different broadcast and cable networks, plus numerous independent stations. Instead of a few hundred magazines, there are now thousands, with scores of new ones appearing each year. These changes make the tasks of the media department more challenging; indeed, media is now considered to be the "second creative department" in many agencies.

There are two main functions in media: planning and buying. **Media planners** put together a schedule of different media vehicles (programs, magazines, etc.), deciding which ones will best reach the target audience and at what cost. Once the plan receives client approval, it is then executed by the **media buyers,** who negotiate with the media themselves for space and time. Both groups work to determine which media will be most effective at delivering the brand's message and at what cost. Some agencies also employ **media researchers,** who help planners and buyers better understand how people use media. Exhibit 2–15 summarizes the key functions of the media department.

EXHIBIT 2-15   Key Media Functions

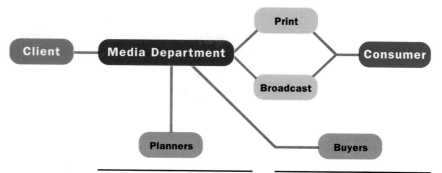

- Discusses the goals of the marketing strategy with the client and agency departments.
- Identifies the potential consumer with the client.
- Considers the types of media used by the target audience.
- Compares various media in order to determine which may be the most effective outlet to the audience.
- Makes recommendations to the creative department and account team regarding the most effective media choices.

- Negotiates print time and advertising space.
- Purchases space in which to display the advertiser's message.
- Negotiates the best price for the advertiser's dollar.
- Monitors the media to make sure that the advertising actually appears in the proper form and at the specified time.

Media Planners.   It is the task of media planners to focus on the media habits and activities of the target to whom the ads are being addressed. Very often that target is determined by the planner, in conjunction with account managers at the agency and brand managers at the client. Once the audience is agreed upon, the planners then have to find out which media forms are preferred by those people. Planners ask questions such as, Does the target audience watch many hours of television, or prefer reading magazines? Which TV shows are preferred, and how many of the target group watches those particular programs? After evaluating the various media alternatives, the media planners come up with a recommendation of which media to use. In addition, the plan recommends how to schedule the media, showing when to use different forms, and for how long. The options are then discussed, first within the agency and then with the client.

Media Buyers. After a plan has received client approval, the media buyers negotiate space in printed media (newspapers and magazines) or time in broadcast media (television and radio). They look for the best rates available to stretch the client's dollar the farthest. After the buy has been made, media buyers are responsible for ensuring that the ads appear when and where they are scheduled. On the occasions that an ad does not appear, the buyers negotiate compensation with the media.

Within the media buying group is another sub-department called *media business services.* This group provides the accounting portion of the media process. It is here that bills are processed and invoices are paid. The people in this unit must ensure that the media are paid for all ads that appear and that the client is billed appropriately for that space and time.

Media Research. A third unit sometimes found within an agency is the media research department. This is a support group for the media planners and buyers (as well as the rest of the agency) that helps answer questions that pertain to how people use media. These questions may be as general as, Are people watching less television? or Do people use coupons placed in magazines? Media research also answers more specific questions, such as, Should I place most of my dollars into the first four weeks of my schedule on cable television, or should I put them into the second four weeks on broadcast TV? Media researchers are involved both in conducting original (primary) research that they undertake themselves, such as a survey or experiment, and in analyzing existing (secondary) data, such as numbers on how many people are watching "E.R." in Las Vegas or how many copies of *Good Housekeeping* magazine are distributed each month. In smaller or midsize agencies, the role of media research is often designated to a media planner.

Specialized Agencies

The traditional ad agency is less and less common, with new forms and organizations being developed almost weekly. There are agencies, for example, that focus on the Hispanic market, while others target African Americans or Asians. Other forms of specialization include high-tech agencies whose primary purpose is to develop advertising messages for companies that appear in some kind of computerized format, whether that means on an online service such as America Online, as a home page on the World Wide Web, or in a kiosk or compact disc. There are also agencies that focus on targeting people directly, through the mail or by telephone or in-person (direct response), and others whose primary business is getting their clients into directories, such as the Yellow Pages. Let's look at some of these specialized agency types.

INTEGRATED MARKETING AGENCIES Some agencies are expanding their scope of activities by involvement in other marketing communications activities, including sales promotions, direct marketing, public relations, or event marketing. These agencies are known as **integrated marketing agencies.** Moreover, agencies that formerly specialized in one of those marketing communication functions are also branching out into others. For example, Frankel & Co., a Chicago-based sales promotion agency, now produces direct-response pieces for clients such as Visa, United Airlines, and Kodak. Rapp Collins, which began as a direct response agency, also handles public relations events for some of its clients, including Bristol-Myers, Gerber, Conde Nast Publications, Delta Airlines, and Hyatt Hotels. Manning, Selvage and Lee, formerly one of the largest public relations agencies, now offers its clients a full array of services, including advertising, sales promotion, and direct response. Exhibit 2–16 shows a list of the top 25 integrated marketing agencies.

REGIONAL AND LOCAL AGENCIES Advertising is not uniquely a big-city phenomenon. Local agencies serve an important purpose in the ad industry, helping small and medium-sized local businesses reach their customers in towns and cities across America. Mark IV Advertising, Inc., in Peoria, Illinois, for example, lists among its clients Caterpillar, a heavy equipment manufacturer located in that city; The Spreader Company, which makes combine attachments; and Hypac, another construction equipment firm in nearby Kewanee, Illinois.

MIDSIZE AGENCIES In between the large and small agencies, there are numerous

EXHIBIT 2–16   The Top 25 Integrated Marketing Communications Agencies

RANK	AGENCY	COMBINED U.S. REVENUE	REVENUE FROM SALES PROMOTION	REVENUE FROM DIRECT RESPONSE
1	Gage Marketing Group	$108,515	$86,812	$21,703
2	Wunderman Cato Johnson	101,007	20,765	80,242
3	Alcone Marketing Group	84,326	80,110	4,216
4	Rapp Collins Worldwide	80,088	—	80,088
5	Bronner Slosberg Humphrey	67,495	—	67,495
6	DIMAC Direct	64,706	—	64,706
7	Ogilvy & Mather Direct	52,000	—	52,000
8	DraftDirect Worldwide	51,688	—	51,688
9	Barry Blau & Partners	49,873	—	49,873
10	Frankel & Co.	47,507	47,507	—
11	Clarion Marketing & Communications	35,005	18,653	16,352
12	Customer Development Corp.	34,387	—	34,387
13	Ross Roy Communications	32,532	20,740	11,792
14	Marketing Corp. of America	31,507	31,192	315
15	Ryan Partnership	29,107	27,361	1,746
16	C-E Communications	28,029	7,007	21,022
17	The Integer Group	27,956	27,956	—
18	Grey Direct Marketing Group	27,915	—	27,915
19	Howard Marlboro Group Worldwide (HMG)	27,800	27,800	—
20	IMPACT	25,500	25,500	—
21	Devon Direct Marketing & Advertising	25,100	—	25,100
22	Targetbase Marketing	24,905	—	24,905
23	D. L. Blair Inc.	24,563	21,370	3,193
24	QLM Marketing	22,780	20,046	2,734
25	FCB Direct	20,400	—	20,400

Notes: Data presented are for calendar year 1995. Figures are in thousands of U.S. dollars.
Figures represent returns only from the U.S. and include internal operations.
Source: Kenneth Wylie, "Marketing Series," Special Report, *Advertising Age,* 5 August 1996, 51.

medium-sized shops that may serve smaller national advertisers or the local businesses in a region. Examples include Valentine Radford, located in Kansas City, whose clients include Ambassador Greetings Cards, Burroughs Wellcome, and Fedex; San Francisco's Goldberg Moser O'Neill, which services companies such as Dell Computer, C&H Sugar, and Kia Motors; and Davis Harrison Dion in Chicago, whose local client list includes Abbott

Laboratories, Chicago Board of Trade, and Pinnacle Bank.

Increasingly, many of these midsize agencies are being purchased either wholly or in part by the larger, New York-based companies to give them greater leverage with one or more of their clients. Omnicom, DDB Needham's parent company, took a 5 percent stake in Fahlgren, a West Virginia agency that happens to have some of the regional McDonald's restaurant operators' business, part of which DDB Needham has at the national level. Interpublic, another holding company, owns Dailey & Associates, a midsize Los Angeles agency, along with Long Haymes Carr in Winston-Salem, North Carolina, which does work with Sara Lee, a client shared by a bigger Interpublic agency, Lintas.

Midsize agencies often find themselves caught in a bind. On the one hand, they can be successful serving midsize companies that feel they would be swallowed up or ignored at a larger agency, where much of the focus is on the "big guys." On the other hand, there are only so many mid-range accounts available. In addition, the lure of the financial security and overall resources of a large parent company are very attractive. That is why agencies such as Bayer Bess Vanderwarker sold out to True North Communications (parent of Foote Cone and Belding), and Griffin Bacal, Inc., became part of DDB Needham Worldwide (itself part of the giant holding company, Omnicom).

NICHE UNITS Another tactic taken by some agencies is to establish smaller, *niche units* within the larger organization. These may specialize in a given area of marketing, such as sales promotions, direct response, or recruitment advertising. Agencies are separating out some of their mainline services as separate entities, sometimes joining forces with competing agencies to serve just one client. For example, True North established the Campbell Media Alliance in 1994 as a media planning, buying, and research unit for Campbell Soup. To form the alliance, employees were taken from all of Campbell's agencies. Similarly, DDB Needham's Team Frito Lay unit, located in Dallas, was designed to serve that client's media needs.

ETHNIC AGENCIES As the U.S. population becomes more and more diverse in its ethnic

> **Loeffler Ketchum Mountjoy (LKM) is a midsized advertising agency based in North Carolina. LKM's accounts include national clients, such as Mannington Floors, Verbatim, and North Carolina Tourism, and local clients, such as the North Carolina Zoo.**

Row,

Row,

Row

your boat

pathetically

whimpering

like a

little weenie

down the

stream.

WHITEWATER IN
NORTH CAROLINA.
1-800-VISIT-NC

CONSUMER INSIGHT

∙∙∙∙∙∙∙∙∙∙∙∙∙∙∙∙∙∙∙∙∙∙∙∙∙∙∙∙∙∙∙

Getting Mileage from Milk

The value of account planning was demonstrated in 1995 in a campaign devised for the California Milk Processors Advisory Board. The problem faced by this generic marketing group was that milk consumption in California had been declining each year from 1980 to 1993 due to increased soft drink consumption and a lack of marketing support. Previous advertising efforts based on a "good for you" strategy had failed to stem the decline.

What the agency discovered from consumer research proved to be crucial to the new campaign. They found that almost 90 percent of milk consumption took place in the home, much of it with a select number of foods (cookies, cereal, etc.). That was the traditional research finding. The account planners then took it one step further—to get inside consumers' minds. They asked a group of people to refrain from using milk for a week, and to keep a diary of all the food and drink they consumed during that time. At the end of the research, they brought the people in for questioning. As the account planners expected, people did not realize how much they missed drinking or using milk until they didn't have any.

The television ads that were subsequently developed stemmed from this discovery, reminding people with the simple tagline "Got Milk?" to check if they had milk in their own refrigerators, and giving them appealing visual ideas of what to eat with it. Radio and outdoor were used to remind them to pick up the milk at the store. Promotional messages in the store also helped.

The results? From 1993 to 1995, milk consumption increased—going up the first year, holding steady the next, and continuing to grow in 1996. And in tribute to the campaign's success in California, it was licensed nationally by dairy producers. All of this came from understanding what was going on in consumers' minds, and translating that into effective and creative communication.

QUESTIONS
How did the addition of account planners help the agency create a better campaign for the California Milk Processors Advisory Board? How else might an account planner contribute to a consumer-focused campaign?

Source: "Got Milk?" Special Planning Section, *Adweek*, 5 August 1996, 6.

The unique research efforts of agency account planners provided the creative spark for the overwhelmingly successful Got Milk? campaign developed for the California Milk Processors Advisory Board.

got milk?

makeup, and as we more readily recognize this diversity, more agencies are specializing in creating advertising for one or more ethnic groups. The two largest of these are ethnic agencies that specialize in advertising for the Hispanic and African American markets, both of which represent sizable segments of the U.S. buying population (10 percent and 12 percent, respectively). The third-largest ethnic group is the Asian American market, which currently represents about 3 percent of the total population but is growing rapidly.

Exhibit 2–17 provides an example of an ad developed by one of these ethnic agencies, Lezcano Associates, in Miami. Notice that this Spanish-language ad for the Chevrolet Cavalier focuses on the importance of safety for one's

family, a topic of particular interest to Hispanic consumers.

There are also agencies that work primarily with one or more *special markets*. Biggs Gilmore Communications, in Kalamazoo, Michigan, for example, focuses on the farm market, while Roberts & Raymond Associates, in Bala Cynwyd, Pennsylvania, deals primarily with business-to-business advertisers.

The debate continues over whether it is better to use a general market or special market shop to reach specific consumers. General market agencies argue that their broader knowledge of the overall marketplace, combined with their larger resources and, in some cases, greater expertise in consumer behavior, means they can handle campaigns designed to reach Hispanic consumers or farmers just as well as a mainstream campaign. In other words, they claim Hispanics or African Americans or businesspeople are simply another type of target audience. In contrast, special market agencies argue that they have the cultural expertise and background that are essential to successful communications with special markets. Exhibit 2–18 provides examples of ads designed to reach two special markets: businesses and disabled people.

CREATIVE BOUTIQUES One outcome of the periodic mergers and acquisitions trends in the advertising industry is the decision by some individuals to break away from their corporate parents and set up their own small shops, known as **creative boutiques**. Frequently, these smaller agencies focus on the creative aspect of the advertising process and consist solely of writers, art directors, and producers. If they are successful, they may gradually expand their repertoire of services until they grow bigger and find themselves buying out or being purchased by other large agencies, thus perpetuating the cycle. Creative boutiques offer advertisers the benefit of a specialized focus on developing creative ideas, but they lack all of the resources and the ability to pull ideas from various disciplines that a full-service agency can provide. In the 1990s, some of the "hot" creative shops included Goodby, Silverstein and Partners (now a unit of Omnicom) in San Francisco; Deutsch, Inc., in New York; and Wieden & Kennedy, in Portland, Oregon.

MEDIA BUYING SERVICES   If an advertiser uses a creative boutique to develop its messages, then it still needs to find a way to get those messages placed in media. This responsibility often gets placed in the hands of a **media buying service,** whose primary purpose is to manage the media buys of advertisers (although some will also create and execute the plans). Media buying services operate just like the very first advertising agents in that they purchase large quantities of advertising space or time on behalf of several clients. By buying in such quantities, they can negotiate large discounts that they can then pass along to their clients, taking a commission or charging a fee for so doing. They also claim greater expertise in media buying because that is their main focus. For smaller advertisers, media buying services offer greater negotiating power than they could find on their own. For larger companies, the services may bring greater cost efficiencies if their goal is the least-expensive space or time available.

The growth of media buying services in the U.S. in the 1990s was considerable, as adver-tis-ers looked for ways to cut down their media expenses. This, in turn, led several major agencies to spin off their media departments as separate operations, working for the agency's clients but also able to solicit independent business on their own. For example, Bozell created BJKE Media; Foote Cone & Belding established True North Media; and Cordiant (formerly Saatchi & Saatchi) set up Zenith Media as a self-sufficient media unit within the company.

This development follows the pattern of what had already taken place in Europe, where media buying services account for more than half of all media dollars placed. In several European countries, competing agencies have joined forces in a given buying operation to give themselves greater negotiating power in the marketplace. Two of the biggest such services are Zenith Media, mentioned above, and Carat Espace, a French company. Both have stated their intentions to expand in the U.S., though it remains to be seen how much impact they will have in the U.S. media marketplace.

IN-HOUSE AGENCIES   The creation of **in-house advertising agencies** was popular during the 1960s and 1970s as part of an effort to save costs and commissions. Companies such as Revlon, Nabisco, and Bristol-Myers all de-

EXHIBIT 2–18   Using their in-depth knowledge of specific consumer groups, special market advertisers create clearly targeted product messages. Businesspeople, such as the engineers targeted by Philips Electronics, and disabled individuals, the target of the General Motors ad, are only two of the many groups on which special market advertisers focus.

veloped their own advertising without the use of external ad agencies. Such operations may cost the company less than hiring outside experts and may be a potential profit center if they also do work for other companies. However, in-house agencies may bring additional problems of their own. One such problem may be lack of initiative or risk taking. Because the in-house operation works for the advertiser, it does not have to worry constantly about possible competitors taking away its business. Its

---

EXHIBIT 2–19   Methods of Agency Payment

TRADITIONAL MEDIA COMMISSIONS

What are media commissions?
Media commissions are rebates offered by media to advertising agencies that place advertisements or commercials with the media. Commissions are typically 15 percent.

How are commissions calculated?
The cost of media placement is multiplied by 17.65 percent. This amount is added to the net cost of media placement in the client's bill. For example, if an advertising page costs $1,000, the client is billed $1,176.50 [= $1,000 + (.1765 X $1,000)]. If you calculate the gross bill to the client, you'll see that the commission, $176.50, is 15 percent of the total bill ($176.50/$1,176.50 = 15 percent).

FEE-BASED COMPENSATION

What are agency fees?
Agency fees are charges to a client that are based on hourly rates of production, plus overhead costs for an advertising agency.

How are agency fees calculated?
Agency fees are established for creative and administrative services. They reflect the salaries of agency personnel, the number of administrative personnel, and the facilities offered to the client. Because agencies are highly competitive, the fees also reflect the nature of competition for a client's work. Fees may be estimated on a project basis, or they may be standardized for continuing client relationships.

MARKUPS OR COST-PLUS AGENCY CHARGES

What are agency markups or charges?
Markups, or cost-plus fees, are standardized fees added to the cost of services that an advertising agency has purchased for a client, such as printing of a client's brochures, or duplication charges for videotapes.

How are markups calculated?
Some agencies use the agency commission percentages to add markups to services purchased from outside suppliers. In other cases, the percentage for marking up services is negotiated by the advertiser and client.

---

budget is fairly secure, too, coming from its own management. This gives the in-house agency less incentive to look for cost savings or innovative means of communication.

A second problem may be an inability to keep up with the marketplace. By focusing primarily on the advertiser's own brands, in-house agencies may be weaker than external agencies because they are less attuned to marketplace changes. They are not able to be as objective as an outside agency, tending to believe instead that whatever the company is doing must be correct. This can lead to a dangerous situation in which the in-house agency fails to notice a new competitor, for example, or to realize that its creative is losing its effect among consumers. While an external ad agency can also be faulted for such short-sightedness or failings, it always stands to lose the business and is therefore more likely to try to stay on top of the situation.

Agency Compensation

From the time NW Ayer established the open contract system and commissions became the traditional method of agency compensation, attempts have been made to change that system to one that is considered more equitable. Today, although the standard 15 percent media commission is the exception rather than the rule, the practice of media commissions has not yet disappeared altogether. A 1995 study by the Association of National Advertisers (ANA) found that only 14 percent of advertisers still use that exact method of payment, although more than half (59 percent) use a variation on it.

In addition to media commissions, agencies can also be paid by way of agency fees or markups. Each of these compensation methods is examined below and is summarized in Exhibit 2–19.

The traditional **media commission** system is fairly straightforward. The agency buys time or space in the media for the advertiser and charges the advertiser the full cost of that time or space. This is known as the *net cost.* The agency then adds a commission rate of 17.65 percent. When the commission and net cost are added together, the sum is the *gross cost.* For example, let's say the cost of a one-page ad in *Cosmopolitan* magazine is $100,000. The agency actually pays $85,000 to the magazine, which is the net cost. That is, it is the gross cost minus 15 percent of the cost ($100,000 − $15,000 = $85,000). The agency then charges the advertiser the net cost of $85,000 and adds on an additional 17.65% commission rate, which brings the total back up to $100,000 ($85,000 + ($85,000 × 17.65%) = $100,000).

The advantage for the advertiser is that it receives the media time or space at a lower rate than if it dealt directly with the media. The drawback, from the advertiser's perspective, is that there is no incentive for the agency to find the lowest cost alternative. Indeed, you might argue that it is in the agency's interest to spend as much of the client's money as possible in media in order to increase the amount generated in commissions. The system is not wholly beneficial to the agency either. If the advertiser demands frequent changes in the advertising copy, that involves increased production costs, and the agency may have to absorb those costs and not make money on the commissions.

Under a **fee-based compensation,** the agency and advertiser agree in advance on how much the agency will receive for the year for working for the advertiser. The fee is usually based on the time involved in producing the ad campaign. This system is considered fairer to both sides for two reasons: (1) It does not reward the agency for spending more money in media, and (2) it does not let the advertiser make unjust production demands on the agency without payment. The chief drawback of this system is that the agency receives no greater compensation if the campaign is highly successful (and profitable) than if it has only moderate success. In addition, it is a fairly expensive system to administer. Because everyone's time must be accounted for, detailed records have to be kept by all those involved on the advertiser's business to ensure that the requisite number of hours are adhered to. It is sometimes difficult for an agency to make money on an account that uses this method of compensation because it is hard to tell a client that you will not work any hours over and above the specified amount—yet in doing so, you are in fact working without pay (or income).

The **mark-up compensation** method is commonly used with smaller advertisers or those who work with an agency on a project basis. Here, the advertiser is charged on a percentage basis for products or services that the agency buys or undertakes for the advertiser. This consists of either a set mark-up charge added to every element or a range of charges, consisting of the net cost plus an additional amount to cover the agency's costs (labor, materials, etc.).

The reality is that a combination of methods is used at many agencies. Some advertisers pay the traditional 15 percent commission; others pay a sliding-scale commission (15 percent on the first $20 million in billings; 12 percent on the next $20 million; and 10 percent thereafter). Some clients pay set fees, or fees plus a mark-up for individual agency services. As advertisers look for more and more ways to keep their costs down, the traditional media commission system will likely fall further and further into disuse.

R E S E T

1. What are the differences between someone working as an account executive and a person who is an account planner? What are the similarities in their roles?
2. What kinds of specialized agencies are there? What are the advantages and disadvantages of each type?
3. How do agencies get paid? How has that changed in the past 10–15 years?

Advertiser–Agency Relationships

The working relationships of advertiser and agency are similar to a marriage. They require trust, openness, and honesty to work well, and they can founder when there is suspicion, discord, or animosity between the two sides. As both agencies and advertisers have grown bigger, each group has voiced complaints that the other party has grown too impersonal or bureaucratic or unresponsive. These generalizations are hard to substantiate, however; while some advertiser–agency relationships have lasted as little as 3 months, many others have gone on for 50 years or more. Exhibit 2–20 lists some of the better-known long-standing relationships between advertiser and agency.

EXHIBIT 2–20   Long-standing Ad–Agency Relationships

LENGTH OF RELATIONSHIP	ADVERTISER	AGENCY
92 years	Unilever	J. Walter Thompson
87 years	Sunkist Growers	Foote, Cone & Belding
82 years	Exxon Corp.	McCann-Erickson
81 years	Hammermill Papers	BBDO Worldwide
66 years	Levi Strauss & Co.	Foote, Cone & Belding
42 years	Marlboro	Leo Burnett Company

Source: Ira Teinowitz, "Why A-B Bounced Bud," *Advertising Age,* 21 November 1994, 1, 8; and Mark Gleason and Laura Petrecca, "Split Decision Grows as Advertisers Seek Edge," *Advertising Age,* 11 November 1996, 20.

But as you saw at the start of this chapter, long-term relationships are becoming far less common. The reasons for breakups between advertiser and agency are many. Sometimes an advertiser has worked with several agencies and found that some are more responsive and creative than others, so it drops the one it finds less effective and reassigns the business to one of the remaining shops. Or it may decide to sever ties with its agency and put the account under **review,** asking several agencies to put a presentation together to solicit the piece of business. This solicitation for business is known as a **pitch.** Occasionally, the current agency is asked to be part of that review, as was the case for Leo Burnett and United Airlines, but it is quite uncommon for an agency to hold onto a piece of business that goes under review.

Less frequently, it is the agency that decides it no longer wishes to work for a particular advertiser. This may occur if the working relationship has deteriorated to the point where it is no longer feasible, or if the compensation received is not acceptable to the agency. In another scenario, an agency will drop an advertiser if it wishes to go after a competing account, such as another brand in the same category. In recent years, the problem of conflicting accounts has grown in the U.S. In this country, advertisers do not like their agencies to work on any business that they perceive to be a competitive threat to their own. They consider it a conflict of interest, as well as a security problem, to let the agency handle sensitive,

proprietary advertiser information. This seems to be less of a concern elsewhere in the world, where agencies may handle brands in different categories even if the parent companies consider themselves competitors.

As both agencies and advertisers expand their reaches, it is almost inevitable that one branch of an agency will end up working on an account in the same industry as that of another branch. Young & Rubicam, for example, does work for both Colgate-Palmolive and Johnson & Johnson in its different worldwide offices. Because both companies manufacture oral care products, a potential conflict would exist if, for example, Colgate decided to introduce a mouthwash into the South American markets where Y&R does the advertising for Johnson & Johnson.

Agencies spend a good deal of time, effort, and money soliciting new business. They may do so by direct contact with advertisers who have publicly acknowledged that they are searching for a new agency for a given brand or brands. Or they may work behind the scenes to develop relationships with key personnel at an advertiser to exhibit their interest in working for that company. Often, a small project conducted either openly or in secret can turn into a new account for the agency. This was the case for Leo Burnett Company, which after working on a piece of the Reebok business, went on to win the worldwide account (although it later resigned the account).

When advertisers ask agencies to participate in a review, they usually ask the agencies to put together a speculative advertising plan, or a **plan on spec.** This means that the agency has to create the plan for free, or with only minimal expenses paid for by the advertiser. While the cost of the preparation may be small compared to the size of the account, some agencies decline to participate if they feel the costs involved are too high compared to their chances of winning the business. Ammirati & Puris, for example, spent an estimated $250,000 to win the creative portion of the Burger King account. The new client compensated the agency about $100,000.[8] Agencies that tried to win the business of Kmart were thought to have spent up to $1.5 million each to obtain the $175 million piece of business.[9]

More and more, advertisers are turning to special consultants to help select their agency partners. These people find out from the company what their needs and preferences are, and then listen to the agency presentations (along with the prospective clients) and advise them on who they believe would be the best match. Consultants maintain that they help make the search process easier, while their critics say they get in the way of a free exchange of ideas and information.

As you saw at the start of the chapter, the advertiser–agency relationship is not as stable today as in the past. One reason behind this is the flurry of mergers and acquisitions that started in the mid-1980s and continues still. Such changes of ownership often result in cut-backs in advertiser spending or agency size. Saatchi & Saatchi, a U.K.–based agency, pur-chased the Ted Bates Agency, Compton World-wide, Dancer Fitzgerald Sample, Backer & Spielvogel, and several smaller shops to create the world's largest agency group, called Cor-diant. It was soon followed by Martin Sorrell's WPP Corporation, which purchased J. Walter Thompson and Ogilvy & Mather. Doyle Dane Bernbach merged with Needham Harper Worldwide to form DDB Needham World-wide, which then, in turn, linked with BBDO under the corporate umbrella of Omnicom. In 1997, in a reversal of that trend, Cordiant was divided again into two separate entities, the Saatchi & Saatchi agency network and the Bates agency network.

On the advertiser side, Philip Morris Com-panies purchased Kraft General Foods (itself the product of the merger of Kraft and General Foods), while R.J. Reynolds bought out Nabisco, to become RJR Nabisco. In 1995, the British pharmaceutical giant, Glaxo, bought out Wellcome to create one of the largest pharma-ceutical companies in the world. Bayer Group, a German company, renamed the U.S. business that had been called Miles and, between 1995–1997, spent $60 million in advertising and promotions to announce the new name to the public. Federated Department Stores now owns Abraham & Straus, R. H. Macy's, Bloom-ingdale's, and Bon Marché. Whenever these kinds of changes take place, it is fairly certain that the advertising, and the advertiser–agency relationship, will be affected too.

The Media: Who They Are, What They Do

Once the advertiser and agency have formed a partnership and worked together to come up with a planned campaign, the ads must then be placed in the media chosen to reach the desired target audience. The role of the **media** is not simply to carry advertising messages to the

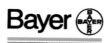

After all these years, we think it's time you called us by our first name:

Bayer

On April 3, Miles becomes Bayer.

You know us as Miles, one of America's largest companies. But in nearly 150 countries, our name is Bayer. Bayer is one of the biggest health care, chemical and imaging technology companies in the world. As such, we've been helping improve people's lives for over a century.

You already know Bayer for aspirin. What you might not know is that our worldwide leadership extends to such diverse fields as pharmaceuticals, diagnostics, imaging systems, crop protection, animal health, fibers, plastics, rubber and coatings. And that results in the creation of over 10,000 products.

You've known us as Miles. Now, as you come to know us as Bayer, we hope you'll realize that we're more than an aspirin company. At Bayer, we cure more headaches than you think.

When it renamed the U.S. busi-ness known as Miles, the Bayer Group spent $60 million on ads and promotions to an-nounce the new name to the public.

reading or viewing or listening public. Its purpose, from a consumer standpoint, is to inform and entertain people with its programming or editorial material.

Most media enjoy revenues from two sources. They sell space and time to advertisers, and they sell programs or content to customers (subscribers, viewers, readers, etc.). Of course, not all media accept advertising. In television, the Public Broadcasting Service (PBS) is funded by a combination of government monies and donations. National Public Radio functions similarly in the radio industry. Several print media are ad-free, such as *Consumer Reports* and *Ms* magazine; for different reasons, both rely primarily on subscriptions for their revenues.

Just as advertisers and agencies expanded and consolidated forces in the 1980s and 1990s, so did media companies. Today's 10 largest media companies, shown in Exhibit 2–21, are noteworthy not only for their size—enjoying annual revenues of $300 million or more—but perhaps even more so for their breadth and diversity. It is rare today to find a media company that is focused solely on one media category. Most have spread themselves across at least two, if not more, looking for ways to enhance their media offer-

ings and possibly create synergies among their properties for both advertisers and consumers.

From the advertiser's perspective, the media industry can be divided into two groups that help the advertiser to place the message in the right space or at the right time. These two groups, collectively know as **media suppliers,** consist of media sales and media audience measurement.

Media Sales

Most media that supply advertising space or time, known as **advertising units,** to advertisers and agencies have dedicated sales personnel whose job it is to sell the advertising units at the best possible (highest) price to the buyers. Often, these people are known as **media representatives,** or **reps.** They may work for a particular TV station, such as WABC in New York, or an individual magazine, such as *Redbook.* They also may sell for a larger organization—a TV network such as FOX, or a magazine company such as Hearst, for example.

Media reps' primary responsibility is to sell space or time to advertisers. To do so, they have to respond to the advertisers' (and agencies') requests and concerns. As an illustration, a rep from WNIC radio in Detroit may try to

---

EXHIBIT 2–21   The Top 10 Media Companies

RANK	COMPANY	HEADQUARTERS	TOTAL MEDIA REVENUE	NEWSPAPER REVENUE	MAGAZINE REVENUE	TV & RADIO REVENUE	CABLE TV REVENUE	OTHER MEDIA REVENUE
1	Time Warner	New York	$11,851.1	—	$2,764.1	$87.0	$9,000.0	—
2	Walt Disney Co.	Burbank, CA	6,555.9	$119.0	321.9	4,425.0	1,690.0	—
3	Tele-Communications Inc.	Denver	5,954.0	—	—	—	5,954.0	—
4	NBC TV (General Electric Co.)	Fairfield, CT	5,230.0	—	—	4,940.0	290.0	—
5	CBS Corp.	New York	4,333.5	—	—	4,323.5	10.0	—
6	Gannett Co.	Arlington, VA	4,214.4	3,335.2	—	685.0	194.2	—
7	News Corp.	Sydney	4,005.0	115.0	660.0	2,500.0	20.0	—
8	Advance Publications	Newark, NJ	3,385.0	2,209.0	1,176.0	—	—	$710.0
9	Cox Enterprises	Atlanta	3,075.3	1,033.0	—	582.0	1,460.3	—
10	Knight-Ridder	Miami	2,851.9	2,851.9	—	—	—	—

Notes: Data presented are for calendar year 1996. Figures are in thousands of U.S. dollars.
Source: "100 Leading Media Companies," *Advertising Age,* 18 August 1997, s4.

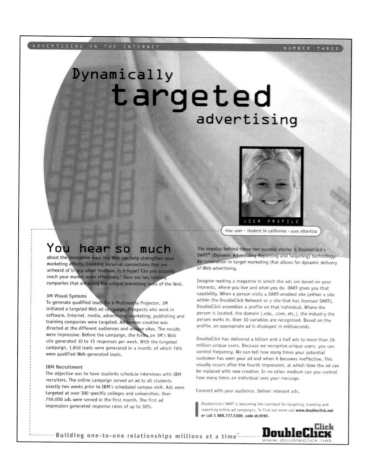

convince Ameritech Corporation that her station can do a better job of reaching adults interested in purchasing cellular phone service from the company, and that it is a superior and more efficient buy than the other Adult Contemporary radio stations in that market. Similarly, the sales rep for *Seventeen* magazine may have to convince the people at Procter & Gamble that his magazine is a more appropriate venue for reaching teenagers who might buy P&G's Cover Girl cosmetics than are *YM* or *Mademoiselle* magazines.

In order to persuade advertisers to buy space or time in their media company, rep firms spend considerable money promoting themselves to others in the advertising industry through their own advertising, known as **trade ads.** Two examples of trade ads are shown in Exhibit 2–22. Rep firms may produce ads for industry trade journals such as *Adweek* or *Advertising Age,* or they may conduct special presentations at agencies that handle the key accounts of advertisers that would be appropriate for their media vehicle.

In an increasingly complex and integrated marketing world, media reps compete not only

against others in their particular field but also against other media and marketing alternatives. For example, a sales rep for Outdoor Systems who sells outdoor billboards may find himself competing with the CNN Airport Network at airports or signage at baseball stadiums, rather than another outdoor company, when he tries to convince Motorola and its agency to buy space on his boards. Similarly, the rep for the *Boston Globe* may have to prove her newspaper's ad effectiveness compared to in-store coupons from Actmedia or electronic online services such as America Online.

The organization of the media sales force varies by company. At some larger organizations, the rep may be responsible for a particular advertising category, such as automotive or fashion, while at other places, he or she may represent the overall title or station or network and try to generate sales across all categories. Sales reps are usually assigned to particular accounts; again, account designations may be made according to advertiser or agency, or by brand, which mixes advertiser and agency.

The sales rep's main goal should be to help advertisers and agencies solve their marketing

EXHIBIT 2-22 Trade ads are one tool used by media reps to convince advertisers of the effectiveness of their media vehicle. As you can see from the ad for DoubleClick touting its Internet services, these ads are not limited to traditional media such as print or television.

TECHNOLOGY WATCH

Selling on the Information Highway

The door opens into a virtual office. Viewers can look around, meet the people working there, and find out about the products being offered. This is not an actual building, nor is it a traditional television commercial. Instead, it is the Internet site for MCI, the number two long-distance telecommunications company, whose fictional publishing company, "Gramercy Press," was so pop-ular on television that it has been transported into cyberspace for interactive enthusiasts. The online version of the campaign lets users find out more details about networkMCI software, the main sales goal behind the entertaining stories. And users do so without necessarily realizing it—testing out functions such as e-mail while they explore the Gramercy offices. To maintain the "realism" of the fictional company even further, MCI announced it would actually publish stories, essays, or poems submitted to the Press by interested readers.

As more and more companies enter the Information Highway with the aim of selling goods and services to interested consumers, they must develop commercial messages that are different from any created for more traditional media forms. While interactive ads can offer some of the benefits of television, such as sight, sound, and motion, they also allow the "viewer," or user, to become far more actively involved in the message, choosing what he or she wishes to look at (and ignore). If the subject does not look appealing enough, it is easy to click to a different site on the Internet or area of an online service.

Part of the reason for all of the excitement about interactive ads is the potential size of the market. By 1998, it is estimated that 34.6 million people will be subscribing to online

---

problems. He or she also works proactively to present ideas to individual advertisers and agencies on how they can solve a particular marketing problem. For example, *Cooking Light* magazine developed a roadshow that it takes around the country to various malls where it gives cooking demonstrations. Advertisers can co-sponsor the tour. Primary candidates for this program might be companies such as Conagra's Healthy Choice or Nabisco's Snackwells divisions, both of which emphasize their healthier food products. Once an order for co-sponsorship has been taken, the rep works with the production team at the ad agency to get the appropriate creative execution in finished form—well enough in advance of the air or issue date—and checks to see that the ad appears as scheduled (and is paid for).

As explained in "Technology Watch: Selling on the Information Highway," the era of new technology is changing the way that media space and time are being bought and sold.

Media Measurement

The other side of the media industry involves audience and brand measurement. In order for advertisers to determine whether their ad campaigns are working, it is essential that they know who has seen it, how often, and to what effect.

There are two types of measurement: competitive expenditures and audience research. Information on **competitive expenditures** shows how much is being spent on each brand and in which media. **Audience research** is information collected from consumers regarding their media usage patterns, product purchases, and demographic and lifestyle characteristics. Both types of measurement are provided by **syndicated suppliers**, which are companies that collect the expenditure and audience information and then sell it to advertisers, agencies, and media. Suppliers also help interpret the numbers or suggest ways to answer specific questions on how to use the data.

services such as America Online, CompuServe, and Prodigy. On the Internet, a global system that links computers up with each other, there are already up to 20 million people around the world who have access not only to parts of the Library of Congress or electronic versions of newspapers but also to advertisers' "home pages," or areas that provide information and sell products and services. Some of the companies testing the Internet waters for selling purposes include J. C. Penney, Lands' End, Sony, Tower Records, and Victoria's Secret.

There are several differences between traditional mass market advertising (i.e., television or newspapers),

direct marketing (i.e., direct mail), and interactive marketing found on online services. Mass-market media rely on high volume to move vast quantities of goods and services. In contrast, both direct and interactive marketing attempt to target their offerings more narrowly—both in terms of the products offered and the individuals to whom they are offered. Moreover, while mass and direct marketing tend to rely on a fairly passive consumer, in the interactive arena, the user deliberately chooses to look at the commercial message. The worst that can happen with mass media is that the consumer does something else while the message appears, such

as change the TV channel or turn the page. For direct marketers, the worst outcome is the trash can. The biggest challenge to interactive marketers is the "shutdown" button; once the user turns off the computer, there is no opportunity to present the message. To combat that potential threat, interactive advertisers must work hard to provide information in a compelling, yet entertaining fashion.

Ford Motor Company, for example, uses a PC-based program called the Ford Simulator that lets people thinking about buying a new car look at different colors, payment plans, or other options for the full line of 25 cars and light trucks. Thousands of Simulator

diskettes are given out each year, reaching the more affluent and educated type of buyer that Ford wants to persuade to buy its vehicles. Although it does not release statistics on how many of those who have received the diskette have subsequently purchased a car, the company seems to be satisfied enough with the results that they are continuing the program alongside the millions of dollars they spend each year on traditional forms of advertising media.

Source: Adapted from Joel Dreyfuss, "Selling in Cyberspace," *Information Week*, 3 October 1994.

R E S E T

1. Why do advertisers and agencies sever their relationships?
2. What are the main duties of the media sales rep?
3. What kinds of information do media measurement companies provide?

Global Advertising

Recall that the advertising industry is fairly small throughout the world. Although advertisers worldwide spend more than $300 billion on advertising, the number of people involved in handling those ads remains fairly small. Despite that, advertising is increasingly a global industry, for advertisers, agencies, and media alike.

Global Advertisers

The pantheon of companies that advertise throughout the world keeps expanding every year. Coca-Cola introduced a new campaign with polar bears into the U.S. market in the mid-1990s and, based on the bears' popularity, started rolling it out to other markets. IBM took the same approach in the 1980s with its Charlie Chaplin character for its line of personal computers, and it has done so again, more recently, with a global campaign in 47 countries that uses identical visuals but unique subtitles for each country. McDonald's takes a slightly different approach. Each country develops its own ads, but the overall emphasis remains on family and friendship, warmth and fun, and a value-for-money theme. Names such as Coca-Cola, IBM, and McDonald's are as commonplace in Melbourne, Australia, as

EXHIBIT 2–23   Top 10 Global Advertisers

			1995 AD EXPENDITURES		
RANK	ADVERTISER	HEADQUARTERS	AD SPENDING OUTSIDE U.S.	U.S. AD SPENDING	TOTAL AD SPENDING
1	Procter & Gamble Co.	U.S.A.	$2,559.6	$2,777.1	$5,336.7
2	Unilever	Netherlands/UK	2,410.1	858.3	3,268.4
3	Nestlé SA	Switzerland	1,415.8	487.3	1,903.1
4	Toyota Motor Corp.	Japan	1,081.9	733.4	1,815.3
5	PSA Peugeot-Citroen SA	France	881.2	0.0	881.2
6	Nissan Motor Co.	Japan	869.4	466.4	1,335.8
7	Philip Morris Cos.	U.S.A.	835.7	2,576.9	3,412.6
8	General Motors Corp.	U.S.A.	812.5	2,046.9	2,859.4
9	Volkswagen AG	Germany	797.8	135.2	933.0
10	Mars Inc.	U.S.A.	734.9	416.1	1,151.0

Note: all dollars in millions
Source: "Global Marketers," Laurel Wentz and Kevin Brown, *Advertising Age International,* November 1996, I15.

they are in Manchester, England, or Miami, Florida. Increasingly, these international advertisers are looking across borders and oceans for campaigns that they can transport successfully from one country to another. Why are they doing so? In the words of Tom Carey, the president of BBDO North America, "Strategic consistency, speed of learning transfer [and] greater efficiencies."

The chief objective in "going global" is to develop a company or brand personality that is identical throughout the world. Xerox wants to be "The Document Company" in every country in which it operates. Andersen Consulting likes to portray itself as a technology leader in each of its 358 offices in 74 countries. And Mobil Oil hopes to convey an image of dependability and reliability in all of its global locations.

Another key reason for expanding globally is to take advantage of economies of scale. Instead of producing different packages or types of detergent for every market it is in, Unilever has been able to consolidate its detergent business into a reduced number of locations, and distribute the product to all markets from those sites. The cost savings it realizes can then be put back into new-product development, marketing, or other parts of the business.

Sometimes one company will be sold to another in order to compete effectively worldwide. Gerber Products Company was purchased in 1994 by Sandoz Pharmaceuticals, based in Switzerland, in order to become a global player in the baby-food market.

Even advertisers that do not use traditional media strategies are pursuing international business. Avon Products, which relies on door-to-door sales representatives in its U.S. base, is attempting to replicate its American success in emerging markets such as Brazil, China, Mexico, and Poland. It employs 170,000 people in Mexico, for example, 25,000 in Russia and the former Soviet republics, and 25,000 in China to sell its makeup products through home visits and special "showrooms."[10]

Globalization is not just a U.S. phenomenon: Marketers in Europe and Asia/Pacific are moving aggressively onto the North American continent, too. Of course, Japanese car and electronics manufacturers are well known in the U.S. In addition, Swedish firms such as the furniture retailer, Ikea, or the bottled water company, Ramlosa, also are expanding westward across the Atlantic Ocean. Just as U.S. companies are looking abroad for additional sales because domestic markets are saturated, so

One of many media corporations extending their reach into newly emerging world markets, Hearst now publishes its *Cosmopolitan* magazine in 32 different countries.

Jahr was able to take its success in magazines in Germany and transpose that to the U.S. marketplace.

As new markets open up in different areas of the world, the well-established players are likely to move in there. Time Warner is heavily involved in developing cable services in several Eastern European countries. News Corporation has taken stakes in various newspapers in that part of the world. The Mexican media magnate Emilio Azcarraga has moved his company, Televisa, into the rest of Central and South America, transferring his expertise in program production and development to these rapidly expanding television markets.

Beyond the moves of media corporations across borders there are more and more instances of companies taking individual titles, programs, or formats from one location to another. Condé Nast's *Elle* magazine, for example, is now published in 29 countries; and

Hearst publishes (or licenses) its popular *Cosmopolitan* magazine in 32 countries. Sometimes, media that are not popular in the home market do extremely well elsewhere. The U.S. TV show "Baywatch" is now seen in 110 countries and often ranks among the top 10 shows outside of the U.S., even though it was canceled by the U.S. network after only one season. Another popular show, "Wheel of Fortune," is sold by license to 24 different markets so that local talent is used to host the game, but the format remains identical to the American version. In addition to this, the U.S. program is aired in 10 other markets.

Globalization of brands and companies also helps domestic media. In 1994, *Forbes* magazine enjoyed a 46 percent increase in advertising pages from foreign concerns, while its chief competitor, *Fortune,* witnessed a 60 percent increase in ads from Asia and a 12 percent increase in those from Europe.[13]

SUMMARY

The advertising industry is not enormous, but it is extremely varied. The three main components—agencies, advertisers, and media—account for fewer than 500,000 jobs in the U.S., about half of which are held by women. The past few years have seen considerable change occurring in the ad industry, prompted by technological and economic challenges. Both advertisers and agencies have striven for greater efficiency, either through cutbacks or mergers and acquisitions.

Advertisers encompass a wide range of expenditures, from Procter & Gamble's $2.4 billion annual national advertising dollars, to local stores that might spend only a few hundred dollars locally. Advertisers are typically structured so that they have product managers, who have line responsibility for a brand, and other support staff, who do not have that responsibility. The organization of large companies may be either centralized or decentralized. This determines where decisions about advertising are made (at headquarters or locally/regionally). The

brand management system developed in the 1930s has evolved into a category management structure, with senior staff responsible for a complete category—such as cereals, detergents, or pet foods—delegating individual brands to brand managers. Smaller advertisers have simpler and less formal organizations

Advertising agencies, which have been in existence for about a century, offer four basic functions: creative, account management, research, and media. All personnel work together to help clients sell their products. Within the agency, creative personnel work at the heart of the agency, developing the artwork and copy messages to sell the agency's clients' products. The creation of ideas is really the cornerstone of an agency's business. The key function of account management is to handle client relations. That means responding to clients' concerns and representing them within the agency. Ensuring that the message is properly communicated to the target is the job of the research department.

Here, the goal is to learn as much as possible about the prospective consumers for a brand. A newer variant of this role is the account planner, who combines the tasks of the account executive with more research responsibilities. He or she is charged with understanding how consumers will respond to an ad. Where to place the communications to the consumers is the task assigned to the media department, which also purchases space and time from the media and conducts research on how people use media.

More and more, however, agencies are offering more specialized choices to their clients, from integrated marketing activities such as sales promotion, direct response, and public relations, to new, high-tech alternatives, such as online services and Internet pages. Agencies vary greatly in size, from the billion-dollar businesses in New York or Chicago to small and medium-sized shops in Peoria or Kansas City. The physical location of the agency may be less important in the future, as agencies rely on new technologies to conduct business in a "virtual world."

Niche units may be set up to serve particular clients, while ethnic agencies focus on particular population groups. Some agencies focus their efforts on the business-to-business or farm markets. Small creative boutiques concentrate primarily on developing ideas, while media buying services deal mostly with placing advertising dollars in different media forms, generally for the lowest cost. Some advertisers maintain their own in-house agencies, but they run the risks of having less initiative to look for cost savings and of not keeping abreast of marketplace changes by focusing only on the in-house brands.

Agencies used to be compensated by a commission (usually 15 percent). More and more, however, they are being paid either by a fee-based compensation or a mark-up on all products or services that the agency buys or undertakes on behalf of the advertiser. At many agencies, a combination of payments is used, depending on the client or on the billings.

Advertiser–agency relationships can last anywhere from a few months to 50 years or more. The reasons for their demise can vary. Increasingly, client conflicts occur when an agency cannot work on one company's business because another client is involved in the same or related business. That client could be served by another office of the agency either domestically in the U.S. or, more and more, at the international level. As a result of this ever-changing business, agencies are always working to develop new business either from new or existing clients.

The media in which ads are placed enjoy revenues from two sources: advertising and consumers. The latter pay to receive certain media, either through subscriptions or fees. Media salespeople, or representatives, call on advertisers and agencies to persuade them to buy space or time in their media offerings for a particular brand. The media use a large number of trade ads to promote their programs or publications to the advertising industry. Media measurement companies provide data on which media consumers are using, while other suppliers focus on offering competitive expenditures that show where companies are placing their media dollars.

The advertising industry operates on a global level. More and more international advertisers are consolidating their marketing and advertising across markets, looking to develop economies of scale and to create a consistent, identical brand personality worldwide. The consolidation results in agencies gaining global responsibilities for a particular brand. This has led agencies to open up offices or create equity partnerships with local agencies in foreign countries to enable them to serve a client in whichever country it wishes to market its products and services. Not surprisingly, as advertisers and agencies spread their wings around the world, so do the media. More media companies are putting together regional or global packages that allow advertisers to distribute the same message across markets. There is also an increase in the number of local programs or magazines that are being moved across borders, either in identical format or as a license to be developed locally.

advertiser, 23

client, 23

brand management, 27

category management, 27

category manager, 27

advertising agency, 28

open contract rate, 28

full-service agency, 29

creative, 31

copywriter, 31

account manager, 32

researcher, 33

account planner, 34

media planner, 35

media buyer, 35

media researcher, 35

integrated marketing agency, 36

creative boutique, 40

media buying service, 41

in-house advertising agency, 41

media commission, 42

fee-based compensation, 43

mark-up compensation, 43

review, 44

pitch, 44

plan on spec, 44

media, 45

media supplier, 46

advertising unit, 46

media representative (rep), 46

trade ad, 47

competitive expenditure, 48

audience research, 48

syndicated supplier, 48

REVIEW QUESTIONS

1. Who are the four key players in the advertising industry, and what are their roles?

2. Explain the difference between a centralized organizational structure and a decentralized organizational structure. What are the advantages of each structure?

3. What are the four functional areas in the traditional advertising agency hierarchy, and what are the roles of each?

4. What is the role of an account manager? How does this person act as a liason between the advertiser and the agency?

5. What are some of the advantages and disadvantages of ethnic and other special-market agencies?

6. Explain the growth of media buying services both in the U.S. and in Europe.

7. How are advertising agencies compensated?

8. What are some of the reasons advertiser–agency relationships break up?

9. What are the two principal groups of media suppliers, and what does each do?

10. Why do advertisers, agencies, and the media want to "go global"?

1. Make an argument for why each of the key departments in a full-service advertising agency is the most important one in the agency.

2. Given the choice, would you rather hire an outside agency to handle your company's advertising or create an in-house agency? Discuss the pros and cons of each.

3. Devise the "perfect" agency compensation plan.

4. Imagine that you are an advertiser who has worked with the same agency for 25 years. Your company is taken over by new owners who demand that you instigate an agency review. Argue both for and against this idea.

interactive discovery lab

1. Select an advertising agency in your place of residence and find out as much as you can about it. Who are the agency's clients? How much money does the agency make each year? How many people does the agency employ? Put together a one-page sales brochure for the agency that it could use to solicit new business.

2. Go onto the World Wide Web of the Internet and look at the Web sites of five well-known companies or brand names. Compare and contrast the information you find on their sites.

Chapter Three

The Advertising Environment:
Social, Ethical, Economic, and Legal Issues

CALVIN KLEIN:
KING OF CONTROVERSY?

When Calvin Klein introduced a new ad campaign for his brand of jeans in August 1995, he did not expect it to cause the controversy that it did.

Consumers were used to the overt and subtle uses of sexuality in his ads, depicting beautiful men and women in seductive poses, wearing their "Calvins." What consumers objected vigorously to in this new campaign was Klein's use of very-young-looking models displayed in TV commercials, print ads, and on outdoor billboards in the typically suggestive poses of a Klein ad. The waif-like models, dressed in little more than their Calvin Klein clothes, were filmed against a backdrop reminiscent of a pornographic photo studio.

Calvin Klein maintained that this was simply one more attempt to generate interest in his products by the youth who are most likely to buy them. However, the campaign was seen by many in society as crossing over the boundaries of good taste and acceptability. As Bob Garfield, ad critic in *Advertising Age,* noted, "This time he vaulted over the line and beyond the pale—and even he has now discovered there are places you dare not go."

After a barrage of complaints, both in the media and from social and religious organizations, the ads were withdrawn. The advertiser took out a

Calvin Klein Jeans

full-page ad in the *New York Times* to apologize for the "misunderstanding." The case did not stop there, however. The U.S. Department of Justice and the Federal Bureau of Investigation began an inquiry to see if the advertiser broke any federal laws banning pornography by using underage models, a charge that Klein vehemently denied.

Despite all of this, Klein benefited from the free publicity and coverage. As Bob Dilenschneider, chief executive officer of the Dilenschneider Group in New York, commented at the time, the TV spots "did not create a negative image of the product or the designer in the mind of the average consumer. They will only remember his name when they go to the store." The controversy was forgotten by the fall of 1995, but the topic will continue to resurface. Only one year later, the TV networks began talking about creating special "zones" for ads that might offend some people, placing them after 9 P.M. and perhaps charging them more for their riskiness.

Sources: Jennifer DeCoursey, "Klein's Apology Wearing Thin," *Advertising Age,* 4 September 1995, 35; Pat Sloan and Jennifer DeCoursey, "Gov't Hot on Trail of Calvin Klein Ads," *Advertising Age,* 11 September 1995, 1, 9; Stuart Elliott, "Calvin Klein to Withdraw Child Jean Ads," *New York Times,* 29 August 1996, C1, C6; Stuart Elliott, "Will Calvin Klein's Retreat Redraw the Lines of Taste?" *New York Times,* 28 June 1995, C1, C6; and Pat Sloan, "Underwear Ads Caught in Bind over Sex Appeal," *Advertising Age,* 8 July 1996, 27.

LOOK BEFORE YOU LEAP

- Does advertising reflect or shape society?

- How are cultural differences taken into account by advertisers?

- How do you handle the advertising of controversial products such as tobacco or alcohol?

- What role does advertising play in the economy?

- How has advertising been treated by the courts?

- Who regulates advertising, and how?

- How does the advertising industry try to regulate itself in the U.S. and worldwide?

3

What happened to Calvin Klein is a good example of the way that advertising has a profound impact on society. The risqué ads were deemed controversial because some critics feared that they would have a harmful influence on the young people to whom they were targeted. Klein, in his defense, maintained that his images simply reflected how young people today look and behave.

There were strong ethical concerns raised, too, because of the quasi-pornographic look of the ads, using childlike models in various states of undress. The controversy was heightened because of advertising's economic role in society, whether as a market force that changes consumer tastes and establishes brand loyalty, or as a source of information that tells consumers what products and services are available. Finally, Klein's campaign led to threats of legal actions by the Department of Justice.

An examination of all of these issues will help you gain a more complete understanding of how the institution of advertising works within the broader social, ethical, economic, and legal environment. This chapter will explore some of the issues and controversies that surround the advertising industry.

The Social Impact of Advertising

The argument over whether advertising is a *mirror* of society, reflecting people's tastes, habits, and desires, or whether it is a *shaper* of that same society, wielding its influence over what people say, think, and do, has existed for almost as long as the industry itself. As early as 1903, in "The Theory of Advertising," Walter Dill Scott questioned what the impact of advertising on individuals might be. Up until that time, advertising had been thought of primarily as a way for companies to keep their name before the public. But with the publication of Scott's book, the concept of advertising as a tool of persuasion became popular. The new definition of advertising, coined by freelance copywriter John E. Kennedy, in 1904, became "salesmanship in print." From then on, the debate over advertising's benefits and drawbacks within society has continued, with some arguing that advertising simply follows social trends, mirroring in the ads individuals or scenes that reflect the social landscape. Others say advertising's role is more definitive, helping to shape the reality that it depicts. For both sides of that debate, advertising is often considered as one of society's "institutions." Before we discuss the mirror/shaper debate any further, let's take a look at the notion of advertising as an institution.

Advertising As an Institution
Advertising's position as an institution in society can be compared with other institutions, such as marriage, family, school, the law, or the church. One purpose of an institution is to provide information and ways to behave appropriately, structure social life, and embody ideas about society.[1] Each kind of institution may be influential on individuals in different ways. The purpose of school, for example, is to teach, while the purpose of advertising is to inform and persuade. Similarly, the institution of advertising is one way for society to answer the question of how best to inform people about the availability of products and services in the marketplace. Institutions also help order human relationships into roles. Marriage puts people into familial roles, while the church creates religious roles for its participants. Advertising establishes the role of the consumer,

helping him or her to make judgments on which goods and services to use or buy.[2]

Advertising really didn't become an institution until the late nineteenth century, when companies that were producing goods began to brand them to differentiate them from the competition. So instead of just selling crackers, the National Biscuit Company named them "Nabisco" crackers. This also gave greater power to the manufacturers. Consumers started asking for the product by brand name, forcing wholesalers and retailers to buy that particular brand rather than a generic one. Moreover, in focusing on the brand name and what it stood for, the manufacturer could shift the emphasis away from price. Even today, brand-name goods generally will cost you more than a generic version. While some argue that the reason is that you are simply paying for the advertising, others will defend the price differential by saying that the branded item is of better quality and more reliable. When you buy a can of Coca-Cola rather than a generic cola, they say, you are also buying some assurance of its taste and quality.

Some critics argue that advertising exerts social control over consumers without any sense of social responsibility.[3] By promoting certain items as desirable, advertising is creating unnecessary demand among people who may not in fact need or be able to afford them. And in depicting individuals in certain ways in the ads themselves, advertising is providing behavioral norms for how society should act.[4] When teenagers look at cigarette ads showing young adults enjoying themselves in various social situations, the message they may take away is that if they smoke, they also will have fun. So while other institutions, such as the church or marriage or even prisons, are attempting to improve the individual, advertising's main purpose, these critics maintain, is to encourage people simply to spend more money. From this standpoint, advertising "tends less to provide the consumer with what he wants than to make him like what he gets."[5]

Critics of advertising tend to focus on one specific area of the practice or industry, objecting to the institution rather than to individual advertisements.[6] Their criticisms also tend to be specific to their own area of expertise, such as economics, but yet are generalized to cover the whole industry. A sociologist might focus his criticism on how "advertising" impedes social relationships, while an economist will show how "advertising" raises the prices of goods and services. But by stating that "advertising is responsible for x" or "advertising does y," they tar everything with the same brush. They ignore, for example, the public service ads that promote organ donation or the United Negro College Fund. They deny the entertainment value of television commercials or the informational value of newspaper ads. Institutional critics also tend to ignore the economic benefits of advertising. Although Honda Motor Company spends $354 million on advertising each year, that is still less expensive than if the company tried to make a personal sales call on everyone interested in purchasing a new automobile. Finally, such generalized criticisms whitewash one of advertising's most basic functions: helping Joe Smith decide which brand of potato chips to buy.

Advertising as Mirror of Society

Proponents of advertising say advertising mirrors society. Many of their arguments are shown in Exhibit 3–1 and are explored in greater detail below.

ADVERTISING REFLECTS POPULAR CULTURE

Advertising's role as a reflection of popular culture is often seen in the use of topical themes or familiar characters or celebrities. The development of the term "yuppies" in the 1980s and "Generation X" in the 1990s was followed by an influx of characters in advertising who reflected

EXHIBIT 3–1   Advertising as a Mirror of Society

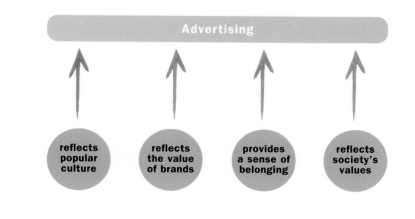

these images. Similarly, Jaclyn Smith's endorsements for Kmart appeal to middle-aged consumers who grew up watching her on the 1970s hit TV series, "Charlie's Angels," and Michael Jordan, the highly popular Chicago Bulls basketball player, endorses everything from Nike shoes to McDonald's, Gatorade, Ballpark Franks, Wheaties, and Chevrolet. In 1995, he earned $38 million from such commercials.[7]

ADVERTISING REFLECTS THE VALUE OF BRANDS Advertising can express the value of a brand among consumers. A dollar value may be placed against the customer "goodwill" for a brand and be made part of the calculation for how much the parent company is worth financially on Wall Street. The $167 million that Gillette spends on advertising its health and beauty aids reflects the value that consumers place on its products.

But it is difficult if not impossible to make a direct relationship between the dollars spent on advertising and how consumers value a brand. While Lexus spent one-fifth of the advertising dollars of Ford in 1993, it was Lexus that ranked higher in customer satisfaction according to the J. D. Power Survey of Potential Car Buyers.[8] Many goods or services advertise very little, if at all, and yet are still highly appreciated and valued by their users. Hospitals typically only spend a few thousand dollars on advertising, yet they are highly valued. In contrast, cable television companies spend a good deal of money on advertising and promotion, but they have low satisfaction ratings.

EXHIBIT 3–2 By focusing on issues, events, or personalities important to a specific consumer group, advertisers attempt to create a sense of direct communication and unity not only with that issue or event but also within that group. These advertisements, one directed to the gay and lesbian community and one directed to the African-American community, are good examples of ads that reflect different cultural or ethnic preferences.

ADVERTISING PROVIDES A SENSE OF BELONGING When Hallmark reminds you to send a Valentine's Day card, "When you care enough to send the very best," your participation in this annual ritual links you to millions of others who are doing the same. Advertising depicts familiar activities or scenes to help consumers feel that they belong to a larger social organization. For example, commercials for Shout stain remover help mothers of young children feel they are not alone in trying to cope with grass or ketchup stains; and Subaru has begun targeting lesbians with creative advertisements designed specifically for that part of the gay market. In each case, the hope is that those individuals will feel that they are being communicated to directly and personally, and will therefore be more likely to consider purchasing from those advertisers.[9]

A sense of belonging is one reason why minority groups argue for specific creative executions for their customers. Major advertisers such as McDonald's and Seagram's have ethnic advertising agencies develop separate ad campaigns to reach African American or Hispanic consumers. These ads show people from those ethnic groups using the product, and they may also reflect different cultural preferences or customs that these minorities will be more likely to recognize and appreciate. Dominick's Finer Foods, a midwestern chain of grocery stores, not only creates ads in Spanish to reach its Hispanic customers, it even shows different cuts of meat in these ads to reflect the pieces that this ethnic group prefers to buy.[10] Two examples of ads that illustrate cultural or ethnic preferences in their messages are shown in Exhibit 3–2.

ADVERTISING REFLECTS SOCIETY'S VALUES Advertising's supporters maintain that the messages it conveys merely reflect the values of society as a whole. In the 1980s, when the United States was enjoying an economic boom and materialistic values became more important, there were numerous ads that focused on having more and buying more. Society's compassionate value is expressed in public service ads that try to raise awareness for some of today's social problems, such as child abuse or AIDS discrimination.

Advertising as Shaper of Society
The critics of the institution of advertising note the ways in which advertising is able to mold society. While they do not claim that advertising is necessarily the sole harmful influence on consumers, they argue that it is powerful enough to give one cause for concern. Their comments often reflect more general dissatisfaction with social values, considering advertising as just one harmful influence among several. Their arguments are summarized in Exhibit 3–3.

EXHIBIT 3–3 Advertising as a Shaper of Society

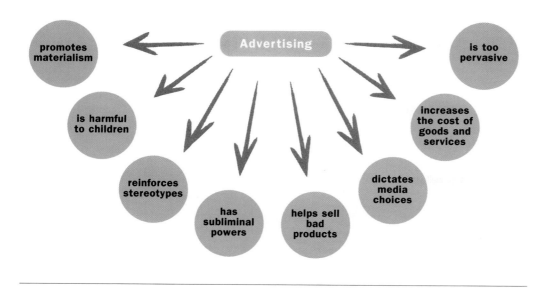

Everyone has something costly hanging round their neck. For the lucky few, it's not a mortgage, school fees or an overdraft.

The estate's all yours. Princeton's paid. The bank manager couldn't be friendlier. So why not visit Asprey? Featured above, an exquisite diamond suite, the necklace of which is set with a heart-shaped emerald in a detachable brooch-pendant. How costly? Well, let's just say the mind's-eye is out of the question. Available from Asprey - Fifth Avenue, New York; Bond Street, London and offices worldwide. For information call 1.800.883.2777 or 44.171.493.6767.

Asprey
LONDON

EXHIBIT 3–4 **This jewelry advertisement is clearly targeted to individuals with a high level of discretionary income. Ads such as this one are seen by some critics as promoting materialism in our society.**

ADVERTISING PROMOTES MATERIALISM

One of the strongest complaints heard about advertising is that it encourages people to buy things they do not need. Do you really have to have a Magnavox TV set or a Motorola cellular phone? Will purchasing Estee Lauder's Alpha Hydroxy Cream really remove all of your wrinkles? Are you an ineffective parent if you do not buy your three-year-old child the Baywatch Barbie doll? This increased materialism further widens the gap between the "haves" and the "have-nots." As society becomes more technologically sophisticated, electronics companies that promote their wide-screen televisions or videogame players as "essential" items for the home may be accused of promoting an unhealthy materialism that will lead lower-income people to spend money on those items

instead of on more essential goods or services such as education or clothing. An example of an ad for a luxury item that is clearly directed to upper-income consumers is shown in Exhibit 3–4.

But one also can argue that advertising is simply part of a market economy and that what these criticisms reflect is a more general dissatisfaction with a capitalist emphasis on materialism. Advertising offers us rewards in the shape of goods and services that we can choose to purchase with our hard-earned money. We are not forced to buy anything we do not want. As Sir Michael Perry, chairman of the global products company Unilever, notes, "It was not the consumers storming the barricades, shouting: 'give us cornflakes!' or 'we demand instant coffee!'" that led to those products being developed. To succeed, companies must find "the competitive edge you achieve by coming up with the better mousetrap, detergent, personal computer, or sports shoe."[11]

ADVERTISING IS HARMFUL TO CHILDREN

Children under the age of seven are too young to make informed purchase decisions or understand the difference between real life and the world depicted in ads. Ads for heavily sugared multicolored cereal puffs encourage children to believe that eating Cocoa Puffs cereal provides a healthy breakfast; dolls that have removable stomachs for holding a baby when "pregnant" lead children to believe that giving birth is as easy as removing one's stomach and taking out the infant; and action figures with guns teach children that weapons are the best way to solve disputes.

Children are exposed to an enormous number of commercials. In 1992, Congress limited the number of ads aired per hour during children's programming.[12] Yet many critics argue that the 10 1/2 minutes per hour limit is still far too high, especially given the large number of hours that the average child sits in front of the television screen (estimated to be about 24 hours per week among children ages 2–11).[13]

While advertising's harmful shaping power over children is fought primarily on television, other media also are considered overly influential in their impact on young audiences. Many localities have restrictions on the types of billboards that can be placed near schools, based on the thought that the large number of alcohol and tobacco advertisers who use the medium should not be allowed to promote their products to children, who cannot legally use them and should not be encouraged to consume them even when they are old enough to do so.

The industry's response to these criticisms is that they are simply targeting appropriate audiences (in the case of children's products) and that for adult-oriented items, they do not wish to encourage irresponsible behavior. There is also a dilemma here for many children's organizations, because advertisers are increasingly willing to provide them with financial support in exchange for promotional opportunities. Several school districts are turning to corporate sponsors to supply them with equipment that their dwindling state or local budgets no longer cover. Products range from serving McDonald's in the school cafeteria, to giving free Nike or Adidas equipment to school sports teams, to selling ads on school buses.[14]

ADVERTISING REINFORCES STEREOTYPES

Advertising can shape society's beliefs by using *stereotypes,* which reduce people or objects into classes based on inferences that are made from an individual or social context. When we say that all professors are absent-minded or that all blondes are dumb, we are simplifying reality by assigning these characteristics to a group of individuals. Many stereotypes prevail about race, age, gender, socioeconomic status, and sexual orientation, among others. For example, studies have shown that when minorities are used in ads, they get stereotyped into roles, such as African American athletes or Asian American engineers.[15]

Advertisers, however, claim that they are merely reflecting society's attitudes towards such groups, or the actual lifestyles of those people. There is considerable evidence to suggest that advertising generally lags behind social trends rather than shapes them. Depictions of working women did not become common in ads until the 1980s, despite the fact that since 1970 half or more of all women ages 18–54 have held full- or part-time employment.[16] Advertising has been slow to include minorities in its commercial messages, although the situation has changed to the point where minorities now may appear as frequently in commercials as they do in real life.[17] However, research has shown that viewers' reactions to racial cues that

Although the number of ads that can run during children's television programming has been limited by Congress, the average child is still exposed to a great number of product messages each day.

appear in advertising can have a definite impact on how people respond to those messages.[18]

Ads may replace one stereotype with another or with unrealistic images. When women were depicted in the workplace in ads in the late 1980s, they were turned into "superwomen" who could not only carry out a full-time job but also have three children, travel on business, and prepare delicious meals in the evening for their loving husbands. Similarly, the increased inclusion of African Americans in ads for luxury cars, computers, or cellular phones may inadvertently suggest that there are more people from this group who are able to afford such products than in fact is the case.

Must advertising depict reality, or can it show a heightened version of that reality? Is it wrong to show the "superwoman" if that is what most women would like to be? By showing people in these situations is advertising inspiring them to achieve those roles, or is it maligning them because they cannot do what the ads suggest—regardless of whether they purchased the advertised product? In addition, because advertising is a form of compressed communication, simplifying a potentially complicated message into 30 seconds or one page, it must reduce that message to its simplest form. This may mean depicting one individual to represent a group, or using one characteristic to signify a personality type.

While stereotyping of one kind or another is almost inevitable, the racial and sexual images that people object to may improve over time. In the 1930s it was not uncommon to see African Americans shown in subservient roles or women in demeaning positions. But as society has changed, so has the advertising that reflects it. Indeed, as the ethnic makeup of the country changes and non-whites represent a larger proportion of the population, more products are being designed specially for them, such as makeup in shades worn by African Americans or foods using spices preferred by Hispanics. Advertising will have to be targeted to a more diverse audience, too. And as women continue to rise through the ranks of corporate America, including the advertising industry, there is hope that ads showing images of women draped over the hoods of cars or running a family and conducting business while working 25 hours a day will disappear.

ADVERTISING HAS SUBLIMINAL POWER

A periodically fashionable criticism made against advertising is that it manages to work at a *subliminal,* or subconscious, level, persuading innocent consumers to purchase goods that they otherwise would not. This was first "discovered" by a marketing researcher, James Vicary. In 1957, he conducted an experiment where the flashing of "Drink Coke" and "Eat Popcorn" messages flashed on a movie screen for 1/3,000 of a second, subliminally suggesting to cinema patrons that they should purchase goods at the concession stand.[19] He eventually confessed the experiment was a hoax. The controversy was resurrected after the publication of several books by Wilson Bryan Key in the 1970s and 1980s that claimed that advertising's subliminal powers were focused on hiding sexual messages in many commercials for everyday products. Key's most famous example was an ad for Gilbey's London Dry Gin, shown in Exhibit 3–5. Key maintained that the advertiser had embedded the word "sex" into the ice cubes to arouse feelings of sexuality, romance, and excitement among the ad's readers.

Despite such claims, there is no scientific or conclusive evidence that shows that advertising can work subliminally, although scientists continue to study the unconscious workings of the brain. A 1996 experiment reported in the journal *Science* found that words flashed before individuals for a few milliseconds did influence their response to subsequent words presented to them, but that the effect lasted only for a matter of seconds and had no longer after-effects.[20]

Some detractors would argue that it is contradictory to say that we can perceive something when it is presented below our threshold of perception. Many psychological studies that look into how people process advertising messages suggest that consumers, for the most part, take an active role in absorbing the information they read, hear, or see in advertisements.[21] Most people will claim they themselves are unaffected by advertising, a phenomenon known as the **third person effect.** If you ask a group of college students whether their clothing purchases were affected by ads for Gap, most would probably say that they were not, but that those ads probably influence others to buy the product. In this way, they feel the ads have an impact on a third, or different, person. Yet a

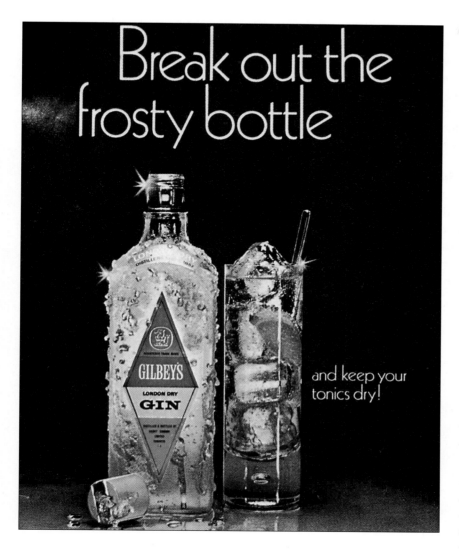

EXHIBIT 3–5 This ad for Gilbey's London Dry Gin, which appeared in *Time* in 1971, was at the center of a subliminal advertising controversy that raged during the 1970s and 1980s.

glance across a college campus will quickly show a large number of students walking around in Gap shirts and jeans.

ADVERTISING INCREASES THE COST OF GOODS AND SERVICES There is little doubt that you will pay more for a jar of Taster's Choice coffee than for store brands such as President's Choice or Master's Choice, but the incremental cost is not solely to pay for advertising. In fact, by stimulating demand for a product through advertising, companies are able to spread the costs of manufacturing and distribution over many more units, which will actually lower the price rather than raise it. This is known as economies of scale. We have witnessed this over the years with many high-tech items, such as VCRs, personal computers, and camcorders. The first VCRs cost several thousand dollars, but it is possible to buy one for less than $300 today.

When only one or a few companies dominate a category, such as breakfast cereals, as soon as one raises its price, the others quickly follow suit. Sometimes this works in reverse, as well. When Post Cereals lowered its prices significantly in 1996 in an effort to boost market share, Kellogg's and General Mills were forced to follow suit, for fear of losing out on the store shelf. If demand increases and supply remains the same, then prices rise. So when advertising leads consumers to think that they have to have Levi's jeans rather than jeans from Sears, the Levi's do cost more. Where advertising is not allowed at all, prices may end up being higher. A study in the 1970s that looked at the eyeglass industry found that in states that permitted advertising, prices were lower than in the states where such advertising was prohibited.[22]

ADVERTISING HELPS SELL BAD PRODUCTS While it is true that the back pages of magazines or late night television hours are filled with ads for "miracle" products that claim they can cure overnight everything from baldness to bad breath to incontinence, for mainstream brands, there are many examples of heavily advertised products that failed to attract consumer interest. One of the classics is the Ford Edsel, a new car model introduced in the 1950s. Despite the great hoopla and energetic ad campaign of the time, the car did not provide the benefits that it promised, and consumers refused to buy it. More recently, Coca-Cola's introduction of New Coke in the 1980s, following substantial consumer research, also died in the marketplace even after extensive advertising. Consumers were quite happy with existing Coke products and were very upset when the company tried to change them. The difficulty of introducing new products, regardless of the extent of the advertising, is seen in the fact that about 70 percent of all new products fail when they enter the marketplace. For most brands, the majority of sales are generated by current users, so if people do not like a product, they are not likely to purchase it again.

ADVERTISING DICTATES MEDIA CHOICES

Advertising is accused of corrupting the media, leading them to make editorial decisions that favor the advertisers rather than the public. A magazine that relies on tobacco sponsors might decide not to publish an article linking cigarettes and cancer or a TV show

in which an oil company has advertised may give only lukewarm criticism of environmental hazards from drilling. Advertisers do vote with their pocketbooks. For example, General Motors pulled its ads from *Automobile* magazine after its vehicles were criticized; Toyota did the same with *Road & Track* when its cars did not make that magazine's "Top Ten" list.[23] In 1994 Kraft General Foods withdrew its TV ads from episodes of "Roseanne" and "Law and Order" that dealt with masturbation and racism, respectively.

The media denies any kind of self-censorship, priding themselves on their role as the "fourth estate" alongside the judicial, legislative, and executive branches of government. They say they are immune from overt influence by advertisers because the large number and variety of advertising outlets weakens the potential harm that one advertiser could inflict.

ADVERTISING IS TOO PERVASIVE
Consumers are exposed to a vast number of commercial

CONSUMER INSIGHT

When Talk Leads to Murder: The Jenny Jones Show

Throughout the early 1990s, one of the most popular television program types, particularly during daytime, has been the talk show. The topics of these shows have grown more outrageous and lurid as competition between programs for more viewers and higher program ratings has led to a

seemingly infinite list of sorrowful people pouring out their hearts on national television. The consequences of this can often be dangerous, and in one case, they actually proved to be fatal.

After being contacted by the "Jenny Jones Show" in Chicago, Jonathan Schmitz agreed to appear on the show in order to learn the identity of a secret admirer. Once on stage for the taping of the show, Jonathan was informed that his secret admirer was not a female, but a male, Scott Amedure, whom he knew slightly. Jonathan expressed his amazement at Scott Amedure's declaration of attraction and noted repeat-

edly that he was not homosexual and was not at all interested in pursuing a relationship with Scott. Three days later, Jonathan Schmitz drove to Scott Amedure's house and shot him point blank with a shotgun, claiming that he could not stand the humiliation and questions about his sexual orientation that had been generated by the TV show.

While this incident was prompted by one talk show, the reverberations that followed indicted the whole genre. As *TV Guide* noted after the Schmitz/Amedure episode, "Watching these shows is the moral equivalent of staring at a train wreck—

messages each day—anywhere from 500 to 3,000, depending on how one defines a "message" and how much the individual chooses to use the media on a given day. The four biggest broadcast TV networks (ABC, CBS, FOX, and NBC) ran more than 350,000 commercials in 1994.[24] During prime time, between 12 and 14 minutes of every hour are devoted to commercials.[25] Although this clutter from ads is generally less offensive in print media (because the reader can more easily ignore it by turning the page), there are many magazines that devote half of all pages to advertising, overwhelming consumers with commercial messages.

The media contend that without such subsidies, the cost to consumers would be considerably higher. Indeed in Germany, where until recently there was almost no commercial time on television, viewers pay an annual fee of about $360 to watch television. And in this country, magazines that do not accept advertising, such as *Ms* or *Consumer Reports,* are priced two to three times higher than those that do.

Moreover, the audience may well enjoy seeing the advertising, or indeed choose a media type in part because of the ads within it. If you are planning to buy a new computer, you are likely to pick up a copy of *PC Week* or *Macworld* not only to read about the different machines available but also to scour the ads in those issues for further information.

Although advertisers' influence on the media is usually indirect, they can still have a serious impact. One might wonder whether the so-called "trash TV" talk shows could exist without advertiser support. As the situation in "Consumer Insight: When Talk Leads to Murder" shows, the media's desperate efforts to keep audience sizes large enough to be attractive to advertisers can sometimes have fatal consequences.

In looking at the institution of advertising, you realize that critics focus more on its social role, while defenders present economic arguments. The debate continues because advertising is so pervasive that it is impossible to be

you know you shouldn't, but it's hard to look away." Advertisers, too, seem to have a fatal attraction to the format. In the 1993–1994 television season, advertisers spent $204 million on the 14 daytime talk shows available, and none, including one of the country's largest advertisers, Proctor & Gamble, pulled out of the "Jenny Jones Show" after Amedure's murder. It is worth noting that children under 18 make up anywhere from 10 to 20 percent of the audience for daytime talk shows, where discussions can range from losing one's virginity, to pornographic movies, to spouses sleeping with friends or relatives.

Jonathan Schmitz is currently serving a 25-year sentence for second-degree murder. In addition to the criminal case, the family of Scott Amedure filed a civil suit against Jenny Jones and her producers, Warner Brothers, seeking $25 million for the "wrongful death" of Amedure, claiming that the TV program was indirectly responsible for his fate.

QUESTIONS
Consider each of these questions from the following viewpoints: the viewer, the TV show producer, the advertiser, and the regulatory authorities: How responsible should a TV program be for the actions

(current or future) of its guests? How much should advertisers care about the exploits on these shows? Who should decide what topics are discussed in this type of public venue?

Sources: Adapted from Michelle Green, "Fatal Attraction," *People,* 27 March 1995, 40–45; Michael Freeman, "Murder by Television?" *MediaWeek,* 20 March 1995, 9-10; Bill Carter, "Television," *New York Times,* 20 March 1995, C5; J. Max Robins, "Viewing the Secret 'Secret Crush' Tape," *TV Guide,* 31 August 1996, 41–42; and Janice Kaplan, "Are Talk Shows out of Control?" *TV Guide,* 1 April 1995, 10–15.

immune from its impact, either harmful or beneficial. Increasingly, we are exposed to advertising messages wherever we turn, from television to train stations, magazines to malls, and billboards to book covers. Not only is our exposure more widespread, it is also more frequent. We are likely to see the same advertising message over and over again in an effort to help us remember the brand name.

Socially Responsible Advertising

Whether you believe advertising is a mirror of society or a shaper of that society (or some of both), it is undeniably an influential force. Because of that, advertising is used quite extensively to promote socially desirable activities.

Environmental standards written in nature's own hand.

Nature always has a hand in writing the standards of our existence, because nature is the standard of all life. Having long embraced measures that preserve and protect the environment, NEC enthusiastically supports the international environmental standards of the ISO 14000 series. These comprehensive guidelines bring a global focus to environmental management issues and allow organizations to compare their efforts against internationally accepted criteria. Written hand in hand with nature, ISO 14000 spells good news for the environment.

http://www.nec.co.jp/english/profile/kan/index.html
NEC'S ENVIRONMENTAL PRINCIPLES: NEC will contribute to a sound environment and a livable society through technology that harmonizes with nature and production that is environmentally friendly. Our vision is a world where our natural environment is preserved, enabling all people of the world to pursue their full potential. For further information, please contact NEC Corporation, Overseas Advertising Division, 7-1, Shiba, 5-chome, Minato-ku, Tokyo 108-01, Japan

EXHIBIT 3–6 In response to both governmental and social pressures, many companies are becoming more aware of environmental issues. NEC, a computer manufacturer, communicates its position as an environmentally friendly company in this advertisement.

These may include ads from chemical companies that tell how they are becoming environmentally responsible or messages from beer companies that remind people not to drink and drive. Exhibit 3–6 shows an example of one such advertisement.

Socially responsible advertising is promoted by the industry as a whole through the private, nonprofit organization of volunteers who make up the Advertising Council. The Ad Council oversees such types of socially responsible campaigns conducted on behalf of nonprofit organizations. The Advertising Council was founded as the War Advertising Council just after the bombing of Pearl Harbor in 1942 as part of the national effort to mobilize the country for World War II. It helped raise $35 billion in war bonds and encouraged 2 million women to enter the job market. After the War ended, it was renamed the Advertising Council, with a new mission to "identify a select number of significant public issues and stimulate action on those issues through communications programs that make a measurable difference in our society."[26]

The Ad Council has been responsible for the creation of such memorable campaigns as "Friends Don't Let Friends Drive Drunk," "Take a Bite Out of Crime," "Only You Can Prevent Forest Fires," "A Mind is a Terrible Thing to Waste," and "Pollution: It's a Crying Shame." In 1994, the Advertising Council helped undertake advertising for 19 causes on a national, regional, or local basis. Such public service advertising may communicate warnings against drug abuse, smoking, and sexually transmitted diseases, as well as support charities such as Save the Children, the Humane Society, and the American Cancer Society. A list of Ad Council campaigns appears in Exhibit 3–7, and an example is shown in Exhibit 3–8.

The Ad Council's advertising, created by agencies for free and placed in media for little or no charge, is known as **pro bono advertising** (in Latin, *pro bono* means "for the public good"). But because media space and time are donated at little or no charge, much of this advertising is aired on the TV or radio station at 3 A.M., or is placed in the back pages of a magazine. Nonetheless, the industry can be credited for considerable success with such campaigns. One of the oldest pro bono campaigns, Smokey Bear talk-

EXHIBIT 3–7   Ad Council Campaigns

CAUSE	CAMPAIGN ISSUE	SPONSORING ORGANIZATION
Community outreach	Blood donation	American Red Cross
	Breaking the cycle of disadvantage	Children Now
	Combating hunger	Second Harvest
	Get out the vote	Federal Voting Assistance Program
Education	Gender equity in education	Women's College Coalition
	Junior achievement volunteering	Junior Achievement
	Head Start	U.S. Dept. of Health & Human Services
	United Negro College Fund	United Negro College Fund
	Value of math and science	National Council for Minorities in Engineering
Substance abuse	Drug abuse and AIDS prevention	National Institute on Drug Abuse
Environment	Clean water	National Resources Defense Council
	Environmental activities	Earth Share
	Forest fire prevention	USDA, Forest Service
Health concerns	Breast cancer detection	American Cancer Society
	Child abuse prevention	National Committee for the Prevention of Child Abuse
	Domestic violence prevention	The Family Violence Prevention Fund
	Healthy start	U.S. Dept. of Health & Human Services
	Infant immunization	Centers for Disease Control and Prevention
	Organ and tissue donation	Coalition on Donation
Public safety	Crime prevention	National Crime Prevention Council
	Drunk driving prevention	U.S. Dept. of Transportation
	Safety belt education	U.S. Dept. of Transportation

ing about preventing forest fires, is credited with saving many lives by educating people on fire safety and prevention. Although the advertising industry frequently cites this work as an example of how it acts in a socially responsible way, the amount spent on such advertising is minuscule compared to the amount spent advertising for-profit goods and services. In 1995, for example, $715 million was spent on nonprofit advertising, compared to $160 billion on for-profit ads.

As the power and influence of other institutions such as church or family weakens, the potential influence of advertising may grow. For example, as children become teenagers and family influence diminishes, heavily advertised brand-name goods become essential to their lives. More markedly, in Eastern Europe in the early 1990s, when former communist countries shifted to market economies and the state's power and control weakened, the importance of advertising rose rapidly.

Recognizing Cultural Differences

As society grows increasingly diverse in terms of its population, the argument over whether advertising is a mirror or shaper of society becomes particularly heated when discussing cultural differences. Immigration to the United States is certainly nothing new—different cultures have been mingling in this country throughout its history. But while the Irish, Italian, and Eastern European immigrants of the nineteenth and early twentieth centuries wanted nothing more than to become as American as apple pie, today's newcomers are more concerned with maintaining their cultural heritage and distinctiveness.

As a form of mass communication, advertising aims to reach as large a group of the target audience as possible, so cultural differences can pose potential problems. Will an ad for MasterCard be understood by Hispanic consumers who are less familiar with paying for products by credit card? Will ads for Humana

EXHIBIT 3–8   In an effort to reduce the number of fatalities resulting from auto accidents, the Ad Council has used variations of its "crash dummy" campaign to promote the use of seat belts and, more recently, airbags in automobiles. This public service advertising is designed to educate and inform the public about significant public issues.

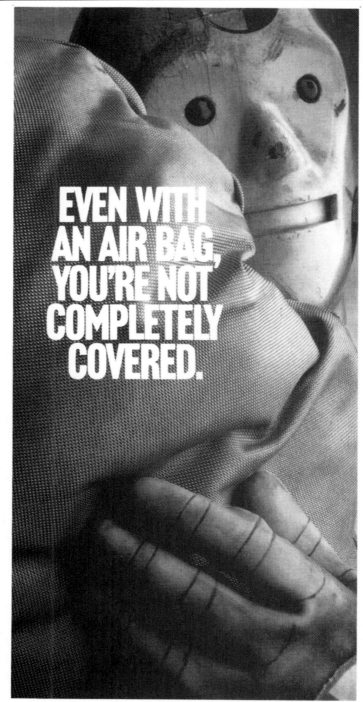

Nursing Homes offend Japanese Americans, for whom the notion of placing elderly relatives in institutions is considered unnatural and immoral? Will newly arrived Polish consumers believe the claims made by an ad for the U.S. Postal Service, given that in their home culture all words spoken by authorities were generally mistrusted?

The solution for advertisers depends on the size and importance of the cultural group to whom the messages are being addressed. In the case of Hispanic consumers, it may require special Spanish-language advertisements in heavily populated Hispanic markets, such as Miami or Los Angeles, that are directed specifically at that group. The solution also depends on the product category. For some industries, for example, it may require ads in the native language that are aimed at a specific nationality. Corona, the Mexican beer, advertises in Spanish in areas heavily populated by Mexican Americans, appealing to them with a brand with which they are familiar in their native language (see Exhibit 3–9).

Cultural differences exist regionally, too. In the U.S., people living on the West Coast tend to be more health and nutrition conscious, for example, than their eastern neighbors. As a result, Yoplait yogurt, which uses a health-based message in its advertising, has typically sold far better on the West Coast than on the East Coast, where its chief competitor, Dannon, uses a taste message. National advertisers can take such differences into account by creating regional versions of their messages. For example, in one campaign, ads for Bud Light were filmed in actual bars of big cities throughout the country and then aired in the regions where they were filmed. An ad filmed in a Dallas bar was shown throughout Texas and the south, while one filmed in a Boston bar aired in the New England area. The bars chosen reflected the culture of that area: cowboy hats and spurs in Dallas, and a young, urban look in Boston.

Even products that are eaten throughout the country exhibit regional preferences. White cheddar cheese is favored in New York and New England, while the rest of the country prefers the yellow variety; chunky peanut butter sells better in the West, creamy elsewhere. And among salad dressing flavors, Southerners like Russian and Thousand Island best, Mid-

westerners choose French, Easterners like Italian, and Westerners pick Ranch. Finally, for soup, Cincinnati consumes the most chicken noodle; Grand Rapids, Michigan, the most cream of mushroom; and Indianapolis, the most chili beef. One flavor, pepper pot, is now sold in just one city, Philadelphia, where it remains extremely popular, with a heritage said to date back to George Washington's time.[27]

Controversial Advertisements

As the opening vignette to this chapter indicated, one area in which advertising themes have provoked controversy is the issue of sex and nudity in advertising. Objections come in two areas: sexual suggestiveness and sexual objectification. People who are strongly religious or have very pronounced moral standards are offended by the use of suggestive, sexual imagery to sell products or services, whether it is a man and woman embracing in a Guess? jeans commercial or bodybuilders flexing their muscles in ads for Soloflex workout equipment. Sexual suggestiveness can even be communicated by insinuation only. Rally's hamburger chain got into trouble for promoting its Big Buford burgers by using the double entendre in its tagline "It's not the size, it's the taste, stupid" in a commercial featuring conversations between men and women.[28]

Women are most likely to be offended by ads involving sexual objectification. Most frequently, this is seen when actors or models are used as adornments to capture viewer or reader

EXHIBIT 3–9 Recognizing the myriad cultures represented in their consumer population, advertisers have begun to tailor their messages to better fit their target markets. This Spanish-language billboard, which highlights a brand with which most Mexican Americans are familiar, is an example of such an advertisement.

attention when they have little or no relevance to the product. Less commonly, handsome men have been used similarly in a decorative rather than functional way. An example of an ad that uses sexual imagery in its sales message is shown in Exhibit 3–10.

The effects of including sexual connotations or appeals in ads may go beyond the consumer audience. In 1992, female employees of Stroh Brewery filed a sexual harassment suit against the company. These workers pointed to the beer maker's campaign at the time, which featured scantily clad women known as the "Swedish bikini team," as evidence of a "hostile work environment." The company settled out of court, and the campaign was quickly dropped.

The depiction of women has been particularly problematic for advertisers. In one in-

stance, Omega Watches temporarily withdrew its own ads from the British version of *Vogue* in objection to the use of the waif-like models found in the editorial content. It expressed concern that the photos were portraying an unhealthy view of young women that could encourage eating disorders in a magazine designed to be highly influential to that group.[29]

Another area where taste comes into play is the use of **fear appeals** in advertising. Some have argued that it is wrong to try to scare people into buying a product, such as by warning them that they will be social outcasts if they don't improve their bad breath with Scope mouthwash, or that they are not adequate parents if they don't buy Northwestern Mutual life insurance to prepare for the worst. The goal of such appeals is to motivate people to take action, but for some consumers this may be offensive. No one likes to be made to feel guilty. Indeed, the effectiveness of such appeals is also debatable.[30] One study of condom ads found that respondents were more positive in their attitudes towards the brand when it was advertised using a moderate-fear appeal than when a high-fear appeal was used. The evidence suggests that the stronger the use of fear in a message, the less likely it is to work, because it ends up turning off consumers and making them dislike the product even though they feel guilty.

One type of advertising that is likely to resort to a fear appeal is advertising for social causes where the aim is to change unhealthy or harmful behavior. This could be to promote safer sex to prevent the spread of AIDS, or to get pregnant women to stop smoking. Although these ads cannot work miracles on their own, it does appear that, together with publicity or public relations efforts, they can help to achieve such socially desirable ends.

Sometimes advertisers find themselves offending the audience by the images they choose. Benetton has created numerous controversies in recent years with its campaigns depicting a man dying of AIDS, a black baby being nursed by a white woman, or the blood-covered uniform of a Croatian soldier. In 1995, a number of German clothing stores that had carried the Benetton line staged a protest at the company's messages. An ad showing a man with a tattoo on his arm that read "HIV Positive" (see Exhibit 3–11) was felt to be too reminiscent of the forced tattoos placed on Jews in Nazi con-

EXHIBIT 3–10 Many advertisements—promoting everything from jeans to bed linens to perfume—use some form of sexual imagery in their product message. Although some ads are overt in their use of sex as a selling tool, this ad sends the more subtle message that consumption of this product is a sensual experience.

BAILEYS®
The Original.
To send a gift of BAILEYS, call 1-800-BE-THERE.

centration camps during World War II, for example. The retailers' protest culminated in a court case, which was ultimately decided in favor of Benetton in March 1996. That campaign was also the subject of legal action in France, where a court ordered Benetton to pay damages to three HIV-positive people who said they were offended by the images shown. The court ruled that the campaign was "a provocative exploitation of suffering."[31]

Oliviero Toscani, the photographer behind many of the controversial images, has argued that these ads are designed to say something beyond the products themselves, to provoke people to think about social issues. Yet unlike other socially oriented campaigns, Benetton's messages have little or nothing to do with the clothes. Whether by creativity or by controversy, or perhaps the combination of the two, the logo showing the United Colors of Benetton is one of the five most recognized logos in the world.[32]

Ethical Dilemmas in Advertising

Ethics are the moral principles and values that govern an individual or group. Critics of advertising claim that the industry overall does not adhere to clear ethical standards. They say it lacks a strong code of professional conduct and does not always distinguish correctly between what is morally right and wrong, instead focusing solely on making money. This can become a very gray area because, unlike a legal issue where the law clearly states what can and cannot be done, the area of ethics is far more subjective.

The criticisms of advertising as unethical range from advertising cigarettes that are known to cause cancer, to implying that the use of a particular perfume will bring hordes of admirers to your doorstep, to claiming that a sugar-coated cereal is "part of a nutritious breakfast" for children when only the accompanying milk or toast has any nutritional value. In some cases, legal issues do become involved. The use of excessive glue or paint to make a product look more appetizing in a TV commercial is not only unethical, it is also illegal. Similarly, there are legal restrictions on the ad-

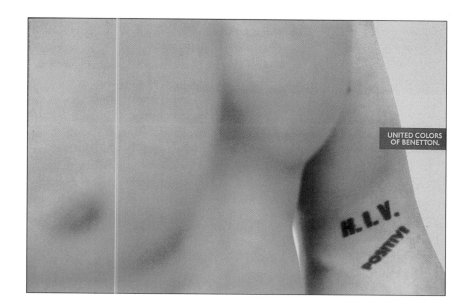

vertising of sweepstakes or lotteries, both of which have been criticized for misleading innocent consumers into believing they have won large monetary prizes.

The question of advertising ethics is clearly linked with the question of the nature and purpose of advertising. Most people can understand that advertisements, at the very least, take liberties with the "truth." This practice of using exaggerations that consumers will know are factually false is known as advertising **puffery.** Most women understand, for example, that they will not look like the models in the commercials simply by buying Salon Selectives hair shampoo. Businessmen realize that when they travel, American Airlines does not literally provide "something special in the air." The use of puffery does not mean that any of those brands is unethical in its advertising. It would only become so if Salon Selectives guaranteed that use of its product would really turn you into a model.

Ultimately, advertising ethics depend to a large extent on your beliefs about the purpose of advertising and your view of consumers. If you believe that consumers are rational, skeptical, and self-aware, and accept that advertising is designed to persuade the audience to think, feel, or act in a certain way in order to increase sales, then you will probably not find advertising inherently unethical in trying to get you to "Be like Mike" (Michael Jordan) and drink Gatorade, or "Have your break today" and eat at McDonald's. On the other hand, if you

EXHIBIT 3–11 This ad, which depicts the way that many people are unfairly labeled or stereotyped, is one of the many controversial ads used by Benetton in its global advertising campaign. Although there were many protests surrounding these ads, the result has been an increased recognition of the Benetton logo, clearly a marketing success.

think that consumers are completely innocent with regard to the ads they see, hear, or read, then you are likely to find advertising, by and large, to be unethical with its promises of leaner bodies, cleaner homes, faster cars, or money-saving credit cards.

In 1997, the Vatican issued a 37-page text on "Ethics in Advertising" in which it emphasized the need for advertisers to adhere to three basic moral principles: truthfulness, upholding human dignity, and social responsibility. It noted that advertising in and of itself is not nec-essarily unethical, but that it "can distort the truth by implying things that are not so or with-holding relevant facts."[33] Importantly, however, the report did not call for increased regulation of advertising; rather, it states that advertisers should work harder at monitoring themselves, with a view to remaining ethically responsible.

Unethical behavior does occur. The most common occasions are advertising to children and the promotion of controversial products such as alcohol, tobacco, and contraceptives. Each of these is considered below.

AdScape

How Cool is the Camel?

In 1988, in an effort to attract more young people to its brand of cigarettes, the R. J. Reynolds Tobacco Company updated the look of its Old Joe Camel character, which had been a prominent feature of the brand for 75 years. McCann-Erickson, Reynolds's ad agency at the time, created a "cool" and more contemporary camel, wearing Hollywood sunglasses or fighter-pilot gear. The goal of the new campaign was to change the brand's image from one people thought their grandfather smoked to one that would be seen as highly desirable among young adult smokers.

Although the change appeared to work rapidly from a marketing perspective—increasing Camel's market share in the cigarette category within six months—the social impact of the campaign created a much bigger fire, leading ultimately to a congressional investigation into the company's promotional practices. Three studies re-ported in the *Journal of the American Medical Association,* a prestigious medical publication, found that the up-dated Old Joe was not only more popular among young adults but also seemed to have a strong potential influ-ence among children. One study claimed that the new advertising had helped in-crease Reynolds's share of the children's cigarette mar-ket from a tiny 0.5 percent be-fore the start of the campaign to 32.5 percent, which trans-lated into an increase in ciga-rette sales to minors from $6 million to $476 million. A sec-ond study found that the high-est ad recognition for the campaign was among 12- and 13-year-olds, while the third study discovered that about 30 percent of 3-year-olds and 91.3 percent of 6-year-olds could accurately link Old Joe with Camel cigarettes. That rate of recognition was com-parable to the link between The Disney Channel and Mickey Mouse.

These stunning findings led health advocates such as the American Heart Association, American Cancer Society, and American Lung Association to demand that the Federal Trade Commission (FTC) "take immediate action" against the campaign. The case went nowhere until 1994, when a subcommittee in the House of Representa-tives asked the FTC to explain the status of the complaint. The reasons for the Commis-sion's slowness to act were several. They had a fine line to walk between regulating ad-vertising and restricting free speech on what remains a legally sold product; and they could not ban cartoon charac-ters from advertising alto-gether. When the FTC finally issued the ruling, the vote was 3 to 2 in favor of R. J. Reynolds, with commis-sioners finding there was insufficient evidence to demonstrate that the cam-paign directly increased smoking among children.

Advertising to Children

Advertising to children is a special case, both ethically and legally. Because children have a difficult time distinguishing between fantasy and reality, they tend to believe everything they see or hear. Most of the ethical debate centers on television, because that is the medium through which most children see commercial messages.

By law, all advertisements directed to children must be crafted so as not to mislead them, deliberately or not, into thinking that a product or service can do something that in reality it is unable to do. Despite this, children find it hard to distinguish between the entertainment of a TV program and the entertainment of a commercial. This is made even harder when a TV show such as "Transformers" is based on a line of toys, or when all of the characters in Disney cartoons are available at The Disney Store.

One of the most controversial ethical areas where children are concerned is with tobacco advertising. Before the Federal Government imposed restrictions on tobacco advertising

Numerous protests have been held across the country to draw attention to the targeting of children in R. J. Reynolds's advertisements for Camel cigarettes. Critics, including the FTC and the American Lung Association, claim that the company has used its cartoonlike character Joe Camel to promote cigarette purchases among minors.

The controversy did not stop there, however. In 1997, in a landmark agreement between the cigarette companies and the government, the companies agreed to severe restrictions on how they promote their product, particularly in media or in areas to which children could be exposed. As part of that settlement, R. J. Reynolds voluntarily killed the Joe Camel campaign, replacing it with a more adult-oriented, subtle image of a camel in all visual media.

QUESTIONS

Consider the arguments raised by this case. How responsible should advertisers be for the impact of their campaigns on people other than their intended target audience, particularly when the unintentional users are illegally consuming the product? Should any restrictions be placed on the use of cartoons to target adults, particularly when the product being promoted is not intended for use by minors?

At what point does the advertiser's right to free speech come into conflict with the consumer's health concerns?

Sources: Judann Dagnoli, "RJR Aims New Ads at Young Smokers," *Advertising Age,* 11 July 1988, 2, 76; Judann Dagnoli, "'JAMA' Lights New Fire under Camel's Ads," *Advertising Age,* 16 December 1991, 3, 32; Steven W. Colford, "House Panel Steps into Joe Camel Problem," *Advertising Age,* 11 April 1994, 1, 46; Steven W. Colford and Ira Teinowitz, "Congressman Douses Threat to Joe Camel," *Advertising Age,* 13 June 1994, 8; Paul M. Fischer, Meyer P. Schwartz, John W. Richards Jr., Adam O. Goldstein, and Tina H. Rojas, "Brand Logo Recognition by Children Aged 3 to 6 Years," *Journal of the American Medical Association* 266, no. 22 (11 December 1991): 3145–48; Joseph R. DiFranza, John W. Richards Jr., Paul M. Paulman, Nancy Wolf-Gillespie, Christopher Fletcher, Robert D. Jaffe, and David Murray, "RJR Nabisco's Cartoon Camel Promotes Camel Cigarettes to Children," *Journal of the American Medical Association* 266, no. 22 (11 December 1991): 3149–52; John P. Pierce, Elizabeth Gilpin, David M. Burns, Elizabeth Whalen, Bradley Rosbrook, Donald Shopland, and Michael Johnson, "Does Tobacco Advertising Target Young People to Start Smoking?" *Journal of the American Medical Association* 266, no. 22 (11 December 1991): 3154–58.

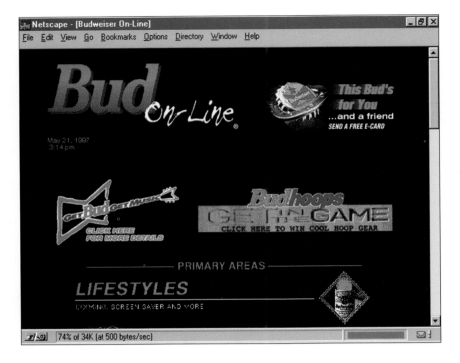

Because the Internet can be easily accessed by minors, the use of this medium by alcohol brands has caused a great deal of controversy. These Web sites, such as the site for Budweiser beer shown here, often include games, contests, and other items of interest to underage youth.

that might be seen by children, RJR Nabisco found itself in trouble for its use of a cartoon mascot called Old Joe Camel to promote its Camel brand of cigarettes. After studies showed how the character appeals to children, and considerable public and government pressure, the campaign was finally dropped. This issue is examined in "AdScape: How Cool is the Camel?".

As we noted earlier, advertisements aimed at children may be ethically suspect by encouraging materialism in the very young, leading them to believe that if they do not have the latest sneakers or makeup set, they will be considered a failure by their peers. This is particularly disturbing where advertising in schools is concerned. The Channel One program has received considerable criticism. It provides a daily 12-minute newscast, including 2 minutes of commercials, to 12,000 middle and high schools and 8 million students across the country. Although schools receive electronic equipment in return for airing these broadcasts, several cities and states have banned the use of Channel One in public schools, arguing that it is wrong to require students to watch commercial messages as part of their education. Other programs targeted to children, such as kids' clubs, product placement in children's movies, or ads on school book

covers, also have come under fire from consumer groups.

In their defense, children's advertisers say they are teaching children at an early age how to be effective consumers. Advertising is one information source among many and can help children in product selections and decision-making behavior. Advertisers also point out that there are many other influences on children, such as family and friends.

Controversial Products

The ethical debate is far louder for certain products than for others. In particular, the advertising of alcohol, tobacco, contraceptives, and pharmaceuticals is singled out as being potentially harmful in the impact it may have on the product user. While advertisers of these products have strong counter-arguments to defend themselves, some advertising agencies and media decline to handle such products, either out of fear of consumer reaction or their personal conviction that these products should not, indeed, be advertised.

ALCOHOL Ever since research studies first started to indicate the harmful effects of alcohol consumption, there has been pressure on advertisers to limit the nature and number of advertising messages. It is deemed unethical to promote products that are known to be partly responsible for health problems such as liver disease and fetal alcohol syndrome, as well as social issues such as increased crime rates and drunk-driving accidents. Alcoholic beverage ads are, in fact, strictly controlled in what they can say and how they can say it. They cannot show the product being consumed, nor can they show people who might appear to be underage holding alcoholic beverages of any kind.

Despite those restrictions, the distilled spirits council, an industry trade group, announced in 1996 that it would reverse a decades-old voluntary ban on broadcasting TV and radio ads for liquor and buy commercial time on radio and TV stations that would be willing to accept them. While that decision prompted many opposed to such ads to push for congressional action to impose a ban on the industry,[34] many radio and TV stations did in fact begin to accept them, with only limited consumer opposition in those markets.

The age of those who might see alcoholic beverage ads is another issue. The product cannot legally be consumed by people under 21, but ads often depict young people enjoying themselves while in the presence of this product, and they sometimes use celebrities who might appeal to young and impressionable minds. Many localities ban billboard ads for alcoholic products within a certain distance of schools or other institutions where young adults congregate. The issue becomes thornier where print ads are concerned. The series of award-winning ads for Absolut vodka have started to become collectors' items among some children, raising concerns that these children may be more likely to be among the half of all children in the United States who will have tried alcohol by the fourth grade.[35] It is also causing controversy on the World Wide Web, where Web sites are accessible by anyone with the appropriate computer equipment, regardless of age. A study undertaken in 1996 found that 35 alcohol brands had Web sites with elements that could be highly appealing to underage viewers.[36]

Alcoholic beverage advertisers argue that they are only trying to influence brand decisions, rather than encourage people to drink more or to drink excessively. Their use of young people as the models for the commercials reflects the fact that much of the alcohol in the U.S., particularly beer, is indeed consumed by younger adults. In showing this age group in the ads, advertisers argue that they are merely reflecting consumer usage patterns. The company that produces Absolut refuses any direct requests from children for ad reprints, telling each underage writer, "You are below legal drinking age. We don't want to encourage you in any way to think about Absolut Vodka."[37]

Advertising of alcoholic beverages to African American consumers raises ethical concerns, too. This population segment consumes above-average quantities of the product, and it also suffers more than the rest of the population from alcohol-related illnesses and diseases. The advertiser must therefore weigh the potential for increased sales from this group against the social responsibility of not encouraging any excessive and debilitating use of the product by

EXHIBIT 3–12 Alcoholic beverages, particularly those with a relatively higher percentage of alcohol by volume, are often promoted in inner-city areas. Are advertisers shirking their social responsibility by promoting these products in high-consumption areas?

any particular group. Despite that, you will often see alcoholic beverage ads on billboards in inner-city areas, where minorities are more likely to live (see Exhibit 3–12).

A powerful argument used by alcoholic beverage advertisers is that there is little evidence to prove any kind of correlation between the amount spent on advertising of alcoholic beverages and consumption of those products. In the former communist countries of Eastern Europe, for example, these drinks were not advertised at all, yet alcoholism was a major problem. In the United States, where billions of dollars are spent on advertising, the rates of alcoholism are relatively low. Those statistics do not, however, take into account alcohol-related social problems. For example, a study released by the anti-alcohol lobby group Mothers Against Drunk Drivers (MADD) reported that more than 17,000 people were killed in alcohol-related traffic accidents in 1995.[38]

TOBACCO Ethical questions surrounding tobacco advertising are equally, if not more, pronounced. Tobacco advertising was completely banned by federal law from all broadcast media (television and radio) after 1970, and there is legislation pending to ban it from all outdoor billboards and magazines that have 15% or more readership among under 18's. There are serious concerns about promoting a product that has been shown to cause cancer; it has been likened to giving these advertisers a license to kill. Unlike the use of alcoholic beverages, there is no usage level of tobacco products that may be considered safe. Yet today, tobacco companies spend at least $1.1 billion on promotions, sponsorship, and advertising.

When tobacco advertisers were banned from broadcast media, they switched their dollars into print instead, providing newspapers, magazines, and billboard companies with an enormous influx in advertising revenues. See, for example, the billboard shown in Exhibit 3–13. This too raises ethical problems. Should a magazine such as *Fitness,* for example, accept ads for products that are by their nature unhealthy? Or given that tobacco is still legally sold, should they willingly accept the additional ad revenues? Tobacco manufacturers now spend heavily on promotions and other forms of integrated marketing. Philip Morris Companies has spent billions of dollars

EXHIBIT 3–13 Banned by federal law from advertising on all broadcast media, tobacco companies now invest their sizable promotion budgets on print media, including newspapers, magazines, and, as shown here, billboards.

each year sponsoring arts companies throughout the country, funding tours, exhibitions, and special events. Critics argue that such expenditures are unethical, considering the products that generate the company's revenues and profits are lethal.

One form of promotion that has led to considerable criticism is the use of stadium signage for sports events. Many critics believe that the main purpose behind such advertising is to have the brand name before the public when the sport is broadcast on television (because tobacco companies cannot buy TV time directly). The U.S. has proposed a complete ban on this type of promotional activity.

The movement against tobacco manufacturers is growing worldwide. While it began in western, developed nations, it has now spread to developing countries in Asia, Eastern Europe, and Africa, much to the chagrin of the tobacco companies, who receive almost as much revenue internationally as they do in the U.S. There are now 27 cities in China that have banned smoking in public places; six Arab countries doubled their taxes on tobacco in 1996 to discourage smokers; and Poland banned tobacco sales in sports arenas and vending machines.[39] Countries as diverse as Latvia, Mexico, and Hungary all have introduced or are discussing further limits on what tobacco advertisers can say, and where.[40] The European Community banned all tobacco TV ads in 1991. Australia, in addition to having a ban on outdoor and cinema tobacco ads, also has limitations on promotions, samples, and point-of-purchase displays.[41]

In 1997, one of the smaller tobacco companies in the U.S., Liggett, agreed to cooperate with regulators in a lawsuit filed jointly by the attorneys general of 21 states. In the settlement, Liggett agreed to put a message on its cigarette packages stating that tobacco can be addictive and can kill. Perhaps even more importantly, it also agreed to hand over confidential documents that reported meetings between the major tobacco companies that could reveal that they have known for many years the damaging effects of their product. This has always been vehemently denied by the bigger tobacco companies, who immediately went to court to ask for an injunction to prevent Liggett from taking such action. When this book went to press, it was unclear how large the ramifications of this first-ever settlement would be on the overall tobacco industry.

Even with this potentially devastating blow, and despite 813 lawsuits in the past 40 years, the tobacco companies have never lost a case (though twice they won only on appeal).[42] The companies are trying to shift their defense, claiming that states receive more than enough money to cover health costs from the heavy taxes imposed on the product. They argue that the industry provides jobs, exports, and marketing dollars for the economy.

In 1996, the federal government declared nicotine an addictive product, thus placing it under the regulation of the Food & Drug Administration (FDA). It also proposed severe restrictions on what forms of advertising and promotion could be used, beginning in 1997. The issue is likely to be tied up in the courts for many months, if not years, as tobacco companies argue that their free speech rights are being violated by the new rules.

The picture is not totally hopeless for the tobacco companies, however. In Canada, the Supreme Court declared a six-year-old total ban on cigarette advertising to be unconstitutional. Tobacco manufacturers responded carefully, creating a new voluntary code that allows them to advertise cigarettes again, although not in broadcast media.[43] Similarly, a Voluntary Agreement in the United Kingdom allows tobacco advertisers there to continue to promote their product, but with some additional restrictions, such as not advertising at bus shelters, near schools, or on storefronts.[44]

Tobacco companies, like alcoholic beverage companies, maintain that until cigarettes and tobacco products are ruled illegal, they should legally be permitted to promote their sale and use, trying to get people who already smoke to switch to their brand. They are supported by advertising trade organizations, who although they may not like the product, maintain they must be "product blind" in any efforts to restrict the rights of advertisers. As O. Burtch Drake, president of the American Association of Advertising Agencies, pointed out, "If the product is legal, then both its producers and its legal users are entitled under our Constitution to the full benefit of truthful, non-deceptive advertising."[45]

PHARMACEUTICALS As regulations on pharmaceutical products are loosened, allowing more of these items to be promoted directly to consumers rather than simply to the medical profession, the ethical issues increase. Does advertising of drugs encourage unnecessary self-medication? How fair is it to advertise highly complex products to people who are not medically knowledgeable? People assume that if a product is advertised, then it must be completely safe. While all drugs sold over the counter or by prescription have indeed passed stringent government tests, they can still cause problems for some few individuals, particularly if not consumed correctly.

In addition to Federal Trade Commission (FTC) regulation, drug advertising is also controlled by the FDA, which protects consumers from deceptive and misleading messages in over-the-counter and prescription drugs. More will be said on this later in the chapter.

CONTRACEPTIVES A controversial product that generates considerable attention from ethicists is contraceptives. Ads for condoms are still routinely rejected by individual television stations, while other forms of contraceptive devices receive very little consumer advertising at all. The problems here are twofold. Some maintain that such ads encourage sexual activity among teens, while others find contraceptive advertising offensive to certain audiences, such as those with strong religious convictions against using the product. On the other hand, given what is known about the benefits of condoms in preventing sexually transmitted diseases, including AIDS, it would seem that there are strong arguments to be made for encouraging more widespread advertising of the product for health reasons.

Global Restrictions

The situation in the U.S. for sensitive products is also seen in many other countries. A survey of 344 U.S. ad agency affiliates in offices throughout the world found that respondents reported restrictions on many of the same products or services: cigarettes, alcohol, condoms, feminine hygiene products, male and female undergarments, sexual information campaigns, and pharmaceuticals. Exhibit 3–14 reports the findings by country.

R E S E T

1. How similar or different is advertising from other institutions in society?
2. What are the ways in which advertising is a mirror of society, and how is it a shaper of that society?
3. Your agency has been asked to develop a campaign to promote malt liquor to African-American young men. Would you take the assignment?

The Economic Role of Advertising

It is clear that an industry that spends upwards of $150 billion per year and represents 2 percent of the gross national product of the United States must have an economic impact on society. Both detractors and supporters would agree that advertising plays a key role in the economy, although they may disagree on whether that role is beneficial or harmful. Again, the argument parallels that of the mirror/shaper distinction. On the one hand, advertising is seen by its defenders as a way to inform people of their choices to satisfy their existing desires. In so doing, it enhances competition and generates demand for goods and services, making society more efficient. Opponents, however, maintain that advertising is a needless expense that simply adds to the cost of those same goods and services, encouraging people to buy things they do not need. Advertising can stimulate consumer activity and increase sales, or it can help large companies shout louder and grow bigger at the expense of their smaller rivals who have a smaller voice because they cannot afford to advertise as much.

The position you take on advertising as an economic force will depend, in part, on the economic system in which you live. There are three to consider: free market, socialized, and controlled. The premises under which each operates has a marked impact on the role of advertising in that society. The *free market system,* developed in the eighteenth century in the U.S. and Europe, is considered an early form of capitalism. It is based on the notion that humans are rational, deliberate, and calculating beings who will not act without some promise of reward. Society is no greater than the sum of its parts, so that the priorities of that society are determined by individuals who together agree on the direction to take. Under such a belief system, the market should operate independently of any overarching control. Although all people are looking out for themselves, the market should not be controlled, but should remain "free" to regulate itself.

The ideals of the free market were constructed before advertising even existed, so today's capitalism is somewhat different from this ideal. Nonetheless, advertising's role in a free market society is to help consumers satisfy their wants and needs by informing them of what is available. By offering consumers choices in goods and services, advertising helps promote competition, making the market operate more efficiently. That, in turn, increases demand for those products, fostering industry to produce and sell more. Countries that fol-

low the free market system include the United States, much of Western Europe (United Kingdom, Germany, Italy, France, Switzerland, and Spain), Australia, and several countries in South America (Brazil, Argentina, Venezuela, and Chile).

In a *socialized system,* although humans are still considered rational and self-interested, it is felt that society's well-being is equally important. The market is not seen as self-correcting and perfect; instead, government is needed to step in to ensure that individuals are not harmed by the market. The role of advertising is still to inform and persuade, but now government has a larger voice in what companies can say or do. The government may restrict, for example, when and where ads directed to children will appear. Government-sponsored messages are likely to be more frequent, encouraging people not to drink and drive, to quit smoking, or to avoid alcohol when pregnant. Although such actions may be found in a free market system, they are decidedly more prevalent in a socialized system. Examples of countries with

---

EXHIBIT 3–14 Television Advertising Restrictions of Sensitive Categories, Select Countries

	CIGARETTES	ALCOHOL	CONDOMS	FEMININE HYGIENE	FEMALE UNDERGARMENTS	SEXUAL DISEASES	PHARMACEUTICALS
Australia	X	X	X	X		X	X
Canada	X	X	X	X	X	X	X
England	X	X	X	X	X	X	X
France	X	X					X
Germany	X	X	X				X
Hong Kong	X	X	X	X	X	X	X
New Zealand	X	X	X	X	X	X	X
Norway	X	X					
South Africa	X	X	X	X	X	X	
Spain	X	X	X				X
Sweden	X	X		X			X
U.S.	X	X	X			X	X

Note: The information presented here was based on surveys of advertising agencies in each country.
Source: Alan T. Shao and John S. Hill, "Global Television Advertising Restrictions: The Case of Socially Sensitive Products," *International Journal of Advertising* 13 (1994): 347–366.

a socialized system include several European countries (Norway, Sweden, Denmark, the Netherlands, and the formerly communist Hungary), Namibia, Israel, and Egypt.

Finally, in a *controlled system* (such as a right-wing dictatorship or communist rule), the State is considered preeminent. The rights of the individual are less important because it is assumed that the State, sometimes personified by an autocratic leader, is working for the greater good of everyone. It is the State, therefore, that makes many of the decisions for people, including where they live, what work they do, and, to a great extent, what products they buy. Advertising's role is therefore far more circumscribed, being limited to State-approved messages that encourage people to buy or do what the State believes is in their best interest. Countries that have a controlled system include Cuba, North Korea, China, and Mozambique.

There are two major schools of thought on the economic role of advertising in a free market or capitalist society. While one school argues that advertising creates market power, the other contends that advertising provides information. Each of these models is examined below.

Advertising as Market Power

In the view of advertising as market power, advertising's main role is product differentiation. In other words, advertising helps change consumer tastes and establishes brand loyalty. Consumers are fairly passive, easily influenced by advertising. They tend to be loyal to a few brands and are therefore less sensitive to price fluctuations. This makes it difficult and expensive for competitors to win over their allegiance. The price of entry into the market remains very high, which leads to a few firms dominating the market and controlling prices. Those companies enjoy higher profits through increased sales. They also charge higher prices for the brand name, further enhancing their revenues. And because people are choosing a product because of the brand name, ads focus on image rather than price.

This model of the marketplace assumes concentrations of power within the market; as a result, it tends to be somewhat static. That is, if a few firms dominate and the price of entry for new competitors remains high, then it becomes difficult for changes to occur or for new products to be offered to consumers. In reality,

however, people's tastes and preferences change, product improvements and innovations take place, and technology changes, all of which can lead to new entrants in the market and shifts in market shares.

Advertising as Information

From the standpoint of advertising as information, sometimes known as the "market competition" model, the economic role of advertising is to provide information to the marketplace. This model assumes that consumers are quite active, seeking new products and brands; they look to advertising for information and are more *price sensitive,* which forces advertisers to be more careful about how much they charge for their products. This holds prices in check and encourages competition as more companies enter the marketplace, using advertising to create awareness for their offerings.

In this school of thought, advertising is considered an incentive for companies to be innovative and compete vigorously. Many new products introduced in the past 10 years have succeeded, in part, because advertising was used to increase consumer awareness of their existence, which in turn increased demand. Examples include personal computers, satellite television, computer online services, and new cars and trucks such as minivans or sport utility vehicles.

As you can see, the distinctions between the two models reflect somewhat negative or positive views on advertising's role in society, respectively. Under the market power model, advertising is helping to shape society by raising the cost of goods and services. Because consumers are less price sensitive, that allows companies to charge more for what they are selling. In contrast, the information model tends to view advertising's role in society more positively, seeing it as a relatively benign influence that merely offers information to consumers. In doing so, advertising is really reflecting the value of brands and allowing consumers to make their own decisions, which will encourage greater competition in the marketplace and keep prices in check. The difficulty with either approach—and with assessing advertising's economic impact in general—is that it is very hard to measure accurately. Because advertising is usually just one of many variables that impact a consumer's decision over which brand to buy, it is almost impossible to determine advertising's precise role in that process.[46]

R E S E T

1. **What are some of the difficulties in trying to measure the economic impact of advertising?**
2. **Find three examples of advertising that reflect the philosophies of the three major economic systems. Discuss the similarities and differences that exist.**

Advertising in the Legal Framework

As we have emphasized throughout this chapter, the institution of advertising has a two-way relationship with all the other social institutions, one of the most important of these being the legal structure. The extent to which advertising should be regulated depends on your viewpoint. From a business or market approach, the desire is to operate as freely as possible, unshackled by rules and regulations imposed by government agencies; from this viewpoint, the market regulates itself through the forces of competition. In contrast, from a consumer standpoint, regulation is needed to protect the consumer against the overwhelming forces of the marketplace.

Advertising regulations are enshrined in the U.S. Constitution because advertising itself is considered a form of speech, protected (either more or less) by the First Amendment, which states that "Congress shall make no laws abridging the freedom of speech or of the press." What that means, in effect, is that advertisers have the right to speak out to promote their products to consumers in society. Advertising is regulated in numerous ways—by federal, state, and local authorities. In addition, the industry attempts to regulate itself. And as communications and technology bring all of the countries of the world closer together, the U.S. advertising industry is likely to be increasingly affected by global advertising regulations, as well.

The First Amendment and Commercial Speech

Unlike someone standing in a park on a soapbox or making a private telephone conversation, advertising is considered **commercial speech** as opposed to noncommercial speech. This means that it has more restraints on it than other forms of speech that the First Amendment protects because its underlying objective is to sell something (a product, a service, or even an idea). Commercial speech was first defined by the Supreme Court in 1942 in *Valentine v Chrestensen,*[47] and this concept was upheld by the courts for 34 years. Advertising received First Amendment protection in 1964 in *New York Times v Sullivan,*[48] a case in which an ad published by a group of Alabama students complaining about the actions of the local police commissioner was deemed to be political rather than commercial speech.

When ads promote discriminatory or illegal practices, they can be regulated (*Pittsburgh Press,* 1973),[49] but if they advertise services that are legal where those services are being offered, then that is considered to be "factual information of public interest"[50] (*Bigelow v Virginia,* 1973).[51]

Even though an advertiser's interest is recognized as being purely economic, that should not prevent the public from receiving the appropriate information. In the case *Virginia State Board of Pharmacy v Virginia Citizens Consumer Council, Inc.*(1976),[52] which concerned prescription drug advertising in Virginia, the Supreme Court acknowledged that "If there is a right to advertise, there is a reciprocal right to receive the advertising." This was the first time that the Supreme Court had given such protection to commercial speech. As Justice Blackmun noted, "Advertising, however tasteless and excessive it sometimes may seem, is nonetheless dissemination of information as to who is producing and selling what product, for what reason and at what price."

Much of the advertising regulation in recent times has been based on a key court decision in 1980, *Central Hudson Gas & Electric Corp. v Public Service Commission,*[53] that established a

TECHNOLOGY WATCH

Free Speech versus Consumer Privacy on the Web

Today, more and more people are connecting to the Internet or signing up for commercial online services such as Prodigy or America Online, and there are several unresolved social and regulatory issues that may have far-reaching impact on the potential for and effectiveness of advertising in these new media forms.

One of the biggest concerns is consumer privacy. Because of the one-to-one nature of communications that these services offer (individuals talking directly either to other individuals or to a company), it is theoretically possible to keep track of every action, every interaction, and most importantly for advertisers, every transaction. Online services such as America Online monitor electronic mail that passes between subscribers to its service, erasing those that it finds offensive. Companies that sell directly through electronic means, such as Land's End and J. C. Penney, not only receive orders on-line, they also know who the buyer is—including their age, sex, household income, and credit history.

While some might argue that such activities are nothing new (TV shows edit phone-in callers to talk shows; companies have been creating data bases for years), what is changing is the speed with which the data can be gathered and the amount of data that is being collected. With regard to the social impact of electronic communications, Howard Rheingold, in his book *The Virtual Community,* pointed out the following:

Yesterday, you might have gone to the supermarket and watched someone total up the bill with a bar-code reader. Perhaps you paid with an ATM card or credit card or used one as identification for a check. Last night, maybe the data describing what you bought and who you are were telecommunicated from the supermarket to a central collection point. This morning, detailed information about your buying habits could have been culled from one database and sold to a third party who could compile it tomorrow into another electronic dossier somewhere, one that knows what you buy and where you live and how much money you owe. Next week, a fourth party might purchase that dossier, combine it with a few tens of millions of others on an optical disk, and offer to sell the collection of information as a marketing tool.[54]

Consumer concerns about the right to privacy are pronounced. A poll conducted by Louis Harris for Equifax, a data base company involved in credit reporting, found that nearly half of those polled (47 percent) were very concerned about threats to their personal privacy. An even higher proportion (59 percent) said that they had at some point refused to give information to a company because they felt it was too personal.

Congress passed the Communications Decency Act in 1996 to prohibit all forms of obscenity and indecency from online communications, although the bill was declared unconstitutional by the Supreme Court because it was an infringement on free speech rights. Some of the most heavily trafficked areas of the Internet involve sexual topics, whether that means user groups where people discuss the subject, or *Playboy* magazine's site on the World Wide Web, which features a digital picture of a nude model. But despite the desire to protect both free speech and consumer privacy on the Web, the pressure to clean up the online environment remains strong.

Sources: Howard Rheingold, *The Virtual Community: Homesteading on the Electronic Frontier* (Reading, MA: Addison-Wesley Publishing Company, 1996); and *The Equifax-Harris Mid Decade Consumer Privacy Survey, 1995* (Atlanta, GA: Equifax, Inc., 1995).

four-part test to determine whether the advertising could be regulated. The four-part test consists of the following four questions:

1. *Is the commercial speech on an illegal activity, or is it misleading?* If the answer is yes, then the speech can automatically be restricted. If the answer is no, then the following three questions must be answered affirmatively:

2. *Is the government interest in suppressing the commercial speech substantial?*

3. *Does the proposed regulation directly advance the government interest asserted?*

4. *Does the proposed regulation go no further than necessary to advance that interest?*

That same test has subsequently been applied in a casino advertising case in Puerto Rico in 1986; in a case involving the distribution of shopping flyers on newsracks in Cincinnati, Ohio (*City of Cincinnati v Discovery,* 1993);[55] and in the right to advertise liquor prices in Rhode Island (*44 Liquormart et al. v Rhode Island,* 1996).[56] In each case, the Supreme Court has gone through the steps of the test to determine whether it is appropriate to regulate and/or prohibit the various forms of commercial speech.

For advertisers, part of the problem is that it remains difficult to determine at times what constitutes "commercial speech." The courts attempt to balance the right of the individual to receive a message with the right of an individual or company to send it. Exhibit 3–15 summarizes some of the major concerns that must be considered when analyzing commercial expression.

Although the Supreme Court has been considering commercial speech issues for more than 50 years, its work is never final. New media and new technologies will ensure that there will be new regulatory issues to consider in the future. As discussed in "Technology Watch: Free Speech versus Consumer Privacy on the Web," nowhere is this currently more obvious than with the rapid growth of the World Wide Web and online services as communications (and advertising) media.

Federal Regulation

Although the most important cases on advertising end up in the Supreme Court, ongoing

EXHIBIT 3–15   Issues of Concern in Analyzing Commercial Expression

THE MESSAGE

Sender	The sender has the right to communicate with targets or with the general public.
Receiver	The receiver has the right to receive information on products, the right to ignore information, and the right to not be exposed to information.
Content	The balance of information versus persuasion in the message and the social importance of the message must be considered.
Medium	The degree of intrusiveness and persuasiveness provided by the medium, as well as the availability and cost of alternative media, are points for consideration.

GOVERNMENT'S ROLE IN PROTECTION

Sender	The government must assure the sender reasonable access to media.
Receiver	The government must maintain the balance of power between the sender and the receiver.
Public	The government must set minimum standards that prevent excessive intrusion and place restrictions on sensitive topics.

Source: Karl A. Boedecker, Fred W. Morgan, and Linda Berns Wright, "The Evolution of First Amendment Protection for Commercial Speech," *Journal of Marketing* 59 (January 1995): 38–47.

regulation is handled by several government agencies. The key authorities, whose jurisdictions sometimes overlap, include the Federal Trade Commission, Federal Communications Commission, Food and Drug Administration, Bureau of Alcohol, Tobacco, and Firearms (Treasury Department), Patent and Trademark Office, and Library of Congress (see Exhibit 3–16). Each agency is discussed below.

FEDERAL TRADE COMMISSION   The primary government authority for regulating advertising that occurs across state lines is the **Federal Trade Commission (FTC).** Under the terms of the 1914 Federal Trade Commission Act, the FTC was given responsibility to protect the marketplace from anti-competitive activities that restrained trade. As such, its powers were defined narrowly to concern itself with "unfair methods of competition." It was not until the passage of the Wheeler-Lea Act in 1938 that the FTC's role broadened to one of consumer protection. The Wheeler-Lea Act amended the FTC Act to

EXHIBIT 3–16   Federal Regulatory Authorities in Advertising

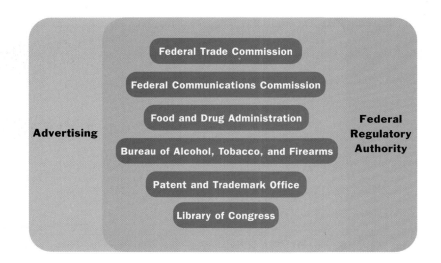

add "unfair or deceptive practices in commerce" to the rubric of the Commission.

The difference between deception and unfairness is worth noting. *Deception* concerns only the likelihood of injury, whereas *unfairness* has to involve actual harm. The Wheeler-Lea Act defined false advertising for the first time, calling it any advertising that contained or omitted content relevant to a consumer's decision or use of a product under ordinary circumstances. This gave the FTC more power to investigate business practices without a complaint being filed, order advertisers to stop misleading practices, and fine companies for not heeding its orders. The FTC was also empowered to guard against deceptive and misleading advertising of food, drugs, and cosmetics, an area of potential jurisdictional overlap with the Food and Drug Administration (FDA). The FDA continues to have jurisdiction over the contents and labeling of food, drugs, and cosmetics, while the FTC regulates the advertising. The FDA will be discussed in detail later in this section.

In the socially active 1970s, the FTC's powers were enhanced by the Magnuson-Moss Warranty-Federal Trade Commission Improvement Act (Warranty Act) in 1975. It could now specify rules for the use of warranties in advertising and promotion, demand substanti-

ation of advertising claims, and rule on "unfair or deceptive acts or practices in or affecting commerce" *before they occurred.* One of the FTC's broadest powers is the authority to issue **trade regulation rules.** Trade regulation rules encompass the Commission's conclusions concerning unlawful trade practices, typically for an entire industry; they can be issued before any violation has occurred and can include legal remedies for any rule violations.

In 1980, the FTC Improvement Act limited some of the Commission's power. New procedures were established for review of FTC actions, and a new requirement was added to stipulate that both deception and unfairness had to be present to support trade rules or legal action.

ORGANIZATION AND PROCEDURES OF

THE FTC   The FTC is divided into three separate areas: the Commission, Administrative Law Judges, and the commission staff, as illustrated in Exhibit 3–17. The Commission is made up of five commissioners appointed by the president. Their role is to make rules, hear complaints, and decide issues. The Judges, who work independently of the Commission and staff, conduct hearings, while the staff members advise the commissioners of potentially deceptive advertising that they have either investigated themselves or about which they have received complaints.

The most common instigator of a complaint is a competing company, although sometimes complaints are brought by consumers. Two types of advertisements that often bring in complaints are comparative advertising and testimonials. In **comparative advertising,** one brand names another brand or company and compares it (usually unfavorably) to itself.

From the consumer's standpoint, comparative ads can be considered helpful and informative because they show the product features of two competing brands. However, the product being compared may object to the way it is portrayed and seek to have such an ad modified or stopped altogether. To do so, advertisers turn to the Lanham Act, which was established in 1946 to prevent an advertiser from making false claims about his own goods and services. In a revised version of the Act, passed in 1988, advertisers were permitted to bring civil suits over false claims about a competitor in com-

EXHIBIT 3–17   **Structure and Organization of the FTC**

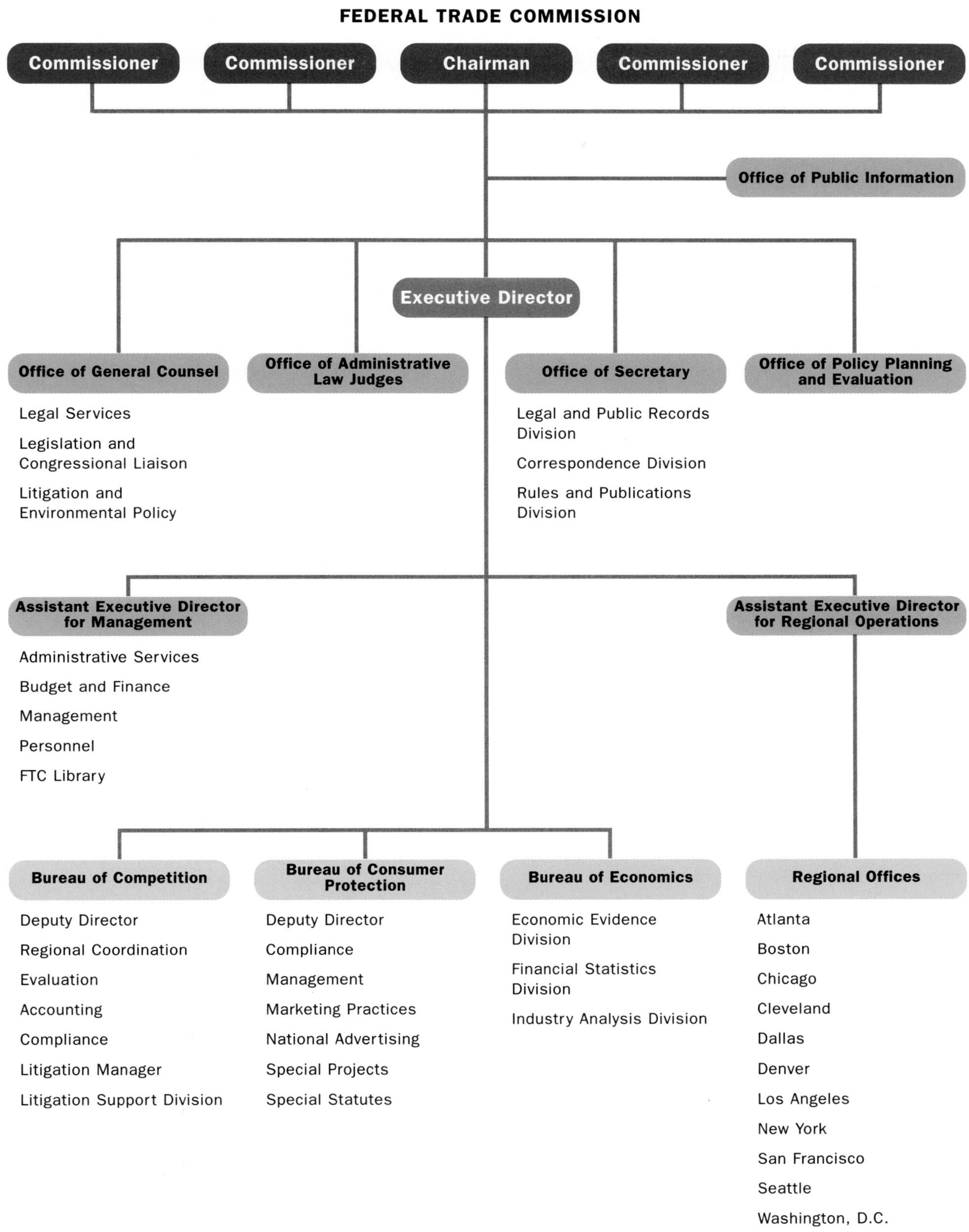

FEDERAL TRADE COMMISSION

| Commissioner | Commissioner | Chairman | Commissioner | Commissioner |

Office of Public Information

Executive Director

| **Office of General Counsel** | **Office of Administrative Law Judges** | **Office of Secretary** | **Office of Policy Planning and Evaluation** |

Office of General Counsel

Legal Services

Legislation and Congressional Liaison

Litigation and Environmental Policy

Office of Secretary

Legal and Public Records Division

Correspondence Division

Rules and Publications Division

Assistant Executive Director for Management

Administrative Services

Budget and Finance

Management

Personnel

FTC Library

Assistant Executive Director for Regional Operations

| **Bureau of Competition** | **Bureau of Consumer Protection** | **Bureau of Economics** | **Regional Offices** |

Bureau of Competition

Deputy Director

Regional Coordination

Evaluation

Accounting

Compliance

Litigation Manager

Litigation Support Division

Bureau of Consumer Protection

Deputy Director

Compliance

Management

Marketing Practices

National Advertising

Special Projects

Special Statutes

Bureau of Economics

Economic Evidence Division

Financial Statistics Division

Industry Analysis Division

Regional Offices

Atlanta

Boston

Chicago

Cleveland

Dallas

Denver

Los Angeles

New York

San Francisco

Seattle

Washington, D.C.

Source: Federal Trade Commission, *Your Federal Trade Commission: What It Is and What It Does* (Washington, DC: Government Printing Office, 1977).

parative advertising. In a 1996 decision, the U.S. Court of Appeals for the Second Circuit sided with Campbell Soup Company in its efforts to show an ad for its Prego spaghetti sauce that compared it favorably to its larger-share rival Ragu. Campbell's TV commercial showed the two brands being poured through a slotted spoon over spaghetti, with Prego being thicker and less runny than Ragu.[57] An example of a comparative ad for the U.S. Postal Service that turned out to be quite controversial appears in Exhibit 3–18. One of the competitors named in the ad, FedEx, threatened to sue the Postal Service (USPS), claiming that unfair comparisons were being made. USPS refused to pull the ads, and later reported that it had seen record increases in the use of its Priority Mail Service, which it attributed directly to the series of comparative advertisements.

The use of a **testimonial,** where a celebrity or product user endorses a given brand, can also result in problems for advertisers. Like comparative ads, testimonials are a very powerful way to enhance a brand's image and gain additional attention and prestige for the brand. However, the FTC has at times held the endorser responsible for damages where the testimonial is false. In addition to not making any false claims in the testimonial, the endorser must actually use the product, and any claims made must be reasonable and understandable by the average consumer.

In a 1978 ruling, the FTC ruled that an ad in which singer Pat Boone gave a testimonial to a topical acne medication was misleading because he implied that all of his daughters had used the product when in fact they had not.[58] A few years later, the actors James Garner and Cybill Shepherd were both showcased as celebrity endorsers for the Beef Council, a trade group that promotes the consumption of beef and beef products. The campaign was fairly popular until it was revealed that neither Garner nor Shepherd ate meat at all. They were rapidly dropped as endorsers, although no FTC action occurred. Exhibit 3–19 shows an example of a testimonial ad.

There are five actions that the FTC has power to take against an advertiser when it upholds a complaint. They are discussed here in order of severity, from least to most serious.

EXHIBIT 3–18 Comparative ads, while informative and helpful to consumers faced with product decisions, are often controversial. This ad from the U.S. Postal Service was challenged by FedEx on the basis that the comparisons in the ad were unfair and misleading.

Work hard. Fix it right the first time. That's when people trust you.

Al Duebber, Shop owner and ASE Certified Automotive Technician, Cincinnati

I've built my business by giving people something they can trust. For me, that means working hard to build relationships with each of them. It also means making sure my technicians have the training and skills to fix their cars right. Because that's what really matters. After all, when customers can trust my shop, they can trust their car.

Snap-on

It takes a lot to be an auto technician.™ To find the best, look for Snap-on® tools and equipment.

EXHIBIT 3–19 Testimonial ads, such as the one shown here, use endorsements from product users to increase brand recognition and improve brand image. These ads have come under increasing FTC scrutiny, however, and as a result, advertisers must verify that all claims made by the endorser are both true and reasonable.

1. *Consent order.* When a company signs a consent order, it agrees to correct or discontinue the questionable practices. Proposed orders are given a public hearing, and consumer comments are taken into account. Companies that violate a consent order can be fined.

2. *Cease and desist order.* If a consent order is not signed, the case goes before an Administrative Law Judge, who may recommend a dismissal or issue a cease and desist order. The accused party must stop the alleged deceptive act immediately, but the order carries no punishment unless the company fails to comply. The judge's decision may be appealed to a Federal Court of Appeals by either party.

3. *Affirmative disclosure.* With affirmative disclosure, the company can say what it wishes to say, but in order to do so, it is required to qualify it with another statement. Warnings on cigarette packages and in ads for that product are examples of affirmative disclosure.

4. *Advertising substantiation.* Similar to affirmative disclosure, advertising substantiation requires that if a company wishes to make a particular statement, it must include proof for that statement. The goal is to let consumers make informed decisions in the marketplace. Responsibility for providing the information rests with the advertiser, its agency, any retailers who might disseminate the ads, and even a celebrity endorser. Substantiation is designed to make sure that advertisers can support their claims before they run the ads.

5. *Corrective advertising.* The most stringent remediation the FTC can impose is **corrective advertising,** which forces an advertiser to rectify misleading statements from previous advertising. The advertiser has to admit publicly that the product claims it had previously made were wrong. This is the only remedy that acknowledges that consumers may still remember the effects of any deceptive advertising.

In imposing corrective advertising, the FTC has determined that simply stopping the deceptive or misleading advertisement is not sufficient to stop the deception. The Commission can specify all of the details of the new message, including content, wording, place-

CONSUMER INSIGHT

In the Soup

In 1968 the Campbell Soup Company was launching a new flavor of soup called Chicken and Stars, a chicken soup with small pasta stars. In filming the commercial, it was found that because the pasta pieces were heavier than the liquid they were in, they fell to the bottom of the bowl. The production staff solved the problem by "propping up" the pasta with pieces of broken glass on the bottom of the bowl to force more of the stars to the surface. At the time, this was an accepted and common technique, a form of artifice practiced by most advertisers. For example, behind the glamorous model's fashionable clothes were pins keeping the garment together; and underneath a tasty-looking hamburger would be plastic or glue to prevent it from collapsing under the hot camera lights.

But this time, Campbell's found itself facing a lawsuit. The Federal Trade Commission requested more information on how the soups were prepared and photographed in both print and TV commercials. It then charged Campbell's with false and deceptive advertising. Campbell's agreed not to continue the practice. In 1969, however, five law students, as part of a class project at George Washington University, reopened the suit under the guise of a corporation they had formed called "Students Opposing Unfair Practices," or SOUP. The group demanded corrective advertising, forcing Campbell's to state in each ad that they had previously used deceptive practices in their advertising. The FTC agreed to investigate further. The proceedings lasted another two years, going all the way to the Supreme Court, before finally ending up at the U.S. Court of Appeals in 1972, where the case was dismissed.

The case set the stage for subsequent justification to impose corrective advertising in cases of deceptive advertising at both the federal and state levels. It also made advertisers and agencies far more wary of how they depict products in commercials. Now the cream-filled cookies you see in commercials are no longer filled with shaving cream, and the head of a beer is real, not created with soapsuds. The onus is now placed on the creative director to shoot the ads as quickly as possible with the genuine product.

QUESTIONS

Do you think the SOUP protesters were right in demanding that Campbell's produce corrective advertising? How else might Campbell's have been punished for their misleading advertisements?

Sources: Adapted from Dick Mercer, "Tempest in a Soup Can," *Advertising Age,* 17 October 1994, 25–29; and Julia Miller, "Shoot Fast, 'Cut Back on Trickery'," *Advertising Age,* 17 October 1994, 9.

The Campbell Soup Company came under fire from the FTC for its use of props in its ads (left). As a result, Campbell's resorted to other less-controversial methods to show its soup ingredients (right). This charge against Campbell's proved to be the impetus for increased federal and state legislation designed to limit the use of deceptive advertising practices.

ment, duration, media mix, and budget. One of the most notorious cases concerning corrective advertising involved Warner-Lambert's Listerine mouthwash. The company had stated for many years that the brand was effective at preventing colds and sore throats. The Commission found this to be a deceptive and misleading claim, as the mouthwash has no medical benefits. In 1975, it ordered Warner-Lambert to spend as much money in corrective advertising as it had spent on the campaign, which amounted to $10 million. The FTC argued that consumers had absorbed the misleading message to such a degree that equally strong corrective ads were necessary. The company's new ads had to include the following statement: "Contrary to prior advertising, Listerine will not help prevent colds or sore throats or lessen their severity." The advertiser's appeal to the U.S. District Court failed, so it had to place the corrective ads.

In recent years, there have been fewer cases of corrective advertising. While advertisers argue that their First Amendment rights to free speech are violated with this remedy, the main reason the action is less commonly used is because research indicates that the remedy is not particularly effective.

In determining whether an advertisement is deceptive or misleading, the Commission often relies on consumer research. In most cases, this research is conducted on behalf of the advertiser and is used to substantiate the claim. Such research may be used to determine the scale or size of the deception, how important the ad message is in influencing the purchase decision, and the impact of regulatory action on changing consumer misperceptions. Problems can arise from this type of research. It tends to be conducted by survey, either in person or via telephone and mail, but if those who complete the survey are not representative of those likely to buy the product and see the ads, then the research findings may not be relevant. Even the way that questions are phrased in the survey can have a strong impact on the responses given by consumers.

While many claims are brought against advertisers each year, most end up being settled at the beginning of the process, via consent orders. Companies fear the cost of litigation, as well as the adverse publicity that may result. In addition, if companies refuse the terms of the consent order, they must go through the full legal process and stand to have the findings go against them. The case filed against the Campbell Soup Company, as described in "Consumer Insight: In the Soup," exemplifies the power that complaints can have in getting companies to change their practices.

THE FEDERAL COMMUNICATIONS COMMISSION The Communications Act of 1934 established the seven-member **Federal Communications Commission (FCC).** Although it has no direct authority to control advertising, the FCC does have jurisdiction over radio, television, and telephone industries and can therefore control some aspects of radio and TV advertising, such as obscenity and indecency in ads. In addition, because it is the regulatory body that issues or renews broadcast TV station licenses, it has the authority to determine whether such an action serves the "public interest, convenience and necessity." If advertising is involved in making such a decision, the FCC can conclude that the license should not be given. Cable television also comes under FCC jurisdiction, but it is less heavily regulated in many ways than its broadcast counterpart, at least in terms of content.

THE FOOD AND DRUG ADMINISTRATION
The **Food and Drug Administration (FDA)** was created in 1906 by the Pure Food and Drug Act. The FDA was designed to protect the nation's health and since 1938 has had jurisdiction over food labeling. Because labels and ads must be consistent in the information provided, the FDA does have considerable influence on advertising. In 1993, food labels were overhauled, bringing standardization and consistency to the nutritional and content information provided on the label. This meant that any advertisements that depicted or referred to that information had to comply with the new regulations, including the use of terms such as "low fat," "low cholesterol," or "high fiber." An example of how the information might be used in an ad is given in Exhibit 3–20.

The FDA also controls prescription drug advertising, whether it is aimed at consumers or the medical profession. As more and more drug companies start promoting their products directly to consumers, they are required to provide as much detailed information as is given to medical specialists. This can increase the ad size by as much as one or two pages, as can be seen in Exhibit 3–21, a consumer ad for Claritin allergy medication.

As noted earlier, the FDA was given regulatory authority in 1996 over tobacco advertising once the product was ruled to be an addictive substance, although a final court ruling has not yet been issued.

BUREAU OF ALCOHOL, TOBACCO, AND FIREARMS   The **Bureau of Alcohol, Tobacco, and Firearms (BATF)** is involved in the regulation of alcoholic beverage advertising through its oversight role in the manufacture and distribution of this product. The BATF issues and renews permits for distillers, vintners, brewers, importers, and beverage wholesalers. In addition, it is responsible for the

EXHIBIT 3–20   This ad for Chef Boyardee ravioli uses the new, simpler presentation of nutritional and content information to support its position as a healthy and nutritious after-school snack.

EXHIBIT 3–21   As is evident in this consumer ad for Claritin, FDA regulations require that a detailed technical product description always appear in conjunction with the creative portion of a drug advertisement.

labeling of such products, including warning messages that, while not yet required on the alcoholic beverages themselves, must be displayed in any facility whose primary business is the sale of such products, such as bars or liquor stores. These messages warn pregnant women about the dangers of drinking while pregnant, along with other health-related consequences of drinking too much.

PATENT AND TRADEMARK OFFICE A **trademark** is defined as any word, name, symbol, or device that is adopted and used by a manufacturer or merchant to identify his goods and distinguish them from those manufactured by others. In order to be official, it has to be registered with the **Patent and Trademark Office,** which was established in the 1946 Lanham Act. Examples of trademarks include the Good Housekeeping seal of approval, the Coca-Cola logo, and the Ocean Spray mark, which represents the collective organization of cranberry growers that make up the Ocean Spray cooperative.

As shown in Exhibit 3–22, there are different kinds of marks that can all be legally registered. A trademark identifies who makes a given product, whereas a *service mark* does the same for a service provider. A *certification mark* is usually given by a trade association or other kind of governing body and affirms that the product meets its set of standards. Organizations can themselves register a *collective mark,* which identifies them as a group that works cooperatively together.

Trademarks are always followed by the word "Registered" or the symbol ®, which means that the mark has been registered and cannot be copied or used by anyone else without permission. If the mark has not yet been registered but an application has been made, the letters "TM" are used instead. One important note about trademarks is that they are category specific; for example, Hyatt Hotels is trademarked separately from Hyatt Legal Services.

Companies are usually very protective of their trademarks and will sue to maintain that exclusivity. A company such as McDonald's, which spends billions of dollars each year to promote a certain image and unique brand quality, does not want its name to be associated with unfavorable products or services. When someone tried to register the name McDonald's

for a Web site on the Internet, McDonald's responded immediately to prevent that from happening. In return for the individual giving the rights back to the company, McDonald's gave a donation to his high school.

In 1995, the U.S. Supreme Court ruled that because a product may be as well known by its color as its name, a company can trademark a color if it is part of the brand identification of that firm, as shown by clear consumer recognition linking the color to the company. The issue arose in 1985 when Owens Corning Fiberglass Corporation was allowed to trademark the pink color of its building insulation materials. Since then, out of the 135,000 applications made each year, 30 companies have registered colors.[59]

LIBRARY OF CONGRESS Copyright is more extensive than a trademark, giving the copyright holder exclusive right to reproduce, perform, or display "original works of authorship." For advertising, this may include photos, TV commercials, video, illustrations, sound recordings, ads, brochures, displays, and literary works. Ideas, facts, slogans, and symbols cannot be copyrighted. Copyrights should be registered at the **Library of Congress** in order to receive full protection under the Copyright Act of 1976. Works that have been copyrighted display the word *copyright* or the symbol © (or ℗ for Audio items).

Advertisers are concerned about copyright protection for two reasons. The first is to maintain ownership over their "property," which is the original work that they have written, photographed, or recorded. Second, with the copyright, the advertiser is given protection and the right to sue if that material is subsequently used without permission. One of the areas that remains unresolved at this point is the issue of copyright on the Internet; once someone places material up on the Internet and it is publicly available to everyone, it is unclear how the copyright can be protected.

State and Local Regulations

In addition to the various federal regulatory bodies, advertising is also monitored and overseen at both state and local levels. While the regulation of advertising at the state level does vary somewhat across the 50 states, there are several areas of commonality. Just as at the fed-

EXHIBIT 3-22

Trademark

Service Mark

Certification Mark

Collective Mark

eral level, most states have laws preventing unfair or deceptive advertising. In addition, most states have some kind of consumer protection law that resembles the FTC Act; however, unlike the federal regulation, these laws also allow consumers to bring civil suits for damages.

The responsibility for enforcing state laws on advertising tend to rest with a state's attorney general. The **National Association of Attorneys General (NAAG)** has worked to bring actions against advertisers simultaneously in several states, particularly if the federal authorities are reluctant to act. This was seen in the late 1980s, when the NAAG attempted to bring numerous state actions against national airlines that were promoting deeply discounted fares that were either restricted or limited in availability. The states had only limited success, however, because the Supreme Court ruled that the 1978 law that had deregulated the airline industry prevented states from enacting regulations covering airline rates.

Individual cities or localities sometimes have their own offices or bodies that step in to regulate advertising. These may reside in the Office of Consumer Affairs or Office of Consumer Protection. The mandate of these offices is usually not restricted to advertising, but includes overall business practices as well. At times, the FTC may get involved in what at first appears to be a local case if it turns out that interstate commerce is involved. For example, if a product sold locally contains parts manufactured in other states, it may qualify for FTC participation in the case.

R E S E T

1. Where in the U.S. Constitution is advertising given legal protection? What legal precedents exist for this protection?
2. What actions can the FTC take to prevent unfair or deceptive advertising?
3. What are the similarities and differences between federal, state, and local regulation of advertising?

Self-Regulation

Given any kind of choice in the matter, the advertising industry would far prefer to regulate itself. Its arguments for doing so are twofold. First, self-regulation is faster and less expensive than government regulation. The industry claims that it knows best how to solve its own problems. Second, advertisers maintain that they are more likely to adhere to regulations they themselves have developed. Critics of the self-regulatory approach argue, however, that such measures are self-serving and ineffective. They point out there is little incentive for advertisers to comply with any regulations if there is no official body ensuring that compliance.

Nevertheless, three groups are involved in helping to regulate the industry: the Better Business Bureau, professional and trade organizations in the advertising industry, and the media.

BETTER BUSINESS BUREAU Self-regulation of advertising began in 1907 when the Associated Advertising Clubs of the World set up "vigilance committees" to expose cases of fraudulent advertising. Today's equivalent at the local level is the **Better Business Bureau (BBB),** which is made up of 137 local bureaus around the country. The BBB is a private, nonprofit organization whose stated mission is to "promote and foster the highest ethical relationship between businesses and the public through voluntary self-regulation, consumer and business education, and service excellence." It does so by investigating consumer or business complaints of fraudulent activity in the local marketplace.[60]

NATIONAL ADVERTISING REVIEW COUNCIL In 1971, the BBB joined with the American Advertising Federation, the American Association of Advertising Agencies, and the Association of National Advertisers to create a self-regulated advertising review system called the **National Advertising Review Council (NARC),** which monitors national advertising and advises advertisers on its findings. The NARC consists of the **National Advertising Division (NAD)** and the **National Advertising Review Board (NARB).**

Two-thirds of the cases brought to the NAD today come from a competitor's complaint. If the NAD and the advertiser cannot come to resolution, the case is taken to the

EXHIBIT 3–23   **NARC Complaint and Review Procedure**

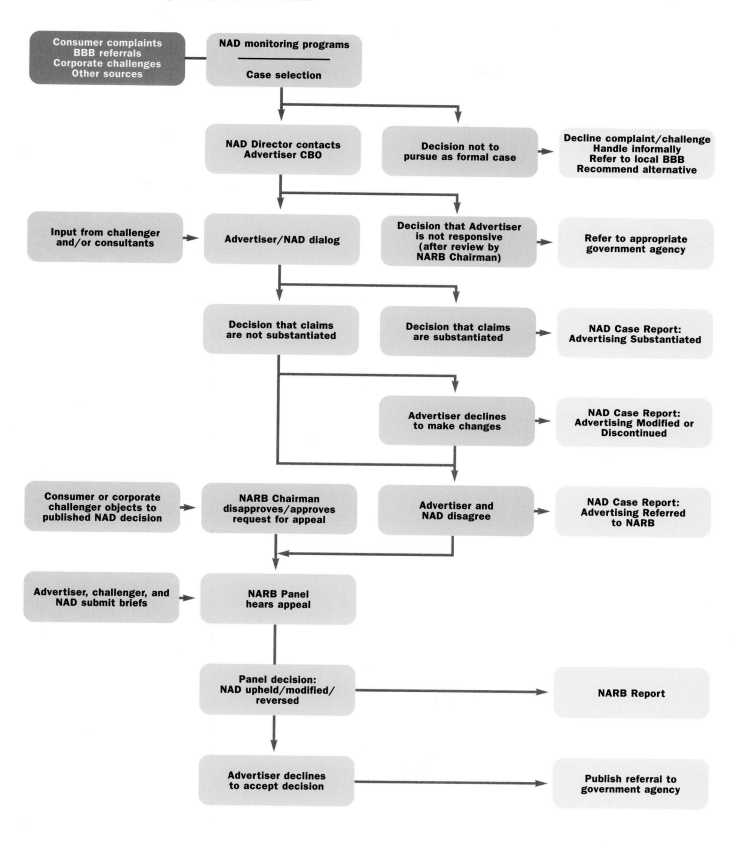

EXHIBIT 3–24   Regulatory Areas Covered by Industry Associations

SUBJECT MATTER OF PROVISION	CODES INCLUDING PROVISION	
	NUMBER	PERCENTAGE
Truth and accuracy	26	100
Substantiation of claims	21	81
Testimonials and endorsements	16	62
Illustrations or television presentations	16	62
Comparative advertising	15	58
Disclosure of complete information	14	54
Price claims	13	50
Puffery	13	50
Taste	12	46
Guarantees and warranties	10	38
Young and immature markets	9	35
Bait advertising	9	35
Use of word *free*	8	31
Layout	8	31
Contests, prizes, and other promotions	8	31
Credit	7	27
Health and safety	7	27
Placement and acceptance in media	7	27
Use of professionally significant words such as *bonded, insured*	6	23
Degradation of societal groups	5	19
Asterisks	5	19
Use of words *factory, manufacturer, wholesaler*	5	19
Fear appeals	3	12
Advertising frequency	3	12
Trade-in allowances	3	12
Abbreviations	2	8
Identification, age, or volume of business	2	8
Advertising space for public causes	1	4

Source: Priscilla A. LaBarbera, "Analyzing and Advancing the State of the Art of Advertising Self-Regulation," *Journal of Advertising* 9, no. 4 (1980).

NARB, made up of 50 representatives from advertisers, agencies, and the general public. The NARB acts as the "court of last resort" for unresolved cases. Each case is reviewed by five people. Exhibit 3–23 illustrates the complaint and review procedure of the NARC.

The conclusions of the NARB are binding on the NAD and the advertiser. If an advertiser then refuses to comply, the only remaining recourse is to refer the complaint to a federal agency, such as the Federal Trade Commission. Between 1971 and 1996, the NAD considered about 3,300 cases, yet only 91 were appealed to the NARB. One-third of those decisions were reversed or changed, and only four were then referred to the FTC.

CHILDREN'S ADVERTISING REVIEW UNIT

The Council of Better Business Bureaus also has a special investigatory arm concerned specifically with children's advertising. The **Children's Advertising Review Unit (CARU)** was founded in 1974 to monitor unfairness in children's advertising. It handles cases in a manner similar to the NAD, calling for substantiation, modification, or discontinuance of the ad in question. In a one-month period, CARU monitors more than 1,000 television commercials, along with ads in print and other media. Only about 10 of these typically raise any issues of concern. CARU accepts ads for pre-broadcast screening, although it will not provide a guarantee that the media will then find those messages acceptable, nor will it guarantee that consumers will not find complaint with the messages.

TRADE AND PROFESSIONAL ASSOCIATIONS

Many industry associations have instituted some kind of self-regulation programs for advertising. The Association of National Advertisers established its own set of codes in 1924, noting the need for truth and accuracy in advertising, and acknowledging problems related to the substantiation of claims, testimonials and endorsements, and comparative advertising. Industry associations may be formed in response to public criticism or to ward off the threat of legal action. The National Infomercial Marketing Association (NIMA), for example, was established in the early 1990s to develop guidelines with the FTC for infomercial labeling. The different regulatory areas covered by such associations are shown in Exhibit 3–24.

The biggest advertising trade organization is the **American Association of Advertising Agencies (AAAA).** The AAAA's Standards of Practice, shown in Exhibit 3–25, includes a creative code that discusses deception, misleading testimonials, price claims, substantiation of claims, and matters of taste. However, in practice, the AAAA rarely imposes sanctions for violations or removes companies from its membership.

MEDIA SELF-REGULATION In addition to media trade associations such as the National Association of Broadcasters or American Business Press, which have codes of conduct for advertising, media self-regulation also occurs at the individual program or newspaper. A television network or magazine must agree to run an ad before it can appear, giving the media an important regulatory role to play in terms of screening and potentially rejecting an ad. This *clearance process* is in contrast to all other forms of regulation (FTC, NARD, etc.), which can only review the advertising after it has run and caused potential harm. Each major broadcast network maintains a "standards and practices" group that clears all ads before they appear on TV. In recent years, the networks have been criticized for their lack of vigilance in what they allow on the air, but they are still reluctant to allow controversial products, or commercials that may offend on the air. Magazines vary in their policing activity. Some, such as *Fitness* or *Self,* refuse to accept any cigarette or tobacco products because they do not fit with the image of those magazines. Others, such as *Good Housekeeping,* refuse to run ads for products that do not meet stringent product-testing standards.

For local media, it is up to an individual station or newspaper manager to decide whether an ad can run. This varies from state to state or even city to city, and may be program dependent. For example, the ABC network drama "NYPD Blue" was considered problematic and too controversial for a number of ABC's local TV stations when it first aired in 1993. Those stations therefore chose to show a different program instead, which meant that the messages of national advertisers who had bought time in "NYPD Blue" could not be seen in cities such as Fort Worth or Dallas, Texas.

EXHIBIT 3–25 AAAA Standards of Practice

We hold that a responsibility of advertising agencies is to be a constructive force in business.

We hold that, to discharge this responsibility, advertising agencies must recognize an obligation not only to their clients, but to the public, the media they employ, and to each other. As a business, the advertising agency must operate within the framework of competition. It is recognized that keen and vigorous competition, honestly conducted, is necessary to the growth and the health of the American business. However, unethical competitive practices in the advertising agency business lead to financial waste, dilution of service, diversion of manpower, loss of prestige, and tend to weaken public confidence both in advertisements and in the institution of advertising.

We hold that the advertising agency should compete on merit and not by attempts at discrediting or disparaging a competitor agency, or its work, directly or by inference, or by circulating harmful rumors about another agency, or by making unwarranted claims of particular skill in judging or prejudging advertising copy.

To these ends, the American Association of Advertising Agencies has adopted the following *Creative Code* as being in the best interests of the public, the advertisers, the media, and the agencies themselves. The A.A.A.A. believes the Code's provisions serve as a guide to the kind of agency conduct that experience has shown to be wise, foresighted, and constructive. In accepting membership, an agency agrees to follow it.

CREATIVE CODE

We, the members of the American Association of Advertising Agencies, in addition to supporting and obeying the laws and legal regulations pertaining to advertising, undertake to extend and broaden the application of high ethical standards. Specifically, we will not knowingly create advertising that contains:

a. False or misleading statements or exaggerations, visual or verbal.

b. Testimonials that do not reflect the real opinion of the individual(s) involved.

c. Price claims that are misleading.

d. Claims insufficiently supported or that distort the true meaning or practical application of statements made by professional or scientific authority.

e. Statements, suggestions, or pictures offensive to public decency or minority segments of the population.

We recognize that there are areas that are subject to honestly different interpretations and judgment. Nevertheless, we agree not to recommend to an advertiser, and to discourage the use of, advertising that is in poor or questionable taste or that is deliberately irritating through aural or visual content or presentation.

Comparative advertising shall be governed by the same standards of truthfulness, claim substantiation, tastefulness, etc., as apply to other types of advertising.

Source: American Association of Advertising Agencies, 1993.

The regulatory environment cannot be looked at in isolation from the social, cultural, and economic arena, either at the national or international level. Ultimately, although advertising is designed to be a creative and inventive process, it is in the advertiser's best interest to adjust to what society considers acceptable, because if that is not done, the message will not be seen or heard and will therefore have no opportunity to help increase sales.

Advertising Regulation Around the World

As we move more and more toward the globalization of advertisers and agencies, issues concerning the regulation of advertising will increasingly arise at the international level. While most countries have some advertising regulation in place, the extent and type of this regulation differs substantially between them. This is not simply a difference in the laws, either; cultural distinctions may mean that what is considered acceptable by one country is thought to be offensive or improper in another. Comparative advertising, for example, is banned or very heavily regulated in several European Union countries and in Japan because it is felt that, in addition to being culturally inappropriate, such ads are inherently misleading and deceptive.

Other countries are starting to impose regulations on advertising, as well. In China, where ad spending has risen 100 times since 1985, the first comprehensive law on advertising was passed in 1994. The State Administration for Industry and Commerce, the government body charged with overseeing the rules for all media forms and all industries in China, screened 1,500 television commercials. Ninety were found to have violated the law and were prevented from being aired until they had been changed.61

Regulations on advertising are greatly influenced by the economic and social structure of the country. Islamic countries, for example, follow the teachings of the Koran. All rules of behavior, including business transactions, must comply with those precepts. The fact that it is illegal to charge interest on loans makes a big difference not only to companies such as Visa or MasterCard but also to retailers or other manufacturers that would otherwise allow consumers to buy goods on credit.

In the former communist countries, where a market system is only starting to be introduced, there is still uncertainty about how best to regulate the advertising industry. In Russia, the decision to ban all advertising on the main television station, Ostankino, resulted in the murder of one of that station's most popular hosts, Victor Listayev. Moreover, one of the fiercest debates between the United States and China in the two countries' discussion on opening up trade links concerns copyright protection. Although China has had such laws on the books for several years, they are rarely enforced, and there is a flourishing trade in the copying of all forms of foreign works, from books to movies to computer software.

In much of the western, industrialized world, legal principles have been developed through court interpretations of statutes, rulings, and legal precedent. These principles are known as **common law.** Advertising regulation in such countries is subject to new interpretations and changes as the times and political and economic landscapes change. Many of the countries of Western Europe have regulations that have been developed following **code law** that evolved from Roman law, where rulings are divided between commercial, civil, and criminal codes.

INTERNATIONAL REGULATION OF ADVERTISING

The highest level of international regulation can be found at the United Nations (UN). Any decisions made by the UN, which are more likely to concern general business practices rather than advertising specifically, are not legally binding on individual countries because the UN is not a court of law. The UN does, however, wield considerable influence on various areas of business enterprise, such as the manufacture, sale, and promotion of foods or the protection of intellectual property rights.

One of the more widely publicized efforts involving a UN organization concerned the marketing and advertising of baby milk formula to Third World countries. Several companies involved in this activity were charged with indiscriminately promoting this product in areas of the world that were ill-equipped to use it, due to illiteracy, lack of sanitation, and inadequate water supplies, among other reasons. Misuse of the formula was blamed for millions of infant deaths in the 1980s. A code was adopted in 1981 that banned the promotion and advertising of this formula. This was supported by every country except the U.S., which objected to the code's rules conflicting with individual country laws. The companies, however, did comply with the ruling.

ADVERTISING REGULATION IN EUROPE On 31 December 1992, economic and social barriers between the member nations of the European Community (EC) were removed with the formation of the European Union (EU).[62] Since that time, some of the concerns that affect advertising regulation have been taken to a supranational level. Issues that were previously only the concern of individual countries must now also gain the approval of the regulatory bodies within the European Union. The main goal of the EC—which originally was formed after World War II by Belgium, France, Italy, Luxembourg, Germany, and the Netherlands—is to work toward complete integration of the member nations' economic and political systems. With the addition of six other countries (Denmark, Greece, Ireland, Portugal, Spain, and the United Kingdom), the EC set up a supranational governmental system consisting of executive, legislative, and judicial bodies.

The European Commission, made up of 17 appointed members, supervises and implements EC policies and regulations. The Council of Ministers consists of a minister from each member country and has responsibility for deciding which Commission proposals shall become EC law or policy. The European Parliament is elected by people in all member countries and consults with both the Commission and Council on legislation, offering recommendations and amendments. Finally, the European Court of Justice is the Supreme Court of the EC. It can challenge laws of the EC or member nations whose laws are not in line with those of the Community.

For advertisers, the primary regulation affecting business is the 1984 Council directive on misleading advertising, which was finally implemented in 1986 after a decade of consultation and wrangling among member nations. Like all EC directives, it is binding on all members, yet must rely on individual countries to enforce it at the national level.

Despite the desire to enact pan-European regulations, in many areas, it remains up to individual countries to implement them. Advertising to children is one such example. Exhibit 3–26 shows how the limits on advertising to children vary from country to country. More recently, the EC has begun discussions on how the it should handle online and computer communications, though as yet, no official papers or proposals have been issued.

EXHIBIT 3–26   Examples of Differences in Regulation of Children's Ads Across Europe

COUNTRY	REGULATION
Austria	No advertising of war toys.
Belgium	Ads for candy on TV must show a stylized toothbrush.
Denmark	No advertising of prizes for children.
Finland	No ads during children's programs.
France	No deception on packaging or contents.
Germany	No ads that encourage children to beg parents to buy product.
Greece	All toy ads banned on TV from 7A.M.–1 P.M.
Ireland	Ads should not encourage the consumption of alcohol.
Italy	Ads aimed at adults not allowed in children's programming.
Netherlands	No candy ads before 7:55 P.M.
Portugal	Ads must not exploit the inexperience of children.
Spain	Size and price of products must appear.
Sweden	Price on ad prohibited.
United Kingdom	Can only show what can reasonably be done with a toy.

Source: Lucy Rouse, Dilip Subramanian, Ia Wadendall, and Fiona McHugh, "A Question of Child Care," *Marketing & Media Europe 1996,* March 1996, 34–35.

SUMMARY

In order to have a complete understanding of advertising and how it works, it is important to examine whether advertising is a mirror of society, reflecting people's tastes, or a shaper of society, influencing what people think, say, and do. Advertising can be considered an institution within the social, ethical, economic, and legal environment. As an institution, advertising helps people make decisions about the goods and services they might use or buy. It helps define people as consumers. Some would argue that the institution exercises social control but has no social responsibility, making people accept what advertising offers rather than giving them complete information on all that is available.

As a mirror of society, advertising can be seen to reflect popular culture, depicting people or scenes in the ads to which the chosen target audience can relate. The reflecting role that advertising plays is also shown in the way it reflects a brand's value, although this erroneously tends to equate dollars spent with customer preferences. Advertising does give people a sense of belonging to a larger society, showing them situations or individuals to whom they can relate. It also reflects the values of society as a whole, such as the materialism of the 1980s or the "value" consciousness of the early 1990s.

In contrast, advertising is also a force that shapes society. It promotes materialism by giving people the idea that they must have the latest car, clothing, or cosmetic item, whether they really need it or not. The impact of advertising on special audiences such as children or minorities indicates the power that the institution can have on society. Children are vulnerable to messages showing sugar-filled cereals as "wholesome" breakfasts, or billboards for alcohol and tobacco showing everyone having a fun time. For minorities or other select groups such as the elderly and disabled, advertising is considered a strong shaping force in the way it can create stereotypes of those groups—always showing African Americans as athletes or musicians, for example. The difficulty lies in creating messages that can be understood and appreciated by as wide an audience as possible without depicting demeaning images of the people in the ads.

One argument for advertising as a shaper of society, that it somehow has subliminal power to make people subconsciously do or buy things they normally wouldn't, has been largely discredited. A more forceful claim, that advertising increases the cost of goods and services, is somewhat true, in that own-label or generic items that advertise little if at all are almost always less expensive. However, the cost of goods depends on other factors as well, including economies of scale, production, distribution, or product quality. It has never been proven that advertising helps the sale of bad products. The relationship between advertising and the media has always been close because most media forms are supported by advertisers. Advertising is said to be corruptive, both in the censorship power it may have on media information it does not like and in the sheer number of commercial messages conveyed. But advertisers are aware of their social responsibilities and use their influence beneficially in many nonprofit campaigns undertaken by the industry at no charge.

Matters of culture and taste are always of concern to advertisers. Messages aimed at ethnic groups, for example, must be easily understood and believed by those individuals. There may also be cultural differences from region to region, whether in product preferences, media usage, or lifestyle activities. These can be reflected in the message content. The use of certain images or themes can be critical, especially where those depictions are of a sexual or controversial nature. Advertisers have to be careful not to offend either their selected target or the public at large, whether through the types of messages they choose (such as fear appeals) or through the images they show.

Advertising is frequently criticized as being an industry without any ethical standards. While it has no industry code of practice, advertisers are aware of their responsibilities, but they also know that advertising's purpose is to promote the sale or use of goods and services. Nonetheless, there is much debate about advertising to certain consumer groups, children in particular, and about the promotion of specific products, including alcohol, tobacco, and pharmaceutical products.

Advertising is an important economic force in society. In most industrialized countries that operate under the free market system, advertising helps consumers to satisfy their wants and needs by informing them of what is available. In socialized systems, found in several European countries, advertising still informs and persuades, but the government has a greater say in what can be promoted or stated. In a controlled system, it is the State that makes many decisions on behalf of the people; as a result, advertising is limited to State-approved messages that exhort people to act a certain way.

In a free market system, advertising is thought either to create market power or to provide information. Those who believe advertising creates market power argue that its main role is to differentiate products, with the focus being on brand images. In this view, competition tends to be among a few larger firms because the price of entry into the market is high. Those who believe advertising provides information argue that advertising, by providing consumers with information, helps keep prices down and encourages competition on price.

Advertising's legal standing begins in the First Amendment to the U.S. Constitution, which prevents Congress from abridging the freedom of speech. Advertising is a special kind of speech, however, known as commercial speech, which means that its protection is more limited. The main federal regulation of advertising comes from the Federal Trade Commission (FTC). The FTC's primary responsibility is to prevent unfair or deceptive acts and practices. The two most problematic areas are comparative advertising and testimonials. The FTC has the power to issue five types of remedies against advertisers: consent orders, cease and desist orders, affirmative disclosure, advertising substantiation, or corrective advertising.

Other national government agencies involved in advertising regulation include the Federal Communications Commission, the Food and Drug Administration, the Bureau of Alcohol, Tobacco, and Firearms, the Patent and Trademark Office, and the Library of Congress. In addition, there are state and local regulatory bodies, many of which mirror the activities of the federal authorities.

The advertising industry tries to regulate itself through the National Advertising Division of the Better Business Bureau. Decisions are placed before the National Advertising Review Council, with appeals sent to the National Advertising Review Board. A special body, the Children's Advertising Review Unit, deals with cases involving children's advertising. In addition, trade and professional organizations have their own standards of practice, while the media impose codes of conduct on their members and set limits on the ads that they will accept.

The regulation of advertising varies considerably from country to country and depends on cultural and economic forces. There are few regulations that cross borders, although the European Community is developing some rules for its 16 member states. The United Nations has also intervened in advertising-related matters where issues of health or economics are at stake.

REVIEW QUESTIONS

1. What is the purpose of an institution? How is advertising considered an institution?

2. How is advertising a mirror of society? How is it a shaper of society?

3. What are some of the choices and challenges that advertisers must consider when deciding whether to include stereotypes in advertising?

4. Why is advertising to children such a sensitive issue? What are the social, ethical, economic, and legal issues to consider?

5. How are the advertisements of alcohol and tobacco regulated in the U.S. and globally?

6. What are advertising's two roles in a free market society?

7. How does commercial speech differ from noncommercial speech? How does this differentiation affect advertising?

8. How is advertising regulated at a federal level?

9. What types of self-regulatory measures are there? How effective are they?

10. What are some of the obstacles preventing effective international regulation of advertising?

1. Is advertising a mirror or shaper of society? Explain your answer.

2. Discuss the arguments for and against a comprehensive ban on all forms of tobacco advertising and promotion. In your response, consider the social, ethical, economic, and legal issues involved.

3. If advertising did not exist, how could people obtain information on goods and services? What alternatives are there?

4. Is regulation of the Internet a violation of free speech rights? Why or why not?

interactive discovery lab

1. Analyze 3 or 4 television commercials or print advertisements in terms of their a) positive recognition of cultural differences, or b) use of potentially harmful stereotypes. Why do you think the particular advertisers made the choices they did?

2. Create a pro bono print advertisement for a product, service, or idea of your choice. Why did you choose this particular product, service, or idea? How is your ad socially responsible?

Chapter Four

The Global Advertising Environment

KODAK DEVELOPS
A GLOBAL IMAGE
WITH ADVANTIX

When Kodak introduced its Advantix product line, a core team was set up that included people from all regions of the world working together from initial research and development through to production and promotion and sales efforts.

The Advantix team relied on Kodak's international ad agency, J. Walter Thompson, to develop global ad concepts. The ideas were initially developed in the United States, United Kingdom, France, Germany, and Italy, with the selected creative concept coming out of the London office. To ensure that the campaign would work internationally, interviews were conducted in 11 different countries, and small-group consumer meetings (focus groups) were held in the U.S., U.K., France, Germany, and Japan to arrive at the best product positioning and advertising copy strategies.

The final campaign depicted individuals discussing how they use photography and why they take pictures, thereby revealing how the new Kodak Advantix system would help improve those pictures. Individuals were filmed in five different countries and seven different languages, enabling Kodak to include several universally recognized beautiful images and offer a sense of localism and cultural variety while still avoiding culturally specific features. In this way, the final global commercials could be used in every Kodak market and still look like they were designed and produced for just that market. The company was not inflexible to individual country needs, however. In Japan, where a popular spokesperson had been used in Kodak's previous ads, they managed to include her in the Advantix spot too, while maintaining the overall look and themes of the global commercial format and staying true to the brand's strategy.

The success of the campaign was evident in several ways. In consumer tests of ad awareness, the campaign scored significantly above the norm. Even better, sales were so high that production had to be increased by 40 percent to satisfy the demand.

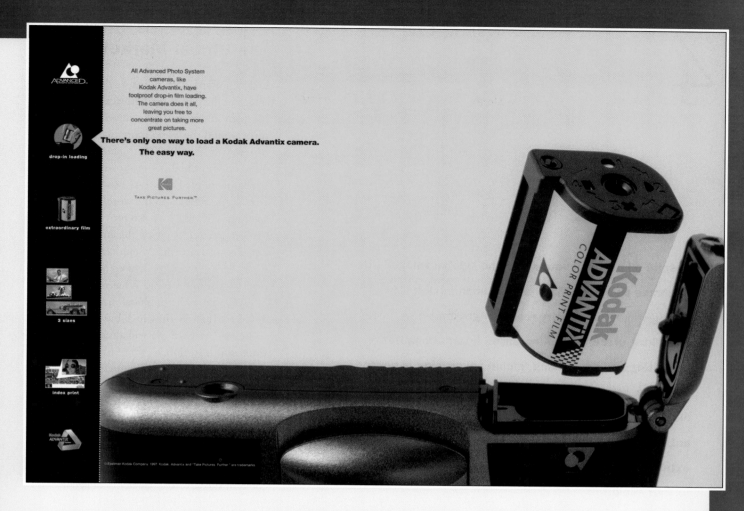

All Advanced Photo System cameras, like Kodak Advantix, have foolproof drop-in film loading. The camera does it all, leaving you free to concentrate on taking more great pictures.

There's only one way to load a Kodak Advantix camera. The easy way.

TAKE PICTURES. FURTHER.™

drop-in loading

extraordinary film

3 sizes

index print

Kodak ADVANTIX

©Eastman Kodak Company 1997. Kodak, Advantix and "Take Pictures. Further." are trademarks.

Success was also found in cost savings from a global effort. In fact, Kodak estimated that it saved $15 million in costs by using this approach.

All of this success does not mean there are no difficulties involved in "going global," however. Kodak discovered that one of the biggest barriers to a global effort may well be the company itself. Internal structures often are designed to foster local autonomy in each market or country, which immediately presents an obstacle to anyone coming in with an idea or campaign developed elsewhere. Second, for advertising to truly succeed on a global level, there must be a strong management commitment to the practice, mandating that it will be used rather than leaving it up to local offices to decide. And third, a company has to resist moving down to the lowest common denominator, developing bland but noncontroversial ads that will not offend any of the parties involved. As James Gallery, manager of worldwide marketing communications at Kodak notes, "To do global advertising successfully, the process itself must be global." Kodak is one company that seems to have achieved such success.

Source: James Gallery, "Global Advertising" (paper presented at the Consumer Insights into Global Advertising Conference, New York, October 1996).

LOOK BEFORE YOU LEAP

- Why are advertisers increasingly looking to global markets?

- How do companies decide whether to use a single advertising campaign worldwide or specific ads in each country?

- What are the benefits and drawbacks of standardized global advertising?

- How are consumer research and media planning different for global campaigns?

- How might a global marketing plan differ from a traditional domestic marketing plan?

4

Despite all of the debate about the "global village" (a phrase coined by Marshall McLuhan back in 1964), and even given all of the very real changes that have been and are taking place toward increased internationalization of marketing and advertising, global advertising is not for everyone, as the Kodak example above suggests. All of the elements considered in the previous chapter—social, ethical, economic, and legal—are present, to a greater or lesser extent, when an advertiser considers spreading its message further afield.

As we will explore in this chapter, although the world is growing smaller thanks to new technologies, the distribution and spread of those technologies is far from even. There also are political elements to any international discussion, with some countries encouraging globalization of business and others trying to control it. This chapter will examine the nature of the global advertising environment—its size and structure; how U.S. firms "go global;" and the cultural, ethical, and legal issues that advertisers need to consider before embarking on a global campaign.

The Global Marketplace

It is important, first, to realize the size and extent of the global marketplace. The growth has been substantial. Total advertising expenditures around the world more than doubled between 1983 and 1993, reaching more than $280 billion. Exhibit 4–1 shows this expansion by region, while Exhibit 4–2 shows the top 10 advertising markets in the world, by total ad spending. Exhibit 4–2 also provides perspective on each market by giving the amount spent per person on advertising, which ranges from a high of $362.40 in the United States to a mere $3 per person in China. What makes a market global? What types of global markets are there? What are the ways in which business can be conducted abroad? We will answer these questions in this section.

While a Rand McNally might show hundreds of countries on its worldwide maps, from an advertising perspective, the globe is somewhat more limited. That is, there are far fewer countries where marketers will actively promote their products and services. *Advertising Age,* in its annual overview of world brands, looks at the advertising activity of agencies on an international level. The extent of that is reflected in Exhibit 4–3, which shows the number of accounts that each major agency has in 10 or more countries in 1996 as compared to five years prior, as well as the percentage of business that comes from U.S. clients. Indeed, if you look at where the top 10 global marketers are spending their money, all but two are spending significantly more outside of the U.S. than within it. Exhibit 4–4 shows the top 10 global advertisers by U.S. versus non–U.S. ad spending.

The first recorded agency to open a foreign office was J. Walter Thompson. It did so as long ago as 1899. The office was set up in London to serve an existing U.S. account. Ironically, it closed its doors in 1916 for seven years due to lack of business. But by the time it reopened in 1923, the practice of international agencies was well underway. Another major international agency, Young & Rubicam, did not open its first non–U.S. office until 1940, in London. Today, it has 331 offices in 64 countries, employing 10,000 people around the world.

Requirements of a Global Marketplace

For a global market to exist, five forces must be in place: 1) production facilities that can generate surplus products; 2) an adequate transportation system to move products; 3) acceptance of outside investments and a stable government; 4) operating an efficient telecommunications system; and 5) acceptance of advertising and consumers with discretionary income. Let's look at each of these forces more closely.

PRODUCTION FACILITIES The emergence of Japan and Korea as manufacturing powers is a demonstration of the link between the ability to produce surplus goods and the ability to send them abroad. Coordinating and encouraging production is often difficult. As seen in the 1990s in Eastern Europe, it can be difficult to overcome political bureaucracy, lack of investment capital, and labor problems.

TRANSPORTATION Not only is there a need for good ground transportation (cars, trucks, etc.), but for international trade to develop, it also is essential to have efficient and economical air and water transportation. Only after raw materials and personnel can be brought in to a country and finished products taken out can international markets be established.

INVESTMENT AND GOVERNMENT STABILITY To speed the rate of economic growth in a country, investment from the government and from outside participants must occur. An infusion of money from outside sources is important because the capital development stimulates local economies, raises the standard of living for nationals, and provides disposable income for consumers. Foreign investment is contingent upon stability in government because multinational corporations want to reduce their financial risk. When Mexico devalued its currency by 45 percent in 1994, many U.S. manufacturers were forced to cut margins or postpone new product launches.

TELECOMMUNICATIONS Coordinated manufacturing, transportation, and trade require communication between producers, sellers, and buyers. Telecommunications must be operating both locally and globally, including telephone, fax, and mail services. Although the level of so-

phisticated technology found in the U.S. (such as computerization, electronic mail, or video-conferencing) is not necessary for a global marketplace to operate, it is important to have the fundamentals in place. In India, for example, direct mail advertising is problematic because of the poor mail service. It can take up to a year to gather all of the responses to a single mailing.

ADVERTISING AND DISPOSABLE INCOME For global advertising to occur, it obviously must be permitted by the receiving country. Differences in government regulations can be a big

---

EXHIBIT 4–1 World Advertising Expenditure Growth, 1983–1993

	1983	1993	% CHANGE
World	$131,280	$282,210	+115%
North America	80,948	150,641	+ 86
Europe	25,985	62,514	+114
Rest of world	24,347	69,055	+184

Note: Figures are in millions of U.S. dollars.
Source: EAT

EXHIBIT 4–2 Top 10 Advertising Markets Worldwide, 1997

RANK	COUNTRY	1997 AD SPENDING ($ BILLIONS)	AD SPENDING PER CAPITA
1	U.S.	$106.0	$362.40
2	Japan	48.1	346.60
3	Germany	24.4	266.00
4	U.K.	17.2	265.90
5	France	10.7	174.70
6	Brazil	8.2	40.80
7	South Korea	8.0	133.60
8	China	6.7	3.00
9	Italy	6.2	94.50
10	Mexico	5.0	32.50

Source: Advertising Age International, May 1997

EXHIBIT 4–3   Agency Growth, 1991–1996

AGENCY	NUMBER OF ACCOUNTS IN 10+ COUNTRIES		U.S. CLIENTS
	1991	1996	
Ammirati Puris Lintas	11	12	39%
BBDO Worldwide	18	23	50
Bates Worldwide	10	17	43
DDB Needham Worldwide	10	21	35
D'Arcy Masius Benton & Bowles	5	15	54
Grey Advertising	14	43	45
J. Walter Thompson Co.	19	25	57
Leo Burnett Co.	11	14	76
McCann-Erikson Worldwide	26	49	54
Ogilvy & Mather Worldwide	27	26	50
Saatchi & Saatchi Advertising Worldwide	23	21	43
Young & Rubicam Advertising	20	25	62

Source: Laurel Wentz and Sasha Emmons, "AAI Charts Show Yearly Growth, Consolidation," *Advertising Age International,* September 1996, I33.

EXHIBIT 4–4A   Global Marketing by Region

	$ MILLIONS	% OF TOTAL
Asia	9,025.2	33%
Europe	15,749.7	57%
Latin America	1,959.2	7%
Middle East	184.6	1%
Other regions	664.1	2%
Total	**27,582.8**	**100%**

EXHIBIT 4–4B   Global Spending by Top Categories

		$ MILLIONS
1	Automotive	8,373.2
2	Personal care	8,056.7
3	Electronics, computers	3,589.3
4	Cleaners	1,033.3

Source: "Global Marketers," Laurel Wentz and Kevin Brown, *Advertising Age International,* November 1996, I19.

roadblock to implementing a global campaign. And in order for the advertising to have any impact on sales, people must have some level of disposable income with which to purchase the goods and services. From a rural, subsistence-level economy in the 1950s, South Korea moved within one generation to a relatively prosperous industrial society with a per-capita income of $5,000. Today, the country is one of the top 10 advertising markets in the world.

Types of Global Markets

As far as global advertising is concerned, one of the biggest distinctions can be made between developed markets, developing markets, and underdeveloped markets. **Developed markets** include industrialized countries such as the United States, Germany, Japan, and Canada. In places such as these, the free market system described in Chapter Three was instituted at least 50 years ago. Consumers in these countries have a broad range of goods and services from which to choose, and they turn to advertising to help them make choices between brands.

Developing markets include a fairly wide array of countries. Places in Eastern Europe that used to be under communist rule, such as the Czech Republic or Hungary, are now moving to the free market system. Many of the Far East countries, such as Indonesia and Malaysia, are also developing in the sense that industrialization and urbanization is increasing in what had previously been primarily agricultural societies. In the process, these countries are starting to allow in foreign companies or brands, giving global advertisers the chance to develop their own markets in these locations. As we shall learn later in this chapter, however, it is not always easy to enter such markets because of stringent political and legal requirements enforced by the local governments.

There are also **underdeveloped markets** for advertising. These include much of the African continent, as well as China and other Asian countries such as Myanmar (formerly known as Burma) or Cambodia. In some cases, the lack of development is due to the terrible internal conditions of the country, such as in war-torn Afghanistan or drought-stricken Ethiopia. In others, such as Ivory Coast, the country may be too small to be worth the attention of foreign marketers. Or the national government could simply refuse any foreign access to its market, as was the case until recently in Albania and Vietnam.

For China, which is just starting to open its doors to foreign investors and advertisers, the main obstacle, until recently, was the communist regime in control of the country. While that type of economic and political force still remains, China is now allowing limited access to its population of 1.2 billion would-be consumers. It has one of the fastest growing economies anywhere in the world, and it also has the fastest growing advertising market, increasing by 53 percent from 1994 to 1995 alone. That potential has already been recognized by several companies. McDonald's opened its first restaurant in Beijing in 1993. Coca Cola, which was thrown out of the country in 1950, returned in 1979 and today is selling 135 million cases of the beverage to Chinese consumers. Procter & Gamble expects its $400 million in sales to quadruple by 1999.[1]

Doing Business Abroad

U.S. marketers conduct business abroad in several different ways. The method they choose depends on numerous factors, including the type of industry, the size of the company, and the length of experience in global marketing. The four most common ways of doing business abroad are to (1) use a local partner, (2) set up a joint venture, (3) create a foreign subsidiary, or (4) use the international unit of a domestic company. Trade shows are a fifth means of doing business abroad.

LOCAL PARTNER One of the simplest ways to undertake international business—and often the approach taken by companies entering a new foreign market—is to find a **local partner** to assist. This may be a local firm or distributor, or even one individual who can represent the foreign concern in the local market. The advantage of this tactic is that it provides the entering company with a local "expert" familiar with the marketplace, customs, and regulations that might impact the business. Bicknell Manufacturing Company, a small manufacturer of industrial drill bits in Rockland, Maine, decided to look at foreign markets during the U.S. economic recession in the late 1980s. The company found a distributor in Mexico and

began selling its products in Latin America in 1993. The deal was so successful that Bicknell is now looking to sell in China and Vietnam. International sales are now accounting for 15–20 percent of the company's total revenue, up from zero just a few years ago.[2]

JOINT VENTURE If the outside company is successful in the new location, it may end up investing with a local firm to create a local business. This is known as a **joint venture.** This is the case, for example, in U.S. cable and telephone companies entering Europe to offer cable TV service. United International Holdings, a cable operator based in Denver, works with the Dutch company Philips Electronics in European cable ventures, and it partners with Globo in Brazil and Century Communications Corporation in Australia to offer cable service in those locations. Other big firms choose to enter a foreign market by buying a local company. Marks and Spencer, the U.K. department store, entered the American retail scene by purchasing Brooks Brothers clothing store and Kings Super Markets in New Jersey.

Joint ventures were critical in establishing an international marketplace in the former Soviet Union. Western aid was given to that country to help overcome some of its major problems, from lack of foreign currency to poor training in labor and management to resistance to change. Soviet consumers had had little to choose from and little money to spend, but several companies recognized the opportunity there and began using awareness advertising to establish recognition of brand names for western products in preparation for when the goods would become available and consumers would have discretionary income.

SUBSIDIARY Sometimes a company will decide to set up its own wholly owned **subsidiary** in another country, staffed primarily by its own personnel. This gives the company greater control over its own destiny, but it also means that the learning curve may be steeper (although local staff are usually hired as well). Subsidiaries are usually the preferred means of entry by larger companies, such as Wal-Mart or Mobil Oil.

INTERNATIONAL UNIT Another way to enter foreign markets is to sell products or services to the international units of domestic companies with whom business is conducted. Thus, the company that sells McDonald's its Russet Burbank potatoes for its French fries was also its initial supplier when McDonald's entered Moscow for the first time in 1990, until a reliable local supplier could be found to grow the same variety.

TRADE SHOWS Trade shows offer another point of entry for a business to check out a foreign market. These may be sponsored by an industry trade group, such as the Food Marketing Institute or American Meat Institute, or by a governmental body such as the Commerce Department, which sponsors trade shows in developing markets such as the former Soviet Union.

One of the obstacles to conducting business abroad can be the various regulations on foreign ownership or activity. In some countries, particularly in those that are just starting to allow international marketers, such as Vietnam, there are restrictions on the kinds of businesses that can have foreign investment or ownership. This is particularly likely to be true of media companies, which are felt to have an important influence on the public and should therefore not be controlled by foreigners. Such a restriction operates in the U.S. as well, with national television networks only allowing a 25 percent foreign ownership. We will discuss the legal considerations of global business in detail later in this chapter.

While most of the attention and activity in the global arena has focused on western coun-

AROUND THE GLOBE

· ·

The Boom in the Pacific Rim

If you ask any marketing soothsayer where most growth in consumer and industrial markets will be coming from by the turn of the century, the answer will probably be Asia. That region has some of the fastest growing economies in the world, along with several underdeveloped markets that many advertisers believe are now or will soon be ripe for exploiting.

The Asia–Pacific region includes affluent markets such as Japan, Hong Kong, and Singapore, where the populations are well educated and relatively affluent; growing markets such as South Korea and Taiwan, where the emerging middle class is starting to demand high-quality goods and services; and emerging markets such as the Philippines, Thailand, Malaysia, and Indonesia, where the population is

younger, poorer, and less educated. Underdeveloped markets, including China, India, and Vietnam, offer large numbers of people but little else (i.e., low incomes, little education, more government control). Finally, the mature markets of Australia and New Zealand come closest to the U.S. in terms of demographics and marketing.

The reasons for the current boom in the Asia–Pacific region are several. The biggest factor is the rapid growth both in population and in industrialization. By 2000, Asia will account for more than half of the world's population of 6.2 billion people. The two largest countries on the continent, China and India, together account for 70 percent of the region's households. As more manufacturing moves to this part of the world and people shift from an

agricultural way of life to a more urban one, they are starting to acquire consumer goods. In 1980, 45 percent of all households in China owned television sets; by 1994 that figure had almost doubled, to 85 percent, and the country now has the largest television audience in the world. Ad spending in China is forecast to rise from $3 billion in 1995 to $22 billion by 2000, which would make it the world's third-largest advertising market, after the U.S. and Japan. In 1995, China recorded the largest percentage advertising increase in the world, with a 53 percent growth over 1994.

There are problems, however. Although the markets are growing, the sophistication of the advertising industry in the Pacific Rim remains far behind the rest of the world. Technology, while rapidly increasing, is

tries in the past 50 years, today's businesses are increasingly looking east to the Asia–Pacific region. "Around the Globe: The Boom in the Pacific Rim" looks at that region's appeal to marketers.

The lessons being learned in Asia are similar to the experiences of international marketers in Europe 10 or more years ago. The key in both regions is to realize that although there are some important similarities between countries, there are as many, if not more, differences between them that must be taken into account. This is particularly true for media choices. Viewers in Hong Kong do not want to see the same programs as people in Thailand or Singapore. Indeed, almost all of the top television programs in each Asian country are locally produced. As Tom Hartje, a media consultant, noted in 1994, "We are finally realizing that the idea of creating a pan-Asian television market, where programming would cross borders as easily as radio waves do, has run smack into a diversity of cultures, peoples, and tastes."3

R E S E T

1. From an advertising perspective, what types of global markets are there?
2. What are the various ways a U.S. company can set up a business overseas?

still not up to western standards, impacting client communications as well as ad campaign development. Economic conditions may be unstable in some Asia–Pacific countries, with inflation creating problems for emerging manufacturers and marketers. Distribution is an especially difficult area, given that for most Asian countries, there are few urban centers and most people live in hard-to-reach rural regions.

One of the hardest Pacific Rim markets for foreign companies to succeed in is Japan, which also happens to be the most affluent nation in the region. While corporations such as Procter & Gamble, Coca-Cola, and Nestlé have done well, it has only been after learning some hard lessons. The Japanese tend to trust information only if it is in their own language. National brands have a strong advantage over foreign ones, and advertising tends to focus on providing solutions to problems, with an emphasis on trust, reliability, and market standing. It is the company's reputation that is featured more than the product itself.

This different perspective on the role of advertising was summed up by Masaharu Matsushita, the chairman of Matsushita Electrical Industrial Company, which markets Panasonic, Technics, and Quasar electronic goods. As he noted in *Advertising Age,*
The ultimate goal of any business enterprise is to make a contribution to the progress of the society in which it operates.... Our advertising policy is therefore from this basic management philosophy.... We have to bring benefits and conve-nience to the lives of consumers. Therefore, we should be absolutely honest.... We want people to be able to understand very easily and clearly about our products.

All of the standard procedures and ways of doing business that are common in the U.S. or European ad industries may not be found in Asia. Ads that are paid for may not appear. The authorities may prevent a commercial from being shown even after giving initial approval. China charges international advertisers up to three times as much as a local brand. In Korea, agencies must buy space in all eight major newspapers because, otherwise, the ones that are left out will write negatively about that advertiser in their pages. The relationship of advertising agency and media differs, too. In Japan, for example, 4 of the top 10 agencies are completely or partially owned by newspaper publishers, making it questionable as to whom they really serve. Consumer research is far less developed, so it is difficult to come up with accurate insights into how people will respond either to brands or to ads.

And finally, as the Asia–Pacific chairman of ad agency Ammurati Puris Lintas, Max Gosling, notes, "Asia is a complex collection of different cultures, and different countries are at different stages of development."

Sources: "Hitching up to the Tiger Boom," in Campaign Report on Worldwide Advertising, supplement to Campaign, ed. Jane Austin, 7 June 1996, 3–12; and David Kilburn, "Masaharu Matsushita Speaks on Advertising," Advertising Age, 8 November 1993, I-3, I-13.

Standardization or Localization

Once a market has been identified and some form of business organization has been established in a foreign country, the marketing mix and, subsequently, the role of advertising must then be defined. The debate over which is the best way to advertise globally has been going on for decades. There are two main schools of thought: Use **standardized advertising** in every market in which the brand is sold, with identical or near-identical campaigns; or, alternatively, adopt a **localized advertising** strategy, tailoring the message and media to each individual market. Many advertisers end up somewhere in the middle, using a similar strategy that aims to create a standard brand image and brand perception, but which also contains varied creative messages that are then customized for local tastes and preferences.

The argument over which approach is more effective really began back in the mid-1960s and has continued to the present day. Its premise, as outlined by Theodore Levitt in 1983, is that "the world's needs and tastes have been irrevocably homogenized. This makes the multinational corporation obsolete and the global corporation absolute."4 Or as John Hegarty, creative director and chairman of British agency Bartle Bogle Hegarty, states it, "We are increasingly living in a borderless world and this applies to the cultural messages we absorb."5

As both advertisers and agencies become more global in their operations, the debate has intensified. This is particularly true in the United States, where companies have been slower to recognize the need to promote their products outside of these borders and hence, to tackle the difficult issues that global advertising raises. In Europe or Asia, where more trade traditionally has come from exports to neighbors in the region or to former colonies, the advertising has been handled mostly on a country-by-country basis. Now, in the current political climate, as borders evaporate and trade barriers come down, companies are looking more closely at finding economies of scale by developing a unified marketing strategy across countries.

Benefits of Standardization

Advocates of standardization point to five key benefits that it offers: 1) unified brand image; 2) appeal to similar basic needs or desires; 3) transfer and sharing of good ideas; 4) lower production, design, and distribution costs; and 5) greater sophistication for less-developed countries. Each of these benefits is discussed below.

UNIFIED BRAND IMAGE   For companies such as Levi's or Coca-Cola, which want to be known throughout the world for a certain kind of brand, global advertising is essential. By using similar or identical messages from country to country, the product becomes strongly associated not only with the values of that message but also with the country itself. Thus, Chanel *is* French, and McDonald's epitomizes America. The Heinz Company established its image 100 years ago when it developed the slogan of "57 varieties"; even though the company now produces more than 4,000 lines of food products around the world, it still uses that moniker in ads and on packages in more than 200 countries, reinforcing its image as a company offering choice and abundance.6 Certain products have even been developed specifically for a global market. Bailey's Irish Cream Liqueur and Rocher chocolates are two such examples.

Some companies have used global ad campaigns to launch new products in order to give them an immediate unified and global brand image. Nike is considered to be one of the first to have done this. It introduced the Nike Air 180 shoe during the 1991 Super Bowl in the U.S., followed by print and broadcast advertising around the world.7 Visa adopted a similar tactic for its bank card, highlighting its worldwide acceptance by using print ads in different languages. Exhibit 4–5 shows a global Visa print ad. Also, as we saw in Chapter Three, Benetton has received a good deal of notoriety, some of it unfavorable, for its global ads depicting controversial scenes or characters. Even when national media reject the ads themselves, Benetton still garners attention and generates awareness for its products from the news coverage it subsequently receives.

It is worth pointing out here that all too often consumers themselves are unaware of the origins of brands. A study conducted in the United Kingdom, for example, found that only 9 percent of consumers knew that Mars was a U.S. brand; 72 percent thought it was a British concern. Similarly, 55 percent knew that Gucci was Italian, but 12 percent believed it to be French.

APPEAL TO SIMILAR BASIC NEEDS OR DESIRES   Global advertising can really only work if the product has a similar appeal across countries and borders. Many youth-oriented products fall into this category. The cable television music network MTV, for example, can satisfy its young audience's desire to be entertained musically in Kansas City, Kansas, Cologne, Germany, or Kuala Lumpur, Indonesia. Similarly, a Volvo automobile, which comes from Sweden, tries to satisfy the safety needs of its customers on a worldwide basis.

TRANSFER AND SHARING OF GOOD IDEAS   For some companies, global advertising offers the opportunity to share and transfer good ideas between markets. This may be ideas about the product, such as introducing breakfast menus at McDonald's, or about the advertising, such as Pepsi's use of Cindy Crawford, an internationally recognized "supermodel," as its spokeswoman in Europe following her success in the U.S. campaign. The infamous cowboy in Marlboro cigarette advertising was first developed in this country, but it is now used throughout the world by Philip Morris to promote this brand, turning it into an American icon in the process.

LOWER PRODUCTION, DESIGN, AND DISTRIBUTION COSTS   One of the biggest arguments made in favor of standardized global advertising is the issue of costs. It makes sense that if you have to produce fewer types of Finesse shampoo bottles or fewer ads depicting them, that your costs are going to be lower. This is probably the biggest incentive for manufacturers to move toward standardized advertising and marketing. Scott Paper, the U.S. maker of paper products such as Scotties tissues and Scott paper towels, is now moving to reduce the number of different brand names it has worldwide in order to lower its

**Para comprar
en su lugar preferido...**

¡Visa es la Tarjeta!

Hay muchas razones para preferir un lugar sobre otro para hacer sus compras. Cualquiera que sea su preferencia, al momento de pagar use la tarjeta preferida por más personas en el mundo... Visa.

La tarjeta Visa le ofrece excelentes beneficios y servicios que satisfacen sus gustos y estilo de vida, por eso Visa es utilizada más que ninguna otra tarjeta.

Visa es aceptada en más de 11 millones de establecimientos en el mundo y le brinda el más amplio acceso a efectivo en las sucursales de los bancos Miembros y en los cajeros automáticos del sistema Visa y Plus.

Infórmese hoy mismo en su banco sobre la extensa gama de beneficios y servicios que su tarjeta Visa le ofrece.

Para comprar en su lugar preferido... **¡Visa es la Tarjeta!**

VISA
PATROCINADOR OFICIAL
JUEGOS OLIMPICOS 1994/1996

production costs. In Britain, for example, the name of its top-selling toilet paper, Andrex, is being changed to Scott Andrex, as the local name is gradually phased out. The Mars candy company has taken similar steps, switching the name of its European candy bar from Marathon to Mars, to be in line with the American product.

It is important to point out, however, that while production, design, and distribution may be consolidated, marketing communications budgets tend to be dispersed across markets. It is estimated that just 5 percent of these budgets in European countries are controlled from one central office, making it more difficult to execute a standardized advertising campaign.

EXHIBIT 4–5   A global ad campaign, such as the one used by Visa, can serve to generate not only worldwide product identification but also a global brand image for the advertiser.

GREATER SOPHISTICATION IN LESS-DEVELOPED COUNTRIES The argument that standardized advertising will bring greater sophistication to less-developed countries appeals to local governments and industry. By bringing in outside personnel or training local people in the craft of advertising as practiced by more-developed countries, advertisers and agencies help to increase the sophistication level of both the local staff and the advertising created for that market.

Drawbacks of Standardization

Critics note that a standardized campaign may create several drawbacks: 1) problems of language, culture, and lifestyle; 2) differences in market characteristics or industry conditions; and 3) local resistance and lower-common-denominator marketing. Each is explored further below.

PROBLEMS OF LANGUAGE, CULTURE, AND LIFESTYLE Language, culture, and lifestyle differences present the biggest stumbling blocks for advertisers that are considering whether or not to use a standardized advertising approach. Language can be a major obstacle. Within India, for example, there are 16 different languages and 200 different dialects. How can an advertiser present a standardized ad campaign to such a linguistically diverse group? Moreover, language distinctions have been known to cause major problems for advertisers trying to use a standardized campaign. One of the most infamous examples is Chevrolet, which introduced its Nova car model to the Spanish market. Sales were meager, and the company finally realized that the name of the car, when translated into Spanish, meant "does not go" (no va). A change of name solved the problem. Pepsi ran into similar language problems using an international campaign in Germany. Its slogan, "Come alive with Pepsi" was translated in German as "Come out of the grave"—hardly an inviting theme for a soft drink!

The cultural problems caused by language are important as well. In Japan, *Newsweek, Time,* and *Business Week* magazines all produce separate Japanese editions, as well as an Asian magazine, having realized that the Japanese will only trust information if it is presented to them in their own language. Sometimes the language that is chosen can mean different things, too. When Procter & Gamble entered Eastern Europe, it found that Polish consumers liked to see detergent labels written in slightly incorrect Polish because they felt that this meant the company was trying to fit in but hadn't quite done so. On the other hand Czech consumers liked English or German labels because they believed that anything in the local language was clearly inferior.[8]

Cultural differences include even the seemingly mundane, such as the way people do laundry. In the U.K., washing machines are front-loaders, whereas the rest of Europe and the U.S. prefer top-loader machines. Europeans prefer to wash clothes in hot water; in Japan, cool water washes are more common. Certain colors or objects may have different significance in different markets; in the Middle East, for example, blue stands for death. Also, objects may have different symbolic meanings in different areas. For example, in general, in Muslim countries, the dog is a symbol for bad luck. Both of these cultural specifics would make it unwise for an advertiser such as Ford to advertise a blue minivan that can hold a large family with a dog. Procter & Gamble had to change the colors on its diapers in Asia from pink and blue to white because women did not want to be seen to be buying or using pink diapers, indicating that they had a daughter.

Even ads that we might consider to be global icons, such as the Marlboro campaign featuring a rugged cowboy, have been shown to have different connotations outside of the U.S. One study found that people in Brazil linked that theme with pollution, while those in Norway associated the cowboy with disease. In Japan, the image conjured up foreignness, and in Thailand, relaxation.[9] Indeed, several studies have found cultural differences in advertising messages that affect the types of appeals that are used. Compared to the U.S., Swedish ads depict more nudity,[10] Japanese ads have been found to have more soft-sell messages,[11] and the British tend to use more humorous appeals.[12]

Humor is one area that is extremely hard to employ on a global or standardized basis. What a Frenchman finds hilarious is unlikely to amuse an Australian or Canadian. According to creative directors involved in international advertising, the ads that travel best across borders are those involving anatomical jokes or visual puns. As Ced Vidler, European creative director of Still Price-Lintas noted, "If a funny ad is going to travel, it has to be visual, because otherwise you get into the idiosyncrasies of what makes different nationalities laugh. Most people share the same visual sense of humor."13 On the other hand, if ads include too many local references, they will be lost on foreign audiences.

Humor is used more in some countries than in others. British and Scandinavian ads are likely to rely more on this appeal than French, German, or Japanese ads. One study that compared food and beverage ads developed for the international market with those created for an individual country found that humor was used far more in the local market ads than in the international ones.14 Exhibit 4–6 shows two ads for Perrier mineral water, one from the U.K. and one from the U.S. While the basic quality of refreshment is clear from each, the way the message is communicated differs. Note the use of puns in the British ad versus the more straightforward image appeal of the American version.

Product use and preference often vary. Toothpaste, for example, is viewed in Spain and Greece as a cosmetic, whereas in Britain and the Netherlands it is considered more of a therapeutic product. Kraft Foods manufactures sliced cheese in Europe, but in Germany the cheese is emmenthal, while in the U.K. it is cheddar. And although Coca-Cola uses global advertising, the product has different sweeteners in different markets, depending on local market food and beverage regulations.

DIFFERENCES IN MARKET CHARACTERISTICS OR INDUSTRY CONDITIONS Given the distinctions drawn earlier between developed, developing, and underdeveloped markets, it is perhaps not surprising that market conditions play a major role in an advertiser's ability to employ a standardized campaign. Sometimes the product category is not equally developed

Having phased out its Marathon brand name in Europe, the Mars candy company is now able to standardize its advertising across many markets, thus allowing it to lower production costs and heighten brand identification among consumers.

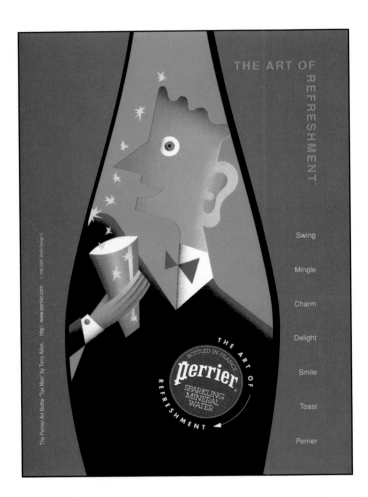

EXHIBIT 4–6 Cultural differences can make it difficult to develop effective global ad campaigns. These ads for Perrier reflect the differences between consumers in the U.S., who prefer an image appeal, and those in the U.K., who respond favorably to humorous ads.

enough. For example, Stouffers would find it difficult to promote its Lean Cuisine frozen entrees in Europe simply because consumers there are far less likely to want convenience foods or weight-loss products. And it makes little sense for a company such as BMW to spend vast sums of money trying to reach large audiences in a country such as India, for instance, because there are very few people who could afford such a luxury car.

Economic differences between markets can have a marked impact. In Brazil, for example, there is a big gap between the "haves" and "have-nots." One-fifth of the homes account for about 70 percent of consumption of all advertised products, but one-third of all Brazilians earn less than $3 per day. Similar disparities are seen throughout the developing world.

Another important area that impacts advertising is the type of media available and how they are consumed. Until recently, very little commercial television was offered in most of Europe, which meant that global advertisers that had relied on TV in the U.S. often found themselves forced to use more print ads in Europe. This, of course, changes the nature and type of message used.

Shopping patterns and retail distribution may harm global efforts as well. A store's own brands (such as Kroger's coffee or Safeway's cereal in the U.S.) enjoy a far higher share of goods sold in Europe (around 30 percent) than they do in the U.S. (18 percent). Two of the most popular U.K. grocery stores, Sainsbury and Tesco, sell far more own-brand goods than brand-name items. It is interesting to note that such own-label products tend to be purchased by more affluent homes in Europe and less affluent people in the U.S. Exhibit 4–7 shows an ad from the U.K. promoting one of Sainsbury's own-label products.

LOCAL RESISTANCE AND LOWER-COMMON-DENOMINATOR MARKETING   For standardized advertising to work, it has to be accepted both by local customers and by local agency personnel. All too often, however, the reaction is one of suspicion or cynicism—the "not invented here" syndrome. Consumer resistance may arise if people feel they are having an alien culture or product imposed upon them unwillingly.

Standardization is only feasible if both client and agency are organized to facilitate the practice. This generally means having some central authority approve the creative campaign and media plan, rather than allowing individual countries to craft it. However, there should be ample opportunity for local markets to provide input and make necessary revisions to be sure that the campaign is in line with cultural or legal requirements, for example.

Even products that do wish to have a unified brand image sometimes do not execute the same campaign worldwide. Chanel, which many would say is quintessentially French, does not use the same creative in its home market as in the U.S. This is due, in part, to the fact that there are internal conflicts regarding who should have creative control of the brand's advertising. One result, in 1994, was that television spots were created in Europe for a new brand, but there was no budget allocated for that medium in the U.S. because there was almost an exclusive reliance on print media in that market.[15]

Think Global, Act Local

Fortunately, the choice for global advertisers is not just black and white—standardized or localized. Instead, more often than not, an advertiser will develop one theme or strategy in one country and then adapt it to other markets. This could be said to be the advertising version of the popular phrase, "think globally, act locally." Many of today's most successful global brands adopt this stance. Levi's jeans, for example, epitomize ruggedness and a cool, "hip" attitude wherever they are promoted and sold, but the messages used to convey that brand image vary from country to country.

Japan is one country that has been notoriously difficult for western marketers. A brand that has succeeded by playing by the local rules is Clorets, the breath-freshener from Warner-Lambert. Because western candy was almost unknown when the brand was first launched in Japan in 1985, the company and its agency, Dai-Ichi Kikaku, decided to adapt the product and its marketing to suit local preferences. That included a change in the product ingredients and packaging. Timing was important, too. The practice of displaying affection in public was just starting to become acceptable in Japan, so the campaign focused on a TV ad that showed a man and woman kissing, something that had rarely been shown before. Now,

Clorets is the leading brand in its category, with a 15 percent share of the total market.

Another U.S.-based company that has done well in Japan is Tower Records, the music and video retailer. The retail industry is particularly tough for foreign companies to crack. Tower's approach was to build on the word-of-mouth that Japanese tourists in the U.S. would take back home with them. It became a fashionable brand name even before it opened its first store in Japan. Then, to sustain its image as the place for young people to shop, Tower started to sponsor a popular TV music show and distributed free copies of a monthly music magazine. This is in contrast to Tower's media strategy in the U.S., which focuses on cable music channels such as MTV, and radio stations preferred by younger listeners. Today, Tower Records has 32 stores in Japan and annual sales of more than $350 million.[16]

As we noted above, even the archetype of global marketing, Coca-Cola, uses different sweeteners and packaging in different markets, although the product positioning is identical. But even Coke is moving towards greater diversity in its global advertising. Having developed more than 25 TV executions using its "Always Coca-Cola" theme line, the marketer gave its local distributors more leeway over which individual spots to air, recognizing the need to speak to people in their own language and culture.

Another company that would seem to epitomize standardization, McDonald's, with

EXHIBIT 4–7   Rather than promoting brand-name items, Sainsbury's uses its ads to promote its own-label products, which are very popular with affluent consumers in the U.K. Advertisers must recognize this type of purchasing-pattern difference when preparing global campaigns.

At last, a meat ad with a bit of meat.

Sainsbury's Traditional Beef is the tenderest, juiciest, tastiest beef you've ever eaten.
Fine words. But as they say, fine words butter no parsnips. The guarantee you see opposite speaks for itself.
It applies not only to our sirloin steak, but to all our Traditional Beef cuts and joints.
How can we be so confident? Because, like all the best guarantees, you'll probably never need it.

GUARANTEE If you are not satisfied with this Sainsbury's Traditional Beef steak, we'll refund your money and replace the steak.

SAINSBURY'S Where good food costs less.

restaurants in 100 countries, caters to cultural differences. In India, for example, the restaurants do not serve beef, in accordance with Hindu religious practices. In Saudi Arabia, the restaurants close five times a day for Muslim prayer. And the chicken sandwich in England is different from the one served in Germany. Indeed, part of the company's success is to position itself as a "multi-local" organization. A large number of its international restaurants are owned by local franchisees, giving people in each country a voice and a financial stake in this quintessentially American company.[17]

The extent to which advertisers are choosing the "think global, act local" route is perhaps shown by the fact that in the European Community just 5 percent of the sales volume of branded products comes from truly standardized brands (identical formulation, packaging, and promotion); 40 percent of that volume is from semi-standardized products (one or more differences); and the remaining 55 percent can be attributed to brands that advertise locally with uniquely designed and packaged products.

R E S E T

1. **Why do advertisers adopt standardized campaigns for their products?**
2. **What stands in the way of success for standardized global campaigns?**

Considerations for a Global Campaign

Whether advertising is to be done on a standardized or a localized basis, there are still many issues that need to be addressed and many choices that have to be made. For any global advertising to succeed, it must face up to the challenge of cross-cultural differences. Just as there are clear distinctions, preferences, and customs between a Californian and a New Yorker, so are there cultural and personal differences between a German and an Italian, or someone from Paris and someone from Nice,

in France. These may be reflected in the marketing mix, consumer research, or media opportunities. In this section, we will look at some of the considerations for planning a global campaign.

The Global Marketing Environment

The practices and tenets of advertising in the U.S. may well be unsuitable elsewhere. This is as true in how advertising and marketing are undertaken abroad as it is in creative or media issues. Here, we will look at the differences within the marketing environment that need to be taken into account when planning or executing a global campaign.

As illustrated in Exhibit 4–8, the traditional marketing mix of a U.S. advertiser is comprised of product, price, place (distribution), and promotion (which includes advertising). These are known collectively as the "4 Ps." For U.S. marketers, all four elements have to be considered as the marketing plan is put together.

If you were attempting to construct a marketing plan in Italy, however, the relative weights given to each of those "Ps" might be very different, due to the fact that there is almost no national distribution of branded goods across that country. Until a few years ago, a national manufacturer, such as Barilla pasta, would have to deal with a different retailer and distributor in each town or region. The place element, or distribution, would therefore be an especially important consideration in the Italian marketing mix. In contrast, Toyota would have an easier time selling cars in Australia than in the U.S. because distribution (place) is more pronounced; Australia has the highest proportion of auto dealers, among all of its retail outlets, of any country (more than 16 percent).

In former communist countries, the price element may remain out of the control of the advertiser, even though communist governments have mostly been replaced by socialist or capitalist ones. A Polish manufacturer of bread, for example, which is considered a staple food in that country, has no control over how much he can charge for the product. Price may be controlled in other ways, too. In many countries in Europe, for example, the telephone system is run by the government, which therefore sets the price that consumers will pay. Unless competition is allowed in such services (which is happening more and more), there is little the advertiser can do to affect any price changes to the marketing mix.

The product itself may be varied, even for a global brand. We have already noted some examples of this. Kraft cheese is sold globally, but it is cheddar in the United Kingdom and emmenthal in Germany. McDonald's does not use beef in Hindu countries. And Coca-Cola varies the sweeteners it uses in certain countries even though the bottles and cans may look almost identical.

The element of promotion offers itself up to a variety of emphases across the globe. It includes all forms that are used to convey a message about a brand to its intended customers. This includes advertising media (radio, TV, or magazines), as well as sales promotions (coupons, store displays), direct response (direct mail, telemarketing), and public relations (publicity about the company or brand). Non-advertising elements may well be far more important in some places than in others. Many advertisers entering Eastern Europe have found that while there is relatively little choice as far as advertising is concerned—a small number of print options, or two to three TV channels, for example—the promotional, public relations, or even direct marketing alternatives are not only numerous but also new to consumers in such places. When Procter & Gamble introduced Head & Shoulders shampoo in Poland, for instance, it used the uncommon method (for that country) of direct mail to send samples to thousands of homes to ensure that people would not only become aware of the brand but also try it.

The diverse tools used in integrated marketing communications vary in their frequency of usage outside of the U.S. Coupons, for example, are used most heavily in this country. In 1994, 310 billion coupons were issued in the U.S., compared with about 27 billion issued in Canada, 9 billion in the United Kingdom, and just 143 million in Spain. The use of direct mail to generate retail sales shows a similar dispersion. While about $70 billion worth of goods were sold this way in the U.S. in 1992, the figures for other countries were considerably smaller. In Germany, about $23 billion was sold through mail order; in the U.K., the figure was $6 billion; and in Switzerland, just

EXHIBIT 4–8   Traditional U.S. Marketing Mix

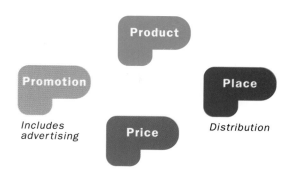

$1.4 million was spent to order goods and services through the mail. Per capita spending on direct marketing tools (mail, telemarketing, and direct TV or radio) varies across Europe—from a high of $252 per person per year in the Netherlands to a low of just $14 per person per year in Portugal.[18]

The relative importance of advertising in the marketing of goods and services can be seen by looking at advertising as a percent of the gross national product (GNP) across various countries. What the GNP shows, in simple terms, is the total value of all goods and services produced by a country in a year. The GNP is often taken as an indicator of a nation's economic activity. The proportion of that figure made up by advertising provides an indication of how much advertising contributes to the national economy. The U.S., perhaps not surprisingly, has the highest level of advertising as a percent of GNP of any country in the world, at 2.2 percent. Exhibit 4–9 shows the figure for other places around the globe. As you can see, even in other highly sophisticated, industrial, and capitalist countries such as Japan, France, or Australia, the level of advertising as a percent of GNP is considerably lower. For marketers, this is encouraging news because it suggests that there remain opportunities in those countries for increased advertising to raise that proportion of the GNP closer to U.S. levels.

Where those advertising dollars will be spent varies by country and region. In the U.S., for example, about 40 percent of all ad

EXHIBIT 4–9   Advertising and Gross National Product

	AD EXPENDITURES	GNP	ADV AS % OF GNP
U.S.	$147	$6,450	2.2%
South Korea	5	346	1.4
United Kingdom	13	1,045	1.3
Canada	7	581	1.2
Brazil	5	479	1.0
Japan	35	3,935	0.9
Germany	17	1,910	0.9
Spain	5	537	0.9
France	8	1,293	0.6
Italy	6	1,141	0.5

Note: Data presented are for calendar year 1994. Figures are in billions of U.S. dollars.
Source: Todd Pruzan, "Top Global Markets," *Advertising Age,* 20 February 1995, I9–I12.

expenditures are devoted to television; in Latin America, this rises to 60 percent; but in the Middle East, television expenditures comprise only about 25 percent of the total. Not surprisingly, this proportion is directly related to the amount of commercial television available. It is also probably not too unexpected to find that when such opportunities arrive, advertisers almost always will switch funds out of other media and into television. As a case in point, when Israel's Channel 2 began offering six minutes of advertising per hour, bringing commercials to Israeli terrestrial television for the first time, Wrigley's Orbit sugar-free gum sales increased by 1,000 percent. Within the first two years of Israeli commercial TV, advertisers shifted 20 percent of their spending to the new medium.

Consumer Research on a Global Basis

While there are several consumer research companies with international offices or affiliates, few of them conduct global studies on a regular basis. The primary reason for this is the large expense involved in conducting such research. The most common method used to find out about consumers' attitudes, opinions, or brand preferences is the survey. Even here, however, differences

exist between countries, with some preferring telephone surveys and others relying on face-to-face, personal interviews with respondents. In addition, even if a product is marketed globally, the differences in the way it is consumed or perceived may require the use of local market studies to support localized advertising efforts.

According to a study conducted by the Council of American Survey Research Organizations (CASRO), the primary reasons that advertisers or agencies conduct global research are to look for international business opportunities or to gain greater understanding of a foreign market. The most popular region in which such research has been undertaken in recent years is Latin America.[19]

There has been some important work done that does attempt to compare attitudes and behaviors across countries. One major study conducted on behalf of *Reader's Digest* magazine in 17 European countries in 1989 interviewed more than 22,000 individuals to find out about their product usage, media consumption, and attitudes. The results revealed many interesting statistics. Microwave ovens, for example, could be found in about half (49 percent) of all British homes but in just 2 percent of Greek households. Floor polish was used by 41 percent of Austrians but only 10 percent of Danes. Nearly all (90 percent) of homes in the U.K. had breakfast cereal, compared to just 17 percent in Italy. Three-quarters of homes in Luxembourg (74 percent) had home insurance, compared to 14 percent in Portugal.[20] Attitudes varied considerably, too. Agreement with the statement that "a woman's place is in the home" ranged from 35 percent in Portugal to 10 percent in Sweden. And while 83 percent of Italians claimed to approve of people who always drive within the speed limit, just 58 percent of Germans did so.

These findings also point out the difficulties of conducting consumer research on a global basis. Interpretations of questions or statements may vary from country to country, even if the literal words are correctly translated. And of course, the distinction between what people say they believe and what they actually do themselves can cause problems as well (even within a single-country study). In the above statement on driving within the speed limit, for example, it is worth noting that Germany has no such limit on its highways, while Italians are not known for keeping to theirs.

Attitudes towards advertising vary from country to country. The *Reader's Digest* Eurodata study reported that confidence in the advertising industry as a whole was found among just one-quarter (24 percent) of people surveyed. As shown in Exhibit 4–10, this ranged from a high of 39 percent in Portugal to a low of 13 percent in Sweden. Again, consideration must be given to the fact that Portugal's ad industry is fairly small, and that in Sweden, the overtly capitalist nature of advertising may conflict with the socialist heritage of that country

In contrast, a study of 22,000 people across five continents undertaken by Gallup International for the International Advertising Association found generally favorable attitudes towards advertising in all 22 countries surveyed. Most respondents, for example, agreed that advertising helps improve the quality of goods and services by promoting competition; in more than half of the countries, 40 percent or more of consumers said that "if advertising were banned tomorrow, I would miss it." Responses did vary widely, however. Only 21 percent of Egyptians agreed with that statement, compared to 78 percent of Japanese.[21] Moreover, as "AdScape: International Brands versus International Advertising" explores, there continues to be a strong loyalty to and preference for locally produced brands and advertising.

AdScape

International Brands Versus International Advertising

Despite the increasing amount of global advertising, research shows that consumers often are reluctant to embrace it. While they may be happy to buy a foreign brand, when it comes down to the advertising, they still prefer the "home-grown" variety. This was shown in a study conducted by *Advertising Age International* and *Yankelovich Monitor*. People in France, Germany, and the United Kingdom were asked about their opinions of brands and their advertising. What the researchers discovered was that the brand most often purchased did not necessarily correspond to the advertising that was liked the most. In the cigarette category, for example, British consumers were most likely to buy Benson & Hedges brand, but they named the advertising for Silk Cut, which is created locally, as their favorite. Similarly, while French consumers purchased Coca-Cola considerably more than any

other soft drink, they named the locally produced Perrier ads as their favorite in this product category.

Consumer perceptions of brand influence and how that impacts loyalty were also different among the three countries. In Germany, just 29 percent of those surveyed felt that "the fact that it is a well-known and trusted brand name" influenced their decision to buy, compared to fully three-quarters (78 percent) of U.K. customers and 53 percent of the French. Yet about half of both Germans and French agreed that "once I find a brand, it is very difficult to get me to change brands." What this study confirms is that liking a commercial does not necessarily translate into sales.

In countries that only recently opened up their markets to global brands, consumer preferences have been slow to change. The most popular dishwashing detergent in Poland remains the local

brand, Ludwig, despite the arrival of global giants Procter & Gamble and Unilever. The locally produced items are generally sold at a lower price, which appeals to consumers who are faced with low wages and high inflation.

While marketers may be working to create global brands, consumers may still resist seeing standardized, cookie-cutter ads for those same products.

QUESTIONS

How important is it for global marketers to use identical campaigns to promote identical products? If they do so, can they or should they overcome the tendency for local customers to prefer locally created advertising?

Sources: Nancy Giges, "Europeans Buy Outside Goods, but Like Local Ads," *Advertising Age International,* April 1992, I1, I26; "Data Watch," *Advertising Age International,* 28 September 1992, I14; and Normandy Madden, "Household Chores," *Media International,* November 1995, 46.

The Global Media Environment

As we saw in Chapter Two, the globalization of the media has been advancing at an ever-increasing rate. U.S. cable networks such as MTV, CNN, and ESPN are now seen in nearly 60 million homes outside of the U.S. *Elle* magazine is available in 29 countries, and *Reader's Digest* can be found in 48. Rupert Murdoch owns media properties in four continents, from Star TV in Asia and the FOX network in the U.S., to newspapers in Australia and Sky TV in Europe (with the U.S. and Japan to follow). This allows him to offer global advertisers multimedia as well as multinational deals if they purchase time and space in his properties.

EXHIBIT 4–10   Confidence in the Advertising Industry

COUNTRY	% OF RESPONDENTS CONFIDENT IN AD INDUSTRY
Germany	19%
Italy	23
Great Britain	26
France	27
Spain	27
Netherlands	17
Belgium	20
Portugal	39
Greece	32
Denmark	18
Ireland	31
Luxembourg	32
Sweden	13
Austria	21
Switzerland	36
Finland	18
Norway	20
Europe (average)	24

Source: Reader's Digest Eurodata Study, 1989.

Nevertheless, global media planning and buying accounts for a minuscule amount of all dollars spent on media worldwide. At MTV Europe, for example, pan-European advertising represents less than 10 percent of the dollars spent on the network's European operation. But altogether, its six international affiliates now account for 28 percent of the network's revenues. Indeed, because of this rush to globalized media, many predict that media planning and buying will inevitably be internationalized in the next decade.

There are two primary reasons for this. First, technology is driving standardization of the media function, primarily through increased computerization. At ad agency BBDO, for example, Macintosh computers are used in Los Angeles, London, and Moscow. DDB Needham Worldwide connects its network of offices through electronic mail, allowing a media planner in Chicago, for example, to ask questions electronically of his or her counterpart in Prague or Istanbul.

A second incentive for more global media activity is on the buying side, where more and more agencies are centralizing the buying function either as an internal unit or as a separate, external division. Cordiant established Zenith Media for this purpose, both in Europe and the U.S. This means that the agency can "unbundle" its local media department into a larger, centralized group that may operate more easily across borders. In creating this larger unit, the agency (or several agencies working together) has greater sales leverage to use against the media sellers, enabling it to obtain more favorable rates for its clients. The growth of specialized media buying units has been most pronounced in Europe. In 1980, the vast majority (87 percent) of media buys in Europe went through a full-service agency; by 1994, that figure had fallen to two-thirds (62 percent).

While global plans and buys are not yet common among packaged goods marketers such as Procter & Gamble or Kellogg's, they are already the norm in certain other categories of products and services. IBM's centralization of its account at Ogilvy & Mather was done, in large part, to facilitate such use of media. And if you fly to any major city today, you are likely to see ads for U.S.-based products such as Digital computers or AT&T telephone service both

inside the in-flight magazine and in posters or kiosks in the airport itself.

Perhaps the biggest problem facing international media planners and buyers is the enormous choice of media available. In Western Europe alone in 1994, media planners could choose from 927 TV stations; 8,808 newspapers; 38,791 magazines; 7,826 radio stations; or 18,863 cinema screens in which to advertise their product.[22] Worldwide, the proportion of advertising dollars going to print versus television or other media is becoming more similar. As Exhibit 4–11 shows, television now accounts for one-third or more of all ad dollars in major advertising markets (U.S., Europe, and Japan).[23]

GLOBAL ELECTRONIC MEDIA The growth of satellites has greatly enhanced the ability of global advertisers to use television to reach people across borders. Although the signals are delivered via satellite, they may be received by consumers via satellite dish, cable television, or other forms of broadcasting. Most of the TV services are distributed pan-regionally rather than globally (with the exception of CNN International). Exhibit 4–12 shows some of the major international cable networks, by region.

Television is growing more international as individual networks or syndicators try to extend their reach to the global level. NBC, for example, now operates CNBC International, a satellite service that reaches 63 million homes in 32 countries in Europe. ESPN International, the non–U.S. version of the sports cable network, has 65 million subscribers in 86 countries outside of the United States. ESPN International tailors its programs to the regions in which it broadcasts; thus, Indians can see more cricket, while Latin Americans view more soccer games and Japanese viewers watch more golf on the network. Commercials are aired in the local language, but global advertisers can buy time on the international satellite feed and appear in different languages in different countries. ESPN International competes against News Corporation's Star Sports service, which reaches 50 million homes across the globe.

The global market for program syndication is expanding rapidly. This allows the produc-

U.S. cable networks are on the leading edge of media globalization. MTV now has six international affiliates, including MTV Latino, from which the network draws 28 percent of its revenues.

ers of a U.S. TV show to sell the rights to air that show or a local version of it to producers or TV networks abroad. There are now 23 foreign versions of "Wheel of Fortune." Oprah Winfrey's popular talk show appears in 111 countries, dubbed or with subtitles. Russian viewers can watch "Dr. Quinn, Medicine Woman," or the soap opera "Santa Barbara."[24] "Sesame Street" is available in more than 60 countries, with local-language versions aired in 14 markets. In Norway, for instance, the show is set in a train station. Mexico's program, "Plaza Sesamo" has been on-air for 22 years. Each local version is slightly different, though all must be approved by the Children's Television Workshop, the U.S. producer of the show.[25] Not all programs translate well, however. German versions of the U.S. situation comedies "Who's the Boss?" and "Married with Children" both failed because they weren't seen to be sufficiently "German."[26]

Despite the increased availability of international TV channels or programs, the amount of truly pan-regional or global advertising remains small. It is estimated that in the European Community, where advertising revenues total

more than $50 billion, pan-European business accounts for just $159 million. Of that, 85–90 percent is generated by just two channels, Eurosport and MTV.[27] At Turner Broadcasting International, which operates CNN, Cartoon Network, and the movie channel Turner Network Television (TNT) both within and outside of the U.S., international advertising accounts for just 14 percent of total revenue. The company is aiming to achieve a 2 percent market share from more than 100 different

EXHIBIT 4–11   Allocation of Media Dollars (percent of total)

	PRINT	TV	OTHER
U.S.	53%	35%	12%
Japan	39	41	20
W. Europe	59	30	11

Source: Internal documents, DDB Needham Worldwide, 1995.

EXHIBIT 4–12   International Satellite TV Services

	NORTH AMERICA	EUROPE	LATIN AMERICA	ASIA-PACIFIC	MIDDLE EAST	AFRICA
BBC Worldwide	•	•		•		
Cartoon Network	•	•	•	•		
CNN	•	•	•	•	•	•
Country Music Television	•	•	•	•		
Discovery Channel	•	•	•	•		
Dow Jones		•		•		
ESPN	•	•	•	•	•	•
MTV	•	•	•	•		
NBC	•	•	•	•		
The Children's Channel		•				
Turner Network Television	•	•	•	•		
Warner Brothers	•		•			

Source: "Who's Where in Satellite TV," *Advertising Age International,* 20 March 1995, l18.

In addition to the extension of networks into markets across the globe, the syndication of individual programs is also growing rapidly. The French version of the Wheel of Fortune is only 1 of 23 foreign adaptations of this popular U.S. game show.

markets. It currently accounts for just 0.001 percent of the worldwide advertising market.[28]

GLOBAL PRINT MEDIA   The opportunities for global advertisers in magazines and newspapers are quite numerous. As with television, there are media designed specifically for the international market. Among newspapers, the most well-known is *The International Herald-Tribune,* a joint venture of The New York Times and Washington Post Companies. *USA Today* also has a separate international version of its newspaper, although that is designed primarily to appeal to Americans traveling abroad.

The magazine industry is moving rapidly into the global arena. *Reader's Digest* is perhaps the granddaddy of this category, having produced its first non–U.S. version in 1938 in the United Kingdom. *Reader's Digest* today has 48 editions in 19 languages and a circulation of 27.5 million worldwide. Today, young women across the world can be reached through the 32 versions of *Cosmopolitan,* 29 of *Elle,* and 26 of *Marie-Claire.* Exhibit 4–13 provides more information on these international consumer magazines.

As with electronic media, the difficulty in developing global print options lies in the strength of local market offerings. France, for instance, has more than 600 different magazine titles (320 for consumers and 210 trade or technical titles), while Italy has a total of 1,800 (114 consumer magazines and 1,686 trade or technical publications).

Other media are less well developed for international planning. Direct mail, for example, is difficult to implement across borders, in part because of dramatic variations in postal rates and standards. Some countries, such as Spain, have privatized their bulk mail service (through which most direct mail is sent), while others maintain a complete postal monopoly that generally keeps postal costs higher and makes direct mail less appealing for marketers.

Opportunities to purchase outdoor billboards internationally are scant. Of the $4 billion spent on that medium across Europe, just 2.5 percent of the expenditures are pan-European. Companies are starting to form alliances to offer centralized buys, but the market remains very fragmented, with differences in poster sizes, display time, and special features.

GLOBAL NEW MEDIA   The growth of the World Wide Web on the Internet should be considered a potentially global new medium for advertisers, as it is likely that other countries will soon see the same rapid expansion of this medium that we have seen in the U.S. in recent years. Although not many Web sites allow for online transactions, either domestic or global, they do offer companies the opportunity to promote their products and services outside of their geographic borders. FedEx, for example,

EXHIBIT 4–13 International Consumer Magazines

MAGAZINE	CIRCULATION	1996 AD PAGES	NUMBER OF COUNTRIES
Cosmopolitan	6.1 million	16,700	32
Elle	4.9 million	27,300	29
Marie-Claire	3.0 million	20,781	26
Men's Health	1.8 million	2,001	9
Auto Bild	1.9 million	n/a	11

Source: *Advertising Age International,* May 1997.

allows its customers to track their packages throughout the world, and the Underground Music Archive already achieves 30 percent of its music sales to people outside of the U.S.[29]

GLOBAL MEDIA RESEARCH   In order to plan and buy media on a global scale, it is important to have information on the audiences reached by both national and global media. Audience measurement poses many problems in the area of media. Because there is no single source of syndicated information on international media usage, planners must rely on local country studies. And although a large number of countries that offer advertising also provide

some kind of measures to show who is reading or watching or listening to the media, there are many differences from study to study as to how the measurements are taken, who is measured, and what is reported.

As a case in point, television audiences may be assessed by asking people to fill out viewing diaries or by electronic people meters, through which viewers record their TV habits on special remote control devices. But there is still no consensus on what constitutes a "viewer." In France, Ireland, and Spain, for example, the person simply has to be in the room. But in Italy, Austria, and Turkey, the person must be in the room and watching the TV set.

The choice of whom to measure can also vary. In the U.K., U.S., and Canada, everyone over the age of two is included in the sample for TV viewing; in Australia and New Zealand, only those ages five or older are admitted; and in Mexico, the local viewing measures exclude every person under the age of eight. At the reporting level, some countries show how many people saw a given commercial break, whereas others only give the audience size for the average minute of a program. Magazine readership and radio listening come either from personal interviews or by telephone surveys. But while Finland measures all listeners that are 12 and older, Sweden has a range of listeners aged 15–70. Radio studies in the U.K. include children aged 4–14 and persons 15 or over.

Like television networks and programs, the print media are now moving rapidly into the global arena. *Reader's Digest,* one of the first magazines to venture into international markets, now has 48 editions in 19 different languages.

What all of this means for the international planner is that it becomes challenging trying to compare how a given schedule of media will perform in different countries. Indeed, studies have shown that if the same schedule is planned for several locations, the maximum number of people who will have a chance to be exposed to a specific ad varies considerably from market to market. As illustrated in Exhibit 4–14, if you wanted to reach three-quarters of all women in the country one or more times with your ad in magazines and newspapers over a four-week period, you would be likely to reach 80 percent of Austrian women, but just 59 percent of Irish females. For a similar goal of reaching 30 percent of all adults age 16–34 with cinema advertising, you would exceed that in France, the United Kingdom, Belgium, and Switzerland, but fall short in the Netherlands, Spain, Austria, Ireland, and Finland.

Currently, there are a few syndicated studies of pan-European media usage available, but none of them are fully representative of the total population of that area. Conducted every few years, the studies are mostly funded primarily by the media themselves. The International Air Travel Survey studies 39,000 air travelers, focusing on newspapers, magazines, and some international TV channels. The European Business Readership Survey, conducted every two

The Underground Music Archive has successfully tapped the international advertising and sales potential of the World Wide Web, with approximately 30 percent of its music sales coming from outside of the U.S.

EXHIBIT 4–14   Differences in Reaching Targets by Country

TARGET	TV	NEWSPAPERS/ MAGAZINES	OUTDOOR	RADIO	CINEMA
	Housewives	Women Aged 18+	Adults	Housewives	Adults Aged 16–34
REACH GOAL (%)	75%	75%	75%	40%	30%
France	75	78	95	48	32
Netherlands	75	75	85	67	15
Spain	86	68	72	41	25
UK	84	77	75	41	31
Austria	75	80	77	60	20
Belgium	75	60	97	64	32
Ireland	75	59	43	64	20
Switzerland	84	66	79	58	55
Denmark	75	77	67	41	30
Finland	84	75	72	67	22
Norway	60	75	75	40	30

Source: *European Planning Guide 1993–94,* supplement to *Marketing & Media Europe,* 1993.

or three years, is designed to measure business executives' media habits. A more general study, the Pan-European Survey, is undertaken every three to four years in 16 European countries. It surveys working executives (male and female), asking about similar media.

It is worth pointing out that some researchers do not want to see media research standardized across borders, arguing that this would reduce the flexibility, and therefore the creativity, of research solutions.

The Global Advertising Environment

Just as marketers in the U.S. have to be aware of ethical, legal, or technological issues that

ADSCAPE

. . . .

Marketing Against Mother's Milk

The creation of infant formula was considered a major breakthrough in the 1950s, allowing women who could not breastfeed their babies to provide them with nutritionally equivalent, healthful substitutes. First introduced in western and developed markets such as North America and Europe, by the mid-1960s the product was being promoted aggressively in developing Third World nations, too.

Along with the promotion came considerable criticism, directed primarily at the Swiss-based manufacturer Nestlé, about the way the product was being promoted, particularly with the distribution of free samples in villages by women who were dressed as nurses. The reason for the outcry was the discovery that hundreds of infants were dying because their mothers were not preparing the product properly, were mixing the formula with dirty or contaminated water, or were not keeping it refrigerated. These poor and often illiterate women could not follow the written instructions provided on the product.

The response from the international community was considerable. Nestlé found itself accused of unethical behavior and malpractice in marketing, and countries urged international action. It took 13 years, until 1981, before the World Health Organization (WHO) issued its International Code of Breastmilk Marketing Substitutes, recommending a complete prohibition on all advertising and marketing of infant formula. Although it carried no force of law, the Code was intended as the foundation for individual countries to develop their own national bans.

At first glance, this might seem to be a wholly acceptable, indeed desirable, response to what was clearly a real tragedy. But further consideration of the issues reveals how ethical decisions cannot be made in isolation from other social and cultural practices. The promotion of infant formula in developing nations was seen by the WHO as an imposition of westernized values and culture on non-western countries, disrupting traditional, more natural means of childrearing. But in trying to protect the cultural autonomy of these countries by prohibiting "unethical" practices, the Code could in fact be said to be harming the people of those nations. One of the key purposes of advertising is to inform and educate consumers about the products available for sale. In not allowing such communication to take place (or rather, recommending that it not occur), the WHO is, in effect, keeping those consumers in continued ignorance. So while it was tragic that infants died as a result of being given the infant formula, it is arguable whether Nestlé should be held responsible for how the product was used (or misused).

QUESTIONS
Because the root causes of the tragedy were social and economic, how responsible should Nestlé have been in changing its marketing practices? Do you think the WHO was correct in taking the action it did? What other consequences might there be, both for consumers in developing countries and for multinational advertisers such as Nestlé?

Source: Adapted from Caryn L. Finkle, "Nestlé, Infant Formula, and Excuses: The Regulation of Commercial Advertising in Developing Nations," *Northwestern Journal of International Law & Business* 14 (1994): 602–619.

may impact their advertising messages, so must global marketers be sensitive to these areas when preparing to disseminate their messages beyond their home countries. This last section examines some of the challenges and choices that have to be made in dealing with global marketing plans.

Ethical Considerations

Marketers wishing to promote their products abroad may have several ethical issues to consider. This is particularly the case with controversial products such as alcohol, tobacco, or contraceptives. Should tobacco manufacturers be allowed to sell their products in developing nations where the people may be ill-informed about the health consequences of smoking? On the other hand, if those products are legally allowed and domestic companies are producing them, isn't it only fair that global companies are allowed to compete, too?

One of the important areas of cultural difference that arises in developing global ad campaigns concerns the use of sex. More specifically, the issue of nudity in advertising has created problems for several advertisers, both within and across national borders. In the U.S., as we explored in Chapter Three, there have been complaints made about the depictions of men and women in various stages of undress in ads for Calvin Klein, Guess? jeans, and Vanilla Musk perfume, among others. Many times, the media impose rules of self-censorship on what they will or will not accept, based on who they believe will be in the audience for such messages. Even spots for Lever Brothers' Lever 2000 soap, which featured models taking a shower and showed pictures of various parts of the body, were criticized in some quarters as being too explicit. De Beers had to modify its international diamond ads for the Middle East, where the silhouetted images of a couple embracing and an apparently naked woman were deemed too risqué for that culture.[30] Exhibit 4–15 shows an example of an ad that uses nudity in its product message.

The area of ethics also comes into conflict with cultural and economic issues at times. As "AdScape: Marketing Against Mother's Milk" explains, the promotion of infant formula in developing countries raised significant ethical issues for global advertisers.

Legal Considerations

Sometimes government restrictions can impinge on global advertisers' wishes. The governments of Singapore and the Philippines, for instance, ensure that all ads have a minimum representation of local people by placing quotas on the types of models that appear in commercials. Governments may also impose restraints on the ownership of advertising agencies or the media. Restrictions on agency ownership can delay or inhibit the international operations and growth of an agency, making it harder to implement a global campaign. Rules about foreign media ownership seem to have less of an impact, because even with less-than-

EXHIBIT 4–15 The failure to recognize cultural differences about the acceptability and appropriateness of nudity has resulted in problems for some advertisers. This ad for Polo, while acceptable in the United States, would most certainly be deemed unacceptable in Middle Eastern countries.

TECHNOLOGY WATCH

....

Satellites

Satellites are launched by spaceship into the sky until they are 22,300 miles up, at which point they are traveling at the same speed as the earth and so remain the same distance from the globe at all times. Signals are beamed up from special sites on the ground to the satellite, and can then be sent down again to a different location, where they are captured by a receiving station that sends the signal on through a wire (for telephone or cable) or by a satellite that is linked directly to a television set (for Direct Satellite Service).

The first communications satellite, Satcom 1, was launched in 1974. Quickly and increasingly, satellites were put to commercial use, beaming television signals across borders and telephone signals across continents. Today satellites are beaming more than 80 TV channels into Europe, 60 into Central and South America, and 69 into Asia. Satellites are essential to the international development of many magazines and newspapers, enabling *USA Today,* for example, to print its newspaper simultaneously in London, Hong Kong, and Lausanne (Switzerland), as well as in major U.S. markets.

Satellites have been instrumental in making the world seem smaller, expanding the horizons of people around the globe. Because satellite signals can be received by anyone who puts up a dish, they have the ability to bring information to people in spite of government attempts to prevent that from happening. Indeed, both Indonesia and Singapore ban the private ownership of dishes.

It is in the less-developed areas of the world where the impact of satellites will probably be felt even more strongly in years to come. By 2005, for example, it is estimated that 256 million households in Asia will be receiving television via satellite or cable TV, a four-fold increase from today's figure of 66 million. And much of what they will be viewing will be provided by multinational companies, such as News Corporation or MTV. This, in turn, will attract more global advertisers to the medium; already, Coca-Cola, Nike, and Procter & Gamble appear on satellite TV.

The first TV network in the U.S. to be relayed via satellite was a local Atlanta TV station, then known as WCKG. Media

majority control, it seems that global media magnates wield sufficient influence on local media properties.

Other regulations that make global advertising campaigns more complex concern which products and services can be advertised, where, and how. As we learned in Chapter Three, this particularly applies to controversial products such as alcohol and tobacco. There also may be legal issues caused by difficulties with distribution. If a product is unavailable in one or more of the markets where the ad is intended to air, then that market must either be blocked out or the ad cannot run at all.

Legalities must be considered from an international media perspective as well. In some countries, such as Germany, coupons are not allowed. And in France, marketers wishing to compile a database must first obtain permission from the Commission Nationale Informatique et Liberté, a national governmental body designed to protect consumer privacy. The process is long and expensive.

An example of how difficult it remains to conduct global advertising is the practice of home shopping in the European Community. Although this form of advertising has been regulated by the European Commission since 1989, the rules nevertheless vary from country to country. Overall, advertising within the EC countries is limited to no more than 15 percent of daily broadcast time, with a maximum of 12 minutes per hour. Home shopping is further limited to three hours per day, and the shopping programs have to be clearly identified as such. In France, home shopping is only allowed on the private, commercial channels, but even there they can only broadcast between 10–11 A.M. or 2–4 P.M. In addition, they are not allowed to air on Wednesday or Saturday after-

mogul Ted Turner put it up on a satellite in the early 1980s so that its programs (and particularly, local sports coverage) could be seen across the country, distributed via cable TV. It was followed shortly thereafter by the premium pay cable movie channel, Home Box Office (HBO). From that point on, the U.S. TV industry was never the same. Today, all U.S. cable and broadcast networks are delivered via satellite.

It is worth noting that satellites have been responsible not only for the growth of cable TV in many countries but also for the delivery of TV signals directly to small satellite dishes located on rooftops. This Direct Broadcast by Satellite (DBS) service is in fact more popular in certain countries, such as the U.K., than cable. In the U.S., the fledgling Direct Satellite Service (DSS) offers as many if not more channels than a cable service provider, but without having to send the signals through cable wires. Currently, about 5 million Americans receive television service this way.

As far as advertising is concerned, satellites facilitate standardized ad campaigns by allowing ad executives in one country to talk to their client in another. As satellites become even more powerful in the future, they will be capable of sending a greater number of signals at one time from point A to point B. This is true both for voice communications, such as telephone, and for video forms, such as television. While the future of communications may not lie in the stars, it probably lies nearby, in the satellites circling the earth.

Source: Suzanne Miao and Kate Burnett, "Rivals in the Skies," *Media International,* September 1995, 26.

deliver the world.

and all of its parts

via satellite. high-quality

communications access

everywhere. voice. data.

broadcast. multimedia.

internet. even ATM.

now. right now.

today.

COMSAT
World Systems
Bethesda, Maryland
301-214-3100
http://www.comsat.com

Satellites have become an integral tool in both communication and media services. As this business ad for Comstat World Systems indicates, satellites have increased access to telephone and electronic mail systems and expanded the reach of advertising media such as television.

noons or on Sundays, which are traditionally children's viewing times, and there can be no mention made of the brand, manufacturer, or retail outlet. In Germany and Spain, the maximum time limit is one hour per day, while in Italy, the product presentations can only last three minutes each. Furthermore, Germany does not allow commercials that last longer than 90 seconds.

Legal issues are perhaps even more complex and contentious in countries that have previously restricted or prohibited advertising. In former communist countries, such as Poland and Czechoslovakia (now the Czech Republic), the authorities have instigated tight restrictions on television advertising. And in China, which until recently had absolutely no regulations concerning advertising, a new advertising code states that all ads must be examined first by the authorities.

This code also bans comparative ads and places partial bans on tobacco ads.[31]

The Impact of Technology

The concept of global advertising, and the subsequent debate over it, have existed for more than 30 years, but the reality of the practice has really only grown significantly during the past 10–15 years. The main reason for that is technology: Although ad agencies were working for clients across the globe as far back as the 1920s, it was only with the development and growth of satellites and computers that global advertising was feasible.

Today, technology facilitates all aspects of the global advertising process, from consumer research to creative development to client relations and media buying. In the U.S., for example, researchers can meet and talk to potential consumers electronically via the Internet or

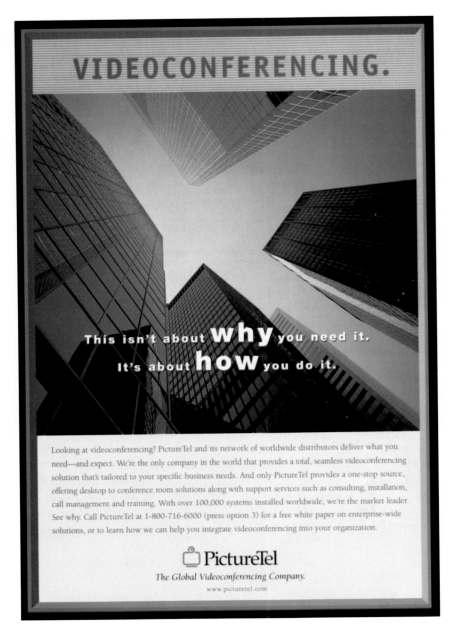

VIDEOCONFERENCING.

This isn't about **why** you need it.
It's about **how** you do it.

Looking at videoconferencing? PictureTel and its network of worldwide distributors deliver what you need—and expect. We're the only company in the world that provides a *total*, seamless videoconferencing solution that's tailored to your specific business needs. And only PictureTel provides a one-stop source, offering desktop to conference room solutions along with support services such as consulting, installation, call management and training. With over 100,000 systems installed worldwide, we're the market leader. See why. Call PictureTel at 1-800-716-6000 (press option 3) for a free white paper on enterprise-wide solutions, or to learn how we can help you integrate videoconferencing into your organization.

PictureTel
The Global Videoconferencing Company.
www.picturetel.com

International creative development has been enhanced by technology. Fax machines and computers allow creative personnel to share ideas across borders with ease, so agencies can work on international business even if they are not part of a global network. Wieden and Kennedy, based in Portland, Oregon, services most of its European Nike business out of one foreign office in Amsterdam. The U.K. agency Bartle Bogle Hegarty (BBH) does international work for clients such as Levi Strauss, Häagen-Dazs, Coca-Cola, and Electrolux, all out of its single London office. Another U.K. shop, Leagas Delaney, uses computers to send its ads directly to its client, Adidas, in Germany.[32]

The effect of technology on client relations at the global level is seen primarily in the ability of technology to bring people together who are physically separated. Videoconferencing has become a popular way to hold meetings between agency and client, even if one or other of the parties is located in a foreign country. Fax machines and electronic mail mean that the time it takes to contact people and provide them with information has been greatly reduced.

Perhaps the biggest impact of technology is in the area of media. As "Technology Watch: Satellites" explains, the development and growth of satellite distribution has made international media both technically possible and much more affordable. Technology has expanded both the types and number of media that are available. Now, instead of viewing just 4 domestic channels, cable or satellite viewers in the U.K. can watch up to 30.

As online services move from their primary U.S. base across the globe, they offer advertisers the opportunity to disseminate their messages across borders. The popular French computer service, Minitel, which has been available for more than 10 years, is starting to expand to the Netherlands and Ireland. This will allow advertisers such as Club Med, which is accessed by 30,000 French people each month, to promote its vacation destinations to other Europeans, too.

The recent explosion of access to the Internet computer network, with its advertising on Web sites, offers advertisers from any country the opportunity to have their message seen by up to 30 million people worldwide. And many of those people may be living in countries where other media are tightly controlled.

As it becomes increasingly more global, advertising is developing a greater reliance on such technological advances as electronic mail and videoconferencing to maintain effective client–advertiser relationships. This business ad for PictureTel promotes videoconferencing as a business tool.

computer online services such as CompuServe and America Online. And researchers in numerous countries can now enter the responses of survey participants directly into their computers rather than having to write down the answers and later transfer them to the computer for analysis. The order in which questions are asked in a survey can now be determined by the computer, depending upon the answer to a previous question. The computer can also provide automatic translation of a survey into different languages (such as English and Spanish in the U.S., or English and French in Canada).

In China, Singapore, Vietnam, and Indonesia, for example, all other types of information are subject to strict censorship, but for the estimated 200,000 households in Asia with access to computers, the Internet offers access to unfettered information from around the world.

In the future, technology is likely to push the global advertising process ahead even faster. The combination of computers and satellites will mean that an agency executive in Sydney, Australia, will be able to talk to his client in Paris and show her examples of creative developed in New York—all live and in real-time (although the time differences may make this less appealing!). It is likely, however, that we will see more and more marketers taking advantage of technology to facilitate their global marketing plans.

SUMMARY

While the world is, in many ways, growing smaller each year, it is still not a fully global village, especially for advertising. Growth of advertising across the world has been considerable in recent years, more than doubling from 1983 to 1993. There are five forces necessary for a global market: production facilities, transportation, outside investments and stable government, telecommunications systems, acceptance of advertising and discretionary income. Differences are seen between developed, developing, and underdeveloped markets. Advertising agencies and advertisers are rapidly expanding their global efforts through local partnerships, joint ventures, subsidiaries, or international units of domestic companies.

One of the biggest issues for global advertising is the choice that has to be made between developing a standardized campaign across all markets or developing a localized campaign that can be customized by market or region. The benefits of standardization include offering a unified brand image; appealing to similar basic needs or desires; transferring and sharing good ideas; enjoying lower production, design, and distribution costs; and providing greater sophistication in less-developed countries. On the other hand, a standardized approach also has several risks. These include linguistic, cultural, and lifestyle differences; differences in market characteristics or industry conditions; and local resistance or lowest-common-denominator marketing. Many advertisers attempt a middle path, planning strategy at the international level but then adapting it to local conditions.

At the global level, the marketing mix elements (product, place, price, and promotion) may be used in different proportions to the way they are combined in the United States. The diverse tools of integrated marketing communications can often play a larger role in certain foreign markets. The role of advertising in the overall economy also varies quite considerably, as reflected in each country's advertising spending as a percent of its gross national product.

For global advertising to succeed, there has to be a solid understanding of how consumers are the same, or different, across markets. Companies rely on consumer research to explore these possible differences. Studies comparing attitudes and behavior in numerous countries have found considerable variations that could impact an ad's effectiveness. The growth of global media opportunities has been substantial, with more and more TV or magazine companies venturing beyond their own borders. This is enhanced by technological advances that lead to greater standardization in media, as well as the centralization of the media buying function at large agencies and specialized media buying companies. The growth of satellites has helped the development of international media, in television for program distribution and in magazines for printing purposes. Television is becoming more international as domestic networks or syndicators extend their reach beyond their own borders. Print titles also are developing partnerships or exporting their titles abroad. The rapid growth of the World Wide Web is likely to offer advertisers a valuable new source of global business. There are major problems in obtaining standardized measurements of media usage and effectiveness. Each country's studies of media usage applies slightly different methods and standards.

The advertising environment needs to be examined from a global perspective. Ethical decisions for global advertisers are found particularly with controversial products such as tobacco and alcohol. The creative message may raise ethical questions, such as the use of nudity in advertisements. More broadly, the issue of a developed nation imposing its beliefs and practices on less-developed countries has caused considerable concern. Global advertisers must be careful to comply with both local and international laws that affect advertising and marketing.

The impact of technology can be seen in all areas of global advertising, from the ability of advertisers to communicate with their agencies across the globe, to the development of creative ideas via fax or computer without any face-to-face contact. Satellite viewing and computer networks will continue to have a major impact on consumer use of media throughout the world.

KEY TERMS

developed market, 112

developing market, 112

underdeveloped market, 112

local partner, 113

joint venture, 113

subsidiary, 113

standardized advertising, 116

localized advertising, 116

REVIEW QUESTIONS

1. What are the requirements of a global market?

2. Why might marketers be interested in advertising their products in developing markets?

3. What kinds of goods and services lend themselves to a standardized ad campaign, and why?

4. Why might a global advertiser such as Nike decide to switch to a more localized approach?

5. How do retail and shopping patterns impact an advertiser's decision on whether to use a standardized or localized approach?

6. Discuss the importance of conducting international consumer research prior to launching a global ad campaign. What difficulties might be encountered?

7. How will international media planners of the future deal with the increased media choices consumers are faced with around the world?

8. What are some of the ethical and legal considerations global marketers must take into account?

9. How much weight would you give the Price element of the marketing mix in former communist countries? Explain your answer.

10. What might a country's GNP tell you about its potential for increased advertising exposure?

1. If you were trying to promote a new brand of shampoo in Eastern Europe, how would you deal with all elements of the marketing mix?

2. For a standardized global ad campaign for the Ford Taurus, which media would you include in the plan, and why?

3. How do you think advertising on the Internet will impact the global advertising environment?

interactive discovery lab

1. Find two (or more) foreign editions of a women's magazine (e.g., *Vandidades* and *Good Housekeeping,* or the Spanish-language version of *Cosmopolitan*) and compare and contrast the ads that appear in the foreign-language editions with those that appear in the U.S. editions.

2. Videotape 4 or 5 TV commercials (or select 4 or 5 print ads) and analyze them in terms of the cultural problems that might arise in using those ads outside of the U.S. Suggest changes that might need to be made.

1900–1925

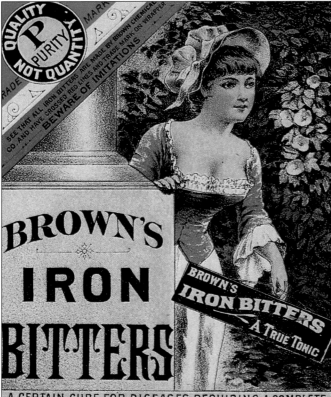

c. 1900

Brand Name	First Appeared
Borden's Eagle Brand Condensed Milk	1866
Campbell's Soup	1869
Levi Strauss Overalls	1873
Ivory Soap	1879
Chase & Sanborn Coffee	1886
Coca-Cola	1894

We begin the history of advertising in the United States with the year 1900 because many of the forces that fueled advertising's growth after the Civil War were in place by the turn of the century. Additionally, by 1925 advertising was becoming a fairly stable economic and social force in the U.S.

Advertising found fertile ground in the United States during the post-Civil War period. Private industry grew by leaps and bounds between 1870 and 1900 due, in part, to a doubling of the population, the building of a nationwide railroad system, and technological inventions that would eventually lead to the development of automobiles, airplanes, and mass communications. Advertising became the primary tool of marketing as these forces fueled unprecedented industrial growth.

Brand-name products were an essential ingredient in the new marketing system that developed after the Civil War. The discovery that trademarks and product packaging could move products better and faster than the old self-serve bulk containers found in most grocery stores resulted in the appearance of the first brand names before 1900. Some of those names still exist today, as shown here.

A new national advertising medium also was growing and developing during these formative stages of our private enterprise system—magazines. By 1900, titles such as *Harper's Monthly, Ladies Home Journal, Cosmopolitan,* and *Saturday Evening Post* were popular among readers and attractive to advertisers. The relationship between advertising and the media was also readily accepted by this time. Magazines and newspapers relied extensively on advertising income and began segmenting their audiences to appeal to advertisers. There were, however, no methods in place to measure the effectiveness of ads.

Advertising for patent medicines, which promised to

1904

c. 1916

cure every kind of ailment, provided a significant source of income to ad agencies and the print media. Concerns about the legitimacy of the claims made in these ads were a primary impetus to the first attempts to regulate and self-regulate advertising content. The Pure Food and Drug Act of 1906 was the first federal law enacted to protect the public's health and to control certain aspects of advertising.

Print advertising in the early 1900s was surprisingly well designed and well produced by today's standards. Pictures were used extensively, and often they were classy pieces of art. Famous artists such as Maxfield Parrish and Frederick Remington were commissioned by ad agencies to create poster-style artwork. These ads were cleanly designed and the copy tended to be simple and clear. Today, many of these early ads are valuable collectors' items.

The 1920s saw the arrival of a new medium, radio, which was among the new inventions of the early 1900s that vastly changed people's lives. Electricity, the automobile, the washing machine, the telephone, and the phonograph all appeared around this time. It was advertising that created national awareness and stimulated demand for these marvels of modern life.

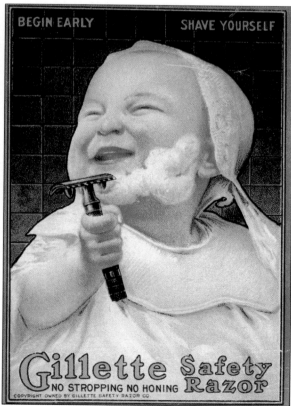

1905

Part One
The Challenging **Business** of Advertising

Part Four
**The Challenge
of Advertising**
Creativity

Part Two

The Challenge of Strategy
in Marketing
and Advertising

Part Three
Media Strategy:
Challenges and Choices

Chapter Five

Integrated Marketing Communications Strategy

IMC:
THE MEAT IN
McDonald's
MARKETING STRATEGIES

The one-size-fits-all advertising and marketing strategies of the television era are rapidly becoming a thing of the past. Today you are more likely to receive product information from videotapes, infomercials, T-shirts, CD-ROMs, World Wide Web

sites, direct response ads, sales promotions, and sponsored events than you are from traditional media advertising. While advertising has long been an important media subsidy, marketers are now finding their way into new domains once thought to be taboo for advertiser-supported messages.

McDonald's advertising and promotion activities provide a case in point, as it works hard to break through the media clutter. No longer is a big, fancy television advertising campaign enough. McDonald's introduced its new Arch Deluxe at Radio City Music Hall with an old-time publicity stunt preceded by a week's worth of teaser TV spots. Ronald McDonald danced with the famed Rockettes while the media were served Arch Deluxe hamburgers and champagne on silver platters. The total bill was $1 million—roughly the cost of two good TV commercials.

McDonald's also uses nonadvertising forms of promotion and public relations to reinforce its wholesome, community-minded image. It runs Ronald McDonald houses for terminally ill children and their families. The company sponsors the McDonald's All American Band and was a major sponsor of the 1996 Summer Olympics in Atlanta. In addition, McDonald's was a corporate sponsor of the Ladies' Professional Golf Association Championship in 1997.

McDonald's is also the leading seller of children's toys, which it uses as a sales incentive to help sell its Happy Meals for kids. McDonald's was so successful with its Teenie Beanie Baby promotion in 1997 that its inventory started running out after only 10 days. McDonald's sales increased by more than 10 percent over the same period the year before for the stores it audited.

All of these messages and activities have to be orchestrated so that each target market gets the right message at the right time. McDonald's has to continuously monitor the marketplace to make sure these marketing communications efforts come together in some synergistic way to sell its image and hamburgers every day. McDonald's knows what is working and what is not because the company knows what and how much it sells every day of the week. For example, when McDonald's found that a 55¢ hamburger promotion was confusing its customers about the value of its meals, it dropped the promotion almost immediately. This is what integrated marketing communications is all about.

Sources: Dottie Enrico, "All the World's a Stage for Marketing Stunts," *USA Today,* 10 May 1996, 1B; Kelley Holland, "A Toy Story at McDonald's," *Business Week,* 9 June 1997, 40; and Bill Shapiro, "Fallen Arches," *Time,* 9 June 1997, 42–46.

LOOK BEFORE YOU LEAP

- What is integrated marketing communications (IMC)?

- What changes in the marketplace and advertising industry have given rise to IMC?

- What are the value of a brand and its brand equity to a marketer or advertiser?

- What are the promotional mix elements and how are each of them used in terms of loyalty, response, and cost?

- What are the four levels of integration in a marketing communications program?

- What are the eight steps in the IMC planning process?

5

The Road To Integrated Marketing Communications

Significant changes in the marketplace over the last 10 years are creating new challenges and choices for advertising and marketing professionals. Advertising and marketing strategists are now being asked to integrate advertising, promotions, direct marketing, and public relations activities so that each contact a consumer has with a brand reinforces the brand image and adds to brand equity. The ultimate goal of marketing communications strategy today is the development of a long-term relationship with consumers.

In this chapter we will present an overview of the key changes in the advertising industry and consumer marketplace that have been the impetus for a more strategic approach to marketing communications. We will then focus on where advertising fits into this larger picture, placing the discussion in the context of why building brand equity for products and services should be the goal of all marketing communications efforts. Finally, we outline the eight-step process of creating a successful marketing communications strategy, leading to the discussion of nonadvertising marketing communications tools presented in Chapter Twelve.

In the past, advertising and its marketing communications cousins—promotions, direct marketing, and public relations—have maintained and protected their own turf. Marketers and advertisers often planned and used each of these elements for very different purposes, treating them as if they were independent forces in the marketplace. Each promotional area became its own industry, competing for its share of companies' marketing budgets. More recently, companies have taken on a more enlightened view of the advertising and promotional tools at their disposal. They have come to realize that it is more effective and efficient to coordinate the use of marketing communications to create a consistent image among their target customers. The term given to the concept and process of coordinating the use of various forms of marketing communications is **integrated marketing communications (IMC)**. IMC is defined as

> a concept of marketing communications planning that recognizes the added value of a comprehensive plan that evaluates the strategic roles of a variety of communications disciplines, for example, general advertising, direct response, sales promotion, and public relations—and combines these disciplines to provide clarity, consistency, and maximum communications impact.[1]

The IMC concept makes common sense to marketers and advertisers today, but this has not always been the case. It has taken some significant changes in the marketplace and advertising industry for IMC to rise to its current level of importance, among which are the demands of a changing marketplace, smarter consumers, more choices, more clutter, and the transition to an information economy. Let's look at each of these changes.

Demands Of A Changing Marketplace

The nature of the consumer goods marketplace has undergone significant and in some cases radical changes since the early 1980s. Fueling these changes has been an increase in the cost of major advertising media such as television, with a corresponding decline in audience size and advertising effectiveness. Advertisers and marketers responded to this erosion of advertising effectiveness by placing more of their dollars into sales promotions and direct marketing activities to produce more immediate sales effects. An increase in competition in many consumer markets also forced companies to put greater emphasis on short-term sales goals. Sales promotion and direct marketing techniques are better suited to these short-term goals than is traditional mass media advertising.

Advertising expenditures accounted for 43 percent of all marketing dollars spent in 1981, with consumer promotions making up 23 percent and trade promotions 34 percent. Today advertising accounts for just about one-fourth of all marketing dollars. Many of these dollars were shifted to trade promotions to get retailers to carry advertisers' brands.[2] There has been some recovery for advertising recently, but it does not appear that the prominence of advertising will ever return to the levels of 15 or more years ago. Exhibit 5–1 illustrates how marketing communications expenditures have changed since the early 1980s.

While advertising effectiveness was declining, changes in the media were leading to more fragmented audiences. Cable television brought more channels and choices to the TV viewer, resulting in a steady erosion of network TV audiences. The average number of channels reaching into our homes in 1980 was 9; today it is 40—and 500 are promised for the near future. The video cassette recorder has added insult to injury. Only 1 percent of homes had a VCR in 1980; today more than three-quarters of all U.S. households own at least one VCR. Video rentals, video games, and personal computer usage have made the competition for the TV viewers' time more intense. Of course, these new media channels also present new challenges and choices for the advertiser.

Consumer magazines proliferated during the 1980s and early 1990s, too, as publishers found smaller and smaller niche markets against which they could target their publications. Consider the fact that magazine titles have grown by a hefty 72 percent since 1980, from just over 4,000 magazine titles in 1980 to just under 7,000 today. You can choose from almost 200 sports magazines, 120 travel publications, and just shy of 100 automotive books.[3]

EXHIBIT 5–1   Trends in Marketing Communications Expenditures

	MEDIA ADVERTISING	CONSUMER PROMOTIONS	TRADE PROMOTIONS
1981	43%	23%	34%
1985	35	27	38
1990	28	25	47
1991	25	27	48
1992	25	27	48
1993	24	27	49
1994	24	26	50
1995	25	24	51

Source: DDB Needham Worldwide, Media Trends 1994, 9; and DDB Needham Worldwide, Media Trends 1997, 10.

At the same time media audiences were becoming more fragmented, retailers were gaining power over manufacturers. This was occurring for two primary reasons. First, manufacturers became reliant on trade and consumer promotions to achieve short-term sales and profit goals while being faced with increased competition from private and store brands. The success of store brands allowed retailers to reduce the number of national brands they carried, thus putting pressure on the national manufacturers to try to buy shelf space that was quickly disappearing. Money formerly used to build a brand's image through advertising was now being redirected toward trade promotions. Secondly, the soft economic conditions of the 1990s have made consumers more demanding. Consumers want better prices and more variety or choices, and they want these things *now*. The consumer's ally in this battle is the retailer, not the manufacturer.

Smarter Consumers

Today's consumers have grown up in the post–World War II consumer products boom in the United States. They also have grown up with television and are experienced viewers who understand its techniques. To some extent, consumers have become desensitized to modern marketing and advertising activities.

"Service" : 60
SFX: Music up and under throughout
(Open on Russ Penick walking through a store)
Woman #1 (VO): Russ Penick? He's the service manager at Saturn of Shreveport.
(Cut to Russ directing cars into the parking lot. Cut to him standing in front of seated customers)
Man #1 (VO): I love barbecues.
(Cut to Russ holding up an owner's manual)
Russ: It's called your owner's manual.
(Cut to barbecue grill in front of picnic tables)
Russ (VO): We're gonna have a good barbecue. Got some spiced spareribs.
(Cut to a man walking with a plate of food. Cut to Russ dishing up more food for the man)
Woman #1 (VO): Every month Russ invites all the new Saturn owners in and tells them about their cars.
(Cut to Russ walking customers through dealership)
Russ (VO): It's like a family deal here (laughs).
Man #1 (VO): It's kind of like a family reunion.
(Cut to customers looking at the underside of a Saturn)
Woman #1 (VO): Everybody here has a new Saturn. Russ just wants to make sure we know how everything works on the car.
Russ: We're gonna cover the right and wrong way to change a flat.
Woman #1 (VO): Thought I'd meet some people and learn a little bit about the car.
Man #1 (VO): He has showed me things on my car that I didn't know.
(Cut to a man and his daughter opening up the sunroof)
Woman #1 (VO): I definitely could change a tire and my oil.
(Cut to the customers looking under the hood)
Man #2 (VO): I could change a spark plug now if I had to.
(Cut to Russ holding up a metallic pad)
Russ: That has to do with these metallic pads. If there's any questions while I'm goin' along raise your hand.
Woman #2 (VO): He's a pretty neat guy. I guess you just have to get to know Russ.
Man #1 (VO): We had a good time when we were out here.
Russ (VO): Did everyone get enough barbecue to eat?
Camera card: A different kind of company. A different kind of car.

They are more savvy, and as a result it takes better products and services, marketing strategies, and promotional ideas to influence people today than it did just five years ago.

The education level of the average American is higher than at any other time in our history. Whereas only 15 percent of the high school graduates in 1960 attended college, today well over half do. This makes the average customer much harder to please. Consumers want to be talked to as if they are the only ones who matter. They want their information and products to be created with their specific needs and desires in mind. They want customization. They want companies to appreciate their patronage and act accordingly. The Saturn Company is a marketer that understood these lessons early on. Saturn studied the common complaints consumers had with car dealers and tried to solve them. Service became the most important component of Saturn's marketing program, which included no-haggle pricing and friendly sales help. The Saturn advertisement in Exhibit 5–2 promotes the importance of service to its customers.

More Choices

There was a time when you could buy only one type of bicycle: a one-speed touring bike. Similarly, whether you were running, walking, or playing tennis or basketball, you wore the same pair of shoes, called "sneakers" by most people. Today, however, population growth, technological change, smarter consumers, and an accompanying affluence have fueled a proliferation of product and service variety in every category imaginable. People expect more, and the marketplace is providing it. You can now buy the bicycle that best suits your needs—racing bikes, trail bikes, and the old-style one-speed. In many places around the world you can rent bikes to ride on local trails and expect to see the same variety you would see in a U.S. bicycle shop. You can also buy athletic shoes for every possible sports activity—running shoes, walking shoes, tennis shoes, and basketball shoes, to name a few. And within each type of shoe you can find multiple brands and a variety of features to meet your heart's desire. The ad in Exhibit 5–3, for example, displays a small portion of Nike's running athletic shoes.

Trends also help to create new products and services. Consider the whole automotive category and what has happened to it over the last 10 years. Passenger cars are no longer the vehicle of choice for many consumers. Sports utilities, vans, and trucks now account for more than half of all automotive sales in the U.S. While Japanese automotive companies have been making serious inroads into the passenger car segment since the 1970s, U.S. auto companies are dominating the truck category, which includes the popular sports utility vehicle. Sports utility vehicles like the Ford Explorer and Jeep Cherokee have fulfilled consumers' desire for something new and more exciting in personal transportation.

More Clutter

Advertising messages appear to be everywhere. They are on T-shirts, sweaters, jackets, race cars, school buses, baseball stadium signs, blimps, luggage, the World Wide Web, sports clothing of all types, and more. More advertising clutter simply means more competition for a marketer's promotional message. Marketing and advertising strategies have to be better conceived and executed than ever before or they will not be noticed. For example, advertisers are flocking to ESPN's broadcasts of extreme sporting events to break through the clutter and reach the elusive teen and Generation X markets. Pepsi-Cola, Colgate-Palmolive, MCI, and Rollerblade are among the advertisers interested in this growing segment of the sports market that appeals specifically to young people jaded by the influence of money on major league sports.[4]

Marketing and advertising have become so much a part of the American culture that the techniques have crept into other types of media content, making for even more competition. News shows such as "HardCopy" and "American Journal" use short, sensationalized stories that play on the fact that our collective attention span is very short. If something does not grab our attention right away, we are quick to zip past it to another channel. Zipping past commercials is one way the average person can deal with the clutter of advertising messages.

There also is more competition at the local media level as entrepreneurship burgeons and small businesses take advantage of the access and flexibility that new media offer. In fact, integrated marketing communications vehicles

Match the correct shoe with the soon-to-be-former world record.*

ZOOM LJ	9.85
ZOOM RIVAL S	1:44.3jr
ZOOM V	3:27.37
ZOOM JAV	26:43.53
ZOOM SD	8' 0 1/2"
ZOOM SUPER FLY	10.89jr
ZOOM HJ	29' 4 1/2"
ZOOM SHIFT	75' 10 1/4"
ZOOM RIVAL D	284' 7"
ZOOM ELDORET	313' 10"
ZOOM ROTATIONAL	12:56.15jr

*Answers found on page 21.

have opened channels for the small business owner while at the same time attracting the attention of big business. Consider the marketing advice for entrepreneurs given in Exhibit 5–4. These ideas are clutter breakers for businesses, whether they are small, medium, or large.

Transition To An Information Economy

Think of the information technology that has become available in your lifetime: fax machines, cellular phones, e-mail, the World Wide Web, overnight mail, and cable and satellite television. What we have experienced in a very short period of time is the transition of our economy from an industrial or manufacturing mode to an information creation and processing mode. The importance of this

EXHIBIT 5–3 Specialization in all market categories has resulted in a plethora of product offerings for the consumer. Nike, for example, has a shoe with features designed specifically for each sport and for each type of athlete.

EXHIBIT 5–4   Clutter Breaking Ideas for Small Businesses

1. **Think community involvement.** Organize community events like 10K runs to raise funds for charitable organizations. Food drives and community beautification programs are other ways you can give back and attract attention to your business.

2. **Sponsor offbeat, memorable events.** Rent out a movie theater for a day in late August and invite kids to a free viewing. Don't do the ordinary; think of ways you can connect to the lives of people in your community.

3. **Set up a Web site.** Set up a Web site and do the little things to make it attractive. Chat it up in discussion groups on the Web. Keep your site current and don't be too pushy. Respond quickly to those who visit your Web site. Finally, market your Web site in other media; let people know you're there.

4. **Stay in touch with past customers.** This is called "relationship marketing" in the world of big business. Invite your customers to see new products; give them discounts and treat them like they are special. Future business will come from your past business.

5. **Use fax cover sheets to promote your business.** Use your fax cover sheet, the first sheet to come through the fax machine, to promote specials. People read these sheets while waiting for the rest of the fax to come through.

6. **Create a handout of handy tips in which your customers will be interested.** People like insightful tips. Lawn care firms can share some of their expert knowledge about landscaping with customers, lawyers can provide legal tips, and health care providers can give home emergency advice.

7. **Hold seminars.** People want good information on things about which they know little. For example, women might like to know more about how to handle simple mechanical problems they encounter with their cars and mature citizens might like to know more about retirement planning issues. The seminars must be good and should be held to about two hours.

8. **Think brand image as well as sales.** Develop a plan for how you want your service or product to be perceived. Build your business around a strong concept; then, pay attention to details like colors, names, package design, and merchandising. Make sure your core concept or value comes through. What does your business mean?

9. **Tell your story in the media.** Bring good public relations principles into your business. Know your local media and how larger issues relate to your business. Make your business newsworthy; keep a scrapbook of articles about your business. Get to know your local news reporters. Try to help them, and they will help you.

10. **Develop a customer appreciation program.** Be the local expert in your business. Be willing to speak at seminars and workshops, and be willing to go the extra mile for your customers. Offer special promotions tied to events of interest to your customers. Remember people's birthdays.

Source: Adapted from Lynn Beresford, Janean Chun, Cynthia E. Griffin, Heather Page, and Debra Phillips, "Marketing 101: Experts Share Their Newest-and-Hottest Marketing Tips," *Entrepreneur*, May 1996, 104–114.

transition for the future is that we are seeing a shift in jobs away from the manufacturing part of the economy and toward the information sector. This shift is similar to the one that took place earlier in the twentieth century when the agricultural sector lost jobs to the growing manufacturing sector. Now it is manufacturing that is on the decline, while the service and information sectors are increasing.

The notion of a well-defined information sector in our economy is important because it influences how we see the growing choices and challenges new media technology provide. This sector also has a profound impact on the entire notion of integrated marketing communications; IMC, as it turns out, is the application of all the information sector has to offer to the selling of goods and services. The information sector can be divided into primary and secondary sectors based on the industry categories that use and create information.

The *primary information sector* is that part of the economy that actually creates and sells information goods and services. This includes such industries as the media, educational institutions, entertainment and film, advertising, sales promotion, public relations, direct marketing, banking, telecommunication, and computers. The *secondary information sector* is made up of companies engaged in noninformation industries that use information internally as part of their business operations. This includes accounting, inventory control, and research firms and departments that service the agricultural and manufacturing industries. Taken as a whole, the elements of the primary information sector provide the foundation for IMC. It is the growth of the primary information sector that has presented most of the choices, challenges, and changes in advertising and promotion that marketers are learning to employ. The increases in entrepreneurship and corporate ventures into global markets are a direct result of the technological means made available by advances in the primary information sector. This also is the sector where the most job growth is occurring. "Technology Watch: The New Advertising Elite" discusses one such new job area, the advertising technologist.

1. Why has paid media advertising decreased in relative importance to other marketing communications elements in the last 10 years or so?
2. How has the existence of more choices brought IMC to the forefront of advertising and marketing thought?
3. How has the transition from a manufacturing economy to an information economy influenced the rising importance of integrated marketing communications to marketers?

Integrated Marketing Communications And The Brand

You should have a sense by now that major changes have taken place in advertising and marketing over the last 5 to 10 years. These changes have made the job of any marketer or advertiser much harder. In short, advertising by itself is inadequate to sell a product. Competition for the consumer's attention and dollar is greater than ever before. At the same

TECHNOLOGY WATCH

....

The New Advertising Elite

To many of us they are known as "nerds" and "geeks." They understand the digital world of *Wired* magazine. Their heroes are more likely to be computer gurus like Bill Gates than the advertisers worshipped by earlier generations of ad professionals. And they were into computers before computers were cool.

In the early days of the computer revolution, ad agencies thought these innovators were nothing more than a nuisance, but times have changed and high technology is in vogue. One of these early visionaries describes his newly found status: "I've gone from nerd to genius to 'the computer guy.'" He likes to introduce himself as "the Webmaster."

Advertising agencies are turning more and more to these new advertising technologists to help them develop sophisticated promotional ideas for cyberspace. What was once a passion among a few "techies" has become the here and now of marketing and advertising. It takes a deep understanding of computers to be able to create the type of interactive messages and Web sites that companies are demanding to stay abreast of the competition. This type of knowledge only comes from years and years of devotion to the computer.

Agencies are finding that to create cutting-edge ideas for their clients, it can be highly beneficial to partner with new-media and technology shops. For example, Leo Burnett partnered with a firm called Giant Step to develop an interactive computer game for Kellogg's Corn Pops. Giant Step (which Burnett subsequently bought) was founded by Eric Hennigan and his brother Adam to help advertisers translate brand identities to cyberspace. The idea is that the child playing the game will become familiar with the Corn Pops brand and message by interacting with it rather than sitting passively in front of the TV screen watching a commercial.

These new advertising elite have become central to what advertisers do. They are needed not only to work the hardware and software, but also to create the dynamic content cyberspace requires. Partnering with firms created by these new media experts can help to integrate cyberspace messages with current brand strategies, as in the Corn Pops example. This new generation of advertising practitioners is no longer relegated to the back rooms of agencies or their garages or kitchen tables. They are rising fast among the ranks of management. They are heading and leading their own technology-based agencies. They are senior vice presidents, presidents, and chief creative officers of specialty as well as mainstream agencies.

Sources: Robyn Griggs, "Up by Their Bootstraps," *Agency,* Winter 1996, 36–42; and Thom Forbes, "Techies and Creatives," *Agency,* Fall 1996, 18–21.

time, there are more opportunities for companies to use new technology and other promotional elements to reach and influence their customers.

The more challenging the situation, the more essential it is that advertisers develop strategies and plans for their marketing communications activities. A primary goal of the marketing planning process has become to coordinate and integrate a wide range of marketing, promotion, and communications tools so that every source of contact consumers have with a company either creates or reinforces a positive and consistent image in their minds. This consistent image is built around a brand. To understand the role of integrated marketing communications in building and maintaining brands, we will first discuss the concept of brand equity. Then we will move on to the roles played by the elements of marketing communications in this process.

Brand Equity

The reason companies have to be concerned about the impression they make in the minds of their customers is that the most valuable thing they own is the name of their company and the names of their products. The name and/or symbol used to identify a product or service and distinguish it from the competition is a **brand.** The value of the brand to the company that owns it is known as its **brand equity,** which is the net total of all assets and liabilities linked to the brand by consumers.[5]

Brand equity is a product quality that exists quite independently from the product or service itself. It resides in the mind of the consumer and gives a firm a certain amount of marketing leverage. Products and services can be copied, but successful brands are unique. For example, all colas may be alike, but Coke and Pepsi are unique in the minds of their loyal customers. As illustrated in Exhibit 5–5, Nike's brand equity is so strong it doesn't even need to identify itself by name.

The aim of most IMC programs is to either create or manage the brand equity of a company's products and services. Even small businesses should be concerned about the equity of their name, as many of the suggestions in Exhibit 5–4 illustrated. The assets and liabilities linked to a brand can be organized into five types, each of which is influenced by marketing communications activities. They are: brand loyalty; brand awareness; perceived quality; brand associations beyond quality; and other assets, such as patents, trademarks, or awards. Exhibit 5–6 illustrates how each of these factors provides value to both the consumer and to the firm owning the brand.

BRAND LOYALTY The degree of attachment customers have to a particular brand is known as **brand loyalty.** It provides the foundation for brand equity.[6] The more consumers you can get to buy your brand on a habitual basis without regard for what your competitors are doing in the marketplace, the stronger your brand equity. These are the customers you can rely on, and the marketing costs of maintaining them as customers are far less than those required to attract new buyers to your brand.

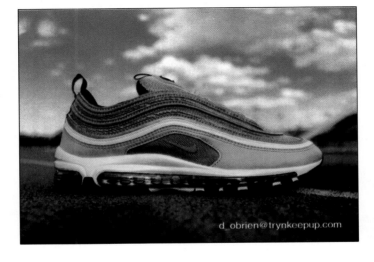

EXHIBIT 5–5   As this ad clearly illustrates, Nike's brand equity is so strong that it merely needs to show the ubiquitous swoop to trigger recognition in the minds of consumers. In short, the swoop speaks louder than words.

EXHIBIT 5–6 The Value of Brand Equity to Consumers and the Firm

Source: From David A. Aaker, *Managing Brand Equity: Capitalizing on the Value of a Brand Name.* Copyright © 1991 by David A. Aaker. Reprinted with permission of the Free Press, a Division of Simon & Schuster, Inc.

BRAND AWARENESS Brand awareness is important to equity because the more recognizable a brand, the more likely it will be purchased over lesser-known brands. Consumers usually have only a small number of brands from which they will select in most product categories. If your brand is not in this choice or consideration set, consumers will likely not purchase it. For example, Bill Gates has been fairly successful at building brand awareness for Microsoft by partnering with the media, such as with NBC to form MSNBC, which brings much needed visibility to the company and thus makes it a more recognizable brand.

PERCEIVED QUALITY Integrated marketing communications also must manage brand equity so that consumers perceive a high degree of quality in the brand without having to know or recall specific product characteristics. Branding and perceived quality go hand-in-hand. A strong brand name should represent consistent and relatively high quality on some important product or service dimension. This is why Intel Corporation promotes its brand name for the computer processing chips it makes—unless you look inside a computer, you cannot see Intel's product and therefore must rely on perceived quality to be influenced to buy computers that have Intel products inside. The bad publicity Intel received when it introduced its Pentium processor chip was of serious concern because its brand equity was at stake. If the perceived quality was not there, consumers would not buy computers with the Pentium chip. Fortunately, Intel was able to overcome initial concerns and restore consumer confidence in the Pentium chip and the company. Exhibit 5–7 demonstrates how Intel approached the perceived quality and confidence issue when it introduced the Pentium processor.

BRAND ASSOCIATIONS Consistent and favorable consumer impressions can be created and managed by developing positive brand associations (beyond quality) for a product or service. A **brand association** is a link in the consumer's mind between your product and just about anything related to it. Brand associations will exist in consumer minds whether you want them to be there or not. IMC strategies should make the creation and maintenance of these associations high priority

because they affect brand equity. The use of Ronald McDonald to appeal to children and create a friendly feeling for McDonald's is a successful example of building the type of brand association you want the customer to have in his or her mind.

There are many ways to develop these brand associations, from the use of trade characters to testimonials and spokespersons to the creation of lifestyle and status appeals. The key to building brand associations is how you position your product in the consumer's mind. **Product positioning** refers to the way a company wants consumers to think of its product or service. The way consumers think about a product is organized in their minds in the form of a network of associations surrounding the brand. Marketing and promotional efforts can and should influence the nature and strength of these associations.

Positioning is employed to give consumers a context within which to interpret their brand associations. A company can position a brand by claiming superiority on a characteristic key to the product category, such as Lee Jeans' claim that it's the brand that fits. It can create a position in reference to the type of customer who uses its brand—such as McDonald's is for families and Red Lobster is for seafood lovers. It can position a product against an entire product category so that consumers associate it with that category, as 7Up did in being the uncola in the late 1960s and *Sports Illustrated* did promoting itself as the third news weekly. A company can also create a product position in relation to the competition. Avis garnered the number two position in relation to Hertz and stole the position away from National car rental when in reality the two companies were virtually tied for that slot.

OTHER BRAND ASSETS Some brands have assets that are not in the minds of consumers but that are tangible and can be employed to protect brand equity. Registered trademarks and patents, for example, can prevent the competition from using similar names, package designs, or symbols to promote their products. These are known as **proprietary assets.**[7] Companies spend a lot of time and effort protecting their proprietary assets. Coca-Cola is very fussy about calling all colas "Coke." A name like Coke, with its long-established equity, is very valuable as a brand

name. However, should it become the generic name for an entire category of products, the brand equity—and everything that went into building the brand—is lost.

The creation and maintenance of brand equity are the key goals of integrated marketing. They are the reasons why the planning and integration of all elements of an integrated marketing communications program are paramount. Negative and inconsistent impressions of a brand can be formed in consumers' minds more easily than consistently positive ones. The potential erosion of brand equity is a problem for all marketers, but particularly so for multinational firms, where awareness levels and the nature of brand associations have to be created and managed in markets that can differ greatly along national and cultural lines. Very often, strong visual execution based on instant brand recognition can overcome language and cultural barriers, as illustrated in the Levi's ad in Exhibit 5–8

that was created for the Spanish market by a Barcelona ad agency.

Advertising Within The Context Of Marketing

Advertising's role in marketing has changed over the last decade or so as we have come to understand how it is that customers develop impressions about products. Consumers do not get their information and images from advertising alone; they get information from every possible type of marketing communications presented to them. Every experience consumers have with a company's products and marketing communications efforts adds to or detracts from the brand associations that are in their minds. To understand advertising's role better, we first have to take a look at its place in marketing.

Marketing is the "process of planning and executing the conception, pricing, promotion, and distribution of ideas, goods, and services to create exchanges that satisfy individual and

EXHIBIT 5–7 By positioning its Pentium processor as the product for the future, Intel attempted to reshape consumer perceptions and restore confidence both in the product and in the company.

LEVI'S 501 JEANS. BORN TO RESIST.

EXHIBIT 5–8 This Spanish ad for Levi's uses a simple visual image rather than a complex message to generate brand recognition. This type of approach allows advertisers to avoid some of the problems often encountered in establishing and maintaining a consistent brand image across international markets.

organizational objectives."8 It is through the marketing process that consumer needs and wants are identified and products and services are created to satisfy these needs. Marketing sets the stage for this exchange of product for need satisfaction by combining four elements—product, price, place (or distribution), and promotion. Together these four elements are known as the **marketing mix.**

Often we find that it is not promotion (including advertising) that really sells a product, but rather the other elements of the marketing mix—the product concept, how and where it is distributed, how well it is serviced, or how it is priced. What is the first brand or company name that comes to mind when you think of photocopiers, chocolate, computers, or athletic shoes? The names most people mention are the companies we perceive as having the best product or service in those categories, in this case Xerox, Hershey, IBM, and Nike, respectively. Similarly, Wal-Mart made its name by building

stores in small towns instead of large metropolitan areas. Enterprise Rent-A-Car stayed away from airports and serviced the in-town replacement car side of the business. And Gary Tharaldson, founder of Tharaldson Enterprises, emphasized both place and price when he built chains of limited-service hotels under the names Fairfield, Courtyard, Comfort, and Hampton Inns. He started his hotel business by building in midwestern towns with populations under 100,000. Without room service and restaurants to maintain, Tharaldson was able to keep his prices down while still offering comfortable accommodations.9

As consumers become more demanding and product choices proliferate, however, few marketers are willing to let their products, prices, and places of distribution speak for themselves. The clutter and competition is too great to let consumer impressions and sales fall to chance. This is where promotion comes in. In order to sell their products and services successfully in today's marketplace, companies must know how to combine the elements of the **promotional mix**—advertising, direct marketing, sales promotion, public relations, and personal selling—into an IMC program that helps them achieve their objectives.

From Promotion Mix To Integrated Marketing Communications

Traditional marketing and promotion planning requires that marketing managers be able to define the roles that the elements of the promotion mix will take in a marketing communications program or campaign. A good way to define these roles is to consider the following three questions:

1. What do we want to accomplish in terms of consumer response?
2. Where are our customers on a brand–loyalty continuum?
3. How targeted do we want our efforts to be in relation to the cost of each promotion mix element?

Exhibit 5–9 illustrates this approach in a loyalty–response–cost–targeting matrix. To a large degree, this decision is driven by budget allocation and payout constraints. However, there also should be some good strategic rationale for how much is spent in each promotional area. A good place to start is with the consumer. Marketing managers must ask themselves where their various groups of customers are with respect to their loyalty to the company's brand. This will help to determine the type of promotional effort they want to make against each group. Those consumers who are nonusers will require different promotional mixes than will more loyal customers.

Next, we need to know where our customers are in relation to where we want to take them (i.e., the response desired). The further we have to take them from unawareness to repeat purchase, the harder our task will be. The harder the task, the more a campaign will cost. Likewise, the more targeted a campaign is in terms of the marketing communications elements we will be using, the more expensive the program will be on a per prospect basis. Most integrated marketing communications programs integrate the promotional mix elements based on what has to be accomplished and the cost of the elements employed.

The final step is to look over all the available promotional elements and what they can help to achieve. The promotional mix elements

---

Exhibit 5–9   Loyalty-Response-Cost-Targeting Matrix

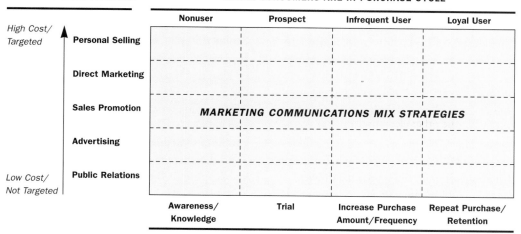

Source: Donald Parente, Bruce Vanden Bergh, Arnold Barban, and James Marra, *Advertising Campaign Strategy* (Fort Worth, TX: The Dryden Press, 1996), p. 225.

IT SEEMS ALL THESE 6TH GRADERS EVER TALK ABOUT IS WHAT IT WAS LIKE TO GROW UP IN THE DEPRESSION.

Not many 6th graders go around reminiscing about the Dust Bowl, soup kitchens, and FDR's fireside chats. For children of that age usually just talk about the things their friends talk about. But, what makes Pamela Schmidt's Shreveport, Louisiana 6th graders so different is that their friends are senior citizens. And their unique relationship began as part of a program Pamela initiated called A⁴ = Altering Attitudes of Aging and Adolescence.

By bringing the two groups together, she had hoped they both would learn from and about each other. In one case, the students interviewed these seniors about their lives, their families and their youth. Then, making the most of their creativity and writing skills, they used those interviews and photos to create individual scrapbooks to present to their new friends. And it was just one of the ways this experience helped to shape the lives of Pamela Schmidt's class and to brighten those of their elderly friends.

For her achievements, State Farm is proud to present Pamela with our Good Neighbor Award, and to donate $5,000 to the educational institution of her choice.

GOOD NEIGHBOR AWARD
STATE FARM INSURANCE COMPANIES
Home Offices: Bloomington, Illinois

The Good Neighbor Award was developed in cooperation with the National Council of Teachers of English.

EXHIBIT 5–10   State Farm's Good Neighbor Award recognizes unique achievements and programs in education. By announcing the winners in ads such as the one shown here, the company can bring its efforts to the attention of the public, thus creating a positive corporate image among consumers.

(excluding advertising) are discussed in greater depth in Chapter Twelve. Here, we describe them briefly in terms of the roles they might play in a marketing communications strategy.

PUBLIC RELATIONS   Traditionally, **public relations** is concerned with how people feel about issues, products, and individual or corporate personalities."[10] However, the rise in importance of IMC has brought about a distinction between corporate and marketing public relations. While **corporate public relations** focuses on the noncustomer goals of a company, such as corporate image or issue-oriented communication, **marketing public relations** activities are designed to support the selling function. Exhibit 5–10, an advertisement for State Farm Insurance that promotes the company's Good

Neighbor Award program, is an example of corporate public relations.

Marketing public relations can make a contribution to the promotional plan by making a company's sales message more credible. Consumers understand that the intent of advertising, direct marketing, sales promotion, and salespeople is to sell them something, but marketing public relations in the form of carefully managed publicity can help create synergy for an integrated marketing program. **Publicity** involves any attempt by a company to get favorable media coverage of its products, services, causes, or events. The tools of publicity typically include press releases, press conferences, informational items in print or video form, product literature, pamphlets or materials covering broader issues related to a firm's business, celebrity appearances, and company-sponsored events. Volkswagen was desperate for good publicity in 1994 when it brought its Concept 1 car to the auto show in Detroit. They asked their California design studio to develop a model of a 1990s version of the famous VW Beetle specifically for the auto show. The publicity generated was so overwhelming that Volkswagen is going to build and sell the new Beetle by 1999 if not sooner.[11]

Public relations activities like publicity are usually less costly than other forms of promotion. The tradeoff is that there is less control over message content, who is exposed to it, and when and how often it will be seen or heard. Nonetheless, marketing public relations should be an important component of most integrated marketing communications plans.

ADVERTISING   **Advertising** is defined as nonpersonal communication for products, services, or ideas that is paid for by an identified sponsor for the purpose of influencing an audience. While paying for a message that you are identified with gives away your intent to persuade people of something, it also provides for more control over content and scheduling than does public relations. This control allows a company to target specific audiences with its message and to plan when and how often it will be run; however, there are other forms of promotion that do an even better job of targeting audiences, as we will soon see. Advertising is best at creating initial awareness of a product or service, building an image, and reinforcing existing impressions consumers have of a brand. Notice how the advertisement for Mercedes-Benz shown in Exhibit 5–11 links its well-known symbol with other easily identifiable icons to underscore the company's reputation of long-standing quality, innovation, and performance.

SALES PROMOTION Companies often want more from their marketing communications programs than the creation of awareness or an image. They want consumers to go out and buy their products or services. To do this, marketing managers have to consider promotional elements that can reach targeted consumers with very little waste exposure and induce them to buy the item being offered. The first of the promotion mix elements we will discuss in this regard is sales promotion. **Sales promotion** is the use of an incentive to buy a product that takes the form of either a price reduction or value-added offer.[12] Sales promotions are of two types, based on whether the target is consumers or the trade.

Consumer promotions attempt to boost sales by encouraging people into the store to buy your product at a lower price or with some kind of special deal. Typical consumer promotions include product samples, coupons, premiums, rebates, contests and sweepstakes, bonus packs, and price-off incentives. For example, M&M/Mars used the Imposter "M&Ms"® Game, an ad for which is shown in Exhibit 5–12, to generate interest in and additional sales of its popular "M&M's"® candies. The growth of the Internet and World Wide Web has provided a new medium for delivering consumer promotions. Consumer promotions can also be used as traffic builders for a Web site in much the same manner as they would be used to build store traffic. American Express, for example, ran a banner on the Internet called American Express University that promoted its Spring Breakaway Sweepstakes targeted to college students. The promotion offered net surfers a chance to win valuable prizes if they visited American Express's Web site.

EXHIBIT 5–11 Although it never uses its name in the copy, Mercedes-Benz successfully communicates its corporate identity in this advertisement.

The important point to consider when assessing the role for sales promotion is how important it is that a campaign or program generate immediate sales or gain product distribution. If short-term sales and distribution are of paramount importance, then sales promotion will play a central role in an integrated marketing plan. Sales promotion programs do tend to be more expensive than advertising and public relations. Some of the expense comes in the form of how extensive the program is, sometimes requiring an inventory of prizes, samples, or premiums. A lot of the costs come from low redemption and participation rates. It takes wide exposure of most consumer promotion programs to achieve reasonable coupon redemption or contest participation rates.

DIRECT MARKETING   Sometimes the ability to target consumers is as important as inducing an immediate response. Selective targeting requires a message delivery system that can pinpoint your best prospects while not wasting your message on other consumers. Direct marketing is the promotion element best suited to this purpose. **Direct marketing,** at its simplest, is "any activity whereby you communicate directly with your prospect or customer and he or she responds directly to you."[13] This definition takes into account the vast changes taking place in direct marketing technology to include computer delivery and database marketing. One only has to watch infomercials, direct-response TV commercials with toll-free telephone numbers, or home shopping channels to see that direct marketing has grown beyond the days when the U.S. Postal Service was its primary vehicle for distribution.

Direct marketing has grown in importance to IMC for a lot of the reasons mentioned at the beginning of this chapter, such as the decline in effectiveness of TV advertising and improvements in media technology (cable TV and Internet) with which to deliver the direct marketing offer. You can add to those broad-based changes in the marketplace the widespread use of credit cards, the convenience of toll-free telephone numbers, advances in computer storage of consumer information and ability to analyze this information, and the desire for better accountability of the effectiveness of a promotional effort. The most

EXHIBIT 5–12   M&M/Mars used this consumer promotion, the Imposter "M&Ms"® Game, to encourage the public to buy more of its very popular product.

Trade promotions, on the other hand, work by offering incentives to retailers and distributors to carry a product or brand and give it added emphasis in their effort to sell it to consumers. Examples of trade promotions include trade allowances, dealer contests, point-of-purchase displays, cooperative advertising, and trade shows. Trade promotions account for almost two-thirds of all sales promotions and half of all marketing dollars spent on promotions and advertising combined. In fact, the growth of trade promotions as the primary marketing tool for gaining distribution of a product has made its most serious impact on advertising expenditures. Thirty years ago, advertising clearly dominated marketing budgets. Today, the roles have flipped and sales promotion gets the lion's share of the marketing pie.

important recent advance has been the ability of many firms to collect a lot of information on their customers in the form of a computer database. This information can be used to profile and target a firm's best potential customers, increasing the likelihood that those who receive your direct marketing offer will respond.

Direct marketing is more expensive on a per-customer basis than public relations and advertising, yet it can yield significantly better results in terms of consumer response. You might be surprised at the types of products and services people are willing to buy from direct marketing efforts. Watch the many infomercials for expensive exercise equipment or pay attention to the price of jewelry sold on home shopping shows. Among the things direct marketers use to bring home the sale are: competitive prices, unusual product options stores do not carry, payment by credit card, toll-free telephone numbers for ordering, incentives like free gifts or coupons, time limits on the offer, quantity limits, and guarantees to reduce the risk of purchase.[14] For example, *The Gundie Weekly Journal* used the series of direct marketing pieces shown in Exhibit 5–13 to generate new subscriptions.

PERSONAL SELLING **Personal selling** is the most expensive element in the promotion mix on a per-customer basis because it involves person-to-person communication to persuade potential customers to buy a company's product or service. Because personal selling often requires face-to-face contact, the cost of this contact can include travel, lodging, meals with prospective buyers, and the salesperson's salary. These costs can be reduced if the contact can be made by telephone, fax, or computer.

The strength of personal selling is that the salesperson can react immediately to feedback from a customer. This allows the salesperson to adjust a sales message as the interaction with the customer proceeds along. On the other hand, the high per-customer cost of personal selling limits its use to high-ticket, complex, or very personal products or services. Personal selling is an important component of the promotion mix for selling automobiles, insurance, financial investments, furniture, real estate, and, as shown in Exhibit 5–14, cosmetics and beauty products as well.

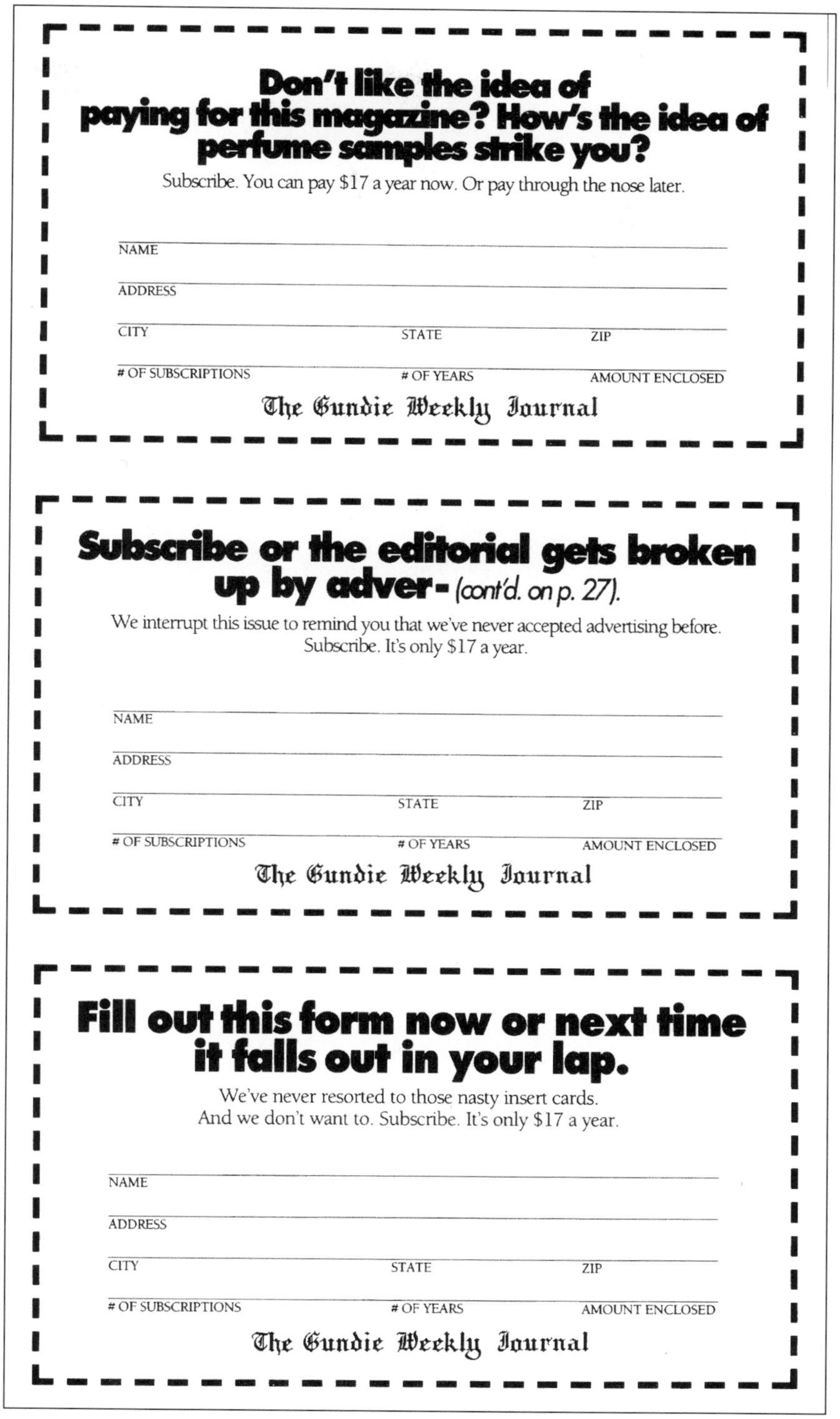

EXHIBIT 5–13 A direct marketing approach allows advertisers to connect directly with their target audiences. This type of promotion was the ideal vehicle for *The Gundie Weekly Journal* in its efforts to secure additional subscriptions.

EXHIBIT 5–14 Personal selling techniques have been used successfully by Mary Kay to sell its line of cosmetics and personal beauty products. By interacting directly with potential customers, Mary Kay representatives can tailor their sales messages to fit the needs of individual consumers.

Briefly review Exhibits 5–10 through 5–14, which show, respectively, a public relations message, an advertising-created image appeal, a sales promotion offer, a direct marketing offer, and a focus on personal selling. Notice that as we move from public relations to personal selling, the content of these ads becomes more directly aimed at making a sale.

R E S E T

1. Why is it likely that advertising is no longer sufficient for selling a product or service?
2. Why is the major aim of integrated marketing communications the creation and maintenance of brand equity?
3. How is the loyalty–response–cost–targeting matrix used to define the roles that the various promotional elements will take in an IMC campaign or program?

The Focus Of Integrated Marketing Communications

Just understanding the roles of the various promotion mix elements and knowing when to combine them into a marketing communications program is not an integrated approach to marketing. Integration of the marketing and promotional mix elements has to start at the top of an organization. While most marketing and advertising planning traditionally occurs at the middle management level of companies, integration of marketing communications requires that the traditional barriers that have separated advertising, public relations, sales promotion, direct marketing, and personal selling be removed. This takes leadership by the top management of companies.

Integration demands that a company change its focus from what it wants to sell to how its customers view its products and services and how they can best be served. Consumers do not share the same view of a company's products, promotion, pricing, and distribution that employees hold. For example, most customers do not differentiate among the various types of promotion a marketing manager has to use in planning a campaign. Consumers only know when they like what they see and when they do not; public relations, advertising, and other promotional efforts are pretty much the same to them. Companies have to learn to know their customers as well as they know their products. This means marketers must place themselves outside of the firm and look at their products the way consumers do.

Successful integration can only occur when the responsibility for all of a firm's communication activities, including marketing communications, is elevated to the highest levels of a firm. This requires the understanding that everything a company does can be thought of as some form of communication. Every contact a consumer has with a company and its products communicates something. Integration requires that a company plan, coordinate, and integrate what it wants that "something" to be.[15]

Integration can occur at four different levels in a marketing communications program. These four levels are illustrated in Exhibit 5–15. The first and most basic level involves the creation of a *unified image.* This is a goal of most traditional advertising campaigns that focus on developing and maintaining a brand image. The projection of a unified image is the minimum requirement for integration to work.

The second level of integration requires that a company be able to communicate with all of its audiences, both internal and external, in a consistent tone or with the same attitude. Regardless of who the audience is and what forms of communication are being employed, the target audience should know right away who the source of the message is; they should be able to recognize a *consistent voice.* Think of some of the most noticeable brands such as Kodak, Coca-Cola, and Levi's. These companies take pains to make sure their image, tone, and attitude are consistent throughout their communications with you.

The third level of integration can be a foundation for the first two levels, but it is a higher-order level of integration when done well: Be a *good listener.* Companies have to learn to be as good at listening to their various audiences or stakeholders as they are at trying

to sell to them. Methods for getting a consistent flow of feedback should be built into any integrated marketing communications program. Today's technology makes this a much easier prospect than in the past. Web sites, toll-free telephone numbers, direct marketing response techniques, and traditional consumer surveys, panels, or focus groups all can be used to develop and maintain long-term relationships with customers.

The fourth level of integration involves being a *good citizen.* This is an area where large firms can learn from small businesses, which have to be good citizens to be successful because everybody in town knows who they are. Large companies, on the other hand, are more anonymous and have to work at demonstrating their corporate citizenship.[16] The Hard Rock Cafe has made being a good citizen part of its corporate philosophy. Its management based the restaurant's concept on providing the freshest food possible at the best value. They decided that all waste would be recycled and water conserved by only serving it on request. The restaurant was founded by two homesick Americans in London, so the decor is rock 'n roll memorabilia to make customers feel at home. The rock 'n roll theme is supported by the sale of T-shirts, hats, and other items sporting the Hard Rock logo. And finally, the Hard Rock further demonstrates its good citizenship by donating leftover food to local charities to feed the homeless. Good value, conservation, helping others, and rock 'n roll have been integrated to form the Hard Rock Cafe. The Hard Rock achieved a synergy that is the goal of all IMC plans: The total effect should be greater than the sum of the individual promotional mix elements. "Consumer Insight: It's All Advertising" describes this goal in more detail.

The move to a more integrated way of thinking about how best to employ marketing communications elements really is a move toward an emphasis on strategic as opposed to tactical thinking. *Tactical thinking* involves the choice and use of marketing communications elements for short-term gains that are limited in scope. Often this type of thinking focuses on one marketing communications element or tactic to achieve a limited result. For example, reducing your price or running a coupon each by itself might help to achieve a

Exhibit 5–15   Four Levels of Integration of Marketing Communications

CONSUMER INSIGHT

. . . .

It's All Advertising

To make integrated marketing communications work, you have to be more concerned with how the consumer views the advertising and marketing communications to which he or she is exposed everyday. The reality is that consumers see all of the promotion mix elements as advertising of some type. The average consumer does not differentiate among the 2,000 or more exposures he or she has to advertising and promotions in a month. Consumers respond to coupons, staged events, image advertising, ads on Web sites, and infomercials all as attempts to sell them a product or service.

Understanding the consumer view of the marketplace is the most important aspect of advertising and marketing today. Consider the diversity in consumer lifestyles and then think about how the expanding diversity in media options might play out. Compare these two possibilities: 1) A person who goes home at night, grabs the daily newspaper, and flops down in front of the television, versus 2) a person who grabs the portable phone, switches on the personal computer, and begins to browse the Internet before doing some serious work at the computer. Add to this scenario the fact that both consumers buy a significant number of items from catalogs. Does the new diversity in media consumption habits affect advertising and marketing strategy? You bet it does. It all comes back to the type and number of contacts consumers have with your brands and company. Think of all these contacts as advertising, promotion, or marketing communications. Every contact sends some type of message and must be considered in terms of the strategies and tactics you employ.

Whether your tactic is one of getting people to use a coupon or buy during a heavy promotion program, you still have to continue to nurture your brand equity. The consumer viewpoint reminds us that no one element of a marketing communications campaign is more important than any other when it comes to the consumer's vantage point. Think of all marketing communications as having some image quotient and some sales impact. This way you always will be integrating your marketing communications.

Sources: Rick Fizdale, "Integrated Communications: The Whole Picture," *The Advertiser,* Summer 1992, 58–62; and "Profile: Leo Burnett Company," PROMO, October 1991 (reprint), 1–4.

---

short-term increase in sales or product interest. But planning only tactically will not produce enduring or long-term competitive value—and it won't add much to your brand equity.

Strategic thinking, on the other hand, is aimed at establishing a coherent direction for a marketing communications plan. The result is a strategy that integrates many elements or tactics in pursuit of marketing objectives. A strategy provides direction to the development of marketing communications campaigns. The best test of an idea for a campaign is against the strategy. Advertising professionals are familiar with the question, But is it on strategy? This is the typical response to what might look like a great idea by itself but which only can be judged against the strategy.

Chevy Truck's plan to change consumer perceptions from its trucks being less dependable and durable than those of Ford and Toyota to being the most dependable and longest-lasting is an example of a well-formulated marketing communications strategy. The strategy was implemented by positioning Chevy Trucks as the most dependable and longest-lasting through the use of rugged images of the trucks and owners. Chevy launched an advertising campaign based on Bob Seger's hit song, "Like a Rock." The song itself does not carry the entire strategy, but when combined with strong visual imagery in television commercials and print ads and tied into an overall brand strategy, it provides an umbrella-like synergy that drives home the dependability and durability message. Chevy Truck's "Like a Rock" campaign was so successful that the company decided to extend the theme and strategy to include other Chevy Trucks like the Blazer and Suburban. Exhibit 5–16 illustrates how Chevy Truck's basic strategy supports the promotion of the Chevy Blazer.

Toward Better Marketing Communications Strategies[17]

Advertising campaign planning and marketing strategy development have been around for a long time. However, the radical changes in the marketplace and emerging computer technologies have both demanded and presented the opportunity for the advancement of these planning processes. Integrated marketing communications planning can be envisioned as an eight-step process, which is summarized in Exhibit 5–17 and described below.

Step 1: Analyze The Target Consumer

The IMC planning process starts with an *analysis of the target consumer.* This involves looking for key insights that can be turned into a key incentive or benefit that will persuade the target consumer to buy your brands. This analysis includes consumer perceptions of the brands in a product category, consumer lifestyles and purchasing behaviors, wants and needs not met by brands in the product category, and media consumption habits.

This type of target analysis led to the discovery that consumers believed Alka-Seltzer actually started working the moment they drank it because of the way it dissolved in water, meaning consumers could expect it to take effect quicker than competitors' brands. This brand quality, labeled "effervescence," became the key product benefit promoted in advertising. "Adscape: Strategic Thinking at Work" says more about knowing your target customer.

Step 2: Analyze The Product

The search for insights does not stop with the consumer. A thorough *analysis of the product* can often yield helpful information that can be used to affect consumer perceptions in advertising and promotion. Find out how the product was made, who invented it, how it works, what its competitive advantages are, how it is stored, how

it is packaged, and who worked on its development and manufacture. If you can, test the product against its competition. Look for all of the brand assets you can find. One of these assets could be highly relevant to consumer purchases.

As a case in point, one of the first things Bill Bernbach did when his agency got the Volkswagen account back in the 1950s was to visit the factories in Germany where the cars were built. While there, he and his colleagues noticed the rigid inspection system used by Volkswagen to make sure all the car parts were in perfect order. They noticed that parts were not inspected once, but over and over again. This observation was the inspiration behind the famous "Lemon" ad shown in Exhibit 5–18, which was one of

EXHIBIT 5–16 Having achieved a great deal of initial success with its "Like a Rock" campaign, Chevrolet decided to extend this message of durability and dependability to its Blazer sport utility vehicle.

WE TOOK THIS IDEA
AND *ran* WITH IT.

The Chevy Blazer has outstanding traction. Its exclusive
Driver Control System sinks its teeth in to give you safety, confidence and maneuverability.
Whether you're on a steep, winding mountain road or on Main Street.
Chevy Blazer: A little bit of security in an insecure world. For a free test drive or brochure
call 1-800-950-0340 or visit www.chevrolet.com/truck.

BLAZER

LIKE A ROCK

EXHIBIT 5–17   Integrated Marketing Communications Planning Process

1. Analyze the Target Consumer

   A. What are consumers' perceptions of brands in the category?

   B. Describe the target consumer's lifestyle and purchase behavior.

   C. What wants and needs have not been met by brands in the category?

   D. Describe the target's media consumption behavior.

   E. What key incentive or benefit will persuade the target consumer?

2. Analyze the Product

   A. How is the product made?

   B. How does the product work?

   C. How is the product used? stored? packaged?

   D. What is the company's reputation?

   E. How does the target consumer perceive the product? quality cost? brand associations (good and bad)?

   F. What are the product's tangible attributes (taste, feel, smell, ingredients)?

   G. Why is the product different?

3. Analyze the Competition

   A. Who is the competition? What business are we in?

   B. How do consumers perceive the competition? What are their impressions of the competition?

   C. How might the competition respond to our efforts?

   D. What are the competitors' weaknesses? Where are they vulnerable?

   E. What is the competition communicating to consumers?

4. Identify the Competitive Consumer Benefit

   A. What consumer problem does the product solve?

   B. What is the one key benefit that makes the product better than the competitors' brands?

   C. Can you state this benefit in one simple sentence? Say it. Write it down.

5. Communicate the Truth of the Benefit

   A. What are the product attributes that support the key benefit?

   B. Which consumer perceptions can we use to support the benefit?

   C. How will the message be presented to communicate the benefit and make it believable?

6. Convey the Brand Personality

   A. What tone and personality will best help to differentiate the product from the competition?

7. Develop Communication/Action Objectives

   A. What should our target consumers know and feel after exposure to our message?

   B. What do we want our target consumers to do as a result of exposure to our messages? Buy the product? Ask for information? Tell others about it? Use it differently?

8. Plan Consumer Contact Points

   A. When and where will our customers be most receptive to our message?

   B. When and where do our customers buy, use, and benefit most from our product?

Source: Based on Don E. Schultz, Stanley I. Tannenbaum, and Robert F. Lauterborn, *Integrated Marketing Communications* (Lincolnwood, IL: NTC Business Books, 1993), 85–86.

the first VW Beetle ads that was based on product insight.

Included in your product analysis should be the issues of consumer perceptions and current brand equity. Find out what the existing perceptions are of product quality, cost, and other associations relevant to the category. Here you are looking for competitive advantages that already exist in the minds of consumers. You want to know whether your brand is just another "me-too" product or perhaps even if it has significant weaknesses that have to be overcome.

The product analysis should allow you to conclude whether or not you can build on a solid brand image. If not, your strategy is more likely to include promotional incentives to get consumers to use your product. These are the two most basic marketing options for a brand: You can either try to differentiate your product based on positive brand associations or take a cost strategy by coming in under your competitors' prices.[18]

Step 3: Analyze The Competition

An important companion piece to your product analysis is the *analysis of the competition.* Ideally, you would like to know as much about your competition and its products as you do about your own company. An important step in this direction is determining against whom you are competing. This is not always so obvious. Logically, you might start with the product or service category in which you are competing; however, this can lead to marketing myopia in that you might not include real competition from outside the category.[19]

You only have to look at the merger between Walt Disney Co. and Cap Cities/ABC to understand that each side in this merger had redefined the business it was in. Disney said that it was not in the movie business but rather in a broadly defined information and entertainment business. Likewise, Cap Cities/ABC had to change its focus from mainstream media like TV and radio and say it too was now in this new all-inclusive information and entertainment business that encompassed the motion picture and theme park industries. Similarly, Las Vegas has broadened its business perspective from an adult entertainment city to a family entertainment city. Amusement parks and resorts complete with golf courses have been built to attract families that might otherwise choose Disneyland or Disney World as their vacation destination.

The key to identifying your competition is to view the marketplace from the consumer's perspective. Do they care whether you are in the entertainment or information business? Probably not, but they do care about the *quality* of the entertainment and information available. From this viewpoint, computer hardware and software companies are in the same business as is Disney.

Step 4: Identify The Competitive Consumer Benefit

After you have carefully analyzed your customer, product, and competition, you are ready to determine the one key benefit that will convince people to buy your brand over a competitor's. The *competitive consumer benefit* must solve a consumer problem better than competitive brands. Remember that a benefit is not simply a product attribute; it is what the product does for the consumer. Arriving at a true benefit, then, demands that you look at the product from the consumer's viewpoint. For example, people buy 1/4-inch drill bits not because they like drill bits but so they can make 1/4-inch holes in things. Lawncare services have burgeoned for two reasons: They save time for busy people and they are experts at making your lawn look beautiful. Both of these are consumer benefits.

Step 5: Communicate The Truth Of The Benefit

Once you have arrived at the key competitive benefit for your product, you have done the groundwork for your integrated marketing communications strategy. Next, you have to determine how you are going to communicate or express this benefit so that it is persuasive and believable. This involves deciding how you can convince your target consumer that your product will do a better job solving his or her problems than will the competitors' brands. This *reason to believe the benefit is true* has to resonate with consumers. It has to contain both the right message content and style.

At the risk of being repetitious, remember that everything a company does conveys a message. Your reason to believe will get its meaning from what it says as well as how it is

EXHIBIT 5–18   Careful product analysis provided the basis for this Volkswagen Beetle advertisement, which plays off of the high level of inspections that take place at the company's manufacturing plant.

AdScape

....

Strategic Thinking at Work

Put yourself in the role of a door-to-door salesperson. Imagine the worst weather you can in the town or city in which you live. You've driven up to the next block of houses on your sales itinerary for the day. There are 10 houses to call on. You have to knock on each door and sell the head of the household at least one bottle of an all-purpose household cleaning agent.

Do you have a strategy or plan in mind? What will you say? Perhaps something like, "Why buy a different brand of cleanser for each cleaning problem? Our brand has been formulated to take care of the toughest problems, yet it is gentle enough for those delicate areas of the house." You'll have to be enthusiastic to bring some excitement to your sales pitch.

But will the one strategy work on all 10 households? Probably not, if each person has a different set of cleaning problems. Maybe one homeowner works on his car at home and has some heavy grease problems. Another

owner could have small children who spill things and track dirt in from the outside. Still another person could have a cleaning business and be interested in a cost-effective cleaner. The point is that if you do not understand each consumer's unique lifestyle and set of problems related to your product, you will try a one-size-fits-all strategy instead of adjusting your strategy to each situation.

The best approach is to customize your sales message and make it personal to each person on the block. Take the time to find out as much as you can about the backgrounds, lifestyles, and problems of the 10 heads of household on the block. Just knowing the general makeup of their households will help. If you can find out something about activities they engage in that create problems your product can solve, that's even better. Information on competitive brands they use and how they feel about them can help you to position your product in your sales message, as well.

The more specific a picture you have of these 10 potential customers, the more specific you can be in tailoring your message to each. Now, expand this example to a large company and you start to see the value of computer databases to understanding your customers. A database with information on needs, behavior, and habits can allow you to build strategies selling to each person as if you know him or her personally. Have a plan before you start to sell. Otherwise, you'll have to fall back on old tricks or tactics.

QUESTIONS

What kinds of information do you think it would be helpful to know about these heads of households as you prepare to sell them your all-purpose cleaner? How might you go about finding this information?

Source: Adapted from an example in Don E. Schultz, Stanley I. Tannenbaum, and Robert F. Lauterborn, *Integrated Marketing Communications* (Lincolnwood, IL: NTC Business Books, 1993), 64–65.

said. The medium or vehicle used to convey the message also will add meaning. A special event sponsorship, for example, will say something entirely different than will a TV commercial. Notice how Nike was able to build consumer confidence in its shoes with the simple yet powerful message, "Just Do It," illustrated in Exhibit 5–19. The bold message instills confidence in the consumer and in the product. The dramatic visual adds to a bold,

confident brand personality. This message has been so powerful that Nike recently has reduced its expression to a dramatic visual and the Nike swoosh logo.

Step 6: Convey The Brand Personality

It should be impossible for the consumer to separate the content of a message from its tone and the brand personality. The *brand person-*

EXHIBIT 5–19 The simplicity and boldness of Nike's "Just Do It" theme generated strong feelings of power in consumers, both about themselves and about the product. In this case, consumers adopted the product benefit so completely as to make it their own to some degree.

ality conveyed is an important part of how a brand is differentiated from the competition in the consumer's mind. The tone and personality have to be integrated throughout a marketing communications program. Package design, store displays, premiums, advertising, and everything else that is planned to present a product to the public must be coordinated so that the message sent is consistent. Once again, Nike is an example of a company that achieves this goal quite well.

Step 7: Develop Communication/ Action Objectives

There are two additional steps you can take in your planning to help ensure that you have a well-integrated marketing communications program. First, set communication objectives that state what it is you want consumers to know and feel, and clearly state what it is consumers are expected to do after they have been exposed to any form of your message. These *communication/action objectives* will help you to maintain the consumer's perspective while providing concrete criteria to guide your plan.

You should know in advance of executing your program what you want people to take away from your messages. You should also be clear about what they are going to do. Do you want your customers to redeem a coupon, buy more of the product, use it differently, send for information, or tell others about it? Know your objectives well. The objective-setting process will be covered in more detail in Chapter Eight.

Step 8: Plan Consumer Contact Points

The second additional step—and the last in the marketing communications planning process—is to plan your consumer contact points. Know when and where your customer will be most receptive to your message. This analysis can—and perhaps will—lead you to a broader consideration of media vehicles and other ways to present your key consumer benefit. The information you need to understand these contact points will come from your consumer analysis. Chapter Twelve will present nonadvertising marketing communications

EXHIBIT 5–20   As is evident in this advertisement, Saturn clearly recognizes the importance of building a relationship between its employees and its customers.

tools that will expand your notion of what is available for reaching and influencing your target consumer.

R E S E T

1. Why must an IMC effort start at the top of an organization, not at the middle management levels where most advertising and marketing planning typically occurs?
2. In terms of successful marketing communications integration, what is the relevance of a company being a good listener?
3. Describe the importance of consumer contact points to IMC planning.

The Ultimate Objective: The Consumer Relationship

We said at the beginning of the chapter that the primary goal of integrated marketing communications programs is to build brands. When all is said and done, however, that goal cannot be achieved without reaching an even higher goal: establishing a relationship with each of your customers. A relationship assumes two-way communication and a consistent effort to respond to your customers' concerns. It should be enduring and mutually satisfying. The idea is not to focus on the discrete sales transaction as your goal but rather to treat customers on a one-to-one basis so that you can form a lasting relationship with them.

The first step toward building relationships is to think of customers as collaborators in your business and not as targets of your promotional efforts. Learn as much as you can about your customers so you can try to meet or exceed their individual needs. Product or service quality is critical to this approach. Consumer feedback should be used to make adjustments and improvements in product or service quality. Relationship building also requires that all employees in a company work toward improving its products and services.

Saturn built its service philosophy not only on the importance of its customers but also on the importance of its employees. Saturn got its employees involved in the company and with its customers. Notice how the ad in Exhibit 5–20 promotes this relationship.

Most of us have had less than satisfactory experiences with companies and products at one time or another. Often these experiences are the result of a company employee not being willing to help us get around obstacles. These types of problems are easy to identify. In fact, a consumer complaint can be the beginning of the road to a strong relationship. Solving a problem and using that experience to eliminate the problem improves the way a business operates. It is the willingness to work toward the type of product or service quality consumers want, establish two-way channels of communication, and eliminate obstacles to consumer satisfaction that are the fundamentals of creating lasting relationships with customers. Every contact with a potential or existing customer is an opportunity to impress. The more consistency a firm maintains in the impression it makes, the more integrated its marketing communications will be.

SUMMARY

Changes in marketing and advertising are creating new challenges and choices for the advertising or marketing practitioner. These changes are putting new demands on the planning and execution of marketing communications programs. Marketing and advertising strategists are being asked to combine advertising, promotions, public relations, and direct marketing into an integrated marketing communications (IMC) program so that each contact a customer has with the brand either creates or reinforces a positive and consistent brand image and adds to brand equity. The ultimate goal of an integrated marketing communications strategy is to build a long-term relationship with the customer.

It has taken significant changes in the marketplace and advertising industry to propel the notion of IMC to the forefront of advertising and marketing thought. Among these changes are: the demands of a changing marketplace, in which the cost of traditional media has increased while corresponding audience sizes and advertising effectiveness have decreased, and retailers have gained more power over manufacturers; a better educated, more demanding consumer who wants better quality and variety at a better price; a proliferation of product and service variety in every category; more advertising clutter and competition for the consumer's attention; and the growth of computer-based technology that has produced more media options and better methods for storing and analyzing consumer information. These changes have occurred as our economy has been transformed from one based on manufacturing to one based on information creation and processing.

The name or symbol used to identify a product or service and distinguish it from the competition is a brand. The value of the brand to a company is its brand equity, which is the net total of all assets and liabilities linked to the brand by consumers. Brand equity is a product quality that resides in the mind of the consumer and gives a company a certain amount of marketing leverage. It is a function of brand loyalty, awareness, perceived quality, brand associations beyond quality, and other assets such as patents, trademarks, or awards. The aim of most integrated marketing communications programs is to either create or manage the brand equity of a company's products or services.

Marketing is the process of planning and executing the conception, pricing, promotion, and distribution of ideas, goods, and services to create exchanges that satisfy individual and organizational objectives. Marketing accomplishes this exchange by combining the elements of the marketing mix—product, price, place (or distribution), and promotion—into a program that sets the stage for the sale of a product or service. Although the product itself, its price, and its place or means of distribution are all important factors in the product's sales, successful integrated marketing programs require knowing how to combine the elements of the promotional mix—advertising, direct marketing, sales promotion, public relations, and personal selling—to help achieve a firm's marketing communications objectives.

A good way to consider how to define the roles of these promotional tools in an IMC is to consider the following three questions: (1) What do we want to accomplish in terms of consumer response? (2) Where are our customers on a brand–loyalty continuum? and (3) How targeted do we want our efforts to be in relation to the cost of each promotion mix element? These questions can be looked at on a loyalty–response–cost–targeting matrix.

To determine how much emphasis should be put on each promotional mix element, start with the consumer and consider where your various groups of customers are with respect to their loyalty to your brand. Next, look at the available promotional tools and consider how they can help you achieve your desired response. Public relations can make a company's sales message more credible and synergize an integrated marketing program. Advertising allows a company to target specific audiences with its message and to plan when and how it will run. It is best used to create initial awareness for a product or service. Sales promotions can help generate immediate sales for a product or service by offering the consumer a discount or value-added offer. Direct marketing goes one step further: It can induce an immediate response from a company's best prospects. Finally, personal selling involves person-to-person communication to persuade potential customers to buy a company's product or service.

An integrated marketing communications program involves more than understanding the roles of the various promotional mix elements and knowing when to combine them. Successful IMC programs must start at the top of an organization, breaking down the traditional barriers between advertising, public relations, sales promotion, direct marketing, and personal selling. Integration also demands that a company focus not on what it wants to sell but rather on how its customers view its products and services and how they can best be served. Integration can occur at four different levels in a marketing communications program. At the base, the program must project a unified image. Second, the company must be able to communicate in a consistent tone or voice. Third, companies with successful IMC programs must be good listeners; they must ensure that they have a constant flow of feedback from their customers. Lastly, these companies must be good citizens; they must project an image of caring about their communities and their consumers. The move to a more integrated way of thinking about how best to employ marketing communications elements really is a move to an emphasis on strategic as opposed to tactical thinking. Tactical thinking involves the choice and use of marketing communications elements for short-term gains that are limited in scope. Strategic thinking, on the other hand, is aimed at establishing a coherent direction for the marketing communications plan.

Integrated marketing communications planning can be envisioned as an eight-step process. The process starts with an analysis of the target consumer, looking for key insights that can be turned into an incentive or benefit that will persuade the target consumer to switch brands. This includes looking at consumer perceptions of the brands in a product category, consumer lifestyles and purchasing behaviors, wants and needs not met by brands in the product category, and media consumption habits. The second step is an analysis of the product that allows you to determine whether or not you can build on a solid brand image. This involves finding out specific information about the product—who invented it, how it is made, and the like; testing the product against its competition; and finding out what existing consumer perceptions are of the product. A companion piece to the product analysis is an analysis of the competition in which you discover as much about your competition and its products as you do about your own. The key to identifying your competition is to view the marketplace from the consumer's perspective.

The fourth step in the IMC planning process is determining your product's competitive benefit—the thing about your product that solves a consumer problem better than competitive brands. Arriving at a true benefit demands that you look at the product from the consumer's perspective. Next you must determine how you are going to communicate or express this benefit so that it is persuasive and believable. This is known as the reason to believe. The sixth step is to develop the tonality and personality you want your IMC messages to convey. Remember that everything a company does—packaging, store displays, advertising, and so forth—conveys a message. The last two steps help ensure that you have a well-integrated program: setting communication objectives that state what it is you want consumers to know and feel as well as what it is consumers are expected to do after they have been exposed to any form of your message, and planning consumer contact points—the times and places where your customers will be most receptive to your message.

The ultimate objective of integrated marketing communications is to forge a lasting relationship with consumers. The objective is not the immediate sale but rather the relationship that will produce long-term business. This is a bond with one's customers that has to be properly cultivated. Companies are starting to view their customers more as collaborators or mutual stakeholders in their businesses and less as mere targets of promotional efforts. Firms are listening better and trying to remove obstacles that lead to consumer dissatisfaction.

KEY TERMS

integrated marketing communications (IMC), 146

brand, 152

brand equity, 152

brand loyalty, 152

brand association, 154

product positioning, 154

proprietary assets, 154

marketing, 155

marketing mix, 156

promotional mix, 157

public relations, 158

corporate public relations, 158

marketing public relations, 158

publicity, 158

advertising, 158

sales promotion, 159

consumer promotions, 159

trade promotions, 160

direct marketing, 160

personal selling, 161

REVIEW QUESTIONS

1. What is integrated marketing communications? How does it differ from traditional advertising?

2. Describe the changes in the consumer marketplace and advertising industry that have made integrated marketing communications an important strategic orientation.

3. What are the two key segments of the information sector in the U.S. economy? Which of these segments is having the most impact on the advertising industry today, and why?

4. What are the key components of brand equity? Explain how each component is important to both the consumer buying the product and the firm marketing it.

5. What three factors must a marketing manager consider when defining the roles of the various promotional elements in an IMC program? How do these factors affect what elements get chosen and in what mix?

6. Briefly describe the types of roles each promotional mix element can play in an IMC program.

7. What are the four levels at which integration can occur in marketing communications?

8. Describe the eight steps involved in planning an integrated marketing communications strategy.

9. Why is it important that an advertiser or marketer forge a long-lasting relationship with consumers? How should this orientation affect a firm's marketing communications strategy?

1. Evaluate the brand equity of your college or university. Include assessments of brand loyalty, awareness, associations, quality, and other assets. Based on your analysis, develop some strategic recommendations for how your college or university can strengthen its brand equity.

2. Choose a consumer service such as dry cleaning, lawn care, or bicycle repair and explain what promotional mix elements you might use to turn nonusers of this service into users, and why. How might you convert infrequent users into frequent users?

3. Using the same consumer service used in question #2, write a brief integrated marketing communications plan following the eight-step process described in the chapter.

interactive discovery lab

1. Write down every exposure to advertising, marketing, or promotion you experience on one weekend day. Write a brief description of the message, medium, type of promotion, and source of message for each exposure. Count the number of exposures to traditional advertising media and compare it to the number of exposures to other media and promotions. Which do you think does a better job of reaching you, traditional advertising or new media and promotional forms? Why?

2. Find and identify the best and worse Web site (from your perspective) sponsored by a major national advertiser. Once you have found the Web sites, print the screens for the first page of each major section identified on the site's menu. Next, analyze the sites and write a brief analysis (2–3 paragraphs) describing why you have chosen these sites as the best and worst. Focus on what you believe the sites are meant to accomplish, how they fit into the larger marketing communications efforts of the sponsors, and specific strengths and weaknesses of the sites.

Chapter Six

Consumer Behavior: Searching for Insights

STARBUCKS BREWS SUCCESS

Many companies get themselves into trouble when they forget about what made them successful.

Companies succeed when they provide products and services that consumers need or want. Add to this a simple maxim to continue to service and listen to consumers' desires, and you have a basic formula for success. The problem occurs when a company gets ambitious and feels that success automatically breeds more success. This typically leads to an attempt to expand into new products or services, which often results in the "unfocusing" of a company's efforts.

Companies lose their consumer perspective and replace it with an ego-centered corporate viewpoint. A good idea or product that people understand and like can get lost in an unfocused growth strategy. The beer industry is full of companies that have created new products and extended their product lines at the expense of customer focus—and even in the face of declining industry sales. For example, Miller Brewing Company made tremendous gains on industry-leader Anheuser-Busch in the late 1970s with the introduction of Miller Lite. However, this success led to a line extension strategy that has lost market share for Miller.

Starbucks, on the other hand, is a company that started with a strong focus and has stuck with that original idea. Starbucks began in Seattle in 1971 when three coffee lovers decided to open a coffee shop that specialized in coffee. Today Starbucks' name has become synonymous with great coffee served in a civilized atmosphere. The Starbucks Coffee Company has grown fast and now has over 1,300 stores in the U.S., Canada, and the Pacific Rim, with a goal of 2,000 stores by the year 2000.

Starbucks has been able to connect with the coffee drinker in ways no other coffee manufacturer has been able to copy. Starbucks thinks it knows why it has had so much success: Its customers are extremely loyal. The company believes one reason for that loyalty is that Starbucks' employees are knowledgeable about coffee; they are a little bit like good bartenders—you can ask for something different and

odds are they will know how to make it. Also, each Starbucks shop is part of a neighborhood. That means the company has to understand the particular area in which it is located. Each site is different, making Starbucks a reliable friend in each locale. The marketing communications dilemma for Starbucks will be how to remain small, local, friendly, and consumer-oriented while becoming a corporate giant.

Starbucks is a real success story, but even the best are vulnerable to the lure of business expansion. Starbucks is considering entering supermarkets with a line of specialty coffees it has been test marketing in Oregon. Supermarkets account for 80 percent of the coffee sales in the U.S., but this is Procter & Gamble's and Kraft Foods' home turf, not Starbuck's. We will have to stay tuned to this new strategic

choice and the challenge it will present to Starbucks. At the same time, Starbucks is making other changes to include establishing smaller retail units in malls and office buildings. We will have to see if these are good consumer-based strategies or risky expansions of a once very focused business.

Sources: Al Ries, *Focus: The Future of Your Company Depends On It* (New York: Harper Business, 1996), 1–23; "Brewing the Perfect Brand," *American Advertising,* Fall 1996, 12–15; Alice Z. Cuneo, "Starbucks Readies Supermarket Invasion," *Advertising Age,* 9 June 1997, 1, 50; and Alice Z. Cuneo, "Starbucks Breaks Largest Ad Blitz," *Advertising Age,* 19 May 1997, 3, 84.

LOOK BEFORE YOU LEAP

- Why is it important to understand consumer behavior as it relates to the advertising and marketing communications process?

- What individual characteristics affect a consumer's purchase decisions?

- What social and cultural influences affect purchasing decisions?

- How do situational variables affect consumer behavior?

- What problem-solving process do consumers follow as they make purchase decisions?

6

A genuine commitment to the customer is a marketing communications principle that a company violates at its own risk. The ability to see things from the consumer's viewpoint is invaluable in developing this genuine commitment. As consumers, we display a wide range of complexity and flexibility in our purchasing decisions and in our use of advertising and marketing communications. We may purchase a bar of soap without much thought, and then spend weeks selecting a gift for a friend; we may zap every commercial that comes on television, and then search through ads in the newspaper to find features and prices on new stereos.

In this chapter we will examine the basics of what we have learned about consumer behavior as it relates directly and indirectly to the advertising and marketing communications process. This chapter introduces three primary influences on consumer decision making: individual characteristics, social and cultural influences, and situational variables. We also will explore consumers as decision makers to illustrate the role these influences play in purchase decisions.

Consumers' Individual Characteristics

The individual characteristics of consumers are important because they often are the starting point for predicting or explaining purchase behavior. Before we can understand why and how groups such as people's families influence what they buy, we have to understand the characteristics of the individual that are the foundation of behavior. These individual characteristics include motivation, perception, learning, attitude, demography and demographics, and lifestyle and psychographics. "Consumer Insight: The Value of Keen Observation" discusses how observing these characteristics in individuals can help you create advertising that really works.

Motivation

The factors that arouse, maintain, and direct our behavior toward the accomplishment of a goal are collectively known as **motivation**. In advertising and marketing communications, the goal we want people to strive for is to buy our brand of product or service. To do this, we try to make our brand the best alternative for the satisfaction or fulfillment of a consumer need. This is why many ads focus on how a product solves a consumer problem. Exhibit 6–1 illustrates how this most basic of advertising tactics works.

The recognition of a need creates a state of tension that arouses a person to do something to fulfill the need. The need often occurs when there is a recognizable difference between our current state and an ideal state we desire. The greater the need or difference between these states of existence, the stronger the arousal and drive to meet the need. The marketplace presents many different ways for each of us to meet our needs. The selection of a particular brand or product to meet a need is based on our wants. Our wants are developed as we grow up, based on individual experiences and influences of the various groups and cultures of which we are members.

A helpful approach to understanding how human motivation works has been the identification and organization of human needs into a typology. One of the most popular ways to classify human motivation and to describe consumer behavior has been **Maslow's hierarchy of** needs,[1] shown in Exhibit 6–2. Psychologist Abraham Maslow suggested a hierarchy of five levels of needs, starting with basic physiological needs, and progressing through safety needs, social needs, esteem or ego needs, and the need for self-actualization. *Needs* have been characterized in this section as driving forces that arise from the lack of something, such as food, love, or self-esteem.

Maslow's hierarchy is important because it provides an explanation of how an individual's needs change. Maslow believed that an individual didn't move up the hierarchy until the previous level had been sufficiently satisfied. For example, as long as an individual was hungry, she wouldn't be concerned with safety. Then, until she was loved, the individual wouldn't be concerned with the need for self-esteem, and so on. Appeals in advertisements can be made to all levels of the hierarchy. For example, the Nissan Altima ad in Exhibit 6–3 clearly appeals to the need for safety, which has not always been a primary need among car buyers. Look through a magazine with an eye toward Maslow's hierarchy and you will no doubt notice how many ads appeal to our needs.

Maslow's hierarchy is not the only typology of needs. Another useful typology is Settle and

We were told that showing an NBA star in our ad would make Sprite more appealing.

CAFFEINE FREE

Sprite

Image is nothing
thirst is everything
Obey your thirst

EXHIBIT 6–1 Turning away from, and actually ridiculing, mainstream advertising's use of celebrities to promote products, Sprite has simplified its message to address the most basic of human needs: thirst.

EXHIBIT 6–2 Maslow's Hierarchy of Needs

	NEEDS	PRODUCTS OR SERVICES
Self-Actualization	need to reach one's full potential	music or art lessons, military recruitment, athletic goods
Esteem or Ego	prestige, status, self-respect	expensive cars, jewelry, personal care products, expensive clothing
Social Needs	affection, friendship, belonging	sports bars, fraternities/sororities, travel clubs, concerts
Safety Needs	security, protection	medical or health services, locks, smoke and theft alarms
Physiological Needs	food, water, air, shelter, sex	homeless shelters, community soup kitchens, Salvation Army

The Quest is equipped with a standard driver's side minivan airbag. Overprotective parents need protection, too.

Three-point safety belts as well as head restraints are found on the outboard positions in both the second and the third rows.

The V6, 151-hp engine rests in front, which gives added weight over the drive wheels, which gives the Quest better driving traction, which gives you added peace of mind.

In the event of a side impact collision, passengers in the Quest enjoy the added protection of thoughtfully designed steel side-door guard beams.

The Nissan Quest features an energy-absorbing front crumple zone, strategically placed safety stops and head buckling creases.

The sliding side door has a child safety lock to help prevent any child-induced accidents.

Overprotective parents of the world, rejoice.

A standard 4-wheel Anti-lock Braking System on the GXE model helps maintain greater steering control during emergency hard braking.

Similar to the front crumple zone, the steering column in the Nissan Quest has been specifically designed to absorb impact energy in the event of certain frontal collisions.

A front stabilizer bar helps keep the Nissan Quest level during cornering or lane changes.

Presenting the 1995 Nissan Quest. It's the first minivan to have successfully combined the handling characteristics of a car with the defensive properties of an armored vehicle (figuratively speaking, of course). For additional information, please call us at 1-800-000-0000.

NISSAN

It's time to expect more from a minivan.

Nissan Motor Corporation U.S.A. Smart people always read the fine print. And they always wear their seat belts. ¹Minivan airbag standard as of 12/93 production and can provide added protection when used with seat belts. Nissan Quest meets '95 Federal Motor Vehicle Passenger Car Safety Standards except models with privacy glass.

EXHIBIT 6–3 Advertisements can appeal to any of the needs in Maslow's hierarchy. The Nissan ad shown here is clearly focused on the issue of safety. How might this advertiser change the message to address other stages in this hierarchy, such as social needs or ego?

Alreck's list of horizontal needs, shown in Exhibit 6–4. Settle and Alreck describe their classification system as a horizontal set of needs, meaning that we can strive to fulfill more than one need at a time without regard to the hierarchical structure proposed by Maslow. Their set includes: achievement, independence, exhibition, recognition, dominance, affiliation, nurturance, succorance, sexuality, stimulation, diversion, novelty, understanding, consistency, and security.[2] With some searching, you could probably find advertisements with appeals from all of the Settle and Alreck categories in much the same way we demonstrated the use of Maslow's hierarchy. The implications for advertising are the same whether needs are considered hierarchical or horizontal.

It is also helpful to distinguish between utilitarian and hedonic needs. Consumers motivated by the ability of products to satisfy *utilitarian needs* will be interested in tangible attributes such as the nutritional content of foods, the durability of clothing, or perhaps the mileage rating of automobile tires. Product attributes that fulfill utilitarian needs usually are verifiable through use of the product. In contrast, *hedonic needs* are more subjective. People motivated by a product's ability to satisfy hedonic needs are looking for product experiences that might provide them with excitement, fantasies, status, or a sense of achievement, for example.

Whether they are hierarchical, horizontal, utilitarian, or hedonic, the bottom line is that consumers have needs. And the existence of needs implies that people are motivated to fulfill them. Advertising that appeals to people's needs is trying to motivate them to fulfill the needs with the purchase of a product or service. If large and identifiable numbers of consumers have similar needs, then those needs can become the basis for segmenting the market into groups of people that have such needs in common. The toothpaste market, for example, can be segmented into groups based on what people want from their brand. Some consumers want to prevent cavities, others want whiter teeth, and still others want fresh breath.

The desire to prevent cavities or to have whiter teeth or fresher breath are different motivations to which advertisers can appeal in selling toothpaste.

One of advertising and marketing communications' roles is to try to show consumers how a particular brand is effective at meeting a consumer need. This is easier said than done, however. There is a lot of clutter in the media marketplace, as we discussed in Chapter Five, so the effective advertiser has to understand how consumers select messages from all of the commotion.

Perception

Perception is the process of selecting, organizing, and interpreting information from the environment so that it has meaning for us. For our purposes, we are concerned with why and how consumers decide to attend to ads or other elements of marketing communications, and why and how they act on those messages. Understanding how consumers select and organize information can then be used to create marketing communications that have a better chance of being attended to and processed.

Perception is an important subject to advertisers and marketers because the process is highly individualistic. Two people can be exposed to the same message under the same conditions yet have entirely different impressions of what they saw or heard. This is true because each person uses his or her own needs, desires, and experiences as a basis for how the message is perceived. Advertisers, therefore, want to know in advance how consumers are likely to process and interpret a message. This is not always easy because of all of the choices people have in today's marketplace.

One area in which people differ is in how sensitive they are to various types of stimuli. The simple and immediate response of our senses to cues from ads, packages, or even brand names is called the process of **sensation.** Sensation can be influenced by our sensory organs, such as hearing or eyesight, and the actual intensity of stimuli. One of the first goals of all marketing communications is to gain attention to the message by people's senses. This can mean creating and delivering messages in such a way as to maximize the consumer's sensory experience. Fragrances in ads, music coming from point-of-purchase displays, three-

dimensional ads, and taste-tests in stores are ways of stimulating people's senses. A quick visit to a new-age store can demonstrate the importance of the senses to marketing and advertising. The music is calm, you can hear running water, and there are soothing fragrances in the air.

The best efforts of advertisers and marketers to be noticed can be ineffective due to the barrage of stimuli to which consumers are exposed. Even on a dull day, we are bombarded with so many stimuli, including advertisements and commercials, that we couldn't possibly see or attend to all of them. As consumers, we use

---

EXHIBIT 6–4   Settle and Alreck's Horizontal Needs

Achievement: The need to accomplish difficult feats; to exercise one's skills, abilities, or talents.

Independence: The need to be autonomous; to be free from the direction or influence of others.

Exhibition: The need to display one's self; to be visible to others.

Recognition: The need for positive notice by others; to show one's superiority or excellence.

Dominance: The need to have power or to exert one's will on others; to hold a position of authority or influence.

Affiliation: The need for association with others; to belong or win acceptance.

Nurturance: The need to give care, comfort, and support to others.

Succorance: The need to receive help, support, comfort, encouragement, or reassurance.

Sexuality: The need to establish one's sexual identity and attractiveness; to enjoy sexual contact.

Stimulation: The need to experience events and activities that stimulate the senses or exercise perception.

Diversion: The need to play; to have fun; to be entertained.

Novelty: The need for change and diversity; to experience the unusual.

Understanding: The need to learn and comprehend; to recognize connections; to assign causality.

Consistency: The need for order, cleanliness, or logical connection.

Security: The need to be free from threat of harm; to be safe; to protect self, family, and property.

Source: Robert B. Settle and Pamela L. Alreck, *Why They Buy: American Consumers Inside and Out* (New York: John Wiley & Sons, 1989), 24–27.

several different methods of simplifying the huge amounts of information. We filter the information and seek out information that interests us or is related to our needs, and we ignore unrelated stimuli. This process is called **selective exposure.**

An advertiser must work hard to capture an audience's attention by using words in a headline, a visual element or color, or both, that will be of interest to specific audiences. For example, the advertisement for Sherwin-Williams SuperPaint® in Exhibit 6–5 uses a humorous photograph of a woodpecker to capture the attention of homeowners.

Selective exposure has an important effect on message delivery. Because consumers selectively seek information, an advertiser must match media choices to the specialized interests of an audience in such a way that will catch their attention. Because homeowners are likely to be interested in home repair, protection, and beautification, many read such publications as *Better Homes & Gardens* and *Good Housekeeping.*

Two other selective processes are important in consumer behavior. **Selective perception** refers to how incoming information is modified or matched to the knowledge, experiences, and expectations we already have. Our interpretation of new information is shaped by what we already know or what we have experienced in similar situations. Think back to the last movie you attended with someone. Did you both come away from the experience feeling the exact same way about the movie? Probably not. Similarly, two people who go to a sporting event and root for different teams always give different accounts of the game. That's because we alter the experience to fit our beliefs and attitudes. We also remember

CONSUMER INSIGHT

....

The Value of Keen Observation

Becoming a keen observer is a little like learning to be a detective, and this skill can be extremely helpful in devising a successful advertising or marketing communications strategy. If you like a good mystery and cannot resist trying to find out "who done it," then you might be a natural at learning to observe people closely. In fact, you probably are a good observer already and simply have not put the skill to use.

When you sit in a park, do you watch people and try to figure out what they do for a living or what their social status might be? Take a look at yourself in a mirror. What would someone watching you be able to deduce from your clothing, jewelry, or hairstyle?

When you visit a friend or colleague, do you take notice of the type of neighborhood in which she lives? What can you tell by the way her house is furnished? You can tell a lot.

Don't forget that there are professional detectives you can talk to in just about any area of business in which you might be interested. Writing ads for cars? Talk to car salespeople. They have learned to tell things about customers from a lot of clues that a less-trained eye might not notice at first. For example, an automobile salesperson sees a male smoking a pipe come into his dealership. He says to himself, "Pipe smoker. Slow, careful thinker. Probably won't buy. Maybe I should help that other customer over there."

Other professional detectives include secretaries, golf caddies, taxi drivers, bartenders, waiters and waitresses, shoeshine men, and barbers. Who do you think invented liquid correction fluid? Not the boss, that's for sure. These people are in jobs where they have to know people well. They are in positions where people will talk to them. Learn from them. Take advantage of their insight.

Whenever you are given a new project, go out and observe people, talk to professional detectives, and look for little clues that can help explain why people buy the brands and products they do. These insights can help you to create advertising that connects with consumers in a real way.

Source: Based on Lisa Fortini-Campbell, *Hitting The Sweet Spot* (Chicago: The Copy Workshop, 1992), 84–92.

only those pieces of information we want to remember. This process is called **selective recall.** Selective perception and selective recall are important to consider when creating advertising messages because an advertiser wants the consumer to interpret the messages as intended.

The interpretation and organization of stimuli around impressions or images is perhaps one of the most important functions of perceptions for advertisers. An **image** may be thought of as an enduring perception of a product, service, or brand. Advertisers work very hard to create and maintain favorable images of their products. An image is a shorthand method consumers use to give meaning to what they know about products and brands. It is not carved in stone and can be changed based on new experiences or information.

Advertisers and marketers often use product positioning strategies (discussed in Chapter Five) to create a distinctive place for their brands in consumers' minds based on an image or how a product is perceived. Notice how Chevrolet reinforces the image of the Lumina as a family car by emphasizing the car's safety features in the ad in Exhibit 6–6.

Learning

Learning is the process by which people acquire knowledge and experience that results in a permanent change in behavior.[3] Applied specifically to consumer behavior, learning is the process by which consumers acquire purchase-related knowledge and experience that affects their consumption-related behavior. It is not too big a leap to view advertising and marketing communications as teaching processes: We attempt to teach consumers about products and their benefits, where they can purchase products, and how to use them. There are numerous theories of how learning actually takes place. These theories can be grouped into two major schools of thought: behavioral theories and cognitive theories.

BEHAVIORAL LEARNING THEORIES **Behavioral learning theories** argue that the only appropriate thing to study is the observable and measurable responses of people to stimuli. In essence, what people do is far more important than what they say. These theories, also known as *stimulus–response theories,* focus their attention on the connection between exposure to a

'Now You Know Why We Call It SuperPaint.®

When it comes to protecting the outside of your home, it's tough to beat Sherwin-Williams SuperPaint. With a 20-year warranty against peeling, blistering and fading, it's one paint that lives up to its name. And there's only one place to get it — your Sherwin-Williams store. Call 1-800-4-SHERWIN (1-800-474-3794) for a store near you.

© 1997 The Sherwin-Williams Company.

SHERWIN WILLIAMS

WHERE TO GET IT.™

stimulus and the corresponding response. When people respond to stimuli from the environment in a predictable manner, the behaviorist concludes that learning has taken place. For example, when you redeem a coupon for a discounted price on a product, that very act indicates that you have learned that this is a way to save money. The two behavioral theories most applicable to advertising and marketing are classical conditioning and instrumental, or operant, conditioning.

Classical Conditioning. *Classical conditioning* is a type of learning that takes place when a situation can be created under which a response

EXHIBIT 6–5 Sherwin-Williams uses a humorous, colorful visual of a woodpecker to grab the attention of consumers who might be interested in its SuperPaint® product. Placed in appropriate media vehicles, this type of vivid imagery can help an advertiser's message rise above the clutter.

Lumina owners have at least one reason to drive a car this safe.

Lumina LS Here are some more: standard dual air bags,

ABS, Daytime Running Lamps, child security rear door locks and power

window lockout. There's even an integrated child safety seat option. Fact is, no six-

passenger car in its class can offer as many standard safety features for

the money as a Chevy™ Lumina® LS. A small price to pay for a lot less to worry

about. That's something that any parent can appreciate.

Genuine Chevrolet
The Cars More Americans Trust.

Call 1-800-950-2438 or visit www.chevrolet.com ˚Excludes other GM products. ©1996 GM Corp. Buckle up, America! ▣

EXHIBIT 6–6   By using a head-line that suggests that all Lumina owners have at least one child, Chevrolet reinforces the position of the Lumina as a family car. Presentation of the car's safety features, an issue of great importance to family car buyers, adds even more support to this image.

natural to an individual comes under the control of a new stimulus. The Russian physiologist Ivan Pavlov demonstrated how this might take place in an experimental setting using dogs as his subjects. He employed a method in which he used the dogs' unconditioned response (salivating) to an unconditioned stimulus (food) to create a conditioned response. Pavlov selected the sound of a bell as his conditioned stimulus. He rang the bell when he knew the dogs were hungry and immediately placed meat paste (unconditioned stimulus) on their tongues to get them to salivate. He repeated this procedure until he was able to stimulate a conditioned response (salivating) to the bell alone. It was the repetition of the pairing of the bell and meat paste that conditioned the dogs to respond to the bell.

In advertising we often select unconditioned stimuli such as celebrity endorsers, famous sports figures, babies, dogs, and other artifacts to place in ads as unconditioned stimuli. We expect a natural, positive response to these people or items. Through repetition, advertising can pair these unconditioned stimuli with conditioned stimuli in the form of products, and services. We want consumers to respond to the brands in the same positive way they respond to the celebrities, sports figures, babies, and so on. The conditioned response we are looking for is the purchase of the products or services. In Exhibit 6–7, for example, State Farm Insurance uses ducklings as an unconditional stimulus in this advertisement for life insurance. This ad successfully creates an emotional connection between the ducklings and the children, both of which need special protection and care.

There have been some modifications to classical conditioning theory that are worth noting because they add insight to how consumers learn. Some behaviorists argue that subjects exposed to paired stimuli actually learn to associate the two stimuli in a way that creates an expectation that when the conditioned stimulus appears it will be quickly followed by the unconditioned stimulus. For this type of learning to take place, the two stimuli must be logically related to each other and the conditioned stimulus should be novel.[4] This modified, or neo-Pavlovian, theory returns the will and motivation to learn to the consumers. The consumer is viewed more as an active learner who uses his or her perceptual skills to select and process information and images from the environment to create a meaningful picture of the world.[5]

Operant Conditioning. The second behavioral theory of importance to advertisers and marketers is the *operant conditioning,* or *instrumental,* theory. Operant conditioning fits in nicely with advertising and marketing because it postulates that we learn to exhibit behaviors that are rewarded and we avoid those that are not rewarded or are punished. Through trial and error we buy products or brands that offer better outcomes than others. The term *instru-*

mental describes how the response exhibited is instrumental in obtaining the reward, which in turn reinforces future behavior. The psychologist B. F. Skinner is closely associated with operant conditioning because he designed experiments using "Skinner boxes" in which animals were able to obtain food by pressing the right keys or levers. Only when they pressed the right keys and exhibited the appropriate behavior would they be reinforced with a reward of food.

Marketers who employ reinforcement as a tactic have found that the reinforcement does not have to be constant or frequent to produce a conditioned response. Trading stamp and frequent flyer programs prescribe the number of responses required to be rewarded. Frequent flyer programs offer other incentives based on the amount of time in which you accumulate points. These reinforcement schedules are usually used as part of customer retention programs. The airlines hope that the rewards keep customers coming back.

COGNITIVE LEARNING THEORY   Most learning obviously takes place under conditions other than those described by behavioral theories. There are times when we learn things that do not lead to some type of response or specific behavior. Additionally, there appear to be mental processes involved in learning that are not accounted for by conditioning approaches. The theory that focuses on the nature of the mental processes of thinking, memory, and information processing we use to learn and solve problems is called **cognitive learning theory.**

For many years, a dominant approach to the study of consumer behavior was the *information processing perspective.* This viewpoint uses the computer as its basic analogy of the human mind. It looks at learning in terms of how information is selected and received at the input stage, how it is processed and retained, and how it is responded to as a form of output. One of the major criticisms of information processing has been that it is too mechanical and rational in its orientation and does not account for the role of emotions and subjective experiences such as enjoyment or frustration in learning. It also tends to discount the influence of the environment on learning and consumer behavior. However, the information processing

perspective still does the best job of identifying key variables and relationships that are a part of the learning process.

Exhibit 6–8 provides a general diagram of what Peter and Olson call *cognitive processing,* which takes the information processing approach and reduces it to three primary processes: interpretation, integration, and knowledge stored in memory.[6] Using Exhibit 6-8 as our guide, we can see that cognitive learning occurs when we are exposed to information of some kind in our environment and, through our interpretive processes, we gain new knowledge or modify existing knowledge in our memory. Knowledge exists in our memory in the form of knowledge structures known as *associative networks*—concepts that are connected to each other. The knowledge structures in memory can be accessed through

EXHIBIT 6-8   Cognitive Processing Diagram

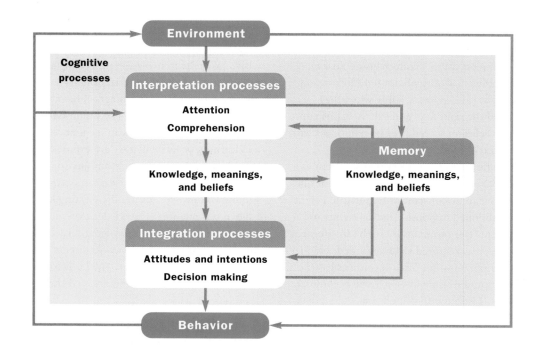

the process of *activation,* which occurs when you are exposed to a stimulus like an ad or when you are just thinking about something. As you think about one or more concepts in an associative network, other related concepts might be recalled. We should remember that our ability to process information at any point in time is limited. However, as we encounter the same situations over time, a lot of processing becomes routine or automatic.

Motivation to learn is an important concern for advertisers and marketers because people will process information differently based on whether or not learning is intentional. *Intentional learning,* also known as *directed learning,* takes place when you want to acquire knowledge. This type of learning occurs, for example, when you are shopping for a big-ticket item

such as a car or computer and want to make sure that you have enough information upon which to base your purchase decision. *Incidental learning,* on the other hand, occurs in many advertising situations, such as when a commercial appears on TV or radio at a time you happen to be watching or listening. When consumers are motivated to learn—that is, when the learning is intentional—they will seek out information. In the case of incidental learning, however, the ad has to find the consumer. Notice the difference in approach and amount of information content in the ads in Exhibit 6–9. The first ad is for a high-ticket item and relies more on consumers finding it, while the second ad has been written to seek out the customer.

We make it
like you would.

If you did.

But you don't.

So we do.

We season. We simmer. We stir. You get to say you slaved in the kitchen all day long.

Heinz. Or is it homemade?

Heinz

THE ABILITY TO SCALE AN

18-INCH VERTICAL WALL. THE ABILITY

TO FORD TWO FEET OF WATER.

THE ABILITY TO MAKE A SEMI THINK

TWICE ABOUT CUTTING YOU OFF.

It's not a car. It's not a truck. It's not another 4X4. It's a Hummer. A vehicle not in a class, but a universe entirely its own. A Hummer is what it is. A wolf in wolf's clothing. A vehicle that looks the way it does because of what it was designed to do. With its 16 inches of ground clearance (twice that of any 4X4), steep approach and departure angles, stable 72-inch track width, and unique geared hub assembly, a Hummer can go places and do things that would be impossible for any other vehicle. A street-legal Hummer can climb a 60% grade, traverse a 40% side-slope, plow through three-foot snowdrifts, and claw its way across even the deepest sand. With its

unique Central Tire Inflation System, you can even inflate and deflate the tires right from the driver's seat for better traction in varied terrain. Of course, a Hummer is also perfectly capable of behaving admirably within the confines of polite society. You'll find parallel parking, going through the bank drive-thru, navigating the city's parking garages, and zipping in and out of rush-hour traffic not only easy, but a blast. In fact, the only problem you are likely to run into in town is working your way through the crowds that invariably form wherever it's parked. For more information or a free brochure detailing Hummer's unparalleled capabilities, call 1-800-732-5493.

HUMMER

The degree to which consumers are motivated to learn about a product or brand is a function of how involved they are with the product or the purchase process. **Involvement** is defined as the perceived personal importance of an object or stimulus in a given situation. By and large, the more expensive or socially significant a purchase—such as a car, gift, or jewelry—the more involved a consumer will be with it. Low-involvement products are those that the consumer purchases without much thought, such as routine household items or low-cost impulse products like gum, candy, or soda. A person who is highly involved with a purchase situation will expend more energy to ensure that he or she makes a good decision. This produces greater motivation to learn more about the purchase options.

The degree of involvement in any purchase, high-ticket or routine, is influenced by the nature of the product or service, how relevant the product is to a consumer's self-image, and the situation in which the purchase occurs. Clothing tends to be a high-involvement category because of how clothes reflect the person. Likewise, products bought to be served, as gifts, or used in public carry more involvement with them. In short, we take more care when we purchase high-involvement products.[7]

R E S E T

1. **Why is it important to understand the consumer's viewpoint when it comes to advertising and marketing products, services, and brands?**
2. **Through what types of selective processes do consumers simplify the huge amounts of information they are exposed to on a given day?**
3. **How does cognitive learning occur?**

Attitude

Once information has been interpreted and stored in knowledge structures in memory, it can be further integrated for use in making decisions. One of the important ways knowledge is integrated is in the formation of attitudes.

An **attitude** is a three-part internal mental structure that integrates a consumer's feelings, knowledge, and intentions to act toward an object, act, or person into an overall evaluation. The three parts are usually referred to as: (1) affect, or positive and negative feelings; (2) cognitions, or knowledge; and (3) behavioral intentions. Attitudes are specific, fairly stable and consistent, and thought to be important predictors for consumer behavior. For example, the belief (cognition) that Japanese cars were made better than American ones was pervasive during the 1980s in the U.S. and resulted in a positive attitude among consumers toward Japanese autos and a negative attitude toward American cars. It took American automobile manufacturers a long time to overcome this attitude and reverse the sales declines of the 1980s.

Beliefs are underlying cognitions, or organizations of knowledge, that represent what the consumer knows about an object about which he or she has an attitude. Beliefs are usually propositional or descriptive in form and connect an object or idea to an attitude through the use of a verb or other relational term.[8] For example, a person may have a belief that there should be a separation between church and state. This belief could be expressed as a statement that says church involvement in politics undermines our ability to govern ourselves. Further, this belief may have an effect on the individual's attitude toward a ballot proposal to partially fund a daycare center that is operated by a local religious group. The person's attitude may be evidenced in negative feelings toward the ballot proposal, knowledge of the specific features of the proposal, and an intention to vote against it based on the belief in separation between church and state. Notice how the belief is more general and descriptive while the attitude is directed specifically toward the ballot proposal and has a positive or negative value associated with it.

People's attitudes can be important to the degree that they use them to evaluate alternatives in a choice situation. The evaluative or judgmental character of an attitude is what makes it the target of a lot of advertising and marketing communications campaigns. Advertisers often try to create or amplify emotions and feelings in their messages as one way to influence attitudes. Public service advertisements, such as the one for the Children's Defense

Fund in Exhibit 6–10, often use emotional appeals to get people involved and to affect their attitudes toward issues about which they might be relatively neutral.

During advertising planning, an advertiser often measures consumer attitudes toward products, services, or issues to determine how messages should be created. Through consumer surveys, an advertiser can identify subgroups in the population that hold similar attitudes. These subgroups can provide the basis for identifying and describing a target audience toward which a campaign might be directed. If the attitudes are closely related to how a consumer behaves, then the advertiser may be able to predict a response to his or her messages.

Attitude change often is a goal of advertising and marketing communications campaigns when there is evidence that such a change can lead to a corresponding change in behavior. Campaigns like Volkswagen's "Drivers Wanted" effort are aimed at changing people's image and attitude toward a product to influence sales or behavior. Volkswagen's sales had declined for years before a new advertising agency was selected to create a campaign that expressed an entirely new attitude about Volkswagen and the type of people who drive VWs. Exhibit 6–11 illustrates VW's new attitude.

Attitudes are among the hardest things for an advertising campaign to change. Part of the reason is that they represent an integration of knowledge, feelings, and experiences that is difficult to undo. Attitudes are learned and are hard to unlearn. New knowledge, feelings, and experiences have to be created to affect an attitude change. Most people are not interested in such a change unless it is very compelling, especially when it comes to attitudes about high-involvement products.

The differences in attitudes and levels of involvement for a particular product raise interesting problems with the individual characteristics that influence consumer decision making. An advertiser doesn't usually have information about the motivations, perceptual characteristics, learning patterns, or attitudes of the consumer. These characteristics are not measured regularly or consistently across the population. As alternatives to the unmeasured individual characteristics, advertisers often use demographic or psychographic information to identify consumer markets and target audiences.

Demography And Demographics

As a science, **demography** originally was concerned with the study of the structure, distribution, and changes in the population using descriptive and quantifiable characteristics such as age, sex, race, marital status, education, income, and geographical region. These population characteristics are called **demographics.** Today, demography has grown beyond the study of these vital population statistics to include interest in areas such as fertility, social class, distribution of wealth, crime rates, and migration patterns. Through popular use in advertising and marketing, the term *demographics* is often used as a synonym for demographic characteristics, the set of variables studied by demographers.

EXHIBIT 6–10 Advertisements can convey powerful emotional messages, and many advertisers hope to capitalize on this ability by using ads to modify consumers' emotions, whether it is for a specific product or, as this ad shows, for a social issue.

It happens to everyone. Sooner or later your sedan gene kicks in. The words "sports car" are erased from your mental hard drive and replaced with "four door sedan." This is usually followed by a cold sweat.

Is there life after four doors? There is in a Volkswagen Jetta GLX. Its 172 hp VR6 engine can take you from 0-60 in about 7 seconds.

It's German engineered so it handles like nothing you've ever driven before.

And those 4 doors? Well, life's a lot more fun when you bring some friends along.

On the road of life there are passengers and there are drivers.

The Jetta GLX: Front wheel drive. Rack and pinion steering. Anti-lock brakes. Dual airbag supplemental restraints. Premium 8-speaker stereo and warranties so the wazoo. 1-800 DRIVE VW or http://www.vw.com. ©1998 Volkswagen. Always wear your seatbelt and we've heard some good things about beta carotene too.

Drivers wanted.

EXHIBIT 6–11 In an effort to change the prevailing perceptions and attitudes about its cars, Volkswagen used the high-energy "Drivers Wanted" campaign to present a new voice and new look to consumers.

Advertisers and marketers use demographic information about us to plan advertising campaigns because perceptions, attitudes, and purchase behaviors often are connected to demographic characteristics. To the degree that we can profile a group that shares some psychological or behavioral trait using demographics, these characteristics become useful in planning campaigns and other marketing communications programs. For example, people with higher education and income levels are more likely to purchase a luxury car than individuals near the bottom of the education and income strata. Similarly, married couples who work tend to have greater purchasing power than unmarried couples. And since some interests and needs vary by gender, there are differences in the products purchased by men and women. It is important to remember that demographic characteristics in populations change over time,

and advertisers and marketers must be aware of these changes both in the present and for the future. These changes often accompany or are accompanied by changes in buying patterns. The result of knowing more about your target market is the ability to customize, as "Technology Watch: Customize, Customize, Customize" describes.

There are a number of important demographic trends that are influencing and will continue to influence advertising and marketing. These include: generational influences, population diversity, aging, gender, and migration. Let's examine each of these trends in more detail.

GENERATIONAL INFLUENCES Baby boomers are the largest cohort group in history to move through society. Because they make up one-third of the American population, baby boomers have received a great deal of attention from advertisers. During the 1990s, baby boomers have become a more attractive target because they are entering their prime earning years. We have to be careful not to approach boomers as if they were one homogeneous market, however. One expert recommends that we subdivide this market into four segments based on education and income. These four subgroups are: (1) a superclass with high levels of education and income (6 percent); (2) elite workers with lower levels of education but high incomes (4.4 percent); (3) would-bes with high levels of education but low incomes (22 percent); and (4) workers with both low levels of education and income (67 percent).[9] The groups most valuable to advertisers and marketers are the superclass and elite workers. These groups are more likely to have swimming pools, multiple TVs, VCRs, computers, and other high-ticket items.

Knowing how to talk to baby boomers—or any demographic group for that matter—as a target audience often requires knowing how one generation is different from the generation that comes before or after it. Yankelovich Partners, Inc., is a research firm that has tracked the changing values, lifestyles, and buying motivations of Americans since 1971 through an annual survey called *Yankelovich Monitor*. Yankelovich has used the results of this survey to compare three generations of consumers—Matures (born 1909–1945), Boomers (born

1946–1964), and Xers (born 1965–present)—in a book titled *Rocking The Ages*.[10] The conclusion of the book is that generationally determined lifestyles and social values influence purchase behavior more than demographics such as income and education. Exhibit 6–12 illustrates, at a glance, some of the differences across these generations that we will briefly describe below.

Matures grew up during a rather difficult era that included the Great Depression of the 1930s, World War II, the Korean War, and the Cold War. Their attitudes toward work, and life in general, were molded by these troubled times. Their expectations are greatly constrained. Their values are what we today term "traditional"—self-discipline, self-denial, hard work, obedience to authority, and financial and social conservatism. Matures approach purchases with a built-in conservatism and are slow to accept new products. They save a larger proportion of their money than do Boomers.[11]

Boomers are the largest and most influential generation in the U.S. today. They were born during the postwar economic expansion of the 1950s and early 1960s and grew up expecting prosperity and educational opportunity. Boomers have been labeled the "Me Generation" because they believed that they were entitled to prosperity and the good life. Both the Matures and Xers see Boomers as self-absorbed people interested more in their personal goals than in relationships with others. The social changes brought about during the formative years of the Boomers were, to some extent, a result of their attitude that continuous economic growth meant that there was plenty of opportunity to share with everybody. Boomers spend a larger proportion of their income than did their parents, and they

TECHNOLOGY WATCH

. . . .

Customize, Customize, Customize

The credo of the 1990s and beyond might be to use technology to customize products, services, and messages to your customers' individual needs. No longer will "one size fits all" suffice. Today, a lot of the inconveniences and "almost-fits" situations that consumers have tolerated for a long time can be rectified by imaginative use of computer technology.

Consider buying shoes as an area where some real progress could be made. How many times have you settled for shoes that almost fit, or bought shoes two sizes too large in order to accommodate a wide foot? Have you bought the wrong size because you liked the style or color and it did not come in your size? Here comes the Custom Foot store to the rescue. The Custom Foot store has no shoes to sell in its store. What it does have is a computerized system that electronically scans your feet to determine the exact size and shape of each foot. The data are transmitted to shoe factories in Italy, where shoes are made to fit your feet at the price of about $140 per pair. Most custom-made shoes from other sources usually cost $500 or more. Levi Strauss offers a similar system for making women's jeans.

The ability to customize products on large scale, as Custom Foot and Levi Strauss are doing, is termed "mass customization." It will eventually result in more and more companies being able to tailor products to individuals for about the same price we pay for products and services today. Another form of customizing consumer products and services is using a database to record preferences that can be used to fit an item or service to a particular person's needs. Upscale hotels are doing this so that preferences such as nonsmoking rooms, king-size beds, and computer hook-ups can be honored without the customer having to ask.

Technology is helping us to know and better understand our customers. Mass customization is not an oxymoron. It is a consumer and marketing reality.

Sources: John Holusha, "Making the Shoe Fit, Perfectly," *New York Times,* 20 March 1996, C1, C6; and Don Peppers and Martha Rogers, *The One-to-One Future* (New York: Currency/Doubleday, 1993).

EXHIBIT 6–12   Boomers in the Middle: Generational Differences at a Glance

	MATURES	BOOMERS	XERS
Defining idea	Duty	Individuality	Diversity
Celebrating	Victory	Youth	Savvy
Style	Team player	Self-absorbed	Entrepreneur
Reward because	You've earned it	You deserve it	You need it
Work is	An inevitable obligation	An exciting adventure	A difficult challenge
Education is	A dream	A birthright	A way to get there
Future	Rainy day to work for	"Now" is more important	Uncertain but manageable
"Program" means	Social programs	Cult deprogrammers	Software
Brands	Converse; Wayfarer	Adidas; Vuarnet	Nike; Oakley
Memories	Marx Brothers	Smothers Brothers	Menendez Brothers
	Hobo	Hitchhiker	Homeless
	Frank Sinatra	The Beatles	R.E.M.
	Orange juice	The Juice runs	The Juice walks
	Pan Am Clipper Fleet	Pam Am Shuttle	Lockerbie
Home stuff	Timex	Casio	Swatch
	Milk and cookies	Milk and Oreos	Milk and SnackWells
	Sex on your honeymoon	Sex in the backseat	Sex on the Internet
Media	*Peyton Place*	*Dallas*	*Melrose Place*
	This Is Your Life	*Candid Camera*	*America's Funniest Home Videos*
Technology	Slide rules	Calculators	Spreadsheets
	Rotary phones	Touch-tone phones	Cell phones

are more likely to be interested in new products and innovations.[12]

Yankelovich labels the Generation X group, or Xers, the "Why Me?" generation. Xers share some of the traits of Matures because they too have lived through a lot of economic, political, and social turmoil. They are more pragmatic than Boomers but still are enthusiastic about the challenges that await them. They exhibit a combination of the social values of the Boomers and the restraint or wariness of their grandparents.[13] If you are reading this text, you are likely to be an Xer ready to take on the changing world scene and new technological challenges ahead.

POPULATION DIVERSITY   Between 1980 and 1990, U.S. Census data indicated that 16 states

had declines in their Caucasian populations and 41 states had double-digit increases in their minority populations.[14] The projections for growth in the minority communities are even more dramatic. *American Demographics* magazine predicts that African Americans, Asians, Native Americans, and Hispanics will make up a majority of the U.S. population by 2050.[15] Exhibit 6–13 illustrates the relative distribution of the non-Hispanic white population by county across the United States. Notice that the minority population is the highest in big cities in the North, the rural Sunbelt, California, and Texas.

As the composition of society changes, advertisers have become more interested in African-American and Hispanic (the two largest ethnic groups) segments of the market.

With this interest in minority segments, advertisers must be aware of the differences within the segment. For example, a study in San Antonio found differences in the way Hispanic consumers searched for information based on their identification with the Hispanic community. Spanish-language Hispanics also differed from English-language Hispanics in demographics, religious tradition, and separation from the cultural mainstream of U.S. society. Research has shown that Hispanics spend 41 percent more time watching television than the general population. Spanish-language TV stations score more points in Hispanic households than English-language TV stations.[16]

Much like the Hispanic population, the African-American population grew by 13.2 percent during the 1980s to 29.4 million in 1990, and it is expected to reach 34 million by 2001.[17] This growth was faster than the general population but slower than Hispanic and Asian minority growth. Most of the growth occurred in the outer-ring suburbs of central cities.[18] The growth in size of African-American segments has been accompanied by an increase in the number of black-owned businesses that cater to the needs of this market. Among these firms are advertising agencies that specialize in targeting the African-American market. With the help of such agencies, many advertisers have learned to target non-whites with their products and services. Companies such as McDonald's and Hilton (Exhibit 6–14) have also created ads that highlight the diversity

EXHIBIT 6–13   Distribution of Non-Hispanic White Population

Source: Brad Edmondson, "The Minority Majority in 2001," *American Demographics,* October 1996, 16–17.

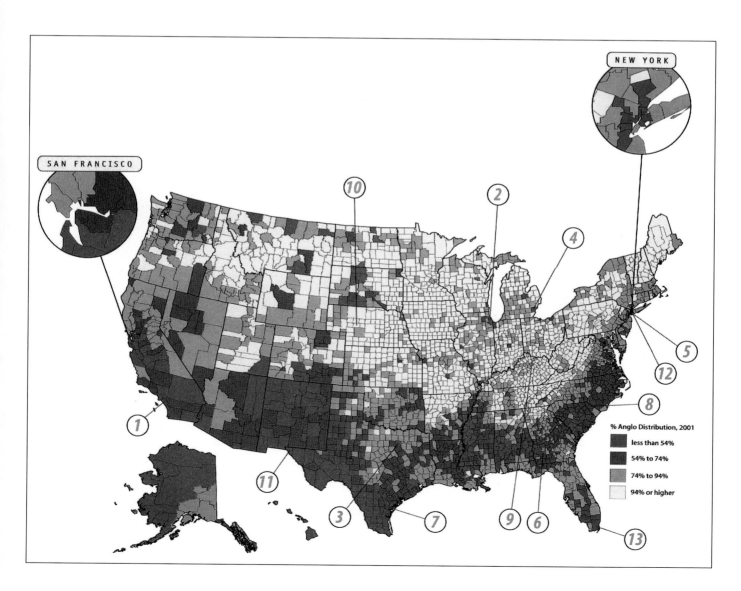

of the consumer groups using their products and services. Advertisers have found targeting minority families profitable because the segment is growing in size and economic buying power.

As the U.S. population becomes more diverse, advertisers must understand ethnic and racial minorities in order to create effective sales messages for their products. Advertisers must demonstrate through the images portrayed that they understand how minorities are different, but also how they are the same as society in general. Media selection and message delivery must consider the unique viewing, listening, and reading habits of minority segments.

EXHIBIT 6–14 Population growth in and increased buying power among minority groups has resulted in increased efforts by advertisers to highlight consumer diversity in their ads.

What Three Romantic Words Would You Love To Use This Weekend?

Do Not Disturb. Imagine. The two of you. Kicking back.
Relaxing. Getting to know each other all over again. But who has the time? You'll find that you do, with Hilton's BounceBack Weekend.® Hilton gives you the perfect hideaway with all the privacy, the pampering, and even a free Continental breakfast. Or for a little extra, have a full breakfast. Now, see how easy it is to make time for romance? You can make reservations online at http://www.hilton.com, or call your professional travel agent, or 1-800-HILTONS.

FROM **$89** PER ROOM PER NIGHT

Program valid Thursday to Sunday through 12/30/97. Offer valid every day of the week at some hotels. Saturday night stay required at some locations. Earlier check-out is subject to payment of lowest available non-BounceBack rate. Kids 18 and under stay free in parents' or grandparents' room. Limited availability. Advance reservations required. Rate does not include tax or gratuities and does not apply to meetings, conventions, groups or other promotional offers and is subject to change without notice. The Hilton logotype is a registered trademark of Hilton Hotels Corporation. ©1997 Hilton Hotels.

Hilton

THE AGING POPULATION Baby boomers are aging and entering a stage in life of maximum earnings, accounting for over $985 billion in purchasing power. This is noteworthy because baby boomers have always been spenders.[19] They also bring with them other important changes to the over-50 consumer segments. For instance, they generally are healthier than their predecessors at this age, they are more financially secure, they have become more active, and they do more leisure travel than other market segments.[20]

Because of such changes—and the fact that the over-50 market segment wants to be viewed positively—advertisers have had to rethink their perceptions of older consumers. People in this market don't think of themselves as "old." In fact, some retired consumers have reentered the work force in order to remain active. Images of over-50 consumers must be realistic and positive. As the boomers move into the over-50 market and are officially labeled "seniors" by the American Association of Retired Persons, owners of new media aimed at this market are struggling to find inoffensive names for their magazines. Words such as *mature*, *prime*, and *horizons* are being tapped as positive euphemisms for old age. Néscafe has successfully used humor to speak to this maturing market's perceptions of itself. The ad shown in Exhibit 6–15 was part of a Néscafe campaign run in Canada.

WORKING WOMEN Since World War II, when women entered the workforce to contribute to the war effort, there has been a steady increase in the number of working women in the U.S. In 1994, for example, 55 percent of women with children under the age of six worked, compared to only 19 percent in 1960.[21] Among certain age groups, the percentage of women working is even higher. About three quarters of women age 45–54 are in the workforce.

The most obvious effect of women working is that two-wage-earner households (households in which both the husband and wife work) have more total income at their disposal than do households where only one spouse works. However, there is a trade-off in terms of time pressures. While men and women are sharing more and more of the household chores, women still bear more than half the

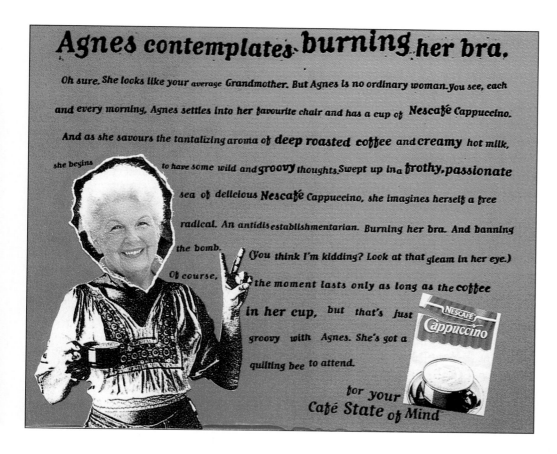

EXHIBIT 6–15 The size and buying power of the aging baby boomer generation has had a notable effect on the representation of older consumers in advertising. This ad for Néscafe Cappucino reflects this new image of the vibrant, active lives of older adults.

burden. Some of the time pressure is relieved by using more convenience products and time-saving services such as maids. Many stores and other businesses have responded to the lifestyles of the two-wage-earner family by remaining open for longer hours and on weekends. Catalogs and other forms of direct marketing also offer convenient ways to purchase things while saving time. And the Internet promises to do the same.

The increased number of working women has run roughly parallel to other social changes. For example, women have become more financially independent. This has changed the nature of many marriages. Whereas in the past women sought financial security in a marriage, today many women want to be financially independent and look more for companionship. With more women in the workforce there also has been an increase in the number of women business owners and senior-level executives. Working women have increased their individual purchasing power while improving the economic status of many two wage-earner families. This new-found financial independence has made women a prime market for durables such as cars and financial services like insurance and investment funds.

MIGRATION TO THE SOUTH AND WEST

While the population center of the U.S. remains in the North, it is shifting to the southern states. This shift adds both political and economic power to those states that have grown the fastest in the past decade and a half. California and Florida gained the most people in the 1980s, with net population growth exceeding 2 million in each state. Texas followed closely behind, growing by 1.2 million people. These three large southern and western states accounted for more than half the population growth in the U.S. since 1980.[22] Look back at Exhibit 6–13 and notice that these three states also are among the most diverse.

There is some truth to the observation that the Atlanta–Dallas–Los Angeles axis across the South will be serious competition to the Boston–New York–Chicago axis for advertisers' dollars in the future. The real challenge here will not only be a shift in numbers of people but also the fact that these new markets are home to large numbers of Hispanics, African

Americans, and Asians. This diversity stands to some degree in contrast to the European heritage of the North. Products, appeals, and media are being created to meet this new demand in the South and West. For example, *Latina* is a new bilingual lifestyle and fashion magazine targeted to over 8 million Hispanic women. *Essence* magazine (which is aimed at African-American women) is partnering with *Latina* to bring its distinctly Hispanic viewpoint to the lifestyle and fashion magazine market.

It is projected that California, Florida, and Texas will continue to add population and be fast-growing states until at least 2010. States adjacent to these also are growing fast. Arizona, Colorado, Georgia, North Carolina, South Carolina, and Virginia will grow substantially by 2010 to make the Southeast and Southwest potentially lucrative markets over the next decade and beyond.

Lifestyle And Psychographics

Creating advertisements for the various generational, minority, aging, women, and regional markets requires sensitivity to the issues that are important to the target audiences. The major growth trends in demographics focus on population changes, but these changes also are accompanied by changes in attitudes, lifestyle, and values in the target population. Attitudinal and lifestyle information provides important insights beyond demographics.

Lifestyle is a concept that has evolved from personality and values research that describes the "patterns in which people live and spend time and money."[23] **Psychographics** refers to a set of quantitative research procedures that we use to measure lifestyle—values, personality, attitudes, and the like. To illustrate the insightful value of lifestyle and psychographics to advertising and marketing, let's return to our discussion of working women. Demographic information can provide statistics about how many women are seeking careers. It can tell us the levels of education women have acquired and what changes in income have occurred for working women. However, demographic information can't tell us how women *perceive* and feel about their new roles. Demographics can't tell us what challenges or problems women have found in their new career environment. Nor can it tell us how

women feel about products and advertising. But lifestyle and psychographic information can. This information adds qualitative dimensions to a demographic description that can help advertisers create messages targeted to, in this case, working women based on their perception of work.

Gathering lifestyle and psychographic information about the target market or target audience can provide more precise planning information for the advertiser. Some of the most widely used psychographic techniques attempt to segment the market on the basis of lifestyle variables. For some advertisers, psychographic analysis has become synonymous with lifestyle segmentation research.

One of the most popular lifestyle and psychographic tools in the 1980s was the **Values and Life-Styles (VALS)** measurement system developed by SRI International in California. The original VALS typology of consumer segments was developed as a combination of Maslow's hierarchy of needs and the inner- and outer-directed categorization of people developed by sociologist David Reisman. For Reisman, outer-directed individuals structured their behavior by watching others; in other words, other individuals provided models for their values and behavior. Possessions for outer-directeds are symbols of a person's worth. Inner-directeds, on the other hand, are self-directed. They set their own goals and are resistant to peer pressure. Combining the two categorizations of behavior, the VALS typology shown in Exhibit 6–16 was created.

The double hierarchy that characterizes this typology was developed to show the independent paths of inner- and outer-directed consumers. As indicated, there are nine categories of consumers: survivors, sustainers, belongers, emulators, achievers, I-am-me, experiential, socially conscious, and integrated. Notice how survivors and sustainers are need driven; belongers, emulators, and achievers are outer directed; and I-am-me, experientials, and the socially conscious are inner directed. Integrated consumers combine values of the inner- and outer-directed consumers.

VALS2 is a revision of the original VALS typology that was designed to incorporate economic and demographic changes into the system.[24] The developers relaxed the connec-

EXHIBIT 6–16   Original VALS Typology

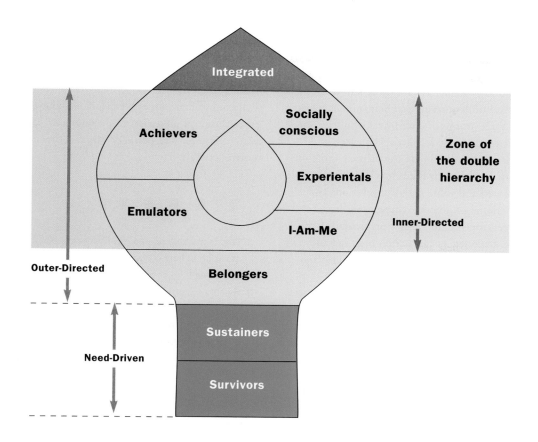

THE NINE VALS TYPES

Need-Driven

Survivors: Elderly females who might be poorly educated and ill, or inner-city or rural families.
Sustainers: Mostly young and unemployed. Almost half are black or Hispanic.
   Struggling to find a place in society.

Outer-Directed

Belongers: The solid middle class; 4 out of 10 Americans. They value security, stability, and group
   identification; they don't like to take risks or be flashy.
Emulators: One in every 10 Americans. They spend ostentatiously, tend to be in debt, and are a
   study in frustrated ambitions.
Achievers: One out of five. Older, wealthy, well-educated, overwhelmingly white, married homeowners.
   Emulators are struggling to join this group.

Inner-Directed

I-Am-Me: Mostly students. Passionate about self-expression, loud music, outrageous clothes, and
   opposition to the Outer-Directed.
Experientials: Believe in education, saving the environment, and having peak experiences. Many are
   former I-Am-Mes.
Socially Conscious: The best-educated group. Early middle-aged adults who moved from flower power
   to Vietnam. Watergate and *The Big Chill*. Although suspicious of large institutions, many make
   comfortable livings and have influential jobs.

Integrated

Combines Outer and Inner values. Mature and psychologically balanced. One in
   50 Americans.

tion between values and lifestyles in VALS2. The revised system, shown in Exhibit 6–17, divides consumers into eight categories on the basis of resources, self-orientation, and action orientation.

Starting at the top of the exhibit and working down, actualizers are successful consumers with abundant resources. Below the actualizers are three groups of consumers who have sufficient resources: fulfilleds, achievers, and experiencers. Fulfilleds are satisfied and comfortable with their lifestyle. They are principle oriented and value practical solutions and functional products. Achievers are status and career oriented and prefer predictability to risk. Experiencers are action oriented and live for the experience. They are young and impulsive.

On the next level are three more categories of consumers with fewer resources. Believers are principle oriented and favor proven brands. Strivers are career-driven and are influenced by the approval of others. Like achievers, they are status oriented. Makers are action oriented and often focus on being self-sufficient because they have fewer resources than experiencers. Finally, strugglers, like survivors and sustainers

in VALS, have a difficult time making ends meet. They are concerned with necessities.

VALS, VALS2, and other lifestyle segmentation techniques are designed to define market segments. If the variables in the lifestyle questionnaires tap the vein of consumer decision making, then the techniques will provide better predictions of consumer behavior. With better predictions, the advertiser can create more effective messages and persuade target audiences more effectively.

R E S E T

1. Why is attitude so important to our understanding of how consumers make purchase decisions?
2. How do advertisers and marketers use demographic information?
3. How do advertisers and marketers use psychographic information?

EXHIBIT 6–17   VALS2 Typology

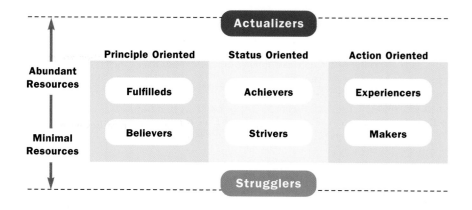

Social And Cultural Influences

We can see from the amount of information and content covered in the previous section that individual characteristics have played a significant role in our understanding of consumer behavior. However, there has been an increasing awareness that social and cultural factors often have more influence on our purchase decisions than previously believed. As we grow and are socialized into society, there are many personal influences upon our life. The first and sometimes most lasting influence is our family or other members of our household. Other influences include reference groups, social classes, and cultures and subcultures.

Household Influences

In the past, researchers have looked at how family units influence purchasing decisions. A family can be defined in several ways, including *family of origin* (the family you were born into), *nuclear family* (yourself, mom, dad, sisters, and brothers), and *family of procreation* (the family you create through marriage). Over the past 40 or 50 years, however, there have been changes in the traditional family structure, and these changes have led researchers to begin studying household influences instead of just family influences. A **household** differs from a family in that it includes all the people living under one roof regardless of their blood relationships. These may include single-parent homes, step-families, people living together who are not married, or people living alone. The household is a basic social and economic unit that serves a number of key functions that influence the products we buy.

Households, and especially traditional families, provide many influences including: (1) economic security, (2) emotional support or nurturing, (3) models for lifestyle choices, and (4) models for the socialization of children as to society's most basic values and sanctioned behaviors. Advertisers, marketers, and society at large are interested in how children are socialized as consumers. The process occurs in a number of ways. One is through social learning or modeling, whereby children mimic the behavior of their parents. Children who go shopping with parents watch how

purchases are made and what is being bought. Many of these purchase-related behaviors stay with children into adulthood. Parents also use forms of reinforcement and punishment to influence their children's behaviors. A lot of these reinforcements involve products. Parents buy things as rewards or withhold purchases as punishments.

Family and household members also play roles in purchase decisions that affect themselves as well as the family or household. One of the most important questions an advertiser asks when trying to sell a product to families is, Who is the primary decision maker in the family? In other words, are product decisions influenced most by a spouse, parent, or child? A contributing factor for family decision making is the structure of the family. In the U.S. in the last 30 years, there has been a decrease in the number of married couples with kids, a decrease in the number of married couples without kids, and an increase in single-parent and single-person households.[25]

In addition to these demographic changes, there have been changes in the roles family or household members play in purchases. For example, men now participate in more of the traditionally female-dominated aspects of household duties, such as shopping or cleaning. Younger men may participate more because of their household duties while single. Blurring of gender roles also has occurred in family decision making. Women are making more decisions that were once joint decisions or decisions made by the husband in areas such as financial services or automobiles.[26]

Decision making may vary by product or service, too. For some decisions, such as dining out, children can influence the decision heavily.[27] Knowing who the decision maker is for a product or service enhances the probability of success. Advertisers often use family influence appeals when they are relevant to their claims. Exhibit 6–18 illustrates how consideration of family members might influence a decision. Notice how Radisson Hotels is targeting families with young children in this advertisement for its Family Magic℠ program.

The needs of a family change as the unit grows through the stages of its life. The *family life cycle* typically includes the following stages:

EXHIBIT 6–18   Recognizing the powerful influence of family life cycle on the purchase decisions of households, Radisson Hotels Worldwide developed its special Family Magic℠ package to target families with young children.

- young-single households
- young marrieds without children
- young divorced without children
- young marrieds with young children
- young divorced with young children
- older married without children
- married with older children
- married with adult children no longer at home
- retired couples
- surviving spouse

You have only to think back on your own growing years at home to understand how family needs change as children grow or household composition changes. A lot of product needs are dictated to some degree by the family life cycle. For example, young singles typically

spend more on audio cassettes, compact disks, and clothing. Young couples without children spend more than others on dog and cat food. Families with young children spend more on diapers, cereal, soft drinks, and videocassettes. Families with older children are good markets for fruit and soft drinks, potato chips, and detergents. Once the children leave home, coffee becomes an important item in a household, along with greeting cards. Older singles buy less of almost everything except items like frozen dinners.[28]

Changes in society have created some alterations to the traditional life cycle stages for many people. Not everybody lives through these stages as they are laid out here. More people are getting divorced, creating households headed by one parent that often limit the family's resources and expenditures. Some couples decide not to have children at all and focus on careers instead. This can lead to a very affluent household without children to consider in purchases. Some people decide to remain single throughout life, while still others have children much later in life after they have accumulated substantial wealth. There also is more cohabitation, thus creating different-sex and same-sex households where the members are not married.

Advertisers must consider how these alternative household structures affect needs and purchase decisions. Effective messages must be delivered to the right family or household members. An advertiser must examine the media habits of family members to match message delivery to the right decision maker. Sometimes the influence on decision makers extends beyond the family boundaries. When it does, the decision maker's reference groups must be included in the target audience.

Reference Group Influences

A **reference group** is "any group with which a person feels some identification or emotional affiliation and which is used to guide and define his or her beliefs, values, and goals."[29] A reference group likewise can influence the products and services people buy at both the category and brand levels. For some purchases, such as computers, trash compactors, and ice makers, just owning the product category is influenced by one's reference groups. Other products or services are more susceptible to influence at the brand level, as can be seen with cars, clothing, and watches. Still other purchases can be influenced at both the category and brand level. Owning a boat can be important in some social circles, and the brand even more important in others.[30]

Reference groups influence our behavior in three primary ways. First, they can use *normative influence* by pressuring us to conform to their standards of behavior. Reference groups do this by rewarding behavior they approve of and punishing behavior that is disapproved of by the group. Once again, products and brands that are socially conspicuous are susceptible to this type of influence. For example, fashion items that identify a person as being a group member can be influenced by a group such as a fraternity or sorority or even a professional group that adheres to a particular mode of dress. Teenagers, as a peer reference group, can wield a fair amount of influence to maintain their group identities.

Sometimes groups have influence over people simply through a *value-expressive mecha-nism,* whereby consumers want to express their group affiliation. This can occur for reference groups that have no official membership but are nonetheless recognized as a social group. Marketers can take advantage of this mechanism by directing their advertisements to these social groups. For example, a reference group for energetic, athletic, outdoor-loving individuals has developed in the 1990s in the United States. Teva sandals (see Exhibit 6–19) have become a badge product with which this social group has identified; thus, wearing these sandals can indicate an individual's affiliation with this group.

Finally, recommendations and endorsements can influence our purchase behavior through the *informational influence* of reference groups. This tends to be strongest when it is difficult to judge the products or brands we are considering. Salespeople in stores as well as trusted celebrity endorsers in ads can influence our acceptance of purchase-related information.

EXHIBIT 6–19 Consumers will often make specific purchases to illustrate or reinforce their social group affiliations. An athletic, outdoor-loving individual, for example, might wear Teva sandals to indicate his or her identification with this reference group.

Storm

©1997 Teva

Experience ACTUAL Reality

TeVa

(800) FOR-TEVA   www.tevasandals.com   Champs Sports   Eastern Mountain Sports

Reference groups vary by whether or not they are primary or secondary, aspirational or dissociative, and formal or informal. *Primary reference groups* have the most influence on our behavior because they are small and involve a lot of individual contact. The family is an example of this type of group. *Secondary reference groups* are characterized by less regular interaction among members. Many professional and community groups such as your local advertising club are of this type.

We also can look at reference groups in terms of whether we are attracted to them or want to avoid them. *Aspirational groups* are groups people strive to become members of or identify with because they want to adopt the norms and values of the group. Professions often have this type of influence on students who want to enter them as they plan their careers. A quick look at how college students dress can identify those who aspire to be accountants or lawyers versus those who want to enter the arts such as theater or music. On the other hand, *dissociative groups* can influence our behavior to the extent that we try to demonstrate our non-membership or affiliation with a group. Groups that attract some people often become dissociative groups for others. Fraternities, sororities, yuppies, and other groups whose members are easy to identify become dissociative groups for others.

The strength of reference group influence also can be a function of whether they are formal or informal groups. *Formal groups* typically have a list of members, require dues, put their rules in writing, and hold scheduled meetings. Local professional groups, churches, and fraternal organizations are examples of formal groups. The group cohesiveness and degree of conformity required of members determine how strong an influence formal groups can exert. By contrast, *informal groups* are based more on collegiality or friendship. Their influence can be strong if people are highly motivated to be identified with these groups.

Reference group influence is acknowledged in ads by including group members in the ads, referring to them in headlines and copy, or using media aimed at these groups. "Adscape: The Gay and Lesbian Markets" addresses the growing effort to advertise and market to these reference groups.

Social Class Influences

Although we like to think of the United States as a country without a formal class structure, there still remains a social stratification of society based on people's education, occupation, and other status-related variables. Thus, each of us has some standing or ranking in society that we call our social class standing. **Social class** is defined as the overall ranking of people in society so that those grouped in the same social class are similar in terms of their social status, occupations, and lifestyles.[31]

The social class concept is important to advertisers and marketers because it is related to how much people spend on products and services as well as to how the money is spent. For example, a working-class person might have a lot of money and decide to buy a snowmobile, while a person of similar means but with a professional job might decide to go on a ski vacation.

Social class groupings are based on a status hierarchy in which some members of society are better off than others. The currency of the status hierarchy can be money, power, or respect. Americans can be grouped into four primary categories—Upper Americans, Middle Class, Working Class, and Lower Americans. These social class categories are illustrated in Exhibit 6–20, along with the relative percentage of the U.S. population estimated to be in each grouping.

One of the ongoing issues surrounding social class membership has been the relationship between income and class standing. While income is one component of a person's class standing, how money is made is a better indicator. A family, for example, can make more money by having a spouse go out to work. The spouse may hold down a clerical job that adds significant income to the household but that does not change the family's social standing. Occupational prestige is another factor that contributes to social status. A college professor has a higher social standing than does a better-paid auto worker.

Education level, neighborhood, and type of house owned are also partial measures of social class. Very often the type of house and how it is furnished are reflective of a person's social class because they demonstrate a person's tastes and lifestyle. Higher social standing is related to having items such as artwork, large potted plants, a piano, or expensive window coverings. Lower social standing corresponds with bright colors for wall coverings and carpeting, family photographs on display, large TVs, artificial flowers, and cheap furniture. Hardwood floors and expensive rugs suggest higher standing while general clutter is found in lower-class households.

More recently, social class and lifestyle measures have been greatly enhanced by the creation of consumer databases that link geography or where people live to these psychographic-type variables. This process can create and profile consumer segments as small as Zip code+4 areas that have 6–25 households in them. This approach to grouping consumers based on lifestyle, social class, and location is called **geodemographics.** The premise underlying geodemographics is that people who live in the same areas or neighborhoods have other important characteristics in common.

There are four major suppliers of geodemographic segmentation systems. They are PRIZM from Claritas, ClusterPLUS from Donnelly Marketing Information Services, ACORN from CACI Marketing Systems, and MicroVision from Equifax.[32] The four systems work in a similar fashion: They combine U.S. Census data with research like that supplied by Simmons Market Research Bureau and data they have collected themselves, and identify and group areas based on common characteristics so that they can be targeted by advertisers and marketers. These computer-based systems also have the ability to use lifestyle information like that available from SRI in its VALS2 typology.

Cultural Influences

Culture and subculture are two of the broadest influences on our behavior. **Culture,** sometimes referred to as a "society's personality,"[33] is defined as the shared beliefs, values, and customs we learn so that we can interact and function within our social and physical environments. You might want to envision culture as a system of codes and rules for behavior that are not passed along genetically but that must be learned. People who share specific codes and rules make up a culture. An example of how we learn the beliefs, values, and customs of our culture can been seen in a cultural change that has taken place and how it has influenced the Xer generation. It is interesting to notice, for example, how almost everybody smokes in the

---

EXHIBIT 6–20   Social Class Groupings

Upper Americans (14 percent of population)

This group consists of the upper-upper, lower-upper, and upper-middle classes. They have common goals that are differentiated mainly by income. This group has many different lifestyles, which might be labeled postpreppy, conventional, intellectual, and political, among others. This class remains the segment of our society in which quality merchandise is most prized, special attention is paid to prestige brands, and the self-image ideal is "spending with good taste." Self-expression is more prized than in previous generations, and neighborhood remains important. Depending on income level and values, theater, books, investment in art, European travel, household help, club memberships for tennis, golf, and swimming, and prestige schooling for children remain high consumption priorities.

Middle Class (32 percent of population)

These consumers definitely want to "do the right thing" and buy "what's popular." They have always been concerned with fashion and following recommendations of "experts" in print media. Increased earnings result in better living, which means a "nicer neighborhood on the better side of town with good schools." It also means spending more on "worthwhile experiences" for children, including winter ski trips, college educations, and shopping for better brands of clothes at more expensive stores. Appearance of home is important, because guests may visit and pass judgment. This group emulates upper Americans, which distinguishes it from the working class. It also enjoys travel and physical activity. Deferred gratification may still be an ideal, but it is not so often practiced.

Working Class (38 percent of population)

Working-class Americans are "family folk" depending heavily on relatives for economic and emotional support, e.g., tips on job opportunities, advice on purchases, help in times of trouble. The emphasis on family ties is only one sign of how much more limited and different working-class horizons are socially, psychologically, and geographically compared to those of the middle class. In almost every respect, a parochial view characterizes this blue-collar world. This group has changed little in values and behaviors despite rising incomes in some cases. For them "keeping up with the times" focuses on the mechanical and recreational, and, thus, ease of labor and leisure is what they continue to pursue.

Lower Americans (16 percent of population)

The men and women of Lower Americans are no exception to the rule that diversities and uniformities in values and consumption goals are to be found at each social level. Some members of this world, as has been publicized, are prone to every form of instant gratification known to humankind when the money is available. But others are dedicated to resisting worldly temptations as they struggle toward what some believe will be a "heavenly reward" for their earthly sacrifices.

Source: Richard P. Coleman, "The Continuing Significance of Social Class in Marketing," *Journal of Consumer Research,* December 1983, 265–280. © 1983 by the University of Chicago.

AdScape

....

The Gay and Lesbian Markets

Many advertisers, including the Miller Brewing Company, are becoming increasingly aware of the size and purchasing power of the gay and lesbian community and, with that, are directing more ads toward homosexuals. This ad is an illustration of Miller's efforts to target the gay male beer drinker.

Respecting and recognizing the burgeoning diversity in the marketplace means addressing the very real advertising and marketing question of how to reach the gay and lesbian markets. Thinking through this basic business decision carries with it some of the same questions companies had 20 years ago as they started to approach minority markets. First, does it make marketing sense to target the gay and lesbian markets specifically, or can they be reached through the general media? Research shows that gays and lesbians want to feel accepted, suggesting that honest appeals and depictions of the gay and lesbian lifestyles can be effective.

The second consideration is one of risk on the part of the advertiser. Acceptance of alternative lifestyles is increasing, but research by Yankelovich shows some reluctance remains in the general population toward homosexuals. However, it may be the very fact that a company is willing to take this risk that can win over gays and lesbians.

It appears that gay men are more likely to reveal their sexual orientation than are lesbians, but this may be changing. The lesbian lifestyle has been addressed on TV shows such as "Friends" and "Ellen," and more mainstream movies have focused specifically on romantic relationships among women.

Some believe that marketing to gays and lesbians is simply a business decision. However, the exact numbers of gays and lesbians is not known, and only now are we starting to learn more about their activities, interests, and opinions through syndicated data. Some advertisers have used nontraditional media such as event sponsorships and the World Wide Web, where anonymity or the comfort of being among like people has made receptivity to appeals more likely. Right now, promoting products and services to this market is done more by hunch than science.

As the social taboos associated with the homosexual lifestyle continue to lift and customizing of products and marketing communications become more prevalent, expect to see more advertising and media aimed at this potentially lucrative market.

Source: Cyndee Miller, "'The Ultimate Taboo' Slowly but Surely, Companies Overcome Reluctance to Target the Lesbian Market," *Marketing News,* 14 August 1995, 1, 18.

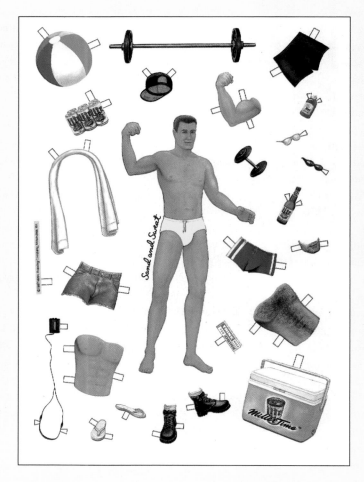

movies of the 1940s. Today, smoking in a movie is more likely to be associated with undesirable or low-class characters. You likely are more health conscious than your parents and grandparents because there has been a cultural shift toward the value of healthy lifestyles. As a result, a huge industry built around products such as vitamins, health foods, exercise equipment, and athletic gear has arisen to meet the needs created by this cultural change.

Within cultures there are smaller social groups based on age, race, ethnicity, gender, religion, geographic region, language, and lifestyles. These groups are called subcultures. A **subculture** is distinguished from a larger culture of which it is a part by having beliefs, values, and customs that are unique to it.

A culture, then, has two components: (1) a set of core beliefs, values, and customs common to all members of a society; and (2) unique beliefs, values, and customs shared by members of specific subcultures. A simple look at regional differences in the United States (a culture) illustrates how subcultures fit within the dominant culture that makes us Americans. For example, there are unique customs in the South that are quite different from those in the North. Thus, while fried green tomatoes, blue grass music, and grits are indigenous to the South, Italian food and rap music are characteristically northern. However, although there are subcultural differences, northerners and southerners share American cultural values concerning equality, opportunity, freedom, and the importance of world peace.

It is important to remember that culture guides behavior because it has been determined over time that certain behaviors are more beneficial to individuals and society than are others. Visiting another culture is a good way to observe differences in how behavior can be molded because you can observe behaviors different from those that you normally see in your own culture. Americans, for example, are seen as being obsessed with personal hygiene, while some other cultures value household cleanliness more. Also, the success of McDonald's in the U.S. is, to some degree, related to our acceptance of the appropriateness of eating beef. Beef cannot be sold in cultures where cows are considered sacred and are not to be eaten, as is the case in India.

A key aspect of culture is that it is both enduring and dynamic. The very survival of a society requires that its beliefs, values, and customs endure. At the same time, societies have to adjust to change or they will die. Notice how the United States has evolved within the last 40 years—its population has become more diverse, women's roles have changed, technology has become more and more sophisticated, and more people have a college education than ever before. These changes require adjustments in our beliefs and values. This is very important for marketers because products, services, and marketing communications have to change to meet new needs and desires reflected in changes at the cultural level. As an example, see how Exhibit 6–21, an ad for New Balance running shoes, reflects

EXHIBIT 6–21 In order to correctly position and effectively promote their products, advertisers must speak with a modern voice—one that reflects current societal views and trends. Note, for example, how New Balance adds power and focus to this product message by communicating a modern view on the roles of women in our society.

You can run to become a better runner.
Or you can run to become a better mother.
Or a better doctor. Or a better teacher. Or a better friend.
You can run to become a better runner.
Or you can run to become better.

Achieve New Balance.

new balance®

The 851, our newest most advanced running shoe, available in multiple widths. For a dealer call 1-800-253-SHOE or visit www.newbalance.com

women's changing roles and the corresponding growth of women's sports.

The growth and expansion of global markets has made culture a very important variable in many companies' marketing plans. As we learned in Chapter Four, a major strategic decision for multinational companies is to what degree can they standardize their marketing communications and save on valuable resources versus customizing messages to every different cultural market. Some products have universal appeal because the product is basic, such as Coca-Cola. Products like blue jeans provide an opportunity for standardization because they appeal to subcultures like teenagers whose interests and desires often cut across national boundaries. Other products, however, require sensitivity to cultural differences. Walt Disney Co., for example, found it more difficult to export its Disney World concept to Europe than it expected because some people in other cultures consider Disney to be the ultimate symbol of the "domineering" United States culture.

Cultural and subcultural variables are becoming more and more important to advertisers and marketers as they work hard to understand what their brands mean to consumers. It is difficult enough to manage your marketing communications programs within your own culture. Advertising and marketing to a different culture require real understanding of how your products will be received, as described in "Around the Globe: Cultural Problems and Opportunities."

R E S E T

1. What types of influences do households provide and how do they affect consumers' purchase decisions?
2. In what three ways can reference groups influence our behavior?
3. Think of a subculture to which you belong. How do the beliefs, values, and customs of this group distinguish it from mainstream American culture?

AROUND THE GLOBE

....

Cultural Problems and Opportunities

As political and economic barriers continue to tumble around the world, more and more companies are looking for marketing opportunities in foreign countries. But along with these new opportunities come some problems that have made more than one company proceed with caution.

Cultural barriers are among the most difficult to overcome once markets open up economically and politically. Consider BMW's launch of its new Series 7 in Europe. The new European Union was supposed to make Europe one market; however, when BMW tried to market the new line of cars with one ad campaign, consumers in other countries resisted. Why? Because the ads showed the car with German license plates.

Cultural resistance is a big problem in many countries. Marketing and advertising efforts on the part of highly developed countries in lesser-developed countries can be viewed as cultural imperialism. Many of these countries also feel that Western nations do not take them seriously and dump inferior products on them.

Standardization or globalization of marketing and advertising efforts still may be a dream. The term "glocalization" has been coined to describe the fact that successful marketing requires a global brand that is backed by

Situational Variables

We all like to think that we control our environment and the decisions we make. In reality, however, environmental factors that are in force at a specific time or in a particular place can have a substantial influence on how we behave and what we buy. Consider, for example, the physical surroundings when you go shopping. Think about the importance of store location, parking, the interior decor of a store, lighting, where and how merchandise is organized, and store cleanliness. Do these factors affect where you shop? Sometimes they do and sometimes they do not. But when they do, these physical characteristics of your shopping environment make a difference.

Think about your social surroundings when you make a purchase. If you are with friends, do they influence what you buy? Does sales help make a difference in your decision-making process? Time constraints can also influence your purchase behavior. The time of day, the day itself, or the month of the year can be a factor in how you shop. Other situational factors such as your mood or financial status at the time of purchase can come into play, as well. Here we will examine the effects of several types of situational influence: purchase situations, consumption situations, time, and communication situations.

Purchase Situations

The purchase situation is extremely important. Store environment plays a very big part in purchase behavior. Stores must be aware of how they present prices and the colors they use in their decor. The presence or absence of help also can impact sales. In fact, stores that used to rely entirely on self-service to offer customers lower prices are reinstituting some sales help as the retail environment becomes more competitive. Where products are placed within a store and at what height make such a difference in sales that manufacturers pay for prime spaces and locations. Notice, for example, how

local advertising and marketing efforts. McDonald's realization that it could not sell hamburgers in its restaurants in India because cows are sacred there has been used as an example of a global brand going local. Instead, McDonald's developed the Maharaja Mac with two all-mutton patties, special sauce, lettuce, cheese, pickles . . . you can finish the jingle!

Other cultural realities include product and brand piracy as well as the stealing of intellectual property. In the U.S. we consider these things to be forms of corruption if not outright violations of the law. It is common, however, to see counterfeit and pirated versions of products on the market in Pacific Rim countries. Often the packaging looks exactly like the legitimate product except for, say, the substitution of a letter in the brand name to confuse consumers who don't speak English. Counterfeiting is a major obstacle to firms that spend a lot of time on research and development only to have their products copied in six months or less.

There appears to be some trepidation on the part of marketers and the countries in which they market to the whole notion of international marketing. Yet opportunities may be lost if companies are not willing to try to understand and overcome political, economic, and cultural barriers. South America and the southeastern corner of Asia are becoming prime overseas markets. They offer large numbers of consumers and growing economies with rising disposable incomes. Some industries that are finding growth flat in the United States have looked to these new markets for a large part of their business. Abbott Labs, for example, generates 60 percent of its sales from its Asian and South American markets. The opportunities are there, but so are the problems.

Source: Cyndee Miller, "Chasing the Global Dream," *Marketing News*, 2 December 1996, 1–2.

children's cereals are located on the lower shelves to reach children at their eye level. Point-of-purchase displays also can make a difference. The easier they are for consumers to use and the better the location in a store, the bigger the influence on sales.

A single important change or addition to the shopping environment can increase sales significantly. One of the most interesting changes in supermarket marketing has been the installation of machines to automatically deduct grocery expenses from a checking account through the use of a debit card. Not only is this a convenience, but it can lead to more sales too. In direct mail advertising, a pen or pencil may be sent with an offer so the consumer doesn't have to look for one before completing an order. If the pencil increases orders by 1/2–1 percent, the extra profit will probably cover the cost of the pencil, and more.

Stores have capitalized on consumer behavior in the purchase situation in different ways. Grocery store managers know that consumers spend a considerable amount of time walking through the aisles, so they use displays to remind consumers of what is available and on sale. Drug store managers know that consumers arrive at the store with a list of products they intend to buy quickly. While drug stores still use displays to sell impulse items, the organization of store displays must assist the consumer in making speedy decisions. According to the Point-of-Purchase Advertising Institute (POPAI), almost three-quarters of all brand selection decisions are made within the store.

Consumption Situations

Consumption situations are those circumstances, places, or settings in which we actually use a product or service. For example, there are important differences between eating a meal in a candlelit restaurant versus at a busy fast-food outlet. If we're in the restaurant, the presence of a special friend may lead to a different product choice than we would usually make. In the fast-food outlet, our decisions may be habitual. Likewise, how we use durable goods such as refrigerators, cars, and stereos may determine how often we replace them. And when we know a product will be consumed in private, we may select a less-expensive brand or an unbranded product to fulfill our needs.

One major change in the consumption situation in restaurants has been the division of dining areas into smoking and nonsmoking sections. This separation of smokers and nonsmokers influences the whole dining experience. Often, smokers who dine with nonsmokers are prevented from lighting up. This alters their level of satisfaction when dining out. The experience, good or bad, may affect a smoker's decision about where to dine the next time he or she goes out.

Consumer behavior is dynamic, and what happens at any particular stage of buying and consuming a product is information that is processed and integrated into one's attitudes and beliefs for use the next time a decision has to be made. Thus, the consumption environment becomes very important to a consumer's experience with a product or service.

Time

Time is an important variable when it comes to making purchase decisions. Time can be thought of in several ways, including the seasonality of sales for particular types of products. Soft drinks sell better in the summer, toys are a hot item around the Christmas season, and cars and houses typically are in high demand in the spring.

Time sometimes can be a restraint on decision making. We have all felt the panic brought on by the car battery going dead, the TV set breaking, or the shower drain clogging up. Emergency purchase situations often restrict our ability to search for information and compare alternatives. Sometimes time pressure can prevent us from making a purchase that we normally would like to consider at greater length. At other times, time pressure may cause us to change our mode of purchase; as shown in Exhibit 6–22, mail order advertisers often try to capitalize on the time crunch that consumers feel by emphasizing the convenient and time-saving nature of their offers.

Time of day can have an important influence on consumer behavior, too. Fast-food restaurants find that they do better at lunch time than they do during the dinner hour. People have more time at the end of the day and either eat at home or in a more leisurely environment; breakfast and lunch hours, on the other hand, are times when people have to eat quickly, so speed is more important.

Communication Situations

Communication situations are of two types, personal and nonpersonal. *Personal communication situations* are characterized by face-to-face contact in which a person's credibility adds or subtracts from the impact of the information being conveyed. Friends and family can influence a purchase through word-of-mouth communication that can carry the added weight of your relationship with them. We implicitly trust some family members and friends and do not trust others. How much weight we give to word-of-mouth communication depends on our experiences with the various sources of that information. However, word-of-mouth communication typically is considered to be more credible than nonpersonal forms of communication.

Nonpersonal communication situations include all forms of marketing communications as well as other mediated communication such as news and entertainment found on the Internet, television, radio, or in print media. Nonpersonal communication lacks the face-to-face interaction and feedback dimension of personal communication. Nonpersonal communication in the form of advertising is influenced by the environment in which the medium that carries it is received as well as the actual vehicle (i.e., TV show, news article, radio program) in which it is placed.

The environment or setting for exposure to a medium is divided into at-home and out-of-home situations. Most people are more relaxed at home, and thus the home is considered to be a more receptive environment for advertising. It also is at home that interruptions can occur and the viewer has more control over exposure to ads. Viewers at home can get up and leave the room or ignore commercials by doing something else when they are on.

There are interesting out-of-home settings that advertisers have tried to use to their advantage. Doctors' offices, airline terminals, the cabins of planes, and movie theaters are unique environments because the audience is captive. In-flight magazines have become very successful because they can deliver relatively affluent audiences to advertisers. And don't forget that you also can be a good audience for advertisers when you are driving your car. One advertising professional once argued for the effectiveness of radio by saying that at 60 miles per hour you cannot leave the room!

A TV or radio program, magazine or newspaper, or outdoor board's surroundings are environments that also have an impact on advertising. Advertisers should be aware of how a program influences the reception of advertising it carries and the impact of an ad's position. We have known for a long time that viewers are harder to catch between programs than within them. Thus, ads run during programs have larger audiences. Similarly, ads placed in the very front or on the back cover of magazines have a better chance of being seen than ads placed in the interior. Newspaper ads that run above the fold of full-size newspapers get more reader attention than those below.

EXHIBIT 6–22 As the pace of modern society continues to increase, so does the impact of time on the purchasing behaviors of consumers and, as the headline in this ad for the Cosmetique Beauty Club illustrates, the efforts of advertisers to capitalize on this factor in their selling messages.

Consumers As Decision Makers

Over the years, many descriptions of consumers as decision makers have been developed by consumer researchers. Understanding consumer decision making helps advertisers provide the most persuasive information at the most appropriate time in the decision-making process. Studying consumer decision making can lead to insights that result in more effective messages. Target audiences can be expanded to include influential individuals. Market segments can be selected to match the attributes of the product to the specific needs of the market segment.

For our discussion we'll use a description of consumer decision makers as problem-solvers, as shown in the diagram in Exhibit 6–23.[34] At the top of the illustration are the three types of influence we've examined so far: individual characteristics, social influences, and situational variables. Each of these factors influences the consumer's awareness of a need or want [1]. For our illustration, consider a jogger who is trying to make a decision about new running shoes.

Our jogger runs five miles every other day and does not compete in races. There may be several reasons she could realize a need for new shoes: the old shoes could be wearing thin on the bottom, new shoe technology may fascinate her, or she may want to purchase a second pair of shoes because running magazines have advocated rotating two pairs of shoes for jogging. Any of these reasons could be sufficient for her to consider new shoes. But let's add a new situational influence: Suppose the maker of her present brand of shoes has discontinued the model she wears.

Once she—or any consumer—is aware of a need or want, there are two choices. First, an automatic or routinized response can be selected [2]. For most routinized responses, the consumer selects the previous brand. In our example, however, the running shoe manufacturer has removed this option by discontinuing her model of shoe. Another routinized response that is possible is to select any brand. Consumers who have little interest or involvement in a product class may use routinized responses to save time.

Consumers also have the option of choosing not to make a routinized response. In this case, once she decides that she must acquire more information, then an information search begins [3]. Depending upon the importance of the decision, she may consult friends, dealers, magazine articles, or advertisements to learn about possible product choices. Suppose our jogger consults four sources: *Runner's World* magazine, a mail order catalog for *Road Runner Sports,* advertisements for Asics and New Balance running shoes, and a retail clerk at the nearest athletic shoe store.

After she is satisfied that she has acquired sufficient information, she must make sense out of the information. At this point, she sets criteria for the decision and evaluates the alternative solutions [4]. The jogger may have decided that the new pair of shoes must come in width sizing to accommodate a wide foot, must have extra cushioning in the heel because she is a heel striker, must cost under $100, and must not be ugly. If she cannot find a shoe model that meets her criteria, then the decision may be postponed [7] until a suitable shoe can be found. Suppose, though, that our jogger has identified four shoe models during the evaluation process: two Asics models, one Nike model, and one New Balance model. From this set of alternative solutions to the problem of replacing shoes, she decides to purchase one of the alternatives [5].

Once a decision has been made, she must decide where to purchase the product. There are many alternatives. Retail advertising and mail order catalogs may influence the jogger's decision about where to purchase the new shoes. Suppose she purchases the new model of shoes at an athletic shoe store [6]. After the purchase, she evaluates her choice [8] using this information to modify her next decision about products—in this case, running shoes.

EXHIBIT 6–23   McCarthy and Perreault's Problem-Solving Model

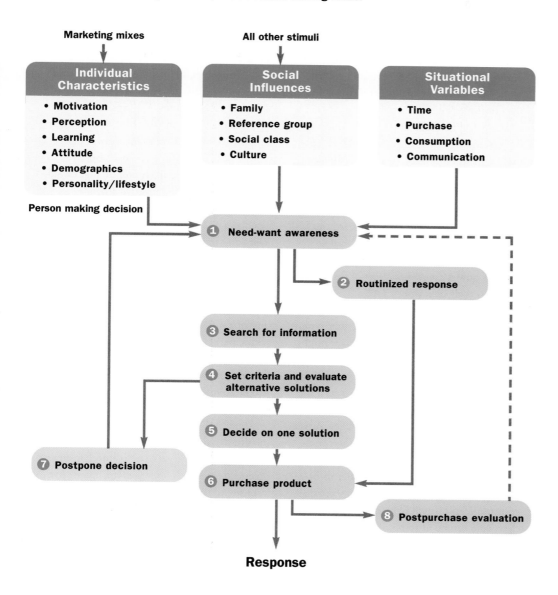

Source: William D. Perreault, Jr. and E. Jerome McCarthy, *Basic Marketing,* 12th ed. (Chicago, IL: Richard D. Irwin, 1996), 184.

An understanding and appreciation of the consumer's viewpoint in the advertising and marketing process is as important as the advertising and marketing skills and expertise one brings to a business problem. Ultimately, it is the consumer who decides to buy or not buy a product. The reasons underlying the purchase decision are critical to the success of any marketing communications venture. Understanding your customer often leads to insights that would be overlooked without a strong belief in the value of the consumer's viewpoint.

Knowing your customer well requires an understanding of the individual, social, cultural, and situational factors that influence purchase decisions. The study of motivation encompasses determining the factors, such as people's needs and desires, that arouse, maintain, and direct their behavior toward the accomplishment of personal goals. Maslow's hierarchy of needs has had significant influence on how we view the effect of people's needs on their behavior.

Selecting, organizing, and interpreting information and images from our environment so that we can assess how alternatives might meet our goals is called perception. Consumers are highly selective in choosing, organizing, and interpreting stimuli because the information environment is very cluttered with competing messages and images. Advertisers and marketers try to make their messages stand out from the environment and appeal to consumers' needs in order to increase the probability that their marketing communications will be perceived the way they were intended to be received.

Most of our consumer-related behavior has been learned. Learning is the process by which we acquire knowledge and experience that results in a permanent change of behavior. There are two major theories regarding how people learn: behavioral and cognitive. Behavioral theorists believe that the only appropriate thing to study is the observable and measurable responses of people to stimuli. Cognitive theorists view behaviorism as incomplete and focus more on the mental processes of thinking, memory, and infor-

mation processing. Behavioral theories can further be divided into classical conditioning and instrumental, or operant, conditioning theories. An important contribution of the cognitive approach is the idea that information and knowledge are organized in people's minds into associative networks of concepts.

Information can have a direct influence on a decision through its simple recall and use, or through its integration into an attitude. An attitude is a mental structure that integrates a consumer's feelings, knowledge, and intention toward an object into an overall positive or negative evaluation. A person with a positive attitude toward a brand is thought to be more likely to buy that brand than a person with a negative attitude.

Quantifiable population characteristics such as age, sex, race, marital status, education, and income are called demographics. The science of demography is the study of the structure, distribution, and changes in these population parameters. The demographics of the United States has been changing in a number of ways over the past 50 years, particularly as related to generational influences, population diversity, aging, the increase in working women, and a migration to the southern and western parts of the United States.

The study of consumer lifestyles brings a qualitative richness to our understanding of how products and services fit into consumers' lives. Lifestyle describes the way people live and spend time and money. People's lifestyles are studied and measured using psychographics. Lifestyle and psychographic research can be used to identify market segments based on consumption patterns, attitudes toward products, and people's activities, interests, and opinions. Two of the best known lifestyle segmentation systems have been VALS and VALS2.

Advertisers and marketers are finding that social and cultural influences can be as important, and sometimes more important, than individual characteristics for a lot of purchases. Important social and cultural influences are families or households, reference groups, social class, culture, and subcultures.

The family is the primary social and economic unit that teaches children how to be consumers. The family is dynamic and its needs change as it grows from a small household unit with no children to a larger unit with older children. Its needs continue to change as children leave home and parents return to an empty-nest stage. There are more single-parent, single, and same-sex partnership households than ever before. These family and household units have some different needs from traditional families that marketers are recognizing and trying to serve.

Reference groups are any social group with which people feel some type of identification or affiliation. Consumers use reference groups to guide and define their beliefs, values, and goals. Reference groups can influence behavior by establishing norms or standards for how their members should act. People may try to buy products that express their group affiliation, or seek out purchase-related information from groups and people they identify with and trust.

Social class is the overall ranking of people in society in terms of variables such as social status, occupation, and lifestyle. Our social class membership does have some correlation with how much money we spend on products and services and what types of items we buy.

Culture and subculture are two of the broadest influences on our behavior. Culture is the shared beliefs, values, and customs we learn so that we can interact in our social system. A subculture is distinguished from the larger culture by having beliefs, values, and customs unique to it. Subcultures are smaller groups within the dominant culture such as religion, region, gender, race, or age. One's culture and subcultures combine to provide each of us with our basic set of values and customs we use to guide our behavior.

Situational variables such as the nature and characteristics of purchase situation, con-

sumption situation, time, and communication situation present very tangible factors that can influence the products and brands we buy. Characteristics of a purchase situation can have a very real effect on our purchases. Store decor and organization, lighting, package and product displays, nature of sales help, availability of parking, and ease of payment can all have an influence on where we shop and what we buy. The circumstances under which we use or consume a product can alter our satisfaction with the experience. Consuming a product at home or in public can affect the brand we buy. Using a product alone or in a group can have a similar effect.

Time can be a restraint on our decision-making ability. Other dimensions of time such as season of the year or time of day can influence the type and quantity of products purchased. The nature of communication and the setting in which it is received influence the effect of messages. Personal communication is considered more credible and effective than nonpersonal communication. Mass-media advertising is nonpersonal communication and can be affected by the environment that surrounds it. The home is thought to be a better environment for receiving advertising messages. There are some interesting out-of-home settings, too, such as in an airplane, where in-flight magazines and videos can reach a captive audience. The environment within a medium and the placement of an ad can have an impact on the message's effectiveness. Location of an outdoor board and placement within a magazine, TV, or radio program should be planned to maximize the effect of the medium on receptivity to an ad.

The individual, social, and environmental variables that influence consumer behavior can be viewed in terms of McCarthy and Perreault's consumer decision-making model. This model illustrates how consumer decisions are made to solve problems. The decision-making process can range from routine, taking little time, to complex decisions that involve extended search processes.

REVIEW QUESTIONS

1. Why is understanding the consumer's individual characteristics important to planning and developing effective advertising and marketing communications programs?

2. How can consumer motivation influence the types of products or services people buy?

3. What is perception? How does it affect consumer behavior?

4. What are the differences between behavioral learning theories and cognitive learning theories?

5. What purpose does an attitude about a product, service, or brand serve for a consumer?

6. Describe four major demographic trends in the United States and what they mean for advertisers and marketers.

7. How are VALS, VALS2, and other lifestyle segmentation techniques used?

8. What types of social and cultural influences affect consumer purchasing decisions, and how?

9. What are the situational variables that affect purchase decisions?

10. Describe the consumer decision-making process. Why is it important to understand this process?

DISCUSSION QUESTIONS

1. Some advertising practitioners believe that advertising is really a game of perceptions. Demonstrate your understanding of consumer perceptual processes by explaining what these practitioners mean.

2. Find and describe an existing advertising or marketing communications campaign that makes a strong appeal to some basic and enduring American cultural values and beliefs.

3. Provide an example of a purchase you have made recently and describe how it both followed and deviated from the process described in Exhibit 6–23.

1. Search through two or three magazines and tear out examples of ads that demonstrate appeals to each of the types of needs identified in Maslow's hierarchy of needs. Select at least one ad for each type of need in the hierarchy and indicate whether or not you believe the appeals are relevant to the brands being advertised.

2. Using the same magazines, find ads that reflect the three different generations identified by Yankelovich. Describe the specific components of each ad that convince you it is appealing to either Matures, Boomers, or Xers.

Chapter Seven

Strategic and Evaluative Advertising Research

HARLEY FUELS ITS ENGINE WITH MARKET RESEARCH

When Harley-Davidson needed to make some tough strategic decisions about how to promote its motorcycles as the market for heavyweight bikes was shrinking in the 1980s, it turned to research.

Harley felt confident that it could hold its core customer, the traditional biker, regardless of where the market was heading. It had been successful in attracting white-collar motorcycle enthusiasts to its brand in the 1980s, but it was concerned about whether or not these "rubbies" (rich urban bikers) would stay with them or move on should another fad or fashion replace biking. The company needed to know if it could find a more universal thread to the appeal of its bikes in order to reach other markets.

Harley started its research program with a series of focus groups made up of current owners, Harley prospects, and competitors' customers. The focus groups were asked to make collages that expressed their feelings toward Harley-Davidson. The themes of enjoyment, the outdoors, and freedom emerged from the groups. Next the company's marketers sent a psychological inventory of questions to 16,000 motorcycle owners. The responses to the survey enabled Harley to identify seven customer types: adventure-loving traditionalists, sensitive pragmatists, stylish status seekers, laid-back campers, classy capitalists, cool-headed loners, and cocky misfits. The universal appeals Harley was looking for also fell out of

Just released. The Harley-Davidson Bad Boy.

Standing there, blinking in the sunlight. Chrome on black. Springer® front end. Ready to run at last on the open road. The Softail® Bad Boy.™ Call 1-800-443-2153 for a dealer near you. Let's talk freedom.

The Legend Rolls On™

the data: Independence, freedom, and power were the attributes that attracted Harley's customers to its bikes. The survey also indicated a high degree of brand loyalty for Harley-Davidson.

The research findings gave Harley the confidence it needed to expand its marketing efforts. By 1996 sales had grown to 105,000, from only 30,000 in 1985. Harley still has a waiting list for its bikes.

Source: Ian P. Murphy, "Aided by Research, Harley Goes Whole Hog," Marketing News 30, no. 25 (2 December 1996): 16–17.

LOOK BEFORE YOU LEAP

- What are marketing and advertising research and why are they important in the planning of advertising and marketing communications campaigns?

- How do advertisers determine whether research should be done?

- What types of research questions can be asked, and when?

- What are the characteristics of each type of research design?

- How are research data collected?

- How are research results analyzed?

- What is strategic advertising research and how is it conducted?

- What is evaluative advertising research and how is it conducted?

7

Research And The Advertising Planning Process

The Harley-Davidson example demonstrates a variety of roles for marketing and advertising research. One role for marketing research is to determine what consumers think and feel about a product, service, or brand. Marketing research also is used to help segment the market into more understandable and identifiable groupings. The large-scale survey conducted by Harley-Davidson accomplished both of these goals.

Once the foundation of information and analysis has been built, **strategic research** can be performed to aid in the development of an advertising or marketing communications program. After an advertising message has been delivered, **evaluative advertising research** can be conducted to assess the effectiveness of specific messages or delivery methods used in a campaign. This chapter will introduce you to marketing research and strategic and evaluative advertising research. It will take you through the key decisions on which research can be brought to bear. It will then discuss the types of research and techniques used to plan, develop, and evaluate advertising and marketing communications campaigns.

When implemented properly, the advertising planning process is continuous and dynamic. After an advertising campaign has been planned, created, and delivered, information gathered in the evaluation phase is used to plan the next campaign. This means information from the first campaign's evaluative research becomes strategic research for the next. The transformation from evaluative information to strategic information further illustrates two important principles: 1) the types of advertising research discussed here are distinguished only by when they occur in the advertising process, and 2) because all types of advertising research use scientific procedures and methods, there are no differences in the procedures and methods used to acquire strategic or evaluative information. While the methods strategic or evaluative research employ are similar, however, there are differences in the types of questions that are asked during each phase of the advertising process.

Exhibit 7–1 outlines the advertising and marketing communications planning processes and lists several common types of research. **Marketing research** is a broad term that refers to the systematic acquisition, development, and analysis of new information used for marketing, advertising, or marketing communications decisions. Because marketing research stretches across a wide domain of marketing problems—from product development to distribution—it includes strategic and evaluative advertising research as subsets. **Advertising research** can be differentiated from marketing research because it is research activity that is performed in support of the planning, development, placement, or monitoring of ads. Before we delve into the research and planning process in detail, we need to take a quick look at each type of research—marketing, strategic advertising, and evaluative advertising—in order to define several key terms and concepts.

Marketing Research

Marketing research's primary contribution to the advertising planning process is in building a foundation of information and understanding of the market situation. Marketing research, which for our purposes can also be called the *situation analysis*, can be broken down into four key areas: product research, consumer research, market research, and competitive analysis research. A situation analysis answers the question, What is the current marketing situation today, relative to the product we are trying to advertise? Marketing research may be totally or partially completed before advertising planning begins. For this reason, these research types are listed as marketing research inputs in Exhibit 7–1.

Typically, the first type of research input into the situation analysis is product research. **Product research** attempts to find answers to questions about the product, such as Which formulation of our new soft drink is favored by consumers? or How important is an automatic sorter to purchasers of our new mail machine? Product research questions often are stated relative to the target market segment or consumers. For example, Procter & Gamble has spent over $200 million to develop and test the fat substitute olestra, which is an ingredient in potato chips and crackers, in order to counter consumers' beliefs that it will make them sick to their stomachs.[1]

Next, **consumer research** asks questions about individuals in the target market, or consumers in general. Consumer research often tries to examine consumer attitudes or motivations toward a product purchase. Questions asked in consumer research might include, What types of consumers purchase electric lawn mowers? or Why do consumers buy packaged soft chocolate chip cookies instead of less-expensive bulk cookies in the supermarket? Consumer research can lead to the repositioning of a product based on consumer usage patterns and attitudes. Beecham of Great Britain repositioned its Lucozade sparkling glucose drink away from the convalescent market and toward healthy consumers looking for heightened physical performance when it found out through consumer research that only 20 percent of usage was by those recuperating from illness.[2]

When individuals are studied as a purchasing group or market segment, the research is called **market research** (as distinct from marketing research). Market research may also

EXHIBIT 7–1   Marketing Research and the Advertising Planning Process

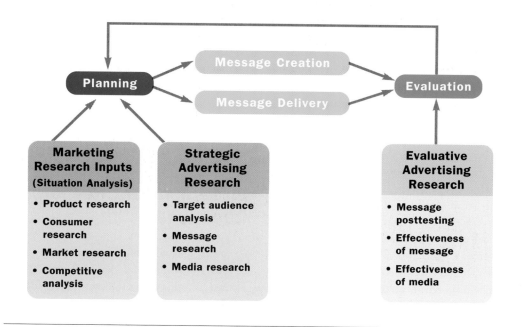

compare the profitability of market segments, analyze the total market based on known market segments, or attempt to find new segments in a market. Market research questions might include, Is there a way to define the market that would give us an advantage over major competitors? or Where is the best potential market for a product or brand? Dell and Gateway conducted market research and discovered the mail-order computer market. By not competing with retail outlets, they have quickly garnered a significant share of the total market.

Finally, in any market, it is important to know what competitors are doing to promote their products. **Competitive analysis,** also known as *competitive research,* attempts to analyze the marketing and advertising strategies of competitors by tracking their advertising and promotion activity. Competitive research answers questions such as, How much do our competitors spend on advertising and marketing communications? In what media do our competitors advertise? What types of promotions do our competitors use? A lot of the initial interest by advertisers in the Internet as an advertising and marketing communications vehicle was based more on competitive activity than on its effectiveness as a marketing tool.

Strategic Advertising Research

Three types of strategic advertising research are usually important for the advertising planner. **Target audience analysis** attempts to identify the target audience, describe its characteristics, and examine the audience's consumption and media habits. A researcher investigating the target audience might ask, Who is the target audience? or How does the target audience learn about a product category? **Message research** examines characteristics of the advertising message and its impact on target audience members before it is run in the media. Sample message research questions might include, Which message has the most effect upon consumer recall of the brand name?, Which sales point has the largest effect upon the target audience's preference for a brand?, or What illustration or visualization is most memorable to the target audience?

The third type of strategic advertising research is **media audience research,** which finds media audiences that match the characteristics

of the advertiser's target audience by investigating the ability of the media under consideration to reach the target audience. Questions from a media researcher may include, How much of our target audience is included in this magazine's readership? or What combination of media vehicles will reach the largest portion of our target audience? Sometimes budget questions relating to how much media weight to use can be an important part of media research.

Evaluative Advertising Research

Evaluation of advertising may include an assessment of the impact of single advertisements, called **message posttesting,** or a comparison of overall campaign results to the objectives of the advertising campaign. By examining the impact of advertising messages on the target audience, an advertiser can determine whether the message had the intended effect or not. Evaluation of the communication effect on the target audience is a test of **message effectiveness,** even though a faulty media plan can also reduce the effect of the message. **Media effectiveness** can be assessed by comparing the actual media placement to the original media plan. In addition, the effectiveness of specific media can be compared to see if one is better at persuading the target audience.

R E S E T

1. Describe some of the different roles for marketing and advertising research.
2. Is the research process linear or dynamic? Explain.
3. How can marketing and advertising research be differentiated?

Five Important Research Questions

For years, the owner of the corner grocery store or drug store found out what customers wanted from his or her business by walking through the aisles and talking to customers. By listening carefully to the compliments and complaints, the owner could shape the business to increase sales and improve the attitudes of customers toward the store. Small store owners who listened carefully and understood were able to flourish; those who didn't listen, or who failed to understand consumer needs, disappeared. In truth, the "facts" obtained by the small store owner are no different from the facts discovered by advanced marketing research methods today. The only difference is that the small business owner could get by with informal research procedures because he or she was closer to the customers and could see them on a more regular basis. In contrast, large and medium-size firms are more removed from their customer bases, making regular contact impossible. Add to this distance and contact problem the high cost of failure and you have a good reason to consider creating a more systematic approach to gathering information on the marketplace.

Few firms have the resources, however, to afford or require a systematic research effort such as that outlined in Exhibit 7–1 every time they embark on a new advertising or marketing communications program. Most firms have to do some real soul searching before they take on a research project. In this regard, Exhibit 7–2 describes a sequence of five research questions that will be made by advertisers, advertising planners, or researchers whenever they are considering an advertising or marketing research project. The answers to these questions determine which research procedures will be used. Because the decisions are sequential, the answer to each question influences decisions that follow. The five questions, each of which is discussed in detail below, are as follows:

1. Should research be done?
2. What is the research question and objective?
3. What research design will provide the best answers to the research question asked?
4. What data collection methods will be used for the selected research design?
5. What conclusions can be reached from analysis of the research data?

Should Research Be Done?

To answer the question, Should research be done? actually requires that another question be answered first: What is the purpose of the research project? Because the purpose of a study has its origin in a management problem, researchers often have to be able to take poorly articulated management problems and identify the true purpose of a project. For example, suppose the city council of a small city near a university is concerned that local residents do not appear to be patronizing local merchants in the city. The council decides to survey residents about why they don't shop in town to provide a basis for a marketing communications campaign to promote the local merchants' businesses. However, while the research project is being designed, it is discovered that the local merchants' committee is not in favor of a special marketing communications program for this purpose. Now the problem has an additional dimension to it that might have to be included in the research project. If the project is to go forward, merchants might have to be interviewed also. This changes the purpose, design, and affordability of the research project.

Once the purpose of a proposed study is known, managers considering the decision to begin a research project should ask themselves two additional questions: Can we afford the cost of research? and Does the information

EXHIBIT 7–2   Research Decisions

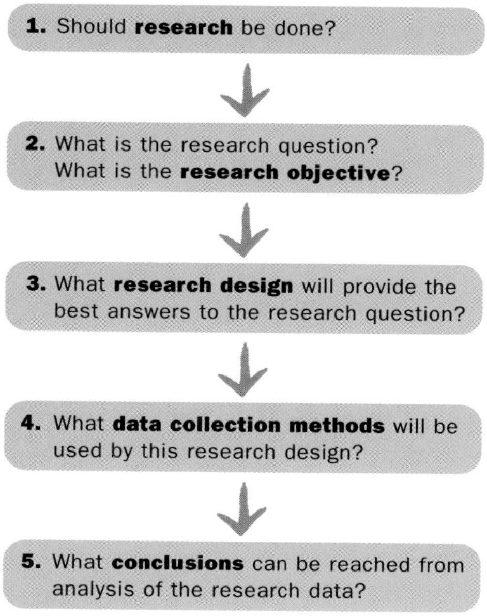

1. Should **research** be done?

2. What is the research question? What is the **research objective**?

3. What **research design** will provide the best answers to the research question?

4. What **data collection methods** will be used by this research design?

5. What **conclusions** can be reached from analysis of the research data?

we're looking for already exist? In answer to the first question, the affordability of research is connected to the cost of the proposed campaign. A research project costing only $500–$1,500 is probably too expensive if the answer will be used to decide the future of a $2,000 advertising campaign (the research costs would make up 25–75 percent of the advertising budget). On the other hand, a $100,000 expenditure on research may be justifiable and affordable if it will increase the effectiveness of several multimillion dollar campaigns. Marketing researchers often use mathematical formulas to estimate the value of research information. These formulas compare the cost of success to the cost of failure.[3]

As for the second question, the advertising or marketing manager has to determine whether the necessary information exists or not. There are two types of information: primary data and secondary data.

SECONDARY DATA Existing information or data is called **secondary data.** If the secondary data exist within the advertiser's organization, they are known as **internal data.** Shipping and billing information, customer account records, sales volume statistics, and past studies of advertising effectiveness are examples of internal data. Information gathered and stored by sources outside of an organization is called **external data.** Examples include media audience studies to which a company subscribes, or large-scale consumer lifestyle studies like the VALS research discussed in Chapter Six. When an advertising researcher systematically searches secondary data, he or she is performing **secondary research.** Improvements in information technology have resulted in dramatic increases in the amount of secondary data available to an advertiser. Some of the most often used sources for secondary marketing information are public library reference collections; government publications, including special U.S. Census services; trade association publications and research reports; online information retrieval systems; publications from marketing and advertising research firms; and Web sites on the Internet. A lot of secondary information is available on CD-ROM, allowing easier access and use than is possible with print documents.

Some large information services, such as Dialog Information Services, Inc., contain over 400 separate databases of information and are available in university libraries. Users typically pay a fee for accessing these fairly costly database services. LEXIS®-NEXIS® is an online service that provides lists of and access to databases such as Claritas' geodemographic service, REZIDE. Exhibit 7–3 shows an ad promoting this service. The editors of *American Demographics* magazine compile a list of "The Best 100 Sources for Marketing Information" every year.

PRIMARY DATA If the information needed by an advertiser is not available in secondary data, then the advertiser may decide that a research project should be initiated to gather primary data. **Primary data** are acquired through original research, also known as **primary research.** As you might imagine, primary research is more costly and time consuming than secondary research because the firm has to undertake the actual gathering of the information, or contract to have it done. An advertiser may contract for original research from a research supplier. This research is called a *proprietary study* because the research is conducted only for the single advertiser. If an advertiser's study is integrated into an ongoing research system such as a national consumer panel to produce results for an individual advertiser or marketer, then the study may also be called a *customized study.* Some research data are gathered continuously and distributed to advertisers by subscription such as the Nielsen Television Index or Simmons Study of Media and Markets. This research is called *syndicated research.* "Technology Watch: The Reality of Virtual Research" discusses the ability researchers now have to conduct primary research online, including the use of virtual reality.

What Is The Research Question And Objective?

There are three basic types of questions an advertising researcher might want to ask in a research project: 1) *explore what and why* questions (exploratory research); 2) *determine what is* questions (descriptive research); or 3) *prove what or why* questions (causal research). The type of question selected will influence the type of research that can be considered and the kind of conclusions that can be made as a result of the research.

EXPLORE WHAT AND WHY QUESTIONS: EXPLORATORY RESEARCH

Explore what and why questions are used when the advertiser has little or no existing information about a research problem or a potential problem. The key term here is the word *explore.* Explore means to make an initial inquiry into what the situation is like or why it is the way it is. For example, suppose the advertising and marketing people at Corona wanted to see if the message approach used in advertisements for Corona Extra Beer in Tokyo would work with American target audiences. The explore what and why research question might be, *What* do American beer drinkers think about the Japanese Corona Beer ads and *why* do they feel the way they do? Answers to this dual question from several members of the target audience could provide information about the interest created or the dangers of using similar messages in the U.S.

Research using explore what and why questions is called exploratory research. **Exploratory research** is an initial attempt to provide insights into a research problem on a small scale and at minimal cost. Because most exploratory research uses small numbers of research participants and informal environments, the results are suggestive only; advertisers cannot draw reliable conclusions from exploratory research. But the research does allow the advertiser to gather information that can highlight research questions to be studied further.

DETERMINE WHAT IS QUESTIONS: DESCRIPTIVE RESEARCH

Determine what is questions are more specific than explore what and why questions. From what is questions, the advertiser can determine what exists in a marketing situation. For example, a retailer may want to know how far his or her customers travel to shop at the store. This could be rewritten into a what is question such as, *What is* the distance customers travel to my store? If the retailer asked customers for several weeks, then a detailed description of the distances could be gathered. What is questions are the focus of **descriptive research,** which tries to describe a marketing or advertising situation. If the research project is extensive and carefully done, the advertiser can be confident that he or she has analyzed the existing situation with some precision. Most consumer surveys are examples of descriptive research in action.

If you got any closer, you'd be living with them.

Claritas REZIDE Database...Now On LEXIS-NEXIS

For a specific geographic region, you'll know how many are married or single. Renting or owning. Blue collar or white collar. You'll get a distribution of their housing type, income, age range, and much more. And you'll get it all – easily – from one single source: Claritas REZIDE, on LEXIS-NEXIS. ■ Claritas REZIDE, the National Encyclopedia of ZIP Code Demographics, profiles every community in the United States served by a ZIP Code. So now it's easier than ever before to plan new store locations...target media schedules...or plan direct mail campaigns. ■ Claritas REZIDE, on LEXIS-NEXIS. The easiest way to get the inside scoop on your target audience. (Without asking them to set an extra place for dinner!)

LEXIS·NEXIS
A member of the Reed Elsevier plc group

For more information on how to access Claritas REZIDE on LEXIS-NEXIS call 1.800.227.4908 or visit our web site at http://www.lexis-nexis.com

LEXIS and NEXIS are registered trademarks of Reed Elsevier Properties Inc., used under license. The INFORMATION ARRAY logo is a trademark of Reed Elsevier Properties Inc., used under license. REZIDE and Claritas are registered trademarks of Claritas Inc. ©1996 LEXIS-NEXIS, a division of Reed Elsevier Inc. All rights reserved.

EXHIBIT 7–3 LEXIS®·NEXIS®, an online service that provides access to information databases such as Claritas REZIDE, is an important source of secondary marketing data for researchers.

TECHNOLOGY WATCH

. . . .

The Reality of Virtual Research

Advances in computer technology have made the gathering, storage, and analysis of vast amounts of information easier and faster. This is fairly obvious. What might not be as obvious is that the most recent advances have opened up different avenues for doing the actual advertising and marketing research. Consider the Internet. Researchers are now doing focus groups and surveys on the Internet. This greatly reduces the cost of research and increases the speed with which a study can be completed. Moreover, responses can be instantly analyzed.

New technology always presents us with trade-offs. We save money and overcome time restraints while opening up the question of how the interaction of people with computers is affecting our results. We might ask ourselves if people change when they are online. This might be more of a problem when we use the Internet for online focus groups. The human interaction we have become accustomed to in live focus groups is lost on the Internet. There is more anonymity online, perhaps influencing how people respond. Some people might be more guarded for fear many others are "listening" in cyberspace. But could the anonymity lead to more honest answers? We don't know at this point.

Another research opportunity presented by computer technology is simulations using virtual reality techniques. Full-scale simulations can put the consumer right into the purchase-related situation you want to test. For example, instead of asking people how they might respond to changes in a McDonald's restaurant, you can show them the changes on a computer, demonstrating menus, shelf displays, and interior design. Once the respondents are involved in the virtual reality simulation, you can ask them what they would do each step along the way. If you were selling stereo systems you could ask a customer to build the system he or she wants right on the computer screen. A store selling sunglasses could scan the customer's picture into the computer and demonstrate how different designs might look on him or her.

It is always expensive to put people into realistic environments to see how they would react. Computer technology provides virtual reality equivalents that get the researcher one step closer to the real thing without spending a lot of money for field research. Computer technology is becoming more and more a part of the design of research projects. Stimuli can be presented on screen, focus and chat groups can yield exploratory information, surveys can be administered, and virtual reality simulations can imitate field research environments. Time and money can be saved by using cyberspace as real space. The major downside is not knowing whether people respond differently online than in real life.

Sources: Margaret Roller, "Virtual Research Exists, but How Real Is It?" *Marketing News* 30, no. 12 (3 June 1996): H32-H33; and Chad Rubel, "Researcher Praises On-line Methodology," *Marketing News* 30, no. 12 (3 June 1996): H18.

PROVE WHAT OR WHY QUESTIONS: CAUSAL RESEARCH Prove what or why questions require research to determine cause and effect relationships between marketing communications activities and consumer responses. In other words, they require more control from the advertising researcher in order to rule out interfering or extraneous factors. By controlling the research environment more carefully, stronger conclusions can be made about the relationship between advertising and marketing activities and the research results. For example, suppose an automotive parts supplier wanted to use a celebrity spokesperson to endorse a line of professional tools. He or she may want to compare the believability of a typical auto mechanic, a sports personality, and a professional race driver. To find out which individual would be a more believable spokesperson, the researcher would have to prepare ads that were identical except for the spokesperson. Target audience members would then rate the believability of the spokesperson in the ad to which he or she was exposed. No target audience member could rate more than one spokesperson because seeing more than one spokesperson could influence how they rated another. Prove what or why questions are asked in causal research. **Causal research** controls interfering factors so a strong conclusion of cause and effect can be determined. Exhibit 7–4 provides several examples of the three types of research questions that advertising researchers might ask.

RESEARCH OBJECTIVES   Once the advertising manager has determined what type of research question needs to be asked, the research objectives can be established. A **research objective** describes the question to be answered, the target audience that will be the focus for the research, and the time frame for the completion of the project. Exhibit 7–5 provides examples of research objectives that have been written to complement the research questions in Exhibit 7–4.

R E S E T

1. Why do we need a systematic approach to research?
2. What sources might you consult for secondary research data?
3. What is a research objective?

EXHIBIT 7–4   Examples of Advertising Research Questions

Exploratory Research Questions (Explore *what* or *why*)

- What role does advertising play in a small business owner's decision to purchase a color copier?
- Why do subscribers to *Better Homes and Gardens* magazine like the publication?

Descriptive Research Questions (Determine *what is*)

- What percent of adults between the ages of 18 and 34 purchase compact disks from mail-order sources?
- What are the relative proportions of heavy, moderate, and light users of public transportation in Northern California?

Causal Research Questions (Prove *what* or *why*)

- Will a coupon or sales promotion premium generate more purchases for a new brand of margarine by women 18–34?
- Which advertising message, a fear appeal or a peer pressure appeal, will result in more recall about AIDS prevention in teenagers?

EXHIBIT 7–5   Examples of Advertising Research Objectives

Exploratory Research Objectives

- To find out what role advertising plays in a small business owner's decision to purchase a color copier.
- To find out why subscribers to *Better Homes and Gardens* magazine like the publication.

Descriptive Research Objectives

- To determine what percent of adults between the ages of 18 and 34 purchase compact disks from mail-order sources.
- To determine the relative proportions of heavy, moderate, and light users of public transportation in Northern California.

Causal Research Objectives

- To determine if a coupon or sales promotion premium will generate more purchases for a new brand of margarine by women 18–34.
- To determine which advertising message, a fear appeal or a peer pressure appeal, will result in more recall about AIDS prevention in teenagers.

What Research Design Will Provide The Best Answers To The Research Question Asked?

A **research design** is a plan for research that guides the collection of data and the methods of analysis that will be performed. The three primary types of research design have already been identified: exploratory, descriptive, and causal. As shown in Exhibit 7–6, each research type has different characteristics in terms of goal of design, flexibility of data collection, representativeness, type of validity, and control of outside variables. Knowing the characteristics and how they impact the research will affect which research type is chosen to answer the research question.

GOAL OF DESIGN   As we have discussed, the goal of exploratory research is to explore what a situation is like and why it is the way it is. A researcher would choose exploratory research, for instance, to get a tentative idea of what the major factors are at work in a situation. Descriptive research describes in more precise fashion what a situation is. This type of research is best suited for when we want to be able to say with some certainty that a particular set of circumstances (such as people's opinions or feelings about a product) do exist in the marketplace. And causal research establishes the nature of cause and effect. A researcher would design this type of research to find out if one variable or set of factors has a direct influence on the observations or measures that follow them.

FLEXIBILITY OF DATA COLLECTION   The level of flexibility in data collection delineates how formal or informal the data collection methods are

used to obtain data must be. Because discovery is the main purpose of exploratory research, a great amount of flexibility is permitted in data collection. For example, an advertising researcher might visit a retail store and conduct a personal interview with a few customers. Or the researcher might use a case study method to analyze how advertising is planned by franchisees. Some research firms, such as Creative Services in Farmington Hills, Michigan, spend hours watching children interact with products and talking with them about brand names. Advertisers using this firm's services hope to find insights into the preferences of children.

Data collection for descriptive research is not flexible because procedures, including sampling and measurement, must be systematic and consistent across all sampling units. Much descriptive research attempts to measure the frequency of behaviors for the target audience. For example, how many target audience members are aware of the brand? How many individuals remembered the sales point in an advertising message? How often do consumers purchase products in the product category? From descriptive research designs, an advertiser can attempt to make accurate estimates about target audience characteristics before and after a campaign.

Causal research requires the same systematic sampling and measurement procedures as descriptive research but adds the requirement that outside influences be controlled. For example, if a researcher wanted to select the most persuasive photograph from four different photographs, he or she would select a group of individuals for the test. Each individual would rate one advertisement. In this experimental setting,

---

EXHIBIT 7–6   Characteristics of Research Designs

	EXPLORATORY	DESCRIPTIVE	CAUSAL
Goal of design	Explore what and why	Describe what exists	Determine cause and effect
Flexibility of data collection	Very flexible	Not flexible	Not flexible
Representativeness	Not representative	Representative	Not representative
Type of validity	Face validity	External validity	Internal validity
Control of outside variables	No control	No control	Strong control

the four different photographs are called *treatments,* experimental terminology for the variable that is being manipulated. To get an unbiased appraisal, the photographs must be randomly distributed to the research participants. **Bias** is systematic distortions or errors in the research setting or data collection method. Causal designs use many controls to eliminate bias.

REPRESENTATIVENESS AND SAMPLING To make accurate estimates of target audience characteristics, the advertising researcher must take precautions so the individuals included in the research study are representative of the entire target audience. Or, if the study intends to investigate a whole geographic region, then participants must be representative of those people living in the region. There are specialized research procedures to control the representativeness of research participants, called sampling.

Sampling is a method of selecting a relatively small number of individuals from a large group and then using information obtained from the small group to make predictions about the large group. In sampling, the large group is called the *population;* the small group is called the *sample.* Research firms often use a photographic representation of sampling to illustrate the concept. In Exhibit 7–7, a photograph is reproduced using different numbers of dots. The more dots selected—that is, the more people selected—the more accurate the photographic representation. There are economical limits to how many people can be sampled for research, however, because the cost of research is proportional to the size of the sample selected.

To illustrate sampling, suppose a national bank wants to know whether or not it should offer a credit card to elderly consumers. The bank wants to determine how many men and women over 65 would be interested in obtaining a credit card with benefits tailored to elderly consumers. Sampling procedures will let the bank find out how much interest there is without asking every elderly person in the country. Even though the U.S. Census doesn't record every person in the U.S., the Census statistics are the population for the bank's sampling task. There are several ways the bank could select a sample for its research. The bank could contract with a research firm, such as Maritz Marketing Research, and have a ran-

dom probability sample drawn from its database. If every person in the population has an equal chance of being selected, then the sample is called a **random probability sample.** This sample would have names distributed approximately like the population of the U.S. If the advertiser wanted to restrict the sample to states or regions where the bank had offices, then the advertiser would ask Maritz for a stratified random sample. A **stratified random sample** divides the population into groups or strata and then selects individuals at random. For a stratified random sample, Maritz would select communities or regions by zip code and then select individuals at random from those areas.

Probability sampling provides excellent samples for descriptive research. Where representativeness is not as important, advertisers often choose to use nonprobability sampling because nonprobability samples are less expensive. In a *nonprobability sample,* not every individual in the population has an equal chance of being selected. Suppose the bank put up signs in its 2,420 branches that said, "If you're over 65, ask us about our new 65+ card." When

EXHIBIT 7–7 These four photographs are used to illustrate the concept of sampling. Note that the fewer the dots, the less clear the overall picture. In other words, the accuracy of your results is directly related to your sample size.

As is evident in this trade ad, Maritz offers a number of different sampling services to researchers.

the bank customer asked about the card, the teller could ask the customer two or three questions about his or her interest. Nonprobability samples can give distorted views of the population. In the bank example, a nonprobability sample such as the one described would only reach present customers. Predictions from the nonprobability sample might not apply to the general population.

Descriptive research designs can provide representative estimates of the target audience's behaviors when strong sampling techniques are used. From a relatively small sample, the advertiser can make accurate estimates of a wide range of behaviors. Because causal research designs try to determine cause and effect, they must attempt to manipulate and control the variables that are being studied. For causal research, the advertising researcher often brings target audience members to an experimental laboratory where outside influences can be controlled; thus, these studies are not always representative of the target audience.

TYPES OF VALIDITY   Researchers use a concept called validity to describe research designs and the social scientific data collection techniques they use. **Validity** means how consistent a research design or data collection technique is with known facts, or how logically consistent the research design or data collection technique is. There are many types of validity. Only three types will be explained here.

Face validity is the most tenuous type of validity. Face validity means that if you look at a research design, a research setting, or a data collection technique, common sense seems to support how well the situation or technique reflects known facts.[4] *External validity* is the degree to which the research results can be generalized to the population, or to the target audience for the advertising researcher. Finally, *internal validity* is the degree to which the research results can prove an unambiguous relationship between two variables of interest to the researcher.[5] Validity is usually discussed in comparative terms. A researcher might say, for example, that descriptive research designs have more external validity than exploratory or causal designs.

For exploratory research designs, face validity is the only type of validity that can be used to describe the setting. The research results cannot be generalized to the population, so external validity is low. Unambiguous relationships cannot be determined; therefore, internal validity is low. Exploratory research such as focus groups are often used because the researchers are willing to sacrifice external and internal validity for what they can save in time and costs. Researchers will try to overcome this problem to some extent by running several focus groups with distinctively different samples of people. Differences in results will then be attributed to the differences in sample characteristics.

Descriptive research usually takes place in settings similar to those to which the researcher wants to project the results (i.e., real life). This means that both the population from which the sample is drawn and the type of conditions that exist when the survey is conducted can be generalized. Because there is no attempt to control any of the outside influences on the results that might exist in the setting, external validity is used to describe it. For causal research, internal validity is used to describe the setting because the researcher is attempting to control anything and everything that is not part of the experiment so that direct cause and effect can be established.

CONTROL OF OUTSIDE VARIABLES **Outside variables** are part of the natural environment, such as the weather, season, size of market, or competitors' promotional efforts. In exploratory research there is no control over outside variables because, by its very nature, this type of research attempts to determine what effect outside variables exert. Descriptive research is concerned less with the influence of outside variables and more with how representative the results are of a population. Thus, the focus in descriptive research is on sampling and the time period in which the data are collected. Causal designs, on the other hand, attempt to control all outside variables in order to determine cause and effect relationships. Tight control extends to data collection techniques in order to avoid bias in the research data. The research setting is also carefully controlled. Participants often are tested in a laboratory setting, but because the research setting is unlike the natural environment, it is difficult to generalize the research results to the target audience. However, causal designs do provide an opportunity for the researcher to find unam-

biguous relationships. Therefore, they are higher in internal validity than exploratory and descriptive research designs.

We should also mention a fourth type of research design, field experiments, that attempts to preserve the advantages of the descriptive and causal designs. **Field experiments** are research designs in which control is exerted over important variables, and data collection takes place in a natural environment. The use of Universal Product Code (UPC) scanner data has improved data collection and resulted in more field experiment research. Field experiments are expensive and are often performed by large advertisers or major research companies, such as Information Resources Inc., and A.C. Nielsen.[6] The research design decision is critical because of its influence on conclusions that can be drawn and the data collection techniques that will be used.

What Data Collection Methods Will Be Used For The Selected Research Design?

Data are collected or gathered in advertising and marketing research using one of two primary techniques: questionnaires or observational methods. A third, less common data collection method is discussed in "Consumer Insight: Projective Research Techniques." How you collect data should always be distinguished in your mind from your research design. In other words, any data collection technique can be used with any research design as appropriate. For example, a survey is a research design that often involves collecting data with a questionnaire. Likewise, you can use a questionnaire in exploratory research and experiments, two other types of research design.

QUESTIONNAIRES The most common data collection technique is the research questionnaire. A **questionnaire** is a data collection instrument that guides the questioning of respondents to obtain information from them. The instrument contains the questions to be asked, the order in which the questions will be asked, and instructions for the interviewer or respondent. Questionnaires are often used in survey research to gather information about consumer attitudes, opinions, and motivations, as well as product usage, media usage, and lifestyles.

CONSUMER INSIGHT

. . . .

Projective Research Techniques

Projective techniques are a series of data-gathering devices that can be used when there is a sense that consumers cannot or will not respond in a meaningful manner to direct questions about a subject. People may not be able to articulate their feelings about products, brands, and ads, or they may be embarrassed or unwilling to reveal their true thoughts or attitudes. The arrival of the account planning function has given techniques like the ones that follow a renewed role in the search for insights into consumers.

The *word association technique* requires respondents to say the first word that comes to mind when presented with a stimulus word. Word association works well when you want to know how people feel about companies or brands. For example, you might ask people to respond to a series of words in which a brand name or names are imbedded. Then you can count the frequency with which certain words appear to be associated with your brand. This will give you a feeling for how people really feel about your product.

Sentence completion tests present the subject with an incomplete sentence and then require that it be completed. You might ask people to complete sentences about attributes of competing brands or how they feel in certain purchase or use situations. A variant of the sentence completion test is the story completion technique. Here a short narrative or cartoon might be

presented and the respondent asked to complete it. For example, you could describe a situation in which two people are walking down the street, stop between two competitive stores, and have to choose which one to walk into. You ask the respondents what they are saying to each other. The only way the person can respond is to project his or her own feelings into the situation.

Role playing is an interesting technique because you can ask a person to assume a difficult role such as selling a product to consumers over their objections. From this scenario you might be able to glean ideas, words, or themes to use in the sale of your product or brand. You gain insight into the consumer's thinking process that direct questioning would not yield.

Picture interpretation tests use ambiguous pictures as stimuli. Line drawings, illustrations, or photos can be presented to subjects who are asked to describe them. Brands and products can be injected into these pictures and consumers asked to express how they feel. Suppose you had a picture with two people seated in a restaurant together. You could create two versions of the scene, one with your brand of wine at the table and the other with your competitor's brand. By comparing subjects' responses to the two scenes you can get a better idea of how people feel about your brand.

Photo sorts are among some newer techniques that

require respondents to sort pictures of people and brands in order to indicate an association between a brand and the type of person thought to use that brand. The purpose is to get at how brands fit into people's lives or express their needs and motives.

Some projective techniques ask people to create collages portraying their image of a product, pretend a product is a person and describe its life, or solve complex case studies. There is flexibility in adapting the techniques to specific research problems. Projective techniques can be helpful in getting past barriers people put up when questioned or in providing a vehicle that allows people to articulate how they really feel.

QUESTIONS
In what types of research situations would a projective technique be the method of choice? Explain your answer.

Sources: David A. Aaker, V. Kumar, and George S. Day, *Marketing Research,* 5th ed.(New York: John Wiley & Sons, 1995), 183–188; and Donald Parente, Bruce Vanden Bergh, Arnold Barban, and James Marra, *Advertising Campaign Strategy* (Fort Worth, TX: The Dryden Press, 1996), 76–77.

There are several ways questionnaires can be administered to participants in a typical survey. Questionnaires are commonly used for telephone or mail surveys. Questionnaires are also used for *mall intercept interviews,* which are direct interviews of consumers in a shopping mall environment. With an increase in new technologies, researchers can now send questionnaires by fax, include questionnaires on computer databases, place questionnaires as magazine inserts, and use the Internet to deliver questions.

The purpose of research questionnaires is to obtain accurate, honest answers from research subjects. In order to do this, the questions included on a questionnaire must be simple, clear, and focused. Consider this question: What type of automobile do you drive? Does "type of automobile" mean body style, such as coupe or station wagon? Does it mean nameplate, such as Pontiac, Isuzu, or BMW? Does it mean the exact model, such as Acura NSX or Cadillac Eldorado? And what does "do you drive" mean? Does this mean own or use frequently, or does it refer to the types of cars you are able to drive? All of these interpretations of the question could result in imprecise answers from the target audience. A better way to ask the question would be: What make, model, and body style of car do you own? Writing good questions takes a lot of practice and know-how. The best questions are short, focused, and simple.

A question like What kind of car do you drive? is an **open-response question** (also called an *unstructured question).* Open-response means the response from the research participant is not shaped or structured by the question; any answer is allowed. If, on the other hand, the question asked, Do you drive a sedan, a station wagon, or a truck? only three answers would be permitted. This second question is called a **closed-response question,** or *structured question.* Exhibit 7–8 compares an open-response question to four examples of closed-response questions.

For the researcher, there are several important differences between open- and closed-response questions. Open-response questions permit more freedom in their answers for participants, but they are more difficult to analyze and summarize. Because they require more effort from participants, answers will take more

EXHIBIT 7–8 Questionnaire Questions

Open-response question

What do you remember about the advertising for Amnesty International?

Dichotomous question

Have you seen a commercial on television in the past week for Kansas City Auto World?

Yes ☐   No ☐

Multiple-choice question

Would you say your advertising for lawn and garden supplies has worked much better than last year, a little better, about the same, or was it a little worse, or much worse than last year?

Rank-order question

Below are five types of information that can be put in advertisements for Xanto Stereo Equipment. Put a 1 beside the information that is most important for you, then put a 2 beside the information that is second in importance. Rank this information from 1 to 5, from most important to least important.

_____ Service policy
_____ Stereo specifications
_____ Special pricing information
_____ Warranty
_____ General system descriptions

Numerical scaling questions

On a scale from 0 to 10, where 10 is very exciting and 0 is not exciting at all, use a number from 0 to 10 to indicate how exciting the Stahl 902 Mountain Bike commercial was for you to watch.

time. Shorter questionnaires hold the interest of research participants, so they will answer more of the questions. Closed-response questions are usually easier to understand, faster to tabulate, and easier for participants to complete. However, open-response questions can yield richer information.

Consider the question, Do you follow your automobile owner's manual and change your car's oil at regular intervals? This question almost suggests that if the respondent didn't follow the authority of the owner's manual, there would be something wrong with him or her. In addition to the issues of validity discussed earlier, questionnaire questions must be reliable. **Reliability** means that, if performed in a similar environment, the same questions or research techniques will produce similar results in the future. In other words, the research technique is repeatable. When questions suggest answers, such as in the oil-changing example, they can result in an entire sample giving similar biased answers. This form of bias is called *question bias.*

There are several other sources of bias that the advertising researcher must understand. In research surveys, *interviewer bias* occurs when the person interviewing respondents gives cues that suggest one answer rather than another. For example, an interviewer expressing interviewer bias might acknowledge agreement with an answer or frown when the respondent gives one specific answer. *Source bias* occurs when a source of the research message, such as a manufacturer, influences the answers given by the respondent. Respondents like to please the researcher, so popular sources of messages may stimulate too many positive responses, while unpopular sources may result in negative distortions of the data. *Sample bias* occurs when the sample is distorted and doesn't represent a good cross-section of the target audience.[7] Finally, *nonresponse bias* is the error caused by large numbers of respondents refusing to answer research questions or respond to questionnaires. Nonresponses may be caused by long questionnaires, difficult research tasks for the respondent to complete, or confusion between research and telemarketing efforts. Advertising researchers believe nonresponse bias may be the major problem facing survey researchers.[8] Whatever the cause of bias, the advertising researcher must attempt to control it.

OBSERVATIONAL METHODS **Observational methods** of data collection describe or count overt human behavior, such as shopping behavior, brand selection, television viewing, or coupon use. Because observational methods of data collection rely on visible human behavior or measurable human response, the major strength of observational methods is accuracy. A summary of six types of observational methods appears in Exhibit 7–9.

There are several reasons why an advertising researcher might prefer observation to a questionnaire to collect data. First, some behaviors, such as how consumers use a point of purchase display in the supermarket, may be so habitual that the consumers don't think about it and can't describe it accurately. Second, some purchase decisions may be personally embarrassing for consumers, such as the purchase of adult diapers or laxatives. Therefore, questioning consumers directly may result in distorted or untrue answers. In addition, some consumers, such as young children, may not be able to verbalize their feelings or attitudes about a product, and some tasks, such as recording entire grocery purchases, may be too difficult or complex to complete without some form of mechanical assistance. Finally, the very act of asking questions might influence the answers researchers get. People often like to please the interviewer, which could result in more favorable findings than exist in reality. In these cases, observational methods of data collection may be warranted.

Observational methods may be structured or unstructured. Using an **unstructured observational method,** the researcher describes human behavior as it occurs. If the researcher has an idea about what behaviors consumers will use, then he or she may have observers record specific types of behavior. For example, suppose an advertiser is interested in the reading habits of mothers while they're waiting in a physician's office. An interesting research question may be, Does the woman select reading material for herself or reading material that interests her child? An observer could record this information from a seat in the waiting room. When pre-established categories of behavior are used, the observational method is called a **structured observational method.**[9] For example, if the observer in the waiting room had a form with predetermined categories of reading on it that could be checked off based on the reading material selected by the woman being studied, this would be a structured observational method.

Observations also may be made in a natural setting, such as the physician's office described above, in which the observer attempts to observe without changing the environment, or in a contrived setting. In a contrived observational setting, the observer becomes an active participant to stimulate a response from consumers or target audience members in order to see how consumers react. For example, a contrived observation may use disguised observers, known as *confederates,* to telephone a computer

EXHIBIT 7–9   Types of Observational Data Collection Methods

OBSERVATIONAL METHOD	DESCRIPTION	EXAMPLE
Structured observation	Classify or count behavior into pre-established categories that provide structure for the observations that are made.	Observing how family members interact while watching TV with a form that has categories on it indicating which family members are interacting during each time segment being studied. The observer simply checks the categories that match what is being observed.
Unstructured observation	Records events as they happen. Observer makes an effort not to impose predetermined categories on the events or the people being observed.	Observer takes notes on how people interact while eating pizza in a restaurant. Observer writes down exactly what is happening.
Natural setting	Observer attempts to observe without changing the environment.	Observer stands in a store window across the street from another to observe how pedestrians are reacting to new signage and remodeled exterior.
Contrived setting	Observer becomes an active participant to stimulate a reaction from the individuals being observed.	McDonald's sends spies into its restaurants to check on cleanliness and service. Spies go to the counter and make unreasonable demands on servers to see how well they handle the situation.
Human observation	Observation performed by individual observers. Because they are human, observers are subject to errors in counting and judgment.	Person in storefront example above uses his or her own judgment to write down the reactions of pedestrians to the remodeled store. Another observer might have a different interpretation of the reactions.
Mechanical observation	Observation made by automated devices that are subject to errors due to mechanical problems, rather than human judgment.	Scanners in supermarket or video camera behind a two-way mirror in a focus group situation.

help line to see how helpful the computer professionals are to customers.[10] Companies might use confederates to go into their stores to cause a fuss and then observe how their employees handle the situation.

Finally, observations may be made by human observers or by mechanical devices. Focus group research makes use of human observation in the form of observers who often watch the sessions from behind two-way mirrors. But since the observers are human, judgment and errors are not uncommon. As such, mechanical devices such as video cameras or tape recorders also are used to preserve the observation of focus group participants for analysis later on. Supermarket scanners that use Universal Product Codes (UPCs) to monitor the movement of brands in the retail store, and Nielsen's people meters that measure television viewership in homes are examples of observation with mechanical devices. The advantage of using a mechanical device is that human error in measuring and recording observations is eliminated. The major disadvantage is that the mechanical device could fail. We have all watched supermarket checkout personnel struggle to get a grocery item scanned only to have to resort to manual entry on a keypad.

Physiological measures, such as voice stress analysis, galvanic skin response, brain wave monitoring, eye movement tracking, and pupilometric measurement of the eye, have also been used to test consumer responses to commercials and advertisements. As sophisticated as the mechanical devices get, they have a very important limitation: Unless observational methods are coupled with other methods of data collection, they cannot provide attitudinal or motivational information about the target audience member's behavior. To obtain data about the attitudes and motivations of consumers, advertising researchers often couple observational data with information obtained from research questionnaires.

What Conclusions Can Be Reached From Analysis Of The Research Data?

The type of analysis performed on the research data is determined by the research design and data collection methods employed in the research investigation, and it should be planned for in advance of collecting data. "Adscape: Enter the Account Planner" looks at this job in more detail as it relates to interpreting and analyzing research.

In exploratory research, for example, transcripts from focus group sessions must undergo interpretation or qualitative analysis to see what insights can be extracted. By *interpretation* we mean that the researcher uses his or her depth of knowledge to draw conclusions from what has been observed or said. Statistical techniques are not appropriate to use in focus group analysis because of the small number of participants, the manner in which the participants are selected, and the lack of quantitative measures taken. Conclusions from focus groups can provide a basis for further descriptive research, or suggest changes in current advertising and marketing communications programs. A researcher should be careful not to place too much weight

AdScape

....

Enter the Account Planner

In Chapter Two we talked about the account planner, a new addition to the account team at many advertising agencies. As you may remember, the account planner's role is to interpret research information in such a way as to provide insights into consumers that traditional reporting of research findings was unable to yield.

The account planning revolution, as it has been called, started in Great Britain in the late 1960s and early 1970s as a response to the expense and stodginess of traditional research methods. Small- and medium-sized agencies were looking for more efficient ways to organize information and bring it to bear on the creative product. The concept of account planning is a major transformation in how agencies view the role of research in the creation of advertising. To make it work requires a commitment to the value of maintaining the consumer's viewpoint throughout the advertising planning process.

Another factor influencing the shift by some agencies to account planning has been the elimination of redundant research efforts between clients and agencies. Most of the heavy-duty foundation research has moved back to the client firms, leaving agencies with the more qualitative efforts that support the development and tracking of the advertising.

The account planner has to bring several strengths to the role that were previously not found in many researchers or account executives. The account planner must not only be well versed in the research techniques covered in this chapter, he or she must also be able to see insightful connections in data and information and inspire the rest of the account team to use the insights in their work. The account planner has to remain in contact with the advertising process long after the research has been presented.

The account planning system, along with reliance on anthropological research that treated consumers as if they were members of a tribe, on the conclusions drawn from exploratory research such as focus groups.

Descriptive research requires the quantitative measurement of variables and answers to questions to make them amenable to statistical analysis. Answers to survey questions, for example, are coded to translate them into numbers that can be analyzed quantitatively. This type of analysis, known as **cross-tabulation**, is a frequently used method of categorizing quantitative data so that two or more variables can be compared to one another. Exhibit 7–10 is an example of a cross-tabulation of a target audience's age with heavy, moderate, and light use of soft drinks. Looking at the data in Exhibit 7–10, we can see relationships such as how soft drink usage correlates with age. Notice that usage declines with age for all three usage groups. Also, there are more moderate soft drink users in all age groupings.

There are numerous more sophisticated types of statistical analysis for descriptive data than are illustrated here. While we need not describe them for our purposes here, you should remember that all of them have underlying assumptions about the nature of the data you have to collect to be able to use them. Make sure you consult a good statistician or researcher during the planning stages of your project so that you collect the data required for the use of the analytical techniques planned for in the research design.

Causal research designs require more sophisticated statistical analysis than descriptive studies. This is because causal research attempts to draw conclusions about a cause and effect relationship between variables. In the soft drink example above, we showed that soft drink usage is associated with age. We cannot say, however, that age causes people to drink certain amounts of soft drinks because there are other factors—such as where someone lives or the season of the year—that also influence soft drink usage, and we have not controlled for these other explana-

resulted in an innovative and insightful advertising campaign for Borders bookstore. Perich + Partners in Ann Arbor, Michigan, found out that loyal Borders customers were passionate about their interests and learning. This exploration and discovery theme was turned into an advertising campaign that asked consumers to "Find out, Borders" in answer to a series of questions such as, "How do you gift wrap the world?"

Agencies' approaches to research are changing as they are being challenged to find more and better creative solutions to their client's problems. Account planning is one of their responses.

QUESTIONS

Why has account planning become a popular addition in advertising agencies? Do you agree or disagree with the concept?

Sources: Lisa Fortini-Campbell, *Hitting the Sweet Spot* (Chicago: The Copy Workshop, 1992), 159–189; Leah Haran, "Borders' Patty Kerr," *Advertising Age*, 24 June 1996, s22; and John Wolf, "Account Planning Moves Up Its Forces," *Agency*, Fall 1994, 39–43.

In creating its "Find out, Borders" campaign, Borders successfully used the account planning process to identify and then speak to the passions of its customers. This dedication to the consumer is evident in this ad from that campaign.

tions. To have confidence in the existence of a cause and effect relationship, we must be able to show a strong statistical relationship among the variables we are studying. Remember, when researchers say one thing caused another, they are concluding that if they can manipulate the cause, a specific effect will follow. If a company bases a campaign on these results, and the researchers were wrong, it stands to lose a lot of money. Causal relationships are the hardest to demonstrate with certainty because of the difficulty of controlling all the variables involved.

Most marketing communications decisions are based on descriptive research, which we know is not conclusive about the exact relationships between the variables studied. There is always risk in decision making. Research is used to reduce the risk of a bad decision, but it cannot eliminate this risk entirely.

R E S E T

1. What is bias and how can it be eliminated?
2. What are the pros and cons of questionnaires and observational data collection methods?
3. What is cross-tabulation?

Strategic Advertising Research

Recall from the beginning of the chapter that strategic advertising research is performed during the planning stages of marketing communications or advertising campaigns. The results can be used in the development of a creative strategy for a campaign. There are three areas of strategic advertising research that may interest an advertiser during advertising planning: target audience analysis, message research, and media audience research. Let's look at each of these in more detail.

Target Audience Analysis

Products, services, ideas, and issues are limitless. Each has an appeal to an audience, and the advertiser must understand the audience to know what that appeal is. Target audience analysis is different from the foundation marketing research a firm might do about target markets in that it focuses on communication and promotion-related issues and problems. Specifically, target audience analysis identifies who the audience is, describes its characteristics, and examines the audience's consumption and media habits.

The advertisements in Exhibits 7–11, 7–12, and 7–13 illustrate three distinct audience communication problems that could require target audience research to help solve. *Business Marketing* magazine, shown in Exhibit 7–11, is an advertising trade publication; part of this magazine's target audience is media planners for business advertising. Businesses that advertise in *Business Marketing* could employ target audience analysis research to help them understand how media planners decide which media vehicles to buy for their clients. They could then build those criteria into their trade ads, thus increasing the effectiveness of their messages. In Exhibit 7–12, Mongoose, a bicycle manufacturer, is trying to connect with its audience in terms of attitude and outlook about mountain bikes. The more Mongoose knows about its audience and their habits, the better it can connect with them. The outdoor board in Exhibit 7–13 presents a different communication problem because it is trying to reach people who abuse drugs. Overcoming and reversing an addiction is probably one of the most difficult tasks advertising can

EXHIBIT 7–10   Crosstabs of Age with Soft Drink Usage

	SOFT DRINK USERS			
	HEAVY USERS (000s)	MODERATE USERS (000s)	LIGHT USERS (000s)	TOTALS (000s)
18–24	736.1	1,030.1	687.0	2,453.2
25–34	578.4	809.7	539.8	1,927.9
35–44	473.2	662.5	441.7	1,577.4
45–54	368.0	515.3	343.5	1,226.8
55–64	289.2	404.9	269.9	964.0
65+	184.0	257.6	171.8	613.4
Totals	2,628.9	3,680.1	2,453.7	**8,763.0**

Note: Heavy = 12+ cans per week; Moderate = 6–11 cans/week; and Light = less than 6 cans/week.

EXHIBIT 7–12   Both the visual and the copy in this ad for Mongoose bicycles reflect the company's knowledge of the habits and desires of its target audience, avid mountain bikers.

EXHIBIT 7–11   The target audience for *Business Marketing* magazine includes media planners for business advertisers. Business advertising in *Business Marketing* could therefore benefit from target audience analysis research to determine key factors that influence the purchasing decisions of media planners.

EXHIBIT 7–13   Because they face such a formidable communication task, public service advertisements, such as the one shown here from Partnership for a Drug-Free America, could benefit from target audience research to help correctly position their messages.

be asked to help accomplish. The more difficult the task you ask of your advertising and marketing communication activities, the more you will want research on your audience to help you develop your messages. In this case, Partnership for a Drug-Free America might want to know if messages aimed at drug abusers' self-concept and low self-esteem could be effective in getting them to take notice of their problem.

Understanding the target audience requires an assessment of its knowledge of the product category, brand awareness, decision processes, and media habits. Advertisers use surveys of the target audience to examine the communication task for an advertising campaign. In addition to surveys, advertisers often rely on the results of industry surveys conducted by trade associations. Exploratory research with focus groups also has been important to the study of target audiences. Assessment of the target audience may also include an investigation of the importance of competitive products or services in the mind of the target audience. The purpose of this part of the analysis is to assess and monitor competitor advertising and marketing activity. A small retailer may simply make a clipping file of competitive newspaper advertisements to keep track of competitors. Larger advertisers often use syndicated research services such as *Competitive Media Reporting* (CMR) or *Nielsen Monitor Plus* to provide competitive expenditure data by brand, medium, and geographical area.

CMR monitors advertising expenditures in 11 media. It gathers data for all national television (network, syndication, and cable) through electronic monitoring of what appears on TV, and compiles data on spot television from local station information. For magazine and outdoor advertising reports, it relies on two trade associations (Publishers Information Bureau and Outdoor Advertising Association of America) to provide the dollar figures. And for newspapers, it monitors ad spending in major markets. Nielsen offers a similar type of service using similar sources. Both companies offer reports in both printed and electronic form, providing advertisers with extensive information on how much their competitors are spending, and where and when they place their media dollars.

In order to find out what messages are being sent, CMR and Nielsen both offer separate services (Ad Detector and Adviews, respectively) that capture all TV commercials on-air and make them available within 24 hours in digital form. In order to review the print messages being presented by their competitors, advertisers can subscribe to a clipping service; Burrell's clipping service, for example, pulls print advertisements from over 18,000 newspapers and magazines. Advertisers can then use services such as those provided by Video Monitoring Services of America, L.P. (VMS) to keep abreast of commercials appearing in electronic media. VMS monitors both standard and cable television networks and radio and will alert users to new commercials appearing in these media. Also, advertisers can subscribe to VMS's Adbank product, which provides a monthly update reel of the commercials appearing in a specific product category. Exhibit 7–14 summarizes the activities of the major syndicated research services. Comparison of commercials will provide some insight into the strength of competitive claims, but message research also may be needed to obtain predictions about what a message can achieve with the target audience.

Message Research

Message research examines characteristics of the advertising message and its impact on the target audience members before it runs in the media. Two types of message research are sometimes included in advertising planning: concept testing and copy testing. Both testing techniques could also be called *pretesting* because they are being applied to the planning stage of the advertising process.

CONCEPT TESTING **Concept testing** is a technique used to evaluate an advertising concept and to improve it. To do this, members of the target audience are exposed to the concept, and their reactions are monitored and recorded. Concept tests may be as informal as focus group analysis or as formal as a quantitative survey questionnaire.[11] An advertising concept is not an advertisement, nor is it advertising copy.

David Schwartz has divided advertising concepts into two types. A *core concept* states the major benefits of a product in a few sentences or paragraphs. A *positioning concept* lists all of the product's major benefits and secondary benefits and is usually longer than a core concept.[12] Exhibit 7–15 illustrates a core concept statement for Secret Solid Antiperspirant, while Exhibit 7–16 shows a positioning concept statement for the same product. Schwartz recommends beginning research with a core concept test. If the results are favorable, he then recommends proceeding to a positioning concept test.

Concepts vary in their success as a predictive tool for the success of an advertising campaign. One of the problems with concept tests is the specificity of the concept statement. Ambiguous concept statements produce unpredictable results. Furthermore, participants in concept tests bring information about competing products and competing advertisements into the testing situation. This competitive information is called a *competitive set,* and it has been shown to influence the results of a concept test. Measuring the persuasiveness of a concept is extremely difficult. These difficulties are not reduced in the copy testing situation.

Concept tests can be effectively employed to determine which concepts from among alternatives being considered are best received by consumers. For example, if you were trying to market a biodegradable tissue product, you might present several key concepts, such as softness, value, and clean water, to potential consumers. You might then ask consumers to rate or rank the importance of each concept to them. The highest-rated concept would then become your best bet as a central idea for ads.

COPY TESTING   Copy testing is the systematic examination of the effect of the verbal and visual elements of an advertisement on members of the target audience. For the advertising planner, copy testing is designed to diagnose problems with advertisements and commercials before they are placed in the media. Over the years, there has been considerable debate over what should be measured in a copy test. Some of the candidates have been: recall, persuasion, copy playback, brand salience, and commercial reaction.

Recall is a measure of how well the participant remembered what was written or shown in an advertisement or commercial. Some tests measure recall when it is aided by the researcher; these tests are called aided recall or recognition. Changes in *persuasion* are mea-

EXHIBIT 7–14   Syndicated Research Services

	INFORMATION PROVIDED	MEDIA MONITORED
Comprehensive Media Reports	Advertising expenditures	Magazines, newspapers, business publications, trade publications
		Network and spot TV, syndicated TV, cable TV, network radio
		Outdoor
Burrell's	Competitor activity	Newspapers, magazines
Video Monitoring Services of America, L.P. (VMS)	Competitor activity	Network TV, cable TV, radio

sured by brand choice, purchase interest, and an overall rating for the brand. *Copy playback* tests ask participants to repeat the copy that was in the advertising or to describe visuals. Tests of *brand salience* attempt to show awareness of a brand. *Commercial reaction* is a measure of overall liking for a commercial.

In 1990, the Advertising Research Foundation completed a major study of the validity of copy testing methods and concluded that all of the current methods of testing could be correlated with increases in sales. *Likability* was a surprisingly good predictor of advertising effectiveness. *USA Today* has used this measure in its weekly Ad Track survey of people's reactions to currently running commercials. Exhibit 7–17 shows how an HBO commercial fared in the Ad Track survey. The study concluded that earlier guidelines established by an industry group, Positioning Advertising Copy Testing (PACT), were still important for effective copy testing.[13] Exhibit 7–18 is a summary of the PACT principles.[14]

Copy testing has been a dynamically changing procedure. To improve copy testing techniques, some industry leaders have suggested a multidimensional set of tools that includes recall, persuasion, and likability. Another innovation has been *continuous testing,* also known as moment-to-moment test-

EXHIBIT 7–15   Secret Solid Antiperspirant Core Concept

Secret Solid Antiperspirant is comfortable to apply to the body because it goes on dry.

It contains a pleasant feminine scent and provides the wearer with effective, all-day protection.

EXHIBIT 7–16   Secret Solid Antiperspirant Positioning Concept

Secret Solid Antiperspirant

Goes on drier than roll-ons, so it feels good on a woman's underarm.

Secret Solid Antiperspirant is different. It goes on drier than wet, sticky roll-ons, so it feels more comfortable when a woman puts it on.

And Secret Solid gives you effective, all-day protection that's strong enough for a man, yet its pleasant, feminine scent tells you it's made for a woman. Secret Solid Antiperspirant.

---

ing. Continuous testing is a qualitative technique in which small groups of participants watch commercials and use hand-held computer devices to record their reactions.[15] Researchers can monitor the continuous recordings superimposed over the commercial to see how summarized reactions relate to commercial content. Tests of reliability for the measuring system, using the Program Evaluation Analysis Computer (PEAC) developed by PEAC Media Research, found high levels of reliability for the copy testing system.[16]

Copy testing is a major message research activity for advertisers and advertising agencies. Exhibit 7–19 provides a summary of the research methods available to advertisers and agencies. Notice that you can vary the following elements: 1) whether or not you are testing finished ads, 2) the number of exposures, 3) how the ads are shown, 4) the setting, 5) the sampling procedures, 6) how wide the scope of testing is, 7) the measures of persuasion, and

8) the nature of the research design. Different research suppliers of copy testing have adopted the methods they believe to be the most valid and reliable for predicting the success or failure of the ads tested.

Media Audience Research

The goal of media audience research is to find media audiences that match the characteristics of the advertiser's target audience by investigating the ability of the media under consideration to reach the target audience. In order to compare media audiences to target audiences, the advertiser must have demographic information about its target audience and the media audiences. Audience measurement is an important activity for the media because it justifies their advertising rates to advertisers and advertising agencies. This section will provide a brief overview of audience research techniques and organizations. The application of audience research to media strategy and planning will be presented in Chapters Nine, Ten, and Eleven.

BROADCAST AUDIENCE MEASUREMENT
Broadcast audience measurement includes the measurement of national television audiences, local television audiences, and radio audiences. The size of national television audiences is measured by Nielsen Media Research's National Television Index (NTI). People meters are used by viewers in Nielsen households to monitor program viewing and audience characteristics on a continuous basis. The NTI system uses a random sample of 5,000 households to represent national viewing patterns. Households are rotated on a 24-month cycle. Because the viewing data are automatically transmitted to Nielsen computers in the early morning, rapid computer analysis produces reports that are available online for subscribers to access the following day.

There is one source of local television audience information, the Nielsen Station Index (NSI). Nielsen draws samples from all markets in the U.S. Sample sizes are larger in larger markets. Participants in the 40 biggest markets have people meters, similar to the national sample. For smaller markets, set meters are used that simply record when the television set is on and to what channel it is tuned. That information is supplemented by viewing diaries,

EXHIBIT 7–17   As this example illustrates, the Louis Harris Ad Track survey from *USA Today* uses likability as the key factor in its advertising rating system.

which people are asked to fill out for a one-week period, noting the station, program, and time of viewing. The most controversial aspect of local audience measurement is the question of how accurate these diaries are, since the data they produce tend to inflate viewing figures compared to people meters, which rely less on human memory.

Another criticism of the Nielsen ratings system at the local level is its practice of sampling most local markets for four-week periods four times a year and generalizing findings to the whole year. These periods are known as "sweeps" months, and TV networks and local stations plan special programming to influence the ratings levels because local advertising rates are based on the results of the sweeps.

Radio's All Dimension Audience Research (RADAR®) measures network radio listening by using day-after telephone interviews. Arbitron Radio uses diaries to monitor listening habits in more than 250 markets for local radio. Radio audience measurement has similar problems to those of TV audience measure-

ment, with local radio stations staging special events and programming to influence the ratings during radio sweeps periods, which occur from one to four times a year, depending on the size of the market.

One of the most interesting applications of new technology to audience measurement in recent years was the joining of UPC scanner data with television audience meters, creating what is known as **single-source data.** In the past, advertisers have had to analyze separate data about product use and media audiences, but the combination of meters with scanning data promised a single source of data for both measurements. In spite of high hopes, however, the implementation of single-source data systems faced tremendous problems. Nielsen's Scantrack® uses a national probability sample to couple media exposure to product purchases. In an effort to challenge Nielsen's national television ratings, Arbitron developed a product called ScanAmerica®. Arbitron's system used scanning wands in the home to measure product purchases. In 1992, because of increasing fi-

EXHIBIT 7–18   PACT Copy Testing Principles

A good copy testing system

Principle I:	Provides measurements that are relevant to the objectives of the advertising.
Principle II:	Is one that requires agreement about how the results will be used *in advance* of each specific test.
Principle III:	Provides multiple measurements, because single measurements are generally inadequate to assess the performance of an advertisement.
Principle IV:	Is based on a model of human response to communications—the *reception* of a stimulus, the *comprehension* of the stimulus, and the *response* to the stimulus.
Principle V:	Allows for consideration of whether the advertising stimulus should be exposed more than once.
Principle VI:	Recognizes that the more finished a piece of copy is, the more soundly it can be evaluated, and requires, as a minimum, that alternative executions be tested in the same degree of finish.
Principle VII:	Provides controls to avoid the biasing effects of the exposure context.
Principle VIII:	Is one that takes into account basic considerations of sample definition.
Principle IX:	Is one that can demonstrate reliability and validity.

EXHIBIT 7–19   Copy Testing Research Methods

The advertisement used
- Mock-up
- Finished advertisement

Frequency of exposure
- Single exposure test
- Multiple exposure test

How it's shown
- Isolated
- In a clutter
- In a program or magazine

Where the exposure occurs
- In a shopping center facility
- At home on TV
- At home through the mail
- In a theater

How respondents are obtained
- Prerecruited forced exposure
- Natural exposure

Geographic scope
- One city
- Several cities
- Nationwide

Alternative measures of persuasion
- Pre/post measures of attitudes or behavior (pre/post attitude shifts)
- Multiple measures of recall/involvement/buying commitment
- After-only questions to measure persuasion (constant sum brand preference)
- Test market sales measures using scanner panels

Bases of comparison and evaluation
- Comparing test results to norms
- Using a control group

nancial pressures on the system, Arbitron had to abandon ScanAmerica®.[17] Another competitor, Information Resources, Inc., developed BehaviorScan® to provide single-source data. Their system uses split cable television systems in 10 markets, such as Eau Claire, Wisconsin, and Visalia, California, to couple scanner data with controlled advertising messages. Different commercials are broadcast to each half of the split cable television system. With the demise of Arbitron, Information Resources and Nielsen have become fierce competitors in the U.S. and European scanning markets.

PRINT AUDIENCE MEASUREMENT   During the early days of advertising, newspaper and magazine publishers often inflated their circulation figures in order to charge advertisers more money for space in their publications. Today, however, a nonprofit organization called the Audit Bureau of Circulations (ABC)—formed by publishers, advertisers, and advertising agencies—establishes standards for reporting circulation. A similar organization, Business Publications Audit of Circulation (BPA) audits over 1,500 business publications. Two research firms, Simmons Market Research Bureau (SMRB) and Mediamark Research, compile extensive syndicated audience data for magazines. Both systems use lengthy face-to-face and mail interviews to obtain information about magazine readership, other media usage, product usage, and demographics. This information is available to subscribers on CD-ROM in interactive form to allow for additional analysis.

Audience data are essential for effective advertising planning. New measurement techniques are being developed continuously. The economics of expensive data collection make audience research a difficult part of the research business. Proprietary research may play a more important role in the evaluation of advertising campaigns.

R E S E T

1. How is target audience analysis different from foundational target market research?
2. Are concept tests always successful as predictive tools? Why or why not?
3. How might you measure a magazine's audience for media audience research?

Evaluative Advertising Research

The purpose of evaluative advertising research is to assess the effectiveness of specific messages or methods of message delivery used in a marketing communications or advertising campaign. Two types of evaluative research will be discussed here: posttesting and before-after tests. Other evaluative methods include *tracking studies,* in which the advertiser monitors the impact of its advertising while it is running, and *telephone coincidentals,* in which the advertiser surveys consumers while or immediately after they have been exposed to a message running in the media.

Message Posttesting

Specific elements of a campaign can be evaluated using a posttest research design. **Message posttesting** is research evaluation of an advertisement or commercial that occurs after the advertisement has been delivered to the target audience. Like the message variables tested during copy tests, posttesting usually measures recognition or recall. Two research firms have played a prominent role in advertising posttesting. Roper Starch Worldwide (formerly known as Starch INRA Hooper) is known for its Starch Readership Survey of magazines. The sample of respondents selected for this readership study are asked whether they have read a particular issue of a magazine that is being used for the test. If they have read the magazine, the Starch researcher then asks questions about the advertising by showing the respondent ads from the magazine.

The Starch Readership Survey is called a *recognition test* because the respondents are shown the ads. There are three scores obtained for elements in the advertisement: Noted, Associated, and Read Most. The Noted score indicates the percent of the magazine readers who remembered previously seeing the ad in the test issue of the magazine used for the study. Associated scores indicate the percent of magazine readers who remembered seeing an element of the ad that indicated a brand or advertiser's name. Read Most scores indicate the percent of magazine readers who read more than half of the material in the advertisement.

A similar readership posttest is offered by Gallup and Robinson. The difference between Gallup and Robinson and the Starch Readership Survey is that recall is the variable for the Gallup and Robinson test. In order to be included in the survey of magazine readers, participants must demonstrate that they have read the magazine. Once included in the test group, participants are not shown the advertisements; instead, participants are asked to select advertisements they've seen in the test magazine by looking at the names of advertisers from the test issue. From the list of advertisements a participant has seen, questions are asked about the advertising. Gallup and Robinson scores record three percentages: Proved Name Recognition is the percent who correctly associate an ad with a brand or company name; Idea Communication is the percent of respondents who recall the main theme or idea of the advertisement; and Favorable Attitude is the percent of respondents who have a favorable attitude toward the brand or company from the advertisement. Gallup and Robinson also provides day-after recall tests for broadcast commercials.

Before–After Testing

A second common method of evaluating both message and media effectiveness is called a **before–after test.** Exhibit 7–20 is a simple diagram of this evaluation procedure. To evaluate message effectiveness, the advertiser starts by writing objectives stating the goals of the advertising message *before* the campaign begins. The advertiser also performs descriptive research to establish initial, or baseline, awareness within the target audience. *After* the campaign, the advertiser measures these goals and compares them to the baseline awareness numbers. Most of the research companies and measurement procedures that were discussed for message research can be applied to determine the before–after effect of the advertising campaign.

To evaluate media effectiveness, the advertiser must compare the media objectives written before the campaign to the audience awareness measurements that were delivered. Suppose media objectives suggested that 70 percent of the target audience should see or hear the advertising message. By examining the audience levels that were obtained by television programs, the advertiser can decide whether 70 percent of the target audience was exposed to the message. If

EXHIBIT 7–20   Before–After Testing

	BEFORE (during advertising planning)	**AFTER** (during evaluation)
Message Effectiveness	Set measurable advertising goals for the message. Measure the baseline values of the message goals.	Measure the message goals after the campaign has run and compare the results to the baseline values.
Media Effectiveness	Set measurable goals for media. Measure the baseline values of the media goals.	Measure the media goals after the campaign has run and compare the results to the baseline values.

discrepancies exist between the audience that was promised by the media vehicle and the audience that was delivered, then the medium should adjust the costs of the media buy (or offer additional ad time as compensation).

The amount of posttesting or evaluation used by an advertiser is proportional to the risk taken in the advertising campaign. Evaluation may be formal or informal. For low-budget advertising campaigns, evaluation is sometimes scaled down. The most important reason to evaluate an advertising campaign is to provide better advertising in succeeding campaigns.

SUMMARY

There are several types of advertising and marketing research. Marketing research, also known as situation analysis, is a broad term that refers to the systematic acquisition, development, and analysis of new information used for marketing, advertising, or marketing communications decisions. It extends to all elements of the marketing program, including strategic and evaluative advertising research. Marketing research can be broken down into four key areas: product research, consumer research, market research, and competitive analysis. Product research is used to find answers to questions about products. Consumer research investigates questions about individuals in the target market. Market research studies consumers as market segments or purchasing groups. Competitive analysis, or competitive research, examines the promotion activities of competitors.

Advertising research can be differentiated from marketing research because it is research activity that is performed in support of the planning, development, placement, or monitoring of ads. Strategic advertising research is research that is performed during the planning stages of the advertising process. The results can be used in the development of a creative strategy for a campaign. Evaluative advertising research is done after a campaign to assess the effectiveness of specific messages or methods of message delivery. The two types of research are distinguished only by when they occur; there is no difference in the research procedures that can be used for the two types of research.

Five research decisions are important for the advertiser: 1) Should research be done? 2) What is the research question and objective? 3) What research design will provide the best answers to the research question asked? 4) What data collection methods will be used for the research design chosen? and 5) What conclusions can be reached from analysis of the research data?

Before deciding whether the research should be done, the researcher must first determine the purpose of the research project. Once the purpose is known, two additional questions must be answered: Can we afford the cost of research? and Does the information we're looking for already exist? Affordability is connected to the overall cost of the proposed campaign. Existing information is known as secondary data. If the secondary data exist within the advertiser's organization, they are known as internal data; information gathered and stored by sources outside of an organization is called external data. If the information does not exist in secondary data, then the advertiser may decide to conduct a research project to gather primary data—information acquired through original research.

Researchers can ask three types of questions in a research project. Explore what and why questions make an initial inquiry into what the situation is like or why it is the way it is. Research using explore what and why questions is called exploratory research, which is an initial attempt to provide insights into a research problem on a small scale and at minimal cost. Determine what is questions are more specific than explore what and why questions. From what is questions, the advertiser can determine what exists in a marketing situation. These questions are the focus of descriptive research, which tries to describe a marketing or advertising situation. Prove what or why questions require research to determine cause and effect relationships between marketing communications activities and consumer responses. They are the focus of causal research, which controls interfering factors so a strong conclusion of cause and effect can be determined. Once the advertising manager has determined what type of research question needs to be asked, the research objectives can be established. A research objective describes the question to be answered, the target audience that will be the focus for the research, and the time frame for the completion of the project.

A research design is a plan for research that guides the collection of data and the methods of analysis that will be performed.

Each of the three primary types of research design—exploratory, descriptive, and causal—has different characteristics, including goal of design, flexibility of data collection, representativeness, type of validity, and control of outside variables. Knowing the characteristics and how they impact the research will affect which research type is chosen to answer the research question.

Data are collected or gathered in advertising and marketing research using one of two primary techniques: questionnaires or observational methods. A questionnaire is a data collection instrument that guides the questioning of respondents to obtain information from them. The instrument contains the questions to be asked, the order in which the questions will be asked, and instructions for the interviewer or respondent. Questionnaires are often used in survey research to gather information about consumer attitudes, opinions, and motivations, as well as product usage, media usage, and lifestyles. Observational methods of data collection describe or count overt human behavior, such as shopping behavior, brand selection, television viewing, or coupon use. Observational methods may be structured or unstructured, natural or contrived, and conducted by human observers or by mechanical devices. Because observational methods of data collection rely on visible human behavior or measurable human response, the major strength of observational methods is accuracy.

The type of analysis performed on the research data is determined by the research design and data collection methods employed in the research investigation, and should be planned for in advance of collecting data. In exploratory research, for example, transcripts from focus group sessions must undergo interpretation or qualitative analysis to see what insights can be extracted. Descriptive research requires the quantitative measurement of variables and answers to questions to make them amenable to statistical analysis. Answers to survey questions, for example, are coded to translate them into numbers that can be analyzed quantitatively by a process called cross-tabulation. Causal research designs require more sophisticated statistical analysis than descriptive studies. This is because causal research attempts to draw conclusions about a cause and effect relationship between variables.

Strategic advertising research is performed during the planning stages of a marketing communications or advertising campaign. The results can be used in the development of a creative strategy for a campaign. There are three areas of strategic advertising research that may interest an advertiser during advertising planning: target audience analysis, message research, and media audience research. Target audience analysis attempts to identify the target audience, describe its characteristics, and examine the audience's consumption and media habits. Surveys of the target audience, industry surveys, focus groups, and competitive product investigations using syndicated research are all ways to analyze the target audience. Message research examines characteristics of the advertising message and its impact on target audience members before it is run in the media. Concept testing

and copy testing are the two most common types of message research. Media audience research, both broadcast and print, finds media audiences that match the characteristics of the advertiser's target audience by investigating the ability of the media under consideration to reach the target audience.

The purpose of evaluative advertising research is to assess the effectiveness of specific messages or methods of message delivery used in a marketing communications or advertising campaign. Evaluative research methods include message posttesting, message effectiveness, and media effectiveness. Post-testing is research evaluation of an advertisement or commercial that occurs after the advertisement has been delivered to the target audience. Message effectiveness is a test of the communication effect on the target audience. Media effectiveness can be assessed by comparing the actual media placement to the original media plan. In addition, the effectiveness of specific media can be compared to see if one is better at persuading the target audience.

KEY TERMS

1. Why are marketing and advertising research important in the planning of advertising and marketing communications campaigns?

2. What are the five important research questions an advertiser must consider when planning a research project? Briefly describe how the answer to each leads to the next question.

3. Explain the differences between primary and secondary research. Give examples of each type of research.

4. Distinguish between exploratory, descriptive, and causal research. Give an example of when each type might be used in the development and evaluation of an advertising or marketing communications campaign.

5. What is a research objective? Why is it important?

6. Why is sampling important? Discuss the differences between probability and nonprobability sampling.

7. What are the major advantage and disadvantage of observational methods of data collection? Give examples of structured and unstructured observation and examples of natural and contrived settings for observation.

8. What is the relationship between data collection and research design? Do some designs suggest particular data collection methods? Explain.

9. What is the purpose of copy testing? Outline several measures of message effectiveness that have been used by advertisers.

10. Name and briefly describe the major sources of audience data for broadcast and print media.

1. There has always been resistance to the role of research in advertising, especially among writers and artists. Based on your understanding of strategic and evaluative advertising research, with which type do you think advertising writers and artists would have the most difficulty?

2. If you had limited resources to spend on research and had to make a choice between spending your money on strategic versus evaluative research, where would you put your money? Why?

3. The states of Michigan and South Dakota and the Chrysler Corporation all developed similar advertising slogans based on focus group research. Michigan's slogan is: "Great Lakes. Great Times." South Dakota's is: "Great Faces. Great Places." Chrysler's is: "Great Cars. Great Trucks." Given the similarity of the slogans, how much confidence do you have in these focus group findings? Would you have recommended additional research? Why?

interactive discovery lab

1. Develop a short questionnaire to find out how your fellow students feel about outdoor advertising in town around your college or university and along the interstate highways. Consider the type of questions you want to ask, how best to ask them, how long your questionnaire should be, and how you might sample your schoolmates. Make sure that you will be able to quantify answers.

2. One of the most interesting data collection methods is simple observation. Develop five research questions that you think might be answered through the observation of consumers. Describe how you might set up this observation and what form your data will take. Consider whether you should use a structured or unstructured approach in each situation.

Chapter Eight

Objectives, Strategy, and Budgeting

GAP INC.'S TWO-TIERED SUCCESS

Strategic planning requires a combination of foresight that comes from really understanding the industry within which your firm operates, and the courage to make changes to respond to new conditions and opportunities.

The idea behind strategic planning is that management must be committed to constantly looking toward the future for changes in market conditions that will provide opportunities to reconsider its product or service offerings, the consumer segments it has been targeting, and the way it is marketing and advertising its products or services.

Consider how Gap Inc. has developed a two-tier marketing and advertising strategy to appeal to both upscale consumers and those at the lower end of the price spectrum. Gap Inc. sells a pair of blue jeans at its upscale Banana Republic clothing stores for $58, while selling a lower-priced version of the jeans for $22 at its Old Navy stores. The Old Navy concept was developed to appeal to customers who were finding prices a little too high for them at Gap and Banana Republic outlets. Gap Inc. has developed this two-tier strategy because it recognizes that the traditional middle-class consumer no

longer exists. The middle class has been evolving into at least two different economic classes since the 1960s—one very affluent and the other losing ground and buying power.

The two-tiered strategy used by Gap Inc. is apparent not only in the pricing of the clothing at their various outlets but also in the layout and design of the stores themselves. Gap Inc.'s approach is also evident in the stores' advertisements. For example, ads for the Gap tend to be clean and sophisticated, while those for Old Navy tend to be less refined, often using tongue-in-cheek humor in their messages.

Other firms also are responding to the growth of the top and bottom ends of the middle class. Walt Disney Co., for example, markets two distinct lines of Winnie-the-Pooh merchandise. On the one hand, Disney sells Winnie-the-Pooh's image on china, pewter, and stationery in upscale department stores such as Nordstrom and Bloomingdales.

Gap store

Old Navy store

Go to Wal-Mart and you will find Winnie-the-Pooh on T-shirts, plastic key chains, and polyester bedsheets. Gap Inc. and Walt Disney Co. are making conscious strategic choices to offer two versions of merchandise to two different emerging price segments.

Source: David Leonhardt, "Two-Tier Marketing," *Business Week,* 17 March 1997, 82–90.

LOOK BEFORE YOU LEAP

- **What is strategic planning and how does it apply to advertising planning?**

- **How are advertising and marketing communications objectives determined, and why?**

- **What is an advertising and marketing communications strategy?**

- **Why is the advertising and marketing communications budget so important, and how is it determined?**

8

Strategic Planning For Advertising And Marketing Communications

The responses of Gap Inc. and Walt Disney Co. to economic and social changes in the marketplace illustrate how reacting to changes leads to new strategies. These strategies became reality in the form of plans to sell different versions of the same merchandise to different consumer markets or to specifically target one of those price segments. In other words, a strategy provides a vision and direction while a plan lays out a course of action.

Chapters Five, Six, and Seven focused on the key ingredients for developing successful marketing and advertising strategies: the integrated marketing communications perspective, consumer insights, and information gathering. Likewise, the fundamental concepts learned in those chapters provide the foundation for creating plans that will make a strategy a concrete course of action and not just a harebrained scheme. In this chapter, we will discuss how the basics of advertising planning—such as target market selection, setting objectives, and developing a budget—are essential to translating a strategy into an actual plan.

The concept of strategic planning combines a vision of where a firm is headed with the reality of a plan of action formed to achieve specific objectives or goals. In marketing and advertising, strategic planning comes down to "the consideration of current decision alternatives in light of their probable consequences over time."[1] To achieve this, a marketing manager/planner must have an external orientation to the marketplace and the changes taking place in it. A planner also has to be adept at formulating strategies and analyzing situations and strategic alternatives, and has to have a commitment to action.[2] In short, then, **strategic planning** involves two important activities: 1) determining the objectives or outcomes expected from a plan and 2) developing strategies that are plans for accomplishing or meeting the objectives. We can think of strategies as the means to the ends, which are the objectives.[3]

Some planners like to distinguish between objectives and goals for a plan or strategy. First, an **objective** is a statement of broad direction for a plan. More specific to our purposes, an **advertising objective** is a statement explaining the purpose and role of an advertising campaign or a particular advertisement. Intel, for example, has an objective for its advertising of reminding consumers of the value of buying computers with its Pentium® microprocessor inside. If Intel wants to be more specific about what it means by "remind," it can establish criteria and a time frame in which it wants this objective accomplished. By doing so, Intel would be establishing a goal for its objective. A **goal** is an objective with specific measurable criteria and a time frame for reaching the criteria stated. Intel's goal might be to make 75 percent of all new computer buyers aware of the importance of buying a computer with the valued Pentium® microprocessor inside within a year of the start of the campaign. This is a measurable goal that Intel could then evaluate after 12 months.

While a **plan** lays out a general course of action, a **strategy** is "a broad plan of action with an objective or goal in mind."[4] Intel's strategy

Video is smoother with a PC that has a Pentium™ processor with MMX™ technology and software designed for MMX technology. The result is a great multimedia experience. With richer color, faster graphics and fuller sound.* Get it all from Intel MMX media enhancement technology. It's the technical term for fun. ▶ www.intel.com

The smoothest performance yet.
Now available in video.

The Computer Inside.™

is to make sure that consumers remember the value of buying computers that use Pentium® microprocessors, while at the same time, it works hard to create the next bigger and faster microprocessor. This is the "Intel Inside" strategy. Finally, the specific ads that are created and the media that are bought, as well as all other marketing communications activities employed to implement a strategy, are called **tactics.** The Intel ad in Exhibit 8–1 is among the tactics Intel has used to implement the "Intel Inside" strategy.

The notion of strategic planning in advertising and marketing communications leads to a consideration of how we set objectives and goals for this part of the overall marketing plan, and how we develop plans to meet these goals. In the next section we discuss how the manager/planner determines the role played by advertising and marketing communications in a consumer's final purchase decision and then uses that understanding to set objectives.

R E S E T

1. Conceptually, what does strategic planning require of management?
2. Define an objective and distinguish it from a goal.
3. Similarly, define a plan and distinguish it from a strategy.

EXHIBIT 8-1 To support its Intel Inside strategy, which is designed to communicate the value of purchasing products that contain a Pentium® microprocessor, Intel has used a series of ads promoting the various advantages that the microprocessor can provide to consumers.

Advertising And Marketing Communications Objectives

Implicit in the process of setting objectives and goals for an advertising or marketing communications campaign is the understanding that planners have segmented the market for a product or service and have selected a specific segment toward which they want to direct or target the program. Objectives are then written in terms of the types of responses expected from the target market selected. Let's look briefly at the process of segmenting the market and selecting consumer targets as it relates to setting objectives.

Selecting A Target Market

The selection of a market toward which to direct your advertising is based on an understanding of how to divide a larger market into its subsets. This process of division is called **market segmentation**—the process by which a large heterogeneous market is divided into smaller, homogeneous subsets of people with similar needs and/or responsiveness to marketing offerings.[5] The group selected by a marketer as the best prospects is called a **target market.** To illustrate, consider that the housing market can be divided into segments based on people's ability to afford a particular type of housing—from apartments to manufactured housing to a house built on-site to a house built according to a person's specific requirements. Knowing to which segment you are renting or selling and what the segment is looking for in housing influences the strategic choices available to you. These fairly large categories can be further subdivided by price and location, which enables home builders, real estate agents, and landlords to hone in on their specific segment's needs.

An important part of the market segmentation process is understanding consumer needs, much along the lines we discussed in Chapter Six. An assessment of the nature of these needs in relation to a product or brand is part of the research process covered in Chapter Seven. By way of example, a company that sells factory-built homes found that it could turn its failing business around by letting its customers select most everything that went into the home, from the color of carpeting to skylights and whirlpool baths. Attention to their consumers' need to not feel as if they were buying cookie-cutter homes or trailers changed the entire manufactured-home industry.[6] Today almost one-third of all new homes are factory built, up from one-quarter 10 years ago.

Another interesting example of how identifying consumer needs leads to target market selection and a unique market position can be seen in the banking industry. While most of us bank at a branch in our neighborhood, some banks target the needs of the wealthy in very specific ways. Bessemer Trust Company targets customers with a minimum of $5 million in investable assets. The bank assigns one knowledgeable account officer to every 14 families in this target group. While the majority of us visit our bank's branches or automated teller machines to conduct our banking business, Bessemer sends account officers to its customers. These officers help Bessemer's clients with everything from managing estates to managing race horses.[7]

Once the market has been segmented based on consumer needs, the segments must be profiled in terms of the demographic, geographic, or lifestyle variables we discussed in Chapter Six. Recall that these can be variables such as age, gender, education, income, occupation, social class, county size, region, or VALS segment. We then correlate need-based segments with these variables to make them accessible with our advertising and marketing communications efforts. Media audiences, for example, are described in terms of demographic and other quantifiable variables, not on the basis of audience members' product-related needs.

Target markets are selected from among profiled segments on the basis of those groups that will best respond to a firm's products or services and marketing communications program. These segments also should be the most profitable. Marketing managers can choose from three basic options when selecting a segment or segments to target. They can target an undifferentiated market, a differentiated market, or a concentrated market.[8]

The **undifferentiated market segmentation strategy** ignores differences across market segments and offers one set of products or services to everybody. This is the strategy Henry Ford followed in marketing his Model A Ford, which he often said he would offer in any color "as long as it was black."[9] In more modern examples, one could argue to some extent that Microsoft wants everybody to use its Windows software and that Coca-Cola wants everyone to drink Coke.

The advantage of the undifferentiated approach is that you can reap tremendous efficiencies from standardizing your marketing and advertising approaches across consumer segments. On the other hand, not segmenting the market can put a company in a position similar to that of Sears and J.C. Penney: When the market changes and is no longer one homogeneous mass of consumers, the old mass-appeal strategy no longer works.

The **differentiated market segmentation strategy** is perhaps the most common approach used today. Companies that differentiate market segments often have more than one brand in a category, and each brand is supported by a different mix of marketing communications specifically designed for its own consumer segment. Many large packaged-goods marketers employ this approach. Procter & Gamble, for example, markets and advertises two brands of diapers for different markets: Pampers and Luvs. Procter & Gamble also markets both Cheer and Tide, which compete for a share of the laundry detergent market.

The primary advantage of using a differentiated market strategy is that it allows the marketer to focus its resources on the segments with the best potential while not wasting money on consumers who are a hard sell. This leads to advertising and marketing communications that do a better job of appealing to

consumer needs and desires than is the case for an undifferentiated market strategy. The disadvantage of the differentiated market strategy is that a company might miss a segment that could turn out to be very profitable. Likewise, given the trend toward smaller and smaller consumer segments demanding more customized versions of products, it is possible that a differentiated market strategy might not go far enough in dividing the market into segments that reflect the true needs of the marketplace.

The **concentrated market segmentation strategy,** also known as *niche marketing,* focuses on winning a significant share of a limited market. The Motel 6 chain of lodges is a good example of a concentrated marketing effort. Motel 6 decided back in 1962 to compete in the economy segment of the lodging industry, but did not advertise a great deal until 1986. Since then, Motel 6 has focused its advertising efforts in outdoor and radio in an effort to get travelers who are making decisions about where to stay while on the road to choose the discount motel.

The advantage of niche marketing is that it allows a firm to zero in on one particular market segment. This is a good strategy when a company is able to identify such a segment and has limited resources with which to market and advertise its product or service. Kentucky Fried

Procter & Gamble employs a differentiated market segmentation strategy in the laundry detergent market, marketing both Cheer and Tide brands. To differentiate these brands within the product category, P&G markets and advertises each brand to a different consumer segment.

Chicken (KFC) went as far as to express this strategy in one of its advertising campaigns by saying, "We do chicken right." The biggest disadvantage is that if the niche segment is no longer profitable due to changes in consumer demand, a company does not have other segments to fall back on. Volkswagen benefited in the 1960s from the cult following of its Beetle sedan, but almost lost its entire business when demand for that model declined in the 1970s. It has taken Volkswagen almost 30 years to reestablish itself with cars that appeal to more than one small segment of consumers.

Setting Objectives

Once the market has been segmented and the appropriate target groups have been identified, planners can turn their attention toward the process of setting objectives—the broad direction for the strategic plan. Advertising and marketing communications objectives tell all those working on a marketing communications program what is expected of them. Some examples of objectives include: to change perceptions of a brand, to increase awareness of a brand attribute, to dispel a false impression, or to educate about new product uses.

The accomplishment of an objective should solve a problem or take advantage of an opportunity discovered in the situation analysis and research phases of campaign development. Objectives, especially when expressed as specific and measurable goals, also establish the standards against which a campaign or program can be evaluated. This evaluative information can then be used to adapt a campaign to changing market forces or as input to new marketing communications efforts. Carefully established objectives also make management and their agencies accountable for their recommendations.

ISOLATING THE EFFECT OF ADVERTISING AND MARKETING COMMUNICATIONS Setting appropriate objectives for advertising and marketing communications requires knowing how these promotional activities influence sales. It's easy to say that all marketing communications activities should help sell a product; however, there are many other factors—both under and not under the control of a marketer—that influence sales. As such, it is difficult to isolate the effects of advertising or any other element

of marketing communications on sales. For example, suppose Kellogg's and its agency plan to advertise Special K cereal with ads that are directed specifically at adults. Here are a few of the variables, aside from the proposed ads, that could influence the sale of cereal during any six-week period:

- The product could receive poor product placement in a large chain of grocery stores, resulting in a decrease in sales.
- A delivery-truck driver strike in two or three states could reduce distribution and sales.
- Expanded personal sales incentives could result in more distribution outlets for the product, increasing sales.
- Unseasonably cool or hot weather could result in more or less cereal consumption, changing demand for the product.
- Product publicity might generate a national magazine feature on health and low-fat foods, which in turn stimulates sales of the health-oriented brand.
- Kellogg's own sales promotion coupons in a Sunday newspaper supplement could increase sales, separate from advertising.

Because of the difficulty in isolating the effect of advertising and marketing communications on sales in light of all the other factors that may also affect it, advertisers have adopted two approaches to the problem. First, they focus their marketing and advertising efforts on situations where it *may* be possible to correlate sales to marketing communications. And second, they use intermediate measures of marketing communications effectiveness that planners believe can be associated with product purchases.

MEASURING THE EFFECTIVENESS OF ADVERTISING: DAGMAR Advertising and marketing communications objectives and goals are most useful when they specify what types of thoughts and feelings people should be expected to have about a product or brand after exposure to communication-related activities. Consumer thoughts and feelings can then be measured using criteria such as awareness, knowledge, interest, attitudes, desire, images, brand preference, brand position, and brand associations.

In 1961, Russell Colley created an advertising measurement system called **DAGMAR** (which was an acronym for the title of his book, _Defining Advertising Goals for Measured Advertising Results_). This system delineated the steps Colley believed consumers must go through en route to buying a product. These steps, known as the **hierarchy of effects,** have become the basic criteria for advertising objectives/goals. Other researchers have established their own hierarchies by changing the labels for the steps (criteria), adding or subtracting steps, or altering how they conceptualize the relationships among criteria, but Colley's approach still has had a wide-ranging effect on how we think about advertising effectiveness.

The hierarchy that provides the basis for DAGMAR is linear, and it conceptualizes consumers going from unawareness to awareness, comprehension, conviction, and ultimately action.[10] The hierarchy, the marketing forces that facilitate a consumer's movement along it, and the countervailing forces that deter a consumer's movement are illustrated in Exhibit 8–2. Colley's main point was that to measure advertising's role in the sale of a product you have to be able to define realistic goals

for it. These goals have to be in the area of communication tasks that advertising could reasonably be expected to achieve.

The important thing to remember is that most advertising and marketing communications programs reach consumers somewhere along the hierarchy. To be effective, the marketing communications must take consumers _beyond_ where they are on any of these communication steps. If people are aware, then perhaps comprehension is important. Or sometimes people have to become aware of something new about a product that the advertiser wants them to know. The order of the hierarchical steps is not as important as knowing how your customers make decisions and how communications can influence them to do what your objectives have set down in terms of a response. In the next section we'll discuss the specific criteria for setting these objectives. "Adscape: When is Sales an Appropriate Goal for Advertising and Marketing Communications?" looks further into the difficulty of isolating the effectiveness of these programs as related to sales.

EXHIBIT 8–2   Marketing Communications Forces and Hierarchy of Effects

- Advertising
- Promotion
- Personal selling
- Publicity
- User recommendation
- Product design
- Availability
- Display
- Price
- Packaging
- Exhibits

MARKETING FORCES
(moving people toward buying action)

| Unawareness |
| Awareness |
| Comprehension |
| Conviction |
| Action |

COUNTERVAILING FORCES

- Competition from other brands within the product category
- Memory lapse
- Sales resistance
- Market attrition
- Competition from other product categories
- Other environmental factors

AdScape

....

When is "Sales" an Appropriate Goal for Advertising and Marketing Communications?

Solomon Dutka, in his revision of Colley's DAGMAR principles, suggested there are only four conditions when advertising expenditures can be associated with current sales figures. These conditions were when: 1) advertising is the only variable; 2) advertising is the dominant force in the marketing mix; 3) an advertisement calls for immediate action, such as the case for direct response or retail advertising; and 4) there is no change in the marketing environment.

It is almost impossible for advertising to be the only variable in a marketing setting. For that to be true, advertising would have to be the *only* element in the marketing mix or environment that is changing. While advertisers may only change the number of advertisements or total advertising expenditures, they cannot control competitive expenditures or disruptive events in the marketplace. About the only place where some level of control over nonadvertising variables is possible is in a sophisticated testing environment. In controlled settings, supermarket scanner data can be combined with other marketing and advertising information to assess advertising's impact. Even when advertisers use two matched test markets to compare advertising results, control of extraneous variables is difficult, and the relationship between advertising expenditures and sales is still likely to be distorted.

As expenditures for sales promotion and direct marketing have grown in the 1990s, isolating the single effect of advertising on sales has become much more difficult, although this is not necessarily the case when an advertisement asks for immediate action. Both direct response and business-to-business advertising use promotional devices to stimulate action. For example, in a direct response advertisement for *Wired* magazine, readers were asked to log on to *Wired's* Web site to buy hats, shirts, and jackets with *Wired* designs and logos on them. Business-to-business advertising often carries the lion's share of the responsibility for producing sales. The simple addition of a toll-free telephone number or a Web site address in a business-to-business ad can help facilitate responses that could lead to sales.

The difficulty in establishing clear measures of advertising effectiveness related to sales has stimulated much discussion and research. The inherent advantages of measuring direct response advertising results have contributed to the growth of direct marketing expenditures. Internet advertising that allows Web users to buy directly from the computer is improving the ability of advertisers and marketers to build response mechanisms into their ads. Yet there is another position that should be considered concerning advertising's relationship to sales: Because the positive effects of advertising last for several years, many advertising experts believe that advertising is a long-term investment in profitability for brands and brand equity. While advertising is treated as an expense on the corporate ledger, these experts believe that advertising should also be considered an investment in future sales. In fact, all marketing communications activities should be viewed this way. Many national manufacturers of consumer products, such as 3M, use the long-term effects of advertising to justify their expenditures for corporate image ads.

Advertising and marketing communications should be developed with both short-term sales and long-term brand image goals in mind. Factors such as the nature of the product or service and the type of marketing communications being employed determine whether or not sales is an appropriate objective.

QUESTIONS

Do you think sales is an appropriate measure for advertising and marketing communications effectiveness? Why or why not?

Source: Solomon Dutka, *DAGMAR: Defining Advertising Goals for Measured Advertising Results* (Lincolnwood, IL: NTC Business Books, 1995).

Criteria For Setting Objectives[11]

Colley set out the notion that advertising objectives should be set for the communication-type tasks that advertising can accomplish. Advertising and marketing communications can reasonably establish, maintain, reinforce, increase, or change variables such as consumer awareness, understanding, conviction, trust, attitudes, images, or preferences. Awareness can further be broken down to include simple top-of-mind awareness of a brand, or awareness of actual properties and characteristics of a product. In addition to this basic understanding of the behavioral steps consumers go through in learning about and purchasing products, there are other criteria that objectives must meet in order to be effective in directing the energy of a company toward their fulfillment. The following seven criteria provide a yardstick for evaluating the quality of objectives that have been set for an advertising or marketing communications plan:

- Identify unit responsibility.
- Link objectives.
- State output, not input.
- Establish a time frame.
- Set realistic objectives.
- Include one result per objective.
- Make objectives specific and measurable.

IDENTIFY UNIT RESPONSIBILITY   Objectives should be set so that each unit involved in the planning process knows what its responsibilities are. Units involved in advertising and marketing communications planning include, at a minimum, the client's advertising and marketing departments and the creative and media departments at the agency. Sales promotion, direct marketing, and public relations firms or departments at the agency or client's company can also be brought in. Unit-oriented objectives allow for those in the unit to see how they have helped achieve the overall objectives of a marketing plan while making them accountable for their work.

LINK OBJECTIVES   Marketing and advertising campaigns require the efforts of a lot of people who do not work together in the same unit; therefore, objectives should be set so that the units are linked together to achieve the primary corporate objective. When the creative team

and media departments in an agency reach the objectives set for their areas of responsibility, it is their expectation that they have helped a company achieve larger objectives in terms of sales and profits. For this to happen, objectives must be connected or tied into others that reach back up the corporate hierarchy.

Exhibit 8–3 demonstrates how objectives are related to each other. This is a hypothetical example for a soft-drink firm that makes the Fruit Juicy brand. Notice how the sales promotion, media, creative, and advertising objectives all are linked back to the sales objective.

STATE OUTPUT, NOT INPUT   It is important in all phases of marketing communications planning to distinguish between objectives and the strategies or tactics used to achieve them. This means that objectives are correctly stated when they are focused on results or output, not on what it takes to get the results, or input. This might appear to be hair-splitting, but consider this example: Suppose McDonald's wanted to promote the fact its restaurants are special places for families to go to eat. An input-oriented objective might state that McDonald's wants to use a warm father-and-son or mother-and-daughter situation to show that McDonald's

---

EXHIBIT 8–3   How Objectives Should Be Linked

1. **Corporate Objective:** To increase the rate of profit from 5 percent to 7 percent of sales by the year 2000.

2a. **Financial Objective:** To secure $10 million in capital to finance the construction of a new production facility within the next six months.

   b. **Production Objective:** To produce 10,000 cases of Fruit Juicy by the end of the first quarter.

   c. **Marketing Objective:** To increase sales of Fruit Juicy 300 percent compared to the previous year by the end of the year.

3. **Advertising Objective:** To establish top-of-mind awareness in 70 percent of the target market by the end of October 1998.

4a. **Creative Objective:** To establish in the minds of the target market an association between the trade character, JUICE MAN, and Fruit Juicy.

   b. **Media Objective:** To reach 85 percent of the target market by the end of the year.

   c. **Sales Promotion Objective:** To get 20 percent of the target market to play the tropical sweepstakes game during the first quarter.

Source: Donald Parente, et al, *Advertising Campaign Strategy* (Fort Worth, TX: Dryden Press, 1996).

is a special place for families. But this is a creative tactic, not an objective. It describes what will be done to achieve the objective. An output-oriented objective, on the other hand, might be stated as follows: to reinforce consumer loyalty among families who eat at McDonald's. Loyalty or repeat business can be measured and is an expected result. The strategy is to build this emotional bond between the customer and McDonald's through the use of tactics such as depicting warm family situations in its ads.

ESTABLISH A TIME FRAME Objectives should indicate by what point in time you expect to see results. These time periods can vary by different type of objective and how they are linked to each other in the firm. You might set an objective for awareness of a brand that can be achieved in a shorter period of time than, say, a brand image goal, which is harder to accomplish and, therefore, takes more time. Time frames may also vary by level of organization, with sales goals taking longer to achieve than advertising-related goals in some cases. Setting a time or date by which you expect to reach your objectives allows you to track and evaluate the effect and effectiveness of your marketing communications activities.

SET REALISTIC OBJECTIVES Objectives should reflect what you really expect to achieve. Some managers like to shoot high and then are satisfied to fall short. Sometimes this is done to get a larger budget for advertising and marketing communications programs, and sometimes it is done to get everybody working on a campaign to work even harder. These are not good reasons to set objectives unrealistically high. The opposite problem is to shoot low and make it too easy to achieve your objectives.

If you set your objectives too high or low, you lose the ability to use objectives to set expectations for the efforts of all who will be responsible for achieving them. This coordination function is important to bringing all of the pieces of a campaign together.

INCLUDE ONE RESULT PER OBJECTIVE Most advertising and marketing communications plans include multiple results that must be accomplished for them to be considered

successful. There is a temptation at times to make several of these results part of the same objective. Suppose that a plan calls for increasing the awareness of two different brand or store characteristics. Let's imagine that Best Buy discount store's objective is to make 75 percent of consumers in its retail markets aware of its overall low prices and the high quality of the computers it sells. One way to tell if these should be separate objectives is to ask if one part of the objective can be achieved without the other being accomplished. Here the answer is yes. So these objectives are better written as: 1) to make 75 percent of consumers in Best Buy's retail markets aware of its overall low prices; and 2) to make 75 percent of consumers in Best Buy's retail markets aware of the high quality of the computers it sells.

Another way to determine if your objective has more than one result is to consider the question you would need to ask in your follow-up (evaluative) research. In the case of Best Buy's objective, the questions might be, "Which store in town has the best overall low prices on appliances and electronics?" and "Which store in town sells a wide range of high-quality computer equipment?" This obviously requires two separate questions, so you should write two separate objectives.

MAKE OBJECTIVES SPECIFIC AND MEASURABLE Objectives are most useful to planners when they can be quantified in terms of specific criteria to be accomplished. When we can do this we are converting our objectives into goals. Indeed, one of the reasons many marketers and advertisers fall back on sales as the goal of their plans is because communication-type objectives are not easy to quantify and measure.

Advertising and marketing communications objectives that speak to issues of awareness, image, attitude, perceptions, beliefs, or intention to purchase can be quantified if we have knowledge of current levels for these variables. Objective setting is perhaps most problematic in the creative area. Here we may not want to quantify our objectives, but rather state our objectives to provide direction for writers and artists.

The more specific we can be in stating our objectives, the better. Knowing how much we want to increase something or what maximizing an objective means makes it easier to evaluate a campaign. The more vague you are in writing objectives, the more difficult it will be to provide direction for those working on a plan. It also makes it hard to hold people accountable or measure results.

Now that we have a better understanding of how to go about setting objectives, let's shift our discussion to the importance of strategy to achieving these objectives. Advertising and marketing communications strategies are often what distinguishes one brand from another in the eyes of consumers.

RESET

1. Why do marketers choose the target markets they do?
2. When are objectives and goals most useful?
3. Explain Colley's hierarchy of effects.

Advertising And Marketing Communications Strategy

The changing marketplace has put a premium on two essential methods companies can use to achieve their objectives. First, companies can become more effective in running their businesses. They can employ the latest technology and use the most current management tools and techniques. We have all heard of these tools. They go by names like total quality management, partnering, reengineering, outsourcing, and benchmarking. This is the approach the Japanese automakers used to out-compete American automobile companies in the 1980s. The basic problem with this method of achieving objectives is that the competition has access to the same tools and can quickly match a firm's level of effectiveness. And while advertising and marketing communications can and do benefit from improvements in technology and other tools, they are essentially areas that rely more on strategic thinking than operational effectiveness. Thus, the second way a

company can achieve its objectives and outperform its competition is through the development of better strategies.

Strategy in advertising and marketing communications is most often about being different from the competition. When a company develops a strategy, it is "deliberately choosing a different set of activities to deliver a unique value" to a targeted group of consumers.[12] A good, clear example of choosing a different set of activities to differentiate a company from its competition is the strategy selected by Southwest Airlines Company. Southwest offers one-class, one-price, short-haul service between large and midsize markets, often using secondary airports in major cities. The airline operates one type of plane, the Boeing 737. By doing so, training, scheduling, and maintenance are all greatly simplified, thereby reducing costs and allowing Southwest to offer low fares.

The interesting aspect of Southwest's strategy is the choices it made and did not make. Southwest made a deliberate decision not to fly great distances or between large airports. As is clearly illustrated in the ad shown in Exhibit 8–4, Southwest consciously appealed to flyers who might have traveled by some form of ground transportation had their airfares not been a good value. Southwest adheres to its strategy by making sure that all of its activities deliver on its low-cost, convenient service position in consumers' minds. Southwest provides fast turnarounds at its gates; it does not offer meals, assigned seats, or different service classes; and to top it off, Southwest has consistently communicated a sense of humor and community.[13]

As you can see from the Southwest Airlines example, strategy is about how a company chooses its business activities. Advertising and marketing communications strategy, therefore, is about deliberately choosing the marketing communications vehicles with which a company can achieve its objectives. These choices are directed by the company's objectives and are often limited by its budget. A marketing communications strategy is always some combination of advertising, public relations, direct marketing, sales promotion, and personal selling. How we put these elements together to achieve our goals is our strategy. "Around the Globe: Reflecting the Local Culture" addresses

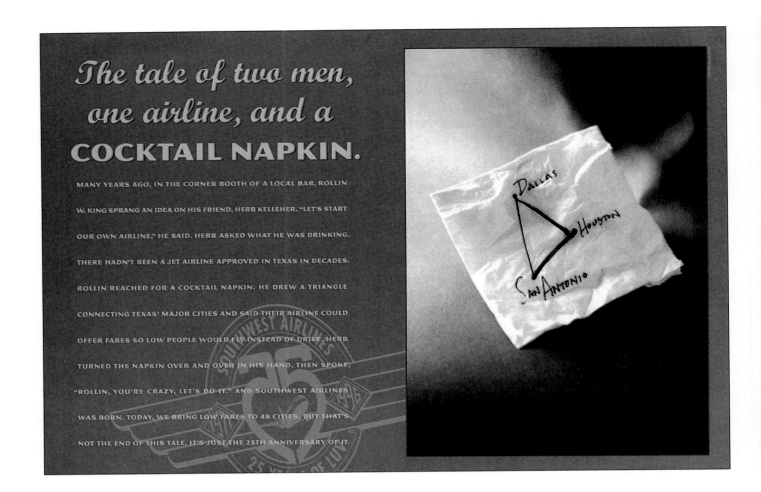

The tale of two men, one airline, and a **COCKTAIL NAPKIN.**

MANY YEARS AGO, IN THE CORNER BOOTH OF A LOCAL BAR, ROLLIN W. KING SPRANG AN IDEA ON HIS FRIEND, HERB KELLEHER. "LET'S START OUR OWN AIRLINE," HE SAID. HERB ASKED WHAT HE WAS DRINKING. THERE HADN'T BEEN A JET AIRLINE APPROVED IN TEXAS IN DECADES. ROLLIN REACHED FOR A COCKTAIL NAPKIN. HE DREW A TRIANGLE CONNECTING TEXAS' MAJOR CITIES AND SAID THEIR AIRLINE COULD OFFER FARES SO LOW PEOPLE WOULD FLY INSTEAD OF DRIVE. HERB TURNED THE NAPKIN OVER AND OVER IN HIS HAND, THEN SPOKE, "ROLLIN, YOU'RE CRAZY, LET'S DO IT." AND SOUTHWEST AIRLINES WAS BORN. TODAY, WE BRING LOW FARES TO 48 CITIES. BUT THAT'S NOT THE END OF THIS TALE. IT'S JUST THE 25TH ANNIVERSARY OF IT.

EXHIBIT 8-4 The decision by Southwest Airlines to focus its business energies on convenient and economical short-haul flights helped to create a unique—and quite successful—market position for the airline vis-à-vis its competitors.

the issue of implementing a strategy in international markets.

Since the early 1970s, positioning has been the most popular type of advertising and marketing communications strategy. **Positioning** is a strategy that attempts to create a unique meaning for a product or brand in the mind of the consumer. Thus, it is a competitive strategy that focuses on how people think about a brand. The elements of marketing communications, including the creative and media strategies, employed to create this position are part of a strategy.

The concept of product positioning was originally espoused by Al Ries and Jack Trout. It referred to how the consumers perceived brands in a category relative to each other. This idea, where the frame of reference is your competition, is the most basic form of positioning.[14] The idea behind positioning has evolved so that any of the sources of difference to be described next can be used to create a position relative to the competition. A brand's position is created by using market-

ing communications as well as pricing, distribution, and packaging to establish unique associations with the brand in people's minds. This position is established relative to how people perceive similarities or differences between a brand and its competition.

Types Of Strategic Positions

The decision to position your brand is a deliberate choice to emphasize some dimensions and not others. If your target consumer is to have a clear picture of your brand, then you must focus your marketing communications and resist the temptation to try to be all things to all people.

Positioning strategies can originate from a number of different sources. For example, positions can come from the following:

- Product characteristics or benefits.
- A price–quality relationship for your brand.
- How a product is used.
- The type of person who uses a product or service.
- The entire product class.

- Cultural symbols.
- Explicit position relative to the competition.[15]

If you can emphasize a characteristic or benefit in a way to make your brand stand apart from the competition, you can create a unique position. Of course, this characteristic or benefit has to be important to your target market for it to work as a position. For example, as shown in Exhibit 8–5, Black and Decker established the uniqueness of its VersaPak™ cordless tools by promoting the interchangeable, rechargeable battery that works with all of the specially designed tools.

The Southwest Airlines example discussed at the beginning of this section demonstrates how a company can employ a price-quality positioning strategy. Revisit Exhibit 8–4 to see how the thinking behind this strategy originated.

How a product is used or the benefit derived from its application can become a very effective position for a brand, as well. Polaroid has occupied the instant camera position for years because of the benefit of using its cameras. The ad in Exhibit 8–6 continues Polaroid's long tradition of its preeminence as "the" instant camera.

Some brands can be sold effectively by showing the type of person who uses the product. The product user can be an ordinary person or a celebrity. American Express has added cachet and status to its credit card by portraying celebrity card users in its ads, as we can see in Exhibit 8–7. Thus American Express has established an exclusivity position among credit cards.

If you can associate a brand with an entire product class, you can establish a position that can preempt any other brand's claim to it. And sometimes a unique distribution system, package, or way you do business can put you in a position all by yourself. When this happens, you might have to position yourself with or against

---

AROUND THE GLOBE

. . . .

Reflecting the Local Culture

Implementing a brand strategy in international markets can become problematic when countries do not have the available media to which we have become accustomed in the United States. Intel ran into this problem when it wanted to build brand awareness for its microprocessors in China using its highly successful "Intel Inside" strategy.

The challenge was to find a way to build brand awareness in a country without a mass media infrastructure. How did Intel get its message out without the use of mass media? The back fenders of the millions of bicycles rolling down China's streets!

Intel's agency in Hong Kong came up with the idea of distributing bike reflectors in Shanghai and Beijing. The reflectors glow in the dark and display the words, "Intel Inside Pentium Processor." Because bikes in China typically do not carry reflectors, Intel also was helping to make bike riding safer. Millions of these reflectors have been distributed to date.

One might question why Intel would make this consumer effort in a country where computers are used mostly by businesses. Intel is looking to the future, to a time when computers will penetrate the home environment in China. When this happens, Intel wants to be ready to win the lion's share of the market. China has the potential to become the world's largest consumer of electronics of all kinds. Intel wants to be first in the minds of Chinese consumers as this scenario unfolds in the next 10 years.

Intel's bicycle reflector strategy is supported by TV and outdoor advertising. Survey research is also being performed in concert with the distribution of the reflectors to see if the brand message is understood. The reflector strategy is unique, and it demonstrates the importance of adapting an overarching brand strategy to the requirements of the local culture.

Source: Fara Warner and Karen Hsu, "Intel Gets a Free Ride in China By Sticking Its Name on Bicycles," *The Wall Street Journal*, 23 July 1996, B–3.

EXHIBIT 8-5 As this ad illustrates, Black and Decker established the uniqueness of its VersaPak™ cordless tools by focusing its advertising message on the versatility and flexibility afforded by the interchangeable, rechargeable battery.

EXHIBIT 8-6 In some cases, a strong market position can be established by emphasizing the uses of a product. Polaroid, which holds a unique position in the camera market, promotes its product by focusing its advertising message on the many benefits that are generated through the use of the camera.

might have to position yourself with or against another product class to get the point across.

Cultural symbols associated with a brand can also help to create a powerful brand position. Leo Burnett, founder of Leo Burnett Company, was an expert at identifying and using cultural symbols to position his clients' brands. Among the cultural symbols his agency created are: the Maytag Repairman, Tony the Tiger, the Jolly Green Giant, Charlie the Tuna, the Marlboro Man, the Pillsbury Doughboy, and the Keebler Cookie Elves.

The symbols are so well known by consumers that they can create instant brand recognition for a product. For example, as Exhibit 8–8 illustrates, Tony the Tiger is so ingrained in popular culture that the mere representation of his stripes can invoke the image of Tony and identify the brand, Kellogg's Frosted Flakes cereal, in the minds of consumers.

Once a clear and defensible position has been identified, planners can turn their attention to the choice of marketing communications activities that can best be combined and integrated to convey the position to the target market. Some of these activities have been discussed in Chapter Five. Integrated marketing communications will also be discussed in greater detail in Chapter Twelve.

Media and creative strategies flow directly from the overall advertising or marketing communications strategy. Media planners and buyers and creative and art directors are involved in developing executional plans that will help a company achieve its marketing objectives. The choice of target market, establishment of objectives, and development of an overarching strategy or position provide important guidance to the advertising agency as it fulfills its role in the marketing communications campaign planning process.

EXHIBIT 8-7 Some brands benefit from showing product users in their ads. This type of approach proved to be quite successful for American Express, which established a position of exclusivity in the credit card market by highlighting celebrity card users in its advertising communications.

R E S E T

1. **What are the key elements of a strategic plan?**
2. **In addition to marketing communications, how is a brand's position created?**
3. **Describe the various ways that advertising can be used to position a product.**

Advertising And Marketing Communications Budget

The amount of money to be allocated to advertising and marketing communications is of strategic interest because it often constrains what can be done in a campaign. Certainly a small budget puts added pressure on creativity and creative strategy decision making, but talented creative personnel can work wonders on small budgets. Media expenditures, however, account for upwards of 80–90 percent of a budget, so constraints here will severely limit the amount of media exposure that can be bought.

The amount of money a firm allocates to advertising and marketing communications is called the **budget appropriation.** While a company cannot achieve its objectives simply by throwing money at them, there is a relationship between the size of an appropriation and what reasonably can be accomplished. A firm should be concerned to some extent with the size of its budget relative to the size of its competitors' advertising expenditures. This is because, everything else being equal, a firm's percentage of the category's media expenditures will have some relationship to its share of market. This assumes that media planners for the competitors' agencies are equally effective and efficient in buying media. It also assumes that

the sales impact of all other marketing elements is relatively equal across competitors.

There is a threshold of expenditure that must be invested in a new or existing brand just to get the advertiser's voice heard above the clutter. It is not always easy to determine what this threshold is, but it is related to the total amount of money spent by advertisers in a product category. It takes appreciably more money to build awareness and favorable brand associations for new products than it does to maintain established levels of awareness for existing products, for instance. This is because the effects of advertising are cumulative and new products have to start from scratch. Any expenditure level below the minimum required to make an impression in the marketplace is wasted. Likewise, there is a point beyond which each additional dollar spent has little or no effect. This is known as the *point of diminishing returns.*

Determining the optimum amount to spend takes good research information and constant attention to how expenditures influence the variables stated in your objectives. The experience of advertisers who sponsored the Summer Olympics in Atlanta in 1996 demonstrates that the sheer clutter of advertisers can diminish the effect of even the best-financed advertising effort. General Motors (GM), one of the two largest advertisers on NBC's television coverage of the Games, planned for extra and unusual marketing communications activities at the Games because it believed its messages would be drowned out by the 200+ companies sponsoring TV coverage, supplying goods and services, or selling licensed products. GM sponsored a car ballet each night in which it hoisted life-size models of cars 60 feet in the air and had them move to music and a laser light show.[16]

Most advertisers fall back on other methods of budgeting because the cost of locating this optimum budget is more than what they might save by doing so. The bottom line in budgeting is that the size of an advertising or marketing communications appropriation is important because it can make a difference in a firm's ability to execute its strategies and accomplish its objectives.

Let's look at four common approaches to determining how much to spend on advertising and marketing communications: percent-

EXHIBIT 8-8 Cultural symbols are extremely effective in creating strong brand images. Tony the Tiger's stripes are so well known among consumers that they generate instant brand recognition for Kellogg's Frosted Flakes cereal.

age of sales, all you can afford, competitive parity, and objective and task. Then we will propose a procedure that incorporates the strengths of these methods.

Percentage Of Sales

One of the easiest ways of deciding the size of an advertising and marketing communications budget is the **percentage-of-sales budgeting method.** As the name suggests, this method involves settling on a percentage of sales to be allocated to advertising and marketing communications activities—such as 3 percent or 5 percent of last year's sales revenue. A variation on this approach is to decide how much per unit sold goes to advertising. Automotive manufacturers and dealers typically arrive at their budgets this way, agreeing that $100, for example, of every car sold will go toward advertising and marketing communications.

The percentage or amount per unit to be used is derived from a company's experience over time. Inputs into this decision include factors such as level of competitors' expenditures, special factors in the current situation, or a new project under consideration. The advantage of this approach is its ease in application. The disadvantage is that, because it most often is based on past and not future sales, advertising becomes a function of sales. When sales are high, advertising and marketing communications budgets will be high. This relationship makes it hard to use advertising to increase sales when they are low. Low sales years will produce smaller advertising budgets in the years that follow these slumps.

All You Can Afford

A simpler but less desirable approach is the **all-you-can-afford budgeting method.** In this type of budgeting, planners figure out what all their necessary expenditures are for running their business and then use what's left for advertising and marketing communications. Small businesses with limited resources plan advertising and promotion expenditures this way. The reasoning here is that a company should not be wasting money it cannot afford on advertising. There is some well-reasoned truth to this argument. The fallacy, however, is that if you truly believe that advertising and marketing communications are essential to your business and its growth, you should consider the money spent

as an investment in your brand equity and future profits. The all-you-can-afford approach treats advertising as an unwanted expense.

Competitive Parity

The **competitive-parity budgeting method** assumes that the best point of comparison for determining the size of a budget is what the competition is spending. Our previous discussion of the relationship between share of a category's advertising expenditures and share of market is principally what drives this method.

The major disadvantage to this method is that it assumes the competition is spending money to promote its products at optimal levels. Because factors such as how well or how effectively competitors are spending their budgets enter into the equation, a firm might find this approach risk aversive but not truly effective. Markets and situations change over time. Opportunities can be lost for firms that get complacent and spend at levels that have been determined by past activity in a category. Competitive parity or matching the competition's activity is a factor to consider, but it is not the only factor.

Objective And Task

The **objective-and-task budgeting method** starts with an assessment of the tasks or programs recommended for accomplishing a firm's advertising and marketing communications objectives. The costs of these programs in total become the budget required to reach the stated objectives. This is a very logical approach to budgeting. Its major shortcoming, however, is that without some sort of starting point such as past expenditures or competitors' expenditures as a reference or benchmark, it becomes difficult to establish the link between advertising and increases in sales or other variables.

The objective-and-task method requires benchmark research to establish current levels of the variables stated in the objectives. If an increase in awareness is called for, for example, current levels of awareness must be known.

A Budget-Setting Procedure[17]

The budgeting methods just described give us a starting point in that they provide factors that should be considered in determining a budget. Each method by itself is inadequate;

however, taken together, they identify good things to consider.

In large firms, upper management has to approve budget requests. Therefore, a planner has to sell them on the affordability of the budget request. The more systematic you can be in presenting how you went about arriving at an appropriation, the better chance you have of getting your request approved. Advertising and marketing communications budgets typically are assumed to be inflated. The better you can link requests to objectives and concrete tasks, the better off you will be.

There is a place for considering the advertising budget as a percentage of sales. This factor works best if a firm thinks about what it will take to achieve future sales rather than appropriating an amount based on past sales. Forecasting future sales requires a strong research program that has tracked past sales and predicted future sales by anticipating changing market conditions.

The all-you-can-afford method is not a realistic approach in large firms. However, if the budget process includes starting with a budget estimate from top management, this can be considered an estimate of what the company believes it can afford.

Competitive activity and expenditures should be inspected more for changes occurring in the marketplace than as a budgeting method. All budgets require adjustments to meet changing conditions. It is foolish to ignore competitive activity, just as it is to follow it blindly.

Most appropriations include budget allocations based on the objectives and tasks that have been identified by marketing and advertising management. This is becoming more and more the case as we approach promotion from a marketing communications perspective. Advertising, public relations, sales promotion, direct marketing, and research all might have their own allocations within a budget. These tasks and what each will cost must be built into a budgeting process.

A prerequisite of a good budgeting method is data. These data should be able to illustrate relationships between advertising and marketing communications and the variables stated in a firm's objectives. Forecasting is at the heart of

budgeting. You have to have a good sense of where you want to go with a program and what it will cost to get there. Here's a budgeting process we like, that really works, and that has a lot of business sense built into it.

ESTABLISH A BASE   A systematic budget process should start with a base budget to which adjustments will be made. The objective-and-task method is a good way to do this. Each task recommended in a marketing communications program should have an expenditure associated with it. The base for the appropriation request is the total of the costs for each task in a program. This is where we start.

MAKE ADJUSTMENTS TO THE BASE BUDGET
The budgeting factors previously considered—competitive parity, affordability, and percentage of sales—can now be checked to see if the base budget is out of line. Some firms have a ceiling for budgets that they will not go beyond. If budget cutting is called for, priorities can be established based on the objective-and-task method used to build the base budget. This way management can see what will be lost if particular programs are cut or reduced.

GET FEEDBACK   Budgeting should be a long-term process in which research is fed back into the procedures used to build budgets. For example, budgets can be tested using statistical models to see if the appropriations were effective and efficient in achieving the objectives set at the outset of a campaign or program. It's important to remember, however, that advertising and marketing communications planning are dynamic processes. New challenges come about as the marketplace changes. Future choices as to which strategies and tactics will best meet objectives should be approached with the best information available. Determining the best appropriation level for advertising and marketing communications activities is an important part of this process. The bottom line is that you have to spend money to make money.

SUMMARY

The advertising and marketing communications planning process has become more strategic as competition for business from a very sophisticated consumer market has become tougher and tougher. Strategic planning involves the determination of objectives or outcomes expected from a plan, and the development of strategies for accomplishing or meeting these objectives. An objective is the statement of broad direction for a marketing communications plan. More specifically, an advertising objective is a statement explaining the purpose and role of an advertising campaign or a particular advertisement. If we can make an objective measurable with specific criteria, then we have stated a goal. A strategy is a plan of action in which specific activities are selected over others for the purpose of reaching an objective or goal. The ads that are created and media that are bought to implement a strategy are a plan's tactics.

The process of setting advertising and marketing communications objectives requires an understanding of the target toward whom the objectives are aimed. The selection of a market or markets toward which to direct marketing communications requires the segmentation of the market. Market segmentation is the process by which we divide a large heterogeneous market into smaller, homogeneous groups of consumers. The purpose of market segmentation is to identify groups of consumers who have needs in common that can be met by a product and its related marketing communications activities. The group a marketer selects as its best prospects is called a target market.

Target markets are chosen because the company believes these groups of people will best respond to the product message. They can be selected using one of three basic strategies: undifferentiated, differentiated, or concentrated. An undifferentiated market strategy ignores differences across market segments and offers one set of products or services to everybody. In a differentiated market strategy, a company supports different brands in a product category by developing a different mix of marketing communications specifically designed for its own consumer segment. The concentrated market strategy, also known as niche marketing, focuses on winning a significant share of a limited market.

Once a target market has been selected, attention can be turned toward setting objectives—the broad direction for the strategic plan. The accomplishment of an objective should solve a problem or take advantage of an opportunity discovered in the situation analysis or research phases of campaign development. Objectives should also establish standards against which a campaign can be evaluated and make management accountable for their recommendations.

After selecting a target market, the next step in setting objectives is determining the relationships between a company's sales goals and the influence of various types of marketing communications. A firm's sales can be influenced by factors other than marketing communications. Thus, it is important to set marketing communications and advertising objectives in terms of those communication tasks that they can realistically accomplish. It is also important to use intermediate measures of effectiveness that planners believe can be associated with product/service purchases.

Russell Colley was instrumental in emphasizing to advertising and marketing strategists that often "sales" is not the best measure of effectiveness for most advertising campaigns. In his advertising measurement system, called DAGMAR, Colley created the idea of a hierarchy of effects—stages that consumers should pass through en route to buying a product. He believed that advertising and marketing communications programs were designed to make consumers aware of products, to teach them information about products, to create brand images in people's minds, to influence consumer attitudes and create conviction toward brands, and ultimately, to get people to purchase a product. We now realize that there is more than one order to these steps depending on the type of product being considered and where along the hierarchy people are in relation to a product.

In addition to the behavioral steps consumers go through in learning about and purchasing products, objectives can be set according to certain criteria that will help ensure that they play their proper role in a marketing communications program. Objectives should: 1) identify unit responsibility; 2) link objectives; 3) state output, not input; 4) establish a time frame; 5) set realistic objectives; 6) include one result per objective; and 7) make objectives specific and measurable.

Strategies are developed as plans to reach the objectives or goals of a marketing communications program. As such, strategy in advertising and marketing communications is about being different from the competition. A strategy is a conscious choice to employ one set of activities over others to obtain stated goals. The most common type of marketing communications strategy is called positioning. Positioning attempts to create a unique meaning for a product or brand in the mind of the consumer. There are several ways a product can be positioned in people's minds using advertising and marketing communications. A product can be positioned using its characteristics or benefits; by focusing on its price–value relationship; by playing up how it is used; through portrayals of the type of person who uses it, relative to the product class it is in; by using cultural symbols; and in direct comparison to the competition.

The determination of the advertising and marketing communications expenditure is important to strategic planning because a budget can constrain creativity and creative strategy development as well as limit the amount of media that can be bought. The overall advertising and marketing communications budget is called an appropriation.

Most companies use some combination of four basic methods for establishing the size of the advertising and marketing communications budget: percentage of sales, all you can afford, competitive parity, and objective and task. The percentage-of-sales method involves settling on a percentage of sales (or amount per unit sold) to be allocated to advertising and marketing communications activities. Using the all-you-can-afford method, planners figure out what all their necessary expenditures are for running their business and then use what's left over for advertising and marketing communications. The competitive-parity budgeting method assumes that the best point of comparison for determining the size of a budget is what the competition is spending. Finally, the objective-and-task method starts with an assessment of the tasks or programs recommended for accomplishing a firm's advertising and marketing communications objectives. The total costs of these programs then become the budget required to reach the stated objectives.

Another budget-setting procedure was also presented. The first step in this procedure is to establish a base budget using the objective-and-task method. The second step is to make appropriate adjustments to the base budget using percentage of past sales, competitive expenditures, and what is affordable as guidelines. Feedback in the form of research data is important to a dynamic budget-setting process that plays an important role in strategic planning.

KEY TERMS

strategic planning, 250

objective, 250

advertising objective, 250

goal, 250

plan, 250

strategy, 250

tactics, 251

market segmentation, 252

target market, 252

undifferentiated market segmentation strategy, 252

differentiated market segmentation strategy, 253

concentrated market segmentation strategy, 253

DAGMAR, 254

hierarchy of effects, 255

positioning, 260

budget appropriation, 264

percentage-of-sales budgeting method, 265

all-you-can-afford budgeting method, 265

competitive-parity budgeting method, 265

objective-and-task budgeting method, 265

1. What is strategic planning?

2. What is market segmentation? What is its importance in setting objectives?

3. What are the three basic strategies marketers use to select a target market?

4. What is the purpose of objectives?

5. How do marketers approach the problem of isolating the effect that advertising and marketing communications have on sales?

6. List and explain the seven criteria to be followed in setting objectives.

7. Explain the real purpose of an advertising or marketing communications strategy.

8. What is product positioning? Describe as many ways as you can of using advertising to position a product. Provide real-world examples of each approach to positioning.

9. Describe four basic budgeting methods for determining the size of a marketing communications appropriation.

10. How does the budget-setting procedure described in the chapter make use of the four budgeting methods you described in Question 9?

DISCUSSION QUESTIONS

1. Think about the stores where you shop or the products you buy. Identify one store or product for each of the following market segmentation strategies: undifferentiated, differentiated, and concentrated.

2. For the examples you selected for Question 1, describe how the store or product is positioned to take advantage of its market segmentation strategy. Describe how these positions are executed in the advertising of these firms.

3. Infomercials are a form of marketing communications aimed at selling products. What makes an infomercial different from a traditional TV commercial? Discuss how the goals for an infomercial differ from the goals of most TV commercials for national brands.

4. Think of some brands that you believe are poorly positioned in consumers' minds. Come up with some better positions for these brands.

interactive discovery lab

1. A small or insufficient budget often is blamed for bad advertising. Identify some good local advertising in your community that appears to be done on a shoestring budget. Identify the characteristics of these ads that make them unusually good. Compare these ads to some national ads you like. What do the local ads and national ads have in common that make them "good" in your mind?

2. Web sites for national advertisers often give you clues as to how they have segmented the marketplace. For example, Hallmark Cards, Inc., includes Web pages specifically geared to its target groups. Search the Web for some good sites that are organized around the advertisers' target groups. Print out the home page or first screen that identifies these groups and write the names of the groups next to where they appear.

3. Find a Web site for a multinational company like Shell Oil Company, Nestlé, or Norelco to find out how it views itself in the global marketplace. What features does your multinational company include in its Web site that instantly identify it as a multinational company?

1925–1950

1926

1934

The rapid growth and development of the advertising industry during the 1920s came to a screeching halt with the stock market crash of 1929 and the ensuing Depression, which lasted a good part of the next decade. In 1929, total ad spending hit a record high of $3.4 billion. Four years later it had plummeted to less than half that amount and stood at $1.7 billion. One effect of the Depression was a cautiousness among advertisers that spawned the growth of research companies offering more accurate measures of advertising effectiveness. George Gallup started polling people on their attitudes and lifestyles, and A. C. Nielsen began the first tracking of actual sales in drugstores. More government regulation, including the Wheeler-Lea Act and the Federal Food, Drug, and Cosmetic Act of 1938, was introduced to ensure that what was said in ads and on packaging was truthful.

The style of ads produced during this time reflected the nation's economic difficulties. Advertising budgets were shrinking, which resulted in less-expensive ads that often lacked the costly artwork that was so prevalent in the 1920s. One cost-cutting measure was the establishment of in-house

art departments in agencies, which remain a part of agency structure today. When World War II broke out in the 1940s, the growth of the advertising industry was further thwarted by shortages of talent, merchandise, and resources such as paper.

The federal government established the War Advertising Council to help mobilize the country behind the war effort. The War Advertising Council's ads were the forerunners of today's public-service advertising. After the war, the War Advertising

1933

Council was renamed as the Advertising Council, which continues to create public-service advertising even today.

Advertising's relationship with and importance to the media was solidified in the middle part of the century. Radio entertainment was dominated by the "soap opera," so-called because of the soap companies who sponsored them. When television arrived shortly after the end of World War II, it followed a similar pattern in that advertisers sponsored an entire show, with all of the messages (delivered by the presenter or an off-camera announcer) being given to one brand.

More new products that we still buy and use today appeared between 1925 and 1950, including cellophane and zippers. Advertising played a major role in explaining to the public what these products were and how to use them. Advertising agencies played a significant part in bringing new products into people's lives by researching consumers' views of the products and identifying difficulties that they might have with them. The agency's role in new-product introductions continues today.

1943

Part One
The Challenging **Business** of Advertising

Part Four
The Challenge
of Advertising
Creativity

Part Three

Media Strategy:

Challenges and Choices

Chapter Nine

Media Strategy and Creative Media Planning

MILK MUSTACHES:
A TESTAMENT TO THE ADVERTISING POWER
OF MAGAZINES

The campaign for the National Fluid Milk Processor Promotion Board in which celebrities (both real and fictional) are photographed wearing "milk mustaches" is likely to be remembered as one of the classic campaigns of the late 1990s.

You can probably list several of the people who have appeared in the campaign promoting the health benefits of milk and making it a more "hip" drink again after several years of declining sales, but can you recall where you saw those ad messages?

If your answer was "everywhere," then that is a testament to the power the media have to impact the delivery of an advertiser's message. In truth, at least for the first year or so of the campaign the ads were placed in just one medium—magazines. Yet the creative use of that medium had the effect of making the campaign seem to be omnipresent.

The agency that developed the plan, Bozell New York, was given a budget of $45 million. Instead of trying to compete with billion-dollar advertisers on television where their message would have been fighting for attention, they instead chose print, placing a total of 813 full-page ads in 56 different national and regional titles, all of which would be read by the desired target of women between the ages of 25 and 44.

The agency went further than that, however. They secured special deals and promotions with a number of the magazines to stretch the media dollars and increase their impact. *People* magazine added a 50-page supplement on celebrity diet and fitness routines, while *Better Homes and Gardens* created a 96-page cookbook with milk recipes.

Lisa, I like that mustache even better than the one you usually have.

Listen, bonehead, experts say calcium helps prevent osteoporosis. So have a cow, man.

MILK
Where's *your* mustache?™

1-800-WHY-MILK

The results were stunning. Not only were there significant changes in how people perceived the product and much greater awareness of its health benefits, but the sales losses were at first halted and then reversed, giving the client its first increase in sales in several years.

Source: T. L. Stanley, "The Gods of Milk," *MediaWeek*, 20 May 1996, 44–45.

LOOK BEFORE YOU LEAP

- How does media fit into the advertising and marketing process?

- How do media planners assess the potential market for their product or service?

- How do media planners find out what media their audience prefers?

- How do media planners select the right media for their target?

- How do media planners determine whether the media plan they put together is any good?

9

Assessing the Market and Audience

The first phase in the media planning process is assessing the market and audience. This phase creates the framework for a media plan that will work. It involves understanding what is happening to your brand in the marketplace in terms of sales and market share, and then determining who it is you are trying to reach with your advertising messages. The tasks in this first step are assessing the overall market, analyzing the competitive situation, understanding budgetary concerns, looking at brand dynamics, and finding the right audience.

Assessing the Overall Market

Before any thoughts can be given to the media objectives and strategies, you must first assess what the overall marketing plan is trying to achieve. What are the specific goals for the product or service? That is, through advertising, how many cars does GM plan to sell? How many visitors does Hyatt Hotels hope to attract to its locations? How many T-shirts does the souvenir shop in Malibu, California, hope to sell? Equally important is the goal as stated in terms of market share. That is, of the total market for the product in question, how much of it does your brand hope to achieve by this time next year? Bud Light, for example, currently has about an 8 percent share of the total beer category. In such a situation, where millions of cases of beer are sold each year and where the competition is fierce, it is unlikely the brand could increase its market share by more than a few decimal points. For a newer brand or for a brand in a smaller and less competitive category, however, market share gains can be quite considerable. Within two years, Arizona Iced Tea went from a tiny brand distributed in just a few markets to a national brand representing 12.6 percent of all units sold in that category.

The media implications of the marketing objectives are twofold. First, they can indicate what the purpose of the advertising may be. Do you intend to bring in new users for the brand or encourage current users to use the product or service more often? If the volume and/or share goal for marketing is very aggressive, it is likely that it will only be achieved if new users are

Bozell's ad campaign for the Fluid Milk Processor Promotion Board is testament not only to a great idea but also to the creativity of how the media were planned and bought. Recall from Chapter Two that media planning and buying constitute one of the major functions within an advertising agency, helping advertisers place their ad messages most effectively, and at a reasonable cost.

For any advertising message to be successful, you need a **media plan.** As Exhibit 9–2 shows, that plan has to fit the overall marketing and advertising process. Based on marketing goals (such as increasing sales, market share, etc.) and advertising goals (such as improving awareness, changing attitudes), the media plan defines **media objectives** to help achieve those goals, outlining how the target audience will be reached, and when. The **media strategy** details where and when messages appear, and at what cost.

This chapter focuses on showing how to design a creative media plan. (See the Appendix.) There are five steps involved: (1) assessing the market and audience, (2) examining media preferences, (3) selecting the right media, (4) executing the media plan, and (5) evaluating the media plan.

found. If that is the case, then the second implication for media may be that a larger budget is required to reach all of those potential new users with your advertising message.

Other elements of the marketing mix must also be taken into consideration. For example, what is happening to the brand in terms of its distribution or price? If Campbell's Soup is rolling out a new flavor in the southwest United States, then there is little point placing any media in the Northeast or Pacific Northwest (and, in fact, it is illegal to advertise a product when it is not available). If a brand has increased in price due to higher production costs, it may help to include some special promotion or event in the advertising, both to encourage sales despite the price increase and to remind people of the value and worth of the brand.

In addition to looking at the marketing objectives, attention must also be given to the more specific **advertising objectives.** These are the objectives that answer such questions as: What is the purpose and role of the advertising? Is it intended to build awareness for McDonald's outlets in Amoco gas stations? Remind people to use their Discover Card

to pay for their purchases? Encourage them to try Nabisco's new SnackWell's yogurts? Or simply maintain their awareness of the strength of the IBM brand name in computers? As we will learn later in this chapter, each of those advertising objectives will lead to important differences in the media strategy that you develop.

Analyzing the Competitive Situation

Before media planners can start putting together a media plan, they must first look at what the other brands in the category are doing. For this analysis, planners need to consider all potential competitors, not just those with similar products or services. For snackmaker Frito-Lay, the competitors to its Doritos tortilla chips include not only the company's own Lays potato chips or Fritos corn chips but also potentially other types of snacks, such as cookies, popcorn, or candy, as well. When Amtrak, the national passenger rail service, started to think carefully about its competition, it realized that it was trying not simply to get people to leave their cars at home but also to switch from using all other forms of transportation,

EXHIBIT 9–1   The Media Planning Process

Marketing Factors	Advertising Factors	Media Planning Factors
Competitors	**Budgeting**	**Competitive Spending Analysis**
Consumer Behavior	**Competitive Activity**	**Geographic Distribution**
Distribution Patterns	**Media Usage**	Local
Environmental Factors	**Message Types/Approaches**	National
Pricing Strategy	**Organization**	Regional
Product Quality	**Research**	**Media Goals**
Promotions	**Target Audience**	**Media Mix**
Advertising	Demographics	**Seasonality**
Direct Response	Psychographics	**Target Audience**
Public Relations	Geographics	Demographics
Sales Promotion	Product Usage	Size
Regulation	Relative Value	**Timing**
Segmentation		Continuity
Society and Culture		Flighting
		Pulsing

Take an Amtrak vacation,

and experience

an incredible high.

(33,000 feet to be exact)

Amtrak must consider travel not only by cars but also by airplanes and buses when evaluating its competitive environment. This ad for a unique program between United Airlines and Amtrak illustrates how Amtrak has turned this situation to its advantage, using its competitor as a positive rather than negative force in its sales efforts.

such as planes or buses. Competition may vary by time of day, too. The National Fluid Milk Processor Promotion Board, which funded the "milk mustache" campaign featured at the start of this chapter, had to face alternative competitors such as coffee or tea in the morning at breakfast, sodas at lunch time, and possibly alcoholic beverages in the evening.

Competitors typically are defined in terms of their spending on advertising, although it is important to include others who may be fighting for the same customers through nontraditional means. In the hair care category, for example, Mane 'n Tail established quite a presence by using public relations. The Body Shop, a retail chain that emphasizes ecologically sound beauty products, uses no traditional ads, instead relying on special events and word of mouth to increase sales.

When planners look at the amount spent on advertising by their brand and their competitors, they analyze historical spending over a two- or three-year period. By doing so, they can spot trends that will help them create their media plan. Some of the questions they consider are: Which firms have greatly increased or decreased spending, either overall or in a particular media category? And what proportion of all dollars spent on a medium by the category does Company A represent?

Competitive spending data are available through syndicated services such as Competitive Media Reporting (CMR) or may be collected independently by the client. Exhibit 9–2 gives an example of the data provided by CMR. Notice that in this example, showing total media spending over a three-year period in the sportswear category, the big players stand out. The top two spenders, Levi Strauss, Inc., and VF Corp. (which makes Wrangler and Lee jeans), are accounting for an increasing amount of total category spending, going up from 15 percent in 1994 to fully 48 percent of the total for 1996. You can also look at the chart to find out which companies have significantly increased or decreased their spending from year to year. In the case of Haggar Apparel, for example, the drop could have been due to a shift from sportswear to other types of clothing categories.

Additional reports would allow you to break down the total company spending further, both by individual brand (Lee jeans for women versus Lee jeans for men) and by media type (TV, magazines, outdoor billboards). This would allow you to determine changes in media strategy (i.e., switching from all television spending to all magazines), creative changes (i.e., moving from 30-second to 15-second TV spots, or full-page to quarter-page print ads), or target audience shifts (i.e., moving from prime-time evening shows to daytime soap operas, or from *Time* and *Newsweek* to *Parents* and *Child* magazines).

Understanding Budgetary Concerns

Planners must know from the beginning approximately how much money they have to spend. This is important because it greatly affects the types of media that can be chosen. Is the budget $500 or $5,000,000? It is also crucial to know from the beginning whether there are any constraints on how the funds can be allocated. For example, must certain TV shows or newspapers be included and others avoided? There may also be sound strategic reasons for making a special case for using one vehicle over another. For example, for years Master Lock put all of its (limited) television budget into the once-a-year Super Bowl because it could be guaranteed that the ad would be seen by a good portion of the 45 million or so viewers who tune in for that one special event. Some companies may have additional funds that are held back for conducting market or media tests, or for special opportunities that come along.

The media budget must be looked at in conjunction with the funds for other parts of the mix, as well. Ideally, for example, promotional moneys will be allocated to tie in with the media spending in order to generate a cumulative impact for both elements. When tire maker BF Goodrich joined up with Timberland shoes for a "Free All-Terrain Vehicle" promotion to link the idea of wearing the best shoes for hiking on foot with having the best tires for "hiking" in vehicles, they placed ads on outdoor billboards, in radio, and in car magazines to support the posters and brochures displayed where both brands were sold. During the two months the campaign ran, tire sales increased 31 percent over the previous year, and 1,000 orders were placed for Timberland shoes at the tire dealerships.

Looking at Brand Dynamics

Perhaps the most obvious area that requires analysis before putting a media plan together is the brand to be advertised. The planner should be aware of when and where the brand is sold, and how often purchases are made. This step is as important for cream cheese as it is for insurance or CD players. There are three elements to

EXHIBIT 9–2   Example of CMR Data

A115: SPORTSWEAR PARENT COMPANY	TOTAL COMPANY SPENDING		
	1994	1995	1996
Bongo	3,038.1	3,829.9	3,120.8
Bugle Boy Industries, Inc.	1,286.8	3,186.5	1,831.2
Donna Karan	1,369.8	580.8	1,540.1
Escada AG	928.0	983.5	1,132.3
Farah USA, Inc.	4,396.2	3,061.7	1,720.6
Farley Industries	11,434.7	4,457.7	8,235.0
Gap, Inc.	20,789.7	17,716.7	15,868.8
Gianni Versace	649.3	873.6	3,025.0
Guess, Inc.	9,663.2	10,629.2	8,400.2
Haggar Apparel Co.	14,522.1	13,389.0	7,526.6
Joop	468.8	1,135.8	1,083.9
Levi Strauss Assoc., Inc.	89,256.7	104,033.0	120,057.8
Nike, Inc.	5,763.2	12,199.1	3,897.6
Pepe Clothing USA	1,599.6	2,589.8	14,987.0
Russell Corporation	11,180.7	12,421.2	12,482.6
Sara Lee Corporation	11,634.6	19,478.0	16,079.9
Sasson Jeans for Men	1,151.9	750.2	1,059.4
Seattle Pacific Industries, Inc.	1,609.7	1,077.0	3,809.8
Starter Corporation	5,999.6	7,646.6	5,529.4
VF Corporation	41,448.2	43,545.1	67,072.4
Walt Disney Corporation	1,031.7	2,115.1	2,128.3
Warnaco Group, Inc.	1,421.3	1,174.8	2,669.0
Total of top 22 companies	240,643.9	266,874.3	303,257.7
Total category	328,028.5	353,254.5	387,324.1

Note: Figures are in thousands of U.S. dollars.

brand dynamics: geography, seasonality, and purchase cycle.

GEOGRAPHY   Because we can usually buy the same goods in stores throughout the U.S., we tend to think that products do not have any geographic limitations. But if you think about the size of the country, it should not be too surprising that there are, indeed, many goods and services whose media plans are impacted by geography. It might be as simple as not advertising scuba diving equipment as much in inland areas as on coastlines, to knowing that four-wheel-drive cars sell better in the more mountainous areas of the country than in flat areas. On a more local level, there is little point in advertising a regional chain of pizza restaurants beyond a given parameter outside the local market.

Even brands that are nationally distributed often choose to have regional executions in their campaign to appeal to local targets. Exhibit 9–3 shows both a regional and a national advertisement for a national brand.

SEASONALITY   The link between geography and seasonality can sometimes be close. Not only would Subaru be less likely to promote its four-wheel-drive car in Baton Rouge, Louisiana, but it would also probably not promote it as much in June in Minneapolis, when

the need for such a product benefit is less pronounced. Obvious examples of seasonal advertising include suntan lotion during the winter months in places where it is below freezing, or snowblowers in the summer when it is 90 degrees. A less obvious form of seasonality may be the brand's name itself. To launch a new French perfume named Parfum d'Ete ("summer perfume"), the advertiser covered the most famous bridge in Paris with 40,000 fresh flowers on midsummer's day. It not only attracted a good deal of attention from passersby, but was also featured on the national television news during prime time.[1]

Many products have a seasonal skew to their sales, so media can be used to do one of two things: either generate as many sales during that peak period or, less commonly, promote the item outside of the heavy selling season to help flatten the peaks somewhat. Even goods or services that one might think would sell evenly throughout the year do, in all likelihood, have some seasonality to them. Hospital birthing departments, for example, are needed and selected by people every day and every week, but there are more births during the summer months, so demand is higher in June and July than in November or December. For this reason, the hospital might want to advertise in winter to promote its child-preparation classes.

EXHIBIT 9–3   National brands will use regional executions of their advertising messages to generate more local appeal for their products or services. As shown here, American Airlines uses both national ads and regional ads, such as this one for the greater Chicago area, to reach consumers who might use its services.

Marketers are increasingly creating seasonal events. The "back to school" period in late August/early September has offered businesses as diverse as shoe stores, luncheon meats, and crayons the chance to reach their customers at a time of the year when their products are more likely to be on buyers' minds. That, in turn, has a significant impact on how the media are planned and bought. Thanksgiving has become an important time of year for the holiday-related foods that are consumed primarily in November. Foods such as whipped cream, green beans, and pie fillings all focus their advertising efforts at this time of year.[2]

Some products that used to have a seasonal sales period no longer do so. Many fruits and vegetables, for example, used to be in stores for just a few months or even weeks. Today, however, one-quarter of all produce that we consume in the U.S. is imported, primarily during the times of the year when we cannot grow it ourselves. In the winter months we get apples and pears from Argentina, cantaloupes and oranges from the Dominican Republic, and asparagus from Peru. That means the local grocery store can advertise and promote its produce specials on a year-round basis, not just seasonally.[3]

PURCHASE CYCLE Knowing how often a brand is purchased is important in determining that brand's dynamics. People buy suntan lotion more frequently in warm-weather climates and/or in summer than they do during the winter in Vermont. For that reason, Coppertone will probably concentrate advertising in the late spring and summer, when most people are more likely to be thinking about being out in the sun. On the other hand, regardless of where someone lives, he or she will probably not buy a washing machine more than once every few years. Thus, Maytag would need to advertise at a steady rate year-round in hopes of catching potential customers as they are considering this purchase. And for Burger King, it is important to try to reach the target audience on a near-daily basis because it is likely that people are making decisions about which fast-food restaurant to go to at that frequency.

Finding the Right Audience

Before thinking about which media will best help achieve the marketing objectives, planners need to know who it is they are trying to reach. Is the brand bought most often by young women, older men, or teenagers? Do they live in urban or suburban areas? Are they affluent or of moderate income? Do these people like outdoor activities or boardgames? Do they consider themselves opinion leaders, or do they ask friends for advice about brands? All of these demographic, lifestyle, and psychographic characteristics help to define a **target audience** for a media plan.

Ideally, the media target is identical to the overall marketing target for the brand. However, there are several important differences to keep in mind. First, when buying media to reach the

Turn the sea green with envy

JANTZEN

Keep
Our
Beaches
Beautiful.

For the retailer nearest you call
1-800-238-SWIM

Special thanks to Hawaii's Ihilani Resort & Spa, located on Oahu's west shore

Purchase cycle is one of the many elements that must be considered when planning media strategy. Jantzen, for example, allocates a good portion of its budget for advertising during the early spring and summer months, when people are more likely to purchase swimsuits.

target audience, it is not possible to specify actual product users, such as "Discover Card owners" or "frequent business travelers." For radio and television, only age and sex demographics can be used, such as "men 25–54" or "women 18–49." With magazines and newspapers, the targetability depends on the nature of those media types. Each magazine will tend to be read by a certain type of person. For example, publications about children and child care, such as *Parents* and *Parenting,* will most often be read by people who have or are interested in children, while people interested in computers are more likely to be reading *PC Week* or *Internet World* than anyone else. With newspapers, the selectivity is geographic. That is, if space is bought in the *Milwaukee Sentinel,* it is because most of the audience is located in that area. Similarly, not many Miami readers can be reached with an ad in the *Gainesville Sun.*

Media planners develop a **target definition** using two primary sources. The first is from the advertisers themselves. Advertisers should have a good idea of who is using their product or who they think is the most likely prospect. Second, and equally important, syndicated sources provide survey data on product purchases across a wide array of categories. The two most well-known syndicated sources are Simmons and Mediamark Research, Inc. (MRI). Both companies ask questions of 20,000 people across the United States on the products and brands they buy, the media they use, and their personal characteristics, and

compile the information in a vast database on CD-ROM. This allows planners to find out, for example, how many people with children under the age of two are reading *Child* magazine, or what proportion of single women are heavy users of facial moisturizers.

Sample Simmons data are shown in Exhibit 9–4. This table shows that 1,175,000 adults with children under the age of two read *Child* magazine. That number is 10.4 percent of all adults with children under the age of two, and 31.8 percent of all readers of *Child* magazine. Compared to all adults in general, those with children under the age of 2 are 441 times more likely to be reading this magazine.

Sample MRI data are shown in Exhibit 9–5. In this table, you can see that there are 384,000 females who graduated college and are heavy users of facial moisturizer. (Heavy users are defined as those individuals who have used facial moisturizer 14+ times in the last 30 days.) This number represents 14.3 percent of all heavy users of the product but only 2.1 percent of all women who graduated college. The college graduate market is, therefore, 23 percent less likely than all women to be heavy users of this product (the index is below 100).

Having a target audience defined on paper for a media plan is only part of the task. The people who make up that target have to be reached effectively through advertising media, attend to the message placed there, and then take the desired action. That's a pretty tall order! As "Consumer Insight: Consumer

EXHIBIT 9–4   Sample Simmons Data

		ADULTS WITH CHILDREN UNDER 2		
	TOTAL U.S. POPULATION (000)	PERCENT OF TARGET USING MEDIA	PERCENT OF MEDIA IN TARGET	INDEX TO TOTAL POPULATION
American Baby	2,146	18.9%	39.7%	674
Baby Talk	1,416	12.5	36.1	613
Child	1,175	10.4	31.8	541
Cosmopolitan	1,113	9.8	6.6	111
Elle	270	2.4	5.8	96
Family Circle	1,503	13.3	6.3	106

Source: Simmons Market Research Bureau, *Study of Media and Markets,* Spring 1997, 67.

EXHIBIT 9–5 Sample MRI Data

| | WOMEN WHO ARE HEAVY USERS OF FACIAL MOISTURIZER | | | |
	TOTAL U.S. POPULATION (000)	PERCENT OF TARGET USING MEDIA	PERCENT OF MEDIA IN TARGET	INDEX TO TOTAL POPULATION
Graduated college	384	14.3%	2.1%	77
Attended college	1,000	37.2	3.6	135
Graduated high school	926	34.5	2.6	98
Did not graduate high school	376	14.0	2.0	74
Northeast	561	20.9	2.7	100
North Central	595	22.2	2.5	94
South	880	32.7	2.5	94
West	651	24.2	3.2	117

Note: A heavy user is defined as a user that has used a facial moisturizer more than 14 times in the last month.
Source: Mediamark Research Inc., *Men's, Women's Personal Care Products Report,* Spring 1996, 102.

Control and Avoidance" explains, getting consumers to pay attention to an advertiser's message is becoming increasingly difficult due to advances in technology.

R E S E T

1. **How do advertising objectives impact the media plan?**
2. **What do you need to know about your brand before you can start putting a media plan together?**
3. **What do you need to know about your target audience?**

Examining Media Preferences

As you have probably realized by now, as much as media planning involves dealing with numbers, there is also room for a good deal of judg-

ment. Once planners have identified the most appropriate target audience for the brand, they then have to think about how best to reach this audience with the advertising messages. That leads to an examination of the target's media preferences. Do they watch a lot of television, or do they prefer to read magazines and newspapers? Are they traveling frequently and therefore reachable through airport and in-flight media? Do they attend sports events where stadium signage could be effective? Are they in high school, where gym bags or book covers might work well? Are they the primary shopper for the household, suggesting the use of in-store media forms?

The key point to remember is that people don't watch "television"; they watch "Friends" or "This Week with David Brinkley." They don't read "magazines"; they read *Wired* or *Vibe.* This distinction is defined as the difference between a **media type,** or category (television, newspapers, etc.), and a **media vehicle,** the specific program or station or title that the consumer uses.

In today's media world, where there are myriad media forms available, the biggest challenge for media planners is to determine which specific media types would do the best job not only at reaching the target but also at doing so when potential buyers are likely to be receptive

CONSUMER INSIGHT

....

Consumer Control and Avoidance

In the halcyon early days of advertising media, the question of how to attract attention to your advertising message rarely came up. And if it did, it was usually answered by saying that if the creative message was good enough, it would be heard, or read, or seen. Today, that answer is probably not sufficient. Because while groundbreaking messages will usually reach the right audience, the sheer number of commercial messages out there has led consumers to look for ways to avoid them and to seek greater control over what advertising they will attend.

No one really knows just how many commercial messages people face each day. Consider that you are exposed to a brand name on the product itself; in paid media forms such as television, radio, newspapers, billboards, and magazines; or in the store. You may also hear the brand referred to in conversations at school or work (Pass me a Kleenex. Did you see that funny Budweiser ad during "Seinfeld" last night? Have

you checked out the new Pepsi Web site on the Internet?). There are newspaper articles on a new Ford car plant being built in Tennessee; interviews with celebrities who are smoking Marlboros or drinking Coca-Cola; and late-night infomercials for Volkswagen. The list is almost endless.

According to a study conducted by the Leo Burnett ad agency in the early 1990s, consumers feel that almost all encounters they have with a brand name constitute advertising. And with so many messages coming at them from all directions, consumers are increasingly looking for ways to control what they are exposed to and to avoid what they don't want to see or hear. For example, they read only those publications whose topics interest them. The general-interest magazines that were popular in the 1950s, such as *Life, Look,* and the *Saturday Evening Post,* have either disappeared altogether or are much smaller. Today's magazines are far more specialized, such as *Tropical Fish, Hobbyist,* or *Chemical Age.*

Consumers also control their TV and radio commercial exposure by ignoring all of the advertising messages that are not relevant to their needs or wants. As a case in point, it is only when they are in the market for a new car that most people start noticing car ads everywhere. They may even pay attention after they have bought one to reassure themselves that they made the right decision. But in one year's time, they will probably ignore Buick's TV spots or Honda's radio commercials. The clear challenge for advertisers and agencies, therefore, is to make sure that the ads directed at a given target are delivered at the most opportune and appropriate time *before* the brand decision has been made. This point is discussed in the next section of this chapter.

Technology is both helping and harming advertisers in overcoming consumer control and avoidance. Magazines can now implement selective binding, which enables them to use computerized printing presses to create hundreds or

to the advertiser's message. Those dual goals can be accomplished by considering two key characteristics of the target audience: the Personal Media Network© and Aperture®.

The Personal Media Network©

From a creative standpoint, it is difficult to design an ad that is targeted at "women 25–54." Just think of the enormous differences that exist between a 25-year-old and a 54-year-old! But if you know that you are writing your ad

to appear in an issue of *Cosmopolitan* rather than in *Woman's Day,* that tells you a good deal more about who your target is. In fact, a target group's media preferences are extremely helpful and informative for both media and creative decision making. Sometimes complete brand strategies can be designed around those choices. Kingsford Charcoal, for example, was targeting middle-aged men, with only mixed results. But when it was discovered that that particular group of people were heavy viewers of baseball

even thousands of different editions of the publication, each one designed to fit the needs and preferences of different subscribers. *Successful Farming* magazine produces up to 4,000 versions of each magazine issue, with both articles and advertisements tailored to the crops that are of concern to the subscriber (cotton for the cotton farmer, wheat for the wheat farmer, etc.).

In contrast, the advertisers' technological bane is the television remote control. Now in more than 80 percent of all television households, viewers can switch channels so easily that commercial avoidance occurs in a matter of seconds. It is not clear whether this really does lower commercial audience numbers, because there is some evidence to suggest that as many people will switch into a commercial break as will switch out. In addition, the way that many TV channels are programmed means that the viewer is likely to find ads on the screen across many networks all at the same time. Nielsen Media Research, which measures set tuning electronically, reports far less channel switching, or zapping, occurring than is reported in surveys. Remote controls also allow people to fast-forward through ads when they are watching programs they have taped, a practice known as zipping. The extent to which these practices are done has been estimated to be as low as 20 percent of the time to as high as 60 percent or more.

Niche magazines such as *Garden Railways* are becoming more and more popular today. These magazines provide readers with articles in a specific area of interest, and in doing so, they also provide advertisers with a clearly targeted market to whom they can direct their product or service message.

As we move into the era of computer interactivity the consumer's ability to control and/or avoid unwanted information, including advertising messages, will only grow. On the World Wide Web, it is up to consumers to decide whether they want to look at any advertising. This challenges the advertising industry to create attention-getting, informative, and entertaining advertisements that will not only bring people to them once but also make them want to keep coming back for more. Unlike traditional media forms, where the ad is placed in a specific program or issue that then has a limited shelf life, ads on interactive media may remain there for as long as the advertiser chooses to pay for the site.

QUESTIONS

How does consumer control and avoidance of advertising affect an advertiser's media choices? If you were developing a media plan for a new car model, for example, what would you do to ensure that your message got to the right target audience at the right time?

games, Kingsford gained a key insight into how to position the brand. Not only were analogies made in the creative message between success at the game and a successful, trouble-free cookout, but those ads were placed strategically during televised baseball games to increase the chances that they would be seen by the right audience.

One of the ways that media preferences can be examined is by analyzing the target's Personal Media Network. This tool, designed at DDB Needham Worldwide, allows media planners to "follow" the target's use of media forms and vehicles throughout the day—from the moment they wake up until the time they are in bed at night before going to sleep. The responses come from an annual national survey of 4,000 consumers.[4] Exhibit 9–6 shows a visual representation of how two people can have very different interactions with media during the course of a day. While both of them use radio, TV, magazines, and out-of-home media,

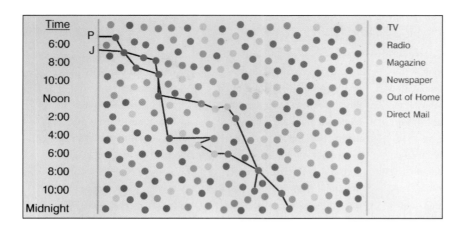

Time		TV
6:00	P	Radio
8:00	J	Magazine
10:00		Newspaper
Noon		Out of Home
2:00		Direct Mail
4:00		
6:00		
8:00		
10:00		
Midnight		

EXHIBIT 9–6   A Visual Depiction of the Personal Media Network©

they do so at very different times of the day, which might well impact the way that they would respond to ads appearing in those media.

There are two important premises behind the Personal Media Network. First, advertisers have a better chance of reaching people with their advertising message if they know which media the target audience uses—or doesn't use—at different times of the day. For example, if teenage users of Clearasil don't read news-papers, then why bother selecting news-papers as the medium for that product? Second, it makes sense to think that people are more likely to be receptive to an advertising message if it appears in the media that they have chosen to look at or listen to. If a Taco Bell ad appears in the late afternoon when the young adult target is watching television and probably thinking about what to have for dinner, not only is it more likely to be seen, but also the chances are increased that the audience can actually be persuaded to visit the restaurant that night.

In addition to indicating which media they use, people who respond to the Personal Media Network questions also state the primary reason for the media use: information, entertainment, or (in the case of TV and radio) background. Again, there are important creative implications here. A copywriter developing a Levi's jeans ad for a target that uses television mostly for entertainment might come up with a different creative strategy than for people who are newshounds, watching TV mostly to gain information.

Of course, it is not enough to know that the target uses a given media type. Planners also must find out which specific programs the target watches or to which station types they lis-

ten. Here, syndicated data can be used to fill in those important blanks. Services such as MRI and Simmons ask exhaustive lists of questions about the individual media vehicles that people use. This information can be compiled for a given target group and than analyzed to see where the best opportunities are to reach that group. Exhibit 9–7 gives an excerpted list of the various media vehicles included in different media categories.

Aperture®: Time, Place, and Circumstance

The second tool to help examine a target audience's media preferences is the concept of Aperture, also developed at DDB Needham Worldwide. This notion is divided into three elements: time, place, and circumstance. The planner has to consider when, where, and in what conditions the target is most likely to be receptive to the advertiser's message. The element of time is not simply time of day; it could be days of the week, weeks of the year, seasons, or any other time period. Similarly, place includes both physical location and where the consumer makes the purchase decision, such as in the store or at the car dealership. The third element, circumstance, is perhaps the trickiest to pin down. It refers to the consumer's frame of mind when he or she is exposed to the advertising message. When Tide is trying to reach a working mother to tell her about its new and improved detergent, it probably won't get a very good reception if she sees the ad at 5:30 P.M. when her children are screaming for dinner. On the other hand, if she is watching "Nightline" after the children are asleep, or reading *Parenting* magazine in bed at night, then there is a much better chance that she will attend to the message and be receptive to it.

Selecting the Right Media

After media planners have thought about, analyzed, and determined which media the target audience prefers, they are then in a position to select the media types and vehicles that will do the best job at reaching the marketing, advertising, and media objectives. This involves message considerations, media availability, nontraditional possibilities, scheduling the media, and evaluating the media.

Message Considerations

In thinking about different media possibilities, it is important to be aware of the inherent benefits and drawbacks of each media type. Television, for example, is good for demonstrating how a product can be used, something that radio is not great for. Some media are better for conveying emotion, while others are thought to be more appropriate for conveying information. Additionally, there are times when it is possible to enhance the message impact by contradicting people's expectation of what they will see or hear in a particular media vehicle. To promote two L'Oreal perfumes in England, for example, the advertiser placed color ads in *The Times* of London newspaper on the pages showing stock prices and classified recruitment ads—not where the reader would expect to see beautiful pictures promoting perfume![5]

The grid in Exhibit 9–8, developed at DDB Needham Worldwide, can provide some help in suggesting "which media do it best."

Media Availability

Just as certain product categories tend to be promoted more at given times of the year, so are some media vehicles seasonal in nature. The nature of those seasons is not always strictly calendar related, however. Television, for example, has an "upfront" selling season, during which time slots are sold for the new season of fall TV shows. This selling season traditionally begins in April or early May, beginning with the major broadcast networks (ABC, CBS, FOX, and NBC), followed by cable networks (CNN, ESPN, MTV, etc.). After those initial commercial slots are sold, advertisers must then make do with what remains (known as the *scatter market).*

Because the U.S. advertising marketplace operates under the laws of supply and demand, it is almost always possible to buy time or space in a media category. The question becomes how much you will have to pay for it. The more demand there is for a particular radio time slot or page position in a magazine, the more those media can charge the advertiser to be there. Thus, availability is not just a matter of whether there is room for another ad, it is also a financial concern.

For print media such as newspapers and magazines, there is less of a problem in expanding the space available for ads if demand increases. Unlike the electronic media, where most programs have to fit into time limitations (30-minute or 60-minute slots), printed media can simply add an extra page or two if they wish. They cannot do so indefinitely, however. If the balance between editorial content and advertising becomes too lopsided, readers are likely to complain or choose a title that is less cluttered with advertising.

Certain issues of a magazine or newspaper are likely to prove particularly popular with advertisers. Often, these are special issues, such as *Vogue* magazine's fall and spring

---

EXHIBIT 9–7   Excerpt of MRI Media List

MAGAZINES	RADIO FORMATS	NETWORK TELEVISION	CABLE NETWORKS
Allure	Adult Contemporary	American Gladiators	Arts & Entertainment
American Baby	All News	America's Funniest Home Videos	American Movie Classics
American Health	All Sports	America's Most Wanted	Black Entertainment TV
American Hunter	AOR/Progressive Rock	Baywatch	The Box
American Legion	Black	Beverly Hills 90210	Bravo
•	•	•	•
•	•	•	•
Working Woman	Religious/Gospel	Washington Week in Review	TV Food Network
WWF Magazine	Soft Contemporary	Wild America	USA Network
Yachting	Spanish	Wings	VH-1
Yankee	Urban Contemporary	WKRP in Cincinnati	The Weather Channel
YM	Variety	The X-Files	WGN-TV

Source: Mediamark Research, Inc., Spring 1995.

fashion previews, *Good Housekeeping's* November holiday issue, or *Time* magazine's "Person of the Year" issue in December. Many local newspapers create special inserts or features periodically throughout the year, such as Entertaining, Summer Dining Guides, Home and Garden, or Bridal Guide. Ad space can sell out for these, too. This is particularly important in the business-to-business arena, when trade publications publish special editions at the time of a key trade show or a peak selling period. As Sue Haggerty, vice president of media services at Koehler Iversen, a New York agency that specializes in health care and business-to-business advertising, points out, "Since there is usually heightened interest around the time of these events (not to mention bonus distributions), an advertiser can benefit from more intense reader involvement. A well-positioned ad in one of these issues can virtually be assured of enhanced readership."[6]

On the other hand, media that had not been considered before but that fit in very well with the target's media preferences and Aperture may become available. For example, a basketball stadium may start to accept advertising above the scoreboard, which would be an appropriate choice for advertising to Reebok's customers. A supermarket chain may add new in-store media signage or instant coupon machines that would help Contadina promote its tomato sauce more widely across the country.

EXHIBIT 9–8   Which Media do it Best

	TELEVISION	MAGAZINES	NEWSPAPER	RADIO	OUTDOOR	PLACE BASED	DIRECT MAIL	PUBLIC RELATIONS	POINT OF SALE	EVENT MARKETING	PACKAGING
Authority	S	S	S	G	G	G	A	G	A	G	A
Beauty	S	S	A	A	S	A	A	A	A	G	G
Bigger-than-life	G	G	G	A	S	G	A	G	A	S	A
Credibility	G	S	G	G	G	A	A	S	A	G	S
Demonstration	S	G	A	A	A	A	G	S	S	S	A
Drama	S	G	A	G	S	G	S	S	A	S	A
Education	S	S	G	G	A	A	S	S	A	G	G
Elegance	G	S	A	A	G	A	G	G	A	G	G
Emotion	S	G	A	G	G	A	G	G	A	A	A
Entertainment	S	G	A	S	S	G	G	A	A	S	A
Excitement	S	G	G	G	G	G	G	S	A	S	A
Flexibility	G	G	A	S	A	S	A	G	A	G	A
Humor	S	G	G	S	S	A	G	A	G	A	A
Imagination	S	G	A	S	S	G	A	A	A	G	A
Immediacy	G	A	S	S	G	S	S	S	S	G	A
Information	G	S	S	G	A	G	S	G	G	G	S
Influence	S	G	G	A	A	A	G	S	A	G	A
Innovation	G	G	A	G	G	S	G	G	G	S	A
Intimacy	G	S	G	S	A	A	S	G	A	A	A
Intrusiveness	S	G	A	G	G	S	S	G	S	G	A
News	S	G	S	G	A	A	S	S	G	G	G
Quality	S	S	G	G	A	A	S	S	A	G	G
Permanence	A	S	A	A	G	G	A	G	A	A	A
Price	G	A	S	G	A	A	G	A	S	A	G
Recipe	G	S	G	A	A	G	S	A	S	S	S
Sensuality	S	G	A	S	G	G	G	G	A	S	G
Spectacle	G	S	A	A	S	G	A	G	S	S	G
Style	G	S	G	A	G	A	A	G	A	G	G
Unconventional	G	S	A	S	S	G	G	A	A	S	G

Key: **S** Superior   **G** Good   **A** Acceptable

Source: DDB Needham Worldwide

Or an advertiser might "create" a new medium, as U.K. agency Abbott Mead Vickers did to promote the financial news-paper, *The Economist,* when they put posters on the roofs of buses to attract the attention of people working in high-rise office buildings, with the message "Hello to all our readers in high office."[7] In all of these cases, the important point for the media planner is to remain flexible and open to considering the variety of choices that are, or may become, available. While this makes the task of the planner more challenging, it also makes the creation of the media plan more interesting and dynamic.

Nontraditional Possibilities

The panoply of media choices extends beyond looking for new TV shows, radio formats, or magazine titles. Indeed, the number of nontraditional media possibilities seems to have increased exponentially in the past decade or so. And many that were once considered unusual or innovative have become fairly standard today. For example, the Leo Burnett team working to promote Samsonite luggage to frequent travelers turned to extensive use of airport media such as posters in the main walkways and baggage claim areas, the Airport Channel at the gates, and *USA Today,* read heavily by travelers. The focus on such nontraditional media proved both innovative and successful. As Lisa Seward, assistant media director on the account noted, "The plan wasn't totally new; it was more evolution than revolution. We've been using in-flight magazines for years, but we just keep adding to that so now we have a powerful, integrated program.... Airports aren't all we do, but they're where we focus."[8]

The same success is likely to be found in the future for several media forms that still seem novel. In-store advertising, for instance, only took off in the 1980s as advertisers realized the importance of reaching consumers right before they made their brand choices. At the same time, stores were looking for new sources of revenues. That resulted in the appearance of companies such as ActMedia, which offers ads and promotions in the aisles, on the shelves, and at the checkout. As for future nontraditional venues, online services and the Internet are two critical new areas for advertising messages. As more and more of the population gains access to or owns a computer

(currently about one-third of homes do so), the attractiveness of these new media forms will grow considerably. Advertisers have even looked beyond earth to promote their products. The movie "The Last Action Hero" paid $500,000 to be emblazoned on the side of an unmanned NASA rocket, perhaps to reach potential viewers in other universes!

Nontraditional media thinking should also incorporate other forms of marketing communications. As we noted earlier, studies have shown that to consumers nearly all encounters with the brand name are considered forms of advertising. When Nike sponsors a triathlon and gives away T-shirts with its logo emblazoned on them, that can be seen as a medium of communications. When street vendors hand out samples of General Mills cereals to

Chicago Tribune Magazine

SPECIAL ISSUES

FASHION
SEPTEMBER 7, 1997

TRAVEL
OCTOBER 5, 1997

HOME DESIGN
SEPTEMBER 21, 1997

Look forward to the Chicago Tribune Magazine's special Fall 1997 issues exploring Fashion, Travel and Home Design. With articles by our award-winning editorial staff and breathtaking four-color photography, these issues offer a unique environment for our advertisers and readers.

DEADLINES:	Publication Date	Space (10:00 a.m.) Deadline	Material Deadlines (Noon) Color	B&W
Fashion	9/7	7/28	8/1	8/8
Travel	10/5	8/25	8/29	9/5
Home Design	9/21	8/11	8/15	8/22

To advertise in the Chicago Tribune Magazine's special Fall 1997 issues, contact your Chicago Tribune Representative or Judi Bowe at (312) 222-3244.

 FOR 150 YEARS IT'S MEANT THE WORLD TO CHICAGO Chicago Tribune

www.chicago.tribune.com

Special issues of magazines— such as the *Fashion, Travel,* and *Home Design* issues promoted in this planner-targeted advertisement by the *Chicago Tribune Magazine*—provide unique opportunities for advertisers. Because they are so popular, advertising space in these issues tends to sell out quickly.

passersby, that too is a media form. Even putting a brand name on keychains or pencils or duffel bags means that future customers will have the opportunity to see your name and possibly remember it the next time they are in the market for that type of product or service. Exhibit 9–9 lists some examples of nontraditional media forms.

Scheduling the Media

Once the media mix has been determined, the next issue to consider is how media time and space should be scheduled. Here, there are three traditional patterns of media distribution: continuity, flighting (or bursting), and pulsing.

The ideal for many companies is to advertise throughout the year, providing a constant media presence. This type of scheduling is known as **continuity.** Because it is often not known exactly when the target customer will be buying a bottle of Pantene shampoo or a Whirlpool refrigerator or Gatorade soft drink, some advertisers want to keep their name before the public as much as they can. In reality, the only firms that can afford to do this are the biggest-spending advertisers, such as McDonald's, Philip Morris, or AT&T. You probably see one or more ads from such companies on a daily basis. For smaller-budget advertisers, continuity is harder to achieve. This leads them to one of the two other scheduling alternatives.

Flighting, sometimes referred to as *bursting,* involves concentrating the media activity into selected periods, or flights. These might last for a week, a month, or several months. Consequently, there are times in the year where no advertising activity occurs. The flights are scheduled in accordance with the marketing strategy and objectives, taking into account people's purchasing habits, seasonality, and product usage, among other factors. For example, Hallmark Cards might flight its media to tie in to major card-giving holidays, such as Christmas, Valentine's Day, or Mother's Day.

A scheduling strategy that offers a combination of continuity and flighting is **pulsing.** Here, a low level of media spending is maintained for much, if not all of the year, but it is supplemented by additional pulses, or bursts, of greater activity at key times. For example, Campbell's Soup might advertise in each month of the year but pulse the schedule to have increased spending during the winter months. Exhibit 9–10 gives a graphic depiction of the three scheduling strategies.

The main advantage of continuity is that it keeps the brand name before the public at all times, reminding consumers to think of buying that brand whenever they might be considering a purchase. Flighting or pulsing can be the most useful when an extra amount of attention is desired, such as for a new product launch or brand introduction, to saturate the media with your product or service. The chief drawback to continuity is its costliness, whereas for the other two scheduling strategies, it is the fear of not having an advertising presence at the moment of brand choice. Research in the early 1990s suggested that for frequently purchased items, such as those that are sold in supermarkets, the most effective scheduling approach for advertising in order to generate additional sales is to maintain a continuous presence in the marketplace.[9]

Decisions about scheduling also need to take into account three additional factors: media objectives, size of the media budget, and product usage patterns. The scheduling strategy that you choose will depend, in part, on your media objectives. That is, one type of schedule will do a better job at reaching a large

EXHIBIT 9–9 Examples of Nontraditional Media Forms

ABC Inflight	Airplanes
ActMedia	Supermarkets
Aislevision	Supermarkets
Aladdin's Castle	Malls
Beyond the Wall	College posters
Channel One	High schools
CineSpot	Cinemas
CNN Airport Network	Airports
Cover Concepts Book Covers	High schools
Go Cards	Health clubs, restaurants
Instant Coupon Machine	Supermarkets
Military MediaBoards	Military bases
Miller Airship	Blimps
Resort Sports Network	Resorts
Roadmark Fleet Advertising	Trucks
Screenvision	Cinemas
U	College newspapers

number of different people fewer times, while another will be preferred if you want to reach more of the same people more frequently. For most advertisers on limited budgets, flighting the schedule is the best alternative. Similarly, for seasonal products such as lawnmowers or ski vacations, it does not make sense to advertise all year round, as people are not likely to purchase these products throughout the year.

Once the media schedule has been determined, the media planner then puts it into a flowchart, giving a visual presentation of all media activity for the brand for a specified time period (typically one year). Exhibit 9–11 shows an example of such a flowchart. Notice how the two different media forms—daytime television and women's magazines—are used differently throughout the year, with television being used almost constantly in every week of the plan, while magazines are selected more in particular months (probably due to the content of those issues).

Evaluating the Media

In order to properly evaluate the various media forms under consideration, it is important to be able to make comparisons both between media vehicles and across media types. These comparisons, known as **intermedia** and **intramedia,** respectively, are done by using some simple, straightforward calculations.

One of the most basic concepts used in media planning is the notion of a **rating point.** This is defined as the percentage of a given population group that uses a specified media vehicle. For example, if the household rating for the television program "48 Hours" is 9.4, that means 9.4 percent of all households in the U.S. viewed that show in a given week. The media planner can compare that rating to the figures for other possible programs in which to advertise. Rating points for individual media vehicles are accumulated to provide the **gross rating points (GRPs)** that form the basic building blocks of a media plan. That is, the planner summarizes the total number of points by media type, and for all media, to show how the ratings will be distributed for the plan. Thus, if "48 Hours" has a 9.4 rating against the target and "Friends" has a 14.3 rating, then the total GRPs would be 23.7 (9.4 + 14.3 = 23.7).

Although the rating point is used in each media category (TV, radio, magazine, and so

EXHIBIT 9–10 Scheduling Strategies: Continuity, Flighting, and Pulsing

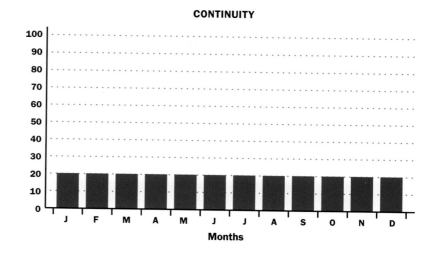

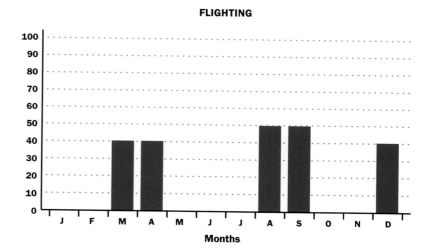

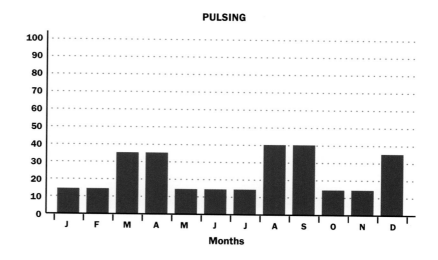

EXHIBIT 9–11   Sample Flowchart of a Media Plan

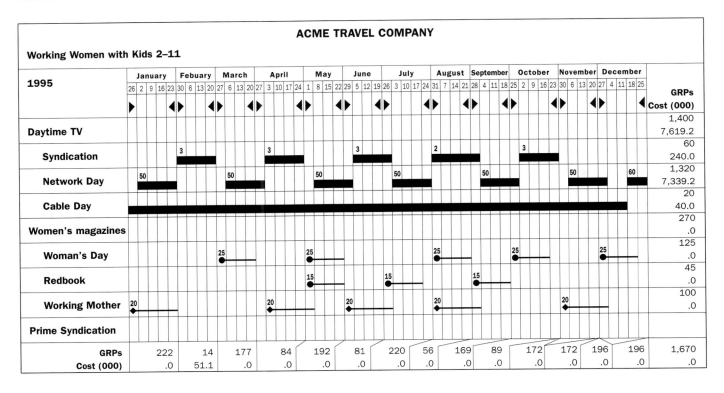

Source: Stone House Systems.

on) it represents something slightly different for each one. Generally speaking, the concept refers to the percentage of people using a given media vehicle in a set time period. But the measurement used to arrive at that figure varies for each media category, making it not quite the same across the board. For radio, the rating is generally provided on a station-by-station basis by time of day; for example, WXRT in Chicago may receive a 2.5 rating in an average quarter-hour during the morning. Meanwhile, that same rating figure for the TV talk show "Oprah" refers to the percentage of people who watched three or more minutes of the show. And for *Outside* magazine, it would mean the proportion of people who read one or more issues within a one-month time period.

Rating points and GRPs can be translated from percentages into people. This is done by converting gross ratings into **gross impressions,** which express the number of audience exposures to a media vehicle or media plan multiplied by the number of times they will see or hear them. This figure includes duplication, because one

person may see several of the vehicles in which your ad is placed, and do so multiple times.

The proportion of the net *unduplicated* audience that has the opportunity for exposure to an ad is defined as a plan's **reach.** This number, usually expressed as a percentage, is the most common evaluation tool in media planning. Reach is defined as the percentage of the target audience that has the opportunity to be exposed one or more times to a specified media vehicle, or media plan, in a given timeframe. The number of times the target is likely to be exposed, known as the **average frequency,** is another key tool for media planning. For a given time period, such as four weeks, or for the full plan's timeframe, such as one year, the average frequency shows how many times, on average, the target will be likely to be exposed to the media in which the ads appear.

Through the use of computers, which can perform statistical calculations quickly, it is relatively easy to determine the percent of the target exposed at each level of frequency, known as the **frequency distribution.** This shows what percent of the target will be exposed to the media 1+ times, 2+ times, 3+ times, and so on.

The relationship between reach and frequency is critical to how a plan is developed. If the objective is to reach a large number of different people and increase awareness of a brand, for example, then the plan must have great reach. In other words, it must use many different media vehicles and types to increase the likelihood of different people seeing the ad in each of those places. On the other hand, if the goal is to remind a select group of people to use a brand more often, then the plan should emphasize frequency, placing more ads in fewer vehicles to reach the same people over and over

again. Given a limited budget, there is usually a tradeoff between reach and frequency because it is too expensive to place many ads in a large assortment of vehicles for an extended period of time. Only the biggest-spending advertisers are usually able to do this. Exhibit 9–12 illustrates the difference between reach and frequency.

In addition to evaluating media possibilities in terms of their audience impact, the media planner must also consider cost implications. There are two key terms to know. **Cost per thousand (CPM)** is a calculation of how much it will cost to reach 1,000 members of the target audience. The CPM is simply the total cost of the schedule, divided by the audience size, and

TECHNOLOGY WATCH

Computers in Media Planning

The famous dictum that we live in interesting times is highly appropriate for media planning. The media planning function has been dramatically transformed by the growth and expansion of computers. In the 1980s, media planners spent hours poring over volumes of printed materials to discover how much a particular brand, and all its competitors, were spending in different media categories; today, that information is available at the touch of a few buttons on the computer. At one time, their target audience analyses were restricted to whatever was on the printed page; now, they can define their targets in any manner they wish to find out the lifestyle, media usage, and demographics of that particular group of people.

Computers also help media planners in crunching the numbers. The standard issue for a media planner in the 1970s was a huge desktop calculator.

Today, although numbers still play a very important role in the life of a planner, the computer can do most of the simple yet tedious calculations that are required in putting a plan together. The key terms of *reach* and *frequency*, which involve sophisticated statistical routines using probability techniques, can be produced by a computer in a matter of seconds!

Having the computer do much of the drudgery allows media planners more time for strategic and creative thinking. Because the computer handles so much of the detail in constructing a media plan, today's planners usually have to consider more alternatives than before. Should radio or television be used? What is the impact of advertising across 15 weeks versus 20 weeks? What happens if some of the television advertising is instead put into magazines? It used to be that the answers to

such questions involved lengthy calculations and were only embarked upon if the answers were considered essential. Now planners routinely go through numerous "what if" scenarios to make sure that the plan that is presented to the client is truly optimal.

In the future, computers will likely play an even larger role in media planning. Already, flowcharts can include digitized images of actual ads, so that as the advertiser looks at when the TV spots are going to run, he or she can also see what those commercials will look like. The continued growth in the amount of data being collected and processed on advertising activity will mean that computers will become even more essential in constructing and executing a media plan.

EXHIBIT 9–12   The Difference between Reach and Frequency

REACH   VERSUS   FREQUENCY

The process by which the media are purchased differs not only by media type but also by geography. For national media such as television and magazines, the media buyer usually works with his or her counterpart at the national office of the TV network or magazine publisher (the media seller or rep). Rates (costs) are negotiated for the specific time or space required in the particular magazine issue or program. The cost for electronic media will vary depending on supply and demand. It is likely to be higher when the economy is doing well and companies are thus spending more on advertising. The cost also depends on how popular the show or title is; an advertiser pays far more to advertise in "Seinfeld" than in "Nightline," for example, because more people watch that situation comedy than the late-night discussion show. The volatility of prices for TV and radio also reflects the fact that what is actually being sold is airtime, which is finite. Unlike the print media, where space can be added to accommodate additional advertising needs, the electronic media have only a finite amount of commercial time available; the commercial time must be sold before the time has expired.

For local media, such as newspapers, local television, or local radio, the media buyer works with the individual representatives at the local newspaper or TV or radio station. In the case of local radio and television, this entails a good deal of negotiation, with the buyer receiving competing bids from a number of possible stations that meet the plan's criteria in terms of reaching the desired target audience at the right cost. He or she will then negotiate directly with the station to find the best deal in each market. With newspapers, where there is generally only one per market, the negotiation typically involves determining where the ad will appear (i.e., in which section). Pricing is less negotiable here. "Adscape: Buying Media" provides an overview of the work of a media buyer.

multiplied by 1,000. A plan that aims to reach 50,000,000 target audience members and costs $5,000,000 would have a CPM of $100 (5,000,000 / 50,000,000 = 0.1; 0.1 × 1,000 = 100). Planners can use the CPM for both intramedia comparisons, such as comparing the cost of one magazine against another, or for intermedia comparisons, such as looking at the CPM of television versus radio.

Another cost comparison planners use is the **cost per rating point (CPP).** This is defined as the cost of purchasing one rating point in a given media vehicle or type. It is calculated by dividing the total cost of the vehicle or type by the average rating for that vehicle or type. Examples of all these calculations appear in Exhibit 9–13. Today, much of the tedious work in media planning is alleviated by computers. "Technology Watch: Computers in Media Planning" explores this in greater detail.

Executing the Media Plan

Once the media plan has been completed and scheduled, it must receive the approval of everyone involved, both within the agency and, most importantly, at the advertiser. At that point, the plan is ready for execution. This means that the media that have been proposed must now be bought—commercial time on radio and television, or ad space in newspapers, magazines, and billboards. Then, the ads begin running.

Evaluating the Media Plan

Once the media plan has been devised, agreed to, and executed, it might seem that the planner's task is complete. In fact, there is one more key phase: evaluating the plan to make sure it worked. There are three tasks involved: posting, monitoring, and measuring the impact. Each task is considered briefly below.

Posting and Follow Up

Following up after an ad has been executed, known as **posting,** works differently for different media forms. In television, the buyer receives an affidavit that shows exactly where the commercial ran—the day, date, time, and position in the program and in the pool of commercials. If it turns out that the ad appeared in a venue or at a time significantly different from the one agreed upon with the station or network, the advertiser can generally request a **make-good.** This means that the media channel agrees either to give monetary compensation or, more commonly, to place the spot again at no charge. Although the data about when and where the spot ran are generated overnight, the advertiser or agency usually will not receive them for a week or longer, which sometimes results in the timeliness of the commercial being lost.

As for posting procedures in other media, radio stations provide affidavits that state when the ads ran. Magazines usually send a copy of the issue to their clients. Newspaper ads can be checked by requesting the **tearsheet,** which is a copy of the actual page with the ad on it. Services are available to provide proofs of purchase to the agency or buyer. For outdoor billboards, it is possible to "ride the boards" with the outdoor company, visiting all or a proportion of the actual boards in each city to verify where they are located and whether all the negotiated terms have been met.

Ongoing Monitoring of the Plan

The media planner has to keep track of possible changes occurring not only in the media but also in all elements of the marketing mix that could potentially harm the plan's ability to impact sales. On the media side, for example, a major international or domestic crisis could disrupt regularly scheduled television programs and/or people's viewing habits, which might mean the chances of your ads being seen are substantially reduced. Other marketing considerations that the planner must watch for in monitoring the plan include unexpected new entrants into the category or a sudden increase in spending by a major competitor.

EXHIBIT 9–13   Media Concepts and Calculations

Audience: Number or percent of homes or persons reading, listening to, or viewing a particular media vehicle.

Rating: The percent of target audience reached by single issue of a publication or episode of a program.

   RATING = AUDIENCE/UNIVERSE ESTIMATE

Coverage: The percent of homes or persons receiving a broadcast signal in a geographic area or receiving a specific magazine or newspaper title.

Households using television (HUT): Percent of homes watching television at a given time.

   NUMBER OF HOUSEHOLDS WITH SETS ON/TOTAL TV HOUSEHOLDS

Persons using television (PUT): Percent of persons watching television at a given time.

   NUMBER OF PERSONS WITH SETS ON/TOTAL TV PERSONS

Share of audience: Percent of homes or people using television at a given time who are tuned to a particular program.

   SHARE = RATING/HUT OR PUT

Gross ratings points (GRPs): Total number of rating points against a specific target for a particular media schedule.

Gross impressions: GRPs expressed in numbers rather than percent.

   IMPRESSIONS = GRPs X UNIVERSE

Reach: Number or percent of different homes or people exposed at least once to a media vehicle or schedule in a given time period.

Average frequency: Average number of times a home or person is exposed to a media vehicle or schedule.

Effective frequency: Minimum number of times a consumer must be exposed to a message to have a positive impact on that individual; this varies according to objectives, advertisers, etc.

Frequency distribution: Reach of media vehicle or schedule at each level of frequency (1, 2, 3 times, etc.).

Circulation: Total number of copies of a publication sold through all forms of distribution.

Readers per copy: Average number of people reached by a single issue of a publication.

Cost per thousand (CPM): Cost to deliver a vehicle or schedule to 1,000 homes or people.

   CPM = (MEDIA COST/IMPRESSIONS) x 1000

Cost per rating point (CPP): Cost to deliver one rating point.

   CPP = TOTAL SCHEDULE COST/GRPs

Universe estimate: Total persons or homes in a given population.

Sources: Northwestern University Integrated Advertising/Marketing Communications Department and Magazine Publishers of America, *A Guide to 19 Key Media Terms* (Chicago: Northwestern University, 1993); and *Nielsen Pocket Guide to TV Terms* (New York: Nielsen Media Research, 1995).

AdScape

....

Buying Media

In order to be successful at buying media space or time, a combination of talents is needed: a thorough understanding of the marketing and media objectives for the plan, complete knowledge of media dynamics, and skill at negotiating with the media sellers (the magazines, newspapers, or radio and TV stations). A media buy must remain in line with the communications objective of the plan, which might be to reach 45 percent of the target within a four-week time frame or to expose the target to the brand's message at least four times within the next two weeks. The buyer also must be familiar with what is happening in the media marketplace at the time the negotiations are held. How much inventory is available, in terms of programs, print space, or billboards? How great is the demand for radio spots in New Orleans, Louisiana, or Orlando, Florida? Because the media industry is driven by supply and demand, the cost of time and space is directly reflective of those terms.

When the negotiating between buyer and seller begins, it is likely that the price offered by the seller will be higher than the amount the buyer is willing to pay. It then becomes a matter of discussion to agree on the price that both sides can find acceptable. Sometimes the seller will make that cost more attractive by including merchandising or "added value" elements. These might be additional mentions of the brand at the beginning or end of a broadcast ("This has been brought to you by your local Midas dealers"), free tickets to a local sporting event, or an extra "free" page in a magazine.

After the buy has been made, the buyer is then responsible for ensuring that the ad runs as scheduled and that the media vehicle in which it appears performs as well as expected or guaranteed.

QUESTIONS

What types of information would help a media buyer's knowledge of media dynamics? How would you approach a negotiation in which the two sides cannot agree on a monetary figure for the buy? What kinds of added value elements might you consider acceptable in a TV airtime negotiation?

Source: Jim Surmanek, Media Planning: A Practical Guide (Lincolnwood, IL: NTC Business Books, 1996), as excerpted in Inside Media, 4 October 1995, 40–42.

Indeed, anything that upsets the marketing arena is liable to have an effect on the media plan. The planner, therefore, should keep a close eye on the marketing and media situation and be prepared to recommend changes in the media tactics to respond to changes in the real world. It is not too uncommon for the plan to be cut midway through the year, particularly if the company does not make its financial targets or a new management team is brought in. In that case, the planner has to revise what has been bought, canceling space and time when possible, or look for relief by selling what was bought to another advertiser.

Measuring the Impact

Although the potential impact of the media plan is calculated upfront in terms of its reach and frequency, media planners also should evaluate the plan's effect based on actual figures. For example, the planner might have planned to buy a total of 585 gross rating points for the year, generating a monthly reach of 45 percent. If it turns out that the plan only got 450 points, that would lower the reach estimate, which means the plan will not achieve its objectives. That, in turn, could have consequences for the overall advertising and marketing plans, potentially impeding them from obtaining their goals, too.

A plan's impact can be measured in several ways. One way is to test consumer awareness of the ad campaign before, during, and after it appears to see if the desired communication objective has been reached. Sales data, such as that given by scanners or sales transactions, can offer another, very tangible indication of how much the media plan has helped generate sales, even though it is difficult to tie sales response directly to most media activity (with the exception of direct response). Finally, the plan's actual reach and frequency figures can be compared with what was proposed beforehand.

One of the results of measuring the media plan's impact is that it gives you an important advantage in preparing the plan for the next year. Based on what is discovered in the assessment of the current plan's performance, the planner may recommend significant changes in, for example, the media mix, the time frame, or even the budget.

SUMMARY

Media planning involves producing a document, called the media plan, that establishes how the media will be used to disseminate the advertiser's message. It lays out the marketing and advertising goals, and then defines what the media will do to help achieve those goals. Media planners put together a schedule of different media to determine how many of the target will be exposed to the advertising messages in a given time period, and how often. The plan shows where and when the messages will appear, and at what cost. Once the client has approved the plan, media buyers negotiate with the media for space and time. The media planning process is affected considerably by the more general advertising and marketing situation.

There are five steps to putting a media plan together: assessing the market and audience; examining media preferences; selecting the right media; executing the media plan; and evaluating the media plan. To assess the market and audience, planners must examine what the competitors have been and are doing in terms of media spending and placement. It is important to know from the beginning approximately what the media budget will be, as well as the amount of funding being allocated to other parts of the media mix. Planners must also gain a comprehensive understanding of the brand's dynamics in the marketplace, in terms of geography (distribution, regional sales), seasonality, and purchase cycle. The identification of the target audience—by demographics, psychographics, and from a strategic sense (product usage)—is achieved by talking to clients and by examining syndicated data resources such as Simmons and MRI.

Once the target audience has been identified, the media preferences of these people can be looked at more closely. The Personal Media Network© helps pinpoint the media vehicles that the target audience chooses to use on a typical day, while identification of the right Aperture® indicates where, when, and under what circumstances the target is more likely to be receptive to a relevant advertising message.

Before selecting specific media vehicles, it is necessary to consider what the advertising message will be. Certain message types work better in particular media forms. The availability of a media vehicle has to be taken into account; space or time in the vehicle may be sold out or the cost may be too high. Nontraditional media forms, such as buses, sports resorts, trucks, or health clubs, should be evaluated as well. This includes other means of disseminating the advertising message, such as T-shirts or on-the-street samples.

There are three strategies for media scheduling: continuity, flighting, and pulsing. Continuity scheduling provides a constant media presence throughout the year. Flighting involves concentrating the media activity into selected periods of time. Pulsing involves a low level of media spending throughout the year, supplemented by additional pulses of greater activity at key times. The scheduling plan is depicted in a flowchart, which gives a visual presentation of all media activity for the brand in a specified time period. To evaluate the various media forms being considered, planners make evaluations both within (intramedia) and across (intermedia) media. They calculate the total number of rating points, or GRPs; the proportion of the target reached by the plan (reach); and the average number of times they are reached (average frequency). The percent of the target exposed to the message at each level of frequency is called the frequency distribution. Given a limited budget, there is usually a trade-off between reach and frequency. Costs are determined in relation to the audience size (CPM) and in relation to the number of rating points being purchased (CPP). Computers are increasingly being used in media planning to perform most of these calculations.

After receiving approval for the plan, it can then be executed by the buyers. This varies considerably, depending on the type of media and whether the buy is national or local. Media time and space costs usually follow the laws of supply and demand. Following the buys, the buyer receives proof through affidavits or copies of the actual ads (tearsheets) that the ads ran as scheduled. When this does not occur, make-goods are negotiated.

The media plan must be monitored throughout its time span to respond to any changes in the brand's marketing situation or in competitors' activities. The impact of the plan can be assessed by testing consumer awareness, by looking at actual sales data where some kind of response mechanism is built into the ad, or by comparing the plan's actual reach and frequency figures with what was proposed beforehand. Based on what was discovered in the assessment of the current plan, the media planner may recommend changes in next year's plan.

KEY TERMS

1. What might be the impact on your media plan of a price increase for your brand?

2. If you saw that all of your key competitors were spending most of their media dollars in network television, what strategies might you consider taking for your own brand's plan?

3. What types of budgetary issues must media planners take into consideration?

4. Explain how geography, seasonality, and purchase cycle would impact the media plan for Tylenol Cold Medicine.

5. You are trying to put a plan together for Pillsbury Cookie Dough Mix. Your target is women 25–54 with children. What do you think would be the best times, places, and circumstances for reaching this group of people with your advertising message?

6. Which media types would do the best job of delivering the following types of message: humorous, innovative, intrusive, unconventional, demonstrative, and bigger than life?

7. What are the different, less traditional ways that advertisers are reaching consumers?

8. If you are advertising laptop computers, how might you wish to schedule your advertising in the media plan, and why?

9. Why is it important to know the reach and frequency of your media plan? What do those terms tell you?

10. Why is it important to monitor and evaluate the plan once all the media buys have been made? How is that done?

1. Given that media planning involves working with a lot of numbers, where do you see opportunities for creativity?

2. How might advances in technology impact the media planning and buying process in the future? Think about the impact of computers both within the agency or advertiser, and for the consumer receiving media messages.

3. What ways can you think of to quantitatively test (and definitively prove) whether your media advertising worked? What difficulties arise in trying to do so?

interactive discovery lab

1. Develop your own Personal Media Network© for yesterday. At which times, and in which media vehicles, do you think you would have been most receptive to an ad message from Reebok? How about one from Diet Coke? Compare your network to those of others in the class.

2. Go through all of the ads in an issue of your favorite magazine and determine who you think the primary target is for each message. Alternatively, tape your favorite TV show and perform the same exercise.

PIZZA HUT STUFFS ITS TARGET WITH FEWER ADVERTISING DOLLARS

How do you launch a new product in an extremely competitive category, yet still get national visibility and demonstrate what makes the product different—and all for just $6 million?

The answer, for Pizza Hut's Stuffed Crust Pizza and its agency, BBDO New York, was to be highly selective in where the ads were placed and stretch the dollars as far as possible.

The introduction of this line extension was a tall order for two reasons. First, Pizza Hut competes for attention not only against other pizza restaurants, such as Little Caesar's and Domino's, but also against other types of fast-food restaurants, including McDonald's, Burger King, and Wendy's, each of which spends vastly greater amounts of money. A second challenge was that the key target for the product was young men, who are notoriously difficult to reach through television.

But the one place this target can be found is sports events, and it so happened that Pizza Hut had already bought time in the NCAA Basketball Tournament Final Four games. So, once the spring product launch date had been confirmed, BBDO recommended promoting the new product there. At the same time, the Fox TV network was anxious to attract sponsors to its first-time coverage of the National Hockey League (NHL) Stanley Cup playoffs. That proved to be a valuable addition to the media plan. By becoming an exclusive sponsor of the games, Pizza Hut got additional minutes in the game, along with 10-second promotional teasers to the ads, with Fox helping to fund them.

Additional spots aired in several high profile spots in prime time shows such as "NYPD Blue" and "ER," and newspapers were used to drop coupons in 12 key NHL markets. The overall effort resulted in store sales increasing by 25 percent compared to the year before,

versus the goal of a 10 percent increase. Sales were also 30 percent higher than the pre-launch period, which was double expectations. And the Stuffed Crust Pizza has become Pizza Hut's most successful product introduction.

Source: W. F. Gloede, "Long on the Right Stuff," Media Week, 2 May 1996, 58–59.

LOOK BEFORE YOU LEAP

- Why do advertisers choose electronic media to convey their messages?

- What are the benefits and drawbacks of television and radio advertising?

- How are television and radio audiences measured?

- How are television and radio time purchased?

- What has the impact of technology been on television and radio?

- What other types of electronic media are available, and for what audiences should they be considered?

10

When the first radio broadcasts were made in 1916, only a few hundred homes could receive them; when the first nine TV stations came on-air, only 7,000 working TV sets existed across the country. Today, the average U.S. household has three radios, nearly all have at least one TV set, 80 percent have a VCR, and a third own a personal computer.

The electronic media account for $55 billion (31 percent) of all U.S. ad expenditures. Today's media planners and buyers must cope not only with the increasing array of electronic media forms, but also the growing number of choices within each one. Thirty years ago, there were just three TV networks; today there are at least 50 TV networks (broadcast and cable), more than 20 radio formats, and nontraditional electronic media. Technology and globalization are important too. Satellites and digitization have facilitated the global dissemination of ad messages.

In this chapter, we consider these electronic advertising media opportunities, looking at what each media type offers, its benefits and drawbacks, how its audiences are measured, and the impact of new technologies on each one. Let's start with the biggest of them all: TV.

Television

The various forms of television make it the biggest player in the advertising marketplace today. In 1996, advertisers spent a total of $43 billion placing their messages in this medium. There are more than 1,500 television stations in the U.S., 80 percent of which are commercial (that is, they accept advertising). The remainder are educational and/or noncommercial.

Types of Television

There are four major forms of television to consider: broadcast network, spot, cable, and syndication. Each of these is explained below.

BROADCAST NETWORK TELEVISION From the first broadcasts that aired in the 1940s, broadcast network television has been the predominant form of this medium. Even today, the four major broadcast networks (ABC, CBS, FOX, and NBC) account for the bulk of both TV audiences and TV ad dollars. But that fact belies the considerably more complex marketplace that exists for the broadcast networks.

Each of these networks is made up of **local station affiliates,** TV stations in individual markets that agree to air a network's programs in return for being paid a fixed amount of compensation, including a proportion of the network advertising revenue. They also usually agree that the programs will air at a specific time, creating a "network" of shows that are seen nationally at about the same time (taking into account geographic time zone differences). This way, viewers in each region know, for instance, that "Murphy Brown" will be on TV on the CBS network at the same day and hour every week. It is this consistency that enables the broadcast networks to amass the largest audiences for single programs of any TV form. For blockbuster events such as the annual Super Bowl football game, nearly half of all households watch at least some of the game each year. As a result of these larger audiences, broadcast networks are able to charge advertisers higher prices because the program ratings are generally higher, too (depending on the program and the time of day).

Because an individual network can only own a limited number of actual stations (regulated by the FCC), changes in station ownership can have a marked impact on the network's performance. In 1994, when FOX bought a number of CBS-affiliated stations, which then switched to showing FOX programs, a domino effect set off a slew of station sales that impacted about 40 percent of all television markets. Not only did viewers have to find where their favorite programs were on the channel lineup or TV dial, but the ratings of network programs in those markets were seriously upset as well.

Broadcast network programs are shown for only a portion of the viewing day. The rest of the time, the local stations must fill the air themselves, either with local shows or with nationally syndicated products.

SPOT TELEVISION   Advertisers have the option of placing their television dollars in individual markets, rather than across the whole country via a broadcast network. So while WMAQ, the NBC affiliate in Chicago, airs network commercials that will appear on all other NBC-affiliated stations across the country at the same time, the station also sells local advertising time to both national and local advertisers. This is known as **spot television advertising** because the advertiser is buying particular commercial spots. Such advertisements air between programs rather than within them, and they provide the local station with the bulk of its revenue. Obviously, the number of people who are watching a specific program in a specific market is going to be smaller than the national figures, which leads to proportionately lower costs. However, if advertisers have to buy commercial time in multiple markets, they may find themselves with greater total out-of-pocket costs than if they were to buy time on the TV networks.

In addition to selling time between network programs, spot TV stations also earn income from advertising that appears in the locally produced programs. The most popular of these is the news. Local newscasts are aired in the early and late evening and, in larger markets, in early morning as well. Many TV stations are affiliated with companies that act as *station representatives,* or *rep firms*. Recall from Chapter Two that these companies put together packages of stations for advertisers, providing "one-stop shopping" to enable an advertiser such as Kraft to air a commercial for its Singles Cheese Slices on all the stations represented by a rep firm. For example, one such firm, Katz Communications, represents 175 different television stations across the United States; this group includes stations that are affiliated with all four of the major networks—ABC, CBS, NBC, and FOX.

The advantage of using spot television is that a marketer can supplement a national TV buy with additional media "weight" (GRPs) in selected markets. It also enables a company to provide TV support for a regional product or a new brand being tested in just a few locations. Other elements of a marketing plan can be tried out, too, such as new creative or different media mixes. And retailer support may be enhanced if the local dealer or distributor is mentioned in the ad. On the downside, buying local time in this way can become expensive, particularly on a cost-per-thousand (CPM) basis. It is also time consuming, requiring negotiations with individual stations (unless a rep firm is used).

CABLE TELEVISION   Cable television first arose in the mid-1940s as Community Antenna Television to enable households in rural areas to receive television signals. People who could not get clear broadcast signals pooled their resources and put up a single, tall antenna that would capture the signals, which were then relayed to individual homes via the cable wires. In this way, viewers could watch programs from stations in outside markets. The growth of the industry continued slowly until satellite launches in the early 1980s allowed those same cables to bring in many more channels whose programs were beamed up from distant locations. Unlike broadcast television, cable is organized into local systems, with different companies operating them. Initially, each locality had a different operator, but the industry has seen enormous consolidation to the extent that the top five *multiple system operators,* such as Tele-Communications Inc. (TCI) and Time Warner Cable, account for nearly half of all cable subscribers.

Another key difference between network and cable TV is that network TV, relying simply on the airwaves, is free to anyone with a television set. By contrast, cable requires homes and sets to be "wired" to receive the signals beamed down from the satellite. As a result, people have to subscribe to the service. That provides the cable industry with dual revenue streams, because it gains income from subscriptions and also from advertising. Today, cable TV accounts for 8 percent of total TV ad spending. Of that amount, the bulk ($2 billion) is spent on national networks, while the remainder ($800,000) is spent on local cable systems.

Another difference between broadcast networks and (most) cable networks lies in the type of programs that they air. Broadcast networks, by their mass audience nature, focus on general interest programs across a wide spectrum, including dramas, comedies, news, sports, and children's shows. In contrast, cable networks tend to focus on more specific topics. Cable shows include Cable News Network (CNN), offering news 24 hours a day; Entertainment and Sports Programming Network (ESPN), with 24 hours of sports; Arts & Entertainment (A&E), focusing on cultural programming; and Nickelodeon, which only shows programs for children. Because of their more specialized nature, cable network audiences are smaller than those of broadcast networks. Consequently, the prices charged to advertisers are lower, too.

The development of more sophisticated cable systems, along with the growth of satellite technology, has meant that more and more cable networks have been launched in the last 10 years, becoming increasingly specialized in their focus. Today, we have The Golf Channel, Court TV, History TV, and the Faith and Values Network, among others. Exhibit 10–1 lists some of the more established cable channels consumers can choose from today, together with the percent of all U.S. households that are able to receive them. Because each cable system serves a unique area, a cable network is not automatically included on every system's lineup of channels. Indeed, many systems have filled their capacity and cannot add more networks until they upgrade the technology by which the cable signals are delivered to the home. That is happening more and more across the country, with the result that instead of a cable system only showing 42 channels, more than one-third of them now have 55 or more channels to offer consumers.

EXHIBIT 10–1   Cable Networks

NETWORK	% OF U.S. HOUSEHOLDS
The Discovery Channel	71
The Nashville Network	71
ESPN	68
Nickelodeon	68
Cable News Network	67
TNT	67
Arts & Entertainment	66
MTV	66
QVC Network	65
Lifetime	64
American Movie Classics	63
CNBC	63
Nick at Nite	63
Headline News	62
The Family Channel	60
The Learning Channel	58
VH-1	57
Home Shopping Network	54
The Weather Channel	53
Black Entertainment Television	45
ESPN2	45
Comedy Central	42
E! Entertainment TV	41
Cartoon Network	39
Courtroom Television Network	39
Country Music Television	39
The Sci-Fi Channel	35
The History Channel	30
The Disney Channel	22
Home & Garden Television Network	22
MSNBC	22
The Travel Channel	21
Home Box Office*	20
Telemundo	18
Animal Planet	17
Cinemax*	9
Showtime*	8

*These are pay cable networks that do not accept any advertising.

Source: Cablevision Database, at http://www.cvmag.com, August 1997.

BROADCAST SYNDICATION   The development of syndication is relatively new for television; it began in the early 1980s as more local TV stations were established, leading to the need for more programs to fill the available airtime. **Syndicated programming** works like this. A show is produced by a company that then sells the show directly to individual stations in each market. The local station is allowed to sell some of the commercial minutes itself, while the syndicator sells the remainder to national advertisers. This system means that a syndicated show may air on an ABC-affiliated station in one market and a CBS affiliate in another. Examples of syndicated shows are talk shows such as "Oprah" and "Ricki Lake," game shows such as "Wheel of Fortune" and "Jeopardy," dramas such as "Star Trek: Deep Space Nine," and news and reality programs such as "Rescue 911" and "Entertainment Tonight."

There are two ways that a syndicated program can be sold. Advertisers either pay for the program in cash, or they agree on some kind of partial or total exchange of their products or services for airtime. This is known as **barter syndication.** Until a few years ago the market was dominated by barter deals, but as syndication has grown and as program producers have realized the additional profits they can generate this way, more and more syndicated programs sell advertising for cash.

Until the mid-1990s syndicated programs tended to focus on the types of shows not being aired by the networks or local stations; in fact, until 1995, the broadcast networks were prohibited from earning profits from their own shows if they went into syndication. With the removal of that ban, however, the networks can now compete with syndication companies. And as "Around the Globe: Watching Baywatch Worldwide" explains, syndication is an increasingly international business.

Dayparts and Genres

From the viewer's perspective, television consists of a lineup of programs, ranging from "Nightline" to "Friends" and "All My Children" to "Mighty Morphin Power Rangers." From an advertiser's perspective, however, television is categorized by dayparts and genres. The **daypart** refers to the different times of day and day of week in which a program appears. Using the above-mentioned examples, "Nightline" is in the late night (sometimes called "late fringe") daypart, while "Friends" is in prime time, "All My Children" is in daytime, and "Power Rangers" is in Saturday morning. Exhibit 10–2 shows the standard dayparts.

The value of dayparts is that they help to categorize audience viewing patterns. More people watch TV during prime time than at any other time. The main audience for Saturday morning is children, whereas most TV-watching men can be found on weekend afternoons, when sports programs are aired. From a media planning perspective, dayparts are what the planner selects, leaving it up to the buyer (for the most part) to negotiate specific programs. Because the audience size for programs will vary by daypart, costs also vary accordingly, with prime time being the most expensive and early morning or weekend afternoon being some of the least costly. One 30-second commercial in "Seinfeld" may run as high as $490,000, while an early morning program such as "Good Morning America" might cost $30,000.

Another way of classifying television shows is by **genre,** or program type. This classification system helps media planners match the right type of show to their target audience. Genres include drama, situation comedy, sports, and news. A fuller list of program genres is shown in Exhibit 10–3.

EXHIBIT 10–3
Program Genres

Animation/Children
Drama/Adventure
Late Night Talk
News
Reality-Based
Specials
Talk
Daytime Serials
Games
Movies
Primetime News
Sitcoms
Sports

EXHIBIT 10–2   Standard Television Dayparts

Early morning	M–F 7:00 A.M.–9:00 A.M.
Daytime	M–F 9:00 A.M.–4:30 P.M.
Early fringe	M–F 4:30 P.M.–7:30 P.M.
Prime access	M–F 7:30 P.M.–8:00 P.M.
Prime time	M–S 8:00 P.M.–11:00 P.M.
	Su 7:00 P.M.–11:00 P.M.
Late news	M–Su 11:00 P.M.–11:30 P.M.
Late night	M–Su 11:30 P.M.–1:00 A.M.
Saturday morning	Sa 8:00 A.M.–1:00 P.M.
Weekend afternoon	Sa–Su 1:00 P.M.–7:00 P.M.

Note: All times are Eastern Standard Time (EST).

Benefits of Television Advertising

Clearly, the medium that accounts for the second-largest amount of advertiser dollars and the greatest share of national ad dollars must have several important benefits, and indeed it does. They include: sight, sound, and motion; mass audiences; and large presence and influence.

SIGHT, SOUND, AND MOTION At present, television is the only widespread advertising medium that offers sight, sound, and motion. While print media have sight, radio has sound, and computers have both, only television can combine those characteristics with the ability to show people or products moving as in real life. Indeed, it is the unique advantage of television to be able to show people using the

AROUND THE GLOBE

· ·

Watching Baywatch Worldwide

It's hard to believe. People in Tokyo, London, and Frankfurt all sitting down on a weekly basis to watch a program about surfers in California. But that is the case for "Baywatch," a one-hour drama that first aired on NBC in the U.S. in 1989. The show was unceremoniously canceled after one season because of small audiences, but the company that produced it made a deal with the Gannett Company to continue producing the show for the U.S. syndication market. Nearly 10 years and more than 100 episodes later, the program is the biggest-selling U.S. TV show ever, selling to more countries even than the 1980s soap opera drama "Dallas."

The show's international distributors, Fremantle Corporation, had been selling the show abroad quite successfully since its inception. Today, "Baywatch" is seen in 144 countries and is translated into 15 different languages. Not only are there new episodes airing weekly, but even the old shows are syndicated to be shown on a daily basis each weekday. The show has been so successful that the producers even created a spinoff, "Baywatch Nights," which fea-

tures the same main character (actor David Hasselhoff).

People who are involved with the program attribute its success to several factors. First, the settings are memorable and appealing. If you are watching television in a place where there is a cold rain falling steadily outside or a gloomy urban panorama around you, it would certainly be enjoyable to watch an escapist soap opera drama set in southern California. Indeed, that far-from-reality feeling puts "Baywatch" in a similar position to other evening soaps, such as "Dallas" or "Knot's Landing," appealing to viewers' desires to follow the lives of a number of different, somewhat unbelievable but always beautiful, characters. A more hard-nosed reason for the show's success is that it is relatively inexpensive to produce. When the program began on NBC, each episode cost more than $1 million. For syndication, that figure was cut to about $800,000. And because the producers own the rights to the show, the sales revenues when the program is sold to other countries come back to them rather than to a TV network.

International syndication barely existed 10 years ago. But today it is a thriving market. For U.S. companies and networks, it offers extremely lucrative opportunities because the costs of production are paid for by U.S. advertising or station revenue, leaving any syndication sales as profit. Syndicated programs that are sold abroad come from a broad spectrum of producers. As we noted in Chapter Four, there are 23 foreign versions of King World's hugely popular "Wheel of Fortune" show, while Oprah Winfrey's talk show appears in 111 countries. ESPN syndicates its various sports programs to 200 international broadcast, cable, and satellite outlets. Even PBS enjoys revenue from the numerous versions of "Sesame Street" that air in 60 countries around the world.

QUESTIONS

Why is international syndication becoming such big business? Aside from those mentioned above, what other U.S. television programs do you think would have success in international syndication?

Source: Bill Carter, "Media," *The New York Times,* 3 July 1995, C5.

product or service, which helps advertisers show consumers what their product looks like or how it is used in real life.

MASS AUDIENCES Although the four major broadcast networks today only reach about half of the viewing audience during prime time, that still represents about 45–50 million households—hardly a negligible number! And even if your ad appears in a program that is seen by 10 percent of TV homes, it has a chance of being seen by 9,500,000 households. Because of its national capabilities, television is the biggest of all mass media. Local newspapers may be read by almost everyone in a particular town or region, but no medium can compare to TV in its ability to reach mass audiences nationwide, carrying the same ad message simultaneously to people in Anchorage, Alaska, and Little Rock, Arkansas. For advertisers that wish to increase awareness of their product, this is a particularly valuable benefit, giving them the opportunity to expose large numbers of people to their ad message.

PRESENCE AND INFLUENCE The importance of television in people's lives is made evident almost every day, from discussions at the office water cooler or in the student dorm about last night's episode of "NYPD Blue" to Congressional debates about the impact of TV violence. Because almost every household in the U.S. has at least one TV set, the presence of television is enormous. And although its precise influence on people's lives has been questioned for almost as long as the medium has existed, it undoubtedly does have important influential properties. If someone hears a speech or sees a product on television, he or she is very likely to assume it is both accurate and authoritative. Clearly, this can be highly beneficial for advertisers, allowing their products to be associated with the medium (People tend to think "It's on TV, so it must be good").

That belief can also provide benefits at the local level, by providing a brand with additional status and prestige. This can help the local or regional sales force merchandise the product to retailers or dealers, giving them additional ammunition with which to make their presentations to current and prospective customers.

Drawbacks of Television Advertising

The main problems of television ads are high cost, ad clutter, and limited viewing time.

HIGH COST As soon as television became a truly mass medium in the late 1950s, the absolute, out-of-pocket cost of placing advertising exploded. Today advertisers pay, on average, $350,000 for a 30-second commercial on the top-rated network prime-time shows. A 30-second spot in the Super Bowl cost $1.1 million in 1996. That's just for 30 seconds of airtime! The high cost can, however, be offset at times by the large number of people being reached, leading to a relatively efficient CPM. Exhibit 10–4 shows the cost of various prime-time programs in 1995–96.

AD CLUTTER The popularity of television for advertisers has been a double-edged sword. As more and more marketers have placed their dollars in the medium, more and more competition has developed between those companies

---

EXHIBIT 10–4   Cost of Prime-Time Advertising, 1997–1998

PROGRAM	NETWORK	COST PER :30
Seinfeld	NBC	$575,000
ER	NBC	560,000
Friends	NBC	410,000
Monday Night Football	ABC	360,000
Home Improvement	ABC	350,000
The X-Files	FOX	275,000
Drew Carey	ABC	275,000
NYPD Blue	ABC	240,000
The Simpsons	FOX	225,000
Ellen	ABC	180,000
Melrose Place	FOX	175,000
60 Minutes	CBS	165,000
Law & Order	NBC	165,000
48 Hours	CBS	70,000

Source: "Seinfeld" Nears Price Ceiling as Sophomore Shows Soar," Joe Mandese, Advertising Age, September 15, 1997, 1/18.

for airtime. For the consumer, this leads to increasingly large blocks of TV time filled with one ad after another. This, in turn, diminishes the chance that an advertiser's ad will be seen and remembered among all of the clutter. Today, about 19 minutes of every hour of daytime programming on the broadcast networks is taken up by material other than the program. This non-program time consists of national or local TV commercials and the network's or station's own promotional messages.

LIMITED VIEWING TIME There are two elements to consider here. First, a commercial is designed to last 15, 30, or occasionally, 60 seconds. That is not a lot of time for the viewer to notice what the brand is and what the message is, and to determine whether the message has any relevance or not. Unlike a print ad, which you can stop and carefully read through when you see an interesting-looking message, the TV ad comes and goes within minutes (VCRs notwithstanding).

Second, viewing time is limited by the viewers themselves. People are finding more and more ways to deliberately avoid watching the commercials. They may go to the bathroom, talk on the telephone or to other people in the room, read, or simply ignore the ads. And with remote control devices in 9 of every 10 TV homes today, one of the easiest ways to give an ad limited or no attention is to switch channels when the message appears. If the message is not relevant and appealing to the right target, it is highly likely the viewer will "tune out"– mentally and perhaps physically, too.

Measuring the Television Audience

Advertisers want to know two things before they spend money on television: (1) Who will see their message? and (2) How many people will see it? The measurement of the television audience began almost as soon as the medium was born. At first, surveys were conducted asking people what they had seen, but given the notorious fallibility of people's memories, it soon became clear that a mechanized technique was required. The development of the Nielsen Audimeter (which had first been used in radio) to monitor when the TV set was turned on and off changed the TV audience measurement business completely. Now advertisers could learn what proportion of the sets were on and to which channels they were tuned.

The Nielsen system, with various improvements over time, is still in place today. A box on the TV sets of the 5,000 households in the Nielsen sample keeps track both of when the TV set is on or off and to which channel it is tuned. In addition, the people in the house use a device that looks like a remote control, called a **people meter,** to record when they are watching TV. The data are sent through the telephone lines to Nielsen's computers, which then tabulates them all to determine what proportion of the population is tuned to each program. This figure becomes the **program rating.**

TV programmers want to know what proportion of all households have their TV sets on at a particular time, a measure known as the **households using television (HUT).** More often, they look at the proportion of *people* with sets on at a given time, which is known as the **persons using television (PUT)** measure. This measure is calculated by adding up all the program ratings against households or people.

Another simple calculation is made to find out what proportion of all TV sets that were on at a given time were tuned to a particular show. This is known as the **viewing share** or **audience share.** If three-quarters of all homes were watching television last night and 15 percent of all homes were watching "Frasier," then that means "Frasier" had a 20 percent viewing share (15 / 75 = 20). Exhibit 10–5 provides examples of program ratings, HUTs, and audience shares. Ratings will always add to the HUT, while shares always add to 1.0 (or 100 percent).

EXHIBIT 10–5   Ratings versus Shares

HOUSEHOLD	PROGRAM	RATING	PROGRAM	SHARE OF VIEWING (%)
Home 1	Program A	10	Program A	25
Home 2	Program B	15	Program B	50
Home 3	Set off	—		—
Home 4	Program C	15	Program C	25
HUT		**40**	**All viewing**	**100**

The Nielsen people meter system is used to measure national TV audiences, but what about the viewing levels for Tulsa, Oklahoma, or Baton Rouge, Louisiana? Here, Nielsen uses a combination of methods. First, it divides the country up into 218 geographical areas, known as **designated marketing areas (DMAs).** The 38 largest of these TV markets are measured continuously using people meters. For the remaining 180 markets, the TV set meter and *viewing diaries* capture local market information. The diaries are filled out by each member of the family and record which channels they viewed for each hour of a seven-day period. Measurement is done four times a year, over a four-week period known as the **sweeps.** These take place in February, May, July, and November. Not surprisingly, both networks and local stations try to reserve their best programming for these months in order to increase their audiences while the measurement is occurring (though they are legally prohibited from any overt tampering with the measurement process).

The measurement of both syndication and cable TV occurs as part of the Nielsen process at both the national and local level, but the information is reported separately from broadcast TV. In the future, as "Technology Watch: Passive Participation" explains, TV viewing may be recorded without the viewer having to do anything.

Planning and Buying for Television

Once advertisers or agencies have determined that they wish to use television, the next step is to figure out the specifics of the media plan, such as the individual program costs and scheduling, and what the plan will deliver against the target. After that has been approved, the television time can be purchased from the stations and networks that have been selected.

TV PLANNING: RATINGS, REACH, AND GRPS

Much as we discussed in Chapter Nine, media planners who are planning and buying for television look at program ratings against a defined target to see how well each show delivers that audience. TV programs live and die by their ratings. If they do not garner high enough numbers, they usually are canceled because larger ratings translate into higher-priced commercial time for the network, station, or syndicator.

STILL GROWING.

Look who has a leg up on household numbers once again. In the 1995-96 broadcast season, The Family Channel was America's fastest growing network. And now? A new year, another growth spurt. We're up 25% in Prime Time household delivery. Up in Early Fringe by an extraordinary 146% among adults 18-49. Late Night? We're up 51% in adults 18-49. And in Daytime, women's numbers are up 22%. More families are discovering we're the network with the kind of quality entertainment they'll never outgrow. Try us on. Bet we fit just right.

Recall from Chapter Nine that rating points are added together to create gross rating points (GRPs), which tell the planner how many ratings, in total, are being purchased. Another critical consideration for TV planning (and, indeed, all media planning) is to analyze the reach of the schedule. Again, as we explained in Chapter Nine, the reach shows how many different people, expressed as a percent of the target, will view the programs or schedule. A single program might reach 35 percent of the target in a four-week period, but if ads are placed in several different shows, then that gives more—and different—target members the opportunity for exposure to those messages, perhaps increasing the reach level in this case to 45 percent.

This planner-targeted ad for the Family Channel touts that channel's growing popularity among specific demographic groups, information that is crucial to media planners and buyers.

TECHNOLOGY WATCH

. . . .

Passive Participation

The idea of passive people meters has been in existence for more than a decade. It sounds ideal: Create a meter that can record when people are watching TV and what they are watching, to remove the need for the viewer to do anything other than watch what he or she wants. The reality, however, is far more complicated. First, there are the simple technical issues of designing such a meter. Early versions proved flawed because they relied on infrared heat detection to identify someone in the room watching TV, which meant that non-people items such as irons or pets were counted in the audience. Newer prototypes use high-powered artificial intelligence routines to capture a viewer's key facial features, which are then matched with a stored database for each family member.

Beyond the technical questions, there are ethical ones. The biggest concern has been privacy. If Nielsen is to measure all TV sets in the house, then what happens if a passive meter is placed in bedrooms or even bathrooms? To many in the industry, this sounds too close to the notion of having "Big Brother" watch your every move. That, in turn, leads to questions about who would be in the measurement sample. Are the people who would agree to having such a device in their home still representative of the total population, as Nielsen's current panel claims to be?

From the TV networks' perspective, a passive meter would not necessarily be a good idea either. When national audience measurement moved from set meters and viewing diaries to people meters in the late 1980s, measured audience levels fell. This could readily be explained by the fact that the people meter was providing a more accurate count of viewership than the handwritten diary. What many at the networks fear, and probably rightly so, is that a passive meter would result in even smaller reported audiences for their shows. That would mean that the networks would not be able to charge advertisers as much money for commercials in those programs.

Nielsen's plans to test and roll out a passive system have been extended over many years. The company has done various tests of the meter and reported success in its implementation. But the passive meter is unlikely to replace the current system anytime soon, because of both the high cost of its implementation and the resistance from the broadcast community.

History is not on the side of a passive system, either. Two earlier attempts in the 1980s to introduce this type of technology both failed. As much as advertisers and agencies call for a change in the way television audiences are measured, complaining about the burden that people meters place on participants in the survey (who, it should be pointed out, are asked to push buttons for two years), the discussion is likely to continue for many years.

Last but not least, the media planner looks at each element of the TV plan and the overall plan in terms of its costs, both the total schedule cost and the relative costs compared to other media (the cost-per-thousand and cost per rating point).

BUYING TV TIME The television market works according to the laws of supply and demand. Advertising time at both the network and local level is based on how much advertisers want that time slot and how much commercial airtime is available. Although this might seem to keep the buyers at a disadvantage, any airtime that is not sold when the program airs cannot be filled in later, so it is in the sellers' interest to sell out as much inventory as possible.

For network TV, much of the airtime is sold during the "upfront marketplace" in May or June prior to the start of the new season in the fall. Advertisers that commit to purchasing airtime early receive more favorable rates that come with locked in, or **guaranteed audience ratings.** This means the TV network will guarantee a minimum number of people who will watch a show. If the actual program rating is higher, it is considered a free "bonus," but if the figure falls short, the network must provide a *make-good*, either by giving money back to the advertiser or, more commonly, offering additional commercial spots at some other time.

For advertisers that choose not to buy during the upfront market, there are two alternatives. First, the **scatter market** allows advertisers to make short-term, quarterly purchases at somewhat higher rates and mostly without guarantees. The best time slots are likely to have been sold during the upfront market, but many advertisers prefer the greater flexibility that scatter buys allow them. The second alternative to purchasing network time upfront is to make an **opportunistic purchase.** This type of buy occurs on a week-to-week basis and often consists of program inventory that other advertisers had bought but then canceled. Opportunistic purchases tend to be much cheaper, but they leave the advertiser with little choice in terms of programs or pricing.

Television commercials are sold on a fixed, preemptive, or run-of-station basis. A **fixed spot** costs the most because it prevents another advertiser from taking that spot. **Preemptive spots** are sold with the understanding that another advertiser can come along, offer more money for the spot, and get it. The station is obligated to inform the first advertiser if this situation arises so that it can try to make alternative arrangements. There are varying degrees of preemptibility; the more lead time that is required by the advertiser, the higher the price. With the **run–of-station-spot**, the message may be aired at any time and preempted at any time. The one stipulation is that the spots are truly "rotated"; that is, they air at different times of the day and are not all shown at 3 A.M.

At the local level, the advertiser or agency contacts individual stations to request what is available, known as the **avails.** The stations then provide the available times, dates, prices, program ratings, households, CPM, reach, and frequency. The buyers compare the different proposals, which may also include additional "added value" promotions or special deals. Spots can be bought on a fixed or preemptive basis, although during prime-time stations will usually only sell time in specific programs at a fixed rate.

Television and Technology

The impact of technology on the world of television has been long lasting and continuous. Whereas cable television originated as a technological means of improving reception for people living in rural or mountainous areas, it has developed a much larger scope thanks to the growth of satellites. Today, it is those satellites, working in conjunction with computers, which are the driving forces behind the changes occurring in the television industry.

DIRECT BROADCAST BY SATELLITE The idea of delivering television directly to a home satellite dish is really a natural extension of or alternative to cable TV. Instead of wires being used to deliver signals that are received by a large satellite dish, direct broadcast by satellite (DBS) takes those signals directly from the geostationary satellites circling the globe at 22,300 miles away from earth. The development of the DBS industry has been fairly slow

Companies such as DISH Network utilize satellite technology to provide direct broadcasting by satellite (DBS). DBS has greatly expanded the viewing options of consumers, allowing for the development of niche TV channels, which like niche magazines, cover specific areas of interest.

in the U.S., in part because of legal difficulties in obtaining rights to program material and in part because of the high cost of the equipment involved. Nonetheless, in 1994, four DBS services were launched to offer packages of networks and programming on a subscription basis. Three of them, DirecTV, United States Satellite Broadcasting (USSB), and EchoStar's Dish Network require users to purchase the satellite dish, while the fourth, Primestar, lets customers lease the dish. Each service offers 100 or more channels of television, including numerous channels that show movies and events which can be purchased on a pay-per-view basis (i.e., you pay for a single movie or concert each time you watch it). By 1996 there were about 5 million households viewing television this way.

One potential drawback of DBS at present is that viewers cannot receive their local broadcast stations as part of the subscription package, requiring a special switch to allow them to view their local ABC-, CBS-, FOX-, or NBC-affiliated stations. This may change within the next few years. Despite this one drawback, because they have so many channels available, DBS providers can offer more special interest or niche programming, such as TV Asia, with programs from the Indian subcontinent, or the Physician's Television Network, which provides medical information and educational programming to doctors and hospitals. Another area where DBS has a potential advantage is in sports. Each service has created special sports packages that permit subscribers to see games from teams across the country, instead of being limited to the one being aired in their region. The National Football League, National Basketball Association, National Hockey League, Major League Baseball, and Major League Soccer all have signed deals with the DBS companies to allow fans of those sports to choose from dozens of different games.

Initially, the DBS providers claimed that they were not competing directly with cable but were aiming their services at rural areas that would never receive cable television because of the high costs involved in laying cable wires. Today, however, with 6 million subscribers, the industry is making more competitive claims against the cable industry. They maintain they have higher-quality pictures and sound, and greater viewing choice—all for a lower price. The advertising opportunities on DBS are only indirect and national at this point. That is, if advertisers place spots on an individual cable network or broadcast network that happens to be carried by the DBS provider, then viewers may see them. As there are no local channels on these services, there is presently no spot advertising.

Even as the DBS companies continue to expand their operations in the U.S., they already are looking at the international marketplace. In 1996 DirecTV launched a service for Latin America and the Caribbean that offers about 200 channels of TV or audio material. Of the 144 TV channels, 72 are in Portuguese, reflecting the importance of Brazil as a market, and 72 are in Spanish. The actual mix of channels varies from country to country, but like the U.S. version, it includes a combination of broadcast networks, cable networks, movie channels, and pay-per-view movies and events.

INTERACTIVE TELEVISION   Although most forms of interactive television remain in test at this point, they are potentially where the future of television may lie. **Interactive television** allows the viewer to respond directly to what he or she sees on the screen. This may involve selecting the camera angle for a sporting event, paying bills directly from home, ordering goods or services through the TV set, or controlling the utilities in the house.

The technical ability to use the TV set in this fashion, rather than sitting passively in front of the programs, has only become feasible within the last few years, primarily because of advances in computer power and speed. For example, as recently as the early 1990s, one test of a video on-demand service that allowed people to order up a movie they wanted to see actually required employees at the central site to physically take the video of the movie that had been requested and put it into one of a host of videocassette recorders, each of which could service a few homes![1] Today, video on-demand tests rely heavily on computers to make it work.

The most ambitious interactive television test took place in Orlando, Florida, in the mid-1990s on a cable system operated by Time Warner. There, several thousand homes were linked to the Full Service Network, which promised to allow the individuals in those homes to do everything via TV—from shopping, to information searches, to programs on demand, to responding directly to classified ads. There would be many potential opportunities for advertisers in such a system, because every area of the service could, in theory, be sponsored by a brand or company. After great fanfare when the project was first announced, the actual deployment and growth of the system was much slower, mostly because it turned into a far more difficult technical proposition than had at first been realized, requiring enormous and highly sophisticated computers to handle all of the requests. The project was finally killed in 1997.[2]

A less complex form of interactive TV was tested in Montreal, Quebec, for several years starting in the early 1990s. Available to subscribers within the Videotron cable system, Videoway allowed viewers the chance to select different camera angles, play along with game shows, or check on sports statistics during a game. The interaction was not truly two-way, as the viewer could only respond to what appeared on the screen, but without any immediate response from the TV set itself.

What interactive television holds out for advertisers is the potential for truly individualized communications via the mass medium of television. That is, with a two-way, interactive link from each home to a central location, advertisers would be able to send discrete messages to neighboring households that are tailored to the wants and needs of each one. With this, Mr. and Mrs. Jones, who live with their three children and a dog, might see a commercial for Pedigree dog food, while their neighbor, Mrs. Smith, who is a senior citizen living with two cats, might at the same time be sent an ad for Pedigree cat food.

A less sophisticated existing version of interactive television is **direct response television (DRTV).** Here, viewers respond via telephone, calling up to purchase an item being promoted or to request information on a product or service. The growth of the DRTV industry has been considerable in recent years as the use of toll-free and 900 phone numbers has flourished, and as people have become more and more comfortable buying goods sight-unseen.

TELEPHONE COMPANIES   The entry of regional telephone companies into television is occurring slowly but surely as regulations that prevented their offering such services have been eliminated. Each of the so-called "Baby Bells" has dipped its toes into testing television service. For example, Ameritech, which serves five midwestern states, is offering cable television to subscribers in selected markets throughout its region. U.S. West embarked on a more ambitious plan to offer a fully interactive TV service to people in Omaha, Nebraska, working with the cable operator, Tele-Communications Inc. (TCI). As the legal barriers separating telephone and cable companies are removed, it is very likely that, in the future, we will be able to receive cable service from telephone companies and telephone service from cable operators. This is already available in other countries, most notably the United Kingdom. There, the introduction of telephone service by cable operators led to a rapid increase in the numbers of people who wanted to have both services provided by the same company. Today about half of all new subscribers to cable television also opt for telephone service from the same company.

COMPUTERS   It is impossible to look at the future of television without considering the role and impact of computers. Not only are they critical to the provision of interactive services, but many believe it will not be long before people will use televisions and computers almost interchangeably. You will watch TV programs on your computer or use your TV set to perform complex computer applications. Of course, this is already possible to a certain extent today in that videogames can be played through both pieces of equipment (using special add-ons in the case of TV). And many computers can already show live action and full motion video on their screens. Cable companies offer cable modem services to allow you to access the Internet along with your cable television service.

In March 1997, Compaq Computers announced that it would begin selling a combination TV-computer in 1998. The new machine would resemble a television set but offer computer features and programs, including access to the Internet. It would appear that the next battle for TV viewers will take place between TV set manufacturers and computer makers as each side tries to figure out what it is that consumers really want and, equally important, how much they are willing to pay for such devices.[3]

Changes in Television Advertising

In many ways, television advertising has not changed all that much since Bulova Watches paid $9 to air the first TV commercial during a baseball game in 1941, yet in other ways, it has changed considerably. The first television advertisers sponsored complete programs, giving rise to such programs as the Hallmark Hall of Fame and the Texaco Star Theater. Although that is almost unheard of today because the cost has become prohibitive, Ford Motor Company was the sole sponsor of the broadcast premiere of the movie "Schindler's List" when it aired on network television in 1997.

Once the notion of multiple sponsors for a show had became popular in the 1950s, it was only logical for program segments to be divided by commercial breaks during which companies could present their sales messages. Although the length of the commercial has decreased since then, with the standard now being 30 seconds rather than the original 60 seconds (or more), the placement of TV ads is still similar. The move to shorter commercial lengths first took place in the late 1960s, when the standard shifted from :60s to :30s. There was another diminution in the mid-1980s when, again, the commercial length was halved in order to make advertising dollars stretch further. Today, about one-third of all network TV ads are 15 seconds in length. National spots are placed both during the program and between two different programs; local spots air only between programs.

At the same time ads were getting shorter, the past few years have seen the growth and development of longer-form commercials, or **infomercials.** These may last anywhere from three minutes to a 30-minute program sponsored by one or a few advertisers. The content of these messages varies widely. Examples of advertisers that have aired infomercials include Ford Motor Company, Eastman Kodak, and Walt Disney World. The real moneymakers, however, have been much smaller operations, such as Nordic Track, the Juiceman, and Soloflex, each of which brought in more than $150 million in revenues in a recent three-year period. The messages often are aired late at night or on smaller cable networks; in each case, it is airtime that would probably be difficult to fill with any other program material. About 60 percent of these long-form messages appear on broadcast stations, with the remainder airing on cable networks.

The infomercial segment of the TV advertising industry has brought in close to $1 billion a year, and it is expanding outside of the U.S. borders. One of the leading producers of these long-form commercials, Quantum, operates in 30 different countries. For a product to succeed in an infomercial at an international level, it must be demonstrable and universally understood, such as a knife set. Second, it must not be culturally bound, such as perfume or clothing, which vary tremendously from coun-

New developments in technology have increased the interaction between computers and television. For example, Toshiba's Infinia™ personal computer allows users to watch television broadcasts on their computer screens and to switch easily between software applications, TV, and radio.

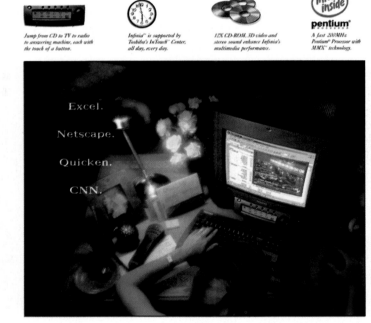

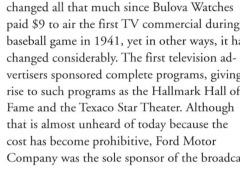

try to country. Logistics have to be taken into account as well, with differences in distribution channels and regulations on what can be said in this type of commercial message. Infomercials in France, for example, cannot name the specific brands.

An extension of this kind of long-form message is seen on **home shopping networks.** Here, TV channels are devoted to selling goods and services to consumers, with the orders placed via telephone. There are two major networks: Home Shopping Network (HSN) and the Quality, Value, Convenience Network (QVC). These networks air their programs on a combination of broadcast stations and cable systems. HSN reaches a total of 60 million households, while QVC reaches 50 million. Together, the two networks can claim to account for $2.5 billion in sales. They differ in the types of merchandise they feature, with HSN dividing its airtime between jewelry (35 percent), home and lifestyle (35 percent), and apparel and accessories (25 percent). QVC features jewelry in nearly half of its programming (49 percent), with the rest of the time being used to sell hard goods (34 percent) and soft goods (15 percent). Between them, they ship nearly 150,000 packages every day, after receiving about 320,000 calls to their phone lines.[4]

The popularity of home shopping is growing worldwide. It is estimated that more than one-third of the $8 billion spent on home shopping worldwide in 1995 came from outside of the United States. The well-known American stain remover, DiDi Seven, is now being sold in 107 countries. Even in China, where annual incomes in the larger cities still only reach about $1,000, millions of people are tuning in to 10-minute infomercials and buying hair spray or stomach exercisers.[5]

R E S E T

1. What is the value of classifying television programming into dayparts?
2. What do people in a Nielsen sample home have to do to record their viewing behavior?
3. How has television advertising changed since its inception?

Radio

While we tend to think of television first when it comes to advertising, radio is, in fact, the older ad medium. There is still a debate over who invented radio. One of the first radio stations to broadcast to a sizable audience was KDKA in Philadelphia. Its first program, with an estimated 1,000 listeners, was the election returns for the 1920 presidential election between Warren Harding and James Cox. Just two years later, the first radio commercial aired on WEAF in New York City for the Queensboro Corporation, which sold real estate. At that time, it was referred to as "toll broadcasting," with sponsors paying a "toll" to use the airwaves. In 1923, WEAF linked with WNAC in Boston to create the first commercial network radio program, "The Eveready Hour." Four years later, in 1927, the RCA company established the first radio network through its National Broadcasting Company (NBC) subsidiary.

Today, radio generates nearly $10 billion in advertising revenue from both national and local advertisers, but local ads make up the vast majority. In its early days, before the growth of television, radio was used mostly by major national advertisers; by 1996, however, 96 percent of its advertising dollars came from spots placed in local markets. The importance of radio at the local level is also seen in the sheer number of radio stations there are. In 1996, that figure stood at more than 12,000, of which 10,000 were commercial.

Not only are there multiple stations in a market, but from the consumer's standpoint radio is an "everywhere" medium. Indeed, 53 percent of all radio listening occurs outside of the home, 27 percent of it in the car. Nearly all cars on the road today (95 percent) have a radio built in. And the invention of the personal stereo in the 1980s has made radio the most portable electronic medium available.

The future of radio remains fairly healthy. In 1995 radio ad revenues reached the $1 billion mark for the first time. And in 1996, after ownership restrictions were removed on the number of stations one company can own, the sale of radio stations grew rapidly around the country.

EXHIBIT 10–6 Standard
Radio Formats

Adult Contemporary

Adult Standards

Album-Oriented Rock (AOR)

All News

All Sports

Alternative

Children's Radio

Classical

Classic Rock

Classic Country

Contemporary Hit Radio (CHR)

Country

Easy Listening

Educational

Ethnic

Gospel

Jazz

Modern AC

New Adult Contemporary/
   Smooth Jazz

New Country

New Rock

News/Talk/Information

Nostalgia

Oldies

Religious

Rhythm & Blues

Seventies Oldies/Classic Hits

Seventies Rock

Soft AC

Southern Gospel

Spanish Contemporary

Spanish Language

Talk/Personality

Urban AC

Urban Contemporary

Urban Oldies

Variety

Frequencies, Formats, and Geographies

For the listener there are two types of radio frequencies available: AM and FM. AM, which stands for Amplitude Modulation, relies on changing the airwave's strength (its amplitude) to convey the sound. Although the quality of the sound is inferior to FM sound, AM wavelengths can travel through the air or the ground, allowing them to go further. AM stations can be picked up a considerable distance from where they originate. This means that stations such as WGN in Chicago can be heard at night as far away as Boston or Atlanta. That distance will vary however, depending on the station's dial position. The lower the signal's operating frequency, the further the signal can travel. So a station that is situated at 960AM will have a broader distribution and reach than one placed at 1500 on the AM lineup.

The higher-quality type of radio frequency, FM, which stands for Frequency Modulation, conveys sound by altering the radio wave's frequency. Because the signals can only travel through the air, they must not be obstructed either by geography or manmade constructions (such as tall buildings). The sound quality is superior to AM, but the listening area of these stations is more circumscribed. The growth of FM stations has been steady and significant to the point where, today, nearly 80 percent of listening is to stations on this wavelength.[6]

Regardless of the frequency, every radio station is assigned unique **call letters,** such as WOI in Des Moines, Iowa, or KKDA in Dallas, Texas. The practice of identifying stations in this way goes back to radio's origins as a means of communication from ships to land. At that time, the ship's signal was given a one- to three-letter telegraphic code to identify to the receivers on land who was "calling" through the airwaves. By 1934, with the passage of the landmark Federal Communications Act, station call letters were increased to four and the country was divided into two regions by the Mississippi River, with the call letters of stations west of the river starting with a K and those to the east beginning with a W. Exceptions were made for existing stations, so today we still listen to WDAY in Fargo, North Dakota, or KDKA in East Pittsburgh, Pennsylvania.

The types of programs that air on radio are usually divided up into **formats,** which are much like TV's genre divisions. Exhibit 10–6 provides a list of those formats. Each year, the list grows longer as new formats are created and older ones are fragmented. Country music, for example, may now be heard on stations that call their formats "old country," "young country," or "classical country." Rock music may be heard on "classic rock," "soft rock," "album-oriented rock," or "alternative rock." And urban contemporary stations, popular with African American audiences, are now splitting into more specialized rap, hip-hop, or light jazz formats. Estimates of the number of different program formats vary. Arbitron currently counts 39 major formats, but some have calculated that there are more than 50.

Because of the superior sound quality that FM provides, certain kinds of programming, particularly music related, are more likely to be found on FM stations. As music formats moved from AM to FM, the AM stations consolidated their program types in two main areas: news and talk. In recent years, both of these have seen a significant increase in popularity again, driven in part by the fact that they are both highly economical formats for a station to run. Ironically, this increased popularity has led more FM stations to switch to those formats, as well. Stations in Chicago, San Francisco, Little Rock, and Dallas all have moved their news or sports broadcasts from AM to FM wavelengths in the last few years.

Like television, radio is divided up into dayparts, although they are broader time periods than for TV. A key difference between the two media is that ad time on radio is usually bought by daypart rather than by program. The most popular dayparts are Morning Drive (6–10 A.M.) and Evening Drive (3–7 P.M.), because that is when the listening audiences are largest as people commute to and from work, listening to the radio in their cars or on their personal stereos. A list of radio dayparts appears in Exhibit 10–7.

Network Radio and Spot Radio

Radio advertising is divided into two types: national network and national or local spot. **National network radio** works in a similar way to television: An advertiser places a spot with a network of radio stations that are all affiliated with the same company. Radio networks, however, provide far less national programming to their affiliates than do television networks. As a result, some stations end up belonging to more than one network (such as one for music and another for news). Another difference from television is that radio networks are usually made up of stations that air the same kind of program or appeal to the same type of listener. ABC Radio has five different networks, including one aimed at younger listeners (ABC Excel) and one focused on older ones (ABC Prime). Westwood's six networks include a business network (Westwood CNN+) and a country music network (Westwood Country). Exhibit 10–8 lists all of the radio networks available. Although network radio only accounts for 5 percent of all radio ad dollars, it does offer a simple and relatively inexpensive form of advertising that will air nationwide.

For advertisers that wish to buy radio time in individual markets, **spot radio** is the answer. This is where the bulk of all radio ad dollars are spent, both by national and local advertisers. For small businesses, spot radio makes a good deal of sense. It is not too costly, yet it allows the message to be heard within the community in which the business operates. In addition, many radio stations are eager and willing to create or provide *added-value programs* to enhance the value of the commercial time. Such programs might involve organizing a sweepstakes or contest, or airing the show from the local business's premises (such as a car dealership) to help draw traffic on that day. For companies that have franchisees or dealers, some radio stations are willing to sponsor special events at the station as a bonus for buying airtime. As with spot televi-sion, representative firms are available to facilitate spot market buys.

One of the trends in radio has been toward more syndicated programming. This began in 1981 when the FCC made news coverage by radio stations an option rather than a mandate. Starting with syndicated or network news shows, stations began buying other kinds of programming from a central source. Two of the growth areas here are music shows and talk shows. In 1994, the top station in Las Vegas aired nothing but syndicated programs.

Benefits of Radio Advertising

As with television, radio has distinct advantages for advertisers. These include low cost, local appeal, imaginative involvement, and targetability. Each is explained below.

LOW COST   Compared to many other media, radio is an efficient and inexpensive advertising medium. Depending on the market, a :30 spot on an individual radio station may run anywhere from less than a hundred to a few thousand dollars. The contrast with television is striking: A :30 radio commercial in Morning Drive, the most-listened-to daypart, may cost $10,000; to buy 30 seconds of TV prime time, on the other hand, could end up costing you more than $250,000. Admittedly the audience sizes are very different, but from a purely financial standpoint, radio has the advantage.

LOCAL APPEAL   With almost half of all ad dollars being spent locally, advertisers have many options from which to choose—they can use spot TV, local newspapers, local or regional magazines, or outdoor billboards. But as we noted above, one of the advantages of buying

---

EXHIBIT 10-7   Radio Dayparts

Morning drive	6:00 A.M.–10:00 A.M.
Daytime	10:00 A.M.–3:00 P.M.
Afternoon drive	3:00 P.M.–7:00 P.M.
Evening	7:00 P.M.–Midnight
Late night	Midnight–6:00 A.M.

EXHIBIT 10-8   Radio Networks

ABC	CBS	WESTWOOD
ABC Excel	CBS Radio	Westwood AC
ABC Galaxy	CBS Spectrum	Westwood CNN+
ABC Genesis		Westwood Country
ABC Platinum		Westwood Variety
ABC Prime		Westwood Young Adult
		Westwood Source

radio time locally is the connection that a station has with its audience in that market. The personalities who appear on the station are often well known and popular, and because of the way people listen to the radio, a station tends to develop a close relationship with its listeners. This can be particularly helpful for advertisers that wish to create some kind of community feeling.

IMAGINATIVE INVOLVEMENT   Given that radio is an aural medium, the creative message has to rely on the listeners' willingness to attend to the message. That does not mean that radio ads are restricted to plain, straightforward

text being read by an announcer, however. In fact, it is quite the opposite. Many radio ads become mini-dramas on the air, with people playing different characters, and sound effects filling in where voices cannot. As such, radio becomes highly imaginative and involving, inviting the listeners to recreate a scene in their minds and to follow along with the story. The radio spot for Little Caeser's pizza shown in Exhibit 10–9 is an excellent illustration of the creative use of sound in radio.

TARGETABILITY   The development and subsequent splintering of radio formats at stations has created one benefit for advertisers in that they are able to better target their messages to the appropriate audience. Instead of placing a message on all stations in Atlanta, for example, America Online might buy time on just those stations that are listened to more by younger adults, such as WKHX or WNNX. This advantage is particularly pronounced for ethnic marketers, because most large markets have stations whose programming is geared to the bigger ethnic populations in that area, such as Hispanics in Los Angeles or Miami, or African Americans in Baltimore and Detroit.

Drawbacks of Radio Advertising
The drawbacks to radio include the fact that it is a background medium, it only offers sound, and the message life is very short. These disadvantages must be considered by media planners as they evaluate radio as a possible medium for their advertising messages.

BACKGROUND MEDIUM   If you think about the way you, yourself, listen to radio, you may quickly realize that you tend not to pay a great deal of attention to it. Unless you have tuned in to hear a weather report, traffic update, or the news, the chances are high that the radio is on in the background while you are occupied with something else—working, driving, entertaining, and so on. Given that most people use radio as a background medium, advertisers may be rightly concerned that their messages can be too easily ignored.

The advertiser's task is to break through the clutter of other advertising and capture the listener's attention. Although it is not easy, this can readily be achieved if the message is reaching the right target at the right time, place, and

Network radio provides advertisers with a relatively easy way to air their advertisements in markets throughout the U.S. This planner-targeted advertisement demonstrates the wide array of programming formats that fall under the large ABC Radio Networks' umbrella.

circumstance when those people are thinking about the product. When McDonald's airs radio spots right before lunchtime to encourage people to take a break at their restaurants, that is a very timely and appropriate venue for reaching people who are hungry and are thinking about where to go for lunch.

SOUND ONLY   The fact that radio offers sound as its only sense is often considered a drawback of the medium. People need to concentrate on the message to absorb its contents, and they can very easily be distracted from this by what they are otherwise seeing or doing. And for many products, the single sense can be limiting. It is difficult to demonstrate the product in use, for example, and the time limit prevents a great deal of detail from being included.

BRIEF MESSAGE LIFE   The combination of background medium and sound only is made more problematic by the brief length of radio commercials. Although the standard radio spot remains at 30 seconds (and it is fairly common to have 60-second commercials), that still does not leave much time to overcome the background nature of the media type and the single sense being used. Unlike print, where people choose to read or ignore an ad, a radio commercial airs and then disappears. And unlike TV, where that is also the case, the radio spot has to work much harder to get the listener's initial attention and then hold it for the spot's duration because it is most often being heard in the background while the listener is otherwise occupied.

Measuring the Radio Audience

The standard method for measuring how many people are listening to radio and for identifying who those listeners are is provided by The Arbitron Company. Using a method somewhat similar to Nielsen's for TV, Arbitron fields seven-day listening diaries in each of the 259 markets that it measures. Ninety-four markets are measured four times a year, 79 just twice, and 86 only once. People are recruited by telephone and are asked to keep a diary that records all of the radio stations they listened to for every 15 minutes of the day for 7 consecutive days. The diaries are then mailed back to the company and the data are processed. The choice of 15-minute segments is an historical

EXHIBIT 10–9   Creative Use of Sound in Radio

LITTLE CAESAR ENTERPRISES: "FAMILY DINNER" (:60)

Father: So how was your day, son?

Son (from a distance): What?

Father (shouting): I said, how was your day?!

Son: Oh, pretty good.

Announcer: Eating a pizza as long as Little Caesars' new Pizza-by-the-foot has its drawbacks.

Father: Great pizza, huh, son?!

Son: Sure is! Hey, dad?

Father: Yeah?!

Son: Is that mom sitting next to you?!

Mother: Good eyes on that boy.

Father: Yeah, that's your mother!

Son: Say hi for me, will you?!

Father: Jimmy says hi.

Mother: Ask him if he'll pass me a slice of pepperoni.

Father: Hey, son?!

Son: Yeah?!

Father: It's your dad again!

Son: Oh, hi, dad!

Father: Hi, son! Listen, pass me a slice with pepperoni!

Son: OK!

(Sound of a pizza slice whistling through the air and landing on the table.)

Father: Boy, has that kid got an arm!

Mother: I'm so proud. (Shouting) Nice throw, son!

Announcer: Little Caesars' new Pizza-by-the-foot—nearly 3 feet of pizza and free Italian bread. Just $10.99 carried out or have it delivered.

Source: "The Best Awards," *Advertising Age,* 21 May 1997, 58.

quirk of fate. Originally, radio programs were 15 minutes in length, so when audience measurement services were first established for the medium the "average quarter-hour" became the industry standard by default. So strong was its influence that the same measure was later adopted for television too, even though TV programs lasted far longer.

What Arbitron actually calculates is the proportion of the sample that listens to at least five minutes of a 15-minute time period to arrive at the station's rating for a quarter-hour, which is then usually compiled across a broad daypart. This methodology has remained basically unchanged for decades, but Arbitron (and others) are working to improve the system based on new technologies that could facilitate widespread changes in how radio audiences are measured. One such tool would be the personal, portable meter, a little device that clips onto a person's clothing and is able to pick up the electronic signals that emanate from a radio that is on. The meter would passively record when the individual was listening to a station and to which frequency he or she was listening.

Network radio listening is measured by Statistical Research, Inc. (SRI). Its Radio All-Dimension Audience Research (RADAR) service uses telephone surveys to estimate audiences for different radio networks by asking about "yesterday" listening. The use of the telephone to collect such information is preferable, according to some researchers, because it requires less effort on the part of the respondent to remember to fill out the diary. Indeed, as "AdScape: How to Measure Radio Listening" describes, the issues surrounding radio audience measurement can be as thorny as those which cause controversy for television measurement.

Planning and Buying for Radio

When media planners are deciding whether to include radio in their media plan, there are several key terms and concepts that they use to compare stations or networks. This comparison is often done in conjunction with the media buyers, who are usually in regular contact with the sales reps at the radio stations themselves.

RADIO PLANNING: AQH, CUME, TSL, AND TURNOVER A media planner who is considering radio in the media plan needs to examine several radio-specific measurements in order to determine which radio stations or networks to include. These are the average quarter-hour (AQH) audience, the cume audience, the time spent listening (TSL), and the station's turnover.

As with television, radio audiences are defined in terms of ratings. The rating represents the percentage of the target that listens to the station in a specific daypart. The actual measurement, as noted above, is on a quarter-hour

basis, giving rise to the **average quarter-hour audience (AQH)**. For the most part, these rating levels are quite low (1–3 percent of a given target group), though that depends on what is being aired at the time. The AQH can be examined on a station-by-station basis within a market or even across markets to find out which one has the largest listenership. To find out how many people in your target are listening to any radio station, these individual station ratings can be combined to arrive at the **persons using radio (PUR)** measure, which is similar to the persons using television (PUT) for TV audience measurement.

Because people usually listen to radio for a sustained length of time, radio audiences also are looked at cumulatively. This **cume audience** represents the total number or percentage of the target group that listened to the station at all in a specified time period. Although it is cumulative, the audience is unduplicated. That is to say, each individual is only counted once, no matter how long he or she listened. A radio station might reach 2 percent of women 25–54 during the average quarter-hour, but across the midday daypart, its cume audience could rise to 15 percent.

To determine whether people are spending most of their time with one station or moving between several of them, planners and buyers can look at the **time spent listening (TSL)** measure. This is calculated by multiplying the number of quarter-hours in a daypart by the average quarter-hour audience, and then dividing that product by the total audience size. For example, if 2,000 men 18–24 listen to station WAAA during evening drive (3–7 P.M.), and there are 10,000 total men 18–24 in that market, then the time spent listening would be 2,000 multiplied by 16 quarter-hours, divided by 10,000, or 32 minutes [$2,000 \times (16 \times .25)/10,000 = 32$].

The TSL can be thought of as a measure of station loyalty; if a station's audience has a higher TSL, that suggests that once people tune in, they stick with it (as might happen with a station airing broadcasts of baseball or basketball games, for example). Music formats are likely to show greater volatility, as people get tired of hearing the same kinds of music or the same songs all the time. Media planners who are trying to reach many different people would look for stations with a low TSL; media

AdScape

How to Measure Radio Listening

Given that radio audiences have been measured for more than 40 years, you might think there would be little debate remaining on how best to do so. But people have more listening options (more stations) and may find it harder to remember which station they heard. They have far more media choices to make, which could again be confusing. And it has become harder to find people willing to fill out a diary for seven days.

Many argue that the responses received are highly error prone. People may not remember accurately a given station's call letters or frequency. Were they listening to WABC or WBCD? Was it located at 101 or 103 on the FM dial? And to have to provide the information for every 15 minutes of the day is also quite burdensome. Furthermore, listening is allocated based on having heard five or more minutes in a quarter hour (the average quarter-hour audience), but that is based strictly on clock time, so if you were listening from 8:11 to 8:16 A.M., then neither quarter hour would receive your listening data.

Then there are sampling issues. Is it reasonable to expect that you will find the necessary number of randomly selected people who will go through this lengthy measurement process? Are enough people's listening habits being surveyed to provide valid and reliable numbers? Arbitron responded to this latter criticism by increasing its sample sizes in more than half of all the markets it measures.

A rival service to Arbitron for local markets, Strategic AccuRatings relies on a telephone survey to ask about "yesterday" listening. Rather than asking people to account for every 15 minutes of the previous day, the service asks which stations were listened to in the past 24 hours, and which of those was the favorite. People then say which was their favorite station six months ago, in order to show how listening preferences either do or do not change. Because of the lower cost of a telephone survey, AccuRatings can afford to sample far more people than Arbitron. This offers greater statistical reliability in AccuRatings' findings.

One of the difficulties for AccuRatings is that agencies and advertisers have grown so used to dealing with traditional types of data, such as average quarter-hour ratings and shares, that it is difficult to convince them to switch to a different service. Birch Radio faced this problem in the 1980s, when it too offered a telephone survey of radio listening. It eventually went out of business. It remains to be seen if AccuRatings can carve a large enough niche in the radio measurement marketplace to be successful. Focusing its efforts at radio stations rather than agencies (to cater primarily to the stations' programming decisions), the company is currently in 33 markets across the country.

QUESTIONS
How do you think the measurement of radio audiences could be improved? What do you think are the most important questions that should be asked?

Source: Strategic Radio Research, *Strategic AccuRatings Overview* (Chicago: Strategic Radio Research, 1995).

planners who are trying to reach the same people over and over again would have a greater chance of doing so with a higher TSL station.

Finally, planners or buyers may wish to know how frequently a station's audience changes. This figure, known as **turnover,** is simply the ratio of the total number of people listening to the station in a given daypart (the cume audience) to the average number listening in a quarter-hour (the AQH). If a station's Morning Drive AQH of women 18–49 is 1,000 and its cume audience in that daypart is 45 percent, then the station's audience turns over about 22 times during that time period (1,000/45). When turnover is high, media planners would need to place their ad more often to reach different people as they tune in and out.

BUYING FOR RADIO   As with television, individual radio stations structure their ad rates based on supply and demand. A station in New York City may charge $800 for a :60 spot, while one in Biloxi, Mississippi, would charge only $150. Nevertheless, in both cases, prices and discounts are based on the size of the audience and the quantity of time being bought. Also, the more time an advertiser purchases, the lower the unit rate is likely to be.

Dayparts affect radio pricing. The most expensive radio time period is Morning Drive (6–10 A.M.), when most people are commuting to work. Second to that is the Afternoon Drive (3–7 P.M.), when people are returning home. Midday and evening or overnight time periods are relatively cheaper. Also similar to television, radio spots may be purchased on a fixed basis, which is the most expensive, or on a preemptive basis, which includes run-of-station (ROS) time.

Radio and Technology

People have been predicting the demise of radio ever since the birth and growth of television, but the medium remains strong and valuable for advertisers. Nonetheless, radio has not disregarded technological change as it strives to prepare for the twenty-first century media world. Two areas under development are digital radio and live Internet broadcasts.

DIGITAL RADIO   With all of the hype concerning digitization of television signals, whether for DBS or for distributing television via computer, little attention has been paid to the efforts of radio broadcasters to offer digital versions of their services, but **digital audio broadcasting (DAB)** has been in test for several years. As with digital TV broadcasts, DAB would allow stations to beam their signals up to a satellite and then send them back down again to a station in another city. This is viewed as a distinct threat by many stations, which are worried that the highly local nature of the medium will be compromised.

Several companies are currently involved in tests, but no formal service has been initiated. One of the main supporters of DAB is a consortium of broadcasters called USA Digital Radio, a partnership of Gannett, CBS Radio, and Westinghouse. One of the difficulties in developing this new form of radio is that it

would require new radio sets. It also is unclear whether consumers can hear a significant enough difference between the digital broadcast and a regular analog broadcast to make them feel that it would be worth the additional expense.

Digital radio is already available in a limited way via cable TV. Two companies, Digital Music Express (DMX) and Digital Cable Radio, both offer a large selection of radio programming for an extra fee to a regular cable TV subscriber.

INTERNET BROADCASTING   The growth and development of the Internet as a worldwide means of communication has been remarkably rapid since the mid-1990s. Although its use has been primarily to display visual information (both text and graphics), as computers gain increased speed and power the introduction of comprehensive sound capabilities is also happening. What this means is that users can listen to their favorite songs or a news program through their computers. Because the sound is carried in digital form, the listener is given complete control over the audio, allowing him or her to start and stop at will—listening to one song again and again, for example, or skipping a news item in which he or she is not interested. One of the first companies to offer Internet radio is ABC. In conjunction with National Public Radio, it is offering live broadcasts on the World Wide Web using RealAudio software that can be listened to, edited, or replayed at the user's convenience.

In addition to the network information, several large markets (New York, Chicago, Los Angeles, and Atlanta) also offer local news, weather, and sports on the Internet. Initially no commercials were included in the digital audio played over the Internet, but this is likely to change.

R E S E T

1. Why is radio considered an "everywhere" medium?
2. What is an average quarter-hour audience? A cume audience?
3. How is radio ad time purchased?

New Electronic Media Forms

A great deal of rapid growth has been taking place in the area of new electronic media in recent years. Advertisers are racing to keep up with changes in this arena, monitoring consumer activities to ensure that their messages will be available in whatever media people are drawn to and choose to spend time with. New electronic media include online services and the Internet, videos and cinema, and televisions in airports, stores, and schools.

Online Services and the Internet

Although only about 8 percent of U.S. households currently subscribe to an online computer service, that figure is rising month by month and week by week. The big three services are America Online (AOL), CompuServe, and Prodigy, closely followed by the Microsoft Network (MSN). These information services provide forums for discussion on various issues and special topic areas for people to explore, such as finance or travel. For advertisers, the options vary depending on the service.

AOL offers sponsorships to marketers so that, for a given fee, the company's name or that of its brands will appear on the screen when, say, the user accesses the travel section (e.g., "sponsored by Samsonite"). AOL also allows advertisers to sponsor chat rooms—areas where people can go to discuss specific topics that interest them, such as recreation or cooking. Prodigy's advertising is the closest to "traditional": The bottom one-fifth of every screen displays an ad message that, if the consumer is interested, can be looked at in more depth and detail. Ads are targeted to the demographics of the specific service user. Thus, if 35-year-old Jill Myers signs on to the Prodigy service, she may see an ad for Hanes hosiery, but if her 37-year-old husband John signs on, the ad that appears may be for a Ford Taurus. CompuServe offers an electronic "mall" of retailers from which users can browse or shop. It also has a monthly magazine available to all subscribers that includes regular print ads.

There are two important differences in the way that people use online services versus other media types. First, these are subscription services; like cable TV, people are paying a monthly fee to access the information. That means online subscribers tend to be more affluent and educated than the general population. They also tend to be ahead of the curve when it comes to using or owning other technologies, such as compact disc players or cellular phones. This affects the kinds of advertisers that have so far been placing their messages in this new media form.

A second difference of online service users is that they are selective in what they look at. Unlike other electronic media, where viewers are fairly passive and commercials are imposed on them, in the online world, a click of the keyboard or mouse can easily get rid of an ad message. Users are completely in control of the information, deciding what they are going to look at and for how long. Advertising messages, therefore, have to work more like print ads, striving to gain attention and then hold it long enough for the user to comprehend the message.

Many in the industry predict that the future of computer-based services lies not with online services but rather with the broader, more global Internet. The Internet allows computers to "talk" to each other, not only in this country but around the world as well. A major breakthrough and advance was made in the 1980s when programmers developed a means of displaying information visually and aurally, rather than just in text-based format. With the use of this system, called *hypertext,* the user can click on a word or subject or picture and be transported elsewhere to find out more about that piece of information. This area of the Internet has come to be known as the World Wide Web because, like a spider's web, it is all interconnected and linked together.

At first, both the Internet and Web were used primarily by government and education, but in the mid-1990s, the commercial possibilities began to be realized, to the point where today a company isn't considered to have "made it" unless it has its own page on the Web. All of the top 100 advertisers now have one or more Web sites. Still very much in its infancy as far as advertising is concerned, the Web is being used primarily as an information resource, showcasing new products or features, or telling users more about the advertiser. In 1996, for example, a total of $300 million was spent in advertising on the Web (compared to the $30 billion spent on television). Moreover, there are still only limited transactional capabilities on the Web, because a secure means of handling financial dealings through what has become known as *cyberspace* has not yet been perfected. For now, people who wish to buy or sell goods and services through the Web must rely on more traditional means, such as telephone and mail, to place an order or make a purchase.

Although advertisers are rushing to set up their sites on the Web, one of the biggest hurdles to overcome is to learn more about who is using the system. Unlike all other major media forms, there is no simple, reliable measurement source that can tell you who is looking at your message. Most of the tracking that is available monitors what is happening on the computer itself, but that cannot be traced back to individuals. One company, Media Metrix, has established a panel of 10,000 households whose computers have a piece of software installed that monitors everything that goes on with the computer, including Web activity. Here, there are demographics available. There are several other companies offering measurement services, as well, including research giants such as Nielsen. The future of online and Internet audience measurement is likely to remain in flux for the next few years.

The impact of these new media forms on traditional media is also still a matter of debate. For example, children's TV viewing has declined by about 18 percent from 1984 to 1995. Some believe this is in large part because children are more likely to be playing videogames or be on their home computers than watching TV, although the latter premise has not been definitively proven. A survey undertaken by the *New York Times,* for example, found that in homes with children, 33 percent reported that the child in the house had used a computer the day before. This discovery has led several major children's marketers, such as McDonald's and Nabisco, to follow their young users to online services and Internet. In turn, that move has provoked criticism among some youth advocacy groups who bemoan the commercialization of such media, particularly in light of the fact that many parents encourage their children to spend time there instead of with traditional media forms precisely because they want to keep them away from the advertising![7]

Cinema and Videocassettes

Cinema advertising has long been a mainstay of the advertising industry in many parts of the world. In several European countries, for example, it accounts for 1–2 percent of total ad dollars spent. In the U.S., cinema advertising has traditionally represented only a very small proportion of ad expenditures (less than 0.5 percent). Although it offers the benefits of a larger-than-life screen, full color, sound and motion, and attractive, young audiences, advertisers raise concerns over their spots being seen in conjunction with questionable movies and about the high out-of-pocket cost to reach relatively small audiences.

There is also the question of audience resistance to the "forced exposure" that cinema ads entail. People have paid up to $9 to see a movie and therefore resent having to sit through commercial messages beforehand. In 1990, Disney Studios and Warner Brothers both took the bold step of banning cinema ads before their movies, supposedly in response to consumer irritation, but subsequent polls of moviegoers could not find that strong of an objection to the commercial form.

For videocassettes, advertising has grown quite significantly in recent years. The first promotional messages were placed on tapes in the early 1980s. Often they were not types of feature films, but rather informational, "how-to" cassettes. The breakthrough occurred when Diet Pepsi put an ad message at the start of the "Top Gun" video. Since then, major marketers such as Nestlé, Mars, Pillsbury, and Kraft all have developed special promotions to coincide with the video release of a movie. Often these promotions involve price reductions on the tape when the consumer purchases a given number of products from the company.

The video market is divided into two types—rental and sales—and there are somewhat disparate benefits and drawbacks to each part. On the rental side, placing an ad at the beginning of the movie gives the advertiser the opportunity to reach a large number of different people. For sales, on the other hand, the same people will likely be reached multiple times. In both instances, however, the viewer is in control and can very easily fast-forward through the advertising to go straight to the feature presentation. In addition, the viewer may be annoyed by all of the promotional ma-

terials. One of the biggest advertisers on video-cassettes is the movie industry itself. Movie studios take advantage of the tape to promote future films, either first-run upcoming cinema features or later releases onto video.

Out-of-Home Television

The use of television as an ad medium is no longer restricted to sets in the home. More and more ventures are being tried to place TV sets in locations that attract a large number of people. These include airports, train stations, schools, and supermarkets.

The CNN Airport Network provides programming from the cable channel Cable News Network in 26 major airports. Sets placed in the departure gate areas give travelers hourly updates of news, weather, sports, and other information. Even when inside the plane, you may be reached via television. United Entertainment Network, for example, airs NBC television programs and CNN News on domestic and international flights of United Airlines. The commuter version of the CNN

Airport Network, called Metrovision, is available at train stations in six major metropolitan areas. Custom programming appears on TV monitors placed on the platform, again designed to reach commuters as they are waiting for their train to arrive. As "AdScape: On the Move—Reaching the Business Traveler" explains, one of the main benefits of out-of-home television for advertisers is its ability to reach the elusive business traveler.

A much younger television audience is the focus of Channel One, a television program designed for high schoolers. Originally launched in the early 1980s by new-media entrepreneur Christopher Whittle, the program today is run by KIII Communications and reaches 12 million students. The premise of Channel One is that the company provides TV equipment to high schools free of charge, in exchange for agreeing to air the program on a daily basis to their students. Each 12-minute news clip includes two minutes of advertising from the likes of M&M/Mars, Pepsi-Cola Co., Reebok International, and AT&T, all of

Much to the dismay of some consumer advocacy groups (and many parents), advertisers such as Nabisco have taken their product messages to the internet. Nabisco's *Nabisco Kids* Web site, which features a game and other items of interest to young people, is clearly designed to generate interest for Nabisco products among children.

which are anxious to reach and influence these young people.

As we noted in Chapter Two, there has been considerable controversy over this program since its inception. Several states, including New York, have refused to allow Channel One into public high schools. Also, research evidence has shown that the students exposed to the news clips are no more aware of the issues being aired than other students who have not seen the programs, thereby questioning the fundamental value of such a system.

The notion of putting TVs into supermarkets was attempted in the mid-1980s by NBC, in conjunction with a major grocery wholesaler, Fleming Companies. Originally designed to be in national operation by 1997, the NBC On-Site program has never expanded beyond a handful of cities and states. Programming consists of snippets from NBC shows, advertising, quizzes and games for consumers, and information and price promotions from the store itself. One of the difficulties the system faces is that it has no audio

AdScape

On the Move— Reaching the Business Traveler

For people who are constantly on the road or in the air, traditional media opportunities are few and far between. Because they are often not at home, they are not in front of the TV set at night watching situation comedies or dramas. They read magazines, but it is less likely to be *Sports Illustrated* or *Rolling Stone* and more likely to be *Time* or *Business Week*. Depending on their mode of transportation, their radio listening may either be constant (road travelers) or almost nonexistent (airline passengers).

Yet business travelers remain a very attractive advertising target. People who spend a lot of time working away from home have an upscale profile. According to Mediamark Research, Inc., adults who take three or more business trips a year are 177 percent more likely than the general population to have a post-graduate degree, 115 percent more likely to be in a professional position, and 372 percent more likely to have a personal income of $50,000 or more. So how do companies such as Nokia mobile phones, Thomas Cook foreign exchanges, or the *Financial Times* newspaper reach this moving target?

They do so by placing their messages at the times and places where the target is most likely to encounter them. For frequent flyers, that means airport media such as CNN Airport News, backlit signage in the airport, or some of the airlines' in-flight magazines. Finnish mobile phone company Nokia used a pan-European airport campaign that included exhibitions in which its core target of frequent business travelers could actually test out the product. Thomas Cook, which offers foreign exchange services in 26 countries, uses airport advertising that directs arriving or departing travelers to their bureaus. And the *Financial Times* newspaper places its airport ads as close as possible to where the newspaper is sold so that traveling businesspeople are not only reminded of the product, but can easily purchase it immediately afterwards.

For roadside warriors, radio is probably the ideal medium. Anyone who has taken a long driving trip knows how much the radio becomes a constant companion. Advertisers trying to reach this group of consumers include hotels, restaurants, and gas companies, all of whom want to encourage the driving traveler to utilize their services. The Motel 6 hotel chain made its name

because of the high ambient noise level in most supermarkets. In addition, although the location would seem to be an ideal one for reaching shoppers as they are making their purchasing decisions, most consumers are trying to get the shopping done as efficiently and rapidly as possible, rather than stopping to watch television en route.

Another failed attempt to introduce television into supermarkets was Turner Broadcasting's Checkout Channel, which placed TV monitors at supermarket checkout lines. Al-though the TVs showed CNN news programming interspersed with commercials, they were not popular with consumers. And their placement at the checkout meant that people were exposed to the message after they had filled their shopping carts.

---

with a folksy radio campaign featuring Tom Bodett, offering to business travelers the benefits of all of the lodging basics at an affordable price.

Outdoor billboards also are key to reaching this segment of the market. They notify the audience of the location of amenities such as a Howard Johnson hotel or McDonald's restaurant at upcoming cities. On roads closer to the airport, billboards feature companies aiming their messages at the airborne executives, reinforcing the ads that appear inside the airport itself.

The other major media form used to reach business travelers is print. This medium offers the benefit of detailed, targeted information, whether that is financial insights for stockbrokers or object-oriented programming for computer consultants.

Unlike electronic media, magazines can be carried around wherever the traveler goes—on the plane, from car to hotel, or on the commuter train. While television is more immediate, it cannot provide the depth and analysis of the magazine.

QUESTIONS

Given what was said about business travelers' demographics, what types of products or services would you advertise to this target? In addition to the methods mentioned above, can you think of any other ways to reach them?

Sources: Mediamark Research, Inc., *Survey of the American Consumer* (Doublebase Study), August 1995; Richard Cook, "Clients' Experience of Airport Ads," *Campaign,* Special Report on Airport Advertising, 1 November 1996, 38; and Anne-Marie Crawford, "Getting Down to Business," *Media International,* September 1995, 29–30.

Motel 6 used a humorous radio campaign featuring Tom Bodett to successfully communicate with its elusive target—business travelers. The script from one of these spots is shown here.

MOTEL 6: "AUNT JOSEPHINE" (:60)

Tom: Hi. Tom Bodett for Motel 6 with good news for the traveler. Well, it's time for the biannual trip to see Aunt Josephine. She's a wonderful lady, but the only problem is her cats. It never fails, the moment you step in the door, the big black one, Muffie, starts that curling thing around your leg, and for the rest of your stay, you're doomed to be the object of Muffie's desire. It makes it hard to concentrate on Aunt Josephine's story about Mildred's cousin's husband's neighbor, who just had her goiter treated. But maybe I've got a way to get you off the hook with Muffie. Motel 6. We'll give you a clean, comfortable room for the lowest prices of any national chain. Plus, you get free local phone calls and there's no motel service charge on long distance ones. And at Motel 6, you'll never wake up to find Muffie flipping her tail in your face. And personally, that's worth the price of the room right there. I'm Tom Bodett for Motel 6, and we'll leave the light on for you.

SUMMARY

Electronic media—television, radio, online services and the Internet, and cinema and videocassettes—dominate the advertising landscape today. The various forms of television and radio together account for about one-third of total ad expenditures. There are four types of television advertising: broadcast network, spot, cable, and syndication. Network TV is the biggest player, consisting of networks of affiliated stations in local markets that agree to air the network's programs in exchange for compensation and ad time. That local time makes up the local, or spot, TV ad market. Such commercials are aired between programs rather than within them, as network ads do. Stations also produce their own programs, particularly news, which appear when the networks aren't on the air. Ads can be bought from individual stations or through station representatives, or rep firms. Cable TV, which arose in the late 1940s but only flourished after satellites expanded in the 1980s, offers consumers subscriptions to more specialized channels of programming. Commercial time is sold by the cable networks on a national basis or by individual cable system operators for their local systems. Syndicated programs, sold by producers to individual stations on a market-by-market basis, offer advertisers commercial time either for cash or in exchange for goods and services (barter syndication). Syndicated programming is becoming important in the international television marketplace.

TV is classified by daypart (time of day) and genre (program content). Both are used by advertisers to help categorize viewing patterns. The price of the commercial will vary depending on the size of the audience. The benefits of television for advertisers include its ability to show sight, sound, and motion; its appeal to large audiences; and its overwhelming presence and considerable influence in almost all American households. The drawbacks for television advertisers include its high out-of-pocket cost (up to $350,000 for an average prime-time 30-second commercial); the increasing number of ads in each commercial break, leading to clutter; and the limited time that people have to see each spot.

The national TV audience is measured electronically via people meters that record when viewers start and stop watching TV. Meters attached to the TV sets monitor when the set is on and to which channel it is tuned. For local market audience measurement, the country is divided into 218 viewing areas, or designated market areas (DMAs). Samples of people in those markets maintain weekly viewing diaries in which they write down their viewing behavior. Some markets are measured on a continuous basis, while the majority are analyzed four times a year in what the industry refers to as the "sweeps." Advertisers are interested in how many people are using television in a given time period, and what each program's audience share is among those with TV sets in use. In the future, viewing may be recorded passively without the need for the audience to do anything to record their viewing activity.

Terms used for television planning include ratings, reach, and GRPs. The television marketplace operates under the laws of supply and demand. Advertisers buy time in the new fall season programs in the upfront market each spring. With that early commitment, they are given guaranteed audience ratings. Alternatively, they can buy time each quarter in the scatter market, where the prices may be higher and there are no guarantees. For last-minute buys, opportunistic slots become available from week to week. Commercials are sold on a fixed, preemptive, or run-of-station basis. At the local level, buyers contact local stations to see what is available (avails).

Technology is having an enormous impact on the television industry. The growth of satellite dishes has been enhanced with the development of direct broadcast by satellite (DBS), which delivers the TV signals directly to each subscriber household. There are currently about 5 million homes receiving TV this way. Further down the road, we may see people talking directly through their television set when interactive TV is more established, either through regular TV sets or computers that also offer TV services. The telephone companies are beginning to experiment with TV services, too, as regulations are loosened to remove the formerly strict barrier between these two industries.

Changes in television advertising in the past 40 years have included the move away from full-program sponsorship to shorter commercials and multiple sponsors (advertisers) per show. Long-form messages are available now through infomercials. Home shopping networks do nothing but air such types of advertising to sell products directly to consumers.

Radio, often considered a poor cousin to television, continues to thrive and attract both national and local advertisers. People listen to radio everywhere, but especially outside of the home. Nearly all cars have a radio built in, while personal stereos are commonplace. Radio signals are distributed on either AM or FM wavelengths. The former can travel through ground or air and therefore go further, but with inferior quality to the air-based FM signals. That has meant that AM stations tend to focus on news or talk, while FM stations have tended to offer music programming. Every radio station has its own call letters. Radio program types are known as formats, and these have fragmented considerably, leading to numerous forms of rock music stations or country music stations, among others. Radio advertising is bought by daypart and is either national (network) or local (spot). The latter accounts for the bulk of all ad dollars. There has been a recent trend toward more syndicated programming.

Radio offers advertisers the benefits of low cost, local appeal, imaginative involvement, and targetability. The fragmentation of formats has meant that each station appeals to a select group of people who like that station's programming mix. Drawbacks to the medium include the fact that it tends to be listened to in the background; it only offers sound; and the message, like a television ad, does not last long (30 or 60 seconds).

Radio audiences are measured by use of a listening diary. The Arbitron Company asks a representative number of people in each market to keep a written record of their listening behavior over a seven-day period. Statistical

Research, Inc. (SRI) collects data on "yesterday" listening, via telephone surveys, to measure network radio listening.

When planning for radio, media specialists have to consider a station's average quarter-hour audience (the average number of people listening in a 15-minute period); the cume audience (the total number listening in that time); the time spent listening to the station; and the station's turnover (how frequently the audience changes). Radio is sold according to the laws of supply and demand. Radio time is sold by dayparts, with spots purchased on a fixed, preemptive, or run-of-station basis.

The future of radio seems assured, thanks to technological improvements on the horizon. These include digital radio (digital audio broadcasting, or DAB) to bring digital quality sounds through the airwaves, and broadcasting via the Internet.

The category of new electronic media has been expanding enormously in recent years. The fastest-growing element within the category is advertising on online services and the Internet. Unlike TV and radio, online consumers control the ad messages they wish to look at. Because of this active involvement, advertisements must be informative and attention-getting, in much the same way as print advertising. The growth and development of the Internet, in particular the World Wide Web, is occurring faster than our ability to truly measure who, precisely, is viewing ad messages on it. Total Web ad spending in 1996 reached about $300 million. It is possible that these interactive media increasingly will cut into traditional media usage time.

A more established type of electronic advertising is offered at the cinema or on videocassettes. Although this type of advertising represents a small proportion of ad spending in terms of dollars, its impact may be greatly enhanced by promotional links between the brand's advertising and the special deals offered to consumers. Finally, television broadcasts increasingly are appearing outside of the home, with ads included. Services include CNN Airport News, Metrovision, and Channel One.

local station affiliates, 302

spot television
    advertising, 303

syndicated programming, 305

barter syndication, 305

daypart, 305

genre, 305

people meter, 308

program rating, 308

households using television
    (HUT), 308

persons using television
    (PUT), 308

viewing share, 308

audience share, 308

designated marketing areas
    (DMAs), 309

sweeps, 309

guaranteed audience
    ratings, 310

scatter market, 311

opportunistic purchase, 311

fixed spot, 311

preemptive spot, 311

run-of-station spot, 311

avails, 311

interactive television, 312

direct response television
    (DRTV), 313

infomercials, 314

home shopping networks, 315

call letters, 316

formats, 316

national network radio, 316

spot radio, 317

average quarter-hour audience
    (AQH), 320

persons using radio
    (PUR), 320

cume audience, 320

time spent listening
    (TSL), 320

turnover, 321

digital audio broadcasting
    (DAB), 322

REVIEW QUESTIONS

1. What are the four types of television available to advertisers? How are they similar? How are they different?

2. Describe the key benefits and drawbacks of television for advertisers.

3. Discuss the relationship between program ratings and advertising in television.

4. What is the difference between a PUT and a HUT?

5. What are the various ways television advertising can be purchased? What are the advantages and disadvantages of each method?

6. From a media perspective, what are the different ways of classifying radio?

7. What are the benefits and drawbacks of radio for advertisers?

8. How is the radio listening audience measured, and what are the problems with that form of measurement?

9. How are advances in technology affecting radio?

10. What new electronic media forms are now available to advertisers? How are these media forms best utilized?

DISCUSSION QUESTIONS

1. Your agency's creative department has just written a witty, humorous, and catchy spot to promote use of the train over other forms of transportation. The writers want to put it on television. Argue for or against this proposal, giving consideration to media planning elements such as

targeting, costs, and the benefits and drawbacks of different media forms.

2. How should advertisers deal with a "500 channel" television universe?

interactive discovery lab

1. Listen to your favorite radio station during a standard daypart (e.g., morning drive, midday, evening drive) and write down all of the commercials that air. Note not only who the advertiser is but also who you think the ad is targeted to and what its key message is. After you have all of the ads listed, try to find ways to categorize them (by target, product category, or type of message appeal, etc.).

2. A similar exercise can be undertaken with television. Record one prime-time evening's worth of television, list all of the commercials that aired, and then try to organize them into some cohesive classification system.

Chapter Eleven

Print Media

NEWSPAPERS AND THE WEB: STOP THE PRESSES?

What do you do as a media vehicle when you have two potentially competing avenues for distributing your content?

This is the situation that hundreds of newspapers now face as they set up Web sites on the Internet, which can be updated far more quickly than the regular press run of their hardcopy newspapers. In some cases, it can lead to rivalry between two parts of the same organization. Back in November 1995 in Philadelphia, the two local newspapers, the *Philadelphia Inquirer* and *Philadelphia Daily News*, refused to cooperate with Philadelphia Online in producing an online version of a breaking story for fear that it would cannibalize the next day's newspaper sales. That forced the online service to rely on standard national news agency wire reports until the local papers went to press.

For all of the talk of the Web's ability to provide constantly updated and instantly available news and information, the reality is that it is only doing so to a limited extent. For most major newspapers with Web sites, the story is similar to the case in Philadelphia; that is, daily updates come from agency reports until the newspaper goes to press. Then, the editorial staff contributes to the Web product, sometimes offering more than what appears on paper. The reason for this is financial. Given the relatively small number of people currently using the Web, it is not economically viable for newspapers to devote their own writers and editors to keeping the Web site material up-to-the-minute at the expense of getting the next day's paper off the presses.

That is not to say, however, that newspapers are not experimenting on

the Web. By having its own Web site, *The Wall Street Journal* is able to cover weekend stories on the Web that previously would have had to wait until Monday morning. And in the Silicon Valley of California, the *San Jose Mercury News* is making a name for itself by breaking technology-related stories on its Web site first, because it knows that the audience for such stories spends more time on the Web than with the daily paper.

Newspapers are also keenly aware that the Internet threatens to diminish their importance as people's primary source of news and information. As a printed newspaper, the *New York Times* competes mostly with other national or regional papers, such as *The Wall Street Journal* or *Chicago Tribune.* But on the Web, it is up against CNN's Web site, *Time* magazine, or one of the countless other news-oriented sites that can now all offer instantaneous, in-depth reporting on breaking stories. Whatever the future of newspapers, it is likely to have more and more of an electronic element to it.

Source: Laurence Zuckerman, "Don't Stop the Presses!" *New York Times,* 6 January 1997, C1, C7.

LOOK BEFORE YOU LEAP

• Why do advertisers choose print media to convey their messages?

• What are the benefits and drawbacks of magazine and newspaper advertising?

• How are magazine and newspaper audiences measured?

• How is magazine and newspaper ad space purchased?

• What has the impact of technology been on magazines and newspapers?

• What other types of print media are available, and for which audiences should they be considered?

11

Newspapers are part of the category of media known as print media. The two major forms—newspapers and magazines—together represent about 30 percent ($55 billion) of total ad dollars. While magazines are considered a targeted ad medium, helping advertisers reach computer consultants in *PC Magazine* or teens in *Seventeen,* newspapers are typically more general in their reach, delivering messages to local audiences (town or region).

Your exposure to print media is not limited to these two forms, however. When you go shopping, you will probably see print media in the form of outdoor billboards or transit advertising. Another print medium—the Yellow Pages—helped you decide where to buy an item. At your destination, in-store signage may influence your purchase decision.

This chapter examines various print media. We look at the different options available in magazines, newspapers, out-of-home, Yellow Pages, and in-store vehicles, the reasons advertisers choose them, and some challenges these media face in an increasingly electronic and technology-oriented world. The chapter also considers how internationalization of media affects each type of print media.

Magazines

In the days before the arrival of television, magazines were considered, like radio, to be a mass medium, able to reach large numbers of people across the country. Indeed, if you placed an ad in one issue of *Life, Look,* and *The Saturday Evening Post,* it would have had the opportunity to be seen by more than half of all adults across the U.S.! Today, however, magazines are considered to reach more selective audiences. Even those publications that are generalist in nature, such as *Parade* magazine or *Reader's Digest,* are likely to reach, at most, about 33 million people, or one-third of the U.S. population. Specialized titles such as *SmartMoney* or *Swimmers World* reach even smaller audiences.

The primary reason for this shift in content and focus from general to specific was the rapid development of television, which could instantaneously bring millions of people together to share in the same experience. In addition, the new medium offered the combination of sight, sound, and motion, adding two important senses to the single one provided by magazines (sight).

Today we tend to divide magazines into three areas: consumer, farm, and business or trade/professional. **Consumer magazines** include all titles that are written for a nonspecialized audience. This would encompass *Time* and *Newsweek, Cosmopolitan* and *Vogue,* or *Rolling Stone* and *Spin.* **Farm magazines** are written to inform and educate the agricultural population; the subject matter may be as general as *Successful Farming* or as specific as *Cotton Grower* or *Wheat Life.* The third sector, **business magazines,** incorporates titles that are aimed at a specialized group of people who work in a particular industry. *Milling and Baking* is read by workers in the baking industry; *Chemical Age,* by those dealing with chemicals; and *Restaurant News,* by people managing or working in the food-service industry.

For marketers, the decision about which type of magazine to use obviously depends on the audience to whom the ad is aimed. In many cases, there may be both a consumer and a business target. Thus, Procter & Gamble may run ads for Ivory Soap in consumer publications such as *Ladies Home Journal* or *Parenting* that extol the brand's benefit of being gentle to the skin. But the company may also put an ad message in *Hospital* that lets hospitals or other institutions know of the antibacterial qualities of the soap that would make it a viable option for use in those facilities. Of all the advertising placed in magazines, the vast majority goes into the consumer sector. In 1996, consumer magazines accounted for over 90 percent of the more than $9 billion spent in the category.

Although magazines have grown increasingly specialized in their editorial content, it is still possible to categorize them into several basic content areas. These include general editorial, such as *Reader's Digest* or *National Geographic,* and women's service books, such as *Good Housekeeping* and *McCall's.* A list of the standard magazine categories and examples of each is provided in Exhibit 11–1.

Magazine specialization affords advertisers increased targeting capabilities. If Red Dog Beer wishes to reach outdoor enthusiasts, it can do so in *Outside* or *Sports Illustrated.* But if it wants to talk to music lovers, then its message can be placed in *Vibe* or *Rolling Stone.* The extent to which magazines have become specialized is reflected in the titles of some of the new magazines that are being published. A few of these titles are shown in Exhibit 11–2. They include *Bird Breeder, Miller's Barbie Collector,* and *GadgetWorld.*

At the same time that magazines are narrowing their focus in terms of subject matter, they have been broadening their reach by extending their brand names into other kinds of products and services. *House Beautiful* now has its own line of paint, *Self* magazine is considering opening fitness-related stores, and *Money* magazine conducts finance-related seminars. For some publishers these non-print ventures represent a sizable proportion of total revenues. For Meredith Publications, which produces *Better Homes & Gardens,* two-thirds of its money comes from these types of activities.[1]

Several magazines also have expanded their sales by moving outside of their initial geographic borders. When *Reader's Digest* published its first non–U.S. edition back in 1940 in Argentina, it was a highly unusual move. By the time its forty-eighth foreign edition hit the Thai newsstands in 1995, there were tens, if not hundreds of potential competitors. Similarly, *Elle* magazine is now available in Shanghai, China, along with nine other countries in Asia. "Around the Globe: Oceans

EXHIBIT 11–1   Examples of Standard Magazine Categories

CATEGORY	EXAMPLES
General editorial	*Reader's Digest, National Geographic*
Epicurean	*Gourmet, Bon Appetit*
Parenting	*Parent's, Parenting*
Shelter	*Better Homes & Gardens, Southern Living*
Women's service	*Good Housekeeping, McCall's*
Teen	*Seventeen, Young Miss (YM)*
Sports and fitness	*Men's Health, Shape, Fitness*

EXHIBIT 11–2   Some New Magazine Titles

TITLE	SUBJECT AREA	PUBLICATION FREQUENCY
Aspire	Religion	Bimonthly
Barney Magazine	Children	Bimonthly
Bike Magazine	Sports	9 per year
Civilization	Arts	Bimonthly
Eco Traveler	Travel	Bimonthly
Elle TopModel	Fashion and beauty	Quarterly
Fine Cooking	Epicurean	Bimonthly
German Life	Travel	Bimonthly
Latin Style	Media personalities	Monthly
Louis L'Amour Western Magazine	Literary	Bimonthly
NetGuide	Computers	Monthly
Realms of Fantasy	Mystery and adventure	Bimonthly
Slam	Sports	Bimonthly
Swing	Youth	10 per year
Yolk	Lifestyles and service	Quarterly

Source: Samir Husni's Guide to New Magazines 1995 (New York: Hearst Magazine Enterprises, 1995).

EXHIBIT 11–3   Who Reads Magazines?

DEMOGRAPHIC CATEGORY	% WHO READ 1+ MAGAZINES PER MONTH	AVERAGE NUMBER OF ISSUES READ PER MONTH
Total U.S. adults	88.4%	11.8
Age 18–44	91.7	13.1
Age 25–44	90.7	12.5
Attended/graduated college	94.1	13.7
Household income $40,000+	92.8	13.4
Household income $60,000+	93.3	14.4
Professional/managerial position	94.5	13.5

Source: Magazine Publishers of America, *The Magazine Handbook 1996/97* (New York: Magazine Publishers of America, 1997), 47.

Apart—*Vanity Fair* and *Cosmopolitan*" offers some insight into the differences between the various versions of these two U.S.-based titles.

Benefits of Magazine Advertising

For advertisers, there are four key benefits of using magazines: attractive audiences, long issue life, opportunities for long copy, and reader involvement.

ATTRACTIVE AUDIENCES   Simply by virtue of the fact that you need to be able to read to understand the content of a magazine, people who do so tend to be somewhat more educated and affluent than the general population. Figures provided by the Magazine Publishers of America (MPA), a magazine industry trade group, show that the average adult reader of an average copy of a magazine is likely to have attended or graduated college, be married, be employed full time, own his or her own home, live in a metropolitan area, and have a median household income of $37,000.[2] All of these demographic characteristics position the magazine reader as an attractive prospect for advertisers, as shown in Exhibit 11–3.

LONG ISSUE LIFE   Unlike television and radio programs or ads, which are aired and then disappear forever (notwithstanding VCRs or reruns), magazines and the ads within them may be kept around the house anywhere from a few days or weeks to several months or years. As Bob Moore, the creative director at Wieden & Kennedy in Portland, Oregon, notes, "You cannot put a television commercial on your refrigerator."[3] That extension of the magazine's lifespan may provide the reader with additional opportunities for exposure to your brand's ad. For many titles, people deliberately clip out articles or ads to keep for future reference. And by keeping an issue beyond its publication date, the reader may also pass the magazine along to a friend or relative, thereby creating what the industry refers to as the **passalong audience,** also known as the **secondary readers.** This again extends the reach of the magazine title and allows more people the chance to see your ad.

READER INVOLVEMENT   Reader involvement can be a double-edged sword, but for the most part advertisers like the fact that the magazine reader is going to be more involved with and pay more attention to the subject matter. The comparison to TV or radio is pertinent here, as well. When you watch a TV show or listen to music on the radio, there's a good chance you are either doing something else at the same time and/or are not paying full attention to what is on the screen or in the airwaves. By contrast, when you read a magazine, you have to deliberately and methodically read the material, and if you selected that magazine, the chances are high that you are also interested in what you are reading. That interest allows advertisers to employ lengthy copy points to explain complex ideas.

Advertisers take this one step further by arguing that if an ad is targeted to the appropriate audience and its message is relevant to those people and is reaching them when they are going to be receptive to it, then the involvement they have with the subject of the magazine is likely to spill over into greater involvement with the ad. It is very difficult to prove such a statement, although researchers have tried. One of the first of these types of studies was the Study of Printed Advertising Rating Methods (PARM), conducted in 1956 under the auspices of the Advertising Research Foundation. This study looked at the different techniques used to measure the readership and recall of print ads. It found that the passalong audience, or secondary readers of a publication, had 85–90 percent of the readership and recall of the **primary readers**—those who bought the copy themselves.

More recently, *Family Circle* commissioned a sophisticated study in the early 1990s in which it ran special ads in half of the copies of its magazine and then monitored sales of the products at the supermarket checkout. Results indicated that the *Family Circle* readers spent 7 percent more dollars in the store than those who had not seen the magazine. For specific brands involved in the study, the findings were even more dramatic. Duncan Hines Frostings saw a 29 percent increase in sales volume during the 28-week measurement period; Nabisco Harvest Crisps found that cumulative sales rose by 39 percent among the test households; and 36 percent more of Keebler's Ready-Crust pie crusts were purchased by the *Family Circle* readers than by the consumers who had not seen its magazine ads.[4]

Drawbacks for Magazine Advertising

The three key difficulties that magazines face as far as advertising is concerned are lack of timeliness, reader disinterest, and excessive specialization.

LACK OF TIMELINESS Even though weekly magazines such as *Newsweek* or *People* claim to bring their readers the latest news and information, it is still impossible to beat the daily nature of newspapers or the instantaneous coverage that TV can provide. In addition to impacting consumers' interactions with magazines, this lack of timeliness also affects advertisers. Because of the lengthy production process, the planning cycle for magazines can become very long. A full-page ad in the November issue of *Fitness,* for example, must be purchased in mid-August. The advent of digitization and computers is helping speed up this process—not just in terms of improving the production process but also in enabling magazines to rely on satellite feeds to wait until the last minute to finalize the editorial content. Nonetheless, the fact remains that magazines, at least in their hard-copy print form, cannot be as timely in their coverage as other media.

READER DISINTEREST As we mentioned above, the fact that readers are likely to be

In the past four years, he's had two promotions, three offers and one business magazine.

For business people, change is a way of life. Yet the typical Business Week reader has subscribed to the magazine for more than five years, spending an average of nearly 1 1/2 hours reading each issue.

These 6.7 million readers depend on Business Week to deliver the timely news and insightful intelligence they need to succeed in their professional as well as personal lives.

Basically, they consider Business Week a must read, every week. And for advertisers, that makes it a very intelligent buy.

For information, call Bill Kupper at (212) 512-6945, or e-mail adsales@businessweek.com.

BusinessWeek
Beyond news. Intelligence.

Sources: 1996 Fall MRI, Business Week Adjusted Audience; Business Week Estimate for International; 1996 Business Week Subscriber Study.

© 1997 by The McGraw-Hill Companies, Inc. A Division of *The McGraw-Hill Companies*

more involved with magazines than with other media types can also be a disadvantage for magazine advertisers. If the message is not placed in the right magazine (in terms of its editorial content) or if it is not relevant to the magazine's audience, then it is very likely that the reader will simply ignore the ad completely just by turning the page.

Disinterest may be caused by several factors. It could be that a reader of *Cooking Light* doesn't like to cook shellfish; as a result, ads for Louis Kemp's Crab Delights will not attract his or her attention at all. Clutter of ads can also lead readers to lose interest in the ads. If your message for Coty nail polish appears as the fifth page of advertising at the front of *Glamour,* then the reader, even if she is interested in

Magazines use trade advertisements to attract advertisers who are targeting consumer groups that fall within the magazine's readership population. This trade ad for *Business Week*, for example, is clearly directed to advertisers interested in targeting business professionals. Notice also that the ad provides a readership total and an estimate of the time spent by readers with each issue, both of which are important to advertisers.

nail polish, may well not see your ad because she has lost interest after paging through the previous four pages of commercial content. Disinterest as a result of ad clutter can be particularly problematic in certain genres of magazine, such as fashion and beauty, where the number of ads bunched together in the fall or spring fashion preview editions is likely to deter all but the most diligent of readers from reading through all of the ads. Lastly, disinterest may surface if the reader is extremely involved in an article and is concentrating so much that he pays no attention to the ad, even if he is the right target for the product. He may even become irritated with the advertising, seeing it as an unwelcome distraction from the article.

EXCESSIVE SPECIALIZATION The benefit that most major magazines tout to potential advertisers today is that they can reach a very particular group of people in whom they believe the advertiser is interested. In doing so, however, they are automatically excluding many others who may also be interested in the advertiser's message. Companies wishing to reach gardeners may target narrowly through *Flower and Garden* magazine or more broadly with *Better Homes & Gardens,* which includes gardening as well as other topics. Even titles that reach millions of consumers claim to be specialized within their overall readership. For example, in the early 1990s, *Redbook* focused its efforts on reaching women it called "jugglers," those in the 25–44 age group who were trying to balance work, family, and relationships. *Ebony,* which reaches 950,000 African Americans each month, distinguishes itself from other black-oriented titles by claiming to specialize in reaching women who are independent, career-

AROUND THE GLOBE

. . . .

Oceans Apart—
Vanity Fair and
Cosmopolitan

The ways that magazines can become global properties varies. Two examples of such different approaches are seen in *Vanity Fair* and *Cosmopolitan,* both of which publish editions in both the U.S. and the United Kingdom. For *Vanity Fair,* published by Conde Nast, the U.K. version is its only non–U.S. product. The editorial content is identical in each country; only the advertising differs. *Cosmopolitan,* in contrast, is published by Hearst Magazines in 32 countries; the editorial is separate for each edition, although some of the U.S. material is transposed at a later date. In many of those countries the name is licensed to another, local publisher. The advertising is also sold on a country-by-country basis.

For both magazines, however, the target audience in each market is the same. *Vanity Fair* is read in both the U.S. and U.K. by an affluent, educated group of individuals. In the States, 74 percent are female. The median age of its readers is 36, and subscriptions account for 67 percent of total sales. *Cosmopolitan's* U.S. audience is 83 percent female, with an average age of 32, and 33 percent of its sales come from subscribers.

So how do these statistics impact the magazines' advertising? To find that out, the U.S. and U.K. editions of each magazine were compared for the same month. Total pages, and ad pages, were examined, and the proportion of ad pages devoted to each major category were examined. Here is what we found, shown in the table at right.

To begin with, *Vanity Fair's* U.K. edition has one-fifth of its total pages devoted to advertising, compared to one-third in the U.S. edition. The top two categories of advertising, however, are the same for both countries: health and beauty, and jewelry and watches. Automotive accounts for twice as many ad pages in the British version as the American one, while apparel is almost three times as likely to be in the U.S. edition as compared to the U.K. one.

The differences were less pronounced for *Cosmopolitan.* For both U.S. and U.K. versions, about 30 percent of the magazine was filled with ads. By far the most important ad category, accounting for more than half of all ad pages for each country, was health and beauty. The next most popular ad category for both magazines was personal care, although it was a distant

oriented, and sophisticated. But does an advertiser such as Levi's or Pantene wish to reach only those two groups of women on which these magazines claim to focus? If the answer is no, and the advertiser is looking for a broader reach, then that may lead it to consider using more general media forms such as television or newspapers.

Planning and Buying for Magazines

In order for media planners to determine whether to include magazines in a media plan and, if so, which ones to select, they must look at several key issues, including circulation, coverage, and composition. Once a decision has been made about which magazine to advertise in, planners must consider what size ads they wish to purchase and where in the magazine they want to place the ad.

MAGAZINE PLANNING: CIRCULATION, COVERAGE, AND COMPOSITION A magazine's **circulation** tells you how many copies are sold in each publication period. For the publisher, this indicates how well the magazine is doing. The figure is calculated by taking the number of issues that are distributed to stores or newsstands or directly to subscribers in their homes, and then subtracting the number of copies that are left unsold after a fixed amount of time. For advertisers and agencies, the publisher will then set a specific **guaranteed circulation**—a promise that a certain number of copies will be sold each period (week, month, two months, etc.).

Circulation figures are regularly audited by an independent third-party organization to verify the sales figures showing whether the magazine *overdelivered* (sold more than guaranteed) or *underdelivered* (sold fewer than guaranteed).

second, representing just 7 percent of all of the U.S. ads and 11 percent in the U.K.

So what do we learn from this simple overview? That magazines targeted at similar audiences will be likely to attract the same kinds of advertisers. And regardless of whether or not the editorial material is the same, the kinds of advertisers are likely to be similar. More extensive analysis would really be needed to extend this study over time and over more magazines and/or issues. But even from this glimpse across one ocean separating two countries with the same language, it is clear that the advertising distance between them is not that great.

	VANITY FAIR				COSMOPOLITAN			
	U.K.	% of Total	U.S.	% of Total	U.K.	% of Total	U.S.	% of Total
Apparel	2	6.1%	9	16.1%	4	5.3%	5	6.2%
Automotive	5	15.2	5	8.9	4	5.3	2	2.5
Entertainment	3	9.1	1	1.8	2	2.6	1	1.2
Financial services	0	0.0	1	1.8	2	2.6	0	0.0
Food and wine	1	3.0	3	5.4	4	5.3	5	6.2
Health and beauty	10	30.3	12	21.4	42	55.3	48	59.3
Household	0	0.0	0	0.0	4	5.3	2	2.5
Jewelry and watches	7	21.2	14	25.0	0	0.0	1	1.2
Miscellaneous	2	6.1	3	5.4	1	1.3	3	3.7
Personal care	0	0.0	0	0.0	9	11.8	6	7.4
Pets	0	0.0	1	1.8	0	0.0	0	0.0
Photography	0	0.0	2	3.6	0	0.0	0	0.0
Technology	1	3.0	1	1.8	2	2.6	1	1.2
Tobacco	1	3.0	4	7.1	0	0.0	6	7.4
Travel	1	3.0	0	0.0	2	2.6	1	1.2
Total ad pages	**33**	**100.0%**	**56**	**100.0%**	**76**	**100.0%**	**81**	**100.0%**
Total pages	**164**		**186**		**256**		**250**	
Total ad pages (%)	**20.1%**		**30.1%**		**29.7%**		**32.4%**	

EXHIBIT 11–4   **Coverage versus Composition**

Ladies' Home Journal

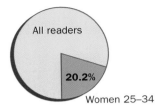

COVERAGE

Percentage of a magazine's audience that is read by a given demographic group. For example, 20.2 percent of *Ladies' Home Journal* readers are women ages 25–34.

Women 25–34

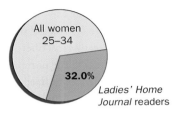

COMPOSITION

Percentage of a demographic group that reads a given magazine. For example, 32 percent of women ages 25–34 read *Ladies' Home Journal.*

Once a magazine starts to overdeliver on a regular basis, the publisher will usually increase the guaranteed circulation level and, subsequently, the price of the ad space (because the ads are reaching more people). For magazines that continue to underdeliver, two results are possible: (1) advertisers will start to avoid those titles, knowing they cannot be relied upon to deliver the audiences they claim to reach, or (2) the publisher will cut down the size of the guaranteed circulation. When the latter is done, it is usually with claims that the publishing house is trying to focus on the "serious" or "real" readers of the magazine rather than those who might occasionally purchase it. Sometimes, too, circulation cutbacks are accompanied by decreases in advertising rates.

Knowing how many copies of a magazine are sold does not tell an advertiser or agency how many people are reading that title. As we have noted, one of the benefits of magazines is their ability to be passed along to other readers. Survey research is able to determine how many **readers per copy** each magazine receives; that is, the average number of people who read a copy of the magazine. This figure is multiplied by the circulation to arrive at the magazine's **audience**. Therefore, while *Redbook* has a circulation of 900,000, 2.3 people read each

copy, meaning its total audience is actually 2,070,000. Audience figures may also be broken down further. They can be classified according to primary versus secondary readership and also according to location of reading: either in-home or out-of-home.

For Jergens Soap, interested in reaching women 25–54 who purchase soap for their household, the total magazine audience is still not enough. What that brand's marketing people really want to know is what percent of *Redbook*'s audience falls into the desired demographic of women 25–54 soap buyers. Again, survey research can determine this, and the end result provides the **coverage** of the magazine against the target audience, which is simply the percent of that target group who reads the magazine. This is also known as the magazine's *rating*.

Another way of examining magazines is to look at their **composition,** which shows what proportion of a magazine's total audience falls into a given demographic group. While *Redbook* might be read by 33 percent of all women 25–54 who buy soap, 47 percent of *Redbook*'s total audience might consist of women 25–54. Composition can be thought of as a way of testing how "rich" a media vehicle is among a certain group of people. Exhibit 11–4 depicts the distinction between coverage and composition.

Media planners analyze the various magazines that might be appropriate for a given brand to see which ones do the best job of reaching that brand's target audience in terms of coverage and composition. Exhibit 11–5 lists the magazines that Cheerios cereal might advertise in to reach women 18–49 with one or more children in the household. Through syndicated resources, a media planner can look at the coverage and composition figures to find the magazines that do the best job of reaching that target. The planner could look at the list of magazines ranked on composition and decide to use only those whose audience is at least 80 percent women 18–49 with children. That would narrow the list to five titles. Then among those top five, the planner could look at the coverage levels and select the two with the highest coverage: *Parent's Magazine* and *Sesame Street Magazine*. The exercise can also be done in reverse, looking first at coverage and then at composition.

BUYING MAGAZINES: AD SIZE AND POSITIONING Magazine space is generally sold in terms of full pages or fractions of pages. The standard size is a one-page, four-color ad, but numerous alternatives are available. Ads may be as small as one-eighth of a page, or as long as a two- or three-page spread. Research has shown that larger ads are more likely to capture readers' attention, although not at a level proportionate to their size; that is, doubling the size of the ad does not mean that it will capture twice the amount of attention. The size of the ad is usually determined in conjunction with creative considerations, such as the length and complexity of the message or the size of the copy.

Magazines have four **cover pages,** three of which are usually available for advertising. The front cover is known as the first cover page, the inside of the front cover is the second, the inside back cover is the third, and the outer back cover is the fourth. The two facing pages in the center of the publication are called the **center spread.** All of these pages cost more than a regular page. Magazines also sell other kinds of special space that are designed to increase readership and sales. A **gatefold** is a three-page spread in a magazine that consists of one full page or part of a page that extends from the original page and folds outward from the center of the book, like a gate, inviting the reader to open it up. Sometimes material is bound into a magazine attached to an advertisement. Called **inserts,** these may be reply cards, coupons, or pop-ups, all intended to attract greater attention than a straightforward ad on the page.

In addition to knowing how big an ad will be, planners must also arrange for where the ad will appear in each magazine. This is known as the ad's **position.** There has been lengthy debate (which is still not fully resolved) regarding the impact of ad position on ad effectiveness. Does a Perdue chicken ad do better when it appears at the front of *Good Housekeeping* or when it is positioned next to the recipe section at the back of the magazine? Some people maintain that ads at the front of a publication are most likely to be noticed, while others claim that the most important factor is the editorial material that the ad appears next to or near. Magazines vary in how much the position can be guaranteed or whether advertisers have to pay additional money to ensure that their pages will appear precisely where they want them.

EXHIBIT 11–5   Magazines to Reach Women 18–49 with Children

TOP 10 MAGAZINES RANKED BY COMPOSITION
(% of magazine readership which is within the target audience)

MAGAZINE	COMPOSITION	COVERAGE
American Baby	86.61%	9.09%
Parent's Magazine	82.77	20.05
Baby Talk	82.17	5.80
Working Mother	81.74	5.57
Sesame Street Magazine	80.24	10.23
Disney Channel Magazine	67.50	9.70
Jet	54.33	6.31
Essence	54.18	6.01
Ebony	53.59	8.89
First for Women	53.09	5.98

TOP 10 MAGAZINES RANKED BY COVERAGE
(% of targeted women reading magazine)

MAGAZINE	COVERAGE	COMPOSITION
Better Homes & Gardens	40.70%	39.79%
Reader's Digest	29.23	42.61
TV Guide	28.44	37.98
People	26.34	45.34
Good Housekeeping	25.36	42.51
Family Circle	24.17	41.41
Women's Day	23.03	42.20
Parent's Magazine	20.05	82.77
Ladies' Home Journal	17.21	40.32
McCall's	15.89	40.92

Source: Mediamark Research, Inc., *Survey of the American Consumer,* Spring 1995.

WRITTEN BY
Official publication of:
The Writers Guild of America

Location ID: 8 MLST 17A   **Mid 063961-000**
Published monthly by Writers Guild of America, West, 7000 W. 3rd St., Los Angeles, CA 90048. Phone 213-782-4522. Fax 213-782-4802.
For shipping info., see Print Media Production Source.
PUBLISHER'S EDITORIAL PROFILE
WRITTEN BY is a magazine written by and for America's screen and television writers. It focuses on the craft of screenwriting and offers a look into the creative process of Hollywood. Readers include those who are interested in writing, studio executives, agents, independent producers and development executives. Rec'd 3/26/97.

1. PERSONNEL
Pub Rep—Dianna Hightower, 818-909-4613; Fax 818-909-4626.

3. COMMISSION AND CASH DISCOUNT
15% commission. No cash discount.

4. GENERAL RATE POLICY
No cancellations accepted after space closing date.

ADVERTISING RATES
Effective January 1, 1997. (Card)
Rates received January 30, 1997

5. BLACK/WHITE RATES

	1 ti	3 ti	6 ti	11 ti
1 page	2160.	2055.	1950.	1938.
2/3 page	1350.	1305.	1260.	1170.
1/2 page	1215.	1170.	1125.	1080.
1/3 page	990.	945.	900.	855.
1/4 page	945.	855.	765.	720.

6. COLOR RATES

2-color, extra	650.
4-Color, extra	800.

7. COVERS

	1 ti	3 ti	6 ti	11 ti
2nd cover	3225.	3120.	3078.	3023.
3rd cover	2700.	2595.	1748.	2385.
4th cover	4500.	4050.	3600.	3150.

9. BLEED
Extra.. 10%

10. SPECIAL POSITION
Extra.. 25%

15. GENERAL REQUIREMENTS
Also see SRDS Print Media Production Source.
Trim Size: 8-1/2 x 11.
Binding Method: Saddle Stitched.
Colors Available: 4-color process; Black & PMS.
Covers: 4-color process.

NON-BLEED
AD PAGE DIMENSIONS

Sprd	16	x	10	1/3 v	2-5/16	x	10
1 pg	7-1/2	x	10	1/4 v	3-5/8	x	4-7/8
2/3 v	4-7/8	x	10	1/6 v	2-5/16	x	4-3/4
1/2 v	3-5/8	x	10	Fractionals	2-5/16	x	2-1/8
1/2 h	7-1/2	x	4-7/8				

16. ISSUE AND CLOSING DATES
Published 11 times a year.
Copy closes 25th of the full month prior to issue date; art closes 5th of the month prior to issue date.
No cancellations accepted after space closing.

18. CIRCULATION
Established 1986. Single copy 5.00; per year 40.00.
SWORN 6-30-96 (6 mos. aver.)

Total	Non-Pd	Paid	(Subs)	(Single)	(Assoc)
12,000	850	11,150	...	...	...

Unpaid Distribution (not incl. above):
Total 700

Magazine rates are based on the publisher's guaranteed circulation figures. The first source planners consult for magazine rates is **Standard Rate & Data Service (SRDS),** a sample page of which appears in Exhibit 11–6. SRDS provides all of the ad size requirements and costs for most magazines, along with a brief editorial description and the names of sales reps to contact. Magazines also issue their own rate cards providing the cost of space in their publications; an example of a rate card is shown in Exhibit 11–7. Nowadays, this is just the starting point for negotiation, however. Large publishers that produce a number of titles, such as Time, Inc., or Conde Nast, may offer special packages available for advertisers that buy space in more than one publication.

Factors influencing the cost of magazine space include the amount of space purchased, the use of color versus black and white, the use of *bleed* (color all the way to the edge of the page), and the purchase of special editions such as regional or demographic breakouts. Advertisers may be given *frequency discounts* for running a given number of ads within a specified time period. *Volume discounts* are given when a large amount of space is contracted. And *page equivalent discounts* allow various different-sized ads to be considered together to determine the rate. Advertisers may also purchase *split-run space,* where alternate ads run in every other issue. This is a more costly alternative, but it can be useful for testing new products or new creative.

Magazines and Technology

As magazines have grown more and more specialized in terms of their content, several publications have begun customizing their issues to select groups or even individuals. Two technologies should be mentioned here. The first, **inkjetting,** allows a magazine to print an individual subscriber's name within an ad. Instead of an ad for Audi simply stating, "Come in for a test drive," an inkjetted version of that ad might say, "Jane Smith, come in for a test drive." This effort at personalization is intended to capture readers' attention and encourage them to read through the whole ad. It is a way of making magazines more like direct mail, delivered personally to each individual. An example of an ad that utilizes inkjetting is shown in Exhibit 11–8. Obviously, inkjetting can only be done on subscription copies because the magazine has no way of knowing the names of people who might buy the publication at the newsstand.

The second technological shift is **selective binding.** Here, different readers of the same magazine might receive different issues, with the content (and even advertising) altered to suit the needs or preferences of those individuals. One of the most aggressive magazines in this area has been *Successful Farming,* which produces several thousand different copies of an issue, varying the types of articles to reflect the crops farmed by each reader. With that, a farmer who grows corn and raises cattle would receive articles on those topics, while his next-door neighbor might instead be reading about soybeans and pigs, if that is what is on his farm.

A more common technological shift in the industry has been the movement of magazines into the electronic arena, primarily online computer services and the Internet. There are now several hundred magazines available on the World Wide Web and through online services such as America Online and The Microsoft Network. The content is most commonly excerpts from the printed version. In addition, a few magazines produce separate and distinct electronic editions. *HotWired,* for example, which is on the Internet, is completely distinct from its sister print product, *Wired* magazine, although both are designed to deal with technological issues from a consumer standpoint. *Omni* magazine moved away from print completely to focus on its electronic product. And several magazines, including *Slate,* have set themselves up solely on the Web without having ever published a hardcopy version. "Technology Watch: *Wired* and *HotWired*" looks at what these publications are doing and what the implications are for both print and electronic magazines.

R E S E T

1. Why have magazines grown more specialized in the past several decades?
2. What is the difference between a magazine's circulation and its audience?
3. How does the position of a magazine ad impact its effectiveness?

Newspapers

The first daily newspaper to appear on a regular basis in the U.S. was the *Pennsylvania Evening Post,* which began in 1783. At that time, newspapers were primarily party organs, voicing the beliefs and stances of the major political forces in the country. This was the legacy of the first European settlers, whose home newspapers were designed to fulfill such a function. Indeed, European newspapers still

fill this role, and with far clearer political orientations than their modern U.S. counterparts. The United States, however, by enshrining in the First Amendment to the Constitution the rights of "free speech and of the press," immediately gave recognition to the powerful role that newspapers play in society as a more neutral force that expresses various points of view and therefore helps to encourage a free, democratic society. About 70 percent of the adult population reads some part of the newspaper on a daily basis, and 90 percent does so during the typical week.

Types of Newspapers

Today there are more than 2,400 newspapers published across the country. Most are pub-

EXHIBIT 11–7 Rate Card for *Disney Magazine*

1997 NATIONAL ADVERTISING RATES

	1X	2X	3X	4X
Four Color				
FULL PAGE	$15,465	$14,690	$13,920	$13,145
2/3 PAGE	$11,560	$10,990	$10,405	$9,825
1/2 PAGE	$9,250	$8,790	$8,325	$7,865
1/3 PAGE	$6,945	$6,600	$6,250	$5,905
Two Color				
FULL PAGE	$13,300	$12,635	$11,970	$11,305
2/3 PAGE	$11,250	$10,690	$10,125	$9,565
1/2 PAGE	$7,985	$7,585	$7,190	$6,790
1/3 PAGE	$5,990	$5,690	$5,390	$5,090
Black & White				
FULL PAGE	$11,570	$10,990	$10,415	$9,835
2/3 PAGE	$8,675	$8,240	$7,810	$7,375
1/2 PAGE	$6,945	$6,600	$6,250	$5,905
1/3 PAGE	$5,205	$4,945	$4,685	$4,425
Covers				
COVER 2	$18,980			
COVER 3	$17,995			
COVER 4	$19,545			

Rate Base: 400,000 BPA Audited

	Spring	Summer	Fall	Winter
AD CLOSE	12/19/96	3/27/97	6/26/97	8/28/97
AD MATERIALS DUE	1/2/97	4/3/97	7/3/97	9/4/97
ON SALE DATE	2/25/97	5/27/97	8/26/97	10/28/97

WE'LL HELP YOU HIT
ONE OUT OF THE PARK
THIS MOTHER'S DAY.

DEAR AMY WINSTON,
SCORE BIG WITH MOM ON MAY 11TH.
BRING IN THIS COUPON FOR
A FREE GIFT WRAP.

Shop at JCPenney for the perfect game-winning hit this
Mother's Day. Choose from an award-winning lineup
of gifts, from sleepwear and jewelry to fragrances and
women's spring fashions. And if you bring in this coupon,
you'll get one free gift wrap with any gift purchase.
It's the perfect way to show your family's MVP just
how much she means to your home team.

Limit one free gift wrap per customer; offer ends 5/11.

JCPenney
I LOVE YOUR STYLE

EXHIBIT 11–8 This ad for JCPenney uses inkjetting to target the sales message to a specific magazine subscriber. Inkjetting allows advertisers to use magazine ads much in the same way as direct mail pieces.

lished on a daily basis, while a smaller segment appear weekly or at other intervals. The sheer size of the continent means that newspapers are considered primarily as a local media form. Thus, if you live in Phoenix, you are most likely to read *The Phoenix Sun;* residents of Jacksonville, Florida, read the *Jacksonville Times Union;* and people living in Buffalo pick up a copy of the *Buffalo News* each day. Larger newspapers may have broader, regional distribution. The *Chicago Tribune* can be found throughout the Midwest, while the *Boston Globe* appears throughout New England. A few select newspapers are considered national in scope. These include *The New York Times, The Wall Street Journal, Los Angeles Times,* and *USA Today.* The latter was really the first newspaper that was originally designed as a national newspaper. It is also one of the few to have been started in the past 20 years. The

trend has, in fact, been in the opposite direction, with many newspapers shutting their doors. Up until the 1970s, it was common for large cities to have two or sometimes even three competing newspapers; today, that competition is found only in the top metropolitan areas. Everywhere else, either two newspapers share production and/or advertising sales staff, as the *Detroit News* and the *Detroit Free-Press* do, or there is just one surviving paper.

Types of Newspaper Advertising

Two principal types of ads in newspapers are classified and display. In addition, national advertising, coupons, and newspaper magazine supplements are also available to media planners who choose to purchase space in newspapers.

CLASSIFIED ADVERTISING   Classified advertising gives consumers and businesses the opportunity to offer information or goods and services for sale directly to other consumers or businesses. The three largest classified categories are employment, real estate, and automotive. Classified ads are small in size, and they are usually sold by the number of words or lines in the text.

DISPLAY ADVERTISING   Ads that are not classifieds are referred to as **display advertisements.** These consist of text as well as illustrations or photos and other visual components. Display ads may be placed by either national or local advertisers. Most newspaper display advertising comes from local businesses or organizations—usually retailers—wishing to reach people in the circulation area of the newspaper. These include supermarkets, banks, department stores, phone companies, and travel agencies. A small proportion of such ads come from national advertisers. Of the 23 percent of total ad dollars accounted for by newspapers, 12 percent is from retail, 8 percent is from classifieds, and just 3 percent is from national display ads.

A sizable portion of display ads from local retailers is funded in part by national manufacturers or distributors. This type of advertising is referred to as **cooperative (co-op) advertising.** Here, the cost of the advertising is divided between the local concern and the national operation. This allows national manufacturers and distributors to increase the

TECHNOLOGY WATCH

....

Wired and *HotWired*

The notion of putting magazines online is not radical. After all, magazines offer a visual display of information and entertainment that fits in very well with the nature of the online medium. But creating separate and distinct magazines for each medium? Now that is certainly different, but it is the route *Wired* magazine took in the mid-1990s—and it was highly appropriate, because *Wired*'s focus is on the relationship between technology and society. Calling itself the magazine for the "digirati" (i.e., people involved with the digital world), the glossy, six-color book looks more like a print version of MTV than a traditional magazine. Text spills over pages and interrupts other articles, every color of the rainbow appears, and computer-generated graphics boggle the mind.

Wired would seem to be a natural for the young, technologically oriented people who surf the Internet or spend hours on an online service.

Instead, the company chose to establish a completely separate entity for the electronic world, called *HotWired*. Although it too provides information and entertainment on the Web, its content is fully distinct from its print sibling. Its focus is solely the online and Internet arena, featuring areas such as Web Monkey, for the most technology-oriented; Synapse, offering comments and interviews; and the Beta Lounge, offering audio and video clips of new bands. Users can look at digital postcards of interesting places around the world, read fiction and essays from up-and-coming writers, or express their opinions to other *HotWired* users about different sites on the Web.

Will all major magazine titles create separate electronic entities? The evidence so far does not point that way. Of the more than 200 magazines that now have some type of electronic presence either on the Web or online

services, the vast majority are simply placing textual versions of the printed copy online. Even some of the biggest publishers, such as Time Warner on its Pathfinder Web site, offer little beyond the reproduction of their magazines, including *Time, People, Money,* and *Entertainment Weekly.*

There are important implications for advertisers. Advertisers to *HotWired*'s very popular Web site receive a discount if they also buy space in *Wired.* Pathfinder advertisers can arrange deals for joint print–electronic ad campaigns. From both the publisher's and the advertiser's perspective, these linked arrangements make a good deal of sense. People browsing through the Web are more likely to visit sites with which they are familiar, such as Pathfinder or *HotWired,* rather than Bill's home page, increasing the opportunity for advertisers on those sites to reach their target audiences. And by publicizing one's Web address in the printed magazine, advertisers such as Joe Boxer, Absolut, or AT&T can encourage the reader to look at the company's electronic message, too. As the growth and expansion of the Internet continues, we will see more connections being made between printed and electronic versions of magazines.

Rather than simply putting the contents of its magazine online, *Wired* created a separate online presence, *HotWired.* Although the general approach of *HotWired* is similar to that of its print cousin, its content is unique and is targeted specifically to Internet users.

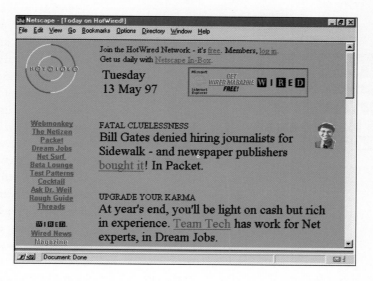

EXHIBIT 11–9 This co-op newspaper ad, which appeared in a weekly circular, shows a combined advertising effort between Ace Hardware and Weber.

impact of their advertising in local markets by arranging for, and also paying for, their messages to appear in the ads of local retailers or dealers. The national advertiser can stretch its budget by splitting the cost of local advertising with a retailer and thereby qualifying for the lower local rate (to obtain local rates, an advertiser must include a local address and/or telephone number).

The system also gives the local retailers or dealers confidence that the national manufacturer is willing to support them. For example, Safeway or Kroger might be paid by Chiquita bananas to feature that product in their local circulars and newspaper ads. The benefit for the local supplier is that people looking for that national brand are more likely to come to his or her outlet to purchase it, thereby increasing sales in that store. In addition to cost sharing, another important advantage of co-op advertising is that it allows for greater customization of the message to the local level. Promotional offers, for example, can be varied by market, product, medium, or season. Thus, Chiquita may have a tie-in promotion with Kraft General Foods and Safeway in San Francisco but put its bananas on sale in A & P in Rochester, New York. An example of a co-op ad is shown in Exhibit 11–9.

NATIONAL ADVERTISING The newspaper industry has been attempting for at least the last decade to increase the ad revenues taken in from national advertisers. One of the main reasons that the medium has not attracted greater interest is the huge price differential for national versus local companies wishing to place their messages in the newspaper. This may be as great as 75 percent (i.e., the national advertiser has to pay up to 75 percent more than the local advertiser for the same space). Another reason is that, historically, the medium was difficult to use because it required placing ads in individual newspapers across the country. To alleviate these problems, the newspaper industry established the National Newspaper Network in the mid-1990s to facilitate national newspaper buys, allowing advertisers to work through a centralized group to place one ad across the country. There are also ongoing efforts to diminish the size of the national–local cost differential.

COUPONS Although it may seem difficult to judge the direct impact of newspaper advertising on sales, the inclusion of a **coupon** provides one way to monitor that link. Coupons, a form of promotion for a brand that will be discussed in more detail in Chapter Twelve, come in several formats. The most common is simply part of the newspaper ad on the page, offering a discount on the price or a special deal if you buy the brand or use the service. One particularly popular type of coupon is the **free-standing insert (FSI)**. This generally appears in the Sunday edition of the newspaper and is not, in fact, sold by the newspaper itself but by a company that contracts with each newspaper to carry these insertions. An example of a free-standing insert is shown in Exhibit 11–10. Today, FSIs account for nearly 90 percent of all coupons that appear in the newspaper.

NEWSPAPER MAGAZINE SUPPLEMENTS
Newspaper magazine supplements are either nationally syndicated or local, full-color inserts placed in the Sunday newspaper. The three biggest titles are *Parade, USA Weekend,* and *Sunday.* These supplements are published independently and then distributed to newspapers throughout the U.S. In addition, several newspapers print their own independent Sunday magazines, such as the *Chicago Tribune*'s or *Los Angeles Times' Sunday* supplements. In both cases, the content and format of these magazines bear a closer resemblance to magazines than to newspapers. They offer the advertiser better color reproduction and have a broader coverage than the daily newspaper. But they also share some of the drawbacks of magazines, such as a fairly long production lead time (about eight weeks) and an audience that may not be particularly interested in the contents.

Benefits of Newspaper Advertising

The three major benefits of newspapers for advertisers are timeliness, readership, and editorial environment.

TIMELINESS   Newspapers, by their very nature, carry the news. If you are an advertiser with "news" of some type to convey to your target, then this medium may be highly beneficial. That news may be the announcement of a new discount plan from AT&T or it may take advantage of a particular recent event or date on the calendar, such as a Labor Day sale. The

timeliness also may reflect news happenings, such as a big storm or an adverse report on the brand. Exhibit 11–11 presents an example of a timely advertisement. In addition, because most papers are published on a daily basis, advertisers have the opportunity to make last-minute changes, if need be, to reflect changes that occur in the world around us.

READERSHIP   As with magazines, the fact that a person has to be literate to read a newspaper means that the profile of the newspaper audience tends to be more educated and affluent than the general population. Newspaper readers are more likely to have been to college, be working full time, have an above-average household income, and own their home. On the downside, however, is the fact that newspaper readers are getting older beyond the overall aging of the population. In the increasingly electronic world in which we live, people find that they have less and less time to spend reading the newspaper each day. Instead, they turn to television or a computer service for their news.

Like magazines, however, newspapers offer advertisers the opportunity to reach an interested and involved audience. This means that newspaper ads can be fairly lengthy or complex because people who are interested in the mes-

EXHIBIT 11–11 The timely nature of newspapers provided the perfect vehicle for Puerto Rico in its attempt to generate tourism in the aftermath of hurricane Hortense.

The sun is coming out and our beaches are as beautiful as ever, despite Hurricane Hortense's short visit.

In fact, there's never been a better time to Discover the Continent of **Puerto Rico.**

Take advantage of our value promotion with the **Endless Summer Breeze packages** available from April 15 through December 20, 1996. For more information, call your travel counselor.

Endless Summer Breeze packages 3 days / 2 nights $329 - $429* including airfare.

Discover what a vacation was always meant to be. **PUERTO RICO**

Prices shown are per person, double occupancy, roundtrip per person from New York / Newark. Other gateways available. For more information and brochures on P.R. call 1-800-866-7827.

EXHIBIT 11–11 The timely nature of newspapers provided the perfect vehicle for Puerto Rico in its attempt to generate tourism in the aftermath of hurricane Hortense.

sage will take the time to read through it, an option that is not offered by broadcast media.

EDITORIAL ENVIRONMENT Again like magazines, newspapers can provide the right environment in which to place an ad. Thus, Drixoral can put its allergy medication ad in the weekly section on personal health and Fidelity Investments' ads for its mutual funds can appear in the Business section. In each case, it is assumed that if people are interested in that topic and are reading articles about it, they are also more likely to attend to the accompanying ads that have related material.

Drawbacks of Newspaper Advertising

The main difficulties in using newspapers are short message life, selective readers, and the lack of color.

SHORT MESSAGE LIFE The fact that newspapers appear on a daily basis is, for an advertiser, both good and bad: While it allows the ad message to be very timely, it also means its message life is very brief. If your readers haven't found your ad by the end of the day, it is highly likely that they will throw the paper out

without seeing it. This is slightly less true for Sunday editions, but even there, most people do not keep the newspaper longer than one week.

SELECTIVE READERS Newspaper readers, like magazine readers, choose what they look at and what they ignore. This is true both for the editorial material and for the advertising. If your message does not reach target consumers when they are receptive to it and thinking about your product or service, the chances are high that the ad will be ignored. Thus, an ad from Midas Mufflers is most likely to be looked at only if the reader is having problems with her muffler, and an ad for Volvo cars probably will be ignored unless the reader is in the market for a new car.

LACK OF COLOR The lack of color in newspapers is gradually being resolved, to some extent at least, by most large newspapers, which are upgrading their production processes to allow for the use of color in ads. Unfortunately, when color is placed on thin sheets of newspaper, the quality remains considerably inferior to that found in other print media such as magazines, direct mail, or catalogs. The best example of color reproduction can be found in *USA Today*, which based much of its early appeal to advertisers on the fact that it was one of the first to offer full-color capabilities.

Newspaper Planning and Buying

When media planners evaluate whether to include newspapers in a media plan and, if so, which ones to consider, they must look at who will be reached by such ads and which areas of the newspaper's publication to purchase. Once the newspapers have been selected, the space can be purchased from individual newspapers' sales reps.

NEWSPAPER PLANNING In order to determine which newspapers to use, there are several basic pieces of information to consider. Like magazines, newspaper circulation tells you how many copies of the newspaper are distributed and guaranteed by the publisher. This information is either provided by the newspaper itself or can be obtained through syndicated resources, such as the Standard Rate and Data Service. Circulation can also be broken down into different geographic areas, informing the planner of the towns or markets in which the newspaper is distributed. Circulation of most major newspapers is verified by the Audit Bureau of Circulations (ABC), an independent auditing group that represents the advertisers, agencies, and publishers.

As with magazines, a newspaper's audience represents the number of actual readers of the paper, based on how many people are likely to read each copy. The newspaper's coverage of a given target group or its composition of that group among its total readership can be examined and compared with other newspapers or other media. Syndicated research from sources such as Scarborough Research or The Media Audit provides this information.

In recent years, newspapers have become increasingly localized in terms of their coverage. Because of computer technologies for printing, it is possible to produce distinctive editions of a newspaper for different areas of the market. The *Chicago Tribune,* for example, prints 21 different geographic versions, or **zones,** of its paper. Advertisers can pick and choose the zones in which they wish to appear, or they can decide to be in all of them.

BUYING NEWSPAPER SPACE Space in newspapers is measured in **column widths,** or the number of columns across the page. The depth (length) of the page is measured in **agate lines per column,** or simply *lines.* Today most newspaper space is purchased in terms of **standard advertising units (SAUs),** a system that was established in the 1980s to standardize ad sizes in newspapers throughout the country. Prior to this, advertisers had to develop separate sizes of their ads to fulfill the requirements of each newspaper. The SAU system, shown in Exhibit 11–12, went a long way to helping newspapers attract more regional and national advertisers, as well as simplifying the process for local advertisers.

As with magazines, the primary syndicated source for newspaper rates is SRDS, to which most newspapers provide rate cards. However, buyers must contact individual newspapers directly to find out the local rate schedules. The

Although the quality of color reproduction in most newspapers is still somewhat suspect, it is improving in some large newspapers. With that, they have begun to promote the use of color as an advertising tool, as this planner-targeted ad from the *Chicago Tribune* demonstrates.

Exhibit 11–12   The Standard Advertising Unit (SAU) System

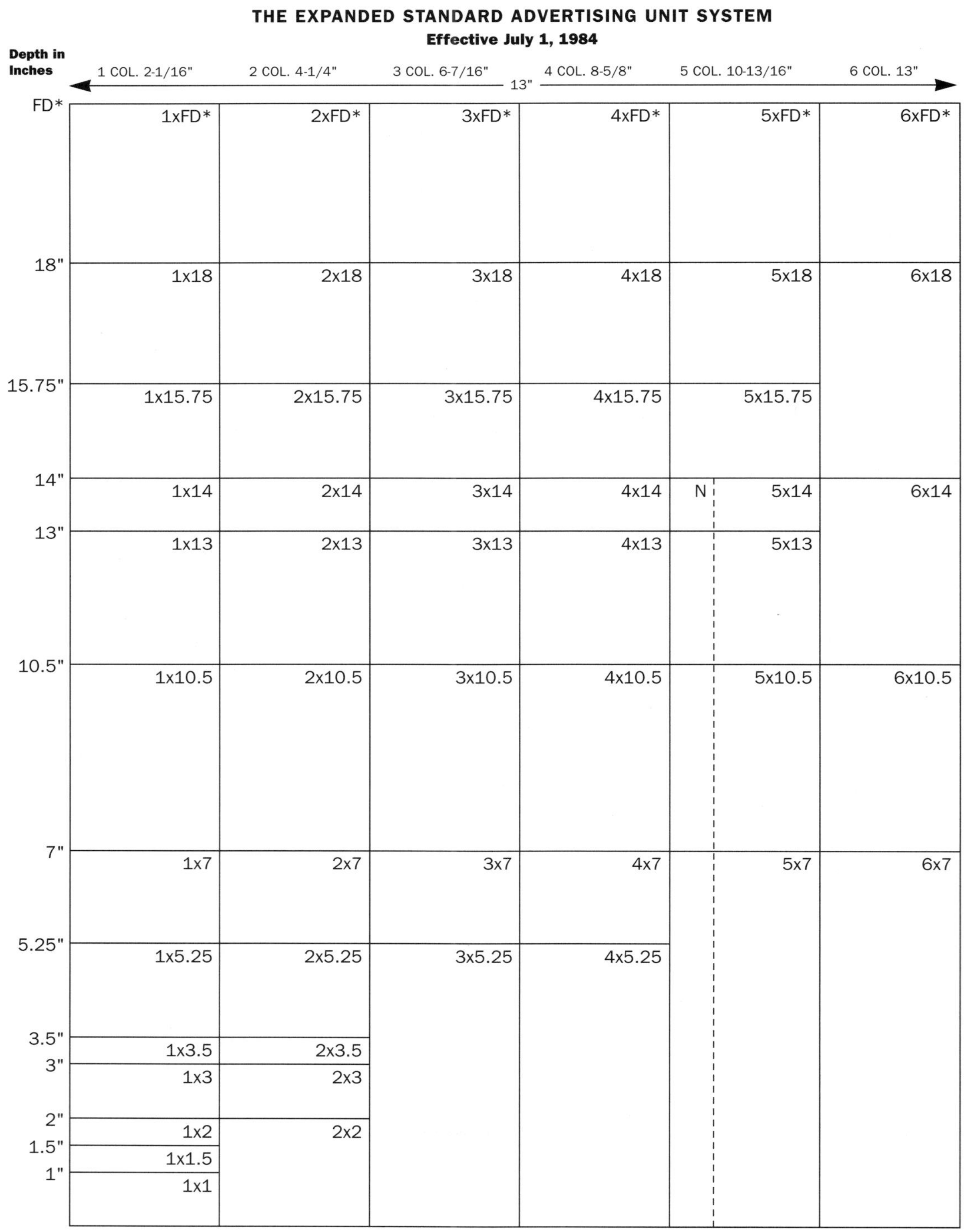

THE EXPANDED STANDARD ADVERTISING UNIT SYSTEM
Effective July 1, 1984

Depth in Inches	1 COL. 2-1/16"	2 COL. 4-1/4"	3 COL. 6-7/16"	4 COL. 8-5/8"	5 COL. 10-13/16"	6 COL. 13"
FD*	1xFD*	2xFD*	3xFD*	4xFD*	5xFD*	6xFD*
18"	1x18	2x18	3x18	4x18	5x18	6x18
15.75"	1x15.75	2x15.75	3x15.75	4x15.75	5x15.75	
14"	1x14	2x14	3x14	4x14	N 5x14	6x14
13"	1x13	2x13	3x13	4x13	5x13	
10.5"	1x10.5	2x10.5	3x10.5	4x10.5	5x10.5	6x10.5
7"	1x7	2x7	3x7	4x7	5x7	6x7
5.25"	1x5.25	2x5.25	3x5.25	4x5.25		
3.5"	1x3.5	2x3.5				
3"	1x3	2x3				
2"	1x2	2x2				
1.5"	1x1.5					
1"	1x1					

13"

1 Column 2-1/16"
2 Columns 4-1/4"
3 Columns 6-7/16"
4 Columns 8-5/8"
5 Columns 10-13/16"
6 Columns 13"

Double Truck 26¾"
(There are four suggested double truck sizes:)
13xFD*   13x18
13x14   13x10.5

*FD (Full Depth) can be 21" or deeper. Depths for each broadsheet newspaper are indicated in the Standard Rate and Data Service. All broadsheet newspapers can accept 21" ads, and many float them if their depth is greater than 21".

Tabloids: Size 5 x 14 is a full page tabloid for long cut-off papers. Mid cut-off papers can handle this size with minimal reduction. The N size, measuring 9⅜ x 14, represents the full page size for tabloids such as the *New York Daily News* and *Newsday,* and other short cut-off newspapers. The five 13 inch deep sizes are for tabloids printed on 55 inch wide presses such as the *Philadelphia News.* See individual SRDS listings for tabloid sections of broadsheet newspapers.

cost of a newspaper ad depends on circulation, position of ad, use of color, and any volume or continuity discounts given to advertisers that buy a large amount of space or place ads on a regular basis.

The **position** of the ad within the newspaper is of key concern to many advertisers. As we have said, one of the benefits of newspapers is their ability to offer editorial compatibility. This has been increasing in recent years as newspapers segment their publications more and more in an effort to attract readers who might not have time to read all of the paper but are interested in, and will read about, selected topics. Some sections appear daily, such as Business or Sports. Others come out weekly, such as a Children's section or Food section. Yet others appear a few times a year, such as a Bridal Guide in the spring or an Entertaining section prior to Thanksgiving and Christmas. For all of these sections, advertisers may be attracted by the opportunity to place their messages in a fitting environment where the ad message matches the content of the section. Newspaper ads are almost always placed with a request for a specific position included, and newspapers will generally try to honor those requests, although they may charge extra to do so.

Newspapers and Technology

Although at first glance it might seem that the electronic era would be most harmful to the oldest print media form, newspapers are, in fact, finding that the Information Superhighway is proving highly beneficial to their existence, both present and future. It is true that newspapers were very slow to adapt to new technologies. In the 1980s, about the only technological offering available to newspapers was **audiotex,** a phone-based service that allows readers to call a local telephone number to get more information on a product or service that appeared in the newspaper, leave voicemail for personal ads, or reach a 900 phone number. Today, more than 600 newspapers offer this type of service. Audiotex was followed by **newspaper fax services,** which provide real estate or car dealer listings, for example, via facsimile. People who are interested in receiving the information have it faxed to them at home or work.

Then in the mid-1990s, as the Internet and online computer services took off, newspapers

found themselves with a potential new lease on life. It is clear that one of the main attractions of these electronic ventures is their ability to provide news and information to consumers—the very reason that newspapers have existed and thrived for several hundred years! At first, newspapers stuck their toes into the online waters warily, but today there are more than 500 newspapers with a presence either on an online service or on a Web site on the Internet. As the opening vignette showed, most newspapers' Web sites provide the same information as that found in the printed edition, but more and more papers are also offering additional details or background on stories. The highly localized nature of the medium is coming to the fore as well, with several newspapers including Little League scores or school lunch menus on their online product. Exhibit 11–13 shows a sample page from the Web site of the *Chicago Tribune.*

At this point, one of the unresolved issues is whether people are willing to pay to receive their news in this fashion. Several papers require users of their Internet sites to pay a regular subscription, just as they would for an online service or cable TV. They have had mixed results so far: Both *The Wall Street Journal* and the *San Jose Mercury News* claim they have had success in finding people willing to pay a monthly fee for their offerings; in contrast, *USA Today* had to drop its fee of $14.95 per month when it found few takers for its

EXHIBIT 11–13 In addition to providing the stories and features found in the newspaper's print version, the Web site for the *Chicago Tribune* allows users to access information and news events specific to particular Chicago suburbs. In this way, the *Tribune* uses its Web page to localize its appeal.

electronic product. Advertising is available on many of these sites.

Most people agree that electronic versions of the newspaper are not likely to replace the printed edition, at least not in the near future. But newspapers are wise to be looking ahead and preparing themselves for that possibility.

R E S E T

1. **What are the different types of newspapers?**
2. **Why would a national advertiser like Visa choose newspaper advertising?**
3. **How is technology proving beneficial to newspapers?**

Out-of-Home Advertising

Various forms of media reach people once they step outside their front doors. Perhaps the best known is the billboard, seen on city streets and suburban highways, on interstates, and by shopping malls. Other forms include transit (train, bus, and stations), sports stadiums, and nontraditional venues such as supermarkets, malls, and schools. Together, these advertising vehicles are known as **out-of-home advertising.**

Outdoor Billboards

The outdoor industry likes to claim that it is the oldest form of media in the world. Pictures on stones that gave people directions or information back in ancient times, they say, are the first evidence of outdoor advertising. Whether you agree or not, it is certainly true that outdoor billboards have been around for a long time.

Outdoor billboards alone bring in $9 billion in advertising revenues a year, and this figure grows by a few percentage points a year. Despite the loss of major sources of revenue (most notably alcohol and tobacco advertisers as they come under increasing attack for advertising anywhere), the industry has found new categories of advertising that more than make up for it. The rest of the out-of-home advertising industry is not measured, but it is certainly expanding as more and more such venues accept advertising messages.

Billboards come in two major formats: poster panels and painted bulletins. The key differences between these two formats are their size and location. **Poster panels** come in different sizes, from small 8-sheets found in local neighborhoods in parking lots or near pedestrian traffic, to 30-sheets that appear on the main arteries of cities. The "sheets" part of the name refers to the number of sheets of paper it used to take to create the full panel. Thirty-sheet posters are typically 12 feet by 24 feet in size. Today, with the help of computers, posters often are generated in one whole section, although you may sometimes still see people pasting separate sheets up onto a board. Most ads remain on posters for a one-month period, though shorter and longer deals can be arranged. Additional flexibility is found in the use of **snipes,** which are special strips on the poster for special or changing messages.

Painted bulletins are larger in size, measuring 14-feet by 48-feet. They are found primarily on major highways, often advertising hotels, eating places, or other attractions at the upcoming towns on those routes. As their name suggests, ads are painted onto these boards and generally remain on them for six months or more. Another option with a painted bulletin is the opportunity to add physical "extras" to the board beyond the standard 14-feet by 48-feet size, such as moving parts. This may allow an ad to become three-dimensional or make the ad seem even bigger than it already is. Examples of these bulletins are shown in Exhibit 11–14. Bulletins often are illuminated so that they can be viewed on a 24-hour basis rather than just during daylight hours.

Until recently, the outdoor advertising industry was primarily a local business, but following extensive consolidation of billboard ownership today the top three players—Outdoor Services Inc., Eller Outdoor, and 3M Outdoor—control more than half of all the inventory. Each company leases display sites to advertisers and is responsible for putting up the messages on the site. It is also up to them to ensure that the structures remain in good shape.

BENEFITS OF OUTDOOR BILLBOARD ADVERTISING   Outdoor billboards offer a number of advantages for advertisers, including message size and impact, neighborhood targeting, and mobile reach.

Message Size and Impact. The fact that an ad on most poster or bulletin billboards is at least 12 feet by 24 feet means that a brand's message is likely to appear larger than life. This is the only traditional medium that can offer such an opportunity. Although people can easily walk or drive by a board without paying full attention, the sheer size of the message creates an impact. Add to that some outstanding creative ideas, and the medium can be highly effective.

Outdoor billboards are used especially for image campaigns, where pictures can tell most of the story. A case in point is the billboard Scott Lumber Company placed at a busy section of Route 40 in Wheeling, West Virginia. The first and last boards in this campaign are shown in Exhibit 11–15. The first board shown was a full-size blueprint of the side of a house. In the next four months, the blueprint was gradually turned into a home, effectively promoting the sponsor, who was finally revealed to be Scott Lumber Company, a local building supply store.5

Neighborhood Targeting. The flexibility in size that poster panels provide means that they can work as part of a national multimedia campaign and still be targeted down to the neighborhood level. Messages can be varied depending on the part of the city or area in which the panel is placed. This is particularly useful for advertisers trying to reach an ethnic group, allowing companies to use boards that are directly aimed at these groups in the areas where they live. The localized nature of poster panels also means that local retailers can offer directions to their stores to people passing by the area.

Mobile Reach. In this hectic and rapidly moving world, outdoor billboards have the advantage of talking to us as we are on the move. Whether we are on foot or in the car, or if we are in an urban or suburban area, there is a good

EXHIBIT 11–14 Taking full advantage of the unique opportunity provided by bulletins, this advertiser uses "extras" to generate additional attention-getting power for its messages. Wouldn't you look twice?

EXHIBIT 11–15 This creative billboard series for Scott Lumber Company generated a great deal of public interest throughout the entire four-month "construction" period.

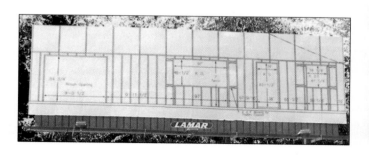

chance that we will have the opportunity to see a poster or bulletin on our travels. This allows advertisers to reach their target closer to the purchase occasion. Ads for Green Giant corn that appear three blocks from the nearby A&P supermarket may be highly effective in reminding people to buy some as they go to that store. Burger King's posters situated on the main roads act as useful reminders to people driving in the morning to pick up breakfast at that restaurant on their way to work. "Adscape: Looking Outside for Insight" discusses how

AdScape

Looking Outside for Insight

Altoids successfully reached its young, mobile target group by placing its advertising message in various types of outdoor media, including billboards and transit advertising.

For the Leo Burnett Company and its client Altoids, a mint distributed in the U.S. by Callard & Bowser-Suchard, outdoor billboards proved highly effective. Research revealed that the key users of these uncommon mints were young and very active, and not easily reached through traditional media such as magazines or television. As Altoids account director Gary Singer noted, "With outdoor, we could place boards wherever these people live and work, and in between. Moreover, computer systems were able to identify precisely for them not only "the markets with the most potential but also the zip codes within those markets where our [target] worked and played."

Outdoor advertising also proved beneficial from a creative standpoint, allowing the product to be the star, in a simple yet highly visual way. Because of the somewhat quirky image of the brand, the selection of billboards helped to "maintain the mystique—people like to think they've discovered Altoids themselves."

The media plan contained various forms of outdoor media—from billboards to bus shelters to buses and telephone kiosks. The results were stunning. In the markets where the plan was used, sales rose by about 50 percent. In San Francisco, for example, after the first six months, awareness had risen 60 percent and usage 40 percent. The success of the medium led Callard & Bowser-Suchard to quadruple the brand's budget, expand the outdoor campaign from 12 percent of the U.S. to half of the country, and employ the medium significantly for two of its other brands.

QUESTIONS

What other out-of-home advertising could Altoids have used, and how? How do you think the use of outdoor helped Altoids "maintain the mystique"?

ALTOIDS
THE CURIOUSLY STRONG MINTS

Sources: "Altoids and Outdoor: Made for Each Other," *Inside Out of Home,* July 1996, 8; and "Altoids: Discover the Power of Outdoor," Special Out of Home Advertising Section, *Advertising Age,* 5 August 1996, A4.

billboards can help smaller brands truly seem larger than life.

DRAWBACKS OF OUTDOOR BILLBOARD ADVERTISING

The outdoor billboard medium does have certain disadvantages for advertisers. These include brief message life, short message length, local medium, and controversial image.

Brief Message Life. Because most billboards are viewed from a car, traveling at 30 miles an hour or more, there is not much time for people to notice a brand's message and absorb the information. Once they have passed by the board, the opportunity for exposure has disappeared.

Short Message Length. The result of the scant time that people spend with a billboard message is that the content of that message has to be extremely brief. One generally accepted rule is that there should be no more than seven words on the board. Thus, brands that need to convey a complex or lengthy message cannot use this medium to do so.

Primarily Local Medium. Although it is possible to use billboards on a national basis, the primary value of the medium is at the local or regional level. Indeed, it becomes fairly expensive to buy boards that cover the whole country. This is only done by larger national advertisers, such as McDonald's or Nike, and even they will buy boards selectively in specific markets.

Controversial Image. Another potential drawback to using outdoor billboards is the criticism that they can draw from the public, either for environmental reasons or, more commonly, because of where certain controversial messages are being placed, such as alcohol or tobacco ads

near schools. "Adscape: Environmental Hazards of Billboards" examines this issue more fully.

PLANNING AND BUYING FOR OUTDOOR BILLBOARDS

There are two key elements to evaluate when planning outdoor billboard messages. The first is the **showing.** This is a number that tells a planner how many boards must be purchased to reach a certain proportion of the population during a specified period of time. If you buy a 100 showing in Philadelphia, that would mean you are buying enough boards to reach 100 percent of the population in that market in a given time period (usually 30 days). Poster panels are mostly bought at the 50, 75, or 100 showing level, while bulletins tend to be purchased at the lower 10 or 25 showing level. Fewer bulletins are needed because they are bought for longer time periods (usually one year). The showing figure can be translated into the number of daily rating points, or GRPs, that are needed to reach that showing level.

To know how many people will be exposed to a billboard message, the **daily effective circulation** (DEC) must be calculated. This is simply the number of cars that pass by a particular board in a fixed time period (usually 12 hours) multiplied by the average number of people per car (which is 1.35). An example of the rates and specifications for buying bulletins in Houston, Texas, is shown in Exhibit 11–16.

In addition to showing and effective circulation, planners must also know the exact location of their intended billboards. Are any of the boards obstructed by either natural or man-made objects? How much traffic really goes by each board? How close are they to the point of purchase or use being advertised? At bigger agencies or for advertisers that use outdoor frequently, the billboard operator will often arrange for a client to **ride the boards,**

Houston		TX	Rotary Panel Size:	14' x 48'	**18+ Population:**	2,891.0
			Panels Available in Plan:	350	**Average 18+ DEC:**	89.0

GANNETT OUTDOOR ADVERTISING
1600 Studemont
Houston, TX 77007

Donna Baker
(713) 868-2284
FAX: (713) 862-7652

Ship to:
Same

TAB
Audited

Daily GRPS	Allotment	Cost per Panel		Monthly Cost	
		Painted	Flex/Posted	Painted	Flex/Posted
5	1	3,400.00	3,150.00	3,400.00	3,150.00
10	3	3,400.00	3,150.00	10,200.00	9,450.00
15	4	3,190.00	2,950.00	12,760.00	11,800.00

Extensions: One time $24.00/Sq.foot Plus maintenance $3.25/Month/Sq.foot
Rotation: 60 Day Frequency **Illumination:** Halophane
Rates: Average monthly costs based on 4-month contracts.

EXHIBIT 11–16 Sample outdoor billboard specifications

where each site is visited to ensure that it is acceptable to the advertiser.

As with other forms of local media, today it is possible to buy outdoor advertising through national rep firms, although you can still buy space directly from an individual market operator. Poster and bulletin rates are determined by the market size and number of posters needed to achieve the specified number of GRPs, and discounts are given for frequency and volume. At one time, advertisers were required to purchase a minimum of 30 days per board, but many outdoor companies are moving away from this, offering advertisers greater flexibility in their buys.

The outdoor advertising industry is unique in that it offers a commission of 16.67 percent to advertising agencies. The extra 1.67 percent traditionally has been used to encourage agencies to consider the outdoor medium in making its media recommendations.

BILLBOARDS AND TECHNOLOGY　The impact of technology on outdoor billboards may not be evident to the consumer, but it is having an important effect on the industry. Computer-generated painting of boards, rather than having individuals actually paint on the message, is greatly enhancing the quality of boards and enables them to look identical from market to market and from site to site. Instead of traditional paper posters, new materials are being used that are better able to withstand the elements. And computer-controlled lighting fixtures mean that boards can be illuminated automatically from a central site at the flick of a switch rather than being constrained to an automatic timer attached to the board itself. Computers also have allowed billboards to incorporate digital elements. MCI has used this capability to keep a continuous and constantly changing message about the amount of money its customers are saving. Many state lotteries

AdScape

....

Environmental Hazards of Billboards

When the environmental movement first grew in the 1960s, billboards were the subject of much debate and criticism. They were scorned for being eyesores on the horizon and blights on the countryside, blocking the pastoral views of drivers along highways or heading into towns and cities. With the passage of the 1965 Highway Beautification Act, billboards were banned in rural areas near a federal highway. Many of these boards were never taken down, and there have been periodic threats to remove them.

Today the environmental criticisms laid against the outdoor industry are of a decidedly different nature. The environment considered under threat is social rather than geographic. When tobacco advertisers were banned from television and radio in 1971, followed shortly thereafter by a voluntary withdrawal from those media by alcoholic beverage advertisers, the outdoor industry rapidly became one of the biggest beneficiaries of the millions of dollars those companies had to spend. And until the mid-1990s, those two categories of advertiser represented the biggest spenders in the medium.

While this might seem like good news for the industry, having a steady and fulsome source of advertising revenues to count on, it soon became problematic. Critics started to focus attention on where those messages appeared and what they said. Why, for example, do so many spirits advertisers place their messages in African

display a digital message featuring the amount available in each week's contest.

NONTRADITIONAL BILLBOARD LOCATIONS

The attempt by advertisers to reach people wherever they may be, both inside and outside the home, has resulted in recent years in billboards being placed in many nontraditional locations. Messages appear on poster panels on college campuses, at ski resorts, and in shopping malls. In each case, the goal is the same: to reach people when they are more likely to be in the frame of mind to be thinking of the advertiser's brand or service. For example, Visa's messages placed at ski resorts are designed to remind people not only that the card is "everywhere you want to be" but also that you should use the card when you purchase items during your vacation. Universal Pictures will advertise its latest movie in the same shopping mall as the movie theater where the picture is playing. And when the Army puts up posters on college campuses to recruit people to its training program, it is placing its messages directly where its target audience is most likely to see them.

A newer arena for outdoor messages is the sports stadium. With the ever-growing popularity of televised sports events, the potential for marketers' messages to be seen not only by those in the ballpark or football stadium but also by television viewers watching the game at home has made stadium advertising extremely attractive. Advertisers can also use electronic billboards inside the stadium, where the message is rotated. Dorna USA's Adtime system can be purchased in 15 major league baseball stadiums, 16 National Basketball Association arenas, and 5 arenas where National Hockey League games are played. These messages are seen not only by people attending the games but also (and often more crucially) by the

American areas? Why do cigarette companies put so many boards near places where young people congregate, such as schools or entertainment venues?

One might argue that they are doing what any good advertiser does. That is, they want to reach their targets in the locations where those people are found. If African Americans are bigger consumers of malt whisky than other ethnic groups, surely ads for those brands should be placed closer to where the consumers live. And if Marlboro wants to persuade young smokers to switch to its brand, then shouldn't it place its messages in areas where young people convene?

But African Americans have a far higher rate of alcoholism and alcohol-related diseases than do whites or Hispanics. Is it socially responsible to promote the use of such products among this segment of the population? Similarly, given the addictive habit of smoking cigarettes, is it right that tobacco companies promote their messages to young people, leading them down a potentially fatal path of cigarette smoking? In 1997, Congress passed a law banning tobacco advertising on all outdoor billboards, in large part to protect children and teens from exposure to these messages. There was uncertainty, however, as to whether this ban would be sustained in the courts, given the First Amendment issues.

Given that the product is still legally available for sale in this country, shouldn't the companies that produce it have the right to express themselves wherever they so wish, using the media that they believe can best deliver their messages? If advertising for tobacco and alcohol are banned now, what will be next? Products with a high fat or cholesterol content, for example?

QUESTIONS

Consider all of these arguments, along with others that you may have, to decide whether billboards—specifically those that advertise "sin" products—constitute an environmental hazard to consumers.

thousands or even millions of viewers watching the broadcast of those games from home.

Transit Advertising

Transit advertising consists of advertising placed on buses and trains or at transit stations, platforms, or terminals. As such, it is primarily an urban and suburban medium offering advertisers the ability to reach a mass audience in metropolitan areas.

Like billboards, bus and train advertising is offered at the local market level. This segment of the industry is fairly fragmented in terms of the number of operators. Each company makes a deal with the local transit authority, which agrees that in return for a percentage of the advertising revenues it will accept advertising on its vehicles. For buses, this may include posters on the sides and back of the bus, as well as smaller *bus cards* inside. Posters can also be

placed on bus shelters. For trains, the ads appear inside the cars and on station platforms. Exhibit 11–17 shows an example of a transit advertisement at a bus shelter; this ad is from a controversial transit ad campaign used by Levi Strauss to promote its Dockers pants.

The advantages of using transit advertising depend in part on the form of transportation being used. For city buses and subway trains, the advertiser is reaching an urban population and messages can even be targeted down to the neighborhood level. This might mean advertising in a foreign language or running an ad along a specific bus or train line to reach the people who live along that route. For suburban trains and buses, the primary benefit is the opportunity to talk to a hard-to-reach target. These people tend to be more affluent and upscale, but because they spend time commuting to and from work each day, they may be harder to reach through traditional media such as magazines or television.

In both cases, transit advertising takes advantage of normal day-to-day travel patterns to build up the message frequency. It is also relatively inexpensive. Transit ads must get attention and make an impact in a relatively brief period of time. A classic example of an outstanding transit ad is the campaign created by Doyle Dane Bernbach for Levy's Jewish Rye, which appeared in major metropolitan areas in the 1960s. The tagline "You don't have to be Jewish to love Levy's Rye" was highly effective in increasing brand awareness and sales for the brand. An ad from this campaign is shown in Exhibit 11–18.

The main disadvantages to transit advertising are the same as those found with outdoor ads in general. People are exposed to the message as they are doing something else and going somewhere, so it is difficult to capture their attention and have them absorb the message. In addition, the message must be very brief and simple because of the size and form in which it appears. And because of the types of locations where transit ads appear, they are unlikely to reach people who do not use public transportation.

The planning and buying of transit advertising follow the same procedures as outdoor billboards, with the advertiser purchasing a number of showings in a market. There is very little research available, however, on precisely who is exposed to particular ads. All that the

EXHIBIT 11–17 To promote its Dockers pants, Levi Strauss placed pairs of the pants behind plastic shields at bus shelters in New York and San Francisco. After receiving numerous complaints (including one from New York Mayor Rudolph W. Giuliani) that the ads invited people to steal the pants, Levi Strauss agreed to discontinue the campaign.

transit authorities can usually provide is the number of passengers using their systems on a weekly or monthly basis.

RESET

1. How do poster boards and painted bulletins differ?
2. How is billboard ad space purchased?
3. What are the advantages and disadvantages of transit advertising?

Yellow Pages Advertising

Although many people consider the Yellow Pages as merely a source for telephone numbers, from an advertising perspective, this medium provides a valuable opportunity to reach a target audience when they are looking for a particular piece of relevant information. For example, of all of the carpet cleaners listed under that heading, a woman who is looking for a company to clean her Indian rug is more likely, everything else being equal, to notice the ad for Magikist Cleaners if its ad is placed prominently on that directory page.

The first telephone directory appeared in 1878 with the names of customers of the New Haven District Telephone Company. Today Yellow Pages advertising represents the fourth-largest advertising medium in terms of revenue, and there are more than 6,000 directories published each year. In recent years, since the breakup of the national phone service in 1984 and the formation of regional Bell operating companies (Ameritech, Nynex, BellSouth, etc.), the Yellow Pages industry has become highly competitive. Not only do the local phone companies distribute directories, but other telephone companies do as well. These may be one of two kinds: *Utility directories* come from the phone companies themselves, while *independent publishers* put out directories aimed at specific segments of a market, such as business-to-business or seniors. The expansion in the number of directories, along with

You don't have to be Jewish

to love Levy's
real Jewish Rye

EXHIBIT 11–18 Using a unique visual and a short but effective message, this classic transit ad for Levy's Jewish Rye successfully increased product awareness and sales when it ran in the 1960s.

a more aggressive sales effort, resulted in Yellow Pages ad revenue rising from $2.9 billion in 1990 to $9.5 billion in 1993. Like newspapers, the bulk of that revenue (87 percent) is drawn from local advertisers.

For advertisers, the benefits of the medium are its widespread awareness and use. People can turn to the Yellow Pages at any time, and when they do so, they are usually looking for a specific item or piece of information, probably because they are thinking of buying a product or using a service. The drawbacks include the cumbersome nature of the directory itself, the long lead time required for production, and the annual publication interval. The latter means that ad messages cannot be changed frequently and prices are usually not included.

As far as consumer use is concerned, studies have shown that nearly all adults (90 percent) refer to the Yellow Pages in the course of a year, and more than half (58 percent) do so in the average week. In a year, nearly 20 billion references are made to the Yellow Pages. The top 10 headings that were referenced in 1992 are shown in Exhibit 11–19.

Because response to a Yellow Pages ad is direct, it can be tracked by the company placing

EXHIBIT 11–19 Top 10 References in Yellow Pages

1. Physicians/Surgeons
2. Restaurants
3. Automobile parts (new and used)
4. Auto repair/service
5. Auto dealers (new and used)
6. Pizza
7. Insurance
8. Attorneys/Lawyers
9. Beauty salons
10. Department stores

Source: Yellow Pages Industry Facts Booklet, 1994–95 (Troy, MI: Yellow Pages Publishers Association, 1994).

the ad. This may be done by simply asking callers where they heard about the company or service, or by using a special phone line in Yellow Pages ads used to count how many calls that ad is able to generate. Some companies, in part in an effort to encourage callers, offer a special deal or discount to people who refer to the Yellow Pages ad when they call or buy.

Technology has not left the Yellow Pages industry untouched. The use of audiotex has become very popular in many directories, allowing consumers to access information directly via their telephones. Many of the information lines are sponsored by advertisers. For example, today's weather might be preceded by a message from Totes, while tips on car repair could be sponsored by the local Pep Boys dealer. More advanced applications of the Yellow Pages include versions on CD-ROM or computer services. The phone companies are putting Yellow Pages listings on the Internet and there are several such directories now available through the World Wide Web (e.g., http://www.BigYellow.com).

In-Store Advertising Media

In an effort to reach consumers right before they decide which brand to choose, advertisers increasingly have been drawn to in-store media. Estimates vary, but some sources claim that more than two-thirds of all purchase decisions are made in the store itself. Combining the elements of both advertising and promotion, in-store media include displays over the aisles, coupon dispensers on the shelf, special coupon kiosks, and ads on shopping carts. Given that just about everyone goes to a supermarket each week, these media forms are seen by a large number of people. On the other hand, their exposure to the message may be very brief. In the cart, for example, the ads may be covered up by items being purchased, while the messages on the shelf are only likely to be seen by those people who go close to pick a particular item.

One of the newer forms of in-store media is electronic couponing. Checkout Coupon issues coupons as the customer pays for his or her items, and the type of coupon that is generated varies according to the customer's purchases. They may be for the same brand just bought, to reinforce brand loyalty, or for the competing brand to encourage brand switching. Sometimes these coupons are in allied areas, so that if people buy Pampers diapers, they may receive a checkout coupon for Sears Photo Studios on the assumption that there is a baby in the household and, therefore, that the home is more likely to want to have photos taken.

One of the drawbacks to Checkout Coupon is that the coupons are issued after purchases have been made, so the discount or offer cannot be used until the next shopping visit. A similar in-store effort, the Checkout Channel, which placed TV monitors at the checkout, failed after a short time because people did not like seeing ad messages after they had collected all their goods in the shopping cart.

SUMMARY

The print media category is comprised of newspapers, magazines, out-of-home advertising such as billboards and transit advertising, Yellow Pages, and in-store advertising. Newspapers and magazines together account for about one-third of total advertising dollars.

Magazines have moved from being generalist in nature, with each covering a broad range of topics, to becoming much more specialized, focusing on highly specific topics and audiences. They are categorized into three types: consumer, farm, and business or professional. Advertisers use magazines for several reasons, namely because of the attractive demographics of their audiences; the fact that they are usually kept around for a fairly long time, offering the opportunity for seeing a detailed ad more than one time; and because readers who choose to look at a specific title tend to be more involved with that publication, showing greater interest in both the editorial material and the advertising. The problems magazines face include a long preparation time for production, which makes it hard for most of the monthly titles to be as timely as other media. Also, because readers choose what to look at, they can readily ignore an advertisement that is not targeted to them. Some critics have argued that magazines have become too specialized and narrow in their focus.

Magazines are purchased based on how many copies are distributed (circulation), how many people read a given issue (coverage), and the demographic make-up of a particular title (composition). Planners also consider the number of readers per copy and whether the readers bought the magazine themselves or read a copy passed along to them. When buying magazine ads, it is important to consider both the size of the ad and its position in the publication (front of book versus back of book, for example). Magazine rates are found in Standard Rate and Data Service (SRDS). They are based on the circulation rate base, a guarantee of how many copies will be distributed. Discounts are available for frequency of advertising, volume, and page equivalencies if different size ads are being used. Inkjetting and selective binding are two techniques that allow advertisers to use magazines to customize their messages and fine-tune them for specific groups or individuals. Technology is moving magazines more and more into the electronic arena, particularly with the development of magazines on the World Wide Web of the Internet and on computer online services.

Newspapers are one of the oldest media forms in the U.S. There are more than 2,400 titles published on either a daily or weekly basis. The medium is primarily local, with national advertisers having to pay a sizable premium over local rates. Advertisers can choose to place either classified or display ads. A large proportion of display ads comes from local retailers; when funded in part by national manufacturers or distributors, this is called cooperative (co-op) advertising. National advertising represents a small percentage of total newspaper ad dollars because the rates are far higher than for local or regional ad buys. Coupons can provide a way to show newspaper advertising effectiveness. In Sunday newspapers, free-standing inserts (FSIs) are popular with consumers, although they are not sold directly by the papers themselves. Sunday editions of the paper often carry magazine supplements, either nationally syndicated or locally produced. They come in full color with broad coverage but, like magazines, have long production times.

Newspapers offer three key benefits. First, because they mostly appear every day, they are very timely, able to change the ad message on a daily basis if necessary. Second, as with magazines, newspaper readers tend to be more educated and affluent than the general population. And also like their print cousins, it is possible to place ads in certain positions within the paper to take advantage of editorial compatibility. Three problems newspaper advertisers encounter are a short message life (usually one day), selective readers who can choose to ignore a message, and lack of color of comparable quality to other print media forms.

To plan for newspaper advertising, it is important to know how many copies are distributed in a market (circulation) as well as how many copies are actually read (coverage). Most newspapers now offer more localized ad sales, breaking out their total circulation into zones. Newspaper space is measured and purchased in column widths, with the length of the page measured in agate lines per column. Pages are usually purchased in terms of column widths, though most are classified according to Standardized Advertising Units (SAUs). Ad position can be critical to advertisers that wish to have editorial compatibility. The future of newspapers remains healthy. After broadening their consumer services through the use of audiotex and fax supplements, many newspapers are developing sites on the World Wide Web, offering information to their readers at little or no extra charge.

The out-of-home advertising industry is dominated by outdoor billboards. These come in two major sizes: poster panels and painted bulletins. The former tend to be within a market and range from 8-sheets to 30-sheets in size, while the latter are found mostly along major arteries and highways and are 14 feet by 48 feet. Outdoor boards offer advertisers the benefits of a large message size, which can create significant impact; the ability to target at the neighborhood level; and the opportunity to reach consumers as they are on the move. Drawbacks include the fact that the message is only seen for a brief time, which means it must be short. Also, billboards are primarily a local medium, making them expensive for national campaigns. They face continued criticism for advertising controversial products.

Billboards are purchased according to the showing, or number of boards required to reach a given proportion of the population in a set time period. The daily effective circulation shows how many people will be exposed to a message in a given time period (usually 12 hours). In order to see the exact location of the boards being purchased, advertisers or their agencies will often ride the boards to visit some of the sites. Technology is improving the look and consistency of billboards, with computer-generated painting and computer-controlled lighting.

New types of outdoor communications are appearing. These include boards or TV monitors at airports, health clubs, grocery stores, sports stadiums, and schools. More traditional means of reaching people outside of their homes are available through transit media, including buses, trains, and commuter rail services. Ads may be placed on the actual vehicles or at stations and bus shelters. Transit advertising is planned and bought in a manner similar to that used for billboards, and it shares many of the same advantages and disadvantages of that medium. In addition, transit ads focus primarily on a commuter audience.

Yellow Pages directories, published by the telephone companies and independent publishers, offer advertising that consumers choose to look at on a fairly regular and frequent basis, making them good opportunities for generating widespread awareness and use, particularly at the local level. Their drawbacks are their annual publication cycle and rather cumbersome size. Responses to ads can be tracked through special codes or phone numbers.

In-store media, such as coupons and displays, reach consumers right before they make a purchase. The message exposure may be brief or, in the case of electronic coupons issued at the checkout, after the purchase has occurred.

KEY TERMS

consumer magazines, 334

farm magazines, 334

business magazines, 334

passalong audience, 336

secondary readers, 336

primary readers, 337

circulation, 339

guaranteed circulation, 339

readers per copy, 340

audience, 340

coverage, 340

composition, 340

cover page, 341

center spread, 341

gatefold, 341

insert, 341

position, 341

Standard Rate & Data Service (SRDS), 342

inkjetting, 342

selective binding, 342

classified advertising, 344

display advertising, 344

cooperative (co-op) ads, 344

coupons, 347

free-standing insert (FSI), 347

newspaper magazine supplements, 347

zone, 349

column width, 349

agate lines per column, 349

standard advertising units (SAUs), 349

position, 351

audiotex, 351

newspaper fax services, 351

out-of-home advertising, 352

poster panel, 352

snipes, 352

painted bulletin, 352

showing, 355

daily effective circulation, 355

ride the boards, 355

transit advertising, 358

1. What are the benefits of magazine advertising? What are the drawbacks?

2. How does a magazine's lifespan extend its reach?

3. Define circulation, coverage, and composition.

4. If you were advertising Soft Scrub with Bleach in *Good Housekeeping,* what are the various positions in which you might try placing your ad, and why?

5. What factors influence the cost of magazine space to advertisers?

6. Explain the different types of newspaper advertising.

7. What are the benefits and drawbacks of newspaper advertising?

8. How are newspaper ads purchased?

9. How do poster boards and painted bulletins differ?

10. How is technology affecting the Yellow Pages?

1. You are the manufacturer of a line of healthy soups designed to appeal to children. Why might you consider using magazine ads? What types of magazines would you select, and why?

2. For a new model of the Toyota Celica, you have to choose between using general-editorial magazines such as *Reader's Digest* and more specialized publications such as *Auto World.* Discuss which types of publications would be preferable, and why, giving consideration to both targeting and cost concerns.

3. You are a sales rep for your local newspaper trying to convince a newly opened home furnishings store to purchase space in your pages. The store's advertising manager complains that newspapers have a short message life, overly selective readers, and poor color reproduction. Explain to her how you can overcome these objections.

4. Consider, from the advertiser's perspective, whether Seagram's should be allowed to promote malt liquor on billboards near places with high concentrations of African-American residents.

interactive discovery lab

1. Take one copy of two different types of magazines (e.g., a parenting magazine versus a fitness magazine). Compare and contrast the advertising that appears in each.

2. Look at an issue of your favorite magazine and analyze the position of each ad. Determine what you think the impact of the surrounding editorial might be, or where you think the ad would be better placed within that magazine.

Chapter Twelve

Integrated Marketing Communications Tools

THE WORLDWIDE DEBUT OF WINDOWS95

When Microsoft decided to launch its Windows95 computer software, it decided to do so on a large scale.

Not only was the $700 million introduction integrated—involving extensive advertising, public relations, promotions, and event marketing—but it also occurred on a global basis. Indeed, the company claims it was the first-ever simultaneous worldwide product launch. The program began at midnight on 24 August 1995 in Wellington, New Zealand, with launches occurring on a country-by-country basis moving westward with the sun.

Some of the events included the following: In Australia, a large, fabricated Windows95 box sailed on a barge in Sydney Harbor, heralded by live musicians. Tommy Lasorda helped promote the product in Japan, and local celebrities helped launch the product in various shopping malls in Hong Kong. In the Philippines, a special ceremony was held to present the new product to the country's president, Fidel Ramos. A launch party for 2,000 journalists took place in Moscow, Russia, while in Poland, journalists were taken into a submarine as a stunt to show them a "world without windows." In Spain, 800 people showed up for a special party that included a live interview with Bill Gates, the president of Microsoft. And in the United Kingdom, the company bought the entire press run of the London *Times* newspaper and gave out 1.5 million copies of the software for free.

Above and beyond these locally based events and promotions, Microsoft also ran a global print and television campaign in more than 20 countries to announce the new product and explain how it would change people's lives. The result of all these efforts was that a million copies of the software were sold worldwide on the first weekend of the product's launch. And as important as advertising is to the company, it is clear that for this global new product introduction, Microsoft's integrated approach was a critical part of its success.

Sources: "Windows on the World," *Promo,* December 1995, 69–70; and Alan Maites and William A. Robinson, "Windows95 Ad Blast Missed a Major Step," *Advertising Age,* 9 October 1995, 14–16.

Look Before You Leap

- Aside from advertising, what tools are available for use in an integrated marketing communications plan?

- What kinds of sales promotions are there, and how do they work?

- What is direct marketing, and why do people respond to it?

- What is public relations, and when is its use most appropriate?

- Why are marketers turning to licensing and sponsorship to promote their products?

12

The various tools that Microsoft employed to launch Windows95 globally were the tactical elements of an integrated marketing communications strategy. As we explored in Chapter Five, integrated marketing communication is designed to use all forms of communication to talk to the customer. By taking an outside-in view of the marketplace—looking at the world from the consumer's standpoint—integrated marketing attempts to offer that consumer a consistent and integrated view of the brand. This helps to build a lasting relationship between customer and brand, enhancing brand loyalty to bring customers back again and again.

This chapter looks at the major tools available to execute an integrated marketing communications strategy. The primary tools considered are sales promotion, direct marketing, and public relations. In addition, we consider event marketing, licensing, and sponsorship. All of these tools are categorized under the "promotion" element of the marketing mix, alongside advertising. Remember, for integrated marketing communications to be successful, all of the elements have to work together toward the common goal of achieving the company's or brand's marketing objectives.

Sales Promotion

Recall from Chapter Five that **sales promotion** is defined as the use of an incentive to buy a product, using either a price reduction or a value-added offer. Its goal is to have a direct impact on the behavior of customers, encouraging additional—and usually immediate—short-term sales. This is in contrast to the longer-term, less direct impact of advertising. Since the 1980s, many companies have come to rely on sales promotions to generate business, leading consumers to adopt the mentality of not wanting to buy items *unless* they are at a reduced price. It is worth pointing out that the U.S. is probably one of the most advanced countries in the world in its use of sales promotions, especially coupons. This may be due to the absence of the necessary infrastructure overseas to handle the couponing process, or it may be a cultural resistance to this type of promotion.

As with other types of integrated communications, sales promotion can be conducted by specialized agencies that focus solely on promotional activities, or it may occur within the broader arena of a general-market agency that has a sales promotion expert or staff. In recent years, more and more of the larger agencies have set up or purchased sales promotions offices to handle the increasing demand by marketers for expertise in this area. The top 10 sales promotion agencies are shown in Exhibit 12–1.

Consumer and Trade Promotions

Sales promotions generally have one of two audiences in mind: consumer and trade. The types of promotions aimed at each group have different goals in mind. **Consumer promotions** attempt to boost sales by encouraging people into the store to buy the product at a lower price or with some kind of special deal. This is known as a **pull strategy** because the promotions are designed to pull the product into the distribution pipeline based on customer demand. **Trade promotions,** on the other hand, work by offering incentives to retailers and distributors, such as additional discounts or deals, so that they will buy more from the manufacturer than they usually do to take advantage of the incentive. This is known as a **push strategy** because the promotion is designed to push the product into the distribution channel based on retailer and distributor demand. An example of a consumer and a trade promotion appear in Exhibit 12–2.

In recent years, marketers have put more of their dollars into consumer promotions, at the expense of traditional media advertising. Part of the reason for this change was the recession of the early 1980s, when marketers moved dollars out of advertising and into promotions in order to speed up sales that had slowed down as consumers found their budgets tightening. Once the financial climate had improved, companies found themselves caught in a short-term cycle of needing promotions to boost sales, which in turn required more promotion to maintain them. In 1995, more than half of marketers' advertising and promotion budgets

EXHIBIT 12–1   Top 10 Sales Promotion Agencies

RANK	AGENCY	1995 REVENUES ($ THOUSANDS)	EMPLOYEES	HEADQUARTERS	AGENCY AFFILIATION
1	Frankel & Company	$ 47,535.6	510	Chicago	None
	(McDonald's, Kodak, Amoco Oil, United Airlines, Visa)				
2	Wunderman Cato Johson	101,007.1	888	New York	Young & Rubicam
	(Blockbuster Video, Chevron, Kraft Foods, Miller Brewing, Sears, Taco Bell)				
3	Alcone Marketing Group	84,325.8	166	Irvine, CA	Omnicom Group
	(Burger King, Coors, Del Monte, IBM, Microsoft, Disney Channel)				
4	Einson Freeman	13,812.0	51	Paramus, NJ	WPP Group
	(Amtrak, Bayer, Kraft Foods, Sony, Tambrands)				
5	Flair Communications Agency	21,157.0	71	Chicago	None
	(Ameritech, Brown & Williamson, Coca-Cola, Dole, Kmart, MasterCard, Mattel, Nintendo)				
6	Marden-Kane	10,485.2	35	Manhasset, NY	None
	(CBS, Campbell Soup, Bank of America, Sony, Kraft Foods, Colgate Palmolive)				
7	The Optimum Group	6,926.4	55	Cincinnati, OH	None
	(Ameritech, Borden, Discover Card, Duracell, Hiram Walker, Iams Pet Food, Procter & Gamble, Valvoline)				
8	US Concepts	7,800.0	60	New York	None
	(Fruitopia, Diet Coke, Kimberly-Clark, Warner-Wellcome, Entenmann's)				
9	Inmark Services	4,600.0	27	Greenvale, NY	None
	(Colgate, CPC, Pillsbury, Perrier, Nestlé, Borden)				
10	Clarion Marketing & Communications	32,742.8	304	Greenwich, CT	DMB&B
	(Heinz, Johnson & Johnson, Nabisco)				

Note: Agencies ranked according to a formula based on revenue size, growth, and longevity.
Source: Promo's Annual Sourcebook, '97.

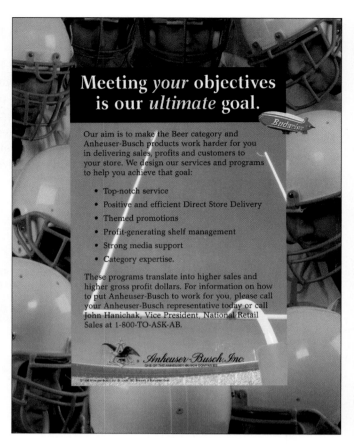

EXHIBIT 12–2 This consumer promotion by Waccamaw attempts to "pull" customers into the store with a "Buy One Get One Free" offer. In contrast, Anheuser-Busch uses a "pull" approach to attract retailers, highlighting the special promotion and support programs it offers to help generate sales of its products.

was allocated to trade promotions (51 percent), with the remainder divided almost evenly between media advertising (25 percent) and consumer promotions (24 percent).[1]

Although sales promotions traditionally have been thought of as tactical add-ons to a marketing plan, their strategic importance should not be underestimated. Consumer promotions can provide some of the most direct contact with the customer of any form of marketing communications, other than the product itself.

Benefits of Sales Promotions

There are three major advantages to using sales promotions: short-term sales gains, measurable response, and brand switching and trial.

SHORT-TERM SALES GAINS When consumers are offered a price incentive to buy a brand—such as 75 cents off on a box of Kellogg's Frosted Flakes or a 25 percent reduction in the price of a subscription to *Snow Country* magazine—they are more likely to buy the cereal or sign up for the magazine than they normally would be, and the company gains sales,

at least in the short term. This has become particularly important for brands or companies that set short-term sales goals that need to be met on a quarterly basis, encouraging the greater use of such promotions in order to achieve those goals. The problem, of course, is that this can become a self-perpetuating cycle when the brand has to rely on the promotions to reach the goals.

MEASURABLE RESPONSE Unlike advertising, where the impact on sales is often tenuous and hard to measure, sales promotions can be assessed fairly easily and directly. When Procter & Gamble places a coupon for Dove soap in the Sunday newspaper, it can know in a matter of days or weeks whether sales volume is up, and, once the coupons have been sent through a clearinghouse, precisely how many were redeemed.

BRAND SWITCHING AND TRIAL It is estimated that more than two-thirds of purchase decisions for regularly purchased supermarket items are *unplanned purchases;* that is, they are made in the grocery store itself.[2] Despite this, the majority of consumers will buy the brands they are used to and familiar with, remaining loyal to those unless something happens to make them dissatisfied. Promotions, therefore, offer one way to persuade people to switch to a competing brand or try a new product. If such an incentive is offered, this reduces the risk involved for the buyers, either by giving them a financial inducement or some other "extra" to compensate them for using a different brand. As a case in point, when Coppertone suntan lotion wanted to promote its Coppertone Sport line, it created a special Sports Challenge promotion in selected markets that participants could enter and win prizes, and then samples of the product were given away at key sporting events. After distributing 1.4 million samples and 1.2 million coupons, and getting 250,000 people to attend Sports Challenge events in six different markets, the brand saw its share increase by more than 10 percent in those markets.[3]

Drawbacks of Sales Promotions

Disadvantages for sales promotions include short-term effect, diluted brand equity, and lower profit per sale.

SHORT-TERM EFFECT While sales promotions do work to boost sales in the short term, that impact is generally only brief; once the coupon expires or the trade deal ends, so will consumer or trade purchases of the product. This may lead to a vicious cycle whereby the brand has to be on sale in some manner in order to encourage purchases, but then sales drop, which then forces the marketer to institute another promotion to generate additional sales. Promotions have, in fact, been blamed for much of the short-term thinking of many American marketers, who, unlike their Japanese counterparts, for example, assess the viability of a brand only in terms of this month or quarter, rather than taking a longer-term outlook that would consider a brand's potential over a year or more.

DILUTED BRAND EQUITY When brands constantly have some kind of sales promotion, consumers may develop an unfavorable image in their minds of what the brand stands for. They begin to see it as a brand for which it is never worth paying the full price. This is what

has happened to some degree in the retail industry in stores such as Macy's or Carson's. Brand dilution also serves to undermine the money being spent on advertising, which typically tries to build up a brand's image and lets consumers know that the money they are paying for the brand name is worthwhile.

LOWER PROFIT PER SALE For each gallon of Tide detergent that is purchased with a coupon, its manufacturer (Procter & Gamble) realizes less profit than if the consumer had paid full price. Thus, while sales promotions can boost sales and profits in the short term, a company may still lose money in the long run. When consumers stock up on the sale item, they are removed from the marketplace for several more weeks or months, which means that the manufacturer loses out on potential future sales to those consumers. This phenomenon also occurs with trade promotions, in a practice known as **forward buying.** Here, the retailer or dealer buys a large stock of the promoted items and keeps them in storage, selling them at a discount for a short while but then raising the price again and keeping the additional profit.

Types of Sales Promotions

Don Schultz and William Robinson, in their book *Sales Promotion Essentials,* identify 12 major forms of sales promotions (see Exhibit 12–3). The most popular types—coupons and sampling, refunds and rebates, contests and sweepstakes, trade promotions, and retailer promotions—are explained in more detail below.

IN-STORE PROMOTIONS: COUPONS AND SAMPLING A large proportion of all sales promotions occurs in the store. This is true for

---

EXHIBIT 12–3 **Types of Sales Promotions**

Coupons	Self-liquidating premiums
Contests and sweepstakes	Refunds
Bonus packs	Trade promotions
Stamp and continuity plans	Retailer promotions
Discount offers	Sampling
Specialty packages	Point-of-purchase materials
Free in-the-mail premiums	

both consumer and trade deals. At the consumer level, in-store promotions may include *displays* (in or at the end of aisles, or on the shelf), *sampling,* and *on-pack coupons.* For the trade, promotions can come in the form of **advertising allowances,** wherein the manufacturer pays the retailer to advertise his product; or **dealer listings,** wherein the manufacturer leaves space on his or her ad to list local retailers or dealers. A list of retail-related sales promotions is shown in Exhibit 12–4.

The reason for the importance of in-store promotions is self-evident: They are likely to be the last type of marketing communication contact with the consumer prior to his or her

purchase. Research suggests that aisle displays, for example, can help increase sales by as much as 20 percent.

Coupons.   A **coupon** is a certificate that may be redeemed for a cash discount. The first coupon ever was issued in 1895 from the C.W. Post cereal company, which offered consumers of its new Grape Nuts cereal one cent off their next purchase of the product. Coupons were not commonly used as incentives until the 1950s, however, when companies such as Procter & Gamble, General Foods, Scott Paper, and General Mills began using them to entice people to try the many new brand-name items appearing on store shelves. In 1965, when coupons began to be tracked systematically, there were 10 million distributed. By 1996, that figure had ballooned to 269 billion.[4]

Coupons represent 70 percent of all consumer sales promotions, and more than half (56 percent) of all shoppers use them in a three-month period. Coupons are distributed in various ways. The most popular method is through free-standing inserts (FSIs) placed within the Sunday newspaper. Nearly 9 out of 10 coupons (88 percent) are distributed this way. Coupons are also placed within the pages of a newspaper or magazine, sent through the mail, or put on or inside the product itself. They may originate with the manufacturer or the retailer. In recent years retailers have become far more active in this area, adding coupons to their weekly sales circulars to promote a given number of items for that week. Results from a survey conducted by R. H. Donnelley found that 88 percent of consumers claimed to have used a coupon for groceries or health and beauty aids in the past month. More than one-third (38 percent) said they often purchase a brand for which they have a coupon.

Many factors can affect the success of a coupon program. The **face value,** or *value,* of the coupon is a key consideration. This refers to the size of the discount on the product for the consumer, such as "50 cents off." In 1995 the average face value on a coupon was 68 cents, although that figure varies by product category. The highest values are found for health and beauty aids. The face value for items such as shampoo, shaving cream, or

---

EXHIBIT 12–4   Retail-Oriented Sales Promotions

CONSUMER

In-store banners: Strips displaying brand name/sales message to encourage purchase.

Bonus packs: Larger size or double packs.

Coupons: Cents-off on brand purchase.

Sampling: Offering consumer trial size of product.

In-aisle/end-aisle display: Special displays with promotions in addition to shelf space.

In-pack/On-pack coupons: Coupons offered inside product or on label for future use.

Price-off labels: Price reduction on current purchase.

Refunds: Money back when set purchase conditions are met.

Shelf talkers: Coupons offered on the shelf.

Tie-in promotions: One promotion covering several products, possibly even from different companies.

TRADE

Buy-back allowance: Money offered for new quantities bought based on amount of initial purchase.

Cash rebates: Cash discount based on total volume purchased.

Cooperative advertising: Manufacturer helps pay for advertising.

Count-recount allowance: Manufacturer pays based on amount sold, not ordered.

Dealer listing: Manufacturer lists retailers or dealers in own ads.

Display allowance: Payment to allow special in-store displays.

Feature advertising allowance: Payment to get brands into retailers' own ads.

Recognition programs: Awards or prizes to motivate salesforce.

Slotting allowance: Payments to retailers to secure shelf space.

Spiffs: Incentives given directly to salesforce to push manufacturer's product.

over-the-counter medications averages more than $1.08 per coupon. The lowest reductions are for refrigerated and frozen products, where the face value for items such as frozen vegetables or dairy products averages about 48 cents per coupon.[5]

Timing is also critical. Distributing coupons for charcoal in the middle of winter when people are far less likely to be using their grills (at least in cold-weather climates) is not a recipe for success. Indeed, research suggests that coupons are most impactful right before and during a product's key sales period. The downside to this is that those are the times when the product would be most likely to sell well without the need for additional promotions.[6]

Although coupons are prolific as a means of promotion, the vast majority goes unused. Of the 269 billion issued in 1996, only 5.3 billion, or 2 percent, were actually used *(redeemed)* by consumers. And that level has been falling in recent years, from a high of 3.5 percent in 1983. The redemption rate does vary by where the coupon appears. It is lowest in newspaper inserts (0.6 percent redemption) and highest for coupons placed on the package (27 percent). When mailed directly to the household, about 3.5 percent of the coupons are redeemed. In the Sunday newspaper, that figure falls to about 1.3 percent.[7]

Another problem is *misredemption,* which includes cashiers accepting coupons for the wrong product, brand, or amount, as well as fraud which occurs when retailers send coupons to the manufacturer that were not actually redeemed by consumers. It is estimated that these types of errors can be as high as 19 percent of all coupons issued, leading to millions of dollars of losses for manufacturers.

In recent years, technology has led to the development of several kinds of electronic coupons. One of the most popular is Catalina Marketing's Checkout Coupon program, which is currently found in 2,800 stores. Checkout Coupon is a system that generates a coupon at the cash register when the shopper's goods are being scanned. The coupons the shopper receives are based solely on his current purchases. That is, if the consumer buys a jar of Smucker's Grape Jelly, he may receive a coupon for Jif Peanut Butter or one for Kraft Grape Jelly. See Exhibit 12–5 for an example of this type of coupon. Although demographics are not directly involved in the coupon generation, they may be implied based on the purchases. When a shopper buys dog food, for example, one can assume that, in all likelihood, she has a dog in her household. This may lead Pedigree to issue that shopper a coupon, because people with dogs represent their desired target. The drawback to Checkout Coupon is in its name: Coupons are issued as the consumer is leaving the store, which means that he or she will have to return with them next time in order to redeem them. However, because 8 out of 10 consumers say they use coupons on a regular basis, this does not seem to present a major problem, and this form of couponing enjoys about a 10 percent redemption rate.

Electronic couponing can also be used by the store itself to increase sales and retain customers. When one retailer saw sales of its baby care items falling due to heavy competition from a mass merchandise (discount) store, it began offering special points to customers who spent money on baby items. When 100 points were collected, they each

EXHIBIT 12–5 The coupons generated by the Checkout Coupon system are unique in that they target specific purchases made by the consumer. For example, this coupon for Nature Valley soft granola bars was generated for a consumer who purchased a different brand of granola bars.

received a $10 store certificate. The results of this program were a 25 percent increase in sales of baby products and a 10–15 percent increase in the number of individual baby items purchased.8

In the not-too-distant future it is likely that electronic couponing will become even more common. In contrast to regular coupons, which tend to be redeemed primarily by current brand users, electronic couponing appears to do a better job at gaining new audiences for new products or cross-promotions. Already companies are testing couponing on computer online services and the Internet. The big advantage here is that the consumers get to choose which coupons they want, based on the brands or services they actually use. At the moment, however, technical difficulties remain, such as the need to have a printer to generate the physical coupon and the problem of preventing one person from printing out hundreds of copies of the same coupon.

Today's electronic in-store coupon machines rely heavily on store scanners. "Technology Watch: Scanning for Gold" looks at how these systems have revolutionized the retail industry and enhanced marketers' knowledge of how promotions work.

While coupons are prolific in the U.S., they are still relatively uncommon in other parts of the world. In the United Kingdom, for example, a household redeems about 16 coupons a year, compared to the 80 or so used by each home in the U.S. Germany makes couponing close to illegal by stipulating that a discount cannot be greater than 1 percent of the value of the item. Similarly, Swedes are only allowed to receive cash from an offer, so two-for-one deals would be considered against the law.9

Sampling.   An increasingly popular form of in-store promotion is product **sampling**. This practice puts the product directly into con-

TECHNOLOGY WATCH

....

Scanning for Gold

In the world of retailing prior to the 1980s, manufacturers and retailers only found out what was selling well several weeks or months after the product had left the shelf. Today, thanks to the technological miracle of scanning systems, they can know in a matter of days and, in some cases, almost instantaneously. Scanning systems are used to electronically "read" the digitized Universal Product Code (UPC) symbols stamped on almost every item that is sold. That code offers a unique identification of the product, recording everything from size and flavor to date sold and location sold.

The development and growth of scanning systems throughout the retail industry resulted in an enormous increase in the power of the retailer over the manufacturer, because it is the retailer who controls the scanning information. Before, the manufacturer would tell the retailer which of its brands to stock, and where to place them. Now the tables have turned, and it is the retailer who tells the manufacturer which brands he will accept in the store and where they will be on the shelf. All of the retailer's decisions are based on knowing how each item is selling on a day-to-day basis.

The amount of data being gathered by scanners is truly astounding. According to the trade magazine *Progressive Grocer,* supermarkets scan an average of 13,900 weekly transactions per store. That data can be used to track product movement, check on sales and promotions, and develop targeted marketing efforts against consumers, based on their individual purchases through the use of frequent shopper cards. It was quickly realized that by linking a shopper's identification to a report of scanned items, retailers would have a very powerful database of information on purchase habits and behavior. That information can then be passed on to manufacturers, which can target specific promotions to different individuals. More than 30 million Americans now carry a frequent shopper card, spending more per store visit than people who do not own one.

sumers' hands, allowing them to try it out with little or no risk involved. It is particularly useful for launching a new product or a line extension. When Taco Bell began its introductory effort for its Border Lights low-fat line, the 4,500 restaurants in the chain offered a total of 8 million free tacos to restaurant patrons, allowing people to try the product immediately. In its first year, Border Lights achieved $800 million in sales.

While the most common form of sampling occurs in the store, it can also be executed in other ways. These include placing a sample in or on an existing package, handing out samples at a special event, or inviting people via a mailing to write or call for a sample. Very often, the sampling is supported by other kinds of marketing communications. Frito-Lay, for example, used a combination of sampling, traditional advertising, and public relations to launch its Rold Gold Fat Free Pretzels. In addition to a commercial in the 1995 Super Bowl and a magazine ad that same day in the Sunday newspaper supplement *Parade,* 5 million pretzel samples were distributed in K-mart stores. The fully integrated effort resulted in sales increasing more than twofold, helping confirm Rold Gold's dominant position in the pretzel category. Sampling may also be used for a select audience, such as children or teens, with distribution in places where that group is likely to congregate, such as schools or movie theaters. The chief drawback to sampling is its relatively high cost not only to produce smaller-size packages but also to distribute them to a select group.

OTHER CONSUMER PROMOTIONS **Refunds and rebates** allow consumers to get back a portion of the purchase price of an item, usually by sending in proof-of-purchase and a cash register receipt. These promotions are often used as early- or late-season incentives to encourage consumers to buy now rather than waiting. Scotts Lawn Products Company often offers rebates early in the year on its fertilizers and herbicides, although the company runs the risk that consumers might stockpile the product and not purchase it again during the summer. An example of rebate advertising appears in Exhibit 12–6.

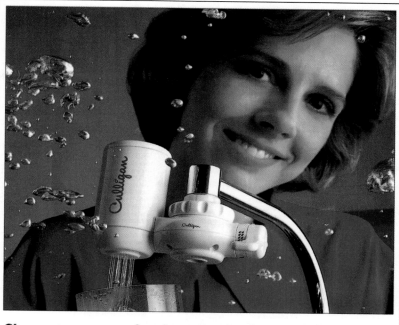

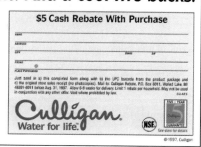

Whenever someone earns miles in an airline's frequent flyer program or collects points by dining in certain restaurants, they are participating in a **continuity program.** The purpose of such a promotion is to encourage people to buy a product or service more frequently in order to "earn" enough points to redeem a gift, such as a free airline ticket or free meal. Another goal of these promotional programs is to increase brand loyalty by enticing people to use the promoter's brand rather than the competitor's to garner more points. Of course, this will only work as long as the promoter's offerings are at least equal to, if not better than, the competition. Quality, value, and convenience all are likely to be more important to the consumer than the continuity program.

One of the most popular forms of promotions among consumers is the contest or sweepstakes. While **contests** are games of skill

EXHIBIT 12–6 Rebate offers are often used to generate immediate sales of a product. This type of promotion may also be used as an incentive for consumers to try a new product.

that have specific criteria on which the winner is judged, **sweepstakes** are completely random, offering prizes based solely on chance. An example of a contest is the Oscar Mayer talent contest in which the hot dog company solicits children for its cute commercials. Thousands of parents bring their offspring to auditions that are held at various locations throughout the country, and hundreds more send in videotapes of their would-be starlets singing the commercial's theme tune. The semiannual Publisher's Clearinghouse program is an example of a sweepstakes that offers prizes randomly. See Exhibit 12–7 for an example of a sweepstakes promotion.

Both promotions enhance the relationship between a company or brand and the consumer, encouraging greater involvement by participants and, in many cases, increasing sales. These promotions can also be helpful for database creation, asking those who wish to enter to supply some additional information, such as demographics or product usage. The main problem with such ventures is that although many people may enter and be excited by the game, only a small proportion of your brand's target audience is likely to take part.

TRADE PROMOTIONS There are a variety of ways that manufacturers attempt to energize

distributors or retailers through promotions. The most common form is the **trade allowance.** This is a special deal or price that the manufacturer offers in order to persuade the retailer to purchase larger quantities of the product. Such allowances are also used to entice the retailer to feature a given brand in his or her own marketing efforts, whether advertising or promotion. The risk for the manufacturer is that the retailer will take the allowance but not pass it on to his own customers, which will not encourage consumers to buy more of that item. To overcome this, manufacturers are increasingly likely to specify in the terms of the deal precisely what the retailer needs to do in terms of features or promotions. Exhibit 12–8 lists and briefly explains the different types of trade allowances.

Companies that rely on a sales force to distribute and/or sell their product may turn to sales force incentives to help boost sales. Contests are used, offering generous prizes to those who sell the most during a specified time period. To encourage rapid sales of a particular model or product, manufacturers sometimes use **spiffs,** which involve giving additional money to the salesperson each time he or she makes a sale of the manufacturer's product. When the British cellular telephone company Cellnet wanted to increase its market share, it chose trade promotions rather than consumer efforts to do so. And rather than using cash, it motivated its sales force with prizes, a sweepstakes to win a new car, and special vouchers for desirable merchandise. The result was that during that promotional period, the number of new connections signed up to the digital network rose 84 percent above what had been forecast, and its market share rose considerably as well.[10]

RETAILER PROMOTIONS Retailer promotions are a hybrid form of promotion conducted by the retailer and directed at consumers. As with any kind of promotion, those done by retailers are designed to persuade people to buy more of the product on sale. The difference is that the retailer wants that purchase to occur in his store only. The most common type of retailer promotion is the *price cut*. Retailers also rely heavily on weekly *feature advertising*, predominantly in local newspapers, to generate store traffic. Certain products are put on sale, priced nearly at cost, to act as *loss leaders* and entice consumers into the store. For example, when Kroger sells apples at just 49 cents per pound, it is cutting the profit it makes on that fruit in the hope that once people come into the store to buy apples, they will also purchase other products.

Whatever type of promotion is being used, it should be appropriate to the product's life cycle. For example, when introducing a new brand a company should use promotions to encourage trial (such as sampling or coupons). For more mature brands, the goal is to increase brand loyalty, perhaps through "buy-one-get-one-free" promotions, or in-pack and on-pack offers.

R E S E T

1. What types of sales promotions might a retailer use to draw customers into her store?
2. Why is the use of coupons uncommon outside of the United States?
3. What types of promotions might a manufacturer use to attract more interest from retailers?

EXHIBIT 12–8   Trade Allowances

ALLOWANCES WITHOUT REQUIREMENTS

Buying allowance: Discount on the product, usually based on volume purchased.

Off-invoice allowance: Discount on purchases made in given time period.

Free good: Extra product given with certain level of purchase.

Dating: Billing for purchases spread out over longer time period.

ALLOWANCES WITH REQUIREMENTS

Cash rebate: Cash discount if retailer fulfills terms of agreement (for promotion, etc.).

Advertising/Display allowance: Discount earned if product is promoted by retailer.

Buyback allowance: Deal to encourage dealer or distributor to stock up on the product.

Source: Don E. Schultz and William A. Robinson, *Sales Promotions Essentials* (Lincolnwood, IL: NTC Business Books, 1992), 162–170.

Direct Marketing

Direct marketing might be considered one of the earliest forms of commercial communication. The first door-to-door salesmen who went from house to house selling Fuller Brush products and Encyclopedia Britannica sets were really practicing a form of direct marketing. **Direct marketing** is defined as "any activity whereby you communicate directly with your prospect or customer and he or she responds directly to you."[11] Its chief purpose is to generate a sale based on one-to-one communications with the target, also called the *prospect* (or prospective customer). Unlike advertising, which is a mass form of communication, direct marketing involves delivering the message at the individual level. It also differs from sales promotion in that the impact may not be immediate but may take anywhere from several days to several months.

Although the response may not be instantaneous, it is highly measurable, particularly if the communication is coded to determine which responses came from which mailings or phone calls or ads. Response rates vary considerably, but it is generally good to obtain a response of at least 2 percent of the total sent. In other words, if 500,000 letters are sent to prospective customers, you are doing well if

10,000 people respond. It is estimated that about 10 percent of all consumer sales and 5 percent of all business-to-business sales are generated by direct marketing communication.

Direct marketing agencies, like sales promotion and public relations shops, today tend to be owned by advertising agency conglomerates such as WPP, Omnicom, and Cordiant. In 1995, $134 billion was spent on direct marketing, and the numbers keep growing.

Benefits of Direct Marketing

The primary advantages of direct marketing are individualized communications, measurable response, database collection, and customer feedback.

INDIVIDUALIZED COMMUNICATIONS In a world where people are inundated by generalized, impersonal commercial messages, most of which are not relevant to their needs or desires, direct marketing can offer a personalized and, if targeted correctly, highly meaningful message that informs consumers about the product and encourages them to act immediately. So rather than delivering an advertising message that is disseminated to thousands, if not millions, of people, direct marketing aims to talk to each person on his or her own. Traditionally, this has been done through direct mail, where letters can be sent to Mrs. Jane Smith or Mr. Ben Jones, but today the World Wide Web offers similar capabilities in terms of sending out unique messages to individual computer users. Because people generally prefer to be called by their own names rather than considered an anonymous group member, direct marketing offers a powerful form of communication with consumers.

MEASURABLE RESPONSE As we noted above, because each message is sent to a known individual, it is possible to find out whether that person responded or not. This is a benefit that most advertising and promotions cannot offer. With most advertising, sales may be generated but we cannot know what caused them. Similarly, promotions are measurable, but not at the individual level. By knowing how many people responded to a direct marketing offer, marketers can plan follow-up messages and future campaigns with a good idea of what kind of response that will generate, making it easier

to predict in advance how many inquiries or sales will result.

DATABASE COLLECTION By gathering the names of all of those who respond to an offer, a company gains invaluable information on its customers. It can also learn who does not respond, and maybe do some follow-up work to determine why. It can classify customers by the types and frequency of response, and tailor future messages more narrowly to appeal to the actual preferences of those people. When someone orders a pinpoint shirt from the regular Lands' End catalog, for example, the company notes that in its database and sends out its specialty catalog, Beyond Buttondowns, which is designed for professional men.

CUSTOMER FEEDBACK In addition to gathering information about customers or prospects, direct marketing allows a company to gather feedback to help it improve its products and services. BankSouth, headquartered in Atlanta, used direct mail to solicit 1,500 of its customers to participate in small-group meetings to discuss the bank's performance and customer satisfaction. After discovering that people disliked the bank's restrictive hours of operation (9 A.M.–4 P.M. on weekdays only) and limited outlets, BankSouth began opening branches in other locations, such as supermarkets, with longer banking hours. It now generates about one-third of its total business from these places.[12]

Drawbacks to Direct Marketing

The main problems with direct marketing are high cost, customer avoidance, and small reach.

HIGH COST Because direct marketing is so individualized, it is far more expensive to deliver a message in that manner than it is to use mass forms of communications such as advertising. Direct marketing messages must be sent to each household and/or to a known name within that household. That requires the development or purchase of a mailing list. Depending on how specialized the target, the total price for developing or purchasing the list may be considerable. To reach people who own or are interested in Arabian horses, for example, you might purchase the list of 48,000 readers of *Arabian Horse Times* magazine and pay $65 per 1,000 names. Similarly, you can buy a list of 100,000 self-employed professionals for $85 per 1,000 names.

CUSTOMER AVOIDANCE Direct marketing represents a more extreme version of print media in terms of how people respond to and process it. That is, they actively filter out the messages that they do not believe are relevant to them, throwing away the "junk mail," putting down the telephone when a telemarketer calls, or changing channels when a direct response TV commercial comes on. If the message being sent does not reach the right target—or does not do so at the right time or in the right place when consumers are likely to be receptive to it—then it is all too easy to ignore, which means that the marketer has wasted his or her money.

SMALL REACH Because direct marketing is so highly targeted, only a small group of people will receive the message. There are exceptions here, such as the mass direct mailings for Publisher's Clearinghouse, but usually, direct marketing is sent to hundreds or thousands rather than millions of consumers. Therefore, it is not considered appropriate for those companies that wish to tell everyone about their product or service, such as McDonald's or Procter & Gamble. That is not to say that large companies do not use direct response, but when they do so, they are probably focusing their efforts on a selected group of their customers rather than trying to reach everyone.

Types of Direct Marketing

Direct marketing generally occurs in one of three ways: by mail, by telephone, or in person. For our purpose, we will focus on direct marketing done by mail and by telephone, as well as database marketing. In-person direct marketing, also known as personal selling, involves such activities as holding Tupperware parties or textbook sales reps knocking on professors' office doors to sell them on the idea of adopting a certain book for their classes.

Mail or telephone direct marketing usually occurs as follows: A company creates or purchases a list of names (and addresses or phone numbers, depending on the method to be used) of people whom the company believes

are good prospects for its product or service. For example, Little Tykes might buy a list of people who have had a child in the last four years, while Columbia Records might create a list of everyone who has purchased a classical music CD or cassette in the last 12 months. From that list, the company or its agency can send out a new mailing or develop a telemarketing effort to encourage those people to purchase its list offering. In these examples, Little Tykes might send out a catalog of its newborn and infant toys to new parents, while Columbia Records could do a telemarketing effort to recruit members to its Classical CD club.

There are many changes occurring in the direct marketing industry, led by technology. In today's computerized world, direct marketing offers an excellent opportunity to gather an electronic database of information on everyone who responds to a message. The challenge is to send the message only to those people who are likely to respond. And because the process is not completely automated there is always room for human error, such as sending a letter to Ms. John Smith or sending an offer for a dog kennel to a cat-owning household. Nonetheless, because it is one of the most "testable" of all media, the experiences of many companies and individuals in this field have made it more predictable in terms of knowing what might work. Exhibit 12–9 offers one such list of guidelines for successful direct marketing efforts.

EXHIBIT 12–9   Direct Marketing Guidelines

1. The word "free" is the strongest, most effective word you can use in an offer.
2. When trying to raise funds for a cause, use lower-quality paper and printing.
3. Enclosures with a direct mail letter should be of different size and color than the letter itself.
4. Limited-time coupons inserted into consumer catalogs boost response rates.
5. Humor does not work well in direct marketing.
6. Emphasize the positive rather than putting down your competitor.
7. Use facts before resorting to testimonials.
8. People who pay for direct marketing orders by credit card tend to spend more money.

Source: Nat G. Bodian, *Direct Marketing Rules of Thumb* (Ithaca, NY: American Demographics Books, 1995).

DIRECT MAIL   Each year about 80 billion pieces of **direct mail advertising** are sent directly to prospects by advertisers, charitable organizations, governmental agencies, and individuals. The U.S. Postal Service (USPS)—in addition to private postal services—realizes considerable revenues from this. To encourage even more direct mail, the USPS decided to promote the use of direct mail over other forms of advertising. This ended up being a highly controversial campaign because the magazine industry objected to the comparisons made. An example from the campaign is shown in Exhibit 12–10. After complaints from the magazine industry, the ads were modified or pulled.

While some direct mail is considered junk mail by critics, overall reaction from consumers tends to be more positive than negative. Indeed, one of the reasons that direct mail is successful is its ability to send relevant messages to interested audiences. Those names are selected from large mailing lists from sources as diverse as telephone directories, credit card purchase histories, state auto licensing lists, and product warranty return cards. Direct mail also can be used for intensive coverage campaigns. Local advertisers may send mail to all postal addresses in a specific geographic area to distribute coupons or special offers. Publisher's Clearinghouse uses direct mail together with network television to achieve widespread coverage and readership for its sweepstakes competition.

The key to the success of a direct mailing depends heavily on the mailing list that is used. The quality of the list is determined by how many *good names* are on it, or the total number of names minus the number of returns. In order to maintain such a list, it must be used frequently and updated regularly to avoid inaccuracies. A significant problem that occurs is *duplicate names,* which must still be paid for by the advertiser. One of the techniques employed to keep a list current is called a **merge and purge.** This involves combining two or more mailing lists together and then removing the duplicates. Thanks to computerization, this task has become fairly simple and routine.

Although it seems as if your mailbox is constantly filled with direct mail, the companies sending it out do so with clear scheduling objectives in mind. For example, you are most likely to receive offers related to book clubs or reading in June prior to summer vacations, whereas products related to self-improvement are sent most frequently near the end of the year, when people think about their New Year's resolutions.[13]

Direct mail can be a highly successful first step in an integrated marketing campaign. Chrysler Corporation sent direct mail to its known owners of Jeep automobiles and invited them to attend the first-ever Camp Jeep weekend in the Rocky Mountains in Colorado. Magazine ads promoting the event appeared along with the mailing. The company selected 500,000 Jeep owners and invited them to spend two days hiking, fly fishing, attending concerts, and receiving training in driving four-by-four vehicles. While they were there, a roundtable discussion of the car was held where owners could talk to the engineers, providing Chrysler with invaluable, one-on-one feedback.

EXHIBIT 12–10   Recognizing the considerable profits that it receives from the use of direct mail, the U.S. Postal Service launched a controversial series of ads promoting the benefits of this type of advertising.

TELEMARKETING Telemarketing is defined as the sale of products or services through direct communication with the customer over the telephone. There are two kinds: outbound telemarketing and inbound telemarketing. *Outbound telemarketing* involves a company making calls directly to customers and prospects, encouraging them to switch telephone companies, sign up for a new credit card, or buy a newspaper subscription, for example. *Inbound telemarketing* refers to the calls made by consumers to the company, primarily through the use of toll-free and 1-900 phone numbers to get information and/or purchase a product or service.

The growth of toll-free numbers has been substantial in recent years. In 1994, more than half of the total population (195 million people) used either toll-free or 1-900 phone numbers. More than two-thirds of all manufacturing businesses now offer the toll-free number, which is free to the caller and paid for by the business. There are more than 750,000 1-800 numbers currently in use. A resulting shortage of numbers forced the Federal Communications Commission to introduce a new toll-free prefix, the 888 code, in 1997.

Most people (71 percent) say they use toll-free numbers to obtain information, while more than half (55 percent) have done so to place an order or make a purchase. The latter action is more likely to be taken by affluent consumers; 70 percent of those with household incomes of $40,000 or more have called a toll-free number for the purpose of purchasing. Toll-free numbers are also appearing in more places. They are about as likely to be seen in print media (newspapers and magazines) as on television, in the phone book, or in brochures and pamphlets.

A specialized use of toll-free numbers is for **telepromotions,** which are defined as automatic calls made in quick succession in order to make a sale. These kinds of promotions are being used more and more by marketers. For example, Pepsi sent direct mail to Diet Coke drinkers, encouraging them to call a 1-800 number and "talk" to the Pepsi spokesman, singer Ray Charles. Fully half of those who received the mailing made the call, and nearly all remained on the phone long enough to complete a survey about their soda-drinking habits. Indeed, toll-free numbers offer another

valuable opportunity for building a database: asking callers some simple questions for subsequent marketing purposes.

The 1-900 number differs from toll-free numbers in two key respects. First, in order to use a 1-900 number, the caller must agree to pay a set fee, usually an initial charge followed by a higher-than-normal per-minute rate. In 1995, 900 numbers brought in $752 million in revenues. The second major difference from the toll-free number is the poor reputation that 1-900 numbers still endure. This is a result of the proliferation of sex phone lines and psychic hotlines, among others. It is worth noting that the greatest interest in 1-900 numbers is actually for referrals to doctors or specialists, as can be seen in Exhibit 12–11.

As the initial step in its Camp Jeep integrated marketing campaign, the Chrysler Corporation used direct mail to distribute invitations to the unique weekend event. Magazine ads such as the one shown here were used to support the direct mail campaign.

EXHIBIT 12–11   Interest in 1–900 Numbers

TYPE OF 1–900 CALL	PERCENT INTERESTED
Referrals to doctors/specialists	73%
Financial tips	66
Dining out recommendations	65
Movie recommendations	58
Sports hotline	57
Computer information	40
Horoscope	29
Dream interpretation	28
Psychic services	24
Dating services	21

Source: Direct Marketing Association, *Direct Marketing Association 1996 Statistical Factbook* (New York: Direct Marketing Association, 1996).

Direct marketing is a well-established practice in the United States, in part because the sheer size of the country encourages marketers to find ways of reaching smaller segments of the population classified by select demographics, psychographics, or product usage. Indeed, more and more companies are realizing the potential of direct marketing for providing additional, often detailed, information on customers. In other parts of the world, however, direct marketing is relatively new, but growing rapidly. "Around the Globe: Talking One-to-One in Europe" looks at how direct marketing is developing in Europe.

DATABASE MARKETING   Database marketing involves collecting computer records, including demographic and financial information on individuals and households that is systematically gathered and updated, then using these records to target advertising to individuals' needs. Databases may be built from credit card information or the U.S. Census; they can also be

AROUND THE GLOBE

Talking One-to-One in Europe

The growth of direct marketing in Europe may be pinpointed to a specific date: 1 January 1993. It was on that date that the 15 member countries of the European Community removed many of the barriers that had previously made it difficult for marketers to consider doing business across borders. Before that date, cross-border taxes were imposed each time a product or service

went from one country to another. The additional costs that these taxes imposed on marketers made the notion of selling directly to customers in another country a mere pipe dream.

Now, however, the situation is starting to change. It is estimated that about 15 percent of the total advertising budget of most large European companies now goes to direct mail. Companies are steadily building up their databases, collecting customer information that will make future sales easier and more effective. Direct marketing offers a unique benefit to European companies (and non-European ones wishing to promote their goods there). It is

the only medium in Europe that is able to speak to each target member directly and individually in his or her own language. That is, while pan-European television or print have to customize their language by region or country, direct marketing can be changed down to the neighborhood level, if need be.

This is an important consideration when you realize how many different languages, and dialects within languages, there are on the European continent. For example, direct marketers have to account for the fact that there are differences between the way French is written and spoken in France, Belgium, and Switzerland, even though all

generated by UPC scanners in supermarkets or other stores. The challenge of database marketing lies in integrating various sources of information into a usable form. One of the industries trying to take advantage of database marketing is retailing. Through the use of department store cards, retailers can know not only basic demographics of their customers but also detailed purchase histories. This has allowed Dayton Hudson Corporation, for example, which owns Dayton's, Hudson's, Marshall Field's, and Target, to conduct sophisticated analyses on the 120 million transactions that occur in its department stores each year. By segmenting its database to reach different people with different messages, the company can send out 400 event mailings each year that are more properly targeted to the recipient. So someone who has purchased furniture at Hudson's may receive a special notice when the next furniture sale is coming or an announcement of an evening event featuring a home design specialist. A person who has purchased cloth-

ing at Target, on the other hand, might receive a flyer announcing when the new spring clothes are in.

A commitment to database marketing as part of an integrated marketing effort requires a shift from short-term tactical thinking to long-term strategic thinking. It can take two to four years to build the database, so the cost of database marketing becomes prohibitive unless that investment can be spread out over a longer time period. The pioneers in database marketing were service industries such as airlines and hotels. Data collection techniques vary, but most are driven by promotions. Consumers therefore select themselves as potential customers when they enter a contest or sweepstakes or write for a product sample.

Three of the biggest names in database marketing are TRW, Equifax, and Trans Union. They are best known in the financial and credit markets, capturing the records of every credit card transaction—from a car loan to a $10 purchase at Sears. These companies have cre-

three countries recognize it as their official language. Cultural differences are perhaps a bigger problem. Time-Life Books had to alter its book, "Home Repair and Improvement," substantially when it was promoted in Europe because the tools and equipment used varied so much by country. Even the way that windows operate can differ; they open inwards in France, outwards in Germany, and move up and down in the United Kingdom! There are also differences in the way that consumers respond to direct marketing methods. The Swiss tend to pay their bills immediately, whereas Greek consumers are more apt to wait as long as possible.

Then there are the physical or technical issues to consider. The mailing or phone lists on which U.S. marketers rely so heavily are far less established in Europe. In the U.S., direct marketers have ready access to motor vehicle lists; this is not the case in most European countries. Moreover, regulations differ from country to country. You cannot advertise books on television in France. In Sweden, a direct response TV ad must elaborate on all of the costs involved in the purchase. For direct mailers, the postal systems and regulations are also varied between countries, even in the way that addresses are structured. Town names may be

spelled differently, depending on where one is from. Mons and Bergen are the same place in Belgium, as named by French and Flemish-speaking inhabitants, respectively.

Compared to the U.S., direct marketing in Europe is generally considered about 10 years behind, but it is catching up rapidly. Although credit card penetration is lower, postal and telephone rates are higher, and fewer commercial TV channels are available, the relative lack of clutter in terms of messages sent directly to consumers opens up many opportunities for both European and U.S. companies to appeal individually to their chosen targets. Already it is estimated that

about one-third of U.S. direct marketing companies sell abroad, many of them to Europe. It seems only a matter of time before others recognize the potential of the market and follow them across the Atlantic.

Sources: Christopher T. Linen, "Marketing and the Global Economy," Direct Marketing, January 1991, 54–56; Nicholas di Talamo, "It's Not What You Do, It's the Way That You Do It," Direct Marketing, August 1992, 25–28; Nicholas di Talamo, "Getting U.S. Catalogs into Europe," Direct Marketing, December 1992, 21–24; Arnold Fishman, "International Mail Order," Direct Marketing, October 1991, 36–41; Wendy Marx, "Foreign Policies," Direct, 15 April 1996, 1, 36–38; and Beth Negus, "They're Not Merry in England," Direct, 15 April 1996, 85–87.

ated enormous databases filled with a wide variety of information, offering databases that specialize in credit cards, homeowners, or new residents, among others. They then sell those names to others that wish to target certain groups. TRW, for instance, has a Families with Children database, which contains information on 19 million such households. Sources for those names and addresses include children's catalogs, magazine subscriptions, book clubs, birth records, and student directories. Exhibit 12–12 shows some of the ways that people in the database can be singled out. Marketers can send their mailing to any one of the categories, such as households with preschoolers, or those with income over $100,000 per year.

EXHIBIT 12–12   TRW Families with Children Database Selections

- Exact age
- Phone numbers
- Established household income
- Length of residence
- Dwelling type

- Gender
- Marital status
- Homeowners
- Direct mail responder
- Geography

Source: TRW Target Marketing Services, *Target Your Market,* Summer 1995.

Database marketing is likely to become even more prominent as marketers and consumers develop and explore the world of the Internet and commercial online services. When people agree to release personal information to companies with pages (sites) on the World Wide Web, that allows the companies to collect vast amounts of information on current and potential users of their products. In 1996, Diet Coke and NBC created an integrated marketing campaign that promoted the cola using the cast of the popular TV show "Friends." The campaign also included a Web site with a game in it. In order to play, however, users had to register their name and electronic mail address. In so doing, Coca-Cola collected thousands of names that it could reach personally in the future through their computers.[14]

One of the issues for database marketers concerns privacy. Should TRW have the right to pass along personal information to another company? Who really owns that information? While some argue that much of the information collected by database companies is available elsewhere—such as car ownership data that are based on driver's license records—when it comes to financial figures such as loans or credit payments, many object to the sale of the information.

The future of all forms of direct marketing looks promising. In particular, many companies are branching out onto the Internet, because the individualized communications offered by this medium are similar to the way that direct marketing operates. One company that has successfully transferred its knowledge and success to the Web is 1-800-FLOWERS. The company began in 1976 as a way for people to order flowers over the telephone. Today it generates $250 million in sales, with 10 percent coming from online users.

It is worth noting that for 1-800-FLOWERS, the people who buy online are not identical to those who pick up the phone. The online buyer tends to be somewhat younger and spends slightly less per order. Also, while telephone orders are split about equally between men and women, online the breakdown is 75 percent male. Not only does online direct selling provide a merchant with a new source of revenue (at significantly lower overhead than a full-time staff of telemarketing operators), it also allows the firm to reach new and different customers who might never have picked up the phone and made that toll-free call.[15]

RESET

1. Name the different types of direct marketing available, and explain their differences and similarities.
2. Why and how is database marketing used?
3. What are the differences between 1-800/ 1-888 and 1-900 phone numbers?

Public Relations

Traditionally, **public relations** is defined as being "concerned with how people feel about issues, products, and individual or corporate

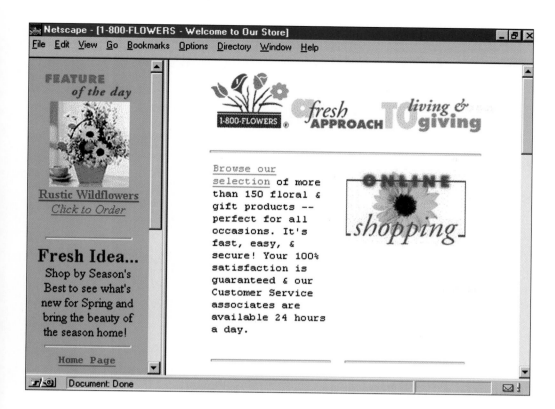

1-800-FLOWERS has successfully tapped the sales potential of the Internet. In addition to allowing customers to order flowers, the Web page also provides 1-800-FLOWERS with a format for promoting specials and displaying product offerings.

personalities."[16] Today, however, that definition really only describes one part of the public relations discipline, known as **corporate public relations,** which looks at a company's relationships with its noncustomer publics, including the media, investors, government, community groups, suppliers, distributors, and employees. People working in corporate public relations typically report directly to the top management of the company. In addition to promoting the company, corporate public relations is responsible for publicizing the company's position on an issue when that becomes necessary. For Nike, this meant taking a stand to refute criticism from labor organizations that its factories situated in southeast Asia were using child labor to produce its sports apparel and footwear. The company agreed to monitor its suppliers more closely to show its firm commitment to supporting good working conditions for all of its employees.

The other type of public relations, which tends to be more involved with integrated communications efforts, is known as **marketing public relations.** Although its basic function is similar to that of corporate public relations—managing the relationship of a company with both its customer and noncustomer publics—

there is one important difference: The purpose of marketing public relations is specifically to help *marketing* interact better with those groups. This type of public relations often works closely with sales promotion, engineering the push–pull effect mentioned earlier. That is, while promotions push a product into the store, public relations helps to pull people in by publicizing the promotion.[17]

When public relations is understood as a means of encouraging people to feel good about a company and its brands, its role in marketing becomes essential. The ways in which public relations works are numerous, involving many of the tools of communication employed by other elements of integrated communication. These tools include simple *press releases* sent to the print media to let them know what is going on with the company or brand, *video news releases* designed to inform television stations, *direct mail* to key opinion leaders in a given field, and *sponsored events* to bring together relevant groups and tell them all about the product.

When McDonald's launched its now-defunct McLean burger in the early 1990s, it used video news releases that had a taped feature explaining how the leaner, lower-fat

Nike's corporate public relations group had its hands full when criticism over the company's use of child labor in southeast Asia ballooned into full-scale protests.

burger was different from the traditional variety. The release was taken up by many TV stations, which aired part or all of the information in their local newscasts as if they had prepared it themselves. More recently, McDonald's made extensive use of this type of communications for the launch of its Arch Deluxe burger. It set up special events in 40 cities across the country, knowing they would generate considerable media interest. These events included a special tasting for reporters, franchisees, and suppliers at Radio City Music Hall in New York City, at which Ronald McDonald appeared on stage.

Press and video news releases are important, but they are not the only ways public relations can be used to help sell a product or service. Some companies send out *newsletters* that can either focus on company events and products or include more broad-ranging material about the overall industry. In either case, these letters are one way to let customers know that the company is working hard and doing a good job. In some cases, a company will produce *books* either directly or indirectly related to its field. The Michelin tour guides are one such example. Although these guides have become famous in their own right as a valuable source of travel information, they, at the same time, help enhance the tire

company's reputation as being knowledgeable about the travel industry.

Anytime a key executive from a company or a famous personality makes a *public presentation* of some kind, that too is a form of public relations, which helps create or enhance the individual's or company's image as important enough to merit an invitation to speak somewhere. Indeed, one of the key roles of an actor's or sports star's agent is to undertake the public relations effort to help his or her client's image (and, thereby, boost the famous person's salary). Exhibit 12–13 lists some of the other kinds of tools used in public relations.

Public relations also can be used to announce changes in other marketing elements. When Pepsi-Cola altered its soda cans in 190 markets outside of the U.S. it spent $500 million over a two-year period to do so, a good proportion of it on integrated marketing efforts that received considerable publicity in the media. For example, to reinforce the new color of the cans—changing from red and blue to all blue—the company spent $200,000 to paint an Air France Concorde plane that same color, mostly to be seen by 400 journalists reporting on the event. It also linked up with Russia's Mir space station, where Russian astronauts consumed the beverage, and it spent $10 million to sponsor programs and events on the global music channel MTV. All of this was part of the company's belief that, in the words of the senior vice president of international sales and marketing, "owning blue will give us a significant competitive advantage in the market."[18]

Public relations efforts are perhaps most evident when a company is in trouble. A classic example of a positive public relations effort in the face of trouble is Johnson & Johnson's handling of the tampering with and tainting of its Tylenol medication in the 1980s. Although the company had to pull the product off all store shelves and lost substantial sales in the short term, its ability to reassure customers that it was taking the necessary actions and putting customer needs and safety above everything else helped to restore people's confidence in the company and its product sooner rather than later.

A contrasting example of how a public relations miscue can hurt a company was seen in the early 1990s from Intel Corporation. Faced with reports of flaws in its Pentium computer chip, which the company had worked very hard to turn from a generic, nameless product into a much sought-after brand, Intel decided that the situation was not that serious and that it did not need to take any immediate action.

Two weeks later, one of its main buyers, IBM, announced that it was holding back shipments of computers with the Pentium chip because of their unreliability. This sent the company into a tailspin as consumer confidence in the product plummeted. Consumers began to voice their complaints, both in person and through the Internet, passing on their unhappy experiences to others, thereby putting off prospective new customers for the company. Intel's failure to respond to the complaints, to react to what both its individual and corporate customers were saying, cost it dearly. By not relating to the public in a time of crisis, the company suffered not only short-term financial losses but also a long-term loss of consumer confidence.[19]

Benefits of Public Relations

There are three benefits to public relations: enhanced corporate image, stronger relationship with customers, and broader dispersion of messages.

ENHANCED CORPORATE IMAGE   When Discover Card issued a press release announcing its support of the Smithsonian's 150th Anniversary Tour, it was not only doing good in sponsoring that nonprofit organization, it was

EXHIBIT 12–13   Tools for Public Relations

Advisory groups
Annual reports
Brochures
Company newsletters
Conferences
Educational materials
Hotlines
Infomercials
Lobbying
Media kits
News releases/video news
   releases
Press conferences
Public service announcements
   (PSAs)

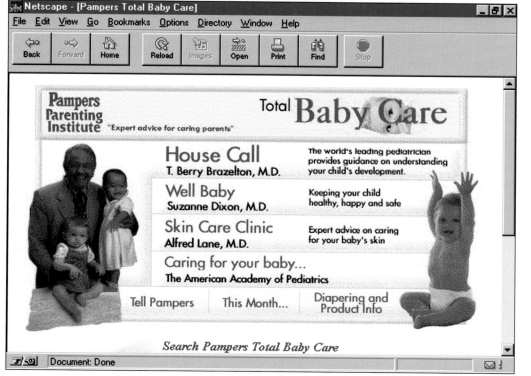

Through the Pampers Parenting Institute's Total Baby Care Web site, Procter & Gamble successfully connects its Pampers product with experts in the field of child care. By communicating concern for and knowledge of the health and welfare of babies, P & G enhances both its reputation and the image of its product.

showing itself to its various publics as a good "corporate citizen." One of the critical uses for public relations is when potential disaster strikes. After AT&T announced that it would be laying off 40,000 employees, it received considerable negative publicity. The company used public relations, in the form of full-page ads in major newspapers explaining that the cuts would probably not be so severe. It included a toll-free telephone number for anyone to call if they were looking to hire white-collar employees. AT&T showed the public that it cared about its soon-to-be ex-employees, thereby hoping to enhance its image as a good corporation.

STRONGER RELATIONSHIP WITH CUSTOMERS

The tools of public relations are diverse enough that they can be used differentially to help a company reach its various audiences. Direct mail to stockholders might be one form of publicity, while promoting the sponsorship of a good cause might help current users feel more loyal to the brand or company. Public relations is a valuable means of reinforcing current attitudes and behaviors, acting as a further reminder (beyond the product itself) that the person has made a wise decision in purchasing the item. This may be as simple as publicizing Campbell's Soup's Labels for Education program, where soup can labels are collected for school equipment, or as complex as generating publicity for the "reunion" for Saturn car owners to reinforce their good feelings about their cars.

BROADER DISPERSION OF MESSAGES

Although it might seem somewhat deceptive, many companies use public relations to place their messages where traditional marketing tools might not be acceptable. Rather than creating an ad that would have to explain in great detail the advantages and disadvantages of its fat-free ingredient Olestra, Procter & Gamble sent out news releases that were picked up by newspapers and TV stations across the country that then produced features about the new products, relying on information supplied by the company itself. In this way, consumers believe they are receiving independent, unbiased information from the media as opposed to receiving what they feel are the known biases of an advertisement.

Drawbacks of Public Relations

Chief drawbacks to public relations are as follows: short message life, difficulty of changing behavior, and lack of measurability.

SHORT MESSAGE LIFE   While a successful ad campaign can continue in only slightly modified form for many years, public relations is premised on producing *news* about a product or company. It therefore requires constant change and new information that must be sent out on a regular basis if it is to have any effect. At the same time, if a company is too predictable in its public relations efforts, the media are likely to ignore the message completely, seeing it simply as just another release from Company X.

DIFFICULTY OF CHANGING BEHAVIOR   If critics of advertising claim that it is hard to make people think or do something different after they receive the message, the problem is even greater for public relations. While an ad or piece of direct mail or sales promotion appeals directly to the consumer to take a certain action, public relations is more indirect, trying to make people feel good about the product or company. It is more likely, therefore, to help change or reinforce attitudes rather than actual behavior—at least if it is not used in conjunction with more direct appeals.

LACK OF MEASURABILITY   Although public relations is used as a marketing tool to help build sales, it is almost impossible to assess the results in a quantitative fashion. Nevertheless, some companies have instituted fairly sophisticated methods to do so. Often, it involves tracking the mentions of a brand or company in the media—either just simple names or analysis of the content itself. Another option is to conduct interviews with the campaign's target audience to assess whether the campaign is helping change attitudes or behavior. And now, with the growth and development of the World Wide Web, there are special "search engines" or software programs and services that can be set up automatically to go through electronic versions of magazines, newspapers, or reports to find instances where a brand or company is cited. It should be noted, however, that these simple numeric counts do not show what kind of effect the message had on the desired audience or, indeed, whether the audience was actually reached by the message.

Other Tools of Integrated Marketing Communications

In addition to the "Big 3" of sales promotion, direct marketing, and public relations, there are several other useful tools available to marketers to communicate with their customers and prospects. Two of these—licensing and sponsorship—are considered here.

Licensing

Product **licensing** is a contractual agreement between a person or company that has a brand, trademark, or personality with sales or promotional value, and another party that wants to use that asset. Product licensing can be used to sell products that feature a legally protected name, logo, design, or likeness. It can also tie in with the owner of the licensed property for promotional purposes. The primary purpose of licensing is to extend and build the life of the brand name or property—a TV show, movie, team, or the like.

This notion of extending the life and power of a brand name or property by licensing it to other companies is certainly not new. Walt Disney's Mickey Mouse and Cinderella characters have been in toy stores for almost as long as their 40+ years of existence. The health care company Bayer has been producing Flintstone's vitamins under license for more than 25 years. In recent times, however, licensing has become a multibillion dollar industry, estimated to be worth $70 billion in 1995. The key is to make the link between the two companies or brands seem as natural as possible. For example, when Celestial Seasonings herbal tea licensed its name to Warner Lambert for a new brand of cough drops, it was expected that consumers would believe that the health product would be as soothing and comforting as the beverage.[20]

As shown in Exhibit 12–14, licensing occurs primarily in two areas: entertainment and

sports. A large portion of licensing deals involve children's products. This is due to two factors. First, the children's market is constantly changing, as older children grow out of kid-oriented products and younger ones start to want them. Second, children are very demanding consumers, even if they do not control the spending directly. When a six-year-old begs his mother for yet another item emblazoned with the Power Rangers, his pleas are frequently not resisted, pleasing one little boy and ringing up another $10 at the cash register—and $1 billion in merchandise sales for "Mighty Morphin Power Rangers" related products in 1994 alone.[21]

Another example of successful merchandising through licensing is the Star Wars trilogy of films ("Star Wars," "The Empire Strikes Back," and "The Return of the Jedi"). From the time the movies were first released back in 1977 until their re-release in 1997, the total revenues generated had reached $4 billion, of which only $1.3 billion came from the box office. Other sources of revenue included videos ($500 million), CD-ROM and video games

---

EXHIBIT 12–14   Licensing Sales by Type of Property

TYPE OF LICENSING	PERCENT OF TOTAL LICENSING SALES	SALES ($ BILLIONS)
Entertainment/Character	25%	$17.22
Sports	20	13.80
Brand names/Trademarks	19	13.15
Fashion	17	12.04
Art	7	4.88
Celebrities	4	2.65
Toys/Games	4	2.73
Publishing	2	1.56
Music	1	1.05
Nonprofit	1	0.68
Other	—	0.26
Total	**100%**	**$70.02**

Source: "The Licensing Letter," *Promo,* June 1995, 34.

EXHIBIT 12–15 Many compa-
nies use licensing agreements
as a way of creating brand
recognition and generating additional exposure and distribution for their products.

Lion King" and "Toy Story" in the mid-1990s not only stole some of McDonald's thunder but also improved its image in the minds of consumers by associating itself with top-quality products. Burger King was so successful with this kind of partnership that McDonald's agreed to sign a 10-year licensing deal with Disney to preempt future successes by its chief rival. Exhibit 12–15 shows a few of the many products that have utilized the marketing opportunity provided by licensing agreements. Part of the power of licensed products lies in the additional distribution and exposure they offer the brand. When McDonald's distributed Gotham City glasses linked to the movie "Batman Forever" in all of its U.S. stores and spent $35 million of its own money to promote them, that was highly beneficial to the movie studio, Warner Brothers.

The use of licensing to take a product into new categories is being tried by more and more brands, beyond those in entertainment and sports. For example, Coca-Cola now has more than 3,000 products bearing its logo, produced by more than 300 licensees in 30 different countries.[23] There is always the risk, however, that a bad match between licensor and licensee can end up harming both parties. For example, the motorcycle manufacturer Harley-Davidson went to court to try to end its licensing relationship with Lorillard tobacco after the company realized that its target audience was no longer attracted to or by cigarettes. The tobacco company, which has spent $75 million on royalties, is unwilling to let go of such a profitable linkage.

($300 million), toys and playing cards ($1.2 billion), clothes and accessories ($300 million), and books and comics ($300 million).[22]

One of the dangers that child-oriented licensees must face is potential criticism for taking advantage of the young. Although the 1990 Children's Television Act prevents toy commercials from being aired during any shows involving those characters, toy companies continue to have widespread influence on what is produced because they often are the largest buyers of commercial time in these programs. However, while toy manufacturers hope that the licensing opportunities from popular children's shows will bring in large revenues, that is not always guaranteed. In the mid-1990s shows such as "Animaniacs" and "Aladdin" proved popular on the small screen, but children were uninterested in the licensed characters sitting on store shelves.

Sports licensing is growing rapidly, too. NFL Properties, the licensing and marketing arm of the National Football League, enjoys $3.1 billion worldwide from its licensing deals. The well-known firearms company, Remington, is attempting to expand its product lines and enhance its image by licensing its name to camping and outdoor equipment.

Some companies look to licensing to enhance their own image. This is evident with Burger King, the perennial second-player in the burger business. Its various tie-ins with highly successful Disney movies such as "The

Sponsorship

As consumers are bombarded with advertising messages in traditional media such as radio or newspapers, marketers are looking for more and more ways to place their brand names before the public. **Sponsorship** offers such an alternative. It is defined as a company paying a set amount of money to have its name or its brand's name placed at the head of an event title or as the designated sponsor of the event. Examples include the Virginia Slims Tennis Tournament, Busch Classic race car event, and the FedEx Orange Bowl in college football. Sponsorship is similar to advertising in that it has a commercial objective: increasing brand or corporate name awareness. But a sponsoring company may also be acting to improve goodwill or enhance its image.

Like advertising, sponsorship tends to be used to reach a wide audience. And often, the sponsor's name appears in all the media where the event is being publicized. A fairly new way for companies to become sponsors is by paying to rename sports stadiums. Pepsi-Cola paid $50 million over a 20-year period to rename the arena in Denver the Pepsi Center; the famous Candlestick Park in San Francisco is now 3Com Park; and the Chicago Bulls play in the United Center in Chicago (named after the hometown airline). The attraction of this type of sponsorship for companies is the chance not only to be seen by people attending the actual event but also by those who watch it on television.

The secondary audiences may be more important than the primary ones. Besides the vast media audience sitting at home, corporate sponsorship can be a powerful form of public rela-

tions. That is, the company sponsoring an event may wish to impress stockholders or community leaders or employees. The tobacco giant Philip Morris is the largest sponsor of dance performances in the U.S., along with many other arts events, a fact which it hopes will help soften antagonism toward it as the seller of a highly controversial, unhealthy product. Increasingly, companies are moving from simply being listed as a sponsor to having their name on the event itself. This is seen clearly in the football bowl games, which now include the FedEx Orange Bowl and the Mobil Cotton Bowl.

Types of Sponsorship

Sports sponsorships account for about two-thirds of the $5.4 billion that marketers spent on this type of marketing communication in 1995. For example, Anheuser-Busch spent $25 million to make its Budweiser beer an official sponsor of the 1998 World Cup soccer championship in France, while its chief rival, Miller Brewing Company, spent $41 million to be the

Tobacco giant Philip Morris reaps public relations benefits from its long-term sponsorship of dance performances in the United States. In addition to improving its image among supporters of dance, Philip Morris can also generate indirect benefits among the general public by connecting its name with this art form.

title sponsor of the Milwaukee stadium for a 20-year period.[24] Music/entertainment tours represent another 10 percent.

In the area of sports, some of the biggest activity occurs every two years with the Olympic Games. Here, companies sponsor everything from a complete event to a team to the broadcast rights in a particular country. In 1996, companies paid up to $40 million to display the five interlinked Olympic rings in their ads that show the public they are an "official" sponsor of something. The reason that firms are willing to pay so much money is that the Games are watched by an estimated 3.5 *billion* people worldwide, making them one of the biggest opportunities for reaching a global audience. The results can be quite impressive. After Fuji sponsored the Olympics in 1984, it saw its U.S. market share in the photographic category rise from 2 percent to 10 percent. Visa saw a 100 percent increase in the number of Norwegian cardholders after its sponsorship of the 1994 Winter Games in Lillehammer, Norway.[25]

Companies that choose not to be official sponsors may take a more devious route into the spotlight by using a practice known as **ambush marketing**. Here, a company may craft its message or bombard the public at the time of the event to make people think that it is in fact the official sponsor. For example, it may sponsor the broadcasting of the event or hold special promotions during that time. This has been done successfully by companies such as American Express against Visa or Nike against Reebok.

Sometimes companies are criticized for taking on commercial sponsors. The Smithsonian Institution, for example, has relied on companies such as Intel, Orkin, and Ford Motor Company to sponsor special exhibitions. Critics dislike the commercialization of a nonprofit museum, particularly if the sponsor takes advantage of the link-up for commercial ends. Ford contributed $5 million to an Ocean Planet exhibition but then placed a Ford Explorer vehicle in the opening area. The concern here is that nonprofit organizations will start to determine their offerings solely by their commercial desirability and appeal, rather than consumer interest.[26]

Another area where sponsorship may be criticized is in the predominance of socially undesirable products as sponsors. Indeed, Philip Morris Companies and Anheuser-Busch are the two biggest sponsoring companies in the country, spending $110 million and $115 million, respectively, in 1995. Critics see this as a way for them to promote their brands via broadcasts when they are not legally allowed to

EXHIBIT 12–16   Cause Marketing Deals in 1995

COMPANY	CAUSE	AMOUNT DONATED
Bayer Corporation	American Heart Association	$ 90,000
Clairol Inc.	National Parks & Conservation Assn.	75,000
Great Brands of Europe (Volvic)	World Wildlife Fund	250,000
Heinz USA (Baby products)	Children's Miracle Network	530,000
Inter-Continental Hotels and Resorts	UNICEF	1,000,000
Lane Bryant	Special Olympics International	50,000
Mattel Inc.	Children's Miracle Network	300,000
Toys R Us	Juvenile Diabetes Foundation	100,000
Tropicana Products (Twister)	Comic Relief	300,000
U.S. Tobacco Co.	National Volunteer Fire Council	1,000,000

Note: Some of these sponsorships were renewals; all were committed in the first six months of 1996.
Source: International Events Group, *IEG Sponsorship Report,* 17 June 1996, 8.

do so through advertising. Several countries are considering broad bans on all forms of promotion by alcohol and tobacco companies, including sponsorship.

The use of sponsorship to enhance a company's "goodwill" among either the general public or special audiences is growing rapidly. Sometimes known as **cause marketing,** this type of sponsorship offers a powerful way to gain visibility by associating with a well-known cause. Examples are shown in Exhibit 12–16. As you can see, while some links might be obvious, such as the pharmaceutical giant Bayer Corporation sponsoring the American Heart Association, or the toy maker Mattel sponsoring the Children's Miracle Network, others are less immediately apparent. We see Clairol, a beauty products company, sponsoring the National Parks and Conservation Association, and Inter-continental Hotels sponsoring UNICEF. Be assured, however, that rather than being simply an expression of corporate largesse, there was probably a strategic reason for these commitments. Clairol can make the claim that it is not only keeping women beautiful but also the land, while Intercontinental Hotels may be promoting both an international and family image by sponsoring an international organization that looks after the needs of children.

Sponsorship is not a practice restricted to large companies alone, nor to just the consumer market. When you open your local newspapers, you are likely to see town festivals or parades sponsored by a local car dealership or hometown firm. Moreover, sponsorship can be extremely valuable for business-to-business marketing efforts, helping involve a sales force or local retailers in a big event or promotion. Xerox, for example, used the 400 hotel rooms it was given for being a major Olympic sponsor in the summer 1996 games in Atlanta as sales incentives for its various business units.[27]

Product Placement

Although technically not a type of sponsorship, the placement of a branded product in a movie or TV show is another way that companies try to increase awareness or prestige for their brands and, therefore, generate sales. From the time that Reese's Pieces first appeared in the movie "E.T." in 1982 and sales of the candy

"Mr. Jenkins and Tanqueray encourage you to support the AIDS Rides."

Tanqueray's American AIDS Rides

Orlando to Miami, May 15-17   San Francisco to Los Angeles, June 2-8
Philadelphia to DC, June 21-23   Twin Cities to Chicago, July 1-6   Boston to New York, September 5-8
For more information, call (800) 825-1000.

subsequently skyrocketed, companies have been using product placement very successfully. When Tom Cruise wore Aviator sunglasses in the 1986 movie "Top Gun," sales rose by 27 percent. Nike witnessed significant sales following the release of the film "Forrest Gump" in 1995, where the lead character, played by Tom Hanks, wore that brand of running shoes when he became a serious runner.[28] In each case, the company paid the movie studio in order to put its product in the scene.

The increased use of product placement has resulted in a hierarchy being developed for the type of placement. The least impactful is when the brand appears somewhere in the scene (such as IBM computers or Budweiser beer).

Cause marketing provides companies with a way to offer financial support to worthy causes. Tanqueray's support of the AIDS ride, for example, enhances the company's visibility and generates goodwill among the general public and among the gay and lesbian community specifically.

More powerful effects are seen when the actor uses the item (such as The Club anti-theft device in "Batman Forever"). The strongest placement occurs when the actor actually mentions the brand, as Hanks did in "Forrest Gump." This is seen as an implied endorsement of the product and will often generate sales. Although some may consider this a form of subliminal seduction (as it is not overtly done, like an advertisement), most consumers do not seem to find it objectionable.

R E S E T

1. **What are some of the tools of communication used by people working in public relations?**
2. **What criticism do child-oriented licensees face? Do you think it is a legitimate criticism?**
3. **What is ambush marketing? Why would a marketer use this tactic?**

Scheduling an Integrated Marketing Communications Plan

Once all of the tools of an integrated marketing communications plan have been agreed upon, scheduling them is not all that different from the way that a "traditional" media plan is arranged and executed. The integrated effort may be more challenging, if only because there could be more diverse elements requiring careful coordination. For example, a luxury car manufacturer such as Lexus might first send out videos to key prospects prior to the official launch of a new model, inviting them to come in for a special preview event at the local dealership. That could be followed with television and magazine ads that introduce the new car to the broader marketplace. Then, personalized invitations could be mailed to those who showed up for the preview party inviting them in for a test drive, followed by a promotional offer of $500 cash back if a new car is bought in the next 30 days.

As we have seen throughout the chapter, timing can be critical for all integrated marketing communications tools—from how long a promotion lasts, to when someone receives a piece of direct mail, to the date that a video news release is issued. Just as with advertising, integrated communications are most likely to be effective if the messages reach the customer when they are receptive to hearing or seeing them. For example, someone is more likely to sample a product in a grocery store if it is close to lunch time. Direct mail offers for a new credit card will probably be noticed more during times of high expenditure, such as before the winter holiday season (Thanksgiving and Christmas).

In sum, the scheduling of an integrated marketing communications plan requires some forethought and consideration to ensure, once again, that all of its elements are truly working together and are presenting the target audience with a consistent message that will lead them to take the desired action.

Measuring the Impact of an Integrated Communications Plan

Depending on the tools used, it is easier in some ways to measure how successful an integrated plan is than one that simply uses advertising. This is because for real integration to occur, there must be some type of direct interaction with the target that requires a response. It could be the redemption of a coupon, attendance at a sponsored event, or a positive response to a telemarketing call. And as we noted at the beginning of the chapter, the savviest users of integrated marketing communications use it to establish or enlarge a database of information on their current or prospective customers. Once that is in place, it becomes fairly easy to monitor the success of various integrated efforts and to see how changes in a plan can impact marketplace results. Although there are still uncontrollable factors, such as the health of the economy or the weather, integrated communications that have some kind of response mechanism built in help marketers establish and maintain a closer relationship with their customers and learn more about what helps sell more products.

SUMMARY

An integrated marketing communications plan is designed to take advantage of the synergy of voices that can be generated by the variety of tools available. These include advertising, sales promotions, direct marketing, public relations, licensing, and sponsorship. In this chapter we discussed the non-advertising methods of communication.

Sales promotions are able to have a direct impact on customer behavior. Designed to encourage immediate, often short-term, sales, promotions may be aimed either at consumers or at the trade (distributors and retailers). The former promotions are designed to "pull" people to the store to purchase the product; the latter aim to "push" the product to the trade users. Spending on promotions has soared in recent years because the short-term results are readily apparent. The response is also measurable at the bottom line. Such promotions are often used to encourage brand switching and trial. The drawbacks are that the effects are brief; the brand's image or equity can be harmed; and profits may in fact be lowered because each unit is sold at a discount instead of full price.

Coupons are the most popular type of consumer sales promotion technique. More than 300 billion are issued each year in the U.S., although only 2 percent of these are redeemed by consumers. Electronic coupons are growing increasingly popular, particularly at the checkout. Another in-store promotion is product sampling, where people can actually try the product. This is particularly popular for new product introductions. Other types of sales promotions include refunds and rebates, continuity programs, and contests and sweepstakes. Trade and retailer promotions usually feature some kind of price discount for those groups.

Direct marketing is designed to sell products or services directly to the customers. Messages are delivered to individuals rather than mass audiences. This is one of the benefits of the approach. In addition, responses are easily measured and can be collected to form a database that may be used on subse-quent occasions. Customer feedback is easy to gather. This approach is expensive compared to mass advertising, and far fewer people can be reached. It is quite easy for the recipients to ignore.

Direct marketing approaches include direct mail, telemarketing, and in-person selling. About 80 million direct mailings are sent each year. If they are not properly targeted, they will be seen as junk mail and discarded. To target correctly, the right list of names must be used. Telemarketing has grown increasingly popular, through toll-free 1-800 and 1-888 numbers or paid-for 1-900 numbers. Telepromotions have developed that make phone calls automatically. Thanks to technological advances, it is simple to create a database, allowing marketers to collect and store demographic and lifestyle information on their current and potential customers. This database can be used later on for future marketing activities. There are privacy concerns, however, regarding who owns such personal information and what use can be made of it.

Public relations can be divided into corporate, which focuses on how a company relates to its noncustomer publics, and marketing, which manages the company's relationships with both customers and non-customers. Its role is to make people feel good about a company and its brands. To do so, it uses tools such as press or video releases, newsletters or other publications, or presentations to key audiences. Public relations is helpful in enhancing the corporate image, strengthening relationships with customers, and disseminating messages more broadly than through traditional advertising. The drawbacks are that the messages tend to be brief, they usually are not able to change behavior, and their impact is very hard to measure.

Other important tools for integrated marketing communications include licensing and sponsorship. Licensing extends a brand's name by selling it to companies to use in other areas or on other products. The link between the two brands or companies should be self-evident to consumers. Entertainment and sports are the two biggest areas where this practice occurs. There is a danger in the licensing of child-oriented products that this will be seen as too commercial and not in the best interests of a vulnerable audience.

Sponsorship is becoming increasingly valued by marketers. Here, companies pay to have their name or a brand's name designated as the sponsor of an event or as the supporter of a location. It helps to increase corporate or brand awareness and to improve goodwill or enhance the company image. In addition to the people who see the sponsor's name at the event or in any publicity generated, sponsorship can be influential with other significant audiences, such as company employees, stockholders, or government officials. The Olympics are considered the premiere sponsorship opportunity in the sports arena. Companies that do not pay to be involved in this may try to benefit from all the attendant publicity through ambush marketing activities. In the entertainment arena, product placement in movies can give brands additional valued exposure that can generate considerable sales if the movie proves popular at the box office.

The scheduling of an integrated plan must be done with care so as to ensure that there is a synergy of communications voices. Timing is everything here, so that all the messages reach the target at the right time and place when receptivity is likely to be greatest. All elements of the plan should incorporate some type of measurable response, such as a 1-800 number, a coupon, or an interactive online ad, in order to determine which elements of the program are most effective in achieving the communication objectives.

KEY TERMS

sales promotion, 366

consumer promotions, 366

pull strategy, 366

trade promotions, 366

push strategy, 366

forward buying, 369

advertising allowance, 370

dealer listing, 370

coupon, 370

face value, 370

sampling, 372

refunds and rebates, 373

continuity program, 373

contests, 373

sweepstakes, 374

trade allowance, 374

spiff, 374

retailer promotions, 375

direct marketing, 375

direct mail advertising, 378

merge and purge, 378

telemarketing, 379

telepromotions, 379

database marketing, 380

public relations, 382

corporate public relations, 383

marketing public relations, 383

licensing, 387

sponsorship, 388

ambush marketing, 390

cause marketing, 391

1. What is the difference between consumer sales promotions and trade sales promotions?

2. What are the benefits and drawbacks of sales promotions?

3. What is the chief purpose of direct marketing?

4. If direct marketing provides greater measurability and accountability than advertising, why don't more marketers use it more often?

5. How do marketing public relations and sales promotion work together to create more sales?

6. What are the benefits and drawbacks of public relations?

7. What types of products or services might be appropriate licensees for a breakfast cereal such as Cheerios?

8. What are the various types of sponsorship opportunities available to a marketer?

9. What are the differences in the ways that sales promotion, direct marketing, and public relations influence consumers?

10. Why is it fairly easy to measure the impact of an integrated marketing communications plan?

DISCUSSION QUESTIONS

1. Imagine you are in charge of media on the Windex glass cleaner account. Consider how you would use the tools of integrated marketing communications to develop a campaign for this brand.

2. As the brand manager for Soft Sheen hair products, which are used primarily by African American women, you have been charged with coming up with an event to introduce a line extension of soaps and hand care items. Present three alternative events that would be effective for this product and target.

3. Imagine your company, a large health care products manufacturer, is being accused by a pressure group of advertising its products in violent TV shows that the group claims are not "family friendly." How might you use public relations (both corporate and marketing) to deal with this situation? What other integrated marketing communications tools might you employ?

interactive discovery lab

1. Save all of the direct mail that you receive in a one-week period and analyze it, looking at how well each company has targeted you and how persuasive the message is in influencing you to take action. For those that are ineffective, explain why.

2. Collect all of the FSIs from your local Sunday newspaper and examine them to find the following: average face value, average time before expiration, and number by product category. Before you undertake the analysis, guess what the numbers will be for each answer and see how close you come!

3. Take a single issue of a newspaper or a magazine and go through it carefully to find every statement in which a company is quoted. Determine whether that statement can be categorized as corporate public relations or marketing public relations.

Discover® Card:
"The American Family. DISCOVERed."

PRODUCT SERVICE CATEGORY

Discover® Card—issued by a business unit of Morgan Stanley, Dean Witter, Discover & Co.—is a general purpose credit and financial services card that is accepted nationwide wherever the NOVUS® sign is displayed.

MARKETING OVERVIEW

The credit card industry continues to be increasingly competitive, as brands seek to differentiate themselves through distinctive card features as well as distinctive brand advertising.

Exhibit A–1

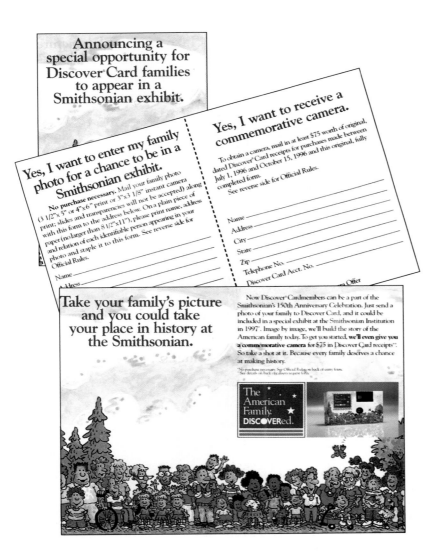

Discover Card's image has been that of a value offering in the marketplace. This positioning was first embraced when Discover Card was introduced over 10 years ago as a wholly owned subsidiary of another value-oriented enterprise, Sears. Although Discover Card has now been independently owned and operated for four years, the Card's core positioning and core feature (the Cashback Bonus® Award) have remained value focused.

"Value" is an attribute that has many positive connotations for consumers, including "smart" and "thrifty." Discover Card research has shown, however, that the Card's Sears heritage has often added a less-than-positive connotation on value.

A sponsorship—a strategic alliance with an entity that would have a positive rub-off effect—was identified as a way to help overshadow the brand's Sears heritage, enhance Discover Card's image, and increase usage of the Card. Special consideration, however, had to be given to the entity with which Discover Card aligned. It had to be one that complemented, while at the same time elevated, what Discover Card stands for to its members. This key insight into Discover Card members would drive this program.

PROMOTION OBJECTIVES

- Elevate Discover Card's image.
- Achieve an above-average response on the direct mail piece, promotional merchandise offer, and photo sweepstakes.

PROMOTION STRATEGY AND TACTICS

The target audience for this campaign was current Discover Card members, both men and women, ages 18–49.

The key Card member insight was identified from Discover Card research undertaken over the past several years. This guiding insight is that, characteristically, Card members have a strong work ethic, have family-oriented values, are very proud, and generally have a strong sense of patriotism. They respect and want to preserve a sense of heritage and community.

This insight into Discover Card members is what guided the selection of an alliance partner, a partner that mirrored many of the values that Card members embrace, thus making members feel better about the Discover Card and, in the process, making them feel better about themselves. The Smithsonian Institution was about to celebrate its 150th anniversary. This was identified as an ideal opportunity for Discover Card to create a strategic alliance that would elevate the Card's image. Key among a number of initiatives, a promotion was created to reach families, drive usage, and raise awareness of the Discover Card sponsorship of the Smithsonian anniversary celebration. The promotion was executed during the third quarter of 1996, and the entire Smithsonian sponsorship ran over a two-year period. Promotion elements included the following:

1. **"The American Family. DISCOVERed." Sweepstakes.** This promotion offered Card members a chance to have their family picture displayed at the Smithsonian. Three thousand lucky families were randomly selected as winners. The sweepstakes event was promoted through television, billing inserts, and national print in the third quarter of 1996. Exhibits A–1 and A–2 show, respectively, a brochure and a print ad announcing this sweepstakes offer. A preliminary sketch of a television ad used to promote the sweepstakes is shown in Exhibit A–3.

TAKE YOUR FAMILY'S PICTURE AND YOU COULD TAKE YOUR PLACE IN HISTORY AT THE SMITHSONIAN.

THE AMERICAN FAMILY. DISCOVERed.

TO APPLY CALL 1-800-DISCOVER

Exhibit A–2

Exhibit A–3

2. **Commemorative Camera Premium Offer.** Card members were offered a free disposable camera when they sent in Discover Card receipts totaling $75. This offer was promoted through television, billing inserts, and national print in the third quarter of 1996.

3. **Back-to-School Shopping Mall Events**. At selected malls, families could have their photo taken and receive a Family Music CD when they showed $50 in Discover Card receipts. At these events, children could draw pictures of their families for a chance to be 1 of 10 selected for exhibit inclusion. One family trip to Washington, DC, was awarded over the course of the mall events. This effort was supported with local newspaper and radio; a newspaper ad promoting one of the mall events is shown in Exhibit A–4.

4. **Celebration on the National Mall.** Discover Card was a lead sponsor of a venue featuring family activities at a celebration for the Smithsonian's 150th anniversary. Celebrities from the Discover Card campaign, including Trisha Yearwood and Scott Hamilton, were at the event site to meet visitors. The activities offered at this celebration included family tree planting, a family mural drawing wall, and hand castings. Exhibits A–5 and A–6 show scenes from the National Mall celebration; a brochure used to promote the event is displayed in Exhibit A–7.

5. **"Great Smithsonian Trivia Challenge" Direct Mail Piece.** This direct mail piece was send to Card members in an effort to make them aware of the Discover Card sponsorship initiative and to encourage them to use their Discover Card. The "Trivia Challenge" grand prize was a trip to Washington, DC. The elements included in

Exhibit A–4

Exhibit A–5

Exhibit A–6

Exhibit A–7

this direct mail piece are presented in Exhibit A–8.

All of these promotions were supported through national and local media. The media strategy and selection were driven by insights into the Card members that identified the circumstances and time at which they would be most open to the messages. National magazines were used for wide exposure and impact. Although most were family oriented, the magazines reflected the diversity of Discover Card's members; the selections included *Smithsonian Magazine, Newsweek, People, TV Guide,* and *Reader's Digest.* Local print was utilized to drive traffic into local mall events. The placement of ads in Friday/Sunday entertainment sections was

Exhibit A-8

all-important because ads in these sections could reach people as they were making their weekend plans. Direct mail included in monthly statements provided extensive program details and special offers for Card members.

RESULTS

Objective: Elevate Discover Card's image.

Results: Roughly 50 percent of research respondents indicated that Discover Card's sponsorship of the Smithsonian made them feel more positive about the Card. Over 25 percent of these same respondents indicated that they would "almost always" choose a product or service offered by a company that was involved with the Smithsonian over one that was not.

Objective: Achieve an above-average response on the direct mail promotion, the promotional merchandise offer, and the photo sweepstakes.

Results: Response to the "Great Smithsonian Trivia Challenge" direct mail piece exceeded goal by 900 percent; response on the camera premium offer exceeded goal by 100 percent; and response on the photo sweepstakes exceeded goal by 45 percent.

SUMMARY

The "American Family. DISCOVERed." promotion maximized Discover Card's $10MM sponsorship investment in the 150th anniversary of the Smithsonian to achieve the following goals: elevate brand image, heighten consumer and trade awareness, and increase usage among existing Card members.

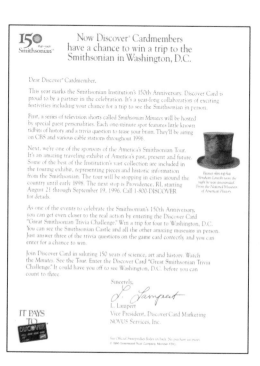

Enter the Discover® Card "Great Smithsonian Trivia Challenge."
Three correct answers could have you flying to Washington, D.C.

Here's your chance to see the amazing Smithsonian and all its treasures up close. Just answer the following five questions by scratching off the square that corresponds with your best guess. If three or more answers reveal the word "correct," you are eligible to enter our random drawing. Simply fill out all the information to the right, fold the card in half and seal. Then, close your eyes, click your heels and send it off for a chance to win the grand prize or one of 20 "America's Smithsonian Exhibition Catalogs."

Please print:

Name

Address

State/ZIP

Phone

Discover Card Account No.

FOLD HERE

1. Who wore these ruby slippers?
   Dorothy   Toto   Grandma Gertrude

2. What stuffed animal was named after a president?
   Garfield the Cat   Teddy Bear   Henry the Elephant

3. Name the world's largest diamond?
   Charity   Old Faithful   Hope

4. Who were the first people to fly across the U.S.?
   The Wright Brothers   The Correctomundos   Wrong Way Tillman

5. Of the original colonies, how many signed the Declaration of Independence?
   Ten   Thirteen   Twenty-four

IT PAYS TO DISCOVER®

FOLD AND SEAL ON ALL THREE SIDES.   © 1996 Greenwood Trust Company, Member FDIC.

1950–1975

The decade of the 1950s was marked by a spurt in desire for all of those material things soldiers and their families had gone without during World War II. The pent-up demand spawned the growth of the suburbs, where homes had to be filled with the latest in appliances, furnishings, and other creature comforts like the newest invention—the television set. Television benefited from this postwar consumer trend and became the country's national advertising medium, replacing radio and magazines as the mainstays of many advertisers' national advertising plans.

Despite the success of advertising in the 1950s, it was the 1960s that proved to be a more important turning point for the advertising industry. Television continued to boom with the advent of color programming, improved production techniques, and widespread use of videotape. Into this burgeoning technological revolution walked three advertising men who would change how advertising was created: David Ogilvy, Bill Bernbach, and Leo Burnett. David Ogilvy believed in the importance of using research to test the impact of advertising content. He was an advocate of presenting serious, informed messages to intelligent people. Bill Bernbach's approach to advertising was in direct opposition to Ogilvy's. He favored appealing to the emotions through the use of humorous, sophisticated visual and verbal messages that stopped people in their tracks. Leo Burnett was a proponent of midwest-style corny but warm advertising. The agency that carries his name has created some of the most memorable trade characters in the history of advertising: The Maytag Repairman, Tony the Tiger, Poppin' Fresh Dough Boy, the Jolly Green Giant, and the Keebler Elves, among others.

1971

The phone company wants more installers like Alana MacFarlane.

Alana MacFarlane is a 20-year-old from San Rafael, California. She's one of our first women telephone installers. She won't be the last.

We also have several hundred male telephone operators. And a policy that there are no all-male or all-female jobs at the phone company.

We want the men and women of the telephone company to do what they want to do, and do best.

For example, Alana likes working outdoors. "I don't go for office routine," she said. "But as an installer, I get plenty of variety and a chance to move around."

Some people like to work with their hands, or, like Alana, get a kick out of working 20 feet up in the air.

Others like to drive trucks. Some we're helping to develop into good managers.

Today, when openings exist, local Bell Companies are offering applicants and present employees some jobs they may never have thought about before. We want to help all advance to the best of their abilities.

AT&T and your local Bell Company are equal opportunity employers.

1974

DRAMATIC EDSEL STYLING is here to stay —bringing new distinction to American motoring

1958

The magazine industry took a heavy hit from television in the 1950s and 1960s. Some large-circulation titles, including *Colliers'* (1957) and the *Saturday Evening Post* (1969), fell victim to television's appeal to national advertisers. The demise of magazines as the primary mass advertising vehicle led the industry to reinvent itself as a more targeted medium. The late 1960s and early 1970s saw significant growth in the development of more specialized, content-focused publications that attracted readers interested in news, sports, or music.

Broad changes in society and the industry during this period of time were evident in the look and sound of ads. Psychedelic colors, Andy Warhol-style pop art, and appeals to the changing role of women in society showed up in advertising. Governmental regulatory activities also reflected the changing times. Outdoor advertising was limited alongside interstate highways, cigarette advertising was banned from television and radio, and corrective advertising was required of advertisers found guilty of making false or misleading claims.

who has a better right to oppose the war?

1969

Part One
The Challenging **Business** of Advertising

Part Four

The **Challenge**

of **Advertising**
Creativity

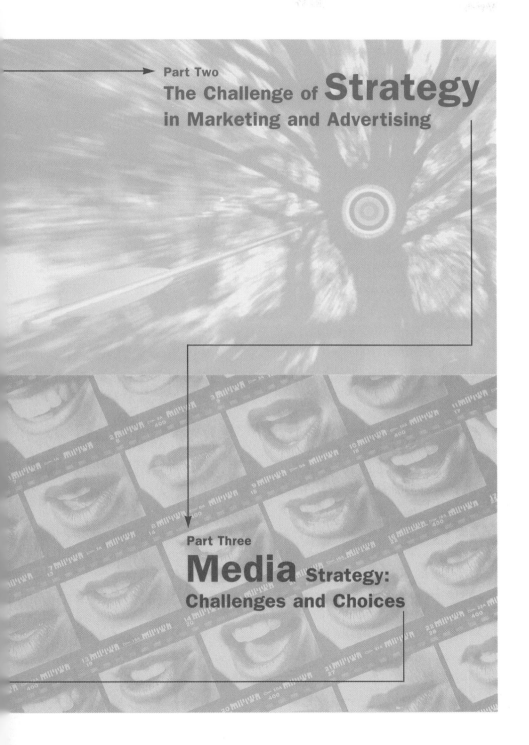

Part Two
The Challenge of **Strategy**
in Marketing and Advertising

Part Three

Media Strategy:
Challenges and Choices

Chapter Thirteen

Advertising Creativity and Creative Strategy

SATISFYING SNICKERS'

BIG NEEDS WITH A SMALL BUDGET

Contrary to popular opinion, some of the most creative advertising has been done under some of the strictest constraints. Constraints can force a writer, artist, or producer to think beyond normal habit and come up with a bona fide Big Idea. Such was the experience of three creative souls at BBDO Worldwide in New York when their client, M&M/Mars, came to them to do five television commercials for Snickers candy bar for under $1 million. That's not much money for a big-time New York City advertising agency–BBDO Worldwide easily could spend that much on one commercial for a lot of their clients! But the agency worked within the constraints and succeeded. One of the spots that was created by BBDO associate creative directors Gerry Graf and David Gray and senior creative director Charlie Miesmer, in collaboration with TV producers Bryan Buckley and Frank Todaro of @radical.media, won *Advertising Age's* Best Television Commercial award for 1996. The creative strategy? Snickers is the candy bar to have handy if "you're not going anywhere for a while."

Here is how the creative team from BBDO Worldwide and @radical.media created the award-winning TV spot: The premise behind the commercial is that the main character, due to circumstances beyond his control, finds himself stuck somewhere for a while without any food nearby. The protagonist in the award-winning spot is an elderly man who paints the end zones

1

2

3

for the Kansas City Chiefs football team's home games. The spot opens with the painter finishing up the "s" in the team's logo in the end zone. As he is finishing, a big football player comes along and says, "That's great, but who are the Chefs?" The painter realizes he has left the "i" out of the Chiefs' name, which is going to take some time to fix. He's stuck there for a while, so he munches on a Snickers.

One of the keys to the success of this spot was the limited budget with which the creative team had to work; rather than see it as a constraint, the "creatives" saw it as a challenge and worked with it. Because of the small budget, the production scope of the spot had to be small even though the idea was big. This type of creative thinking won BBDO an award—and undoubtedly made the client very happy.

Painter: Humming.
SFX: Football practice background noise.
Player: Hey, that's great, but who are the Chefs?
VO: Not going anywhere for a while?
Painter: Great googlie mooglie.
VO: Grab a Snickers.
Player #2: Your spelling's....
Painter: Yeah.

Source: Bob Garfield, "Best TV: Snickers," *Advertising Age,* 26 May 1997.

LOOK BEFORE YOU LEAP

- **What does it mean to be creative?**

- **What are the various types of creative thought processes?**

- **What is a creative strategy and how does it guide creativity?**

- **How do creativity and strategy work together to lead to effective advertising?**

- **What is the career path for a writer or artist in advertising?**

13

Renewal and reinvention are at the heart of the creative spirit. Sometimes those of us in advertising have to look deep within ourselves for the source of this renewal. At other times, changes in the marketplace present opportunities for a creative revival. Currently, new technology and media forms such as the Internet, cable television, and CD-ROM are offering new opportunities to spread our creative wings.

The new focus on integrated marketing communications is also taking the creative person beyond traditional media and into sales promotion, event marketing, direct marketing, and public relations. The challenges provided by these changes are the fuel that keeps the creative fires burning.

This chapter covers three important components of the creative process in advertising: creativity itself, a creative strategy, and the combination of the two. The discussion of creativity speaks to the fundamental importance of the creative process to thinking of advertising ideas. Next we show how the development of the creative strategy provides critical direction to the creation of ads. The combining of creativity and strategy is the final component: the big idea.

Advertising Creativity

The very term *creativity* is at the root of the controversy over its importance to the process of writing and producing advertisements. There is no one definition shared by even a reasonably large group of people. However, James Webb Young, in his classic book, *A Technique for Producing Ideas,* has described the creative person as one who "is constantly preoccupied with the possibilities of new combinations."[1] This basic description, when converted into a definition of creativity, is neither too lofty nor pedestrian for advertising's purposes. It is useful both as a guide to understanding the creative process and as a tool for embarking upon the process itself.

Leo Burnett defined **creativity** as follows:

> I have always felt that perhaps the real key to this nebulous thing called "creativity" is the art of establishing new and meaningful relationships between previously unrelated things in a manner that is relevant, believable and in good taste but which somehow presents the product in a fresh new light.[2]

Burnett's definition describes two important aspects of creativity to the business of advertising. First, it tells us that nothing in the world really is new, but if we look hard and long enough at some old yet previously unrelated ideas, we might find a new relationship that has not yet been discovered. Secondly, it tells us that advertising creativity has a purpose. It is disciplined creativity aimed at saying something new, important, and relevant about a product. Burnett's definition combines the search for the creative fire with the reality of "getting the ad out" for the client.

Writers and artists are forever on the lookout for inspiration. Knowing this, we have included Exhibit 13–1 to give you a peek at the creative act and what it means to some well-known people from many different walks of life. These quotes provide insight into the creative process and teach us that creativity is a constant search for new and different viewpoints. These expressions of what is at the heart of creativity also should leave you with the understanding that no one has cornered the market on discovering new ideas. A great idea can come just as easily from a writer or an artist at a major advertising agency as it can from a three-person design studio. A great idea knows no language or cultural barriers. When you think of a good or great idea, it is yours.

The Five Stages Of Creativity

In spite of the fact that it is so hard to define, there actually is more method to creativity than many aspiring advertising writers and artists might realize. James Webb Young is credited with providing a model of the creative process based on the *Art of Thought* by Graham Wallas. The five-stage model describes the passage of the writer or artist through a problem-solving process of preparation, digestion, incubation, illumination, and application.[3]

At the *preparation stage,* the creative person immerses himself or herself in the problem. It is at this stage that the writer (or artist) gathers the raw material that will become the substance the creative mind will use as its fodder. Some of this material already should exist in the mind of the creative person in the form of previous experience. This is general material that will be combined with specific knowledge of the product and consumer during subsequent stages of the process. The result of this combination of general knowledge about life and specific knowledge about the product is an *advertising idea.* And all good creative people have an insatiable appetite for knowledge of both types.[4] In fact, David Ogilvy has been known to say that when he is looking for new creative people, he always looks for someone with a well-furnished mind—that is, someone with a lot of general knowledge to mix with the specific product knowledge that will then be applied to advertising and marketing communications problems.

Once the raw material has been gathered, the creative person's mind takes over and begins to work on the material constantly and vigorously, trying to find that elusive new relationship that is the foundation of an idea. This is the *mental digestive stage.* This often is the most exhausting part of the process and sometimes appears to be a hopeless stage.

When the creative person reaches the point of exhaustion and hopelessness, it is time to put the problem out of his or her mind and turn it over to the unconscious mind to work on while he or she turns to something else. This is called the *incubation stage.* The incubation stage has been called daydreaming by some. We all have different activities that allow

EXHIBIT 13–1   Ten Enlightening Views on What It Means to Be Creative

A person who never made a mistake never tried anything new.
—Albert Einstein, *scientist*

Creative thinking may simply mean the realization that there is no particular virtue in doing things the way they have always been done.
—Rudolph Flesch, *educator*

Anyone can look for fashion in a boutique or history in a museum. The creative person looks for history in a hardware store and fashion in an airport.
—Robert Wieder, *journalist*

From one man, I learned that constructing a business organization could be a creative activity. From a young athlete, I learned that a perfect tackle could be as aesthetic a product as a sonnet and could be approached in the same creative spirit.
—Abraham Maslow, *psychologist*

Think of writing in terms of discovery, which is to say that creation must take place between the pen and the paper, not before in thought or afterwards in a recasting . . . It will come if it is there and if you will let it come . . . So how do you know what it will be? What will be best in it is that you really do not know. If you knew it all it would not be creation but dictation.
—Gertrude Stein, *writer*

Chaos breeds life, when order breeds habit.
—Henry Adams, *historian/philosopher*

You have to be with the work and the work has to be with you. It absorbs you totally, and you absorb it totally.
—Louise Nevelson, *sculptor*

In every work of genius we recognize our own rejected thoughts.
—Ralph Waldo Emerson, *poet*

The noble men and women of this world are those rare and wonderful ones who not only propose unique ideas but also have disciplined themselves to the patience, the sense of the imperative, the doggedness, and often the lonely drudgery of fulfillment. In the long run, they're the only ones who matter.
—William Marsteller, *advertising agency founder and CEO/advertising writer*

To live, to err, to fall, to triumph, to create life out of life.
—James Joyce, *author*

Source: Compiled from Daniel J. Boorstin, *The Creators: A History of Heroes of the Imagination* (New York: Random House, Inc., 1992), 231; Don Fabun, *You and Creativity* (Beverly Hills, CA: Glencoe Press, 1968), 5, 10, 14; Daniel Goleman, Paul Kaufman, and Michael Ray, *The Creative Spirit* (New York: Dutton, 1992), 14, 18, 35; William A. Marsteller, *Creative Management* (Chicago, IL: Crain Books, 1981), 38; and Roger von Oech, *A Whack on the Side of the Head* (New York: Warner Books, Inc., 1990), 61, 108.

us to mull over a problem with a minimum of the normal daily distractions going on around us. For some it's the shower; others prefer gardening, long walks on the beach, or some type of activity that allows them to passively consider solutions to a nagging problem. Still another way to trigger incubation is to turn to another problem, thus blocking out the present one. This also will allow the unconscious mind to bring its tremendous store of knowledge to bear on the problem.

The fourth stage of the creative process as described by Young is called the *illumination stage* because, when you least expect it, a new idea will appear as if out of nowhere. This is the stage of the process that most people associate with the creative act. It is where the exhilaration of coming up with an idea motivates and energizes you for the rest of the process. "Adscape: Where Ideas Come From" presents a good example of an illuminating moment.

The final stage, known as the *application stage,* requires that the creative person take his or her idea out into the real world to test it against reality—to see if it really works. This stage requires patience and persistence to see the implementation of the idea through to its final success. Many people enjoy thinking of ideas, but few have the patience and tenacity to fight the hard fight to see an idea put into action. Indeed, many a good idea has been lost through sloppy application to the problem.

Exhibit 13–2 tells the story of how the creative process unfolded for the creative team of Michael Patti, Don Snyder, and Ted Sann as they developed the Pepsi "Security Camera" spot that aired during the 1996 Super Bowl telecast. Notice that the story identifies many of the stages of the creative problem-solving process described by James Webb Young, from the first spark of an idea through to its actual development into a complete concept.

Creative Thought Processes

Creating advertising ideas involves a different type of thought process than is commonly found in other advertising activities, although creativity is not confined to just the task of creating advertisements. Four widely recognized and employed routes to the new idea are divergent, associative, lateral, and analogical thinking.[5] A fifth creative process is brainstorming. These thought processes are not mutually exclusive of each other, but they do warrant separate treatment because they have been identified with and developed by important contributors to what we know about the creative process.

DIVERGENT THINKING **Divergent thinking** has as its goal the generation of as many original alternative solutions to a problem as are possible. The thought process is considered divergent because the mind diverges, or moves down many different paths from one common point in a nonlinear pattern, as is illustrated in Exhibit 13–3. Here divergent thinking is compared to *convergent thinking,* in which the line of thought is linear, with each new idea representing a logical conclusion based upon the previous ideas generated. Convergent thinking leads to logical conclusions. Divergent thinking, on the other hand, seeks alternatives, not conclusions.

Illumination can occur anywhere—often when you least expect it!

"Please tell me you didn't throw out that napkin with the whole ad campaign sketched out on it."

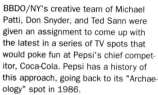

BBDO/NY's creative team of Michael Patti, Don Snyder, and Ted Sann were given an assignment to come up with the latest in a series of TV spots that would poke fun at Pepsi's chief competitor, Coca-Cola. Pepsi has a history of this approach, going back to its "Archaeology" spot in 1986.

Don and Michael worked closely together on the assignment, with Ted poking his head in from time to time to throw ideas around. On one such occasion, Ted came in and said, "Security camera. I don't know what it means, but security camera." Don and Michael thought it was a stupid idea at first.

Then Ted came back and they worked on developing the concept around the "security camera" idea. They talked about a single-take spot with no cuts. They decided to put the Coke and Pepsi coolers next to each other. A few days later they came up with the idea of having the Coke guy go for a Pepsi. Then they let the idea sit for a week.

Don drew the initial storyboard frames above to illustrate the essence of the spot. These frames show the Coke guy going for a Pepsi and being caught by a woman shopper. He is embarrassed and leaves the frame. A few seconds later he returns and grabs a Pepsi and runs like heck.

An alternative ending was added after the client thought the spot could be a little funnier. The result was the Coke guy grabbing the can of Pepsi and all of the cans in the cooler falling on him.

The spot was TV viewers' favorite Super Bowl commercial in *USA Today's* annual rating of commercials on that program.

Source: Paula Champa, "The Moment of Creation," *Agency* (Spring 1996), 12.

EXHIBIT 13-3   A Comparison of Divergent and Convergent Thinking

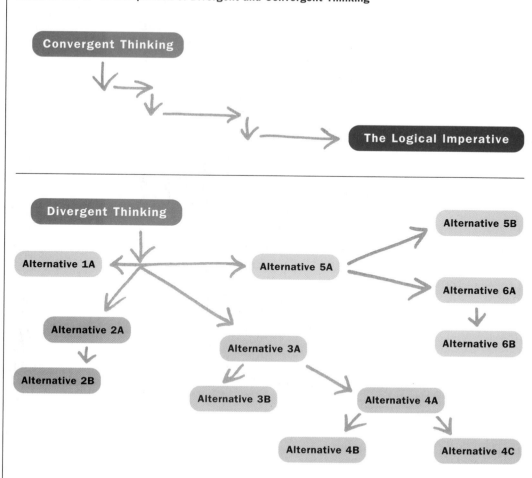

AdScape

....

Where Ideas
Come From

This is the story of copywriter Robin Raj of Chiat/Day Inc. and how he came upon the idea of using verbal/visual puns to advertise NYNEX's Yellow Pages. The campaign slogan, "If It's Out There, It's In Here," had already been in use in radio spots called "Oddities" in which people in unusual businesses such as necktie renovations were interviewed. The new problem faced by Robin was how to transfer this basic approach to television.

The idea of using the now well-known verbal/visual puns such as "Rock Drills," "Furniture Stripping," and "Dumb Waiters" came to Raj and his art director while they were eating lunch at a local tavern. They brought their phone books with them to lunch and kept noticing the curious headings such as "Civil Engineering," which could be taken literally or in a pun-like way.

Raj relates that one of their first ideas was based on the heading, "Manholes." From there, they wondered what would happen if they could get viewers to guess the puns as the commercial unfolded. Raj recalls, "We knew we were sitting on something that, if translated right, could be very powerful because of the interactive nature of it. We spent three hours at that lunch, and we knew we had something. It was one of those rare times when you feel a little magic happening."

Source: Paula Champa, "The Moment of Creation," *Agency,* May/June 1991, 31–37.

A punny thing happened to Robin Raj at a local tavern, and the NYNEX Yellow Pages television commercial series was born.

The notion that creative abilities can be grouped around an aptitude labeled divergent thinking is the work of J. P. Guilford. Guilford also identified three traits that highly creative people share: fluency, flexibility, and originality. *Fluency* is the ability to generate ideas quickly, *flexibility* is the skill to produce unique ideas across many different areas, and *originality* is the talent to come up with ideas that nobody or very few people have thought of previously.[6] Divergent thinking appears to have been behind the classic Volkswagen Beetle campaign created by the writers at the Doyle Dane Bernbach advertising agency. They decided to counter American car manufacturers' penchant for making and advertising big cars with the simple philosophy, "Think small."

ASSOCIATIVE THINKING   Leo Burnett's definition of creativity has at its heart the associative thought process that some call "free association" or "bi-association." In the **free association technique,** words are used as stimuli to make the mind think about something else that it associates with the word, no matter how illogical the relationship. Free association is based on the metaphorical nature of language that allows us to transfer one idea to another by connecting them through characteristics that they have in common. For example, think about a peach and an electric razor. What do they have in common? Suppose you were trying to think of a demonstration for a television commercial for a new electric razor and you started your free association with words such as face, stubble, or beard. Then, you might have called a man's beard "fuzz," as in peach fuzz. Next, you might have noticed that you could demonstrate how closely the razor shaves by shaving the fuzz off of a peach. The ideas "peach" and "razor" only make sense once the free associative process takes you to the last relationship.[7]

LATERAL THINKING   In *Lateral Thinking: Creativity Step by Step,* noted authority on creative thinking Edward de Bono contrasts two styles of thinking that he labels vertical and lateral.[8] The distinction de Bono makes roughly parallels Guilford's convergent and divergent thinking comparisons. For de Bono, *vertical thinking* is analytical, selective, judgmental, se-quential, negative, careful, and follows likely paths. In contrast, new ideas are more likely to come from **lateral thinking,** which is generative, provocative, positive, not judgmental, probabilistic, and explores least-likely paths. Lateral thinking cuts across established ways of seeing things, while vertical thinking stays along the path of the tried and true.[9]

The advertisement in Exhibit 13–4 certainly was not created by going down the tried and true paths of advertising for shoes. This off-beat and funny advertisement uses a unique, creative play-on-words headline to attract the reader's attention. Would you buy a pair of Florsheim shoes based *solely* on this ad? Laterally speaking, why not?

ANALOGICAL THINKING   William J. J. Gordon took the rather loosely organized associative

EXHIBIT 13–4   The explorative nature of lateral thinking gives rise to unique creative ideas such as the one shown here.

THE SOLE OF SUCCESS

FLORSHEIM

Overhead Slam! is the only way to describe Luke and Murphy Jensen's approach to life. From their French Open win to entertaining at a photo shoot for their favorite shoes — the Jensens know how to have fun. It's their style, it's their success.
http://www.florsheim.com, for locations call 1-800-446-3500.

thinking process and structured it using forced analogies into a program called *synectics*.[10] Central to Gordon's approach is the use of analogy—a comparison based on a similarity of distinct objects or concepts to make a familiar problem strange—so that the creative person can see it from a new perspective. Thus, **analogical thinking** is the thought process we use to solve a problem by looking for similarities between our problem (which has some relatively unknown properties) and concepts, objects, situations, or ideas from areas outside of the problem area that have some known characteristics in common with the problem we are trying to solve. Our hope is that this comparison will reveal some aspects of the problem we could not otherwise see and suggest a creative solution. Gordon proposes four types of analogies to aid this process. They are: 1) personal analogy, 2) direct analogy, 3) symbolic analogy, and 4) fantasy analogy. Here are some examples of how to use each of these analogic thinking processes to get creative ideas.

Personal analogy involves identifying oneself with the problem. If the creative person can put himself or herself inside the problem as one of its components, he or she will be able to establish a new viewpoint that releases the individual from seeing the problem in a conventional manner. In advertising, this might be accomplished by becoming a raisin in a bowl of cereal in a breakfast cereal commercial, an engine part in a motor oil ad, or one of the fruit items on the underwear label in a Fruit-of-the-Loom commercial. The storyboard in Exhibit 13–5 demonstrates how a personal analogy might work as an actual television commercial. Notice how the change in perspective provides a different vantage point from which to view the product.

A *direct analogy* is performed by comparing a problem to a similar problem that was solved by a potentially parallel technology from a different area. The creative process itself has been described using direct analogies. For example, consider a jazz ensemble as a model for how a creative team might collaborate on the development of an ad in an advertising agency. Each musician is on his or her own, but together, they must produce "a single weave of sound."[11] Once the process starts, according to jazz musician and composer Benny Golson, "It is very much like iron sharpening iron. When you rub

two pieces together they refine each other."[12] Golson describes the rest of the process this way:

> You tend to fill in the gaps that the other person didn't consider. One person becomes a barometer for the other. And one person encourages the other. Mutual trust is what lets a jazz ensemble take off. You are going into another zone now, and you are not going alone. You are going with other people, and the purpose is to create.[13]

Symbolic analogies are employed to bring into play a more aesthetic and less-technical view of the problem. An advertising writer might look for analogies for marketing and advertising problems in the animal kingdom, insect world, or nature itself. For example, note how Murphy's Oil Soap makes effective use of an analogy to a natural phenomenon in the ad shown in Exhibit 13–6.

Finally, the use of the *fantasy analogy* requires the creative person to willfully suspend reality and enter an ideal world where the problem can be solved by simply making it so. A fantasy analogy allows you to solve a problem without regard for the conventional restrictions of the real world. Once the solution can be fantasized, other types of analogic thinking can be used to make the solution fit the real-world requirements. The movie *Crazy People* certainly was someone's fantasy of what advertisements might be like if the writers could be forthright about the products. Remember the headline for a Volvo advertisement, "It's Boxy, But It's Good"? Such blatant honesty might not be good business sense, but the fantasy could help a writer to hone in on the true advantages of the product. Then, he or she could refine the fantasy into a very good ad.[14]

BRAINSTORMING The discussion to this point has focused more on individual creativity than group processes (the only exception being synectics). But group dynamics can bring quite a bit to the creative process. Alex F. Osborn, one of the founders of the advertising agency Batten, Barton, Durstine & Osborn (BBDO), developed the principles of a group creative process known as brainstorming in his book, *Applied Imagination*.[15] **Brainstorming** is a group creative process that relies on the ability of people to generate many ideas by playing off of each other's ideas. Put simply, many heads are

1. CUSTOMER: Hey, how tough is this Pinnacle tire?
   SALESMAN: Let me show you.

2. MUSIC UP AND UNDER.
   VO: If you faced what your tires face,

3. you'd know why you need the Pinnacle tire from ProCare.

4. So tough, it comes with the only free Road Hazard Warranty.

5. Plus, a 50,000 mile Tread Warranty

6. and free replacement during the first year in case of any failure.

7. CUSTOMER: I'll take 'em.
   SALESMAN: Good, I'm glad you liked them.

8. VO: The Atlas Pinnacle from ProCare.
   Another way we keep our word.

EXHIBIT 13–5   Personal analogy can be used as part of the creative process to provide the creative person—and ultimately the consumer, as shown here—with a fresh, unique perspective on a product.

Something New From Old Faithful.

Introducing an easy way to take beautiful care of your wood floors. New Murphy Just Squirt & Mop. Just one squirt cleans your wood safely and gently, while preserving your floor's finish and natural glow. Trust an old friend like Murphy to make cleaner wood floors just a squirt away.

LOVE YOUR WOOD.

EXHIBIT 13–6   Using a symbolic analogy that draws on the Old Faithful geyser, this ad for Murphy's Oil Soap effectively communicates, both in the copy and in the illustration, the benefits and key characteristics of the new Just Squirt & Mop product.

Some typical brainstorming questions are: Can you modify, minify, adapt, magnify, substitute, rearrange, reverse, or combine ideas mentioned? These questions can push the group's thinking off into a new and fresh direction. A typical brainstorming session consists of 6–10 people. The atmosphere is kept lively and upbeat to encourage people to say anything and everything that comes to mind. In fact, research shows that the looser the group, the more successful it will be at generating unique solutions to problems.[16]

Who Is The Creative Person?

Now that we have discussed the nature of the creative process, you might ask if some people are more creative than others and if they have any identifying characteristics that set them apart from the rest. In fact, there are some general individual characteristics that might help to identify these people. There are also some qualities that are specific to advertising that make some people better writers and artists than others.

Individual characteristics of the creative person might include inherited sensitivity, early encouragement, liberal education, asymmetrical ways of thought, personal courage, sustained curiosity, not feeling time-bound, dedication to tasks, and a willingness to work hard. Add to this list the likelihood that creative people in advertising are imaginative, intelligent, perceptive, objective, empathetic, curious, determined, persistent, self-disciplined, patient, interested in people, self-confident, honest, verbal, and humble. They can also take criticism and have stamina.

To be sure, possessing these characteristics does not necessarily mean that you are creative. And, conversely, if you do not have all of these qualities, it does not mean that you are not creative. A lot of these orientations can be learned, too. The common denominator across most creative people is that they think they are creative. The following passage from Don Fabun's book *You and Creativity* gets at the heart of the matter of what it is to be a creative person:

Yet, somehow, the creative person does seem to be different from most other people. For one thing, of course, he (she) exhibits creativity at a fairly high rate. He (she) is the one society instinctively turns to when it needs 'new' ideas. It doesn't matter, of course,

better than one. Groups also can be inhibiting, however, so procedures were developed to encourage the free flow of ideas in a group setting. The two guiding principles of brainstorming are as follows: 1) Criticism is prohibited while ideas are being generated (i.e., anything goes), and 2) the quantity of ideas is directly related to the quality of ideas (i.e., the more the better).

Brainstorming has some characteristics in common with analogical thinking. Both processes use a series or set of questions that attempt to get participants over mental blocks by asking them to see the problem differently.

whether society asks or not; the creative person will turn them out anyway. If one studies the life stories of highly creative people, it appears obvious that there are certain similarities in their background and in their personalities. But, being creative, they are also quite different from each other.[17]

Creativity is but one part of the process of creating successful advertisements. The idea-generation process described also must be based on a sound plan or strategy. The nature of this plan or strategy and how it guides creativity will be discussed in the next section.

R E S E T

1. How is the current marketplace presenting opportunities for a creative revival in advertising?
2. How are analogical thinking and brainstorming similar? How are they different?
3. Can a creative person be identified solely on the basis of individual characteristics? Explain why or why not.

Creative Strategy

Chapters Four, Five, and Eight discussed the importance of strategy to marketing and advertising planning. The marketing plan includes an advertising plan that speaks to the responsibility advertising has in the creative and media areas. The advertising plan can be further subdivided into both a creative strategy and a media plan. The media component of the advertising plan was discussed in Chapter Nine. Here we will focus on the creative strategy.

The **creative strategy** is the part of an advertising plan that tells the writers and artists what the advertising is going to say and provides some direction about how it will be said. Writing a creative strategy is not just an exercise, it has a purpose: to guide the creation of ads. To achieve this purpose, the creative strategy must be clear and leave no room for confusion or misunderstanding. The best and most useful creative strategies are those that are the sim-plest, clearest, and have a definite focus. A clear, dramatic message or position stands out from the crowd because it does not try to do everything. Decide what your message or position is going to be and then stand by it in your strategy statement.

A well-written creative strategy is also short—one page or less is sufficient. As Roman and Maas say in their book *The New How to Advertise,* "If you can't get it on one page, the chances of getting it into a 30-second commercial are slim."[18] Indeed, if the creative strategy is clear you should be able to say it in one or two concise sentences. For example, the Absolut Vodka strategy was ultimately reducible to: "We wanted to make this a fashionable product . . . like perfume."[19]

A good example of a clear and long-running advertising strategy is that of the lonely Maytag repairman. This character was introduced in 1967 as a symbolic expression of a simple, focused strategy to communicate the dependability of Maytag appliances. "Ol' Lonely" is in constant pursuit of companionship from an owner of a Maytag appliance who needs a repair done. But, as we all know by now, Maytag appliances are so reliable and dependable that the frantic repair call never comes.[20]

The creative strategy should flow logically from the marketing and advertising strategies. It should not be developed in a vacuum; rather, it should help the other components achieve the overall objectives of the marketing strategy. The creative strategy should not go marching off to its own tune. The advertising campaign for Absolut Vodka demonstrates the tie between marketing and the creative strategy in the advertising plan. Absolut's advertising had to overcome what some people thought were marketing obstacles—the facts that the product was from Sweden and it came in a clear glass bottle with the label painted on it. Turning a potential negative into a positive, the creative team at the TBWA agency decided to make the bottle's shape a fashionable part of the product. It was turned into the brand's signature by playing off of the bottle's shape with two-word headlines that associated it, tongue-in-cheek, with everything from the best in art, fashion, and dance, to fashionable locations (see Exhibit 13–7). As competition increased in the vodka market, Absolut introduced flavored versions of its product, and the company

ABSOLUT PARIS.

ABSOLUT VODKA. PRODUCT OF SWEDEN. 40 AND 50% ALC/VOL (80 AND 100 PROOF). 100% GRAIN NEUTRAL SPIRITS. ABSOLUT COUNTRY OF SWEDEN VODKA & LOGO, ABSOLUT, ABSOLUT BOTTLE DESIGN AND ABSOLUT CALLIGRAPHY ARE TRADEMARKS OWNED BY V&S VIN & SPRIT AB. ©1994 V&S VIN & SPRIT AB. IMPORTED BY THE HOUSE OF SEAGRAM, NEW YORK, NY. PHOTOGRAPHER: GRAHAM FORD.
THOSE WHO APPRECIATE QUALITY ENJOY IT RESPONSIBLY.

EXHIBIT 13–7 Absolut Vodka's unique creative strategy, which connects its vodka with popular artists, dancers, and locations, has succeeded in creating a fashionable image for the product. This approach has also been successful with brand extensions, such as Absolut Citron.

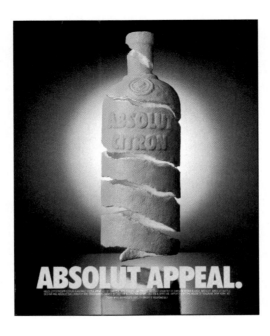

ABSOLUT APPEAL.

found that the original strategy could be extended to these brand extensions as well.[21] Absolut's creative strategy is so strong that it has produced enough advertising executions to fill a popular book, entitled *Absolut Book*.

Components Of The Creative Strategy

Creativity and strategy go hand-in-hand toward the development of effective advertisements. William Bernbach, legendary copywriter and agency head, used the analogy of a locomotive and its tracks to describe this vital relationship. Think of the locomotive, he said, as the creative engine just waiting to create, and the railroad tracks as the strategy providing the direction for the creative train. Once the strategy has been set down, the creative engine can run full-speed ahead down the tracks to effective and outstanding advertising execution.[22]

Developing a creative strategy is the same as the preparation stage identified by James Webb Young in his creative problem-solving process. First, the writer must understand the product, competition, and consumer, answering the questions Why? and How? Some of the necessary information will come in the form of research results from the marketing and advertising plans. You may also want to seek out more information if the existing research suggests new questions that require answers. In this regard, you might work with an account planner whose job is to provide insight into the consumer that then can be used in developing your creative strategy. "Consumer Insight: The Product that Works Before It's Working" describes an account planner's insight that led to a successful campaign for Alka-Seltzer.

The names given to the various components of a creative strategy will vary by agencies to fit their own style and preferences, but most contain the following elements: 1) advertising objective, 2) target audience profile, 3) key consumer benefit, 4) strategic approach, 5) support, and 6) tone, manner, and style.

ADVERTISING OBJECTIVE Recall that an **advertising objective** is a statement explaining the purpose and role of an advertising campaign or a particular advertisement. It should describe what you want the target audience to think, feel, or do. An example of an advertising objec-

Consumer Insight

The Product That Works Before It's Working

Foote, Cone & Belding (now part of True North Communications) was working on a campaign for Alka-Seltzer Plus Cold Medicine that required some small-group research to gain insight into what the product meant to consumers. One of the things that Karen Randolph, the account planner on the account, wanted to know about Alka-Seltzer Plus Cold Medicine was what consumers thought of the meaning of the word "effervescent." She used projective techniques such as profiling and storytelling in these research sessions to get the consumers to describe what it was like to use the product and to identify potential product users.

Once the research sessions were completed, it was Randolph's job to analyze the findings. She found that consumers thought that "effervescent" meant that the product was working the moment the tablets were dropped into water—*before* they drank it.

To them, the word had a magical connotation. With Karen Randolph's help, the creative team was able to use this insight as they worked on the ads for the campaign. The TV spot titled "Sculptor" demonstrates how this consumer insight was turned into an effective commercial for Alka-Seltzer Plus Cold Medicine.

Source: Karen Randolph, personal interview, 20 June 1994.

The product insight gained from projective research techniques provided the basis for this effective and creative advertisement.

Alka-Seltzer Plus Cold Medicine "SCULPTOR" :30 TV

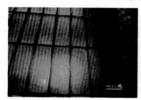

<u>SFX:</u> RAIN

<u>A VO:</u> Carrie Novak won't waste a minute

battling her cold.
<u>SFX:</u> SNEEZE

Pills take time to dissolve…

so she'll rush relief

with the effervescent power of

Alka-Seltzer Plus Cold Medicine.

It's ready the moment you take it.

Rushing powerful medicines to soothe your aches…relieve your runny nose…

free your breathing.

Nothing rushes relief like Alka-Seltzer Plus.⸲

FCB

tive is: to convince consumers that Saturn is a well-designed, high-quality, expressive, and affordable automobile.

The advertising objective should also be written in terms that an advertisement can reasonably achieve. Some of these achievable objectives were discussed in Chapter Eight. For example, advertising is much better suited to achieving communication-related objectives than sales objectives. The exception to this principle is direct response forms of advertising, in which the ads ask consumers to purchase products by using a coupon or toll-free telephone number. Likewise, interactive advertising can be developed with a built-in consumer response mechanism. However, traditional media advertising is often employed with communication objectives in mind.

For example, the objective of the Absolut Vodka advertising campaign discussed earlier was to get the consumer to associate the brand with the well-known and fashionable people, places, and ideas shown in the ads. This is something advertising can do for a marketing plan; it is basically an image-building objective, and advertising can help to build and maintain a brand image. And by doing what it can do, advertising helps the other marketing activities to sell more of the product.

TARGET AUDIENCE PROFILE   The creative strategy should include a profile of the target audience so that writers and artists can understand the buying habits, lifestyles, and motivations of the people who will be reading, watching, or listening to their ads. Recall that a **target audience** is the group of individuals for whom an advertising campaign is specifically devised, as defined by demographic, lifestyle, and psychographic characteristics. In the creative strategy, it is important to try to go beyond a purely demographic description of the

AROUND THE GLOBE

· · · · · · · · · · · · · · · · · · · ·

Cathay Pacific's Challenge in Asia

Cathay Pacific Airlines is one of the five most profitable airlines in the world, linking the western world with Hong Kong and Asia. As the favorite airline of westerners, Cathay has maintained a decidedly western flavor in its advertising and service over the years. However, with the return of Hong Kong to China and a general increase in the number of Asian travelers it serves, Cathay has had to reassess its advertising strategy to meet the needs of its new audience.

Cathay Pacific's new strategy is to create an image for itself as the preferred airline of the discerning Asian passenger while still maintaining its positive image among westerners. Cathay Pacific changed its advertising agency and overhauled its advertising to get this job done. A key change was a redesigned company symbol. The old symbol consisted of its name and a stylized tail of a plane. The new design takes on a stronger Asian identity, using a bird in flight. This new symbol is carried through in all of Cathay Pacific's advertising. The copy in the ad follows through on the Asian theme of strength through flexibility.

The new advertising strategy for Cathay Pacific includes television spots that focus on Asian dance and music and the slogan "Heart of Asia." Business people are also the target of Cathay Pacific's campaign, with ads that promote the availability of such services as TV systems, phone, and fax facilities on board, and the quality of the food and drink.

target audience to a profile that will help the advertising writer to establish the consumer's viewpoint of the product. This is where any insight gained from studying the consumer can bring the target audience alive and lead to good creative solutions to the advertising and marketing communications assignment. "Around the Globe: Cathay Pacific's Challenge in Asia" demonstrates how knowing your target audience can affect your creative strategy.

Some creative strategies are supplemented by a **personal profile,** which is a composite of the key characteristics of the target audience. This profile is a dramatized version of a typical target group member. Its purpose is to help the writer communicate with an individual as opposed to a mass audience. Exhibit 13–8 is an example of such a profile for the typical target audience member for The Marine Corps recruitment campaign. Notice how the personal profile expands on the target audience descrip-

tion; it helps the writer to understand the person to whom he or she is writing. These profiles are not imaginative; they are based on research, and each characteristic mentioned should have documentation behind it.

KEY CONSUMER BENEFIT   A **key consumer benefit** is a product benefit that is important, relevant, and unique to your target group of prospects. This is the reason that your target audience should buy your product—what the consumer gets from buying and using your product. McDonald's friendly family atmosphere in their restaurants is a key consumer benefit, as is Maytag's dependability. The lifestyle image of Polo clothing and the fashionable image of Absolut vodka also are key benefits. These benefits, whether tangible or psychological in nature, are important, relevant, and unique to the target consumers who buy or patronize these brands.

The changing market in Asia and its importance to the region and the world is at the heart of Cathay Pacific's new advertising strategy. After all, half of the world's population is within four hours' flight time of the airline's hub in Hong Kong.

Source: Pamposh Dhar, "Cathay Pacific Seeks to Make Itself More Asian," *Advertising Age,* 16 January 1995, I–4.

CATHAY PACIFIC

JFK 2 HKG

HONG KONG WITHOUT THE SCHLEP.

AAdvantage

Same-plane, daily direct service to Hong Kong. Fly Cathay Pacific. The Heart of Asia.

Cathay Pacific has modified not only its primary product message but also its company logo and image in order to more effectively communicate with its changing customer base.

Target Audience: High school seniors of good character who are uncertain about their futures.

Personal Profile: Hi. My name is Jerry Jones and I'm from Jackson, Tennessee. Well, not Jackson exactly, but from a farm a couple of miles outside. We have a small farm and a big family. Mother, Dad, five brothers, and three sisters. I'm the fourth-oldest boy and I'll be finishing at Jackson High this spring. Don't know what to do after that. I'm a pretty good baseball player, but not good enough to earn a living at it. There really isn't much for me to do on the farm, and there sure isn't anything for me to do in Jackson. Pump gas, maybe. Or clerk in the supermarket. My grades are good enough to get me into college, but we haven't got that kind of money. And besides, I'm not sure I'm ready to hit the books again just yet. I'd really like to get away for a while and see what life is like in the outside world.

Source: W. Keith Hafer and Gordon E. White, *Advertising Writing: Putting Creative Strategy to Work* (St. Paul, MN: West Company, 1989), 42–43.

Your creative strategy will be much stronger and it will be much easier to break through the media clutter if the product you're working on has a genuine key benefit; however, there are creative strategies for situations in which you do not have a key benefit with which to work. Notice that Exhibit 13–9, which will be discussed in more detail shortly, includes some strategic approaches that do not rely on a key consumer benefit.

STRATEGIC APPROACH   The **strategic approach** is a statement of how you will position your product, what appeals will be used, or how your key consumer benefit will be presented. The creative strategy, by implication, is a competitive plan. Its purpose is to articulate how the advertising for the brand will help the brand to compete successfully in the marketplace. Most creative strategies assume that the marketing strategy is to differentiate the brand from the competition in some meaningful way.

Descriptions of some possible strategic approaches for the creative strategy can be found in Exhibit 13–9. Many creative strategies are a combination of these basic strategic approaches, although you can certainly use any one of them individually as well. The point to remember is that a creative strategy is seldom a pure example of one approach; rather, it is an out-

growth of a strong understanding of the market conditions.

SUPPORT   The creative strategy should provide the advertising writer with supporting details or selling points that explain the reasons that the audience should believe the primary message of an advertisement. These selling points will give the writer tangible information about the product with which he or she can then write persuasive copy that will flow naturally from the ad's main idea. For example, the ad in Exhibit 13–10 for Breathe Right nasal strips provides support to the main idea by telling the reader in the copy below the illustration how the product works.

TONE, STYLE, AND MANNER   The tone, style, and manner of the advertising is a statement of the product personality to be conveyed or the manner and style of the advertising campaign or individual ad.[23] This statement should support the basic selling premise and provide the appropriate personality or feel to the advertising. Without these characteristics, the ads created can become what some call "walking strategy statements." This means that the ads are simply the content of the strategy statements arranged to look like an ad. Note how the tone, style, and manner of the ad shown in Exhibit 13–11 instantaneously conveys the desired feel to the customer.

Putting The Strategy In Writing

As we said at the beginning of this section, one of the most important reasons for developing a creative strategy is to use it as a guide during the creation of the actual campaign or ads. The document that contains the strategic elements we have been discussing is called either a creative platform or copy platform. Although these terms can be used interchangeably, the term **creative platform** suggests a plan for more than one ad, while each ad in an advertising campaign can have a **copy platform** or plan of its own. Exhibit 13–12 shows three different outlines for copy platforms, from a short version to a long version. Exhibit 13–13 illustrates a completed copy platform for a hypothetical non-alcoholic beer product.

EXHIBIT 13–9   Basic Strategic Approaches for the Creative Strategy

The Generic Strategy	The generic strategy is best employed when your brand is a leader in the category or when an increase in product category sales would benefit your brand. This approach forgoes claims of superiority or brand differences in favor of promoting the category as a whole. The goal for the brand is to make it synonymous with	the category. Miller Lite did this effectively by inventing the light beer category and then using advertising ("Great Taste, Less Filling") to persuade consumers to associate Miller Lite with the entire concept of light beer. Subsequent competition eroded this effort, but the early years of light beer belonged to Miller Lite.
The Preemptive Claim	Many products are parity or "me too" products that do not offer a distinctive feature upon which to base a creative strategy. However, if a firm can advertise its brand first and persuade consumers to associate its brand with the category, it can preempt the competition's claims. The Philip Morris Company has had unusual	success at preempting other brands or being the first to claim something. Marlboro has become "the" masculine cigarette, Virginia Slims is "the" female cigarette, and Miller Lite is still the first name associated with light beers.
Product Positioning	Product positioning establishes a place for your product in the consumer's mind relative to the competition. Product positioning is a brand differentiation strategy and can be employed in a number of different ways. A firm may wish to position its brand as the best in the category, as Hertz and IBM have. It may seek a position against the category leader, as Avis did with its classic	"We Try Harder" campaign based on its Number 2 position in the car rental business. Or an advertiser might focus on a small market or niche and position itself as "the" product for a particular market segment, as Kentucky Fried Chicken has by offering one basic product and not competing against the entire range of offerings in the fast-food industry.
Brand Image Strategy	Brand image strategy is another strategy for differentiating a brand from its competition, especially when the brands in the category have strong psychological or social significance for the consumer. Brand image strategy also is used when brands have few real physical	differences but offer extrinsic rewards that can become the basis for a unique brand personality. Particular categories of products such as cosmetics, jewelry, soft drinks, beer, cigarettes, and automobiles lend themselves to this approach.
The Unique Selling Proposition (USP)	The use of a USP requires a product with distinctive features that can be translated into meaningful and relevant consumer benefits that then can be expressed in a unique manner. Rosser Reeves promoted this approach in his book *Reality in Advertising* in 1961 and influenced a generation of advertising professionals as to the soundness of this strategy. Of course, not every product has distinctive features that can be advertised	this way. The case of M & M candies is a good example of how the USP works. The hard outer shell of the bite-sized candy is its distinctive attribute. The benefit to the consumer is that because of the hard outer shell, the candies will not melt in his or her hands. The unique expression or USP is the now classic line, "M & M Candies Melt in Your Mouth, Not in Your Hand."
The Resonance Approach	The resonance approach uses experiences with which consumers can identify on an emotional level and then places the product within that experiential context. McDonald's has done this consistently in its slice-of-life commercials. One such McDonald's commercial, called "Perfect Season," depicts heartwarming, realistic	portrayals of various pee-wee football scenes, capturing emotional and humorous moments to which parents can relate. In one scene, the coach is exhorting his team to try harder as the kids decide to run after a grasshopper. In another scene, two parents spread their arms to form a goal post for a field goal try.
The Affective Strategy	This emotion-based approach is often used to break through consumer indifference and change perceptions of a product or service. Public service advertising lends itself to an affective strategy as it tries to break through audience indifference toward a particular cause. The affective strategy for brand advertising employs appeals to the intuition and aesthetic sensibilities rather than	rational criteria. Some products that are unusually well-suited to the affective strategy include greeting cards, flowers, jewelry, clothing, cosmetics, travel, and soft drinks. Coca-Cola's Mean Joe Green commercial in which the young kid shares his Coke with the famous football player is a good example of an affective approach.

Source: Compiled from Bruce Bendinger, *The Copy Workshop* (Chicago, IL: The Copy Workshop, 1988), 26–27; Charles F. Frazer, "Creative Strategy: A Management Perspective," *Journal of Advertising* 12, no. 4 (1983): 36–41; Rosser Reeves, *Reality in Advertising* (New York: Alfred A. Knopf, 1961); Al Ries and Jack Trout, *Positioning: The Battle for Your Mind* (New York: McGraw-Hill Book Company, 1986); and Tony Schwartz, *The Responsive Chord* (Garden City, NY: Anchor Books, 1974), 23–25.

MAKES BREATHING SO EASY, YOU CAN DO IT IN YOUR SLEEP.

A stuffed up nose doesn't go away when your head hits the pillow. At best, you might get an uneasy night's rest. But a drug-free Breathe Right strip lifts and pulls open nasal passages, comfortably and without pinching, so you'll breathe easier all night long. Open up your stuffed nose with a Breathe Right nasal strip. Find them in cough and cold sections everywhere.

Say it with softness.

Downy

For the most fluffy softness, in a bunch of fresh scents. Come on in to Downy.

1. Describe the relationship between creativity and creative strategy. How do the two processes fit together to produce advertising?
2. What are the key elements of a creative strategy statement?
3. What is the difference between a creative platform and a copy platform?

Combining Creativity And Strategy: The Big Idea

Thus far we have discussed the excitement of the creative thought process and the discipline of putting your thinking down in writing in the form of a creative strategy. The trick now is to combine the two processes to come up with the idea or concept that is going to make the advertising work. This part of the process is called *visualization* or *conceptualization*. This is the time when, through a flash of insight or leap of intuition, the solution to the creative problem presents itself to you as an idea. But in advertising you have to be able to come up with more than an idea. The idea must be bold. It must link a consumer benefit to a unique product characteristic and present it in a visual, friendly, and simple yet unexpected way. The idea has to get the audience to stop and take notice because it is a fresh new way of looking at the product. In short, it must be a *big idea*.[24]

EXHIBIT 13–12   Examples of Copy Platform Formats

Short Version

1. Key benefit
2. Target audience
3. Advertising/communication objective

Medium-Length Version

1. Advertising/communication objective
2. Target audience
3. Major selling idea or key benefit
4. Supporting selling points or benefits
5. Creative strategy

Long Version

1. Advertising problem
2. Advertising/communication objective
3. Target audience
4. Competition
5. Product positioning
6. Message strategy
7. Key selling points
8. Supporting selling points
9. Message execution (tone, manner, and style)

Source: A. Jerome Jewler, *Creative Strategy in Advertising*, 3rd ed. (Belmont, CA: Wadsworth, 1989), 45–46; and Sandra E. Moriarty, *Creative Advertising: Theory and Practice*, 2nd ed. (Englewood Cliffs, NJ: Prentice Hall, 1991), 96–97.

EXHIBIT 13–13   Copy Platform for Barley Light Non-Alcoholic Malt Beverage

Advertising Objective: To create awareness among young males ages 21–45 that Barley Light is the only domestic brand of non-alcoholic malt beverage that has a unique combination of imported beer taste with low caloric content that will provide them with a great tasting brew that also is a healthy and responsible way to drink malt beverages.

Target Audience:

Age: 21–45 years old
Gender: Male
Household income: $40,000 plus
Educational level: High school plus

The target audience will be men who make up the majority of beer drinkers but still believe that responsible drinking is important. As well, they are an active, sports-minded group that is concerned about their health. They like the taste of beer and drink it for that reason, not to get drunk.

Major Selling Point (Key Benefit): Barley Light is the only domestic brand of non-alcoholic malt beverage with the unique combination of an imported beer taste and low caloric content.

Supporting Selling Points: Responsible drinking shows that you care for others. Will tie in with Seven-Eleven's responsible drinking promotion.

Creative Strategy: Barley Light will be advertised as the non-alcoholic, premium brew with the taste of imported beer but without the alcohol and calories for the young, active male who is health conscious and concerned about his responsibility to others.

The big idea takes the writers and artists beyond the strategy to a dramatic, involving, relevant, memorable, and fresh viewpoint about the consumer's relationship to the product. For example, the strategy for All Temperature Cheer was simple: to demonstrate its cleaning power in even the coldest of water temperatures. But it took a big idea to make that strategy work. The big idea resulted in a television commercial in which a dramatic live demonstration was performed using ice and Cheer in a cocktail shaker to successfully clean a lipstick stain off an ascot.

Organizing The Creative Task

Chapter Two provided a brief description of how a typical advertising agency organizes its activities. Recall that there are two primary approaches to agency organization that affect how the creative function will be handled. Some agencies like to organize their business functions into departments such as account services, creative, media, and research and then assign people from the departments to work on different client accounts as needed. Other agencies prefer to set up account teams or groups from the outset so that group members feel an affiliation to the clients they work for first and to their functional areas second.

In either case, there generally is a hierarchy of positions in the creative area from executive creative director all the way down to the junior copywriters. In between, there are creative directors, copy supervisors, and copywriters. *Creative directors* who are assigned to supervise the creative work of specific account teams and manage the copy supervisors on these teams report to the executive creative director. *Copy supervisors* work directly with the *copywriters* in the development of advertising concepts. *Junior copywriters* are people who are new to the profession. They are given limited responsibility as they learn the craft of copywriting.

The career advancement track on the writing side is from copywriter to copy supervisor to creative director to executive creative director. The track takes a person on the creative side from the job of writing to the job of supervising other creative people. Some writers

enjoy the advancement into management and others do not. Some of the better known agency heads started as writers. This includes people such as Bill Bernbach, Leo Burnett, David Ogilvy, and Hal Riney.

On the art side, the *art director* works with copywriters on concepts for ads and reports to the creative director. He or she is responsible for the design and production of the advertisements created by the account teams. Art directors also work directly with *layout artists* on designing ads for specific accounts. Art directors can advance to become creative directors, but the special nature of their talent usually keeps them in the art and production area.

Two key factors influence the quality of work produced by the creative staffs of an agency: 1) the talent in the creative area, and 2) how well the creative personnel work with other areas of the agency, such as account services. As for the first, the quality of talent is a key limiting factor to what can be produced by the writers and artists in an agency. The better the talent, the greater the potential for outstanding work. A difficult task is how to identify the truly talented people to hire. William Marsteller offers the following advice on who the really creative people are:

> Being creative is both pleasurable and easy, pretty much like sex. The labor pains come later. Or to draw an analogy from a different recreational form, Tommy Henrich, the one-time Yankee outfielder, said, "Catching a ball is fun; it's what you do with it after you catch it that's a business. . . ."[25]

Now to bring us full circle, William Marsteller (as you'll recall from Exhibit 13–1) completes his thought about who the truly creative folks happen to be:

> The noble men and women of this world are those rare and wonderful ones who not only propose unique ideas but also have disciplined themselves to the patience, the sense of imperative, the doggedness, and the often lonely drudgery of fulfillment. In the long run, they're the only ones who matter.[26]

The second key factor is how well people in different specialty areas collaborate with each other. It is simple to say and hard to do, but the key to good working relationships is open lines of communication within the administrative hierarchy as well as across specialties. Advertising is a communication business, but at the same time a very ego-involving business. And the egos of writers and artists can be among the most fragile. A genuine appreciation of what the writer and artist bring to the advertising table probably is the best way to establish a successful working relationship with these talented people. At the same time, advertising is a business with real deadlines and bottom lines that cannot be ignored. But then, Marsteller has already told us the importance and nobility of getting things done.

SUMMARY

Advertisers must search constantly for renewal and reinvention in their creativity. Current changes in the marketplace are making this easier, as new technology and media forms and the focus on integrated marketing communications allow advertisers to explore new opportunities in their creativity. The creative process involves three important components: creativity itself, a creative strategy, and the combination of the two in the form of a big idea.

The creative process in advertising employs some of the same mental processes that have been used by many great thinkers and artists to achieve superior levels of achievement in their fields. However, the application of creativity to advertising problems requires a discipline to focus one's imagination on advertising ideas that are relevant, believable, and in good taste but that present products in a fresh new light.

No single definition of creativity stands out above the others; however, there is a method to the creative process that has been outlined and agreed upon by advertising and nonadvertising people alike. The basic stages to the creative problem-solving process include the preparation stage, the mental digestive stage, the incubation stage, the illumination stage, and the application stage. The preparation stage involves gathering all of the available information that bears on the problem at hand. The mental digestive stage focuses on the conscious effort to solve the problem with the information that has been gathered. Incubation occurs when the creative person turns the problem over to the workings of the unconscious mind. At some point during the incubation stage an idea or ideas will rise to the conscious level as if out of nowhere. This is called illumination. The application stage requires implementation of the problem-solving idea.

The creative thought process has been studied widely, yielding four prominent views on how creative people get their ideas. These views or schools of thought include: divergent thinking, associative thinking, lateral thinking, and analogical thinking. These approaches are not exclusive of each other and do overlap in some areas. Divergent thinking has as its goal the generation of as many original alternative solutions to a problem as are possible. Associative thinking occurs when a new relationship is created by associating words or items or ideas that normally are not associated with each other. Lateral thinking is a style of thinking that cuts across established ways of looking at things and explores the least likely paths to a solution. Analogical thinking makes use of various types of analogies to force a new perspective on a difficult problem to stimulate new ideas and solutions. The different types of analogies include personal, direct, symbolic, and fantasy. In addition, advertising has contributed its own method to the creative thought process called brainstorming. Brainstorming is a group creative process that relies on the ability of people to generate many ideas by playing off of each other's ideas.

There are some general individual characteristics that can be used to describe the creative person. For example, there does appear to be a general predisposition toward creativity that is inherited and nurtured during one's upbringing. Additionally, creative people in advertising have empathy, determination, self-discipline, confidence, humility, a capacity for criticism, and stamina—qualities that allow them to apply their creative predisposition to advertising.

To be useful in advertising, creativity must be harnessed and guided. The key guiding tool is the creative strategy. This tool is the part of the advertising plan that tells the writers and artists what the advertising is going to say and provides some direction about how it will be said. To achieve this purpose, the creative strategy must be clear, simple, short, and have a definite focus. It should also flow logically from the marketing and advertising strategies, helping the other components achieve the overall objectives of the marketing strategy. To develop a successful creative strategy, the writer must understand the product, competition, and consumer.

The key elements of the creative strategy are an advertising objective; target audience profile; key consumer benefit; strategic approach; support; and the tone, manner, and style of the advertising. The advertising objective is a statement explaining the purpose and role of an advertising campaign or a particular advertisement. It should describe what you want the target audience to think, feel, or do, and it should be written in terms that an advertisement can reasonably achieve. The target audience profile helps writers and artists understand the buying habits, lifestyles, and motivations of the people who will be reading, watching, or listening to their ads. Some strategies are supplemented by a personal profile, which is a composite of the key characteristics of the target audience dramatized as an individual. A key consumer benefit is a product benefit that is important, relevant, and unique to the target audience; it is the reason that the target audience should buy the product or service being advertised.

The strategic approach is a statement of how you will position your product, what appeals will be used, or how the key consumer benefit will be presented. Supporting details or selling points that explain the reasons why

the target audience should believe the primary message of the advertisement should also be included in the creative strategy. These selling points give the writer tangible information about the product that he or she can then use to write persuasive copy that will flow naturally from the ad's main idea. Finally, the tone, style, and manner of the advertising is a statement of the product personality to be conveyed or the manner and style of the advertising campaign or individual ad. This statement should support the basic selling premise and provide the appropriate personality or feel to the advertising. When all of these elements are put together in writing, they are known as a creative platform (when referring to a creative strategy for more than one ad) or as a copy platform (when referring to a plan for one ad).

Combining creativity and creative strategy to come up with the idea or concept that is going to make the advertising work is known as visualization or conceptualization. This is the part of the creative process when the solution to the creative problem presents itself to you. To be a big idea—one that will sell your product—it must be bold, link a consumer benefit to a unique product characteristic, and be presented in a visual, friendly, and simple yet unexpected way.

The creative jobs in an advertising agency start at the top with that of the executive creative director, who manages and supervises the creative directors. The creative directors in turn supervise the creative work of specific account teams and manage the copy supervisors on these teams. Copy supervisors work with copywriters in the development of advertising concepts. On the art side, art directors work with copywriters and copy supervisors on the design and production of advertisements. Art directors also supervise layout artists, who do the actual design and mechanical work on ads.

The key ingredients to becoming a successful writer or artist in advertising are creative talent, the fortitude to work well with other areas of the agency, and the ability to see projects, ideas, and solutions through until they are successfully implemented.

creativity, 408

divergent thinking, 410

free association
    technique, 413

lateral thinking, 413

analogical thinking, 414

brainstorming, 414

creative strategy, 417

advertising objective, 418

target audience, 420

personal profile, 421

key consumer benefit, 421

strategic approach, 422

creative platform, 422

copy platform, 422

REVIEW QUESTIONS

1. What is creativity?

2. List and describe James Webb Young's five stages of the creative process. How does this process work to result in the creation of an idea?

3. Describe the five widely recognized creative thought processes. Compare and contrast them. Which best explains the advertising creative process as you know it? Why?

4. Generally speaking, who is the creative person? More specifically, who is the creative advertising person?

5. What is a creative strategy? How does this document guide the creation of advertising?

6. Describe the six key components of a creative strategy.

7. Why is the key consumer benefit so critical to a creative strategy?

8. In what situations might you use a generic strategic approach? A brand image strategy? A unique selling proposition? Explain and give examples for each.

9. How does a writer get from a creative strategy to the creation of a big idea for an ad or campaign?

10. Describe the career path for an advertising writer.

DISCUSSION QUESTIONS

1. Explain how the inherent freedom required to be creative can be reconciled with the discipline needed to produce effective advertising.

2. Some of the best advertising ideas of all time have lasted the longest and are still running, yet most advertisers change their campaigns very frequently. Why do you think that happens?

3. In your opinion, what are the key consumer benefits for the following products/services? Justify your answers.

    Kinko's photocopying service
    Isuzu Trooper automobile
    Gold's Gym
    Taco Bell

interactive discovery lab

1. Identify two of your favorite books, poems, pieces of music, works of art, architectural designs, or movies. Then select two of your favorite ads or advertising campaigns. Compare and contrast your first selections with the ads you picked. Can you find creative similarities? Differences?

2. Describe your own creative thought process. Describe the stages and nature of each stage you go through to come up with your best ideas. How is your technique similar and/or different from those described in this chapter?

Chapter Fourteen

Advertising Copywriting

CONCEPT TROUBLESHOOTERS: THEIR AIM IS TRUE

Copywriter Harry Cocciolo and art director Sean Ehringer, creators of the "Got Milk?" campaign for the California Fluid Milk Processor Board, are concept troubleshooters for their agency, Goodby, Silverstein & Partners of San Francisco.

As concept troubleshooters, Cocciolo and Ehringer move from account to account and brainstorm with creative groups to help them develop concepts for individual ads or a campaign.

For example, they were brought in on the Polaroid account with a challenge to "think of times where nothing will do but a Polaroid camera when you need *instant* images." One of their first ideas was a TV commercial in which an architect finds a risqué photo of his bride in his briefcase.

Their job for the "Got Milk?" campaign was to think of "the most desperate, eternal milk moments." To gain insight into the problem, Cocciolo and Ehringer spent a week without milk. Cocciolo relates, "When you want a bowl of cereal [and you don't have milk], you're bummed." This revelation was put to work in a series of spoofs like the one in which police interrogators pressure an uncooperative suspect for an admission of guilt by withholding the milk from him while he eats a dry cupcake he's been eyeing.

Cocciolo and Ehringer both have degrees in commercial art. Sean also has a psychology degree. Harry says that if he hadn't gone into advertising he would have been a writer, while Sean thinks he would have been an architect. Their boss, Jeff Goodby, says that "they're like a couple that invites you over to dinner, argues in front of you, and asks you to take sides." Nonetheless, as their ads demonstrate, it's a collaboration that works.

Source: Melanie Wells, "Agency Trouble-Shooters Click with Polaroid," *USA Today,* 17 June 1996, 3B.

California Fluid Milk Processor Advisory Board

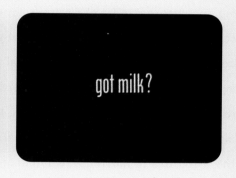

got milk?

"Interrogation": 30
(Open inside the interrogation room of a police precinct house. Two detectives are with a suspect. It's a tense scene)
Detective 1: Why don't you help yourself out?
(The suspect is sitting at the table. There's a brown paper sack, a half-eaten sandwich and two snack-type chocolate cupcakes. The suspect's face looks tired, but defiant and uncooperative. The first detective looks at the suspect, looks down at the table, then at the suspect)
Detective 1: Are you lookin' at my cupcakes?

(The suspect eyes the cupcakes)
Detective 1: Go ahead! Take a bite!
(The suspect grabs one of the cupcakes and starts munching. The suspect chomps on the cupcake. He's got a whole mouthful)
Detective 2: 'Attaboy.
(Cut to the first detective starting to pull something from the paper sack on the table)
Detective 1: All right now . . .
(The suspect, still eating, looks up and sees what the detective pulls out of the bag. His eyes register shock)

Detective 1: . . . we can do this the easy way . . .
SFX: Something is set on the table.
Detective 1: . . . or we can do it the hard way.
(Cut to the first detective sliding a carton of milk back away from the suspect, closer to the camera. Cut to the face of the suspect. Now he looks completely defeated)
Suspect: Gulp.
Camera card: Got Milk?
Anncr. (VO): Got milk?

LOOK BEFORE YOU LEAP

- **What is the job of a copywriter?**

- **What are the basics of writing for print media?**

- **How does writing for television and radio differ from writing for print media?**

- **What are the principles of copywriting for new advertising forms such as infomercials and Web sites?**

- **What are the demands of writing across cultures?**

14

As Cocciolo and Ehringer demonstrate, advertising copywriting encompasses a lot of different activities, all of which start with the creation of an idea that solves a marketing communications problem. The general process of advertising writing varies by the type of advertising medium in which a writer is called upon to work. Each advertising medium has its own set of mechanical requirements that the writer has to master. New forms of advertising further stretch the writer's imagination and add to the challenges of the job.

In this chapter we will discuss the job of the copywriter and the challenges of the major advertising media from the writer's perspective. After outlining in detail the job of the copywriter, we discuss the basics of writing for print media. Next, we examine the fast world of writing for outdoor, transit, and direct mail. The chapter also presents the major types of radio and television formats with an eye (or ear) toward what makes writing for these media effective. Finally, we explore new advertising forms and the demands of writing across cultures.

The Job Of A Copywriter

Just as the word "creativity" might be a poor choice to describe the process of creating ads, so too, the word "copywriting" is a less-than-accurate label for what the copywriter really does. The job of the copywriter is not restricted to the production of the actual words, or **copy,** that make up a good portion of print ads, TV and radio commercials, or interactive messages. The **copywriter** is responsible for much more than copy; in fact, the copywriter is responsible for creating, writing, and managing the entire advertisement development process from concept to headlines, subheads, slogans, logotypes, pictures, sounds, voices, computer icons, and other elements that constitute an ad.

This responsibility for the entire creation process is perhaps demonstrated best not in the large companies and ad agencies but in small companies, where a few generalists do the job that many specialists might handle in a big shop. Eric Meyer, founder of the Simple Shoe Company, is one such generalist. He is the client, ad agency, designer, and copywriter all rolled into one package. Computer technology gives him the ability to create ads like those shown in Exhibit 14–1. Meyer uses a Macintosh computer and graphics software such as Quark and Photoshop to create ads from concept through to finished product.[1]

The typical larger advertising agency has many specialists on hand that the small agency does not have on its payroll. This does not change the goal of the copywriting process, but it does alter the number and types of people with whom the writer works. In the traditional agency, the copywriter collaborates with an art director on the development of an ad. Collaboration is an important part of the team effort through which advertisements are created. While the art director provides expertise in art and design, it is the copywriter's job to be able to visualize the completed ad.

This ability to see the final ad in the mind's eye is called conceptualization or visualization. **Conceptualization** is the application of intuition and imagination to everything we know about the advertising problem on which we are working in order to create an advertising idea. Conceptualization is the copywriter's job, whether creating an entire ad alone or collaborating with an artist. **Visualization,** which is the forma-

Dress down for success

What defines success anyway? My guess is that one's happiness is probably the best measure.

Eric Meyer

Simple®

the Clog™

U.S.A. & CANADA: 495-A South Fairview, Goleta CA 93117   (800) 611 0698   EUROPE 31 174 388 500   AUSTRALIA, NEW ZEALAND 61 0 44 41 5055   JAPAN 81 3 5421 3041

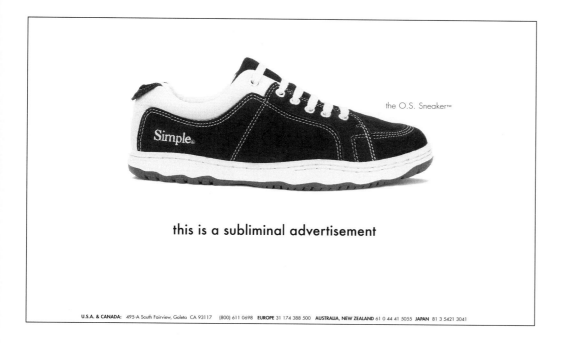

the O.S. Sneaker™

this is a subliminal advertisement

U.S.A. & CANADA: 495-A South Fairview, Goleta CA 93117   (800) 611 0698   EUROPE 31 174 388 500   AUSTRALIA, NEW ZEALAND 61 0 44 41 5055   JAPAN 81 3 5421 3041

EXHIBIT 14–1 These ads for Simple shoes are illustrative of the creativity and production capabilities of Eric Meyer, Simple's founder and the company's one-man advertising group.

tion of a mental image of an ad, usually comes before the designing and writing of an ad, or it may occur concurrently with these processes as artist and writer strive to create a big idea around which they will complete the ad. Visualization differs from designing an ad, which is an art function. The copywriter does not have to have art talent, but he or she is helped by the ability to sense the overall look of an ad. Exhibit 14–2 tells the story of how writers, artists, and production talent collaborate and the importance of visualization. "Adscape:

Stealing Ideas/Concepts" discusses the downside of collaboration and sharing.

The creation of interactive ads typically requires an additional collaborator known as the computer artist. A **computer artist** must be an expert in computer use and know the design and word-processing software required to put an interactive ad together once the copywriter and art director have come up with the concept. The computer artist is essential in the actual production of interactive ads that consumers access through their computers.

The Assignment: The W. B. Doner advertising agency had been given the assignment of creating a television commercial for the University of Michigan Hospitals highlighting their brand-new facility. The assignment did not come without its problems, two of which were the most troublesome. First, the U of M Hospitals are among the world's most preeminent teaching hospitals. As such, they carry the stigma of patients being treated like experiments. Secondly, the new facility housed the latest in medical technology. This information was hard to discuss without the commercial sounding like a medical journal or looking like every other TV spot for hospitals.

The Collaboration: Two of the creative team members, Debbie Karnowsky and Jim Dale, were among the collaborators on the project. Karnowsky says that the idea was to turn people's preconceived notions "inside out." She continues, "When Jim Dale came up with the theme line, that set us in the right direction. It instantly made a plus out of the teaching hospital. In just two words, 'Knowledge Heals,' we had come upon (in our opinion) one of the best ideas ever to come out of the agency."

The Visualization: A third creative team member, Cindy Sikorski, remembers that problems still remained after the theme line was established. The team started to think in terms of crucial medical discoveries that took place at the U of M Hospitals. They wanted to establish U of M Hospitals as a leader in medical technology culminating from all of its previous medical breakthroughs. Sikorski asks, "How do you visualize something like that?" She continues, "We ran the gamut: floating matrices, charts, timelines. We finally hit on rapidly moving pathways with pictures of medical breakthroughs embedded in them."

The Commercial: The television photoboard shown here is a 30-second review of man's medical history that concludes at the new University of Michigan Hospitals.

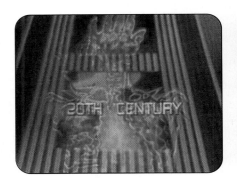 

Source: Likable Advertising (Southfield, MI: W. B. Doner and Company, 1988), 46–47.

AdScape

·······················

Stealing
Ideas/Concepts

Funny thing, ideas. So ephemeral—here one minute and gone the next. And just as intangible—hard to hang your hat on an idea. Yet ideas are the most important thing a writer can bring to an advertising problem. They can bring fame and fortune to a writer, and they are often the envy of others who could profit from stealing them.

Ideas are also what agencies sell to clients. Some agencies put their ideas on the line in new business presentations. But because ideas are so valuable and so hard to protect, other agencies are more guarded and merely show a prospective client past work.

There are three important situations in which ideas can be and are stolen in the adver-

tising business. The first consists of lifting an old idea, dusting it off, and using it in a new situation. Sometimes this happens unbeknownst to the person who has appropriated the idea because some ideas are quite commonplace and can be thought of by more than one person. Sometimes, enough time has gone by and the chance of someone remembering the previous use of the idea is slim.

The second situation is when an advertising agency makes a new business pitch, does not get the account, and the client uses the agency's ideas anyway. This is the risk of offering speculative ideas in the competitive arena of new business presentations. For this reason, some agencies will

not do campaigns on spec for prospective clients.

Ideas also get stolen in a different sense when someone takes credit for an idea created by someone else. This happens in social settings, when someone looking for a job takes credit on a resumé, or in the heat of competition for promotions and raises.

QUESTIONS
Consider these three situations in which ideas might be stolen. Which do you consider the most grievous situation from an ethical perspective? Why? Are there any situations in which stealing ideas is just part of the business? If so, why?

Every writer must rely on collaboration not only with an art director or computer artist but also with the production people in the print, broadcast, or computer fields who will be involved in the actual completion of the finished advertisement. Exhibit 14–3 illustrates the three major parts of the message creation task—copywriting, art direction, and production—and how this chapter is related to the next two. The remaining sections of this chapter will present elements of advertisements with which the copywriter has to work in creating effective ads.

Writing For Print Advertising

We start our discussion of copywriting with the elements of print advertising because the mastery of writing magazine, newspaper, outdoor,

transit, and direct mail ads is fundamental to the ability to write for all media, including the newly emerging interactive media. In fact, it has been said that the creation of interactive ads and promotional materials for the computer, as with other more traditional media, demands good ideas, good writing, and an understanding of how words and pictures work together. The copywriting discipline starts with a firm understanding of how to write a print advertisement.

In print advertising, the elements of importance to the copywriter are: headlines, overlines and underlines, subheadings, captions, illustrations or visuals, body copy, slogans and taglines, and logotypes or signature cuts. These elements make up the copywriter's toolbox for creating effective print advertising. Illustrations and visuals, and logotypes and signature cuts are important to the entire visualization process and will be covered in Chapter 15, "Symbols, Images, and Art Direction."

Headlines

The **headline** is the most important verbal element in a print advertisement because it is the principal statement of benefit or promise in an ad.2 David Ogilvy, in his now classic book *Confessions of an Advertising Man,* said, "Five times as many people read the headline as read the body copy."3 Readers often decide whether to read an ad based on a headline. These points are generally held to be true even in this day of strong reliance on the visual elements of an ad to gain the reader's interest.

THE HEADLINE'S JOB The headline has a very specific job to perform in an advertisement: to gain the reader's attention. Most readers of newspapers and magazines are not looking for your advertisement, so it must find *them.* David Ogilvy offers these research-tested techniques for grabbing the reader's attention:4

- Promise a benefit—a whiter wash, more miles per gallon, freedom from pimples, fewer cavities.
- Inject news into your headline, such as the announcement of a new product.
- Provide helpful information.
- Put your brand name in the headline.
- Flag your audience with words such as "asthma sufferers," or "women over 35."
- Be specific about your offer.

Exhibit 14–4 presents some examples that meet Ogilvy's principles for an effective headline.

Headlines can be used effectively as the primary graphic element in an advertisement. In cases where the budget is limited, an ad or campaign based on unique headlines can provide quite a lot of creative leverage, even in a very small space.

In interactive media, a headline is used to attract the reader's attention to the computer screen in much the same way as it is used in a print ad. Notice that the screen from the Ford Web site shown in Exhibit 14–5 uses a headline to get you interested in the information that follows.

TYPES OF HEADLINES An important principle for advertising in general is that people respond to things that are in their best interest or self-interest. One way to trigger a reader's self-interest is through the use of a **benefit headline.** A benefit headline promises the consumer something personally rewarding in return for buying the product. This reward or benefit should be presented in an interesting and involving manner. The headline in Exhibit 14–6 promises readers that using Neutrogena's New Hands product will give them hands that are softer and more youthful looking.

The **news headline** plays to people's natural inquisitiveness by promising the reader that there is important information to be found by reading the ad. Many news headlines start with the words, "How to . . . ," and then the rest of the ad proceeds to tell the reader how to do or get or experience something new. The advertisement in Exhibit 14–7 illustrates how a new product can be effectively promoted through the use of the word "Introducing" in a news headline.

The **curiosity headline** uses an intriguing question or a creative play on words to pique the curiosity of the reader. This type of headline functions primarily as a "hook" to pull readers into the body copy, where the product benefits and details are provided. For this reason, curiosity headlines must be very well done in order to be effective. Notice, for example,

EXHIBIT 14–3   Copywriting and the Advertising Process

MESSAGE CREATION TASKS

Copywriting   Art Direction

Production

EXHIBIT 14–4   Headline Principles for Attracting the Reader's Attention to an Ad

Include a Benefit	"When was the last time you met a stranger and knew he was a brother?" *Harley-Davidson*
	"You're at a stoplight. It will last twenty seconds. This may be the only time some people ever see you. How do you want to be remembered?" *The New Lexus Coupe*
	"I Hate Sit-Ups. I Hate Sit-Ups. I Hate Sit-Ups. I Hate Sit-Ups. I Hate Sit-Ups." *Rollerblade*
Inject News	"Announcing the most significant fleet to enter the Caribbean since the *Nina, Pinta,* and *Santa Maria.*" *American Airlines*
	"Why Ultra Pampers is Officially Accepted by These Experts." *Ultra Pampers*
	"Announcing the World's First Interest-Free Home Loan." *Chase Bank of Singapore*
Provide Useful Information	"I know I should quit. Don't tell me why, tell me how." *Nicoderm*
	"How the hex on a Crescent can take the curse off a job." *CooperTools*
	"Don't lose another hair without getting the medical facts." *Rogaine*
Include the Brand Name	"The Ultimate Porsche. (Isn't that redundant?)" *Porsche 911 Turbo*
	"Nupe It, Jimmy." *Nuprin*
	"The Good News is Jeep Grand Cherokee is Now Available with a V8. There is No Bad News." *Jeep Grand Cherokee*
Select Your Target Audience	"Arthritis Pain Relief." *Extra-Strength Tylenol*
	"No One Believed I Would Ever Really Quit Smoking." *Habitrol*
	"Exactly how mad is she?" *American Floral Marketing Council*
Be Specific	"When We Roll Out the Red Carpet, It's 250 Miles Long." *North Carolina*
	"Fifteen dealerships into their search for a new car, Barry and Cynthia Nelson felt like throwing in the towel." *Saturn*
	"The world's only 1860s British Fife and Drum Drill isn't in Britain. It's here." *Ontario Canada*

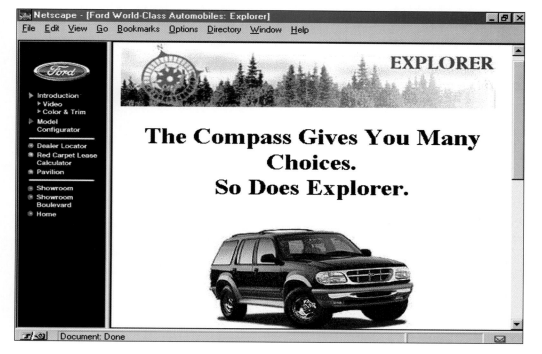

EXHIBIT 14–5   Just as they can draw readers to print advertisements, effective headlines can draw Internet users to particular Web pages. This eye-catching headline in the Ford Web site encourages visitors interested in the Explorer to continue their investigations, thus giving Ford an opportunity to provide those individuals with detailed product benefits and details.

how well the headline shown in Exhibit 14–8 works to pull readers into the body copy of the advertisement.

Other types of headlines that are somewhat less frequently used are the question, selective, and command headlines. The **question headline** can be considered a version of the curiosity headline in that it asks a provocative question to get the reader to read on. The risk is that if the writer is not careful, the reader could answer the question in the negative and not read on, in which case the writer has lost a potential customer for the advertiser.

The **selective headline** attracts the reader who has a particular problem, is in a situation, or is the type of person who has been deliberately identified in the headline. These headlines tend to be very direct in their approach to readers. Two advertisements for the product Cortaid run the simple yet direct headlines, "Eczema: Cortaid Helps Cure It" and "Allergic Rash: Cortaid Helps Cure It." If the reader has either of these problems, these selective headlines have a good chance of getting him or her to read the ads.

The **command headline** does just what it says it does: It commands the reader to do something. The command headline can be used with emotion, fear, or humor to motivate readers to find out more about why they are being ordered to act. It probably is appropriate that a headline for an ad from the U.S. Armed Forces carried this command headline: "If You Never Thought Of Your Child As The Military Type, Think Again."

Subheadings

Subheadings are organizational headings used to break up the body copy into more digestible bites for the reader and to emphasize important points in the copy. Subheads are indicated in bold type or in type that is slightly larger than that used in the body copy. Overlines and underlines are types of subheadings. An **overline** appears above a headline as a lead or teaser to get the reader to read the headline. An **underline** appears after or just under a headline as a transition into the body copy. Overlines and underlines are typically set in a type size that is smaller than that used for the headline but larger than that used for the body copy. The advertisements presented in Exhibit 14–9 illustrate the use of these three types of subheadings.

Captions

Captions typically are used under or next to photographs or illustrations to help the reader interpret them. Captions are among the most read elements in an advertisement after headlines. David Ogilvy believed that the reading of captions was a habit people carried over from reading the newspaper. He also believed that every picture in an ad should have a caption.[5] As Exhibit 14–10 illustrates, the writer can also combine the lure of the caption with that of the headline and use the headline as a caption under an engaging illustration or photograph.

Body Copy

The **body copy** is the heart and substance of an advertisement. It is set in smaller type than the headline and subheadings, and it should follow through on the theme established in the headline and illustrative elements of the ad. The body copy is where the writer can expand on the main idea of the ad and offer supporting selling points and arguments to the reader.

The principles of good writing should apply to body copy just as they apply to writing in general. Exhibit 14–11 lists the important principles of effective copywriting that specifically apply to the writing of body copy. If there is one principle that is paramount for copywriters, it is that the copy must be written as if the writer is talking to one person. Some have called this the *you approach.* As a copywriter, you want thousands or even millions of people to respond to your ad, but you do not write to this abstraction of an audience. To get thousands to respond, your copy should say to each individual reader, "This is only for you."[6]

STRUCTURE OF BODY COPY   Body copy is made up of a lead paragraph, the interior or actual body of the copy, and a closing paragraph. The **lead paragraph,** or *lead-in,* is a transition paragraph that acts as a bridge between the headline and subheads and the rest of the body copy. It continues the main idea and brings the reader into the specific selling points to be covered in the body copy. The *interior body copy* is where most of the selling takes place. This is where specific copy points can be presented to support the ad's central idea. The **closing paragraph,** or *close,* provides the writer with the opportunity to ask for the order or to move the reader to action.

THE BEST WAY TO STOP SUFFERING IS NEVER TO START.

Would you sacrifice 1 minute a day in order to spend the entire allergy season without the sneezing, congestion and runny nose that have always wrecked your summers?

Then consider a new kind of allergy treatment, Nasalcrom.®

Nasalcrom prevents allergy symptoms.

Allergies erupt because the natural immune system in your nose goes haywire.

Nasalcrom is the only medication that *prevents* this over-reaction. So you react like a person without allergies. The best plan is to start a week *before* allergy season hits.

One gentle spray in each nostril when you get up, one around noon, one before bed is all it takes--60 seconds tops.

No drowsiness, no other nasty side effects

Nasalcrom works at the site of your problem, in your nose. So it causes no drowsiness or jitters. There's no dependency and no interaction with other drugs. And you can use it throughout the entire allergy season.

Prescription no longer needed

Because it is so safe and effective, Nasalcrom has now been made available without a prescription. It's not like nasal sprays you could buy before. It's not like *anything* you could buy before. It's prevention, pure and simple.

NASALCROM
For prevention of allergy symptoms

For more information about Nasalcrom and the coming allergy season, call 1-800-395-STOP. (1-800-345-7867)
Individual results may vary. Use only as directed.   © 1997 Pharmacia & Upjohn Consumer Healthcare

THE TROOPER POWER PLANT: 195 LB.-FT.®
OF TORQUE GETS YOU GOING QUICKER THAN
YOU CAN SAY "EIGHTEEN WHEELER."

EXHAUST   AIR

Automakers are fond of giving you lots of technical information about acceleration. Well, here's a little tid-bit about speed you can actually relate to: Big rigs don't slow down. Hence the Trooper's beefy, 190 horse, twin cam, 24-valve, fuel injected, V6 engine.® Even that's more technical than

you really need. How about this, it will put a lot of road between you and lead foot pretty darn quick. There, that works. The Isuzu Trooper. Life's an adventure. Be prepared. (800) 726-2700

ISUZU
Practically Amazing

Maybe potatoes weren't meant to be frozen.

In the Dairy Case.

EXHIBIT 14–11   Principles of Effective Advertising Writing

1. **Place yourself in the background.** Write to draw attention to the product, service, or idea, and not to yourself.

2. **Stay focused.** Do not try to say too much or make too many points. Stick to one main idea and the necessary supporting points.

3. **Keep it simple.** Here are some quick ways to simplify your approach.
   - Write headlines that use familiar combinations of words in familiar sequences.
   - Use key words that are instantly understood by readers.
   - Write in short simple sentences.
   - Use active verbs.
   - Relax and be yourself. Write to express, not to impress. Be natural.

4. **Be specific.** Avoid writing that sounds like advertising. Avoid generalizations and exaggerations in favor of informative, specific copy.

5. **Establish your voice and who you're talking to.** Write from the reader's perspective. Use pronouns such as "you" and "your." Avoid saying "we," "they," or "us."

6. **Establish a rhythm.** All good copy has rhythm. Simple sentences, active verbs, nouns and pronouns, few superlatives, and an ear for pace and rhyming can help to establish a good rhythm.

7. **Write and rewrite.** Read your copy out loud. Let other people read it. Don't be afraid to rewrite. Good copy seldom flows from one's mind perfectly intact. Revisions make good copy.

8. **Follow the copywriter's creed:** *Start with a basic selling idea or concept that succeeds at linking a consumer benefit and product exclusive . . . then think visually, talk friendly, keep it simple, prove your point, stay on track, strive for the unexpected, seek a recurring theme, be yourself.*

Source: Compiled from: Anthony Antin, "Checklist: The A, B, C of Effective Print Advertising," handout, 1985, 1–6; Bruce Bendinger, *The Copy Workshop* (Chicago, IL: The Copy Workshop, 1993), 176–203; W. Keith Hafer and Gordon E. White, *Advertising Writing: Putting Creative Strategy to Work*, 3rd ed. (St. Paul, MN: West Publishing Company, 1989), 119; William Strunk, Jr., and E. B. White, *Elements of Style*, 3rd ed. (New York: Macmillan Publishing Co., Inc., 1979), xvi.

The advertisement for the Water Filtration Pitcher from Brita shown in Exhibit 14–12 illustrates this typical print ad structure. The lead-in paragraph successfully connects the body copy with the headline, and the interior paragraph that follows provides specific information about the product benefits. Finally, the last element in the ad is a tagline, "Tap into great taste." A **tagline,** or *slogan,* is a memorable line or phrase that is repeated in all ads in a campaign to provide continuity from one ad to the next. It also summarizes the major selling premise of the ad and campaign.

BASIC TYPES OF BODY COPY   While the copywriter's style is a combination of his or her own method and the specific demands of the writing assignment, copy styles fall into three general categories: straightforward, narrative, and dialogue. **Straightforward copy** follows through on the main idea as expressed in the headline and illustration. The goal is to stay on track with the headline idea and expand upon it by getting more and more specific until right before the end of the ad. The closing will then offer a summation of the copy points. This is the basic structure described previously in which the theme of the ad is carried from headline to lead-in to interior copy to closing in an orderly manner.

Narrative copy, also known as *story copy,* uses a story to get across the ad's main points. A classic example of narrative copy is the ad written by Nelson Metcalf, Jr., for the New Haven Railroad during World War II. The headline used in the ad reads, "The Kid in Upper 4." The ad is a story about how important it was for civilian railroad riders to be patient while the railroad helped transport the troops for the armed forces. The ad is a slice-of-life story about one particular soldier, what he is thinking about, his fears and hopes.[7] The ad shown in Exhibit 14–13 provides a more current example of narrative copy.

Dialogue copy is best suited for radio and television but can be used effectively in print advertising if the writer has a good feel for the natural way in which people speak. The typical dialogue is between two people; however, it can also be written in a monologue form, where the person making a testimonial speaks directly to the reader.

EXHIBIT 14–12   This ad for Brita's Water Filtration Pitcher is an excellent illustration of standard body copy structure and elements. Notice how the paragraphs of the body copy achieve, in succession, the goals of transition, communication, and call to action.

We can't bring you here.

But we can give you a taste.

How far do you have to go for clear, fresh, wonderful water? As far as your faucet. All you need is the Brita® Water Filtration Pitcher. Just fill with tap water. The remarkable filter does the rest, reducing chlorine taste, sediment, water hardness and copper. It even removes 93% of lead. You'll get some of the best tasting water in the world. And you don't have to go anywhere.

BRITA
Tap into great taste.

Brita offers a money-back guarantee* and is available in half-gallon and two-gallon models.
Find Brita at: The Bon Marche, Burdines, Carson's, Dayton's, Dillard's, Famous-Barr, Foley's, Hecht's, Kaufmann's, Lazarus, Lechters, Linens 'n Things, Macy's, Marshall Field's, Rich's, Stern's, Robinson-May, JC Penney, and other fine retailers. For the retailer nearest you, call 1-800-44-BRITA.
Substances removed may not be in all users' water. *Details in box. © 1996 The Brita Products Company.

R E S E T

1. We've said that the job of a copywriter involves more than writing copy. Can you think of a better job title for what a copywriter really does?

2. Think of a benefit headline that might run in an ad for your college or university to recruit new students. What major benefit does your college or university offer that makes it different from other schools?

3. Why is it important to write copy as if it is written for one individual?

Writing For Outdoor, Transit, And Direct Mail

The principles of writing copy for print ads also apply to writing for media such as outdoor, transit, and direct mail. The goals of attracting attention, following through in the copy, calling for action at the end of an ad, and writing clearly do not change. However, depending on the media, different emphasis is placed on these principles. Outdoor and transit, for example, are read by people in cars, buses, and trains moving quickly past the ads. Therefore, the principles of headline writing are put to a real test. The copywriter has to grab the passerby's attention quickly while getting across the entire message in nutshell form, so the headline or one-liner and visual must work together to communicate the message.

New technology in outdoor and transit can provide new ways to try to reach an audience. Notice in Exhibit 14–14 how technology has made it possible to use the entire exterior of a bus, including the windows, back, and top, for an advertisement. Rather than being limited to a relatively small side-mounted poster, an advertiser can now use larger, more eye-catching images to attract the attention of its audience. The basic rule of thought for outdoor or transit headlines is seven words or less.

David Ogilvy called direct mail advertising "my first love and secret weapon."[8] The reason he liked direct mail so much was that everything a direct mail writer does can be tested. The words, appeals, visuals, length, calls-to-action, or any element that makes up a direct mail piece can change—and the response may change as a result. Some of the best writers in the advertising business were good direct mail writers first. Direct mail disciplines writing in ways general advertising cannot.

The two most important things a writer has to do in direct mail are 1) get the reader to notice and open up the piece to read it, and 2) respond to the advertiser's offer. The envelope, cover, and headline will decide whether or not the reader will open up the direct mail piece. The interior copy will be the deciding factor in the reader's decision to respond to the offer. As a general rule, a **call-to-action,** or request for the order, must come at the end of the interior copy.

BORN TO ZIG.
(CONFESSIONS OF A CATERA OWNER.)

By the time he was 25 years old, my father had spent more time behind the controls of a B-17 than driving a car. Since 1945, however, the gap has grown considerably the other way. The turning point was probably the two days it took him and my mother to navigate to, around and through Terre Haute in a '49 Kaiser after a heavy snowstorm. It was their honeymoon.

His whole working life involved cars, although he had nothing to do with the automobile industry. He was a salesman, mostly; continually patrolling territories of a scope that would have intimidated Lewis & Clark. Judging by the wide variety of expensive toys that surrounded me in my childhood, followed by a free five-year college education, I would say my father was pretty good at what he did.

Before cell phones and e-mail and v-mail and fax machines, the one machine that mattered most to a salesman was a car. My father owned a lot of cars, each one progressively larger.

I learned to drive in one of his more immense land monsters. I know from personal experience that it could not zig. (It could, at times, however, be coaxed into doing some very un-luxury-car things, always with me behind the wheel and my father nowhere to be seen.)

Of course, this was at a time when one couldn't say "luxury" and "fun" in the same sentence, unless one could read 223 pages of Webster's Dictionary without pausing for breath.

Now there's Catera.

Catera scrambles your preconceptions and turns out to be a whole new omelet. Instead of pinching an idea or two from a performance car and putting it into a luxury car, Catera brings innovative thinking direct from the auto racing circuit, a rich and often under-utilized source of zig. Like sodium-filled exhaust valves. (It means more engine power; the whys and wherefores belong in a tech manual.)

Catera gives you full-range traction control, which means you can have Terre Haute or anywhere else quickly in your rearview mirror, even in a snowstorm.

Catera even comes with its own college. Not for you, for Catera salespeople. They learn the body, soul and vision of Catera. So you get a completely new kind of buying experience. My father would approve.

Am I my father's child? Surely. I've spoken in his voice too many times for there not to be a genetic connection. But there are some differences. My eclectic disposition looks for that that says luxury and fun, together. I need a car to do some un-luxury-car things as part of its nature, without coaxing or coercion. I need my zigs.

CATERA.
THE CADDY THAT ZIGS.

Writing For The Radio Commercial

Advertising professional and creative soul Bruce Bendinger says about writing for radio, "It does not play on a piece of paper. It plays between the ears."[9] Comedian and advertising writer Stan Freeberg gets credit for having said of radio, "Radio is a very special medium because it stretches the imagination, while television stretches it up to 21 inches."[10] Radio's ability to play on the listener's imagination is called *theater-of-the-mind* because a good copywriter can create any image or situation he or she desires through the dramatic use of voices, music, and sound effects. The dramatic effect takes place entirely in the listener's mind.

EXHIBIT 14–13 This narrative ad for the Catera is one in a series of ads that Cadillac has run to promote the new, sporty model. In the course of the storylike presentation, each of these humorous ads reveals new product benefits and features.

EXHIBIT 14–14   New technology has been developed that allows the full exterior of a bus to be used as the canvas for an advertisement. As you can see, this transit ad for the television show "Central Park West" takes full advantage of this new opportunity.

Radio producer George Moore of the Leo Burnett advertising agency gives the following example of letting the listener conjure up a vision from a radio spot. He says:

> One of my favorite commercials, called "Workday," has a man enjoying an omelet as he's being shot out of a cannon. It would be impossible to do that spot on television; nor would anyone want to attempt it.[11]

Elements Of The Radio Commercial

Above all, the radio listener's imagination is stretched by the style in which the commercial is written. Radio copy should be written the way people actually speak. Short sentences, fragments, and phrases are closer to actual speech than are complete sentences. The best test to see (hear) if radio copy sounds natural is to read it. Always time your spot as you read it aloud to make sure it fits the allotted time. A general rule is not to write more than two words per second. The radio commercial in

Exhibit 14–15 is a good example of copy that has been written to be spoken.

The radio commercial in Exhibit 14–15 does some other things well beyond its style of writing. For example, it focuses on one simple idea, using a classic "boy-meets-girl" plot to promote the product's name and beer drinker's enthusiasm for its taste. The spot also is relevant to the target audience. It takes place in an apartment complex and uses the awkwardness of the first meeting of a new neighbor to inject humor into the spot. And finally, it registers the brand name with seven product mentions that have been integrated into the humorous dialogue.

The copywriter can employ a wide variety and combinations of voice, sound effects, music, and timing to create effective and imaginative advertising. Good casting of voices can help create the drama in radio. Voices of children, a grandmother, an authoritative teacher or banker, or the friendly postman can all be planned for and cast accordingly. Remember that characters in a radio spot do not have to describe what is going on. A doorbell here, breaking glass there, a vacuum cleaner sound, a dog barking, and a car engine starting are all more vivid ways to let the listener know what is happening. And music in a radio spot can range from a jingle to background music. Sometimes no music at all is the best way to gain the listener's attention in a radio environment filled with music.

All of these elements should be choreographed in such a way as to give a spot a sense of timing, or tempo. Sometimes the tempo should be fast, especially when the writer wants to create a sense of urgency about the offer. Or if a soft, compassionate, or romantic mood is the goal, then the tempo should be slower. It is within the writer's control to create the right tempo to go along with a commercial's message.

Radio Commercial Formats

The elements at the radio commercial copywriter's disposal can be used to create some basic radio commercial formats. Three standard formats are: 1) pitch or straight announcement, 2) situation or slice-of-life, and 3) musical or song.[12]

In the straight announcement or **pitch format** the copy is read by an announcer with little embellishment from sound effects, music, or voices. Sometimes music will be played in the background to establish a mood or attract the listener's attention. Announcer-read copy can be very effective when read by a well-known or local personality. Radio disk jockeys who have strong followings in a market make good announcers for this format.

The slice-of-life or **situation format** is only limited by the writer's imagination. Typically, the radio spot is based upon a slice-of-life situation that can be anything from gritty-real to fantasy. The radio spot in Exhibit 14–15 is a situation commercial. Notice that an announcer does come in at the end of this spot to make the final "pitch" for the product.

The **song format** has several variations. This format can be as simple as a **jingle,** which is a song built around key selling points of a product. Or, more typically, the music or song is played and then lowered in volume so that an announcer can read the copy for the product. The industry term for this format is a **donut.** A jingle, song, or music can also be placed in a situation radio spot.

R E S E T

1. **Why is short copy important for outdoor and transit advertising?**
2. **Why is radio called the "theater of the mind"?**
3. **What types of products or services lend themselves to the pitch-format radio commercial?**

Writing For The Television Commercial

Television provides the copywriter with more ways to create exciting advertising than any other medium. At the same time, television clutter has reached an all-time high, and viewers can easily "zip" past commercials with their remote control devices. And, if they really do not want to watch commercials, they can record programs and "zap" out the television spots altogether. Breaking through this clutter demands a strong visual aptitude and choreog-

rapher's mind for detail and coordination. A flair for the dramatic or theatrical will not hurt the television copywriter either.

Television writers usually write their copy in script or storyboard form. A **storyboard** is a series of panels, or pictures, that indicate the main action of a commercial accompanied by written descriptions of what is in the panels (video) and what will be heard (audio). Audio instructions for music and sound effects complement the written copy, which appears under each panel in which it is to be spoken. Storyboards have become an important vehicle for communicating TV advertising ideas because

---

EXHIBIT 14–15   **Radio Copy Written to Be Spoken**

TITLE: MOLSON GOLDEN, "FRIDGE" (:60)

SFX:	Doorbell
HER:	Hang on
HIM:	Hello?
HER:	Hello.
HIM:	Hi, I'm your neighbor, next door neighbor.
HER:	Yeah.
HIM:	I missed you when you moved in, I guess.
HER:	Really?
HIM:	I wanted to explain about that shelf in your refrigerator.
HER:	The shelf? Oh, you mean the bottom shelf. The one with the whole case of Molson Golden. Boy, what a great surprise that was moving in.
HIM:	It was my Molson Golden, my Molson Golden.
HER:	Your Molson Golden.
HIM:	Yeah, I had an arrangement with the person who lived here before you.
HER:	Oh yeah?
HIM:	I sort of rented one shelf in her fridge.
HER:	You don't have a refrigerator?
HIM:	Yeah, I'm a photographer. Mine's full of film and I needed someplace to keep my Molson Golden.
HER:	Oh yeah, I see.
HIM:	Cool, clear, smooth. I'm sure you understand.
HER:	Oh yeah, I love it. It was terrific.
HIM:	It was terrific.
HER:	Uh-huh.
HIM:	What do you mean *was*?
VO:	Molson Golden, from North America's oldest brewer of beer and ale. The #1 import from Canada. Molson makes it Golden.
HER:	It really was a shame you missed the party.
HIM:	I feel like I was there in spirit.
VO:	Martlet Importing Co., North Hills, New York.

Source: Bruce Bendinger, *The Copy Workshop* (Chicago, IL: The Copy Workshop, 1993), 249.

they contain both the visual and verbal elements of a commercial.

Storyboards come in a number of formats, from a roughly sketched storyboard to a finished *photoboard* that contains still photographs from the scenes in the finished commercial. Most of the storyboards used as examples in this text are photoboards. Storyboards can be videotaped to produce *animatics* that give the writer, client, and consumers an approximation of what the finished TV spot might be like. The animatic is a cost-effective form to use in pretesting the commercial. The current state of video technology has added another rough-cut format called, partially in jest, the *stealamatic,* in which the writer can steal footage from other commercials and edit them together to form a new commercial concept.

As the copywriter approaches the television advertising assignment, he or she must understand that this is a visual medium in which some principles lead to success more often than others. We will discuss some of the basic goals and principles of effective television commercials before moving on to the types of TV commercials.

Principles Of Television Copywriting

The effective television commercial must let the pictures tell the story. A good technique to test whether or not a commercial is communicating is to cover the copy on the storyboard or turn down the volume on the finished spot. If the video portion of the spot is doing its job, the commercial should be able to get the message across without the help of the audio. Among the top TV spots of recent years are the Polaroid commercials that demonstrate situations in which only a Polaroid camera will do. The Polaroid commercial in Exhibit 14–16 relies heavily on the visual part of the message. Notice how little dialogue there is in the TV spot.

Kenneth Roman and Jane Maas, in their books *How to Advertise* and *The New How to Advertise,* also suggest that a writer or client should be able to select one frame from a storyboard that encapsulates or sums up the entire commercial visually, perhaps with an enduring visual symbol in it. This frame is called the **key visual symbol,** or simply *key visual.*[13] The presence of this key visual is a good way to ensure

that the viewer will get the intended message. Look back at the Polaroid commercial presented in Exhibit 14–16. Which panel would you identify as the key visual?

Whereas the headline grabs the reader's attention in print advertising, in television, it is the first five seconds that determine if the viewer will stay with a commercial. The copywriter must offer the viewer a reason to watch the whole commercial from start to finish. This is especially important today, when viewers will go zipping past your commercial at a moment's notice. Offer news, entertainment, a problem to be solved, or a conflict. It is rare that a television commercial that starts out slowly and builds to a climax will be effective.

Beyond these important criteria, television advertising is like all advertising. It should be single-minded, register the name of the product, show people to whom viewers can relate, be consistent in tone with the brand's image, and build on past advertising. Everything else is technique and can be learned. It is how the writer employs the techniques to achieve these basic goals that will result in good television advertising. "Adscape: A Writer's Story" tells such a tale.

Types Of Television Commercials

It is hard to find a classification system for television commercials upon which everyone agrees, so we have selected six types of commercials that are frequently seen on television: 1) demonstration, 2) testimonials, 3) presenters, 4) slice-of-life, 5) lifestyle, and 6) animation.[14] Additionally, we will also discuss the use of humor, music, and emotion in commercials.

DEMONSTRATION   The demonstration commercial perhaps makes the best use of the impact of television. Over the years, there have been all types of demonstrations, from cars leaping over canyons to a truck being driven over a cardboard bridge. Home cleaning products lend themselves well to this type of presentation. Recently, a series of ads promoting Glad-Lock Zipper Storage Bags presented the fail-proof nature of the product's yellow-and-blue-make-green seal. In these ads, messy or dangerous items are placed both in a Glad-Lock bag and in another, competing bag. As the announcer holds both bags upside down, one of

"Dog & Cat" :30

(Open on shot of a kitchen garbage can which has been knocked over. Trash is all over the floor. Cut to a dog being scolded by owner)

Woman (VO): Very bad dog. Bad, bad dog!

(Cat is up on the sink in the background. Cut to a repeat scenario. The dog looks up at the cat on the sink. The cat looks over the edge. The garbage can is full of trash. The dog remembers the woman scolding him. He looks around the kitchen at a rolling pin, a meat cleaver and finally to a Polaroid One Step on the table)

Title Card: Polaroid. See what develops.

(Cut to a shot of the dog as he sits in front of the entry way, tail wagging. The dog has the Polaroid photograph of the cat's mischievous venture in his mouth. The woman's hand reaches down to receive the photograph)

Woman (VO): Oh, dear.

AdScape

....

A Writer's Story

A winner of the 1994 Cannes Grand Prix Trophy, Jeep® marketing's "Snow Covered" TV spot resulted from a collaboration by the members of Gary Topolewski's creative team.

* Jeep® is a registered trademark of Chrysler Corporation.

Gary Topolewski is a managing partner in charge of creative for the Detroit office of Bozell Worldwide Advertising. He oversees the creative direction for all of the agency's clients, including Chrysler Corporation's corporate and international accounts, the national and dealer Chrysler/Plymouth and Jeep® business,* and the agency's multiproduct nonautomotive accounts, such as Cellular One, The Hush Puppies Company, and Rockwell International Corporation. It was in his role overseeing the Jeep brand account that Topolewski worked on the "Snow Covered" Jeep TV spot that won the 1994 Cannes Grand Prix Trophy, the most prestigious

international creative honor in the world.

Topolewski says that the most satisfying aspect of creating advertising is when you can come up with advertising that is unique and fun yet still meets all of the client's objectives. So it was with the Jeep brand spot, which was developed after Chrysler told Bozell to create a memorable TV spot for the 1994 Winter Olympics.

Topolewski entertained hundreds of ideas from his creative team by posting them on his office walls. It was senior art director Andy Ozark who had sketched a visual idea showing a Jeep vehicle burrowing a tunnel through the snow. In the final spot, the Jeep vehi-

cle is depicted under the snow stopping at a stop sign and flashing its turn signal before turning left.

Topolewski started his career in 1981 as a junior copywriter and has risen steadily to his present position at Bozell. His experience as a writer taught him not to dictate ideas to his colleagues. As he says, "Nobody is that good that he has a lock on creativity."

QUESTIONS

Why do you think the "Snow Covered" Jeep® spot was so successful and memorable? What types of creativity and collaboration do you think it took to come up with this idea?

"Snow Covered" :30
SFX: Music and singing under throughout.
(Open on snow and mountains. As the camera pans we see movement under the snow, like a mole underground. The moving continues and then stops. Snow falls from a covered stop sign. Red taillights glimmer through the snow and then the moving vehicle, still covered by snow, turns)
Super: There's Only One Jeep.

the characters is forced to select which bag is to be held over the head of his or her counterpart—invariably a cranky coworker or the school bully. Because the person can verify that the Glad-Lock bag is closed by looking at the color of the seal, it is the obvious choice. These ads effectively achieve the basic goal of demonstration advertising: to show how well your product performs. If the product's performance can be demonstrated, you should demonstrate it.

TESTIMONIALS Testimonials come in three basic varieties, each with its own purpose. The most credible of the three is the *ordinary person testimonial.* Ordinary people do not have the polish that actors do and therefore are much more believable. In fact, it is often the little mistakes they make in front of the camera that add to their effectiveness. *Expert endorsers* are appropriate when their expert knowledge is relevant to the product. Engineers can endorse cars or computers, doctors can endorse health products, and teachers can endorse educational services and products. The *celebrity endorser* can bring attention to a product and help sell it when his or her celebrity is relevant to the product. Bill Cosby is known to love kids, so he does well with children's products such as Jell-O.

PRESENTERS The stand-up presenter is the most basic television format. While agencies might not find this approach very creative, a good personality such as Ed McMahon can be very persuasive on behalf of the product. The presenter can be very believable if he or she goes beyond the prepared script and offers an endorsement based upon personal experience with the product. Today, this format is derisively known as "the talking head."

SLICE-OF-LIFE A **slice-of-life commercial** is a story or staged playlet that involves characters and the product. The setting is realistic, such as a diner, barber shop, beauty salon, or supermarket, and the characters act out a scene in which the product is the hero. Some of these spots demonstrate the product solving a common problem such as unclogging the drain. Others employ trade symbols or characters like white knights, doves, or lonely repairmen as mnemonic (memory) devices. "Consumer Insight: Real Life, Real People" describes how to find ideas for these commercials in everyday situations.

LIFESTYLE **Lifestyle commercials** focus on the consumer's interests and activities as opposed to the product itself to show how the product fits into that lifestyle. Many McDonald's, Hallmark, and Kodak ads, as well as many of the beer commercials on television, emphasize lifestyle over product. Lifestyle commercials can be very effective for socially conspicuous or relevant products.

ANIMATION **Animation** can be used effectively, but it should be approached carefully. Claymation, a form of animation, is very popular due to its unique ability to make the clay figures look very much like real-life characters. Animation is one of those techniques that goes in and out of style. While it is limitless in what it can portray, animation lacks the realism that many consumers look for in television advertising.

HUMOR, MUSIC, AND EMOTION Humor is a technique that David Ogilvy refused to acknowledge for years because he believed Claude Hopkins (the father of advertising), who had said, "People don't buy from clowns."[15] However, more recent research shows that humor is effective. Humorous commercials are among the most difficult to write, however. Care should be taken not to let the humor or jokes overwhelm the product. And, because humor tends to wear out, the advertiser and agency will need to create a large pool of commercials, as Miller Lite did in its "Tastes Great, Less Filling" campaign.

Music can be used in two ways in commercials. First, it can set the mood of the spot. We have seen this use of music, for example, in a series of TV commercials for Mercedes-Benz, all of which used fun, boogie music to set a lighthearted tone to the spots. Secondly, musical jingles can be used as memory devices to improve the memorability of the product such as the use of the song, "Play That Funky Music," in Intel's MMX Technology "bunny suit" advertisements. Also, more recently, Burger King has used a series of advertisements featuring various popular "oldies" to promote its fast-food fare.

Emotional appeals can cause the audience to remember your product by associating it with the feelings conveyed by the ad. Clients tend to err in favor of rational appeals, but consumers like the strength of feeling projected by a good emotional commercial. Hallmark and Kodak are two companies that have used emotion in their ads to sell memories, which are based entirely on emotions.

Writing For New Forms Of Media

The expanding number of television channels available on cable and satellite TV and the ever-increasing penetration of personal computers is creating a new media landscape that is presenting fresh challenges to the advertising industry. New TV programming forms such as the infomercial, and advertising on the Internet and online services are two examples of new formats that are challenging the imagination of copywriters.

Writing The Infomercial

The best way to approach any new form of advertising is to ask yourself why you are using it; then a lot of the answers about how to approach writing for that form will fall into place. The infomercial's purpose is to sell a product or product line directly to viewers. Because an infomercial must maintain its audience's interest longer than typical commercials, it must have some drawing power. Thus, the writing should be both entertaining and interesting while at the same time calling for the audience to buy the products being promoted. The infomercial industry is still young, with most of its growth occurring since 1990. This means that there is room for improvement in the infomercial form.

An infomercial should be involving. The product or service being sold should appeal to audience members' self-interests. This explains why early growth in this industry has included products such as those in the health and

CONSUMER INSIGHT

. . . .

Real Life, Real People

You may be familiar with McDonald's TV spot called "Perfect Season." In it a group of fathers is coaching a peewee football team while another group is serving as human goal posts. Still other dads are devotedly videotaping the action while their sons bungle play after play. Not a very hip commercial by today's standards, but it was good enough for Stephen Spielberg to turn it into a feature-length film entitled "Little Giants."

Cheryl Berman of Leo Burnett writes and supervises a lot of heartwarming ads like "Perfect Season." Where does she search for these dramas espousing eternal truths? From real life. Berman believes that living life contributes in a big way to her ideas. In fact, she claims that every time she had

a child her work got better and better.

Luke Sullivan of Fallon McElligot has a similar take on the value of observing real people. He recommends going to focus groups, where you can watch real people react to your work. The value of this experience extends to the time after the focus group is over; each time you get a new idea, those people are still in your head. Sullivan says, "You can see their faces light up at the right idea and wrinkle up at a stupid one."

The worst thing you can do in trying to inject insight into your ideas is to pretend you know your audience. Sullivan believes that self-consciously customizing your message adds nothing to its persuasiveness. It's like fishing with a

lure the fish like: You don't have to add little signs to the lure that say, "Hey! This is your kind of lure, isn't it?"

The best source of ideas that resonate with consumers is the consumers themselves. Be observant of life's little truths. Listen to real people. Then be natural; don't try too hard.

QUESTIONS

Think of some of your own real-life situations. What kinds of commercials could you imagine fashioning after them?

Sources: Luke Sullivan, "The Gospel According to Luke," *Advertising Age's Creativity,* December 1994, 14-15; and Brenda Wilhelmson, "Mrs. Warmth," *Advertising Age's Creativity,* December 1994, 18–19.

fitness, beauty and personal hygiene, and personal finance categories. Additional involvement is often provided by using celebrities as hosts or guests on the infomercial. The writer's task is to write a TV script for a show that is really a sales pitch or long commercial for the product.

The script for the infomercial should be written with the following direct-response advertising goals in mind:

- Create urgency by regularly asking viewers throughout the show to call in to buy the product.
- Make sure the offer is clear.
- Create exclusivity by including the fact that viewers cannot buy the product in a store.
- Limit the time period in which viewers can buy the product.
- Limit the number of products or versions available.
- Emphasize installment amounts to be paid as opposed to total amount.
- Demonstrate the product and/or results of using it.

The length of an infomercial actually requires more simplicity than a typical TV spot because you do not want the viewer to become confused over the time it is on the air.

Writing For Interactive Media

Consumers are surfing cyberspace in ever-increasing numbers, and advertisers are scrambling to learn how to use the Internet, online services, and CD-ROM to reach and engage the audience in their messages. Writing and designing for these new interactive applications are in their infancy, so this section will provide some guiding advice, with the recognition that things are changing even as you are reading this section.

Interactive messages can be as simple as banners or as complex as entire Web sites. A **banner** is a short, graphic device that acts as a gateway to another page or Web site. They can be static or they can include motion that makes them dynamic. The purpose of a banner is to attract attention and to get the Internet user to click on it to go to another page or location for additional information.

Web sites are a series of screens or pages with an Internet address, organized to allow the Internet user to move through them in an easy and organized manner. For this purpose, Web sites should be organized in layers. You can provide a lot of information while still making access easy by creating options that allow users to bypass some information in favor of that in which they are more keenly interested. This is achieved by starting with a *marquee ad,* which is really a billboard that introduces the user to a larger information space. Then, subsequent screens can be selected and additional options provided that allow each consumer to customize your message to his or her own needs and interests.

The writer of interactive ads has to be sensitive to the time it takes to retrieve information because the consumer can easily move on to something else before information and graphics are downloaded. Information text is more flexible than graphic devices, which take longer to download. Thus, text or words become very important in an interactive ad. Text is retrieved faster, saving time and money for the consumer.

Response or feedback mechanisms should be built into your interactive ads. Be mindful of the importance of feedback to the refinement and updating of information in your ads. Consumers not only want a lot of information from interactive ads, they also expect these ads to be dynamic. The feedback you get from interactive ads will demand frequent responses. Electronic suggestion boxes can be reinforced with files that contain answers to frequently asked questions, or discussion areas where customers can see what other people are thinking about and asking.

When you go online with your ads, remember that you are opening up your access to the entire world. This will result in a wider variety of responses than you normally get from domestic advertising, and as a result, your strategy for using interactive ads should include the likelihood of receiving responses from around the world. This will put pressure on your ability to service the global community. More will be said about global advertising in the next section.

As with any other medium, interactive ads and Web sites should not be thought of in isolation; rather, they should be part of a larger marketing communications plan. Building traffic at a Web site, for example, requires using other media to announce and direct consumers to the site. Additionally, high-traffic areas of the Web itself can be employed through the placement of banners that entice and direct Web surfers to your site.

In some ways, writing and designing interactive ads such as Web sites is no different than creating traditional advertising. You have to have a clear idea of the ad's purpose in mind. Among the common reasons for building a Web site are: 1) reinforcing your brand's image by making your Web site fun, hip, cool, or technologically sophisticated; 2) providing easy and cheap access to product information; 3) improving customer service; and 4) building a community of consumers for your product or service. Your goals will direct how your Web site is constructed and kept up-to-date. "Technology Watch: The Writing Demands of Interactive Messages" says more about writing for the interactive world.

R E S E T

1. Why do you think television is the medium of choice for most copywriters? What does writing for television offer that the other major advertising media do not?

2. In what ways does writing an infomercial differ from writing a standard 30-second advertisement?

3. Why is it still important to understand the purpose of the elements of print advertising in this age of interactive computer messages?

TECHNOLOGY WATCH

·····························

The Writing Demands of Interactive Messages

Creating and writing advertising for the interactive computer environment has been likened to returning to the pre-industrial age, when the consumer was more in control of exposure to advertising simply because there was less of it competing for his or her attention. In this cottage-industry era, advertising was meant to inform in an impressive manner. So it might be today for interactive messages.

The challenge in writing interactive messages is not just to build sites filled with product information but to make the information so interesting, involving, and compelling as to convince the consumer that these ads are the best source of product information. Rather than being asked to create a 30-second image commercial, the writer

will be asked to create 30 screens of enticing information or a 300K catalog or copy for 30 Mb of video.

Among the pioneering efforts on the Internet are World Wide Web sites sponsored by advertising agencies such as Ogilvy & Mather and advertisers such as the Miller Brewing Company. Ogilvy & Mather's Web site contains guidelines on using the Internet, while Miller's Tap Room offers information on the latest in music, fashion, night life, art, sports, food, and social issues. And this is only the beginning.

Bookstores have also taken to the Internet in a big way. Amazon.com bookstore sells its books entirely through the Internet—it has no stores. Barnes & Noble has also taken to the Internet to compete di-

rectly with Amazon.com. In 1997 Amazon.com demonstrated that the Internet is a good place for contests and promotions by creating a writing contest called "The Greatest Tale Ever Told" that asked Internet users visiting its Web site to participate in the writing of a murder mystery, one paragraph at a time, over a 45-day span of time. Each day judges selected a winning additional paragraph to the story from among entries submitted at the Web site on the previous day. Each winner received a $1,000 prize. There also was an opportunity for any participant—whether a writer or a non-writer— to win $100,000 at the end of the contest by simply entering an e-mail address at the site (a great way to build a mailing list). Amazon.com kicked off the

Writing Across Cultures

The advertising process—from research to strategy development to the actual creation of ads—should be the same regardless of the type of product or service being advertised or any cultural differences between the advertiser and target audience. This does not mean that the process we have been describing has always been followed or that the same standards have been applied across different advertising situations. The evolution of advertising targeted to the Hispanic market in the United States provides an example of how the advertising process should work across cultural boundaries.

There is an old way to advertise to the Hispanic market and there is a new way. The old way is to take your general-market advertising and slap a Spanish-language soundtrack over it,

or to shoot another take of a general market ad with Hispanic-looking talent in it. In other words, the changes are made at the execution stage of the advertising process, with little thought given to research or strategy development for this culturally different market.

The new way is to build the advertising plan from the ground up the same way you would develop your advertising for the general market. This method of developing advertising for the Hispanic market results in alterations in the advertising rather than just alterations in the soundtrack or talent. As a case in point, the Spanish-language version of the Toyota advertising slogan "I Love What You Do For Me" is "Estas Hecho Para Mi," which means, "You Were Made For Me" in English. This version of the slogan avoids a potential obscenity, is more relevant to the Hispanic culture, works

contest by getting John Updike to write the opening and concluding paragraphs. This was a very creative and involving use of Amazon.com's Web site, and it demonstrated the interactive possibilities of the Internet.

Writers, advertisers, and agencies are all meeting on the Internet. Good writing, well-organized information, and compelling approaches will prevail just as they do in conventional media. The difference will be that you will know when your ad, promotion, or Web site does not work. And you will get feedback on how to improve your messages and keep them up-to-date. In essence, the consumer will become your producer.

Amazon.com, the online bookseller, has successfully tapped both the sales and marketing opportunities provided by the Internet, as evidenced by the success of its "The Greatest Tale Ever Told" mystery story contest.

better in the jingle, and was created from a marketing strategy developed by a Hispanic advertising agency in Los Angeles.

But this new way of creating ads for different cultures has its detractors. Jo Muse, executive creative director at Muse Cordero Chen, Los Angeles, is an opponent of different standards for advertising created for ethnic groups. He says:

> We do ourselves a disservice when we break advertising up by ethnic groups, when we "Balkanize" advertising and look at it separately. When you do, it seems to invent different standards, and if you subordinate ethnic advertising from general standards, the work naturally decreases in its excellence and standards.

Muse goes on to say that his agency develops its Hispanic work the same way it develops its general-market advertising. He continues:

> We don't do it any differently. We develop the best possible ideas and we work rigorously to make sure, whether it's radio, television, or print, that it meets our individual standards.[16]

Regardless of which side you take in this argument, the bottom line is that the advertising writer—whether writing in French, English, Spanish, Japanese, Korean, Chinese, German, Italian, Swahili, Amharic, or Hausa—must have the same writing standards in mind. And one of these standards, offered by E. B. White, is true in any culture. White describes the writer's true relationship with the audience in this anecdote about his college English professor and co-author of *The Elements of Style*, William Strunk, Jr.:

> All through *The Elements of Style* one finds evidence of the author's deep sympathy for the reader. Will felt that the reader was in serious trouble most of the time, a man floundering in a swamp, and that it was the duty of anyone attempting to write English to drain the swamp quickly and get his man up on dry ground, or at least throw him a rope.[17]

It's the duty of any writer writing in any language to drain the swamp quickly, so do not be afraid to explore the challenges of writing across different cultures.

SUMMARY

The job of a copywriter requires the ability to collaborate with other people on the creation of advertisements. The copywriter's primary contribution to this collaboration with artists, production people, and other writers is that of a conceptualizer or visualizer of an advertisement's central idea. Conceptualization or visualization is required for the creation of advertising in any and all media. Conceptualization is the application of intuition and imagination to everything we know about the advertising problem on which we are working in order to create an advertising idea. Visualization is the formation of an image of the advertisement as a whole in the mind's eye.

Although the writer must be able to visualize an advertisement as a whole, ads are made up of elements that have functions that help the entire ad do its job. In print advertising, perhaps the most important of these elements is the headline. It is the headline's job to stop the reader and attract attention to the ad. Headlines can be made more effective if they promise a benefit, offer something newsworthy, provide helpful information, contain the brand name, flag the right audience, and are specific about the offer being made. The basic types of headlines coincide with the characteristics of good headlines. They are the benefit headline, news headline, curiosity headline, question headline, selective headline, and command headline.

Subheadings, overlines, underlines, and captions are additional print elements that can help to give added emphasis to key copy points in an ad. Subheadings break up the body copy into more digestible bites and emphasize important points in the copy. Overlines typically appear above headlines to lead the reader into the headline, while underlines appear under headlines and act as a transition into the body copy. Captions are used under or next to visuals to help interpret the meaning of the visuals for the reader.

The heart and substance of a print advertisement is the body copy. The body copy should follow through on the idea expressed in the headline and visuals and continue to sell the reader on the offer. The principles of good writing should apply to body copy just as they apply to writing in general. It is paramount that the copy be written as if directed at one individual. This is known as the "you approach." Body copy can be organized into three key sections. They are the lead paragraph, interior body copy, and closing paragraph. Most print ads also include a tagline or slogan that summarizes the key idea of the ad and/or the campaign. The tagline provides thematic continuity from one ad to the next in an advertising campaign.

The three types of copy found most frequently in print advertisements are the straightforward sell, the narrative, and the dialogue or monologue. Most print advertising uses a straightforward sell approach. Storytelling ads follow the narrative format. Dialogue copy is found more often in radio and television writing; however, the monologue, in which a character in the ad talks to the reader, is fairly common.

With few exceptions, writing for outdoor, transit, and direct mail follows the general principles of writing for all print advertising. Outdoor and transit put more emphasis on the headline and visual, while direct mail demands good interior copy and a strong call-to-action.

Writing for radio is unique because there is no visual element with which to work; thus, the writer must create the images and visions in the listener's mind through the use of voices, sound effects, music, and timing. This is called "theater of the mind." Because radio copy is written to be spoken, it should be conversational. Good radio copy is written in phrases and sentence fragments much the way people talk.

There are three basic radio formats that can be combined to make additional types of radio commercials. The basic types are the straight announcement or pitch, the slice-of-life or situation, and the song or musical. The pitch format is read by an announcer with little if any background music, sound effects,

or the like. The situation format is typically based upon a slice-of-life situation that the listener must imagine in his or her mind's eye. The song format can come in either the form of a jingle, which is a song built around key selling points of the product, or a donut, in which the music is played and then lowered in volume so an announcer can read the copy for the product.

Television copywriting affords the writer the largest range of dramatic devices with which to create ads. However, increasing television clutter and viewer control of television content puts a premium on the writer's ability to make the TV spot stand out. Television is primarily a visual medium in which the visuals or picture must tell the story. A strong television commercial should have a key visual or visual symbol that sums up the commercial's message. Additionally, a good television commercial should be able to make an impression without the aid of the audio component.

Television commercial formats roughly follow those found in radio. Six important types of television commercials are the demonstration, testimonial, presenter, slice-of-life, lifestyle, and animated spot. Humor, music, and emotion can also be present in television commercials. The demonstration is perhaps the most effective type of television commercial. The old adage is: Demonstrate it if you can. Testimonials are effective, especially if done by a real person who actually uses the product. Celebrity presenters such as Bill Cosby or Ed McMahon bring instant attention to the television spot. Slice-of-life and lifestyle commercials provide good vehicles for fitting the product into the consumer's life. Animation can help the writer to conjure up ideas that could not be executed in real life. Humor can work in advertising if it is done well and does not overwhelm the product. Music can either set the mood of the spot or be used as a memory device. Emotional appeals can also be used as a memory device, causing your audience to associate your product with the feelings conveyed in the ad.

The emerging world of infomercials and interactive messages will put new demands on the ability of the writer to provide information in a format that maintains an audience's attention and compels it to return to an advertiser's message over and over again. Infomercial writing must be both entertaining and interesting while also presenting the viewer with a call-to-action. Many infomercials sell products that appeal to audience members' self-interests. They also provide extra involvement by using celebrities as hosts or guests. Infomercial scripts should create urgency, make a clear offer, create exclusivity, limit the buying time period, limit the number of products available, emphasize installment payment plans, and demonstrate the product or the results from using it.

On the Internet, consumer control over the information selection process coupled with instant feedback creates a dynamic environment that produces two-way communication between advertiser and customer. Interactive messages have to be kept up-to-date and additional feedback mechanisms maintained in cyberspace. The writer provides and creates the initial information environment, but the consumer, along with the writer, changes it as they communicate back and forth over the Internet.

Access to interactive messages around the world will necessitate that those who create these messages be sensitive to how they are used by the global community. Additionally, traditional advertising writers will have to create ads that are developed from the ground up with local cultural nuances in mind. Literal translations of copy from language to language will no longer suffice in the international marketplace.

KEY TERMS

copy, 432

copywriter, 432

conceptualization, 432

visualization, 432

computer artist, 433

headline, 436

benefit headline, 436

news headline, 436

curiosity headline, 436

question headline, 439

selective headline, 439

command headline, 439

subheading, 439

overline, 439

underline, 439

caption, 439

body copy, 439

lead paragraph, 439

closing paragraph, 439

tagline, 442

straightforward copy, 442

narrative copy, 442

dialogue copy, 442

call-to-action, 443

pitch format, 444

situation format, 445

song format, 445

jingle, 445

donut, 445

storyboard, 445

key visual symbol, 446

slice-of-life commercial, 449

lifestyle commercial, 449

animation, 449

banner, 451

Web site, 451

1. In general, what are the responsibilities of a copywriter in a small to midsize advertising agency?

2. What is the importance of collaboration in the creation of advertisements?

3. Why is the headline so important to a print advertisement?

4. Describe the basic structure of body copy in a print advertisement. How do these copy elements work together to guide a reader through an ad?

5. Compare and contrast how the process of visualization works in writing for television as opposed to writing for radio.

6. Describe and provide examples of how a copywriter can use a listener's imagination to create a situation around a product or service in a radio commercial.

7. What are some of the ways copywriters can overcome the problem of increasing advertising clutter on television?

8. Explain how each of the six television commercial formats might be used to sell a product or service of your choosing.

9. Describe the characteristics of interactive media that a writer should take into consideration in the creation of advertising. Which of these characteristics does the new medium have in common with traditional advertising media? Which ones are new?

10. How is writing for multicultural audiences different from writing for one homogeneous audience?

1. Reconcile the fact that a print advertisement should be visualized as a whole entity, yet each element in the ad has a specific function and is written separately. How can a writer guard against an ad becoming merely an assemblage of parts?

2. If most readers do not read the body copy of an advertisement, why write it? Explain your position and provide examples that demonstrate how this copy exhibits the principles of effective advertising writing.

3. Provide an example of the best demonstration commercial you have seen on television. Do the same for testimonials, slice-of-life, presenters, lifestyle, and animated spots.

interactive discovery lab

1. There are ads all around us. Often we don't look at them very closely, so we miss how well or poorly they are written. Select a product category in which you are interested and gather 10 magazine ads for products in the category. Cosmetics, fashion, automotive, pharmaceuticals, and food products are some possibilities. Read these ads carefully and create a list of words that you think are specific to the type of product being advertised. Now select a product category that is very different from your first choice and do the same thing. Compare your two lists and notice the differences between the two vocabularies.

2. Watch television for at least half an hour and try not to change channels or leave the room during the commercials. Watch the commercials closely. Count the number of commercials you watched in half an hour. Also, keep track of how many of the different types of commercials described in the chapter you see. What was the most prevalent type of commercial? Which types did you not see? Think of some reasons why a particular type of commercial dominates. Is it the program and audience? Time of day? Product category? Some other possible reasons?

Chapter Fifteen

Symbols, Images, and Art Direction

BRAND SYMBOLS SPEAK VOLUMES ABOUT THE POWER OF ART AND DESIGN

A product or brand's identity is often a result of package, logotype, and advertisement designs along with the words used to convey a message. Consider some of the enduring symbols, designs, and images portrayed in the composite photo on the cover of *Advertising Age.* How many of them do you recognize? The fact that many of them are familiar to you demonstrates the power of art and design to advertising and marketing communications.

For example, there are three brand design elements that, taken together, form the identity for Betty Crocker's cake mixes and, more recently, cereals. First, there is the simple red spoon, introduced in 1954 by Lippincott & Marguiles, with Betty Crocker written on it in handwritten letters to convey the feeling of home cooking. Second, there are those now famous cake mix boxes with the four-color illustrations of the cake you are about to make. And third, there is the fictional Betty Crocker, who is the corporate identity symbol created to reflect the company's target consumer—the contemporary housewife. Together, these elements have created a strong brand identity for Betty Crocker products among consumers.

It has taken a little proselytizing over the years to elevate art and design to its current position in advertising and marketing communications. In 1921 Fred R. Barnard, for example,

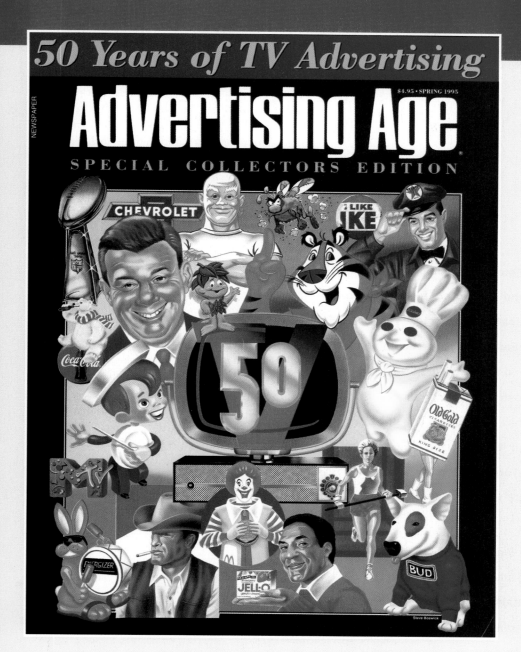

wrote in *Printers' Ink,* "One look is worth a thousands words." Six years later he changed it to "One picture is worth a thousand words," and attributed it to "a Chinese proverb so people would take it seriously."

Source: Ellen Lupton, "Thoughts on Identity at the Century's End," *Communication Arts 1996 Advertising Annual,* December 1996, 248–252; and Justin Kaplan, ed., *Bartlett's Familiar Quotations,* 16th ed. (Boston: Little, Brown and Company, 1992), 782. Original quotes from Fred R. Barnard in *Printer's Ink,* 8 December 1921, 96; and 10 March 1927, 114.

LOOK BEFORE YOU LEAP

- Why is art direction important?

- What is the job of an art director?

- How does art direction fit into the overall advertising process?

- How do corporate symbols, brand logotypes, packaging, and the design of marketing communications work together to create a brand image?

- What are the steps involved in designing print advertisements?

- What is a good design?

- How is design important in the production of television and radio commercials?

15

In today's multimedia environment, we cannot underestimate the importance of art and design to a message or to an entire marketing communications campaign. Think of some of your favorite companies and their products and promotions. How long have you been awake in the morning before you see the Nike swoosh logotype? What about Coca-Cola's basic red and white designs? We might take these designs for granted, but it takes painstaking attention to detail to make sure that every time you see a Nike or Coca-Cola product or message you have instant brand recognition.

In this chapter we will discuss the job of art directors, as well as the importance of advertising design to the process of building and maintaining corporate and brand images, and to the creation of print and broadcast ads. The role of advertising design in the creation of print ads is further broken down by the stages an artist goes through in designing an ad. We also illustrate how art direction applies to the creation of television and radio commercials.

The Job Of An Art Director

The word "art" in advertising refers to a wide range of artistic applications and to several groups of artistic professionals, including art directors, graphic designers, and illustrators. The central artistic role in an advertising agency is played by the **art director.** Based on their background in graphic design, art directors determine how messages will be visually presented to the target audience. As a critical member of the creative team, the art director works with the copywriter to make sure that the visual and verbal elements of ads and promotional pieces work together to convey a clear and consistent message to the target audience. The most important quality an art director can bring to an advertising problem is a "good eye." By this we mean that he or she intuitively knows what looks right and what does not. Even after all of the formal training an art school can provide, the art director relies heavily on experience and a personal sense of what will work with a particular target audience given the constraints of the elements with which he or she is working.

In addition to interacting with copywriters, the art director must often coordinate the work of several other artists and support personnel. In large advertising or marketing communications campaigns, art directors may have to coordinate the services of graphic designers, illustrators, photographers, cinematographers, computer graphics specialists, casting directors, photographic models, and production artists. Sometimes these artists and designers are hired from outside the agency for the special expertise they can bring to a problem. In many cases, agencies own or have long-standing relationships with outside suppliers such as design studios, illustrators, photographers, film production houses, and computer graphics specialists. The relationship between the art director and the illustrator can be a complex one; as described in "Adscape: Art Directors and Illustrators," it is not uncommon for these two professionals to differ in their views of how things should be done.

For advertisers that don't use an advertising agency, the art director's role and responsibilities may be performed by one or more people. Some advertisers have a staff of graphic artists in their advertising departments to provide art direction, rather than advertising agency art directors. Smaller advertisers may hire a local graphic artist or rely on the services of the art staff for the advertising media, such as the layout artist at a local newspaper. When broadcast commercials are used, radio or television production personnel may provide art direction for the commercials. "Technology Watch: Designers and the Web" discusses the role of graphic designers in another advertising vehicle, Web sites.

Whether art direction is provided by an art director or the art staff of local media, the ultimate responsibility for establishing and maintaining visual effectiveness rests with the person approving the creative product. This "person" may be the advertiser or a series of managers at different levels in a corporation or organization. By understanding the broader context of visual communication as it relates to the total marketing and advertising effort, these advertisers and managers can maintain visual continuity in their advertising and mar-

AdScape

. . . .

Art Directors and Illustrators

The advertising business is difficult primarily because it requires the talents and egos of a lot of different specialists to create good advertising. Each one of these specialists—from writers to artists and designers to producers—brings a different perspective and set of personal needs to a project. Two such specialists who often can be thrown into a situation where they might lock horns are the agency art director and the illustrator he or she hires.

Illustrators frequently are freelance artists who work on projects as agencies need them. They have invested a lot of time, energy, and skill perfecting their craft and want to be taken seriously. And they bring to the table a conflict most creative people carry around with them: They consider themselves artists first and advertising people second.

Art directors, on the other hand, work for clients who are seeking the best solutions to their marketing communications problems. The differing perspectives of the illustrator and art director have been

characterized this way for those with a sense of humor:

Two Illustrators Talking
Illustrator #1: "If it weren't for all those idiot art directors, I'd be a big star by now."
Illustrator #2: "They just stifle me from doing great work. They're always compromising my vision, man."

Two Art Directors Talking
AD #1: " I can't believe the gall of that guy. One lousy sketch is all I got and he says, 'take it or leave it.'"
AD #2: "Sounds like the arrogant jerk that I had to deal with recently. He wanted to know why I called him if I wouldn't let him do his *vision.*"

While these conversations have been exaggerated to be funny and make a point, they do speak some truth. Art directors can get better work from illustrators if they do a good job communicating the client's problem and have the confidence to give the illustrator some room in which to work. On the other side of the rela-

tionship, illustrators have to accept that illustration is a business and find other outlets for their true art. Additionally, illustrators will be happier when they have the confidence to know when to say no to jobs that simply do not provide good vehicles for their skills and styles.

Furthermore, art directors can expand an illustrator's perspective and help him or her to grow as an artist. Illustrators should try to work for art directors in whom they have confidence and who they know will go to bat for them. Often art directors establish relationships with specific illustrators they work well with. These long-standing working relationships result in the best work because they represent an appreciation of each other's job.

QUESTION
As an art director, what could you do to foster a good working relationship with your illustrators?

Source: Barry Fitzgerald, "Illustration: The Whole Picture," *Communication Arts: Illustration Annual,* July 1995, 184–192.

keting communications programs. To construct the most effective messages, advertising professionals must also understand the art direction tasks associated with the creation of print and broadcast messages.

Let's now examine the role of art direction in the advertising process and extend its effects to building corporate and brand images.

Art Direction And The Advertising Process

Art direction is the middle of the three message creation tasks (Exhibit 15–1). As is often the case with a "middle person," the relationship between art direction and copywriting is differ-

TECHNOLOGY WATCH

....

Designers and the Web

The popularity of the World Wide Web has opened up new choices and challenges for companies, agencies, and talented graphic designers and computer programmers. In fact, the demand for people who can navigate the Web and bring cutting-edge design work to advertising, marketing, and communication problems has far outstripped its availability. Designers and computer experts can choose from a number of specialties, including video game creation, Web page and site design, on-screen design, and special effects.

While creating a Web site does not demand any special skill, it does take skill and training to create one for which a company is willing to spend an initial $1 million and then allocate an additional investment to hire 10 staff designers in order to maintain it. Designing the architecture for informational hierarchies provides the opportunity to combine print design skills for organizing information with video production expertise.

The growth of Web sites has attracted former print and magazine designers much the

way television attracted radio writers in the 1940s. The very best Web sites are designed by teams of graphic designers and computer programmers. The designer brings traditional art skills to the table, while the computer expert can write the code, create the hypertext links, and manipulate digital files to bring the designer's work to life on the computer screen.

The newest generation of digital artists will no doubt come to the Web and other digital applications with both the design and technical know-how. Small, medium, and large firms specializing in this new digital world are opening up shop everyday. Most companies and agencies have been slow to acquire the necessary expertise, thus leaving the field open to talented and enterprising young artists.

The names of these new firms themselves convey an image of technological innovation bordering on craziness. For example, there's Avalanche Systems, which has designed Web sites for NBC and Super Bowl XXX. And Convergent Media Systems and Razorfish are two

of many shops in the Northeast specializing in Web site design work. What does the future hold? One designer put it this way: "The most qualified designers for Web sites may be those who design rides at Disneyland."

A good example of the dynamic nature of a Web site is the site created for the Discovery Channel. Each week the Discovery Channel sends out a writer and photographer with its team of scientists to locations all over the world specifically to send back content for the Web site. One week it might be the Galapagos Islands and the next the heart of Africa—all available from its Web site. The opportunities created by these technological changes are mind boggling.

Source: Glenn Rifkin, "Increasingly, Top Designers Are Drawn to the Web," *New York Times,* 27 November 1995, C7; and Trip Gabriel, "The Meteoric Rise of Web Site Designers," *New York Times,* 12 February 1996, C1, C5.

ent from the relationship between art direction and production. On the one hand, art directors and copywriters collaborate to explore how to translate an advertising or marketing communications strategy into an effective advertisement or campaign. The copywriter, of course, is primarily responsible for what and how something is said in an advertisement or commercial, and the art director is primarily responsible for how that message is presented. But the final advertisement may not reflect such a clear division of responsibilities. In some cases, art directors make insightful additions to advertising copy. In other cases, visually talented copywriters offer new approaches to advertising artwork and design.

On the other hand, the art director's role in production is to guide and control production processes to ensure that the visual and verbal messages in finished advertisements or commercials are communicated as the art director intended. By monitoring the production of advertisements and commercials, the art director can fine-tune the message to enhance its effectiveness. For example, if color proofs of a product brochure appear lifeless and dull, an art director may enhance the color or substitute visual elements where necessary. With more technical tasks, such as filming a television commercial or overseeing the production of computer graphics, the art director must know how to use the expertise of production personnel to achieve the desired effects.

Creating And Changing Product, Brand, And Corporate Images

The art director's responsibilities for controlling production go beyond the creation of a single advertisement or advertising campaign. Art directors also play a broader role in developing corporate and brand images, trademarks or logotypes, and product packaging that become the centerpieces of entire integrated marketing communications programs.

As firms communicate about themselves or their brands, they attempt to create associations between their messages and their brands in the mind of the consumer. Recall from Chapter Five that these associations are called *brand associations*. Thus, a **brand image** is a set of brand associations that consumers use to organize information about a brand.[1] For example, Carnation is a brand name for which

EXHIBIT 15–1   **Art Direction in the Advertising Process**

MESSAGE CREATION TASKS

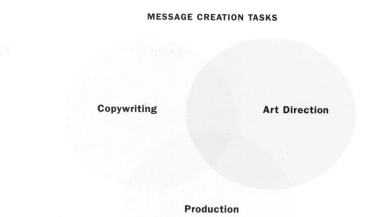

consumers have many brand associations. Similarly, the set of images referring to a corporation is called a **corporate image.** Carnation's parent company, Nestlé, has a corporate image that stands over all of its divisions, each of which has its own brand image.

You can think of the relationship between a firm's corporate and brand images as a hierarchy. Within each of Nestlé's brand divisions there are also product line brands; for Carnation, these include Carnation Instant Breakfast, Carnation Evaporated Milk, and Carnation Baby Formulas.[2] These product line brands can be further delineated into subbrands, such as Carnation Instant Breakfast Swiss Chocolate.

Because of the complexity of this relationship between corporate, brand, and product images, maintenance of the continuity and clarity of the brand message—particularly its visual components—is of the utmost importance. This visual consistency creates a stronger connection between each brand image and the overall corporate image. Because advertising is a highly visible form of corporate communication, establishing and maintaining visual consistency is one of the main functions of art direction.

The role of art direction in creating visual consistency is evident in the graphic changes made by Coca-Cola in the early 1990s. After

reviewing the presentation of their logotypes, product photographs, advertising, and displays, Coca-Cola found widely different presentations of the product and the corporation. To build consistency, Coca-Cola introduced the wave design around the world. Exhibit 15–2 demonstrates some of the ways this design was executed. The overall impact of the wave design art program and its presentations strengthened the brand and corporate images for Coca-Cola worldwide.[3]

By 1993, Coca-Cola sensed a need for something different and bold in its advertising strategy. Through its partnership with Creative Artists Agency and McCann-Erickson, it ran against convention and abandoned what has been called the "one sight, one sound, one sell" approach to advertising and integrated marketing. Instead of basing commercials on a common look, Coca-Cola began preparing its commercials independently to appeal to different markets through fragmented media. The overall theme of the commercials, "Always Coca-Cola," was used consistently across all of the ads, but the commercials were often distinctly different in look and tone.[4] Two of these ads, one featuring polar bears and one depicting scientists attempting to "deprogram" a Cola-Cola drinker, exemplify the different types of approaches used by Coca-Cola in its new strategy. The polar bear commercial conveys a friendly and endearing feeling, while the

deprogrammer spot has a decidedly darker, edgier style.

More recently, Coca-Cola has embarked on a product-licensing program in which its logo and other company images have been made into everything from Christmas ornaments to collectibles. This has helped Coca-Cola extend its designs from its entire corporate history into the very living rooms of its most loyal customers.

The art director's guidance and control is also important when product, brand, or corporate images are changed. By creating fresh images, a business or entire industry can reach new target audiences. New images can change consumer perceptions about an existing product or business. New images can also be used to show how a product can meet consumers' needs in ways they might not have previously considered. Recall, for example, the recent television campaign launched to advertise Kellogg's Frosted Flakes cereal. In this series of ads, adults, shown in half-shadow to hide their identities, confess their love of and cravings for Frosted Flakes. These ads, which clearly target adult cereal eaters, attempt to change adults' attitudes about the cereal by presenting it as a food that is appropriate for and desired by adults as well as kids.

Regardless of the direction of change, an art director is centrally involved in creating and presenting a consistent visual image of the product, brand, or corporation. One of the earliest centers of involvement for an art director is the creation of corporate symbols, trademarks, and logotypes.

Creating Corporate Symbols And Logotypes

A **logotype,** or *logo,* is a symbol or phrase that identifies a brand, a business, or an organization.[5] An obvious symbol associated with a business is its name. Some symbols are graphic or nonverbal, rather than verbal. When logotypes are incorporated into the design of business stationery, signs, and truck identification, for example, they become part of a **corporate identity program.** The purpose of a corporate identity program is to provide a consistent display of corporate symbols. It aids consumers in recognizing brands. As we discussed in Chapter Five, this is a minimum expectation for an integrated marketing communications program.

Through advertising and package design, logotypes become associated with a brand or service. Once learned, consumers use these graphic indicators to speed product or service selection. Because names and logotypes change less frequently than advertising and other forms of corporate communication, these symbols aid recognition and provide continuity for brand and corporate images. When advertising and package designs change, a recognizable logotype reassures the consumer that he or she is selecting his or her favorite brand. For example, no matter how many new products or package designs Kraft produces, they reaffirm your confidence with the classic red and blue logotype, such as the one displayed on the package in Exhibit 15–3.

Certain characteristics of logotypes aid recognition. In *The Design of Advertising,* Roy Paul Nelson suggests five of these that an art director should strive for in designing a logotype or trademark. Nelson asserts that logotypes should be: 1) original, 2) legible, 3) stimulating, 4) appropriate to the product, and 5) easy to remember.[6] Exhibit 15–4 shows examples of logotypes that were developed for companies that are, most likely, unfamiliar to you. In your opinion, do these logotypes meet Nelson's criteria?

Companies thinking about changing a logotype must consider how much equity has accumulated in the brand. For example, if 90 percent of consumers recognize a brand or cor-

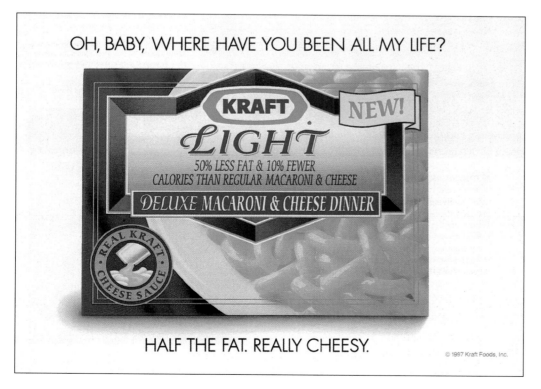

OH, BABY, WHERE HAVE YOU BEEN ALL MY LIFE?

KRAFT

LIGHT

50% LESS FAT & 10% FEWER CALORIES THAN REGULAR MACARONI & CHEESE

DELUXE MACARONI & CHEESE DINNER

NEW!

· REAL KRAFT · CHEESE SAUCE

HALF THE FAT. REALLY CHEESY.

© 1997 Kraft Foods, Inc.

EXHIBIT 15–3   Although its product packaging has changed over the years, Kraft has consistently displayed its classic red-and-blue logotype. In addition to helping consumers identify Kraft products, this easily recognized logotype benefits Kraft in new product introductions and product line extensions, as the logotype communicates a strong message about Kraft quality that carries over to new products.

Wyndham Music   **Comfort Coil Company**   **Hexagraph Fly Rods**

porate logotype, dramatic changes in the logotype will require re-education of consumers to the new symbol. For this reason, art directors usually choose to evolve logotypes gradually, rather than make sudden dramatic changes. Exhibit 15–5 shows how the John Deere logotype has evolved since its introduction in 1876.

Influencing Package Design

Packaging refers to the physical characteristics of the container that holds the product. Product packaging has become a more important part of marketing and provides a more important role for art directors for several reasons. For one, with nearly 100,000 brands on retailer shelves, intense competition for shelf space demands attractive and persuasive product packaging in order to stimulate impulse sales. Product packaging changes, such as the change from the 5-by-12 inch "long box" to the 5-by-5 1/2 inch "jewel box" for CDs, have been made to eliminate the waste of unnecessary packaging material.[7] In addition, global distribution of products requires package designs that can communicate instantaneously across cultural boundaries. This was the primary concern when Minute Maid decided to make the package design for its many branded products more contemporary. The design had to be extendable to more than 100 items carrying the brand name. The design also had to say "Minute Maid" the moment you saw it. Exhibit 15–6 illustrates how this new design works.

Packaging decisions include the choice of shape, color, design, and materials for the container. In collaboration with art directors, package designers attempt to create a design

that successfully meets the marketing needs of the product. At best, package design decisions can be used to support a brand or corporate image; at worst, they can confuse consumers. The editors of *Food & Beverage Marketing* identified five critical areas for successful package design: 1) graphic personality, 2) precise positioning, 3) directional selling, 4) the persuasion factor, and 5) planned simplicity.[8] The *graphic personality* of the package highlights the visual expression of the brand and its most important attributes. *Precise positioning* refers to the coordinated effort by both packaging and advertising messages to establish a clear distinction between the product and its competitors. *Directional selling* is the ability of the product to attract consumer attention without diverting attention away from the selling message on the package. The *persuasion factor* is the ability of a package design to stimulate an impulse purchase. *Planned simplicity* is the elimination of unnecessary information and design elements from the package design.

Using these five criteria, the art director must adjust package designs to accommodate the strength or weakness of a brand name while creating interest in the selling message. "Company names and/or logos can be important—Apple, Lotus and Microsoft, for example," says one computer package design consultant, "but they should never be the major design element."[9] Product names are usually not the major selling message unless they describe a product benefit, such as Word-Perfect (word-processing software) or Satis-FAXtion (fax software). The single most important element in design is a "compelling

EXHIBIT 15–5 As shown here, the logotype for John Deere has gone through a series of modifications to reach its current presentation. This slow evolution of the image has helped to retain the integrity and recognizability of the logotype throughout the years.

EXHIBIT 15–6 Minute Maid's new package design was developed not only to create a fresh image for the company but also to aid in the generation of brand recognition among customers.

phrase that communicates a product's positioning. This message tells why one vendor's product is better for them than a competitor's product."10

As mentioned earlier, the overall role of an art director is to control and guide the presentation of visual messages for an advertiser in order to create and maintain the most effective and consistent brand or corporate image. Because package design is so important, the art director's role in controlling this part of an integrated marketing communications program is significant. This and other activities, however, are often overshadowed by the art director's two primary responsibilities: designing print advertisements and directing broadcast commercials. In the next section, we'll see how art directors design print advertisements.

R E S E T

1. **Describe the major responsibilities of an art director.**
2. **What are the criteria for a good logo design?**
3. **What does an art director try to achieve in designing a product's package?**

Designing Print Advertisements

Because most art directors have training as graphic artists, one of their primary tasks is designing print advertisements. During the design process, an initial idea for an advertisement moves from the thumbnail stage to a piece of finished artwork that will be sent to a magazine or newspaper for reproduction. Although not as linear in practice, for the purposes of this discussion the work process of an art director in designing ads has been divided into four stages: thumbnail sketches, rough layouts, comprehensive layouts, and mechanicals or finished artwork. Exhibit 15–7 shows the design process involved in the development of an advertisement for The VCU Ad Center at Virginia Commonwealth University. It should be noted that the use of computer

design software has given art directors a newfound flexibility that allows them to streamline the design process as the situation warrants. Client demands and situation requirements may necessitate that design stages be combined or skipped entirely. However, even when the designer streamlines the process, he or she often still goes through the steps mentally.

Thumbnail Sketches

The design process begins with many small picture ideas for an ad, referred to as **thumbnail sketches,** or *thumbnails*. These rough sketches, which can either be drawn on paper or conceptualized with a computer, allow designers to create and experiment with many design ideas before committing to a particular design approach. The best ideas are selected from among the thumbnail sketches to be redrawn as full-sized rough layouts.

At the thumbnail stage, art directors are interested in exploring different layout design possibilities. They consider the size and shape of advertisements to be produced, whether the text in an advertisement requires columns of space or simple copy blocks, and what type of visuals are needed to communicate the message effectively. Art directors also use thumbnail sketches to help decide how elements of the advertisement will be arranged.

CREATING A DESIGN FROM AD ELEMENTS

Before an art director picks up a pen (or a mouse) to begin the controlled doodling that accompanies thumbnail sketches, he or she must decide what design elements will be included in the advertisement. Will the advertisement include a headline, subheads, blocks of body copy, photographs, drawings, backgrounds, coupons, logos, or taglines? The number of elements included in the design is important because the more elements, the more complex the design. Complex designs can be confusing to the consumer if they don't present information in an organized manner.

In addition to the number of elements in an ad, there are several important design variables used by art directors to capture and direct consumer attention, including white space, balance, eye movement, proportion, and color. Expert use of these principles also

EXHIBIT 15–7 The Design Process

Thumbnail sketches explore many arrangements
and elements for a design.

Rough layouts test several designs and the arrangement
of their elements at actual size.

Comprehensive layouts show one or two layouts as
they would appear in print.

Mechanicals include all type, visuals, and instructions
for the printer or magazine.

will add to the overall impact and feel of the ad. These design principles apply to the design process regardless of whether the designer is using a marker and layout pad, or a computer. "Around the Globe: Design and Culture in South America" (page 475) tells us about another element: designing images that represent the local culture.

White Space.   **White space,** or the blank areas in a layout, is important for several reasons. Large areas of white space can convey richness, openness, exclusivity, or simplicity in a message. An art director may also add or remove white space in an advertisement in order to make an advertisement stand out from competing ads on a newspaper or magazine page. In the advertisement for Hallmark cards in Exhibit 15–8, the white space helps dramatize the ad's strong but simple message. In contrast,

the K2 ad in Exhibit 15–9 uses up most of the available white space, filling it with funny, intriguing questions and small drawings. The busyness of this design successfully generates both excitement and curiosity, qualities that K2 hopes will attract hip, young readers to their ad.

Balance.   The distribution of elements around an imaginary vertical line that divides a layout or advertisement into two equal halves is known as **balance.** Designers and artists refer to balancing the weight of objects on either side of this vertical axis. A. Jerome Jewler summarizes some of the relationships between objects in his widely used book *Creative Strategy in Advertising* as follows:[11]

- An irregular shape has more weight than a regular shape.
- Dark has more weight than light.
- Larger elements appear heavier than smaller ones.
- A shape with texture has more weight than a smooth shape.
- Color has more weight than noncolor.

The most commonly used design distinction occurs between formal and informal balance. A layout with *formal balance* is symmetrical; it has equal weight on each side of the vertical axis. Formal layouts are often used to represent tradition and formality. The advertisement for Aveda's Self Control™ Hair Styling Stick shown in Exhibit 15–10 uses a formal layout in its presentaion. Notice how a vertical line bisects the image, the headline, and the copy. On the other hand, *informal balance* in a layout or advertisement occurs when there is an asymmetrical relationship between elements on each side of the vertical axis, such as the Café de Columbia advertisement in Exhibit 15–11. Informal balance is often used to convey movement or excitement.

Eye Movement.   **Eye movement** refers to the sequential processing of information in an advertisement by readers. Art directors can influence how readers process the information in a layout or advertisement. They use lines, shapes, or characteristics of visuals to direct the reader's eye in the advertisement. Art directors are intuitively aware of the *optical center* of an ad as they create their designs. This point is about two-thirds up from the bottom of the ad and

Looking for this on the back has become a national institution.

EXHIBIT 15–9 In this advertisement for its line of women's skates, K2 uses a lack of white space to create an intriguing visual confusion. This unique presentation is designed to pique the interest of readers and draw them into the body copy.

EXHIBIT 15–10 Notice that all of the elements in this advertisement for Self Control™ by Aveda are centered on the page. This formally balanced presentation is particularly effective in that it communicates a clear message of precision and control, thus underscoring the product name.

slightly to the right of the vertical axis. Art directors often use objects or models to point readers to the advertising copy or to the visuals of the product. Notice in Exhibit 15–12 how the curved presentation of the headline in the ad for Pepperidge Farm Raisin Cinnamon Swirl Bread directs your eye into the swirls of the bread, the center of which is positioned at the optical center of the page.

Proportion. The relationship in size between elements in an advertisement is known as **proportion.** The more important an element to the selling message, the more space that should be given to the element. The Parker pen advertisement shown in Exhibit 15–13 is designed to communicate a strong message about the quality of this precision writing instrument. Appropriately, the close-up product photo illustrating the delicate nib of the pen dominates the ad.

Color, Intensity, and Contrast. While an emotional headline and advertising copy can create a mood for the product, three other factors also can contribute to the mood created by a layout design: color, intensity, and contrast. Designers often associate certain colors or hues with emotional states. Reds create excitement, while browns and earth tones produce warmth. Greens connote nature and earth friendliness, while blacks build richness and sophistication. **Intensity** indicates the brightness or dullness of a color. Bright colors create excitement; subdued colors may suggest peacefulness. **Contrast,** also called *value* or *tone,* is the relative lightness or darkness of colors to one another. Contrasts in colors or in gray tones can be used to suggest differences in importance for elements in an ad. The Neiman Marcus advertisement in Exhibit 15–14 shows an interesting use of color, intensity, and contrast. A moss green backdrop suggests a sophisticated yet casual mood, while complementing the store's name. The subdued colors and relative lack of contrast between the various colors and tones enhance this sophisticated country cottage setting. White type on the green background plays off the pitcher and delivers a subdued message from Neiman Marcus.

An art director may postpone final decisions about color until the rough layout or comprehensive layout stages of design. Similarly, final decisions about the visuals to be included in an ad may also be made during later stages of design. Nonetheless it is important to consider the types of visuals to be used during early design stages.

SELECTING VISUALS FOR THE DESIGN As an art director produces thumbnail sketches, he or she should start to think about the types of visuals that will be used in the layout. It's important to think about visuals early because visuals have the critical task of capturing the attention of the target audience and helping to deliver the central idea of the ad. An art director's choice of visuals ranges from no visuals at all to multiple visuals of different types. Visuals may be created or acquired from an outside supplier such as a photographic studio or freelance artist, and include color and black-and-white photographs, illustrations or wash drawings, and line art.

EXHIBIT 15–11 The informally balanced presentation in this ad for Café de Columbia helps to add power and excitement to the headline and striking visual.

"Grab life by the beans."

EXHIBIT 15–12 Art directors will often modify the layout of an advertisement in order to take advantage of the natural eye movement of the reader. The curved headline in this Pepperidge Farm ad, for example, in addition to mimicking the swirl pattern in the bread, also leads the reader's eye directly to the middle of the product photo.

EXHIBIT 15–13 As indicated by the relatively large amount of space dedicated to the close-up product shot, the precision and delicate structure of the nib is the primary focus of this Parker pen ad.

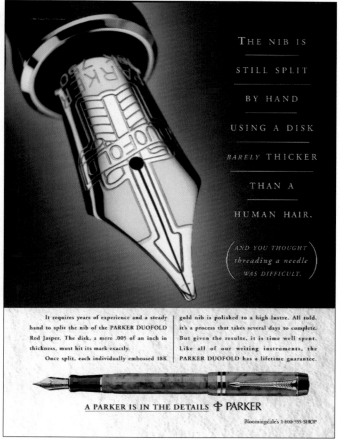

Each type of visual has advantages and disadvantages. Often the limiting factor is cost. A small retailer may be forced to use the inexpensive art services provided by a newspaper, or large advertisers may be unwilling to spend huge amounts of money for original artwork or photography. The availability of stock artwork and photography on CD-ROM (or downloaded from an art or photography studio Web site) is another way to obtain visuals for an ad short of hiring illustrators or photographers to do original work. Regardless of the type of visual selected, advertising visuals must achieve the following:

- Grab the attention of the target audience.
- Be able to fulfill the goals of the creative strategy.
- Be relevant to the message, the product, and the target audience.
- Communicate clearly.
- Be reproducible in or adaptable to each advertising medium that will be used in the advertising campaign.

EXHIBIT 15–14 **This advertisement for Nieman Marcus uses dark, subdued colors to set a sophisticated tone for the message and to highlight the pitcher and the store name, both of which are presented in a lighter color.**

As with the previous decisions made during the thumbnail stage, decisions about visuals may be tentative at first; these concepts can then be refined during later stages of layout development. Several of the thumbnail sketches typically will be used as the basis for the design of rough layouts.

Rough Layouts

A **layout** is a piece of artwork or rendering showing how advertising elements—such as headlines, visuals, and photographs—will be arranged in the final printed advertisement. **Rough layouts** are called rough because they often use quickly drawn illustrations to represent finished drawings or photographs; penciled-in headlines to show headline placement; and lines, squiggles, or unreadable (greeked-in) type to represent advertising copy. The purpose of the rough layout is to identify several different ways to communicate the advertising message effectively. Rough layouts are reviewed by the creative team in an ad agency or by managers in an advertiser's organization. One or two of the layouts will be reproduced as a more finished representation of the final advertisement, called a *comprehensive layout*.

For an art director, the production of rough layouts provides an opportunity to test several layout designs in the same size and shape as those that will appear in magazines or newspapers. Several arrangements of the elements in the ad will be attempted in order to get feedback about the designs. The use of computers to move around design elements has greatly improved the ability of the designer to "play" with design alternatives at the rough layout stage. Because headlines will be used with visuals in rough layouts, the artist generally begins thinking about selecting typestyles for the headlines and text in the advertisement.

TYPESTYLE AS A KEY DESIGN ELEMENT The selection of typestyles for the design of an advertisement is important because type can add or detract from the look, feel, and readability of an ad. The art director has to be very precise in how he or she goes about selecting type. One of the art director's goals in selecting typestyles is to specify the exact typeface, the size of type, and the width of the type block for every piece of type in the layout. The type selection process has been made significantly easier by

AROUND THE GLOBE

....

Design and
Culture in
South America

The importance of design to business communication in South America and around the world tends to both reflect and influence the local culture. As you travel to the key cities of South America, you experience different cultural patterns. For example, São Paulo, Brazil, has a reputation as a sensuous city of colors, signage, and window displays played out against a background of old gray cement and exposed industrial iron. Notice the rich and vibrant design work on the cover of *Placar,* a Brazilian soccer magazine.

In contrast, the colors of the buildings and architecture in Santiago, Chile, remind one of the southeastern coast of the United States. The colors are pastel, bright, and sun-washed, and the hotels are of the high-rise variety. The feel is one of sophistication and the designs extend this feeling to advertising and marketing communications. Notice the poster design that reflects the color and urbane sense one gets from being in Santiago.

As this quick excursion has illustrated, design is important in that it attempts to solve real communication problems. And to do so, it must reflect its cultural context while influencing the values and aesthetic norms of consumers.

Source: Rick Torreano, "Creativity in South America," *Communication Arts* 38, no. 2 (May/June 1996): 109–123.

In each of these designs, the colors and presentation style clearly reflect the character and culture of the city in which it was created—São Paulo, Brazil, and Santiago, Chile, respectively.

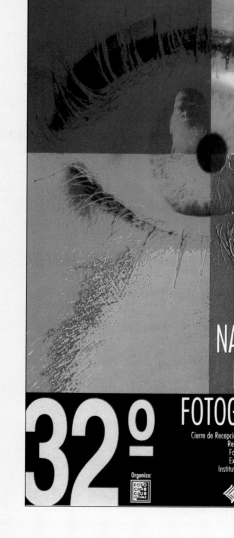

the sheer number of typefaces available for use on the computer. Nonetheless, in order to understand this selection process, we will review some of the characteristics of type that an artist must consider.

In the layout, the larger and bolder type that appears in headlines is called *display type*. Type that is used for small text is called *text type*. There are five broad categories of type: 1) Roman or serif; 2) Gothic, or sans serif; 3) slab serif, or square serif; 4) cursive, or script; and 5) ornate. Within each type category, there are many different type families. These categories and several families from each one are illustrated in Exhibit 15–15.

Roman type is the most commonly used type category because of its interesting variations and readability. Roman type is also called *serif type* because of the small tails or flourishes, called *serifs,* at the end of the major strokes. Another distinguishing characteristic of Roman type is the difference in thickness of the strokes in each letter. *Gothic type* is a contemporary type category characterized by its lack of serifs. It is also called *sans serif* type, because *sans* is a French word meaning "lacking or without." The strokes in gothic letters are uniform in thickness. *Slab serif type* can be distinguished by its square-looking serifs.

Some designers call these types square serif, antiques, or Egyptian type.

Cursive, or script type, appears to be handwritten. While a small amount looks elegant on invitations or awards, cursive type is difficult to read. Because of this characteristic, it is not often used in advertising. *Ornate* or *ornamental type* is a heterogeneous category with many unusual families. These type families are distinguished by their unusual designs and strokes. Some of the type families can be used to match the theme of an advertisement. Retail store headlines may use unusual faces such as Accord or Shothru to create an unusual effect in their advertisements.

Type families in each of the categories may include several individual typefaces or fonts. A **typeface,** or **font,** is a complete set of letters in one size and face. Exhibit 15–16 shows some of the individual fonts in the Futura family. Notice how some of the fonts are bold, while others are light and airy. Art directors will use the heavier fonts for headlines and emphasis; lighter type fonts will be used for text.

Once the font for each piece of copy has been selected, the type size must be specified. The size of type used in the layout is directly related to the amount of copy prepared by the copywriter. In some situations, art directors

---

EXHIBIT 15–15   Five Type Categories with Representative Families

Roman	Characterized by serifs and differences in thickness in the strokes	This type family is Times Roman.
Gothic	Characterized by the absence of serifs and uniform thickness of strokes	This type family is Helvetica.
Slab Serif	Characterized by the presence of square serifs	This type family is Memphis.
Cursive	Characterized by the handwritten appearance	*This type family is Nuptial Script.*
Ornate	Characterized by the unusual formation of characters	This type family is La Bamba.

will choose type sizes based on the amount of copy provided by the copywriter. At other times, especially during the production of catalogs or brochures, the converse will be true, and the art director will ask a copywriter to write a specified amount of copy about a product to fill a gap in the layout. When selecting type, the art director is primarily interested in three measurements: the height of the font's letters or point size, the amount of space between lines of a block of type, and the width of the block of type.

Type font size is measured in *points;* thus, it may also be referred to as the point size of type. There are 72 points in an inch, so type that is 36 points is approximately one-half inch high. Text type is usually set between 6 and 14 points; display type is usually 18 points or larger. Exhibit 15–17 compares the sizes of frequently used text and display type.

In blocks of text type, the amount of space between lines of type, known as *leading,* is important. Changing the leading can make type more or less readable and interesting. Leading is also measured in points, but art directors usually specify text type size and leading at the same time. For example, if 12-point type is to be spaced on 12-point leading, it would be specified as 12 on 12, which is written as 12/12. As the width of a type block increases, leading is usually increased to aid readability. The width of a type block is expressed in *picas.* There are 6 picas to the inch, and 12 points per pica.

Once point size, leading, and width measurements have been specified by the art director, the alignment of type with column margins must be described. One of four types of alignment can be chosen. *Justified alignment* means both the left and right ends of a line of type are aligned with the left and right column margins. To justify type, space at the end of a line of type is redistributed between words in the line of type. When only the left end of a line of type is aligned with the column margin, the alignment is called *flush left* or *ragged right.* On the other hand, when only the right end of a line of type is aligned with the column margin, the alignment is *flush right* or *ragged left.* Finally, a line of type may be *centered,* so that neither the left nor the right end of the line of type is aligned with the margins.

EXHIBIT 15–16   **Fonts in the Futura Family**

FUTURA

FUTURA BOOK

FUTURA BOLD

FUTURA BOLD OBLIQUE

FUTURA HEAVY

FUTURA HEAVY OBLIQUE

FUTURA LIGHT

FUTURA LIGHT OBLIQUE

FUTURA EXTRA BOLD

FUTURA EXTRA BOLD OBLIQUE

EXHIBIT 15–17   **Type sizes**

6 point	TYPE size
8 point	TYPE size
10 point	TYPE size
12 point	TYPE size
14 point	TYPE size
18 point	TYPE size
24 point	TYPE size
36 point	TYPE si
72 point	TYP

Specifying alignment and type size characteristics, called *spacing type,* is a much easier task for the art director today because of computers and desktop publishing. Art directors can manipulate type sizes and alignment on the computer screen and immediately see the effect of changes. Because most type fonts can be scaled by the computer, many software packages allow fractional sizes of type. By removing the time-consuming task of fitting copy to type by hand, the computer allows the art director to focus on aesthetics and readability in type selection.

Several guidelines can improve the readability of type in layouts and advertisements. For one, simple type fonts are more readable than ornate type fonts. Using upper- and lowercase letters makes reading easier; all uppercase letters should only be used in short headlines. Using *reverse type,* in which white letters appear on a black or colored background, can make reading difficult unless the reverse type is large and bold. Large bold letters in the white can be dramatic as well as readable, while smaller reverse type, especially when filled with a color, becomes less readable. Printing type over a color or image, called *surprinting,* can present problems in readability if the background is muddled or if there is little contrast between the background and the type. Finally, matching type fonts to the product, when possible, can improve the overall impression of the advertisement. For example, a Western-wear store may select a Western style of type, such as Desperado, to maintain the Western theme in its advertisements.

During the rough layout stage, headline type is the most important consideration because, even with the ease of computers, art directors rarely include text type on a rough layout. During that stage, art directors want the creative team and managers to evaluate the overall effect of the design, rather than specific details of the advertising copy. Also, rough layouts may be part of a proposal for an advertising project, rather than directed work from an advertiser or agency client. Finally, for projects that have been initiated by the advertiser, finished advertising copy may not be approved at the time of the rough layout.

If copy is provided at the rough layout stage, it is usually typed and presented separately from the rough layout, so the acceptance or rejection of one does not affect the acceptance or rejection of the other. Showing finished copy is an important part of the next stage of development, the comprehensive layout.

Comprehensive Layouts

Comprehensive layouts, or *comps,* are more finished versions of the final advertisement because they show all of the elements that will appear in the final advertisement in their correct positions. Actual photographs or illustrations, accurate type style and size selections, and precise borders and graphics are used in the comprehensive layout. Once again, the use of the computer has given the designer the ability to make the comprehensive layout a very close copy of the final ad. The general purpose of the comprehensive layout is to show, as nearly as possible, how the finished advertisement will look when it is reproduced. Once the comprehensive layout has been approved, finished artwork must be prepared for the printing requirements of a magazine or newspaper.

The specific purpose of comprehensive layouts varies according to who is looking at them. For advertisers, comps are the last stage before final production of an advertisement. Therefore, photographic details, advertising copy, color selection, and layout design must be reviewed and approved before final production begins. Changes made to an advertisement after the comprehensive layout stage were at one time very expensive. However, the use of the computer has made the design process more flexible at this stage; changes to comps can be made on the computer at very little expense. When comprehensives are used for final approval of the advertisement, only one comprehensive layout is prepared. In some organizations, these layouts are done electronically, so they can be reviewed and approved on the computer screen by upper-level executives and managers.

In advertising agencies, comprehensive layouts may be used for new business presentations. The high quality of laser printer output in black and white and color has made it much more economical to prepare comprehensive layouts. Because of improved technologies in printing and scanning, the agency can use the persuasive power of advertisements with a finished look in client presentations. In these presentations, an advertising agency may choose to dramatize one creative approach, or they may prepare comprehensive layouts for a second, more conservative, "fall back" position.

Art directors also prepare layouts that are similar to comprehensives for catalogs and product brochures. These multipage layouts, called **dummies,** are used for design and copy approval before a project is sent to the printer. Preparing materials for a magazine, newspaper, or printer is the purpose of mechanicals, the last stage in layout development.

Mechanicals

The layout that has been prepared to meet the printing requirements of a magazine, newspaper, or printer is called a **mechanical,** or *paste-up.* On mechanicals, the type is pasted into exact position, and any special preparations for illustrations or color reproduction are made. These may include preparation of overlays, sizing of photographs, or notation of special instructions for the printer. Because mechanicals are prepared for the printer, all of the elements in the layout must be **camera-ready.** This means the printer can make photographic printing plates from the mechanical.

Most mechanicals have a base layout with the major elements of the advertisement indicated. Color printing layers are produced on acetate overlays, sometimes called rubyliths or amberliths. The outermost layer is usually tracing paper with instructions to the printer. Photographs are mounted separately, cropped, and submitted to the printer with the mechanical. From these mechanicals, printing plates are made and the advertisement is reproduced. Some magazines and newspapers may request that an advertising agency or advertiser provide printing negatives rather than mechanicals.

Computer technology, when appropriate, allows a designer to send a finished ad to a printer or publisher electronically over the Internet, or on disk. However, many finished ads are still provided on film, in the form of black-and-white photostats, or in mechanical form.

The printing process will be described in Chapter Sixteen, "Advertising Production." While mechanicals are the final stage of layout development, the art director must supervise and monitor advertisements throughout the production process. It is only after an advertisement has appeared and been evaluated that the art director has some evidence for the success of an advertising design.

Effects Of Good Design

What constitutes "good design"? Is it a measure of peer respect? Accolades from national contests and reviews? The popularity of an ad with consumers? Some classic designs, such as the Volkswagen campaign created by Bill Bernbach, an ad from which is shown in Exhibit 15–18, attracted attention, created an image, and are still recognized today for their simplicity and creativity in communication.

EXHIBIT 15–18 Bill Bernbach's Volkswagen campaign, an ad from which is shown here, is still recognized today for its creativity and effectiveness.

Good design can affect response for all levels of advertisers. For example, a good advertisement can increase sales or store traffic, or it can generate consumer interest and awareness. Good designs coupled with good copy create results. But the effects of a good design cannot be separated from the effects of good copy or from the effects of good marketing choices. And, as "Adscape: An Appreciation for Clients" explains, good design is also partially about a good client/agency relationship.

With training in graphic design, the art director's role in the creation of print advertising is clear; there are many applications of graphic skills in the development of advertising layouts. The art director's capacity for visualization is also important for the production of outstanding television and radio commercials. We'll examine how art directors shape and influence the production of these commercials in the next section.

R E S E T

1. **Think of a magazine ad that you like and believe is well designed. Work backward in your mind and imagine what the rough layout and thumbnail must have looked like for this ad.**
2. **How does the art director work with the key principles of design to create effective and exciting layout designs?**
3. **What are five characteristics of type to which the art director should pay close attention?**

Directing Television And Radio Commercials

For television and radio commercials, art directors are members of a creative team that may include copywriters, creative directors, producers, and directors. This team is responsible for creating commercials that transform the creative concept—the big idea—into the images, experiences, and fantasies of the target audience. Because the creative process is a team effort, it is not always possible to determine which member of the team was responsible for a specific image or idea in the final commercial. The art director's role in the production of television commercials is more evident than the role he or she plays in the development of radio commercials, however.

For each television commercial, the art director prepares a storyboard that presents illustrations of key visuals in the commercial, the advertising copy, and instructions for the producer. In the storyboard shown in Exhibit 15–19, the setting also is described. Sound effects and special effects are indicated next to the script, and highlight visuals capture the essence of the important visual ideas in the script.

Even though visuals are absent from radio scripts and radio commercials, the need for clear mental images is apparent, as the "Ironhead/Skillet" script for the Atlanta Falcons football team in Exhibit 15–20 shows. In this example, the sound effects create instant attention and make us wonder what is going on. This humorous setup is followed by the punch line, in which Craig "Ironhead" Hayward's mother asks him to give her the skillet so she can make dinner. Now we know why he's called Ironhead!

Scripting Television And Radio Commercials

Regardless of the individual's level of involvement, all members of the creative team and advertising managers need to understand how scripts are developed for television and radio commercials. For some smaller productions, an advertising manager, a copywriter, or an art director may have to supervise commercial production. By understanding the technical aspects of script development, the production process can be accomplished more effectively and efficiently.

In Chapter Fourteen, we examined the principles of good copywriting for the broadcast media. Each type of broadcast commercial begins with a script that includes instructions written in the vocabulary of broadcast producers. Because the production process is very expensive, less expensive forms of commercials may be used for client or advertiser approval and for copy testing and refinement. Some advertisers and agencies use only storyboards produced from scripts to obtain approval for a television commercial. This is because a storyboard is the least expensive presentation of a TV commercial concept that also includes the key scenes and instructions for the spot. Most

"Ferry Boat" :30

SFX: Great, romantic song throughout.

(Open on a wide shot of a VW driving on a ferry boat in Seattle. The VW is dusty and loaded down with suitcases. Tight shot of a beat-up Ohio license plate. It is dirty and covered with smashed bugs. A beautiful young woman gets out of the VW. She stretches, as if she has been on the road forever, revealing her Lee Jeans. She begins to walk toward the front of the boat. The ferry is getting ready to leave the dock. Suddenly, another car comes tearing into the parking lot and stops)

SFX: Squealing of breaks.

(Cut to a handsome young man. He leaves his car and leaps onto the boat. He begins to try to catch up to the young woman who is still casually walking toward the bow. She looks very good in her jeans. He finally catches up to her. He is out of breath. She turns toward him. He holds out his hand. There is a small locket in his hand)

Man: (Breathlessly) Excuse me, but...you dropped this back there.

Woman: Where?

Man: In Nebraska.

(Cut to boat's wake with the super)

Super: Lee. Cut to fit.

EXHIBIT 15–20   Atlanta Falcons Radio Script

"Ironhead/Skillet" (:30)

SFX: Sound of metal banging against something over and over. Slow and steady banging of metal continues throughout.

Anncr.: How did Falcons fullback Craig "Ironhead" Heyward get his nickname?

Woman: Craig, honey, give Momma the skillet now so I can start supper.

Anncr.: Let's just say . . . he earned it. Atlanta Falcons '95. Order your season tickets now. Call (404) 233-8000.

Woman: (To herself) I swear. Someday that boy's gonna hurt someone with that head of his.

---

advertising managers can grasp what will be involved in producing a TV spot from a storyboard. However, TV production costs have been known to escalate beyond estimates prepared from storyboards. This possibility is hard to ascertain from a storyboard alone.

Large advertisers often request that animatics be prepared. Recall from Chapter Fourteen that animatics are combined audio and video presentations of a commercial that attempt to simulate the look and feel of the finished commercial. The form of animatics varies considerably. Some animatics are prepared by combining the audio portion of a commercial with video shots of the storyboard visuals. Other animatics are prepared using multimedia software to couple images and sound on desktop computers.[12] Advertisers may also be shown film or movie clips of actors or actresses with animatics

AdScape

An Appreciation for Clients

Whenever you see or hear an advertisement you really like, what do you think or ask yourself? The obvious first question might be, Wow, I wonder how the writer or artist came up with that idea or picture? Another thought could be, I wish I had thought of that. The seasoned art director, writer, creative director, photographer, or illustrator quite frequently will ask a different question: How did the creative team or account executive or agency principal get the client to buy an idea like *that*?

Think of some of the really good advertising out there, such as that from Nike, Saturn, or Coca-Cola, to name a few. It took some really skilled people to do those ads. It also took some very good and trusted agency presenters to sell the ideas to the client.

The client is in a very key position. The client puts up the money and gets to call the shots. Some creative souls see the client as the obstacle to great work and stardom. But the reality is that the client is the opportunity. Great advertising people like Hal Riney understand this. It takes great work and the ability to get the OK from the client to produce great ads.

How does the work get sold? By people the client trusts. Creative directors, account executives, and agency presidents who have taken the time to establish a trusting relationship with clients can sell great work. Otherwise, a lot of potentially great ads get left on the drawing board.

It also takes good clients. Good clients understand their business and the advertising

business. They have the experience and expertise (and trust in it) to take risks when appropriate. They know that lukewarm ads are not worth the money to run them.

So the next time you see advertising that inspires you, think of the people who sold the idea as well as those who created it. And have an appreciation for the client who had the courage and conviction to approve the idea. Clients, after all, are people too.

QUESTION

What types of qualities would you expect to find in a successful agency presenter?

Source: Carl Warner, "Clients Are People Too," *Communication Arts,* September/October 1996, 38.

to aid in casting personalities for the commercial. The relatively low cost of animatics, some as low as $2,000, makes them an attractive substitute for storyboards. But an animatic may be as difficult for an advertiser to evaluate as a storyboard.

Intermediate forms of radio commercials are often more realistic than television animatics. For radio commercials, sound effects and a skilled reader can effectively simulate the finished commercial. In fact, most advertising experts believe that radio scripts should be evaluated from audiotapes, rather than a typed script on paper, because radio is an aural medium.

Intermediate forms of radio and television commercials are important for preproduction approval and for copy testing the message. To understand script development, let's look at the technical features of television scripts, storyboards, and radio scripts.

TELEVISION SCRIPTS AND STORYBOARDS

Scripts for television commercials are usually prepared with two vertical columns. One column describes the audio portion of the script while the other column describes video instructions. Once the script has been completed, it goes to the art director.

Art directors prepare storyboards on presentation boards that contain between six and 20 television screen windows with accompanying boxes for advertising copy and instructions to the producer. Key visuals are selected for the storyboard because one function of the storyboard is to sell the idea of the commercial to the advertiser. In order to guide the production of the commercial, the art director must specify the camera shots that will be needed and determine how the camera should move when filming the commercial.

There are two types of camera shots that art directors will describe in the video instructions that accompany a storyboard. First, there are distance shots, which vary from extreme close-ups to extreme long shots. Most producers have shorthand names for these shots, such as "head shots" or "shoulder shots" that indicate how much of a person he or she wants in the shot.

The second type of camera shot art directors are concerned with is camera movement. Varying camera shots, one of the main advantages of television, creates interest and helps tell

the visual story in sequence. Exhibit 15–21 lists several commercial production terms that describe camera movement. Additional video effects can be added in the editing process. Among the more important of these are the transitions from one scene to the next. The two common transitions are cuts and dissolves. Effective producers use *cuts* for exciting changes and *dissolves* for softer mood effects.

Like storytellers, television producers use the technical tools of video and audio mixing to tell an advertiser's story. The art director must make sure the technical effects of the video and audio elements complement, rather than obscure, the message to the target audience. Effectively engaging the target audience requires creating involvement. Roman and Maas suggest four ways involvement can be created in television commercials:[13]

1. Provide information the audience wants.
2. Present a problem to which you have the solution.
3. Present a situation with which an audience can identify.
4. Provide appropriate entertainment.

EXHIBIT 15–21   TV Camera Movement Terms

Pan: Turning the camera from right to left ("pan left") or left to right ("pan right").

Tilt: Making the camera point up ("tilt up") or down ("tilt down") gradually and smoothly.

Pedestal: Raising ("pedestal up") or lowering ("pedestal down") the camera's pedestal.

Tongue: Moving the whole camera left ("tongue left") or right ("tongue right") with the boom of a crane.

Crane or boom: Moving the whole camera up ("crane up") or down ("crane down") with the boom of a crane.

Dolly: Moving the camera straight toward an object ("dolly in") or away from an object ("dolly out") on its mount.

Truck or track: Moving the camera laterally to the right ("truck right") or to the left ("truck left") on its mount.

Crab: Moving the camera sideways on its crane or crab dolly. Camera movements may vary with the lateral movement.

Arc: Moving the camera in a slightly curved arc to the right ("arc right") or the left ("arc left").

Zoom: Changing the focal length of the lens to get closer to ("zoom in") or further away from ("zoom out") an object, rather than moving the camera.

Source: Adapted from Herbert Zettl, *Television Production Handbook*, 5th ed. (Belmont, CA: Wadsworth, 1992), 110–113.

Sometimes it takes only one or two of Roman and Maas's guidelines to engage the audience. For example, a television spot for Hallmark cards opens with a wife unexpectedly finding her husband at home during the day. The audience also wants to know why he's home. Suspense builds until the husband gives the wife a Hallmark card identifying her as a "very special mother." Then, the audience finds out that an adopted child has arrived for the couple. Even if members of the target audience do not have children, they can imagine the joy and emotion surrounding this moment. The audience becomes involved and sees the relevance of the Hallmark card.

RADIO SCRIPTS   Radio scripts, such as the one for the Bay Area Suicide and Crisis Hotline in Exhibit 15–22, are written in a single column with voices identified and sound effects noted. Roman and Maas suggest that radio commercials should:[14]

1. Talk to the audience one-to-one.
2. Focus on one idea.
3. Stretch the listener's imagination.
4. Be topical by connecting with immediate events, people, or seasons.
5. Register brand names.
6. Use the power of music.

Relevance and involvement are also important in radio scripts. The commercial for the Bay Area Suicide and Crisis Hotline begins with the dialogue of a Vietnam veteran expressing his feelings of depression. These feelings can easily be imagined as real by those in the target audience because even though the target audience is not Vietnam veterans, publicity about the plight of Vietnam veterans has probably made the target audience aware of the problem. The immediacy of the message is designed to generate responses from the sensitized audience. Radio commercials such as this one must create images that are recognizable. Because radio messages are sometimes used to reinforce print advertisements, effective art direction contributes to the success of all aspects of the campaign.

EXHIBIT 15–22   Bay Area Suicide and Crisis Radio Spot

"Veteran" (:60)

Veteran: Hello, hello…you still there?

Crisis Hotline Woman: I'm here.

Vet.: Well, I don't know…don't know if it's worth it.

Crisis Hotline Woman: Can you tell me where you're staying?

Vet.: We go over there, drag our…

SFX: Beep.

Vet.: …butts in the mud…nobody listens.

Crisis Hotline Woman: I'm here.

Vet.: Been twenty years, now.

Crisis Hotline Woman: Do you have a friend you could call… to be with you?

Vet.: Ain't got no friends.

Crisis Hotline Woman: Would you like us to send some help?

Vet.: No cops, don't want no cops.

Anncr.: Some 55,000 Americans were killed in Vietnam. Since then, more Vietnam veterans have committed suicide than died in the war. Call the Suicide Crisis Hotlines to find out what you can do. If you aren't there for us, we can't be there for them. Send help. Don't let them die.

Vet.: You know, I kept my gun.

SFX: Breathing.

(Live tag with phone number)

In this era of sound, special effects, and computer-delivered images, the importance of art and design to a message is more significant than ever. The central artistic role in an advertising agency is played by the art director. Art directors work cooperatively with the creative team to translate an advertising strategy into an effective advertisement or campaign. Art directors also guide and control the advertising production processes to ensure that the verbal and visual messages in the finished advertisements or commercials are communicated correctly and effectively.

Visual images are important for the creation of brand associations between a message and a consumer. Brand associations combine to form brand images that consumers use to organize information about a brand. Brand images are also important contributors to the overall corporate image. As part of the task of creating or changing a product, brand, or corporate image, the art director may be asked to design corporate trademarks or logotypes. These logotypes become important elements of the corporate identity program. An art director's influence may also extend to package design, where he or she coordinates aesthetic elements of the package. Successful package designs have graphic personality, precise positioning, directional selling, the persuasion factor, and planned simplicity.

One of the primary tasks of the art director is to design print advertisements. The development of print advertisements progresses from small picture ideas, called thumbnails, to rough layouts, comprehensive layouts, and finished mechanicals that are ready for a printer. A thumbnail sketch is a small, rough picture idea of a possible ad. During the thumbnail stage, the art director must decide what elements will be included in the advertisement. Will there be headlines, subheadlines, photographs, illustrations of the product, text copy? How will the elements be arranged? In addition, the art director must decide how to use several other design variables, including white space, balance, eye movement, proportion, and color. The art director must then select the visuals for the design, considering the economic constraints and the goals of the advertisement, and who will produce the visuals. Visual elements include color and black-and-white photographs, illustrations, and line art.

A rough layout often uses quickly drawn illustrations to represent a finished advertisement, including penciled-in headlines and unreadable type. The purpose of rough layouts is to identify several different ways to effectively communicate the advertising message. At this stage, the selection of typestyles for designs is important because type can add or detract from the look, feel, and readability of an ad. The art director must decide what typestyles will be used in the layout; what font, font size, leading, and type width will be used for both headlines and body copy; and whether the headline and text copy will be typeset as centered, flush right, flush left, or justified.

Comprehensive layouts are more finished renderings of the final newspaper or magazine advertisement; they show all of the elements that will appear in the final advertisement in their correct positions. The purpose of the comp is to show, as nearly as possible, what the finished advertisement will look like when it is reproduced. For advertisers, comps are the final review stage before production; for ad agencies, comps may be used for new business presentations. Comps for catalogs and product brochures are known as dummies. The final stage of print production is known as the mechanical. On a mechanical, or pasteup, the type is pasted into exact position and any special preparations for illustrations or color reproduction are made.

Art directors are also instrumental in translating campaign images into television visuals, called storyboards. Storyboards are used to get preproduction approval and to test approaches to the commercial. Storyboards describe key visuals, movements or camera shots, and the advertising copy. Animatics, or audio-visual presentations of the storyboard, are sometimes requested by the client.

Finally, art directors have a role in the creation of radio scripts because they are part of the creative team and because radio commercials must often be coordinated with print advertisements.

KEY TERMS

art director, 460

brand image, 463

corporate image, 463

logotype, 465

corporate identity
program, 465

packaging, 466

thumbnail sketch, 468

white space, 470

balance, 470

eye movement, 470

proportion, 472

intensity, 472

contrast, 472

layout, 474

rough layout, 474

typeface, 476

font, 476

comprehensive layout, 478

dummy, 479

mechanical, 479

camera-ready, 479

REVIEW QUESTIONS

1. Describe the broad communication role of the art director and the specific design tasks that he or she performs.

2. Discuss the relationship between brand associations, brand images, and corporate images. Give an example that illustrates each.

3. Describe what a logotype is and why it is important to the corporation.

4. Explain why art direction is important when logotypes or brand images are changed.

5. Outline the sequence of the layouts that are made in the development of print advertisements.

6. Discuss the relative difficulty of designing print advertisements as it relates to the number of elements in the layout.

7. Describe how a rough layout differs from a comprehensive. What differences would a reviewer identify?

8. What is a good design?

9. Discuss how storyboards are used by an advertising agency. How are storyboards different from animatics?

10. What should the script of a good radio commercial convey to the listener?

1. What are some of your favorite branded products or services? What images do you associate with each of these brands? Can you point to specific design aspects of the marketing communications for these brands that have been instrumental in creating the images for you?

2. What are some of the current trends in graphic design that you can identify in prints ads or broadcast commercials? What types of graphic designs would you be attracted to on a Web site?

3. Think of an ad for a favorite long-standing company and one for a relatively new company. What is it about the design of the ad for the long-standing company that is consistent with its longevity in the marketplace? What is it about the design of the ad for the newer company that tells you it is a newer company?

interactive discovery lab

1. Many illustrators and photography studios display their visual work on Web sites. Search the Web for companies that sell stock artwork. Print the screens of at least two companies whose work you like. Now search for illustrators and photographers who do original or on-location work. Select one illustrator and one photographer whose work you like. Keep their Web addresses on file for future reference.

2. The next time you are commuting to school or work, pay attention to the outdoor boards you pass. Which ones grab your attention best? What is it about the designs of these boards that attracts your attention? Can you think of how to use these design approaches in other media? How would you transfer the best outdoor board you saw into a radio commercial? What sound devices would you use to get across your point?

Chapter Sixteen

Advertising Production

CLONING SHAQ WAS NO SLAM DUNK

Creating advertising ideas often requires thinking "outside the box" and allowing one's imagination a fairly free reign.

Once it gets down to the nitty-gritty of turning the idea into a finished ad, however, it takes some real attention to detail to bring an ad to life.

This painstaking attention to production detail is nowhere more evident than in the shooting of a Reebok television spot in which Shaquille O'Neal plays basketball against a team of Shaqs. The production problem was to put Shaq's head on the bodies of other players. The solution was provided by Leo Burnett Company and R/Greenberg Associates, working with Silicon Graphics Indigo II workstations.

The first step was to scan Shaq's head with a Cyberscan laser while he sat still for 30 minutes. This resulted in a three-dimensional map of his face displaying a variety of expressions that would be used for the other players. The next step involved shooting the scenes where Shaq plays against five of himself. This required finding actors roughly the size of Shaq—who is 7 feet, 1 inch tall and weighs 300 pounds.

Before Shaq's scanned head could be placed on the bodies of the actors in the scenes, it had to be modeled. It was rotated in space and viewed from a number of angles so shots could be

selected to match the positions of the actors in the spot. Next, features were added to the digitized head. Then it was time to graft the heads onto the actors' bodies; the computerized heads were rotated and matched to the angle of each actor's head.

Once the heads were on the actors, they were colored, textured, and blurred to make them look like they were in motion. The process of digitally inserting the heads into each frame of

the TV spot took 10 people 2 months to do. The next time you see an ad you like, think of the attention to production detail required to make it a reality.

Source: "Making a Multitude of Shaqs," *New York Times,* 22 March 1995, C3.

LOOK BEFORE YOU LEAP

- **What is advertising production and how is it important?**
- **How does the cost of production affect the advertising creation process?**
- **What is the relationship of production to the rest of the message creation task?**
- **How are print advertisements and collateral materials produced?**
- **How are broadcast commercials and videotapes produced?**

16

The live-action cinematography and computer-generated special effects used in the making of the "multiple Shaqs" commercial are just two of the countless techniques used in the final stage of the advertising process: advertising production.

By understanding the steps in print and broadcast production, an advertiser can evaluate and monitor production costs more effectively. David Perry, director of broadcast production at Saatchi & Saatchi, New York, estimated that 75 percent of the cost of producing a commercial is built into the storyboard.[1] Similar cost projections could be made for a comprehensive layout and the production of a print ad.

In this chapter we will first examine why production procedures and costs are such an important part of the message creation process, looking specifically at the influence of production on the advertising process. Next, we examine the sequential production tasks required for print advertisements and collateral materials, and for television and radio commercials.

Production And The Advertising Process

Advertising production is the phrase used to describe the physical tasks of preparing print advertisements, collateral print materials, and radio and television commercials. The production process is the third and final stage of the message creation task that we see depicted in Exhibit 16–1. The ad concept has been created, the copy elements have been written, and the design or art program has been developed and approved by management. Now it is time for the creative director and art director to turn their attention to how the ad is going to be produced. At this stage, the directors have three concerns: 1) how to enhance or maintain the quality of an ad as it was conceived; 2) how to control costs; and 3) how production can influence a campaign's effectiveness. We should point out that, in reality, the process is not so linear; all good writers and artists call on their experience during the ad creation process so that they do not come up with ideas that cannot be afforded or produced because of production limitations. However, for our purposes, let's assume the stages are defined this way.

The Influence Of Production On The Advertising Process

Production decisions can produce positive and negative effects throughout the advertising process. Exhibit 16–2 summarizes some of the influences production has on the quality of the message created, the budget available for message delivery, and the results obtained in the message evaluation process.

Effective production techniques can dramatically increase the effectiveness of the created message. Unsatisfactory techniques, such as poor reproduction of a product photograph or type that is unreadable because of a weak background, can destroy the effectiveness of the advertising message. Production problems that arise during message creation are often correctable, however, if production processes are monitored carefully. The issue of production's role in the message creation task is so important that we will address it in more detail shortly.

The influence of advertising production on message delivery is more indirect. Consider the small-scale example of a local advertiser with a

$2,000 budget illustrated in Exhibit 16–3. If this advertiser spends around $75 per week for a small advertisement in a weekly newspaper, the advertising budget will support 26 advertisements. Suppose this same advertiser is unhappy with the quality of photography that the weekly newspaper provides for free. To improve his or her advertisements, the advertiser hires a professional photographer to take a set of photographs. If the photographs cost $450, then only $1,550 is left to purchase space in the newspaper. This means the advertiser can place only 20 advertisements instead of 26, a reduction in message delivery of about 23 percent. In short, increasing production costs can shrink a media budget. These reductions in media expenditures can have a significant effect on store traffic and sales for both large and small advertisers. In this case, the advertiser must make a choice between improving the quality and potential effectiveness of each ad versus the number of ads that can be run. It could turn out, for example, that fewer but better ads can more than offset the reduction in the number of ads. Only experience or evaluation can tell.

The effects of production techniques on message creation or of production costs on message delivery can be detected during the evaluation stage. If production techniques are effective and cost efficient, the results of a campaign may surge beyond expected levels; on the other hand, poor production can result in marketing communications and sales goals not being achieved. Similarly, because predicting advertising performance is not easy, advertisers monitor production costs carefully. By distributing costs across different applications or geographic areas, the unit cost of producing a single advertisement is reduced. In addition, photographic visuals and illustrations may be standardized for use in several different advertisements, several different media, and several different regions or countries.

Production As A Message Creation Task

When an advertiser or an art director specifies a production procedure, he or she does so with the belief that the production technique will enhance the message. An outstanding photograph may create more awareness for the brand. Multicolor printing may help con-

sumers understand a complex message. Dramatic video footage may heighten a consumer's desire to own a product. In all of these creative roles, advertising production is a fundamental task of message creation.

How a message is transmitted can be as important as what is said in an advertisement. Indeed, how an ad is produced can sometimes

---

EXHIBIT 16–1   Production in the Advertising Process

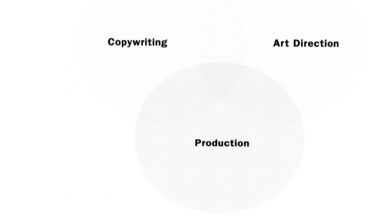

MESSAGE CREATION TASKS

Copywriting   Art Direction

Production

EXHIBIT 16–2   Influence of Production on the Advertising Process

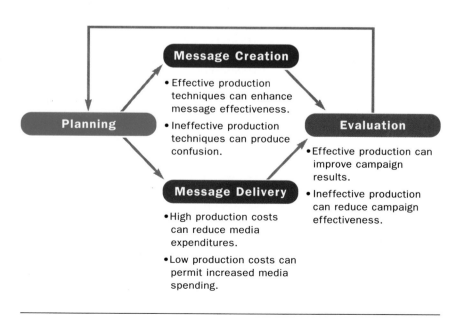

Message Creation
• Effective production techniques can enhance message effectiveness.
• Ineffective production techniques can produce confusion.

Planning

Evaluation
• Effective production can improve campaign results.
• Ineffective production can reduce campaign effectiveness.

Message Delivery
• High production costs can reduce media expenditures.
• Low production costs can permit increased media spending.

EXHIBIT 16–3   Small Advertiser Budget Example

TOTAL BUDGET $2,000

**Local media provides
free production**

$2,000
spent for media

26 ADS
at $75 each
(Total = $1,950)

Advertiser hires photographer

$450 spent for production
photography

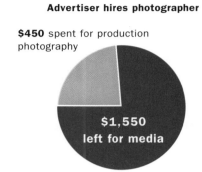

$1,550
left for media

20 ADS
at $75 each
(Total = $1,550)
23% less spent
on media

become the central idea behind the ad. For example, in 1986 Transamerica used a pop-up advertisement of the San Francisco skyline showing the Transamerica "pyramid" building to create awareness for the corporation. A photo of this famous ad is shown in Exhibit 16–4. The advertisement, which appeared in *Time* magazine, was controversial because the production costs for this single advertisement were estimated at $2.7 million. In addition, another $300,000 was used to purchased the space in *Time*. From the 5.5 million issues of *Time* that carried the advertisement, Transamerica estimated that the ad was seen by 23 million people.[2] An evaluation of the ad showed that the pop-up advertisement had provided instant reader identification of the Transamerica pyramid.

Advertisements with unusual production techniques can heighten consumer interest and improve readership. When the selected production technique showcases a product feature or benefit, the results can be even more dramatic. As a case in point, in late 1989 Texas Instruments (TI) incorporated a new speech synthesis chip into a four-page advertisement in *Business Week*. A teaser headline on the first page enticed readers to a two-page spread with a lift-and-listen tab for the message. The fourth page described the benefits of TI's MegaChip Technologies. Production of the advertisement

was coordinated by Intervisual Communications (Los Angeles). The insert was used in 140,000 copies of the *Business Week* business and technology edition, and in 760,000 issues of the European edition of the magazine.[3] It cost approximately $4 to put a piezoelectric speaker, battery, and switch in each of the hand-assembled advertisements, and total production costs were about $3.6 million.

Both the Texas Instruments and Transamerica examples illustrate the high-cost drama in an advertising message that can be created by unusual production techniques. These innovations in print production really began in the early 1980s with fragrance strips in the form of small perfume packets or scratch-and-sniff strips. Some cosmetics advertisers have tried color strip samples of eye liner, lipstick, and blush inserted into print ads. Microchips have appeared in ads playing everything from seasonal greeting messages to birthday songs. Holograms are in their technological infancy, but they present a potential for bringing a more accessible version of 3-D ads to magazines and outdoor. Advertisers and their agencies always have to weigh the gains in attention and other marketing communications objectives against the high cost of these production techniques.

Most of the creative advantages achieved through intelligent production decisions are more subtle. Some are surprising. The Starch Advertisement Readership Service examined black-and-white advertisements that achieved high readership scores. Starch looked for similarities in the ads and concluded that many of them pictured people in dramatic situations, and that the use of black-and-white photography added realism to the ads. The Starch researchers concluded that color photographs are sometimes more distracting because they show depth and individualize objects in a photograph. Black-and-white photographs, they argued, had the power to focus the readers' attention.[4] Subtle production changes can have a dramatic effect upon the creative effectiveness of an advertisement.

In local and national advertisements, many of today's production improvements are the result of innovations in computer technology and desktop publishing. Using desktop technology, small businesses have access to high-resolution typestyles, high-quality clip art, and professionally prepared layout designs. The

major creative advantage of improvements in production technology is the ability to produce more attractive and effective advertisements. From a management perspective, new technologies also have resulted in reductions in the production costs and in the time required to produce a completed advertisement.

R E S E T

1. How does advertising production fit in with the other steps in the message creation process?

2. How can production enhance an advertising idea? Think of an example of an ad you believe has been enhanced by its production value?

3. How do production costs affect the other elements of the advertising creation process?

Producing Print Advertisements And Collateral Material

As we said earlier, the print advertising production process can be viewed, to some extent, as one continuous process that begins the moment a copywriter and art director tackle an assignment. From the beginning, they will have in mind the technical aspects of producing an ad that can either be a springboard to a great idea or limit what they can do. However, the real technical part of the process begins once the conceptualizing, designing, and writing of an ad are completed and a mechanical version of an ad is turned over to a printer. Here we outline the traditional print production process and the newer, computer-aided method. Then we will discuss the print production cost decisions by stage. "Adscape: Murphy's Law and Production" tells the story of how the production process does not always go as smoothly as planned.

Traditional Print Production

The traditional production operations for print advertisements and brochures are divided into three distinct stages, shown in Exhibit 16–5 and discussed in greater detail in the next section. During the **design stage**, which may also be called *copy and art preparation,* copy and layouts are prepared, typesetting is done, photographic sessions are finished, and art and photographs are prepared for the printer. As we discussed in Chapter Fifteen, the last design task is the preparation of mechanicals for the printer.

From the mechanicals, the printer moves on to the **prepress stage.** Prepress tasks must be

EXHIBIT 16–5   Stages and Tasks of Print Production

TRADITIONAL

Design Stage	Prepress	Presswork
• Copywriting • Comprehensive layouts • Typography • Photography • Mechanicals	• Graphic arts photography • Stripping • Platemaking • Prepress proofs	• Press proofs • Printing • Cutting • Binding

completed before printing can begin. Included in prepress operations are: 1) graphic arts photography, to convert mechanicals into negatives; 2) film assembly or stripping, to arrange the negatives for platemaking; 3) platemaking, to convert negatives to printing plates that can be used on a printing press; and 4) prepress proofs, to check the position of layout elements and to check color images.

Once the proofs have been approved, corrected, and reapproved, the advertisement or brochure is ready for the **presswork stage.** Presswork includes "pulling" press proofs, printing, cutting and trimming, and binding. After binding, the production operations for a brochure or magazine are finished.

Computer-Aided Print Production

Dramatic changes in computer technology have had an impact on all areas of produc-

AdSCAPE

Murphy's Law and Production

You know the old saying, "If anything can go wrong, it will"? We would not be surprised if the person who first uttered those words worked in some aspect of advertising production. The success or failure of the production process can severely alter the effectiveness of an ad or an entire campaign. And it can happen to the best of us. Just ask the folks at one of today's hottest advertising agencies, Wieden & Kennedy in Portland, Oregon.

The story starts just after Wieden & Kennedy successfully pitched Subaru's business back in 1991. The agency won the account with a speculative campaign that satirized the hyperbole and exaggeration commonly found in most automotive advertising. Volks-

wagen had done this successfully in the 1960s with the "Think Small" theme, and Wieden & Kennedy thought a West Coast version of this basic anti-advertising angle would work well for Subaru. It was an anti-status status campaign for sure.

With the business in hand, Wieden & Kennedy now had to create and produce the ads. The first production challenge was to produce in a few weeks two television commercials that would normally take months to complete. Deadlines have been blamed for a lot of lousy advertising, but in Wieden & Kennedy's case the deadline problem was real: In about three weeks the agency was expected to find a director, scout Subaru's factory, record the voice-over and

music, shoot and edit the commercial, and present the two commercials.

One major problem was with the concepts for the spots for Subaru's sports model, the SVX, and its luxury car, the Legacy. The spots were best shot in Subaru's factory in Japan in order to call attention to the way the cars were engineered and manufactured, but the deadline problem forced Wieden & Kennedy to instead send a crew to Tippecanoe, Indiana, where they thought they could fake it with close shots. In addition, from the outset, the director and agency art director disagreed on how to shoot the commercial footage. The art director wanted to focus on the machinery, and the film director

tion, including the production of print materials. Exhibit 16–6 illustrates how print production occurs with the assistance of commercial in-house electronic prepress computer systems and, usually, a single piece of sophisticated software that coordinates the whole process. First, page layouts (prepared on the computer) organize elements on the printed page. Copy or text is then entered into the computer and copy is fitted to the page. Graphics are scanned into the computer using high-resolution scanners. Once the layout, copy or text, and graphics are in the computer, the elements are combined during page composition. From these pages, two types of proof can be viewed and corrected. A *soft proof* is a proof viewed on the computer screen; a *hard proof* is printed on paper. Finally, plates are made and the material goes to press.

Desktop publishing computer systems differ from commercial systems in that they need several pieces of software to coordinate the prepress printing tasks. Software such as QuarkXpress® and Aldus PageMaker® is used to prepare the page layout. Copy or text is input into the computer through word-processing programs such as Microsoft Word®, WordPerfect®, or MacWrite Pro®. Graphics can be scanned into the computer using several different types of scanners, such as hand-held, flatbed, or slide scanners. Graphics can also be created in drawing and illustration programs such as Aldus Freehand® and Adobe Illustrator®, or in paint programs such as Deneba's Canvas® and Aldus Superpaint®. After photographic images are scanned into the computer, they can be manipulated and changed with Aldus Digital Darkroom® or Adobe Photoshop®. Both QuarkXpress and

wanted to focus on people working in the factory.

As the shooting progressed, another problem surfaced. The detailed shooting boards put together by the commercial production company were not faithful to the agency's original storyboards submitted to the firm. The director had, among other things, changed the composition of scenes and added the idea of a split screen that was not in the original storyboard. These types of disputes between the director and the agency continued throughout the shoot. The moment agency personnel turned their heads, more people and less car would creep into the shots.

After the Indiana shoot was over, it was the job of the art director to supervise the post-

production process back in Los Angeles. The job was to take four hours of footage—thousands of feet of film—and cut it down to two minutes of the best shots. This was the part of the process that could really save the day. But the initial review of the footage by an editor and art director was disappointing. The shots were not what they wanted. Too "goodwrenchy" was the term they used to describe scenes that were "fakey." The film was jumpy and the lighting was inconsistent. Still, they thought they could fix it in the editing stage.

In the meantime, other agency personnel were working on typesetting for type that would scroll over the factory shots, voice talent to deliver the no-nonsense copy, and

other postproduction tasks. And each task presented more problems, many of which were created by the time crunch. Wieden & Kennedy found itself between a rock and a hard place: They needed the scrolling type to save the footage, but it couldn't be set before the pictures and voice-over were done. They also needed a soundtrack to determine which pictures and voice to use. Not enough time.

The footage was frantically edited into at least three rough cuts that tried to do different things with the footage. The agency tried everything and finally settled on a version for each car. These selections were sent to agency principal Dan Wieden—who promptly shot them down. In the end, the spots underwent more

editing at another studio and an outsider was brought in to save the day. The art director finally came up with spots with which everybody thought they could live. The scrolling type started with, "A car is just a car. And its sole reason for existence is to get you from Point A to Point B." It ended with "May the best machine win."

QUESTIONS

Do you think Wieden & Kennedy could have handled this touchy situation any better? How? Could the client have handled it better? How?

Source: This is a compressed version of the problems Wieden & Kennedy experienced in creating and producing Subaru ads. It is based on Randall Rothenberg, *Where the Suckers Moon* (New York: Alfred A. Knopf, 1994).

EXHIBIT 16–6   Electronic Prepress Computer System

ELECTRONIC PREPRESS

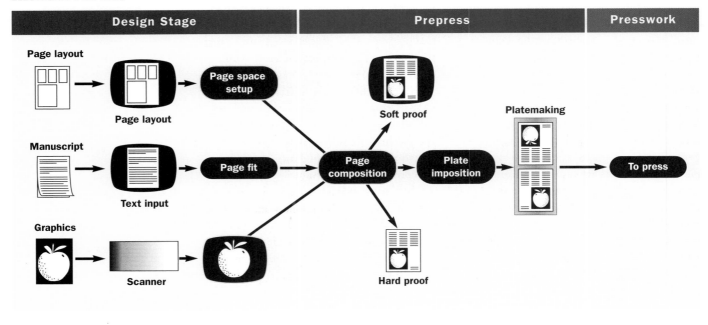

Aldus PageMaker can make lithographic, or printing, negatives as output from their programs, but these negatives must be prepared on high-resolution imagesetting equipment.

The most important factors an advertiser or art director must consider when deciding how to prepare advertising materials for production are resolution and quality of output. **Resolution** refers to how clear and crisp the printed image will be once all the prepress work is completed and an ad is printed. The quality of resolution is directly related to the number of *dots per inch (dpi)* that make up an image and how many dots per inch a printer can print. Exhibit 16–7 illustrates several different resolutions for type, from the 72 dots per inch (dpi) resolution of a computer screen to the 2400 dpi resolution of a high-resolution imagesetter.

While everyone would agree that the 2400 dpi imagesetter quality is far superior, the 300 or 600 dpi resolution of a laser printer may be sufficient for low-budget productions such as newsletters, price sheets, or single-page brochures. By using laser printer output, the cost for high-resolution imagesetter prints or negatives can be avoided. Art directors often use desktop publishing computers to send color layouts to a color laser printer (300 dpi) for comprehensive layouts or sample package designs. For finished advertisements with type and black and white photographs, images are usually sent to high-resolution imagesetters (2400 dpi). The increasing sophistication of desktop computers and output devices has resulted in an adoption of these devices as the standard tools of the trade for advertising production. Advertisers and advertising agencies use desktop computers for all but the most difficult tasks in design and the prepress stages of production.

Print Production Stages And Cost Decisions

The importance of understanding and controlling production costs cannot be underestimated. In the end, an advertisement or campaign that is good from a creative standpoint is not successful unless it stays within the bounds of the advertiser's budget. Production estimate sheets may be prepared for an advertiser by an advertising agency or printer. Their purpose is to provide reasonable estimates of the costs of print production. These cost estimates reflect the choices that an art director or advertiser made during each stage of production. Let's review the stages of production and the decisions that influence production costs beginning with the design stage.

DESIGN OPERATIONS AND COST DECISIONS

Five principal design stage decisions have an important effect upon the costs of print advertisements and brochures. These design decisions are: 1) the size and length of the advertisement or brochure; 2) the number and type of visuals used; 3) the number of printing inks required; 4) the typographic characteristics of the printed piece; and 5) the type of paper selected.

As you might imagine, the more pages in an advertising insert or brochure, the greater the production costs. More pages require more type, more visuals, and more paper. The **trim size,** or actual size, of a brochure is related to paper costs; large, tabloid-size flyers require more paper than 8½-by-11-inch flyers. The quality of paper and inks also can result in increased production costs. For example, heavy paper is more expensive than lighter-weight paper, and particular types of printing (such as raised printing) are more expensive than conventional flat printing. Thus, the longer or larger an ad or brochure, and the higher the quality of the design elements, the greater the expense. Combine these two factors and the increases in costs start to multiply.

Along the same line, when a brochure or advertisement requires more visuals—whether they are photographs, drawings, or illustrations—costs increase. The type of visual used influences production costs in several ways. Some visual types require more prepress and printing operations. Visual types also differ in costs depending upon the services required to obtain the visual. For example, hiring a professional photographer to take a photograph is usually more expensive than renting a photograph from a stock photo service. Exhibit 16–8 illustrates a progressive scale of visuals that ranges from a low-cost, type-only ad with no visuals to expensive ads that include custom photography and original illustrations.

As more printing ink colors are required for an advertisement or brochure, costs also increase. A two-color printing job has two colors of ink and, naturally, it costs more than a one-color printing job. When color photographs are reproduced in a brochure or an advertise-

ment a method of printing called **four-color process printing** is needed. In four-color process printing, separate plates are prepared for each of the four inks: magenta, yellow, cyan, and black. To make these four plates, a separate negative is prepared for each color. These negatives are called **color separations.** The techniques for making color separations will be explained in the next section. As you might imagine, using four-color process printing with color separations is considerably more expensive than one- or two-color printing.

Matching and coordinating ink colors can also present problems for the art director and graphic artists. Many businesses specify exact colors of ink for their stationery and publications. To standardize colors, graphic artists use the **Pantone Matching System®**. This system provides artists with standardized color chips

---

EXHIBIT 16–7   Type Resolution Samples

	At actual size	Enlarged 6 times
At 72 dpi		
At 150 dpi		
At 300 dpi		
At 2400 dpi		

EXHIBIT 16–8   Scale of Costs of Visuals

This scale of costs is based on rough per picture estimates. The costs for each type of visual vary considerably.

All type	In local media, the advertiser is not likely to be charged separately for typography in an advertisement.	**Free**
Ad slicks	Ad slicks are sample ads or visuals prepared by a national manufacturer, and provided free to retailers.	**Free**
Clip art	Clip art may be provided for a nominal fee or free from local media. Individual advertisers can order clip art on computer disk for the fee described.	**$1–10**
Stock photos	Stock photos are rental photographs for a single or specified use.	**$1–10**
Original photos	The original photo estimate is based on a commercial photographer's single shot charge.	**$300**
Original illustrations	Original illustration is much more expensive because of the number of hours required.	**$1,000**

from which to select and identify solid and process color inks, as shown in Exhibit 16–9. Specifying PANTONE MATCHING SYS-TEM colors can increase production costs, but most advertisers believe it is important to use an ink color specified by their graphic artist regardless of a slight increase in cost. PANTONE MATCHING SYSTEM colors are now available for the Macintosh in the form of a program called Pantone ColorDrive®, which allows the designer to achieve more consistent color matches across design software applications.

As we discussed earlier, costs for typesetting can be reduced by using desktop computers to output type to a high-resolution imagesetter. On the other hand, type charges can increase for an advertisement or brochure if exotic hand-set type is used or if type is artistically altered by the graphic artist.

Finally, when a graphic artist specifies a weight and type of paper for a brochure, there can be tremendous differences in the costs of printing papers. These differences become more significant as the number of brochures produced increases. To avoid inflationary paper costs some large advertisers and agencies purchase large supplies of paper to have on hand for brochures that are frequently reprinted. Planning is essential during the design stage to maintain quality and produce cost efficiency. "Adscape: Do You Know As Much As You Should About Recycled Paper?" brings up some important points to consider as you make decisions related to paper.

EXHIBIT 16–9   Pantone Matching System Chips

Pantone® and other Pantone, Inc. trademarks are the property of Pantone, Inc.

AdScape

....

Do You Know As Much As You Should About Recycled Paper?

What goes into the making of the paper you are using for that slick brochure? Are there alternatives that could make a difference to our environment and to the management of our precious natural resources? Consider these facts:

- The U.S. comprises only 5 percent of the world's population and takes up 6.5 percent of the world's landmass. Yet U.S. consumers use about 33 percent of the world's supply of paper and discard 20 percent of it through incineration or in landfills.
- It takes 31 million BTUs to produce one ton of paper—that's enough energy to power a U.S. suburban home for two months. It also takes between 12,000 and 22,000 gallons of water to produce the same ton of paper.
- Approximately 40 percent of trees cut down in the U.S. each year are turned into pulp for boxes, tissues, and paper.
- Nearly one tree for every person in the U.S.—272 million trees—are felled each year to produce our newspapers and magazines. The world's demand for paper is expected to double in the next 15 years.
- It is estimated that almost one-half of the 12 billion acres of forest that once covered the earth has been destroyed.
- Upwards of 50–70 percent of all printed material is never used.

The message is clear: While we are working hard on our integrated marketing communications strategies, creative ideas, and brilliant design schemes, we should not ignore the environmental impact of a decision that might appear routine and without consequence. We should consider the possibility of using alternative sources of paper.

So the answer is to use recycled paper, especially if its use is relevant to our marketing and advertising strategies, right? Not necessarily. You might be surprised to learn that recycled paper does not avert all waste and contamination problems; the de-inking process uses harsh chemicals that add to the toxic sludge in our rivers and lakes. Ecology-minded designers and printers can and do specify the use of chlorine-free papers. And most recycled paper is actually a combination of recycled fibers and virgin wood pulp from tree farms and forests. The use of recycled paper helps, but other alternatives are being sought.

One of these is the use of tree-free paper. Tree-free paper is made from a variety of sources, including cotton and a plant called kenaf. Kenaf grows to maturity in five months versus the 60 years it takes for a pine tree to reach maturity. Kenaf is related to the hibiscus family of plants and is an annual growing plant from Africa. While tree-free paper represents less than 10 percent of the world's paper supply, it is growing in popularity.

Communication Arts magazine runs a feature called ECO that keeps track of progress on the environmental front and how it impacts designers. The September/October 1996 issue has a list of companies that produce recycled, chlorine-free, and tree-free papers. The next time you select paper for a project, think about the possibility of environmentally friendly papers as an alternative.

QUESTIONS
What kind of paper do you currently use for your projects? Can you think of any alternatives you might try?

Sources: Daniel Imhoff, "Tree-Free: Moving beyond Wood-Based Paper," *Communication Arts,* September/October 1994, 103–106; "Taking Paper to Task," *Communication Arts,* May/June 1996, 105–108; and Jack Weiss, "It Isn't Easy Being Green," *Communication Arts,* September/October 1996, 121–124.

EXHIBIT 16–10   Halftone Illustration

Halftone dots enlarged

PREPRESS OPERATIONS AND COST DECISIONS   The purpose of prepress operations is to transfer mechanicals, including artwork, photographs, and type, to printing plates for the printing press. These tasks include graphic arts photography, film assembly, platemaking, and printing prepress proofs. As mechanicals are passed to the printer, many of the production costs have already been predetermined by the design of the advertisement or brochure. By understanding the capabilities of the printer during prepress operations, an advertiser or art director can make use of the specialized printing services a printer offers. In addition, understanding prepress operations also makes it easier to see how late changes in an advertisement or brochure can destroy a production budget.

Prepress operations are influenced by an inherent limitation of the printing process that is illustrated most effectively with black-and-white photography. As you look at most black-and-white photographs, you'll see a range of tones from pure white to black with many shades of gray. The wide range of grays and the pure blacks and whites that make up the realistic-looking images in black-and-white photographs are called **continuous tone images.** Oil paintings, color photographs, or wash drawings are also continuous tone images because they have a wide range of intermediate tones. Unfortunately, printing inks applied to paper do not have the same characteristics as continuous tone photographic images. Printing ink only has one tone, making it impossible to directly duplicate a photograph, painting, or wash drawing.

An alternative method for printing continuous tone images, called **halftone photography,** was developed to take into account the limitations of printing inks. Halftone photography converts a continuous tone photograph into a pattern of small and clearly defined dots of various sizes. The **halftone principle** is an optical illusion created when continuous tone images are represented by small dots of varying sizes and equal spacing printed with a printing ink of uniform density.[5] Halftone reproduction of a black-and-white photograph is illustrated in Exhibit 16–10. Notice the difference in dot sizes for the light and dark areas of the photograph.

Printing presses differ in their ability to reproduce halftone dots. These differences are characterized by the number of lines in the photographic screens that are used to make halftones from continuous tone images. These numbers represent the number of rulings per inch in the halftone conversion screen. Older newspaper presses usually use 65- to 85-line screens; newer newspapers use 100-, 120-, or 133-line screens. Magazines frequently use 133- or 150-line screens. These differences are important for an advertiser or art director because the quality of reproduction is related to the number of lines in the halftone screen. For example, Exhibit 16–11 illustrates the differences in resolution in images printed with a 65-, 100-, and 150-line screen.[6]

Because newspaper halftone images may not be as crisp and clear as magazine images, an advertiser or art director may use a different method of graphic arts photography called **line art photography** to create visuals for newspaper advertisements. Line art photography converts an image into solid black and white rather than halftone dots. The images in Exhibit 16–12 illustrate an example of line art photography. Interesting textures can also be introduced into the black-and-white image by using one of many different line screens. In Exhibit 16–12, straight line, mezzotint, and random line screens have been used to make line art images more attractive. Line art photography and line screens can be used to create more artistic images for advertisements, brochures, and packages.

An art director or advertiser can create a more interesting brochure or advertisement with two ink colors, instead of one color. If a single color is used for a brochure or flyer, it may be more unusual if it is printed in a dark-colored ink other than black. When type or lettering is placed over a color, an artist may consult a production handbook, such as the *Pocket Pal* prepared by International Paper, to see what the finished printing effect will look like. Samples of color with type overprinted on the color and type that has been "dropped out" of the color are provided to help the artist select appropriate colors. *Dropped out type* means there is no printing ink where the type appears, so it appears as white type on a color. The type is actually formed by the absence of printing ink in a field of color.

The most challenging use of color is in four-color process printing. Reproduction of color photographs requires that color separations be made. By photographing artwork or color prints through blue, green, and red filters, color separation negatives produce yellow, magenta, and cyan prints, respectively. By photographing these halftone negatives at different angles, yellow, cyan, magenta, and black dots overlap to produce the natural colors that we see in an advertisement. Because printing inks do not produce color combinations as well as transmitted light, a fourth correction filter is used to produce a black plate. The presence of blacks enhances the contrast and gray tones in the final advertisement.

Making color separations adds considerable cost to advertisements and brochures.

While computer processing of color separations has improved over the years, an advertiser or art director should check the color reproduction during the prepress operations. Prepress proofs of color separations are often made on overlay film, such as 3M Color Key, or as integral (single sheet) proofs with products such as DuPont Cromalin. Even though these proofs do not produce exact color representations of the final printed product, they offer an opportunity to inspect the four-color artwork before it goes to press.

Once a printer has prepared halftones and color separations, the negatives must be assembled for the printing press. If there are separate

EXHIBIT 16–11   Line Screen Sizes

65-line screen

100-line screen

150-line screen

EXHIBIT 16–12   Line Screen Patterns

Straight line

Mezzotint

Cross line

elements, such as type and halftones, the negatives must be joined. Then they are attached to a printing flat. The **printing flat** is the assembled artwork from which printing plates are made. Joining negatives and attaching them to the flat is called **stripping.** A stripper also looks for pinholes in the printing negatives and applies opaque to them to stop light transmission from creating unwanted spots on the printing plate.

Transferring the images from the printing flat to printing plates is the last step in prepress operations. At this stage a special proof of images from the printing flats may be prepared. These proofs are called **bluelines** or **silver prints.** Their purpose is to check the placement, orientation, and accuracy of text and photographs. Bluelines are fairly inexpensive, especially when compared to the cost of reprinting an error-filled brochure. After the bluelines have been corrected, presswork can begin.

PRESSWORK OPERATIONS AND COST DECISIONS Although several different methods of printing are available to the advertiser, the final choice of a printing method may be determined more by the availability of a printing supplier than by a desire for a certain type of printing press. Presses are either sheet fed or roll (web) fed.7 **Web-fed paper** is a continuous sheet of paper on a roll that is cut after it has been printed; **sheet-fed paper,** on the other hand, is precut to size.

Commercial Printing Processes. While the methods of transferring ink to paper may differ by printing press, there are several common features. For example, printing presses must have an image carrier that holds the plate or original securely in place. They must have a method of positioning paper during printing and a method of transferring paper as the printing process continues. Presses must be able to store and apply ink. Most have a method of setting pressures for the application of the image to paper.

Advertisers generally use one of four major printing processes: 1) letterpress, 2) rotogravure, 3) offset lithograph, or 4) screen printing or serigraphy. **Letterpress printing** uses a metal or plastic printing plate on which the printing image is raised from the surface. The raised image is created by sensitizing the plate with the printing negative. An applied emulsion protects the image while acid is used to etch away nonprinting areas of the plate. The image on the printing plate must be reverse-reading, because contact between the printing plate and paper will reverse the image.

An opposite approach is applied with **rotogravure printing.** Plates for rotogravure presses are prepared by etching the image into the plate, rather than etching the nonprinting areas. As ink is applied to a rotogravure plate, the plate is wiped and ink remains in the depressed area of the printing plate. Unlike the other printing processes we are discussing, rotogravure uses printing plates on which both type and illustrations have been screened. The resulting image cannot be distinguished with the naked eye because a fine (150-line) screen is used. These screened images are reverse-reading like letterpress, but the image is a positive rather than negative image. Because making rotogravure plates is a complex operation, most rotogravure presses are web fed and specialize in long-run printing jobs, such as magazines, catalogs, and packaging materials.

Offset lithography printing is the most common printing process used by advertisers. Offset lithography platemaking is similar to letterpress platemaking except the image is only slightly raised, rather than etched. The image on the offset lithographic plate is straight-reading instead of reversed. A straight-reading image is required because the image is transferred to a rubber drum, or blanket, that transfers the image to paper. Speedy printing centers, in-house print shops, newspapers, and some magazines are printed with offset lithography.

Screen printing, or *serigraphy,* is used to print large outdoor signs, small irregular objects such as coffee cups, and many types of posters. Instead of printing plates, screen printing uses stencils made from nylon or stainless steel mesh. Like the silk-screen printing used for T-shirts, ink is pressed through the stencil to the paper or object. For commercial screen printing, rollers replace squeegees for the inking process.

Presswork Production Decisions. One of the first decisions to be made during the presswork stage of production is whether or not to request press proofs. **Press proofs** are color proofs taken from the printing press before the press run begins. These proofs are used to make sure the color and print quality are acceptable. They are not proofs to be used for checking copy accuracy or photographic placement; by the time press proofs are made, it is too late to change copy or visuals without incurring tremendously large production costs.

A second decision related to the presswork stage of production is cutting and trimming. For a simple job, such as a half-page coupon, printing costs can be reduced by printing two coupons on a page. If a nonprofit advertiser wanted 2,000 coupons for a spaghetti dinner, for example, he or she could make a master with two coupons on a page. After 1,000 sheets were printed, the printer would then cut the sheets in half to make 2,000 total coupons (it costs much less to cut than to print an additional 1,000 coupons). Similar savings are possible for large-scale printing jobs. When several copies of advertising artwork are printed on a single print master, the process is called **gang printing.**

Additional cutting charges are incurred for the production of bleed advertisements or brochures with bleed borders. A **bleed advertisement,** or a *bleed border,* has printed images that extend to the outside edge of the page in a magazine or brochure; in comparison, a non-bleed ad uses a white border around a smaller image or uses a white background for the type and images. Take a minute to peruse some of the ads reprinted in this text. Can you identify bleed versus non-bleed ads? Bleed ads cost more money and have unique printing requirements because printing presses cannot print to the edge of a printed sheet. To produce bleed advertisements, the artist must usually prepare a mechanical that extends the visual ¼- to ½-inch larger than the page size. After the page is printed, the printer will trim the brochure or magazine so the advertisement appears to bleed off the page. To find out whether bleed advertisements are allowed, and to find all of the printing specifications for a magazine, an art director should consult the Standard Rate and Data Service *Print Media Production Data.* This guide reports the printing requirements for most print advertising media.

Another presswork expense is the charge for binding large brochures and booklets. To reduce costs, the advertiser or art director should use machine binding operations rather than hand binding, when possible. Hand assembly of advertisements, such as the Transamerica pop-up and Texas Instruments speech synthe-sizer ads discussed earlier in this chapter, can also be very expensive. At times the creative impact of a special mailing package is worth the extra cost of hand assembly.

These general guidelines for reducing costs must be evaluated against the creative impact of higher-cost production methods. For print production, as well as the broadcast production techniques to be discussed in the next section, advertisers must consciously monitor costs and attempt to create maximum effect for their advertisements.

R E S E T

1. Consider the tradeoffs involved in trying to balance print production costs against quality. How important is print production quality to advertising effectiveness? How important is it to keep print production costs down to improve advertising's efficiency?

2. What is halftone photography? How does it help us in printing continuous tone images? How does halftone photography differ from line art photography?

3. Describe the four major types of printing processes. In your campus environment, which of these processes are you most likely to find? Have you used any of these processes in the past?

Producing Broadcast Commercials And Videotapes

An advertiser's, art director's, or agency producer's role in producing broadcast commercials for radio or television is similar to their role in print production: to get the maximum creative effect at the lowest cost. While costs vary from the lowest-priced, locally produced radio commercials to the highest-priced television extravaganzas with large casts and multi-million-dollar budgets, there are production process similarities for both types of commercial.

Any successful broadcast commercial begins with a solid creative idea that is translated into an excellent script. As the script progresses from an idea on paper to a commercial on audiotape or videotape, there are three identifiable stages of production: 1) the **preproduction stage,** when questions of script, casting, and plans for special production effects are discussed; 2) the **production stage,** when the actual video- or audiotaping of commercial elements is done; and 3) the **postproduction stage,** where elements of the commercial are combined into the finished commercial.

Preproduction and postproduction stages normally require more time than the production stage. One of the purposes of preproduction meetings is to discuss efficiency during the production process. Studio time, talent costs, and professional producers are tremendously expensive; thus, reductions in production time can significantly reduce the total costs of a commercial. Postproduction, especially in television, can take considerable time because of the complexities in editing and incorporating special effects.

Throughout the three stages, an advertiser, art director, agency producer, or independent producer must monitor the production process. Decisions must be made daily as the commercial evolves from an idea and script to an aural or visual sales message. As we will see in the next two sections (and as we saw in "Adscape: Murphy's Law and Production" earlier in

the chapter), television production is much more complex than radio production. Nevertheless, production techniques for both types of commercials must convey the advertising message clearly and not obscure it with distracting audio or video effects. Radio production will be examined first.

Radio Production

Radio advertising has been somewhat of an anomaly in the 1990s. A writer for the *Hollywood Reporter* noted how sweeping technological changes in television had left radio ads in the "age of Marconi." He further pointed out, however, that despite radio's lack of technological sophistication, radio advertising revenues had not fallen. In fact, while other forms of advertising had declined, radio seemed to be growing because of its flexibility and low production costs.[8] This is especially true for business-to-business advertisers and advertisers that are trying to reach specialized audiences.

With the growth of radio for specialized audiences, new pressures were put on producers and advertising agency creatives to meet high standards of production. A new annual radio creative awards program, called the Mercury Awards, sponsored by broadcasters and the Radio Advertising Bureau, was established in 1992. Part of the lure of radio for "creatives" is the relative ease of production for radio commercials and the creative potential of the medium.

Exhibit 16–13 illustrates the steps involved in producing a radio commercial. During the preproduction stage, a production company is selected, casting for voices is done, and music and special effects are discussed. Production costs, including charges for the rights to music and talent, are reviewed. If an advertiser wants to create a new jingle for a commercial, it may be produced during the preproduction stage of the radio commercial. For smaller advertisers without writing skills, preproduction meetings with a production company or the media may include script writing. Radio stations do provide writing and production assistance to smaller advertisers.

After the details for production have been approved by the advertiser, production can be scheduled. Studio time is booked and talent hired. Because most radio commercials are part of an advertising campaign, it is usually much

---

EXHIBIT 16–13   Steps in Radio Commercial Production

Preproduction	Production	Postproduction
1. Advertiser sends commercial out for bids	**6.** Recording of commercial in the production studio	**8.** Production staff edits and joins elements of commercial
2. Studio responds with production estimate	**7.** Recording of music, jingles, and sound effects	**9.** Production staff mixes sound on audiotape to produce a master tape for approval
3. Advertiser selects production studio		**10.** Advertiser approves commercial master tape
4. Advertiser and studio production staff meet for a preproduction meeting		**11.** Duplicate audiotapes produced for media
5. Talents are selected jointly by advertiser and production staff		

more cost efficient to record several commercials during one taping session. During the studio session, sound effects, music, and other commercial elements are taped.

Elements taped during the production stage are assembled and edited during postproduction. Sounds and music are added to the narrative script in a process called **sound mixing.** Tapes, called **sound masters,** are reviewed and approved by the advertiser before being duplicated. Duplicating audiotapes is called **dubbing.**

The production cost process is very straightforward for radio. Exhibit 16–14 is an estimate sheet for radio production that arranges charges by the stage of production. This estimate sheet is similar to the sheet shown for print production in the previous section. For elaborate radio commercials, production costs may be more than $5,000. Local commercials, or spots, may cost less than $100 when prepared by a local radio station. Production costs can be avoided completely by providing a script to the radio station that on-air personalities will read during their programs. Unfortunately, the advertiser loses control over the quality of the script when an audiotape is not provided. Quality control is essential, regardless of how expensive or inexpensive production costs may be.

Television Production

Television production costs have always been a major source of concern for advertisers and ad-vertising agencies. According to a survey of production costs by the American Association of Advertising Agencies, the average cost for producing a national television spot in 1995 was $246,000.[9] When combined with the costs of television time that can run upwards of $500,000 for a 30-second spot, you can see that TV production costs cannot be allowed to get out of hand. A guideline is not to let your production costs run more than 10 percent of your media budget.[10]

During the 1990s several advertising agencies, such as Young & Rubicam, Foote, Cone & Belding Communications, Bozell, and D'Arcy Masius Benton & Bowles, added television production units to their organizations. In addition to providing more control over production costs, these in-house production units were designed to produce original programming for their clients. To some extent, this was a return to the early days of television when advertisers and their agencies actually wrote and produced many of television's programs. In this current wave of agency interest in TV production, Bozell co-produced the *Chrysler Showcase* for Chrysler Corporation and two national driving-test programs on CBS for Valvoline Oil. Young & Rubicam eventually abandoned its production unit because of a lack of interest by its clients.[11]

There have also been changes in many advertising agencies without production units, including adding television producers to the

EXHIBIT 16–14   Radio Production Estimate Sheet

	REF #	Service	Est. Price	Rev. Price
Preproduction	1	Preproduction meeting		
	2			
Production	3	Recording/studio		
	4	Talent charges		
	5			
Postproduction	6	Editing/mixing		
	7	Music & rights		
	8	Cassette duplication		
	9	Shipping & postage		
	10	Overtime		
		Total production charges		

creative departments of agencies for which television production is a major activity. There are several advantages of having an agency producer that are related to past arguments about who can create the best television commercials. Some professionals have argued that the copywriter and/or creative director are most responsible for great advertising because they have the best knowledge of what they're trying to communicate to the target audience. Others have argued that television producers know how to make the best television drama, so their role is most important. The agency producer represents a compromise between the two extreme positions; he or she knows television and is exposed daily to the creative goals of advertising. Agency producers may coordinate production with another producer at an outside production studio, or the agency producer may work with an outside director who works with his or her own production staff.

It is important to point out here that there are significant differences between the producer and director roles. A **television producer** coordinates all of the technical and nontechnical personnel involved in the production process. This person is responsible for overseeing scheduling for people and studio time,

budgeting, and monitoring the costs of production. A **television director,** on the other hand, is responsible for the direction of talent and technical staff as they convert a storyboard into film or videotape. The director oversees the editing process until the final commercial is produced. There are many related titles that may be associated with the production process. Associate or assistant producers assist the producer, for example, while associate directors assist directors.

Regardless of the role assumed by the creative staff, the goal of the production operation is to achieve the most effective communication for a specified production budget. Some creative attempts have been very unusual. For example, commercial producer Phil Morrison has been called "no-frills Phil" for his real-life spots often based on the humor in everyday occurrences. His offbeat approach works best for offbeat products like the soft drink Fresca. One such ad for Fresca illustrates what Phil Morrison likes to call "miniaturism." In the spot, "A young girl sitting in a diner gets grilled by the waiter for ordering a Fresca only because a hunk at the counter is drinking one."[12]

STAGES OF TELEVISION PRODUCTION   The television production process involves the same three stages as radio production: preproduction, production, and postproduction. An overview of this process is shown in Exhibit 16–15.

The production process begins when an advertiser or advertising agency solicits bids for production from a production studio. The preproduction stage begins with this request for estimates. Studios that receive the request for bids prepare estimates based on the approved storyboard, production notes, and specifications for the commercials. After the estimates are received, the advertiser or advertising agency selects a studio.

Following selection, a preproduction meeting is scheduled for the production team that will work on the commercials. This team may include a copywriter, an art director, creative director, account executive, agency producer, studio producer, and director. The preproduction meeting is used for discussions of the creative aspects of the commercial, such as the commercial's objective, the theme or emotion

EXHIBIT 16–15   Overview of Television Production Process

Preproduction	Production	Postproduction
1. Advertiser sends commercial out for bids	**7.** Recording of primary visuals in the studio or on location	**11.** Production staff edits and joins elements of commercial
2. Studio responds with production estimate	**8.** Recording of sound and music elements of the commercial	**12.** Production staff mixes sound and video effects to produce a master tape for approval
3. Advertiser selects production studio	**9.** Preparation of video effects, graphics, and animation	
4. Advertiser and studio production staff meet for a preproduction meeting	**10.** Acquisition of stock video footage, if necessary	**13.** Advertiser approves commercial final tape
5. Auditions scheduled and held for talent prospects		**14.** Release tapes produced for media
6. Talents are selected jointly by advertiser and production staff		

desired, and the range of visuals that will be needed. Technical aspects, such as location selection, special effects, procedures for casting, music availability, legal rights and clearances, and schedules, are also reviewed. From this meeting, a production schedule is prepared. Auditions and cast selection are the final preproduction tasks at this stage.

During the production stage, the sound and visual elements of the commercial are captured on film or tape. Production may include studio or location cinematography or videotaping; acquisition of stock film footage from stock film suppliers; preparation of visual effects, such as animation or computer-generated images called *digital video effects (DVEs)* (for more on computer animation in television production, read "Technology Watch: Animation in the Computer Age"); and the preparation of sound tracks for sound effects or music. Once all of the elements have been collected, postproduction begins.

The first postproduction task is editing the visual elements for the commercial into the sequence specified by the storyboard. Through sound mixing, sound effects, background music, jingles, and narration are coupled to the film track or videotape to produce an approval copy of the commercial. After the commercial has been approved, duplicate prints, or dupes, are made and sent to the media.

Exhibit 16–16 shows a television production estimate sheet arranged by the stage of production. To keep production costs down, there are important details and decisions to be made by the advertiser or advertising agency during each stage of production. These decisions begin before the materials are sent for studio bids.

EXHIBIT 16–16   Television Production Estimate Sheet

	REF #	Service	Est. Price	Rev. Price
Preproduction	1	Preproduction meeting		
	2	Casting services		
	3			
Production	4	Recording/studio		
	5	Cinematography		
	6	Talent charges		
	7	Product props/styling		
	8	Art & optical effects		
	9	Electronic transfers		
	10	DVE, graphic effects		
		Animation		
		Tape/film transfers		
		Set design		
		Wardrobe		
Postproduction		Editing/mixing		
		Music & rights		
		Licensing fees		
		Videotape duplication		
		Shipping & postage		
		Overtime		
		Total production charges		

TECHNOLOGY WATCH

· ·

Animation in the Computer Age

"Inner Tube" :30
SFX: Sound of waves, seagulls squawking.
(Camera pans in on a young kid drinking a bottle of Pepsi from a straw. His sister sits in the sand. The camera pans in on the Pepsi bottle as the young boy sips the soda. The bottle is down to the last drops of soda as he continues to drink. When he finishes, the top of his hat starts to move)
SFX: Sucking noise.
(The camera pans in with a close-up of an old woman as she looks around. As the young boy sips through the straw his ears start to wiggle. Suddenly the boy's head is sucked into the bottle along with the rest of his body. The bottle bounces off the inner tube and we see a close-up of the young boy inside the bottle. His sister runs over and stares at the bottle.She picks it up and turns it upside down to try and get her brother out)
Little Girl: Mom, he's done it again!
Super: Nothing else is a Pepsi

Animation is certainly not new to filmmaking or advertising. Walt Disney pioneered the technique using pen-and-ink drawn cells in which the tiniest change in scene or character expressions could be drawn and filmed. Stop motion animation is another technique that is rather crude in its effects. It employs real-life models that are repositioned for each shot. This basic technique was employed with clay characters in claymation commercials such as Will Vinton Studios' "Dancing Raisins" commercial for the California Raisin Advisory Board in the 1980s.

Computer-generated animation effects like morphing made a big splash in the early 1990s in movies and ads.

Arnold Swarzenegger's *Terminator 2* featured actor Robert Patrick as a robotic nemesis who could move freely between liquid and solid forms. Michael Jackson made effective use of this technique in his music video, "Black and White," in which the faces of people of different races and nationalities transformed into one another.

Advertisers picked up on the popularity of the morphing technique and used it to demonstrate changes in car styling, to illustrate shaving problems and differences in men's faces, and to get a cow to sing. To some extent morphing replaces other types of editing transitions such as cuts and dissolves. It is

Real-life and computer-generated sequences were successfully integrated in the production of this eye-catching Pepsi spot.

smoother and can produce dramatic effects.

Morphing is now considered passé, however, and the advertising industry has turned more to refining the computer-generated animation process. Among the current trends is the attempt to make real-life images and computer-generated images work together and appear seamless as you move from one to the other. The Pepsi commercial in which the little boy is drinking Pepsi with a straw and gets sucked into the bottle is an example of this merging of computer-generated and live-action techniques. *Toy Story*, created by Steve Jobs' Pixar Animation Studios, was the world's first full-length film that relied entirely on computer-generated animation techniques.

Animation brings a tremendous amount of flexibility to the creation of advertising effects. It also is expensive and time consuming, and it takes a lot of talent and technical knowledge. The expectation is that the day is not far off when computer-generated animation will be done on personal computers. For now, it takes high-end equipment that only the likes of Pixar and Disney can afford.

Sources: John Krampner, "Technology: New Software Lowers Costs of Morphing Effects," *Electronic Media,* 24 February 1992, 14; Dana Norvila, "Graphics: Computer-Generated Metamorphoses Evolve," *IEEE Spectrum* 4 (April 1992): 11; and Ty Ahmad-Taylor, "Beyond the California Raisins," *New York Times,* 27 November 1995, C–7.

Preproduction Decisions. Before the bidding process is initiated by an advertising agency, the script and storyboard must be approved by the advertiser. In order to standardize the bidding process, production notes are usually included with the script and storyboard. **Production notes** summarize the characteristics of the commercial to be produced. These notes are used to guide the production staff and to prepare the quote. While production notes may be prepared differently, most include the following:

- General descriptions of the objectives for the advertising campaign and major copy points.
- Important video needs, such as locations, settings, cast and wardrobe needs, prop requests, special instructions for handling the product, visual effects, and information about logo placement and preparation of materials for the character generator.
- Audio requirements, such as music and sound effects, and characteristics for talent and voices included in the commercial.
- Specifications of the time frame and type of materials needed from the studio, such as number of videocassettes that need to be duped.

When the studio gets a request for a bid, it usually contacts the advertising agency for clarification of unclear specifications, and then it submits the bid. The bid usually specifies filming locations, number of shooting days, crew requirements, director's fees, equipment rental, editing fees, and charges for visual effects.[13] From the bids, prior experience with a studio, an assessment of the studio's talent and past record of success, and location, the agency makes a decision about which studio to use. A preproduction meeting is then set.

At the preproduction meeting, the commercial is explained. Questions about the substantiality of claims may be asked. Estimates are reviewed. Decisions are made about the shooting schedule and how casting will be done. Talent requirements and contractual obligations for talent are discussed. Residuals, for example, are paid to actors based on the audience size and the number of times a commercial plays. Decisions are also made about how the cast will be selected, and dates for auditions may be chosen. As soon as the auditions are finished and the talent is selected, production can begin.

The Production Team. A television production team is comprised of a large group of people, all of whom have vital and specific roles. Along with the producer and director roles that were described earlier, the production team also includes individual production engineers, who are responsible for video or camera functions, the audio console, and videotape machines. A maintenance engineer may be needed for technical support and repair operations. Character generator (CG) operators input textual and graphic material into the computer so the director can transfer it to videotape or film at the appropriate time. "Talent" is a term that may be applied to an actor or performer in the commercial. Actors portray other people; performers portray themselves. An *announcer* narrates off-camera and is not considered talent unless he or she appears on camera.

A studio setting may have a floor manager, who cues the talent and manages floor personnel. Floorpersons are responsible for holding cue cards, moving sets, makeup, and other physical activities on the set. When available, a teleprompter operator is used to operate the teleprompter. A *teleprompter* is a mechanical or electronic device that moves the script so the talent can read it.

In addition, computer graphics specialists create visual effects, build animated sequences, do renderings of 3-D objects, and can transform objects with a technique called morphing. R. Greenberg, well-known visual effects specialist and owner of R. Greenberg Associates (the company that did the Shaquille O'Neal spot described in the vignette at the beginning of the chapter), predicted that personal computers would become powerful enough to replace existing professional computers in the visual effects industry within the next decade.[14] Likewise, music composers use computers to compose, arrange, mix, and reproduce music.

Postproduction Editing and Approval. There are four editing functions that can be done during postproduction editing: combining, trimming, correcting, and building. *Combining* elements involves hooking two segments together. An in-studio segment about a product may be combined with footage shot on a test track, for example. A second editing function is *trimming* taped segments from the large amount of footage shot into the standard 30-, 60-, or 90-second commercial formats. Another editing function is *correcting*. This may be necessary to eliminate or replace bad segments in a piece of videotape. Sometimes background sounds may need to be erased or subdued, for example, or some video shots may not provide the continuity the director wants in the commercial and may need to be eliminated. The final editing function is *building* a commercial. From segments gathered during production, the editor builds the story that becomes a commercial. If the director knows a commercial is going to be built from segments gathered during the production stage beforehand, he or she may tape the commercial differently during production. Several additional and related segments may need to be taped so the edits can move smoothly from one location or shot to another.

All of the editing functions are performed on editing equipment with several video sources and recorders. Exhibit 16–17 shows a multiple-source editing system on which A and B source videotape recorders play tape to a record videotape recorder. Digital effects can be added through the video switcher. Audio is mixed through an audio mixer. The entire editing process is controlled by the computerized editing control unit.

Using the four editing functions and computerized controls, the director's postproduction goal is to produce a commercial that can be viewed, evaluated, and approved by the advertising agency and the advertiser. There are two different paths for the production of an approval copy determined by whether videotape or film was used during production. When film is used during the shooting, the editing and sound mixing operations produce separate pieces of film for visuals and sound. These separate pieces of film are combined with extra effects on the answer print. The **answer print** is the finished commercial from film that needs client approval. When approved, answer prints are duplicated for release to stations. These dupes are called **release prints.** When a commercial is shot on videotape, on the other hand, sound, video, and special effects are merged on the final tape. The **final tape** is the approval copy for a videotaped commercial. Videotape duplicates are sent to stations after approval. The release of videotapes or release prints marks the end of postproduction.

WHEN PRODUCTION GOES RIGHT: CHEVYS MEXICAN RESTAURANTS Television productions don't have to be as large in scale or as expensive as the process we have just described in order to be creative and effective. In this final section, we will examine the production aspects of the highly acclaimed but low-budget and small-scale "Fresh TV" campaign for Chevys Mexican Restaurants.[15]

In 1991 Chevys Mexican Restaurants was using the headline "Chevys Fresh Mex" to tell consumers that all ingredients at Chevys were fresh. But the copywriter and art director for Chevys' ad agency, Goodby, Berlin & Silverstein, didn't think consumers believed such an advertising claim from a restaurant chain—at least the claim hadn't excited consumers to that point.

It was copywriter Steve Simpson's idea to create, produce, and air instant TV spots to couple the "Fresh Mex" theme with the idea of "Fresh TV." The question, according to Rich Silverstein, co-creative director, "was not whether we should do fresh TV. The question was, could we do it?"[16]

Fifteen spots were produced by Chevys' agency, Goodby, Berlin & Silverstein. The production problems were a logistical nightmare. Simpson and art director Tracy Wong would

EXHIBIT 16–17   Multiple-Source Editing System

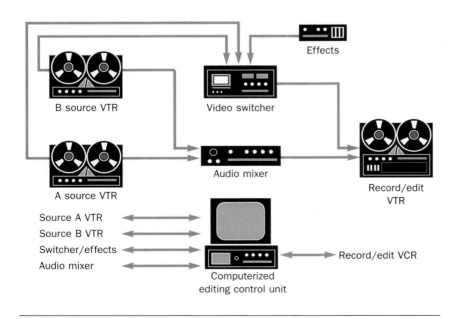

meet at 4:30 A.M. to look for late-breaking stories in the newspaper to use in the spots. "By daybreak, the crew would be filming; at 7:30, they would be editing; by 9:30 the client would approve the spots; and by 10:30 A.M. the spots were at San Francisco stations for airing that evening."[17]

The style of commercials the creative team achieved was a combination of MTV-like graphics, home video clips, and late-breaking news. In look, the spots appeared spontaneous, but many of the imperfections were built in. One spot showed that day's newspaper to prove the commercial was fresh; in another spot, a priest was questioned about the date while he was hooked to a lie-detector machine.

Several facts about the productions were unbelievable. Each spot cost only between $7,000 and $15,000 to produce. With a campaign goal of increasing sales by 10 percent in the San Francisco and Sacramento regions, the consumer sales increase of 13.8 percent exceeded goals. And because of the campaign's creativity, many local news shows were covering the campaign. This added public relations support helped change the attitudes and behaviors of Chevys' customers. The production and execution of the Chevys strategy did what every advertiser and agency would like to do: create the most effective message at the most reasonable price.

SUMMARY

Advertising production is the phrase used to describe the physical tasks of preparing print advertisements, collateral print materials, and radio and television commercials. Production plays a central role in how a message is communicated. Production costs must be balanced against the creative effect of the production technique.

The production process is the third and final stage of the message creation task. At this stage, the creative and art directors have three concerns: 1) how to enhance or maintain the quality of the ad as it was conceived, 2) how to control costs, and 3) how production can influence a campaign's effectiveness.

Advertising production has an influence throughout the advertising process. Effective production techniques can dramatically increase the effectiveness of the message, while bad technique can render a message ineffective. The influence on message delivery comes in the form of production cost versus media budget: The higher the cost of production, the less money that is available for media expenditures. The effects of production technique or production costs are evident during the evaluation stage. When technique is effective and cost efficient the results of the campaign will be positive; poor production, on the other hand, can result in goals and objectives not being achieved.

Advertisers and art directors choose a production procedure with the belief that it will enhance the message. Photographs, multicolor printing, or dramatic video footage can all help an advertiser reach its audience with its intended message. But creative production techniques do not always have to be high cost; used in the right context, a subtle black-and-white photo can sometimes be just as effective.

There are three stages of production for print advertising. During the design stage, copy and art are prepared for the printer. Next, a series of prepress operations are performed by the printer, including graphic arts photography, film assembly or stripping, platemaking, and prepress proofing. Presswork operations include press proofs, printing, cutting, trimming, and binding.

Computers have had an important effect on the production process. Sophisticated electronic prepress systems allow for complete input and page composition, and may be used to output lithographic negatives or film. Desktop publishing systems use multiple pieces of software with a page layout program to output print masters or lithographic film or negatives.

Decisions made during the design stage have a direct effect upon production costs. These decisions can be categorized as: 1) the size and length of the advertisement or brochure; 2) the number and type of visuals used; 3) the number of printing inks required; 4) the typographic characteristics of the printed piece; and 5) the type of paper selected.

By understanding the capabilities of the printer during prepress operations, an advertiser or art director can make use of the specialized printing services a printer offers. In addition, understanding prepress operations also makes it easier to see how late changes in an advertisement or brochure can destroy a production budget. During prepress operations, continuous tone artwork must be changed to halftones—optical illusions that appear to have gray tones but are actually black-and-white dots. Line art photography doesn't make halftones. Instead, it photographs artwork in all black and white. Textures and graphic effects can be added with

line screens. In addition, prepress strippers attach printing negatives to the printing flat. From the flat, plates are made. Prepress proofs, called bluelines, can be prepared from the printing flats.

Presswork operations may be done using one of four different printing processes: letterpress, rotogravure, offset lithography, or screen printing. A printer may prepare press proofs for color approval. Cutting is usually done so materials can be gang printed. Cutting is also the reason bleed artwork is prepared ¼- to ½-inch larger than its trim size.

Broadcast production may be divided into three distinct stages: preproduction, production, and postproduction. The stages are similar for radio and television production. During preproduction, scripts and storyboards must be completed and approved. Production operations include studio taping and collecting all audio and visual elements for the commercial. Postproduction editing and mixing operations assemble the pieces of commercials in order to prepare an approval print for the client.

KEY TERMS

advertising production, 490

design stage, 493

prepress stage, 493

presswork stage, 494

resolution, 496

trim size, 497

four-color process
  printing, 497

color separations, 497

Pantone Matching System®
  (PMS) , 497

continuous tone images, 500

halftone photography, 500

halftone principle, 500

line art photography, 500

printing flat, 502

stripping, 502

bluelines, 502

silver prints, 502

web-fed paper, 502

sheet-fed paper, 502

letterpress printing, 502

rotogravure printing, 502

offset lithography
  printing, 502

screen printing, 502

press proofs, 502

gang printing, 503

bleed advertisement, 503

preproduction stage, 504

production stage, 504

postproduction stage, 504

sound mixing, 505

sound masters, 505

dubbing, 505

television producer, 506

television director, 506

production notes, 509

answer print, 510

release print, 510

final tape, 510

1. What is advertising production?

2. How is advertising production interrelated with copywriting and art direction in the message creation process?

3. Sometimes a production technique can become the actual idea behind an ad. Provide an example of an advertising idea that was derived from a production technique.

4. What are the three stages of production for print advertising materials? Describe the major tasks that are required during each stage.

5. Why and how are halftones made?

6. How does four-color process printing change continuous tone color images into printed four-color advertisements or brochures?

7. What are the three major stages of production for broadcast commercials?

8. Trace the steps necessary for the production of a radio commercial.

9. How are television commercials made? Include descriptions of the roles of producer, director, engineers, talent, and postproduction editors.

10. What is the art director's responsibility throughout the TV commercial production process?

1. Identify a print or broadcast advertisement that you think is highly effective but that looks like it did not cost much to produce. Now think of a print or broadcast advertisement that you believe is equally effective but that looks like it was expensive to produce. Discuss the reasons why you think one concept was expensive to produce and the other was not.

2. Fashions and trends influence advertising much the way they influence other parts of our popular culture, such as music and graphic art. Identify some of the current trends in advertising production and where they come from.

3. Create a print ad from idea through copy and design on a computer. Describe the stages you went through to create this ad. Which of the traditional print production stages were you able to bypass?

4. The production of a print or broadcast ad always has serious budget implications. Discuss some of the stages of producing a television commercial at which you believe errors could result in serious increases in the production budget.

interactive discovery lab

1. Search the World Wide Web for commercial production studio sites. Look for common services and facilities provided. Also look for unique features such as animation capabilities or special computer-based services. You can take notes or print pages from the sites. Once you have all this information, design your own studio and write a brief description of its facilities. Give your commercial production house a name.

2. Create and produce a rough radio or television spot for a product or service of your choosing using stereo or video equipment that you or a friend might have. Think of the idea, write the copy, recruit talent, think of special effects you can do simply, and direct and produce the process. Have some fun!

1975–2000 and Beyond

The last quarter of the twentieth century has illustrated one of the themes of this text—that the advertising business is characterized by change that creates new challenges and choices on a rather consistent basis. Sometimes the advertising industry causes change, and other times it is influenced by change.

The 1980s was a decade in which the industry was obsessed with consolidations, mergers, buyouts, and change. Agencies joined forces, broke apart, renamed themselves, and folded on a seemingly endless trail to become the biggest and best. To some extent, the merger mania simply mirrored a trend in corporate America. One of the more famous of the mergers was that of Saatchi & Saatchi with Ted Bates in the 1980s, which eventually resulted in them breaking up again in 1997.

Fragmentation, integration, and globalization are the bywords of this era. Audiences became more fragmented as advertisers mourned the end of the mass market. Network television audiences declined due, in part, to the growth in the number of channels available from cable operators. Personal computers and videocassette recorders also provided more competition for the consumer's attention.

The very definition of advertising was broadened in the 1980s and 1990s to include all means of communicating with potential customers, a practice known as integrated marketing communications (IMC). It uses public relations, direct marketing, sales promotion, and various forms of nontraditional media (such as advertising in health clubs, airports, sports stadiums, and clothing) to build up brand equity. Advertising now appears to be everywhere.

1983

1976

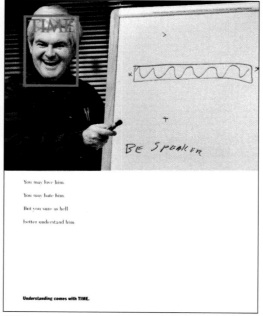

1995

The chance that cosumers would see the same ad in many different countries also increased considerably. The 1980s and 1990s were marked by a rapid increase in the efforts of advertisers to create global ads, using either identical pictures in all markets or adapting a similar theme line and strategy to local customs, tastes, and language. This period also marked the development of the first truly global medium, the Internet, which promises to offer marketers and advertisers direct, immediate, two-way communications with their customers. Advertising is becoming truly interactive as consumers select and respond to those messages that are of interest and ignore the rest.

And what about the future? What will historians say about advertising in the twenty-first century? It is impossible to say. But what we do know for certain is that the advertising professionals—and students—of the next 100 years are likely to face as many, if not more, choices, challenges, and changes as were faced from before 1900 to today.

1985

Getting Started:
A Career Guide to the Advertising Industry

After reading this book and learning about the principles of the business, we hope that you have come away with as much enthusiasm for it as we possess, and that you are interested in pursuing a career in advertising. The subtitle of this book, *Choice, Challenge, and Change,* applies equally well to the job-hunting process. In this appendix, we outline a few ideas for how to find your ideal job in advertising.

Identify Your Goals

CHOICE   First, you should understand that there are a myriad of choices available to you within the advertising industry. The broadest breakdown of the industry—into advertisers, agencies, and the media—should help you to see that. While there is nothing to prevent you from pursuing positions in all three fields, it is to your advantage to focus your efforts on one particular type of job where you feel your talents will be best suited.

Indeed, before you start applying for positions, your first step should be to sit down and figure out what you would be happiest doing, and why. Do you feel your biggest strength is your leadership capability? Are you most satisfied when you have completed an analysis of a large spreadsheet? Do you enjoy working with numbers? Are you a "people person" who enjoys spending most of your time helping others solve their business problems? Many jobs in advertising will require a combination of these attributes—and more! The hardest part for you is to determine for which position you are best suited; armed with that knowledge, you can then pursue all avenues to get there.

CHALLENGE   As you are probably already aware, the advertising business is extremely competitive. That is especially true for entry-level jobs in the industry. You may have to send out 50 copies of your résumé to get any kind of response. You might need to consider relocating, either to a bigger advertising market such as New York, Chicago, or Los Angeles, or possibly to a smaller market where you could begin your career with a specific advertiser or with a local media operation (TV station, newspaper, etc.). Keep your options as wide open as possible to be sure that you find the best position for you.

CHANGE   As this book emphasizes, the advertising industry is premised on change. In fact, if people were not willing to change their buying habits, partially in response to advertising, the industry would not even exist! In terms of career guidance, there are two areas where change is important. First, the *types* of positions that are available will change over time. Ten years ago, it was almost impossible to find an account planning job in the United States. Today, although still not too common, an increasing number of agencies are adding staff in this area. Five years ago, there were practically no jobs in the area of interactive media; now, that is one of the most rapidly expanding areas of the industry. The moral here is to keep abreast of what is happening in the industry. Identify the trends, and see where they are heading.

The second type of change is one that takes place in yourself. That is, you may have been convinced from the age of five that you were a born copywriter, and that is all you would ever consider. As you learn more about that field, and the other areas of the industry, consider seriously whether there are other jobs that might be equally appealing. Given the competitiveness of the business, you may discover that your love of writing could be put to equally good use, and bring as much job satisfaction, as a marketing analyst or account executive preparing reports or summarizing research findings.

Your First Steps

Following those general notions, here are a few specific pointers to starting your career in advertising.

1. Find the available positions. After you have decided what type of job you want to do in the industry, the next step is to find out where those openings exist. This is the correct order to move in—don't simply look at the "Help Wanted" ads and choose to go wherever they are. Work the other way around, or else you may end up taking a job that is very quickly unsatisfying and boring for you. As Chapters Two and Twelve showed, there are a large number of companies out there who employ advertising staff. To find out what positions are available, you can either send out letters to them directly, inquiring about openings, or scrutinize the "help wanted" ads in the local newspaper or advertising-related trade publications (e.g., *Advertising Age, Adweek, Brandweek, Promo, Direct, Folio, Editor & Publisher, Broadcasting & Cable*).

2. Find out who is in charge. Often, you will get a better response by contacting a specific department or, better yet, an individual within a company to learn if there are openings. Two valuable resources to help you in this approach are the *Standard Directory of Advertisers* and the *Standard Directory of Advertising Agencies*. These books are commonly referred to as the industry "Red Books" (due to the color of their bound covers); they provide listings of key personnel at specific companies, along with information about who is responsible for the advertising. Address your inquiries to the person who seems most directly in charge of the area in which you are interested (i.e., agency media director for media positions, station manager for TV or radio station positions). Even if your inquiry is passed along to the personnel department or another individual, you will at least have had your name noticed by someone at the top.

3. Sell yourself. You should think of your résumé and accompanying cover letter as a small foot in a very large door. While it may be tempting to be as "creative" as possible in order to distinguish yourself from the hundreds of other résumés the company receives, keep your information factual, straightforward, and to

the point, unless the position requires a zany or offbeat approach. The résumé and cover letter are designed to pique the reader's interest enough to persuade him or her that you are both interesting and qualified enough to merit an interview.

4. The résumé. Your résumé should be limited to one page in length, except for names of references, which can be attached. There are numerous ways to construct an effective résumé; your college career office probably has someone on staff to help in this area. Do not feel obliged to list everything you have ever done. It is more critical to include those activities and previous positions that you believe reflect those qualities that make you most suited for the position. On the other hand, you also want to avoid leaving long chronological gaps, which can either confuse the reader or make him or her think that you are hiding something in your past.

5. The cover letter. Begin your cover letter by telling the recipient why you are writing to him or her; then, explain what qualities you have that you feel could be of benefit to the company (and its clients, where relevant). In the words of S. William Pattis, author of a career guide in advertising, the question you should be trying to answer for the reader is, "What can I do for you?" rather than "What can you do for me?" As you outline your key traits in your cover letter, make sure they are relevant to the position for which you are applying. You probably want your future employer to know that you are hardworking, but it is much more impressive if you note on your résumé that you paid your way through college by holding down two jobs and a full courseload. Don't use your letter as a lengthy exposition on your résumé; providing too many details in your cover letter can, in your prospective employer's mind, eliminate the need to ask you in for an interview.

6. The follow-up. In the closing of your cover letter, inform the reader that you will be calling him or her on a specific date if you have not been contacted by that date. And if you write that you will call, then be sure that you do. Be persistent in those calls; keep in mind that advertising executives tend to be extremely busy and may not have a chance either to get your message or to respond to it. Most people, however, will appreciate your bothering to call back (within reasonable limits, of course), and will see your actions as showing initiative, which could help you to land the job of your dreams!

Key Positions In Advertising

ACCOUNT MANAGEMENT   Account management is where the agency and the advertiser come together. It is the job of the agency's account manager to act as the key liaison between the agency and the advertiser. The account person is also responsible for ensuring that everything is done within the agency to serve that client. That requires excellent communication skills, as well as leadership abilities. This position is something of a "jack of all trades," in that it is up to the account manager to coordinate all of the research, creative, and media, and to ensure that all of these elements are in line with the advertiser's brand strategies and are working toward achieving the agreed-upon brand objectives. That might involve everything from checking on print production schedules, to helping to analyze focus group findings, to negotiating with radio stations for additional promotional support.

The entry-level job at an agency is usually called the Assistant Account Executive. In that position, your primary responsibility will be to help the account executives fulfill their duties. With that, everything from the mundane (phone calls, typing, duplicating reports) to the critical (developing strategy documents) may fall within your purview.

As we noted in Chapter Two, a hybrid position between account management and research is the Account Planner. This individual's key task is to ensure that he or she represents the consumer's position within the agency and for the advertiser. So while an account planner might get involved in interviewing consumers and seeing how they interpret an ad campaign, much as a researcher would do, the planner is then responsible for delivering those findings to the rest of the agency's client team in a way that will help move the brand forward in terms of its advertising and marketing objectives.

In terms of college degrees, account managers come from various disciplines. At some agencies, business or marketing degrees are preferred, but at others they are not essential.

Some of the larger agencies like advanced degrees (such as a Master in Business Administration degree). Previous business experience is definitely preferred (and sometimes required).

CREATIVE   Creative is the area of the agency that is often seen as the place where fame and fortune are made. After all, without the ideas generated by the creative team, what would an advertising agency have to offer? It sounds pretty inviting to spend your days dreaming up catchy taglines or devising cute and witty ads and commercials. The truth is that the creative positions require a good deal of hard work and effort, as well as a thorough knowledge of the advertiser and brand. Although we tend to think of creativity as something innate, or a "natural" talent, in reality it needs to be honed and perfected through long years of training and experience.

The two key positions within the creative department of an agency are Copywriter and Art Director. Generally, these individuals work together in pairs (or sometimes teams), with the copywriter being responsible for the words, and the art director handling the visuals. To be successful in either role, in addition to being able to write or draw well, creatives must have a curiosity about everything. They are the ones who could look at the bright pink color of Owens-Corning fiberglass insulation and come up with the link to the Pink Panther character (same color) to use as the spokes-character for a long-running ad campaign. They would envision the "lonely repairman" in the Maytag appliance ads who stands for the reliability of those machines, but is lonely because he is never needed. Of course, because creativity can't be programmed, creative folks are often found in the office at unusual times. Theirs is definitely not a "routine" job.

The copywriter and art director work together to come up with ideas that could be developed into an advertisement. Most often, it is not a rapid process! In order to create an ad, the creatives are usually working from a strategic blueprint (developed by the whole team, sometimes in conjunction with the client, but always with client approval) that outlines the brand objectives, target audience, brand benefits, and key insights. Those ideas are conceptualized and put into the format of the ad—print executions, radio commercials, or

TV storyboards. Once accepted internally by the agency team, these ideas are then shown to the client to obtain approval. They are usually tested among representative target audience members before being finalized and executed. The entire process can take anywhere from a few weeks to several months (and occasionally, even years!).

There are no degree requirements for these positions, although art directors often study the visual arts in some fashion (such as graphic design or art history). Copywriters have diverse backgrounds, usually within the liberal arts (journalism, English, or communications, for example).

MEDIA Once thought of as the place for math geniuses or numbers fanatics, media is one of the most exciting areas of the agency to work in today. An ever-increasing list of new media options has made life in media increasingly complicated and challenging. There are two key avenues to pursue for careers: media planning and media buying.

The key role of the media planner is to determine where and when the ads should be scheduled, and how often they should run. That involves consideration of the target audience for the ads, which media those people tend to prefer, and what days and times the target audience is likely to be using those media. Once the general media forms have been selected, the planner then needs to look at the various programs or publication titles within those media. Depending upon the size of the agency, the planner may select specific vehicles to deliver the ad messages, or indicate the general type of program or magazine to which the buyer then tries to adhere, such as "family entertainment shows," or "parenting magazines." The planner is also responsible for figuring out which combination of media forms to use, and how to schedule them during the planning cycle (typically a one-year period). Having done that, he or she estimates what the impact of those media will be, in terms of the numbers and frequency of the target audience reached.

After the plan is approved, it is up to the media buyer to execute it. The main talent required of a buyer is good negotiating skills (which are founded on good communication skills). The buyer works with the media to deliver the plan as proposed, buying the time and space in the most appropriate media vehicles at the best possible price. Once the deal has been made, it is the buyer's responsibility to ensure that the media deliver on it, airing or printing the ads when and where they were scheduled.

One of the more specialized areas within media is that of media research. Here, the task is to find out more about how people use media by analyzing research data on consumers. This is typically a supporting role within the media department.

Most agencies do not require a specific degree for these jobs, though sales experience is helpful for both areas (especially buying), and a marketing background is also useful.

RESEARCH The primary role of a Researcher at an advertising agency or advertiser is to learn as much as possible about the consumer. The focus and application of this work varies, falling into such categories as consumer research, strategic planning, and market research. That might involve sending out surveys, conducting personal interviews, or buying syndicated data on a specific group of people. Researchers study everything about consumers—their likes and dislikes, their opinions and attitudes, their lifestyles and habits, and most importantly, their purchase behavior. They also investigate consumer reactions to ad campaigns, both actual and potential, to see if the work being developed to promote the brand is "on strategy" and likely to be effective enough to impact sales.

This is the one area of the agency where specialized college degrees can help. Having studied consumers in some way, whether through psychology or sociology or anthropology can be beneficial (though being able to apply those fields to a marketing arena is probably equally important). Advanced degrees are often helpful too.

A Few Last—But Not Least—Suggestions

Even after you have worked through all of the steps listed above and have identified the position you are aiming to get, there are a few more things you can do to begin a career in the advertising industry.

1. Immerse yourself in advertising. Would you hire someone to service your car who rarely looked under the hood of one? Or ask someone to redecorate your home if he only occasionally picked up a paintbrush? Well, the same holds true for advertising. If you want to get a job in this business, you need to know it inside and out. Make sure you keep up with the industry trade press to know who is in, who is out, and which accounts have just been won or lost. For the agencies or companies in which you are most seriously interested, study them as if you were taking a test on them (and consider your interview as the test!). Know as much about their brands as possible. Examine the ads themselves—who they are targeting, what they are saying, where and when they appear. Formulate your own opinions about their effectiveness (but be careful in delivering your opinions!). And look more generally at the ads that appear all around you. Start noticing them with a critical eye, paying particular attention to those aspects that are relevant to your specific area of interest. Researchers, for example, should consider how effectively the ads are communicating a message; media folks will want to know whether the messages are placed appropriately; account executives should determine if there is a clear strategy; creatives can critique the verbal and visual effectiveness of the message.

2. Talk to people. As with many industries, to get your foot in the door in advertising, it can help to know someone (or someone who knows someone who knows someone) who already works in the field. Once you have identified that contact, try to get in to talk to that person (even if you don't know him or her very well). Most people are willing to give you 10 minutes of their time to explain what they do. Find out what this person likes best and least about his or her job; how he or she got started in the industry; who this person recommends you talk to next to learn more. Start by trying to talk to as many people as you can in as many different places in order to get various perspectives on a number of available avenues and companies. Then, narrow down your search and your conversations as you determine the path that is best for you. But keep talking (and writing and calling) until you have zeroed in on the position, and/or place you want to be.

3. Gain a variety of experience. Very often, people who end up in advertising come in having had seemingly unrelated experiences. They took care of children. They were volunteer tutors to illiterate adults. They spent a summer studying the Incas in Peru. They helped organize a charity fundraiser. Yet all of those experiences could be useful and applicable to advertising positions. If you can take care of a bunch of rowdy five year olds, then as an account manager, handling a difficult client should be easy. Teaching people how to read might be helpful for aspiring copywriters, who must develop a talent for studying language closely. If you spent significant time studying an ancient, foreign culture, then your curiosity about and interest in people would stand you in good stead in a research position. And if you were able to organize a charity fundraiser, with all of the scheduling and promotions involved, then a career in media planning could be in your future. The important thing here is that you want to get as much experience as you can, in a variety of places working with a variety of people and learning a variety of things. In short, all of your experiences are relevant on some level, but you must be able to identify what you have learned and be prepared to discuss those skills and their applicability in an interview with a potential employer.

4. Don't give up. The final piece of advice for making a career in advertising is, Don't give up! Be persistent. Keep making those phone calls and sending out those résumés. Keep talking to people and gaining experiences. Keep trying to get in somewhere in the industry. Just remember, most of the biggest names in the business today had to start somewhere. And so can you!

Appendix B
Advertising Organizations

Advertiser Syndicated Television Association
1756 Broadway, Suite 3J
New York, NY 10019
(212) 245-0840

Advertising Council
261 Madison Avenue, 11th Floor
New York, NY 10016
(212) 922-1500

Advertising & Marketing International Network
255 N. Meade St.
P.O. Box 11009
Wichita, KS 67202
(316) 263-0124

Advertising Research Foundation
641 Lexington Ave., 11th Floor
New York, NY 10022
(212) 751-5656

American Advertising Federation
1101 Vermont Ave. NW, Suite 500
Washington, DC 20005
(202) 898-0089

American Association of Advertising Agencies
405 Lexington Ave., 18th Floor
New York, NY 10174
(212) 682-2500

American Business Press
675 Third Ave.
New York, NY 10017
(212) 661-6360

American Mail Marketing Association
1333 F St. NW, Suite 710
Washington, DC 20004
(202) 347-0055

American Marketing Association
250 S. Wacker Dr., Suite 200
Chicago, IL 60606
(312) 648-0536

Association of Independent Commercial Producers
11 E. 22nd St.
New York, NY 10010
(212) 475-2600

Association of Incentive Marketing
1620 Route 22
Union, NJ 07083
(908) 687-3090

Association of National Advertisers
155 E. 44th St.
New York, NY 10017
(212) 697-5950

Association of Promotion Marketing Agencies Worldwide
750 Summer St.
Stamford, CT 06901
(203) 325-3911

Audit Bureau of Circulations
900 N. Meacham Rd.
Schaumburg, IL 60173
(847) 605-0909

BPA International
270 Madison Ave.
New York, NY 10016
(212) 779-3200

Business Marketing Association
150 N. Wacker Dr.
Chicago, IL 60606
(800) 664-4262

Cabletelevision Advertising Bureau
830 Third Ave.
New York, NY 10022
(212) 508-1200

Cable & Telecommunications: A Marketing Society
201 N. Union Ave., Suite 440
Alexandria, VA 22314
(703) 549-4200

Center for Exhibition Industry Research
4350 E. West Highway, Suite 401
Bethesda, MD 20814
(301) 907-7626

Cosmetic, Toiletries & Fragrance Association
1101 17th St. NW, Suite 300
Washington, DC 20036
(202) 331-1770

National Advertising Division, Council of Better Business Bureaus
845 Third Ave., 17th Floor
New York, NY 10024
(212) 705-0100

Direct Marketing Association
1120 Avenue of the Americas
New York, NY 10036
(212) 768-7277

Eight-Sheet Outdoor Advertising Association
P.O. Box 2680
Bremerton, WA 98310
(800) 874-3387

Electronic Media Ratings Council
200 W. 57th St., Suite 204
New York, NY 10019
(212) 765-0200

Food Marketing Institute
800 Connecticut Ave. NW, Suite 500
Washington, DC 20006
(202) 452-8444

Grocery Manufacturers of America
1010 Wisconsin Ave. NW, Suite 900
Washington, DC 20007
(202) 337-9400

**Incentive Manufacturers
Representatives Association**
1805 N. Mill St., Suite A
Naperville, IL 60563
(708) 369-3466

Interactive Services Association
8403 Colesville Rd., Suite 865
Silver Spring, MD 20910
(301) 495-4955

Interactive Television Association
1019 Nineteenth St. NW, 10th Floor
Washington, DC 20036
(202) 408-0008

**International Advertising
Association**
521 Fifth Ave., Suite 1807
New York, NY 10022
(212) 557-1133

International Exhibitors Association
5501 Backlick Road, Suite 105
Springfield, VA 22151
(703) 941-3725

**International Federation
of Advertising Agencies**
1450 E. American Lane, Suite 1400
Schaumburg, IL 60173
(847) 330-6344

**International Licensing Industry
Merchandisers' Association**
350 Fifth Ave., Suite 2309
New York, NY 10118
(212) 244-1944

International Radio & TV Society
420 Lexington Ave., Suite 1714
New York, NY 10170
(212) 867-6650

**Leading Independent Agency
Network**
1515 S. Flagler Dr., Suite 2603
West Palm Beach, FL 33401
(407) 655-6973

Magazine Publishers of America
919 Third Ave., 22nd Floor
New York, NY 10022
(212) 872-3700

**Mutual Advertising Agency
Network**
25700 Science Park Dr.
Cleveland, OH 44122
(216) 292-6609

**National Association
of Broadcasters**
1771 N St. NW
Washington, DC 20036
(202) 429-5300

**National Association of Television
Programming Executives**
2425 W. Olympic Blvd., Suite 550E
Santa Monica, CA 90404
(310) 453-4440

**National Automobile Dealers
Association**
8400 Westpark Dr.
McLean, VA 22102
(703) 821-7000

**National Cable Television
Association**
1724 Massachusetts Ave. NW
Washington, DC 20036
(202) 775-3550

**National Infomercial Marketing
Association International**
1225 New York Ave. NW, Suite 1200
Washington, DC 20005
(202) 289-6462

**National Newspaper Publishers'
Association**
3200 13th St. NW
Washington, DC 20010
(202) 588-8764

Newspaper Association of America
11600 Sunrise Valley Dr.
Reston, VA 22091
(703) 648-1000

**North American Advertising Agency
Network**
245 Fifth Ave.
New York, NY 10016
(212) 481-3022

**Outdoor Advertising Association
of America**
12 E. 49th St., 22nd Floor
New York, NY 10017
(212) 688-3667

**Point of Purchase Advertising
Institute**
1660 L St. NW, 10th Floor
Washington, DC 20036
(202) 530-3000

**Private Label Manufacturers
Association**
369 Lexington Ave., 3rd Floor
New York, NY 10017
(212) 972-3131

**Promotion Marketing Association
of America**
257 Park Ave. South
New York, NY 10010
(212) 420-1100

**Promotion Products Association
International**
3125 Skyway Circle North
Irving, TX 75038
(214) 252-0404

Public Relations Society of America
33 Irving Place
New York, NY 10003
(212) 460-1400

Radio Advertising Bureau

1320 Greenway, Suite 500

Irving, TX 75038

(800) 232-3131

Retail Advertising & Marketing Association International

333 N. Michigan Ave., Suite 3000

Chicago, IL 60601

(312) 251-7262

Society of Incentive Travel Executives

21 W. 38th St.

New York, NY 10018

(212) 575-0910

Specialty Advertising Association of Greater New York

523 Route 303

Orangeburg, NY 10962

(800) 722-4691

Television Bureau of Advertising

850 Third Ave.

New York, NY 10022

(212) 486-1111

Toy Manufacturers of America

200 Fifth Ave., Room 740

New York, NY 10010

(212) 675-1141

Traffic Audit Bureau

420 Lexington Ave., Suite 2520

New York, NY 10170

(212) 972-8075

Worldwide Partners

2280 S. Xanadu Way, Suite 300

Aurora, CO 80014

(303) 671-8551

Yellow Pages Publishers Association

820 Kirts Blvd.

Troy, MI 48084

(810) 244-6200

Glossary

Note: The parenthetical number at the end of each definition indicates the chapter in which the term is discussed.

account manager   The individual within an advertising agency who represents the agency to its client and vice versa. (2)

account planner   Particularly in the United Kingdom, the individual who is the advertising team's primary contact with the outside world and who brings strong consumer focus to all advertising decisions; a merger of the account manager and researcher functions. (2)

advertiser   A company or individual that spends money to convey a persuasive advertising message to the public. (2)

advertising   Nonpersonal communication for products, services, or ideas that is paid for by an identified sponsor for the purpose of influencing an audience. (5)

advertising agency   A business that assists advertisers in all stages of the advertising process, from account management and planning to message creation, media planning, and research. (2)

advertising allowance   A type of in-store trade promotion wherein the manufacturer pays the retailer to advertise his product. (12)

advertising objective   A statement explaining the purpose and role of an advertising campaign or a particular advertisement. (8, 13)

advertising production   The physical tasks of preparing print advertisements, collateral print materials, and radio and television commercials. (16)

advertising research   Research activity that is performed in support of the planning, development, placement, or monitoring of ads. (7)

advertising unit   Advertising space or time supplied by the media to advertisers and agencies. (2)

agate lines per column   The depth (length) of a newspaper page; also known as lines. (11)

ambush marketing   A tactic used by a company that is not an official sponsor of an event that involves crafting the advertising message or bombarding the public at the time of the event to make people think that it is in fact an official sponsor. (12)

American Association of Advertising Agencies (AAAA)   The largest advertising trade association; AAAA's self-regulatory Standards of Practice discusses deception, misleading testimonials, price claims, substantiation of claims, and matters of taste. (3)

answer print   In television production, the finished commercial from film that needs client approval before it can be released to stations for broadcast. (16)

art director   As a critical member of an advertising agency's creative team, this person determines how messages will be visually presented to the target audience. Works with the copywriter to make sure the visual and verbal elements of ads and promotional pieces work together to convey a clear and consistent message. (15)

attitude   A three-part internal mental structure that integrates a consumer's feelings (affect), knowledge (cognitions), and intentions to act toward an object, act, or person into an overall evaluation. (6)

audience   The number of people who read a magazine; the readers per copy multiplied by the circulation. (11)

audience research   Research information collected from consumers regarding their media usage patterns, product purchases, and demographic and lifestyle characteristics. (2)

audience share   The proportion of all TV sets that are on at a given time and are tuned to a particular show; also known as *viewing share*. (10)

audiotex   A phone-based service that allows newspaper readers to call a local telephone number to get more information on a product or service that appeared in the newspaper, leave a voicemail for personal ads, or reach a 1-900 telephone number. (11)

avails   A list of available television times, dates, prices, program ratings, households, costs-per-thousand, reach, and frequency provided to advertisers or agencies by individual stations. (10)

average frequency   Average number of times a consumer is exposed to a media vehicle or schedule. (9)

average quarter-hour audience   The percentage of the target that listens to a radio station in a specific daypart as measured on a quarter-hour basis. (10)

balance   The distribution of elements around an imaginary vertical line that divides a layout or advertisement into two equal halves. (15)

banner   A short, graphic device that acts as a gateway to another page or Web site. The purpose of a banner is to attract attention and get the Internet user to click on it to go to another page or location for additional information. (14)

barter syndication   A method of compensation in which advertisers agree on some kind of partial or total exchange of their products or services for airtime during a syndicated program. (10)

before/after testing   A common method of evaluating both message and media effectiveness. The advertiser starts by writing objectives

stating the goals of the advertising message before the campaign begins. The advertiser also performs descriptive research to establish initial, or baseline, awareness within the target audience. After the campaign, the advertiser measures these goals and compares them to the baseline awareness numbers. (7)

behavioral learning theories   Learning theories that argue that the only appropriate thing to study is the observable and measurable response of people to stimuli; in essence, what people do is far more important than what they say. Also known as *stimulus-response theories*. (6)

beliefs   Underlying cognitions, or organizations of knowledge, that represent what the consumer knows about an object about which he or she has an attitude. (6)

benefit headline   A type of advertising headline that promises the consumer something personally rewarding in return for buying the product. (14)

Better Business Bureau (BBB)   A private, non-profit organization made up of 137 local Bureaus from around the U.S. The BBB investigates consumer or business complaints of fraudulent activity and promotes a high ethical relationship between businesses and the public. (3)

bias   Systematic distortions or errors in the research setting or data collection method. (7)

bleed advertisement   An advertisement that has printing images extending to the outside edge of the page in a magazine or brochure. Also known as a *bleed border*. (16)

bluelines   A special proof of images made from printing flats for the purpose of checking the placement, orientation, and accuracy of text and photographs. Also called *silver prints*. (16)

body copy   The heart and substance of an advertisement, this is where the writer can expand on the main idea of the ad and offer supporting selling points and arguments to the reader. (14)

brand   The name and/or symbol used to identify a product or service and distinguish it from the competition. (5)

brand association   A link in a consumer's mind between a company's product and just about anything related to it. (5)

brand equity   The net total of all assets and liabilities linked to a brand by consumers; the value of a brand to the company that owns it. (5)

brand image   A set of brand associations that consumers use to organize information about a brand. (15)

brand loyalty   The degree of attachment customers have to a particular brand. (5)

brand management   A type of organizational structure for an advertiser in which some marketing and advertising decisions are made at the corporate level—either by a corporate marketing staff or by management at the corporate level—while the day-to-day activities are handled by staffs that are responsible for individual brands. (2)

broadcast audience measurement   A media audience research method that measures national television audiences, local television audiences, and radio audiences. (7)

Bureau of Alcohol, Tobacco and Firearms (BATF) Federal bureau involved in the regulation of alcoholic beverage advertising through its oversight role in the manufacture and distribution of alcohol. (3)

business magazines   Periodicals that are aimed at a specialized group of people who work in a particular industry; examples include *Milling and Baking* and *Chemical Age*. (11)

call letters   The unique letters identifying a radio station, such as WOI in Des Moines, Iowa. (10)

call-to-action   A request for the order. (14)

camera-ready   A mechanical proof from which a printer can make photographic printing plates. (15)

caption   Short descriptions that are typically used under or next to photographs or illustrations to help the reader interpret them. (14)

category management   A type of organizational structure for an advertiser in which people who work on individual brands report to more senior staff who are responsible for a particular category. (2)

category manager   An individual responsible for a particular type of product category for an organization. (2)

causal research   A type of research design that controls interfering factors so a strong conclusion of cause and effect can be determined. (7)

cause marketing   A type of sponsorship that offers a powerful way to gain visibility by associating with a well-known cause. (12)

center spread   The two facing pages in the center of a publication; because of its location, this is premium advertising space. (11)

Children's Advertising Review Unit (CARU)   A special investigatory arm of the National Advertising Review Council specifically concerned with unfairness in children's advertising. (3)

circulation   A figure that indicates how many copies of a periodical are sold during the publication period. (11)

classified advertising   Newspaper advertising that gives consumers or businesses the opportunity to offer information or goods and services for sale directly to other consumers or businesses; generally small in size and sold by the number of words or lines in the text. (11)

client   The person or company that has contractually solicited the help of an advertising agency. (2)

closed-response question   A questionnaire question for which only certain answers, such as yes and no, are permitted. Also known as a *structured question*. (7)

closing paragraph   In the body copy of an advertisement, this provides the writer with the opportunity to ask for the order or to move the reader to action. Also known as the *close*. (14)

code law   Legal principles evolved from Roman law, where rulings are divided between commercial, civil, and criminal codes. (3)

cognitive learning theory   The learning theory that focuses on the nature of the mental processes of thinking, memory, and information processing that we use to learn and solve problems. (6)

color separations   Negatives that are prepared for each color in the four-color printing process. (16)

column width   The number of columns across a newspaper page. (11)

command headline   A type of advertising headline that commands the reader to do something. (14)

commercial speech   Speech with the underlying objective of selling something; this type of speech has less First Amendment protection than noncommercial speech. (3)

common law   Legal principles that have been developed through court interpretations of statutes, rulings, and legal precedent. (3)

comparative advertising   Advertising in which one brand names another brand or company and compares it (usually unfavorably) to itself. (3)

competitive analysis   Marketing research that attempts to analyze the marketing and advertising strategies of competitors by tracking their advertising and promotion activity. Also known as *competitive research*. (7)

competitive expenditure   Measurement information that shows how much is being spent on each brand and in which media. (2)

composition   The proportion of a magazine's total audience that falls into a given demographic group. (11)

comprehensive layout   More finished renderings of a final advertisement which show all of the elements that will appear in the final advertisement in their correct positions; the general purpose of the comprehensive layout is to show, as nearly as possible, how the finished advertisement will look when it is reproduced. Also called *comps*. (15)

computer artist   An expert in computer use and in the design and word processing software required to put an interactive ad together once the copywriter and art director have come up with the concept. (14)

concept testing   A research technique used to evaluate an advertising concept and to improve it. To do this, members of the target audience are exposed to the concept and their reactions are monitored and recorded. (7)

conceptualization   The use of intuition and imagination applied to everything we know about the advertising problem on which we are working to create an advertising idea. (14)

consumer magazines   All periodicals that are written for nonspecialized audiences; examples include *Time*, *Cosmopolitan*, and *Rolling Stone*. (11)

consumer promotions   Sales promotions that attempt to boost sales by encouraging people into the store to buy the product at a lower price or with some kind of special deal. (5, 12)

consumer research   Marketing research that asks questions about individuals in the target market or consumers in general; often tries to examine consumer attitudes or motivations toward a product purchase. (7)

contest   A game of skill that has specific criteria involved on which the winner is judged; a type of consumer sales promotion. (12)

continuity   A media scheduling pattern in which media activity is constant throughout the year. (9)

continuity program A type of consumer sales promotion that encourages people to buy a product or service more frequently to "earn" enough points to redeem a gift, such as a free airline ticket or free meal. Another goal of these promotional programs is to increase brand loyalty by enticing people to use the promoter's brand rather than the competitor's to garner more points. (12)

continuous-tone images The wide range of grays and the pure blacks and whites that make up the realistic-looking images in black-and-white photographs. (16)

contrast The relative lightness or darkness of colors to one another; also known as value or tone. (15)

cooperative (co-op) advertising Display ads from local retailers that are funded in part by national manufacturers or distributors. (11)

copy The actual words that make up an advertisement. (14)

copyright Registration that gives the holder exclusive right to reproduce, perform, or display "original works of authorship." For advertising, this may include photos, TV commercials, video, illustrations, sound recordings, ads, brochures, displays, and literary works. (3)

copy testing A message research technique in which the effect of the verbal and visual elements of an advertisement on members of the target audience are systematically examined. For the advertising planner, copy testing is designed to diagnose problems with advertisements and commercials before they are placed in the media. (7)

copywriter An individual in an advertising agency responsible for creating the idea—what to say and how to say it—for an advertisement. (2, 14)

corporate identity program The consistent display of corporate symbols (logotypes) in the design of business stationery, signs, and truck identification, for example. (15)

corporate image A set of brand images referring to the corporation. (15)

corporate public relations Public relations that look at a company's relationships with its non-customer publics, including the media, investors, government, community groups, suppliers, distributors, and employees. (5, 12)

corrective advertising Advertising imposed by the Federal Trade Commission in which the advertiser is forced to rectify misleading statements from previous advertising. (3)

cost per rating point (CPP) A calculation of the cost to purchase one rating point in a given media vehicle or type. Total schedule to 1,000 members of the target audience. (9)

cost-per-thousand (CPM) A calculation of the cost to deliver a media vehicle or schedule to 1,000 members of the target audience; (media cost/impressions) × 1000. (9)

coupon A certificate that may be redeemed for a cash discount. (12)

coverage The percentage of a particular target group that reads a magazine; also known as the *rating*. (11)

cover pages The inside front, inside back, and outside back covers of a periodical; because of their location, these are considered premium advertising space. (11)

creative An individual who works in the creative department of an advertising agency. (2)

creative boutique An agency formed by individuals who break away from their corporate parents and set up their own small shops. Frequently, these shops focus their efforts on the creative aspect of the advertising process. (2)

cross-tabulation A frequently used method of categorizing quantitative data so that two or more variables can be compared to one another. (7)

culture The shared beliefs, values, and customs we learn so that we can interact and function within our social and physical environments. (6)

cume audience The total number of a target group listening to a particular station during a specified time period. (10)

curiosity headline A type of advertising headline that relies on the reader actually reading the rest of the advertisement to find out what is so interesting. (14)

daily effective circulation The number of cars that pass by a particular billboard in a fixed time period (usually 12 hours) multiplied by the average number of people per car (1.35). (11)

database marketing Collecting computer records—including demographic and financial information on individuals and households that is systematically gathered and updated—and then using these records to target advertising to individuals' needs. (12)

daypart Different times of day and day of week in which a television or radio program appears. (10)

dealer listing A type of in-store trade promotion wherein the manufacturer leaves space on his ad to list local retailers or dealers. (12)

demographics Descriptive and quantifiable characteristics of a population such as age, sex, race, marital status, education, income, and geographical region. (6)

demography A science concerned with the study of the structure, distribution, and changes in a population's demographics as well as with areas such as fertility, social class, distribution of wealth, crime rates, and migration patterns. (6)

descriptive research A type of research design that tries to describe a marketing or advertising situation. (7)

design stage (of print production) The first stage of print production during which copy and layouts are prepared, typesetting is done,

photographic sessions are finished, and art and photographs are prepared for the printer. (16)

designated marketing areas (DMAs) Geographical areas into which the country is divided for Nielsen ratings purposes. (10)

"determine what is" questions Questions used during descriptive research and from which the advertiser can determine what exists in a marketing situation. (7)

developed market An industrialized country with free market systems in place at least 50 years where consumers have a broad range of goods and services from which to choose and can turn to advertising to help them make choices between brands. (4)

developing market An increasingly industrialized and urbanized country that is moving toward a free market economy and giving global advertisers the chance to develop their own markets within the country. (4)

dialogue copy A type of advertisement body copy that is best suited for radio and television but can be used effectively in print advertising if the writer has a good feel for the natural way in which people speak. (14)

digital audience broadcasting (DAB) Radio that allows stations to beam their signals up to a satellite and then send them back down again to a station in another city. (10)

direct mail advertising All forms of advertising sent directly to prospects via the U.S. Postal Service or private mail services. (12)

direct marketing Any activity whereby you communicate directly with your prospect or customer and he or she responds directly to you. (5, 12)

direct response TV A less-sophisticated version of interactive television in which viewers respond via telephone, calling up to purchase an item being promoted or to request information on a product or service. (10)

display advertising   Newspaper ads that consist of text as well as illustrations or photos and other visual components; the majority of display ads are placed by local retailers and other businesses, but they may also come from national advertisers. (11)

donut   A radio commercial format in which the music or song is played and then lowered in volume so that an announcer can read the copy for the product. (14)

dubbing   In broadcast production, the process of duplicating audiotapes for distribution. (16)

dummy   A layout for catalogs and product brochures that is used for design and copy approval before a project is sent to the printer; similar to a comprehensive layout. (15)

evaluative advertising research   Research that is performed to assess the effectiveness of specific messages or methods of message delivery used in a marketing communications or advertising campaign. (7)

exploratory research   A type of research design that makes an initial attempt to provide insights into a research problem on a small scale and at minimal cost. (7)

"explore what and why" questions   Questions that are used during exploratory research, when the advertiser has little or no information about a research problem or potential problem. (7)

external data   Secondary information gathered and stored by sources outside of an organization, including media audience studies or large-scale consumer lifestyle studies like VALS research. (7)

eye movement   The sequential processing of information in an advertisement by readers. (15)

face value   In coupons, the size of the discount on the product for the consumer, such as "50¢ off." (12)

farm magazines   Periodicals written to inform and educate the agricultural population;

examples include *Successful Farming* and *Wheat Life*. (11)

fear appeals   Advertising that tries to scare people into buying a product or service. (3)

Federal Communications Commission (FCC) Created by the Communications Act of 1934, the FCC controls the radio, television, and telephone industries and therefore has some control over aspects of radio and TV advertising, particularly obscenity and indecency in ads. (3)

Federal Trade Commission (FTC)   Created by the 1914 Federal Trade Commission Act, the FTC protects the marketplace from anti-competitive activities that restrain trade, protects consumers from "unfair or deceptive practices in commerce," specifies rules for the use of warranties in advertising and promotion, and demands substantiation of advertising claims. (3)

fee-based compensation   An agency compensation method by which the agency and advertiser agree in advance on how much the agency will receive for the year for working for the advertiser, usually based on time involved in producing the ad campaign. (2)

field experiment   A type of research design in which control is exerted over important variables and data collection takes place in a natural environment. (7)

final tape   In television production, the approval copy for a videotaped commercial. (16)

fixed spot   A type of television commercial that is sold with the understanding that another advertiser cannot take that spot. (10)

flighting   A media scheduling pattern in which media activity is concentrated into selected periods of the year, or flights; also known as *bursting*. (9)

Food and Drug Administration (FDA)   Created by the 1906 Pure Food and Drug Act, the FDA has jurisdiction over food labeling and, thus, ensures that advertising is consistent with the information provided on labels. (3)

font A complete set of letters in one size and face; also known as a *typeface*. (15)

format A type of radio program, such as Classic Rock or Urban Contemporary. (10)

forward buying A phenomenon related to trade promotions in which a retailer or dealer buys a large stock of the promoted items and keeps them in storage, selling them at a discount for a short while but then raising the price again and keeping the additional profit. (12)

four-color process printing A method of printing that involves preparing four separate plates for magenta, yellow, cyan, and black inks. (16)

free-standing insert (FSI) A popular type of coupon that generally appears in the Sunday edition of newspapers. (11)

frequency distribution Reach of a media vehicle or schedule at each level of frequency (1, 2, 3 times, etc.). (9)

full-service agency An agency that offers its clients all elements of advertising: message creation, media placement, research, and account management. (2)

gang printing The process of printing several copies of advertising artwork on a single print master and then cutting them to size. (16)

gatefold A three-page spread in magazines that consists of one full page or part of a page that extends from the original page and folds outward at the center of the book, like a gate, inviting the reader to open it up. (11)

genre A type of television program, such as drama, comedy, or sports. (10)

geodemographics Consumer databases that link geography or where people live to psychographic-type variables; the underlying premise is that people who live in the same areas or neighborhoods have other important characteristics in common. (6)

gross impression The number of audience exposures to a media vehicle or media plan multiplied by the number of times they will see or hear them; gross ratings points expressed in numbers of people rather than as a percentage. (9)

gross ratings point (GRP) Total number of rating points against a specific target for a particular media schedule; expressed as a percentage. (9)

guaranteed audience ratings The minimum number of people the networks guarantee will watch a particular show. (10)

guaranteed circulation A publisher's promise to an advertiser to sell a certain number of copies of a periodical during the publication period. (11)

halftone photography A method of printing continuous-tone images that converts a continuous-tone photograph into a pattern of small and clearly defined dots of various sizes. (16)

halftone principle An optical illusion created when continuous tone images are represented by small dots of varying sizes and equal spacing printed with a printing ink of uniform density. (16)

headline The most important verbal element in a print advertisement because it is the principal statement of benefit or promise in an ad. (14)

home shopping network A television network dedicated to selling goods and services to customers, with the orders placed via telephone. (10)

household A unit of measurement that includes all the people living under one roof regardless of their blood relationships; a basic social and economic unit that serves a number of key functions that influence the products we buy. (6)

households using television (HUT) The proportion of all households that have their TV sets on at a particular time. (10)

image An enduring perception of a product, service, or brand; a shorthand method consumers use to give meaning to what they know about products and brands. (6)

infomercial   A long-form commercial, lasting anywhere from 3 to 30 minutes, usually sponsored by one or a few advertisers. (10)

in-house advertising agency   An advertising agency housed within a client corporation that develops its own advertising instead of using an external agency. (2)

inkjetting   A process that allows a magazine to print an individual subscriber's name within an ad. (11)

insert   Material bound into a magazine that is intended to attract greater reader attention than a straightforward ad on the page; may be reply cards, coupons, or pop-ups. (11)

integrated marketing agency   Agencies that have expanded their scope of activities by involvement in other marketing communications activities, including sales promotion, direct marketing, public relations, or event marketing. (2)

integrated marketing communications   A concept of marketing communications planning that recognizes the added value of a comprehensive plan that evaluates the strategic roles of a variety of communications disciplines—for example, general advertising, direct response, sales promotion, and public relations—and combines these disciplines to provide clarity, consistency, and maximum communications impact. (5)

intensity   The brightness or dullness of a color. (15)

interactive television   Television that allows the viewer to respond directly to what he or she sees on the screen, including taking such actions as changing camera angles, paying bills, ordering goods or services, or controlling utilities in the house. (10)

intermedia   Between media, as in intermedia comparison. (9)

intramedia   Among media, as in intramedia comparison. (9)

internal data   Secondary data that exist with the advertiser's organization, such as shipping and billing information, customer account records, or past studies of advertising effectiveness. (7)

involvement   The perceived personal importance of an object or stimulus in a given situation; generally, the more expensive or socially significant a purchase—such as a car, gift, or jewelry—the more involved a consumer will be with it. (6)

jingle   A radio commercial format in which a song is built around key selling points of a product. (14)

joint venture   An agreement between a foreign company and a local firm to do business together; a method of doing business abroad. (4)

key visual symbol   One frame from a storyboard that encapsulates or sums up the entire commercial visually, perhaps with an enduring visual symbol in it. Also known as a *key visual*. (14)

layout   A piece of artwork or rendering showing how advertising elements—such as headlines, visuals, and photographs—will be arranged in the final printed advertisement. (15)

lead paragraph   In the body copy of an advertisement, this is a transition paragraph that acts as a bridge between the headline and subheads and the rest of the body copy. It continues the main idea and brings the reader into the specific selling points to be covered in the body copy. Also known as the *lead-in*. (14)

learning   The process by which people acquire knowledge and experience that results in a permanent change in behavior. (6)

letterpress printing   A type of printing process that uses a metal or plastic printing plate on which the printing image is raised from the surface. The image on the printing plate must be reverse-reading, because contact between the printing plate and paper will reverse the image. (16)

Library of Congress   Oversees the registration of copyrights in the United States. (3)

licensing   A contractual agreement between a person or company with a brand, trademark, or personality that has sales or promotional value, and another party that wants to use that asset. (12)

lifestyle   A concept that has evolved from personality and values research that describes the patterns in which people live and spend time and money. (6)

lifestyle format   A television commercial format that focuses on the consumer's interests and activities as opposed to the product itself to show how the product fits into that lifestyle. (14)

line art photography   A method of graphic arts photography that converts an image into solid black and white rather than halftone dots. (16)

localized advertising   Specific, tailored advertising and media usage for each market in which the advertised brand is sold. (4)

local partner   A local firm or distributor, or even one individual, who can represent a foreign concern in a local market; the simplest method of doing business abroad. (4)

local station affiliate   A television station in an individual market that agrees to air a network's programs in return for being paid a fixed amount of compensation, including a proportion of the network advertising revenue. (10)

logotype   A symbol or phrase that identifies a brand, a business, or an organization; also known as a *logo*. (15)

make good   Monetary payment or a re-aired TV spot placed at no charge by the media channel as compensation for an ad that did not appear at the agreed-upon date or time. (9)

market research   Marketing research that studies individuals as a purchasing group or market segment; may also compare the profitability of market segments, analyze the total market based on known market segments, or attempt to find new segments in the market. (7)

marketing   The process of planning and executing the conception, pricing, promotion, and distribution of ideas, goods, and services to create exchanges that satisfy individual and organizational objectives. (5)

marketing mix   Four elements—product, place (distribution), price, and promotion—that are combined to create marketing exchange. (5)

marketing public relations   Public relations that help a company's marketing interact better with both its customer and noncustomer bases; often works closely with sales promotion to engineer the push–pull effect. (5, 12)

marketing research   The systematic acquisition, development, and analysis of new information used for marketing, advertising, or marketing communications decisions. (7)

mark-up compensation   An agency compensation method by which the advertiser is charged on a percentage basis for products or services the agency buys or undertakes for the advertiser; commonly used by smaller advertisers or those who work with an agency on a project basis. (2)

Maslow's hierarchy of needs   A hierarchy of five levels of needs developed by Abraham Maslow, starting with basic physiological needs and progressing through safety needs, social needs, esteem or ego needs, and the need for self-actualization; a popular way to classify human motivation and to describe consumer behavior. (6)

mechanical   A layout that has been prepared to meet the printing requirements of a magazine, newspaper, or printer on which the type is pasted into exact position and any special preparations for illustrations or color reproduction are made. Also known as a *pasteup*. (15)

media   The means by which advertising messages are carried to the reading, listening, and viewing public, and by which consumers are informed and entertained. (2)

media audience research   Advertising research that finds media audiences that match the characteristics of the advertiser's target audience by investigating the ability of the media under consideration to reach the target audience. (7)

media buyer   The individual within an advertising agency who negotiates with the media for space and time. (2, 9)

media buying service   A company whose primary purpose is to manage the media buys of advertisers. (2)

media commission   The traditional agency compensation system by which the agency buys time or space in the media for the advertiser and charges the advertiser the full cost of that time or space plus a commission of 15 percent. (2)

media effectiveness   Evaluative advertising research that compares the actual media placement of an advertising message or campaign to the original media plan; in addition, the effectiveness of specific media can be compared to see if one is better at persuading the target audience. (7)

media objective   A statement explaining how to achieve the goals outlined in the media plan; it usually states how many of the target will be exposed to the advertising messages in a given time period, and how often. (9)

media plan   A document that establishes how the media will be used to disseminate an advertiser's message, including objectives and strategy. (9)

media planner   The individual within an advertising agency who puts together a schedule of different media vehicles and determines which ones will best reach the target audience and at what cost. (2, 9)

media planning   One of the major functions within an advertising agency, media planning involves putting together a schedule of different media vehicles and deciding which ones will best reach the target audience at what cost. (9)

media representative   An individual with a media supplier whose job it is to sell the advertising units at the best possible (highest) price to the buyers. (2)

media researcher   The individual within an advertising agency who supports media planners and buyers by conducting research on how people use media. (2)

media strategy   A statement in the media plan that outlines how the objectives will be accomplished; it shows where and when the advertising messages will appear, and at what cost. (9)

media supplier   A service organization that helps the advertiser place a message in the right space or at the right time; usually a supplier provides either media sales or media audience measurement. (2)

media type   A media category, such as television, newspapers, or radio. (9)

media vehicle   The specific television program, radio station, magazine title, etc., that a consumer uses. (9)

merge and purge   In direct mail advertising, the task of combining two or more mailing lists together and then removing the duplicates in order to keep a list current. (12)

message effectiveness   Advertising research that evaluates the communication effect of an advertising message or campaign on the target audience. (7)

message research   Advertising research that examines characteristics of the advertising message and its impact on target audience members before it is run in the media. (7)

message posttesting   Evaluative advertising research that assesses the impact of single advertisements or compares overall campaign results to the objectives of the advertising campaign. (7)

motivation The factors that arouse, maintain, and direct our behavior toward the accomplishment of a goal. (6)

narrative copy A type of advertisement body copy that is used to tell a story to get across the ad's main points. Also known as *story copy*. (14)

National Advertising Division (NAD) Investigates and monitors advertising industry practices; one arm of the National Advertising Review Council. (3)

National Advertising Review Board (NARB) A council made up of 50 representatives from advertisers, agencies, and the general public, NARB reviews advertising-related disputes that are not resolved by the National Advertising Division and presents binding decisions; one arm of the National Advertising Review Council. (3)

National Advertising Review Council (NARC) Formed by the Better Business Bureau and several advertising industry organizations, NARC monitors national advertising and advises advertisers on its findings; consists of the National Advertising Division and the National Advertising Review Board. (3)

National Association of Attorneys General (NAAG) National group of states' attorneys general; has worked to bring actions against advertisers simultaneously in several states, particularly if federal authorities are reluctant to act. (3)

national network radio A type of radio advertising in which an advertiser places a spot with a network of radio stations across the country that are all affiliated with the same company. (10)

news headline A type of advertising headline that plays to people's natural inquisitiveness by promising the reader that there is important information to be found by reading the ad. (14)

newspaper magazine supplement Either nationally syndicated or local, full-color magazines placed in the Sunday newspaper. (11)

observational methods Data collection methods that describe or count overt human behaviors, such as shopping behavior, brand selection, television viewing, or coupon use. (7)

offset lithography printing The most common printing process used by advertisers, offset lithography uses plates that are only slightly raised, rather than etched. The image on the plate is straight-reading instead of reversed because the image is transferred to a rubber drum, or blanket, that transfers the image to paper. (16)

open contract rate Financial terms agreed upon by both the advertiser and advertising agency for purchased space. (2)

open-response question A survey question for which the response from the research participant is not shaped or structured by the question; any answer is allowed. Also known as an *unstructured question*. (7)

opportunistic purchase A method of buying TV time in which the purchase occurs on a week-to-week basis and often consists of program inventory that other advertisers had bought but then canceled; these tend to be cheaper buys, but they also leave the advertiser with little choice in terms of programs or pricing. (10)

out-of-home advertising Media such as billboards, transit advertising, and nontraditional advertising such as that found at sports stadiums and malls that reach their target audience outside the home. (11)

outside variables Part of the natural environment, such as the weather, season, size of market, or competitors' promotional efforts. (7)

overline A type of subheading that appears above a headline as a lead or teaser to get the reader to read the headline. (14)

packaging The physical characteristics of the container that holds a product. (15)

painted bulletin A type of billboard typically measuring 14 feet by 48 feet that displays a message that has been painted on; meant to remain intact for long periods of time, painted bulletins are usually found on major highways advertising hotels, restaurants, or other attractions in upcoming towns on those routes. (11)

Pantone Matching System® (PMS) A system that provides artists with standardized color chips to select and identify ink colors. (16)

passalong audience Readers of a publication who have received it from another person rather than purchasing it; also known as *secondary readers.* (11)

Patent and Trademark Office Established by the 1946 Lanham Act, this office oversees the registration of patents and trademarks in the United States. (3)

people meter A remote control device that automatically records what channel a television set is tuned to; works with a device that people use to record when they start and stop watching TV. (10)

people using television (PUT) The proportion of people with TV sets on at a given time. (10)

perception The process of selecting, organizing, and interpreting information from the environment so that it has personal meaning. (6)

personal selling Person-to-person communication intended to persuade potential customers to buy a company's product or service. (5)

persons using radio (PUR) The proportion of people with radios on at a given time. (10)

pitch A presentation made by an advertising agency to a potential client in the hopes of soliciting its business. (2)

pitch format A radio commercial format in which the copy is read by an announcer with little embellishment from sound effects, music, or voices. (14)

plan on spec A speculative advertising plan put together by an agency for free or for minimal expense in the hopes of winning an advertiser's business. (2)

position The location where an ad will appear within a magazine. (11)

poster panel A type of billboard, poster panels range in size from small 8-sheets found in local neighborhoods to 30-sheets that appear on main arteries of cities. (11)

posting Ensuring that an advertisement ran at the intended, preestablished day and time or position, usually confirmed by affidavit or tearsheet provided by the media. (9)

postproduction stage The third stage of broadcast production, during which elements of the commercial are combined into the finished commercial. (16)

preemptive spot A type of television commercial that is sold with the understanding that another advertiser can come along, offer more money for the spot, and get it. (10)

prepress stage The second stage of print production, prepress operations include graphic arts photography, film assembly or stripping, platemaking, and prepress proofs. (16)

preproduction stage The first stage of broadcast production, during which questions of script, casting, and plans for special production effects are discussed. (16)

press proofs Color proofs taken from the printing press before a press run begins. These proofs are used to make sure that the color and print quality are acceptable, not to check copy accuracy or photographic placement. (16)

presswork stage The third and final stage of print production, presswork includes "pulling" press proofs, printing, cutting and trimming, and binding. (16)

primary data Information or data acquired through original research. (7)

primary readers Readers of a publication who have purchased it themselves. (11)

primary research The systematic search for primary data. (7)

printing flat The assembled artwork from which printing plates are made. (16)

pro bono advertising   Advertising "for the public good" created by agencies for free and placed in media for little or no charge. (3)

production notes   Summaries of the characteristics of the commercial to be produced, including general descriptions of the objectives for the advertising campaign and major copy points, important video needs, audio requirements, and specifications of the time frame and type of materials needed from the studio. (16)

production stage   The second stage of broadcast production, during which the actual video- or audiotaping of commercial elements is done. (16)

product manager   The individual held responsible for the success of a brand or product line. (2)

product positioning   The way a company wants consumers to think of its product or service. (5)

product research   Marketing research that attempts to find answers to questions about the product; often stated relative to the target market segment or consumers. (7)

program rating   The percentage of the population that is tuned to a given television program. (10)

promotional mix   Five elements—advertising, direct marketing, sales promotion, public relations, and personal selling—that marketers combine into an integrated marketing communications program to help them achieve their objectives. (5)

proportion   The relationship in size between elements in an advertisement. (15)

proprietary assets   Assets that are not in the minds of consumers but that are tangible and can be employed to protect brand equity. (5)

"prove what or why" questions   Questions used during causal research to determine cause-and-effect relationships between marketing communications activities and consumer responses. (7)

psychographics   A set of quantitative research procedures that are used to measure lifestyle—values, personality, attitudes, and the like. (6)

publicity   Any attempt by a company to get favorable media coverage of its products, services, causes, or events. The tools of publicity typically include press releases, press conferences, informational items in print or video form, product literature, pamphlets or materials covering broader issues related to a firm's business, celebrity appearances, and company-sponsored events. (5)

public relations   A promotional mix element concerned with how people feel about issues, products, and individual or corporate personalities. (5, 12)

puffery   The practice of using exaggerations in advertising that consumer will know are factually false. (3)

pull strategy   Sales promotions that are designed to pull the product into the distribution pipeline based on consumer demand. (12)

pulsing   A media scheduling pattern in which media activity is maintained for much, if not all, of the year but is supplemented by additional pulses, or bursts, of greater activity at key times. (9)

push strategy   Sales promotions that are designed to push the product into the distribution pipeline based on retailer and distributor demand. (12)

question headline   A type of advertising headline that asks a provocative question to get the reader to read on; can be considered a version of the curiosity headline. (14)

questionnaire   A data collection instrument that guides the questioning of respondents to obtain information from them. The instrument contains the questions to be asked, the order in which the questions will be asked, and instructions for the interviewer or respondent. (7)

random probability sample   A sample in which every person in the population has an equal chance of being selected. (7)

rating point   The percentage of a given population group that uses a specified media vehicle. (9)

reach   The percentage of the target audience that has the opportunity to be exposed one or more times to a specified media vehicle, or media plan, in a given time frame. (9)

readers per copy   The average number of individuals who read a copy of a particular periodical. (11)

reference group   Any group with which a person feels some identification or emotional affiliation and that is used to guide and define his or her beliefs, values, and goals. (6)

refunds and rebates   Consumer sales promotions that allow consumers to get back a portion of the purchase price of an item, usually by sending in proof-of-purchase and a cash-register receipt; often used as early- or late-season incentives to encourage consumers to buy now rather than waiting. (12)

release print   In television production, the approved film commercial that is released to stations for broadcast. (16)

reliability   A characteristic of research design that describes whether the same questions or research techniques, if performed in a similar environment, will produce similar results in the future—in other words, whether the research technique is repeatable. (7)

research design   A plan for research that guides the collection of data and the methods of analysis that will be performed; the three primary types of research design are exploratory, descriptive, and causal. (7)

research objective   Describes the question to be answered, the target audience that will be the focus for the research, and the time frame for the completion of the project. (7)

researcher   The person with an advertising agency who learns as much as possible about how consumers have, do, or will interact with the client's brand and how it fits into their lifestyle. The researcher also assesses how effectively a message is communicated. (2)

resolution   The term that refers to how clear and crisp the printed image will be once all the prepress work is completed and an ad is printed. (16)

retailer promotions   A hybrid form of promotion conducted by the retailer and directed at consumers to persuade them to buy more of the product on sale at the retailer's store. (12)

review   The process that occurs when an advertiser severs ties with the agency and asks several ad agencies to put together a presentation to solicit the advertiser's business. (2)

ride the boards   A method of ensuring that billboards are acceptable to the advertiser wherein the agency or billboard operator escorts the advertiser to each billboard site under contract. (11)

rotogravure printing   A type of printing process that uses plates that are prepared by etching the image into the plate, rather than etching the nonprinting areas. As ink is applied to a rotogravure plate, the plate is wiped and ink remains in the depressed area of the printing plate. (16)

rough layout   A quickly drawn presentation of an ad that uses sketches to represent finished drawings or photographs, penciled-in headlines to show headline placement and lines, and squiggles or unreadable type to represent advertising copy; the purpose of the rough layout is to allow experimentation with and identification of several different ways to communicate the advertising message. (15)

run-of-station spot   A type of television commercial that is sold with the understanding that it may be aired at any time and preempted at any time. (10)

sales promotion   The use of an incentive to buy a product, using either a price reduction or a value-added offer. (5, 12)

sampling (a)   A method of selecting a relatively small number of individuals from a large group, and using information obtained from the small group (the sample) to make predictions about the large group (the population). (7)

sampling (b)   A type of in-store consumer sales promotion that puts the product directly into consumers' hands, allowing them to try it out with little or no risk involved; particularly useful for launching a new product or a line extension. (12)

scatter market   A method of buying TV time that allows the advertiser to make short-term, quarterly purchases at somewhat higher rates and mostly without audience ratings guarantees. (10)

screen printing   A type of printing process that uses stencils made from nylon or stainless steel mesh. Like silk-screen printing used for T-shirts, ink is pressed through the stencil to the paper or object; also known as *serigraphy*. (16)

secondary data   Existing information or data. (7)

secondary readers   Readers of a publication who have received it from another person rather than purchasing it; also known as *passalong audience*. (11)

secondary research   The systematic search of secondary data. (7)

selective binding   A process that allows a magazine to print different issues of the same magazine, altered to suit individual subscribers' needs or preferences. (11)

selective exposure   The process of filtering information and seeking out information that interests us or is related to our needs, and ignoring unrelated stimuli. (6)

selective headline   A type of advertising headline that attracts the reader who has a particular problem, is in a situation, or is the type of person who deliberately has been identified in the headline. (14)

selective perception   The process of modifying or matching new information to the knowledge, experiences, and expectations we already have. (6)

selective recall   The process of remembering only those pieces of information we want to remember. (6)

sensation   The simple and immediate response of our senses to cues from ads, packages, or even brand names; can be influenced by our sensory organs, such as hearing or eyesight, and the actual intensity of stimuli. (6)

sheetfed paper   Paper used for printing that is precut to size. (16)

showing   A number that tells a planner how many boards must be purchased to reach a certain proportion of the population during a specified period of time. (11)

silver prints   A special proof of images made from printing flats for the purpose of checking the placement, orientation, and accuracy of text and photographs; also called *bluelines*. (16)

single source data   The joining of universal product code (UPC) scanner data with television audience meters, creating a single source of data about product use and media audiences. (7)

situation format   A radio commercial format in which the radio spot is based upon a slice-of-life situation that can be anything from gritty-real to fantasy; also known as a *slice-of-life commercial*. (14)

slice-of-life commercial   A radio or television commercial format that is a story or staged playlet that involves characters and the product; also called a *situation format*. (14)

snipe   Special strips found on a poster panel for special or changing messages. (11)

social class   The overall ranking of people in society so that those grouped in the same social class are similar in terms of their social status, occupations, and lifestyles. (6)

song format   A radio commercial format that can either be in the form of a jingle or a donut. (14)

sound masters   In broadcast production, tapes that are reviewed and approved by the advertiser before being duplicated. (16)

sound mixing   In broadcast production, the process of adding sounds and music to the narrative script. (16)

spiff   A type of trade sales promotion in which the manufacturer gives a retail sales person additional money each time he or she makes a sale of the manufacturer's product. (12)

sponsorship   A company paying a set amount of money to have its name or its brand's name placed at the head of an event title or as the designated sponsor of the event. (12)

spot radio   A type of radio advertising in which advertisers buy time in individual markets. (10)

spot television advertising   A television commercial that is sold by an individual station and that runs between programs rather than within them; may be either local or national advertising. (10)

standard advertising units (SAUs)   A system that was introduced in the 1980s to standardize ad sizes in newspapers across the U.S. (11)

standardized advertising   Identical or near-identical advertising and media usage used in every country in which the advertised brand is sold. (4)

Standard Rate & Data Service (SRDS)   A syndicated service that provides all of the ad size requirements and costs for most media, along with a brief editorial description and the names of sales reps to contact. (11)

storyboard   A series of panels or pictures that indicate the main action of a commercial ac-companied by written descriptions of what is in the panels (video) and what will be heard (audio). (14)

straightforward copy   A type of advertisement body copy that follows through on the main idea as expressed in the headline and illustration. The goal is to stay on track with the headline idea and expand upon it by getting more and more specific until right before the end of the ad. The closing will then offer a summation of the copy points. (14)

strategic advertising research   Research that is performed during the planning stages of a marketing communications or advertising campaign. (7)

stratified random sample   A sample that divides the population into groups or strata and then selects individuals at random. (7)

stripping   The process of joining negatives and attaching them to the printing flat. (16)

structured observational method   A data collection instrument in which preestablished categories of behavior, such as a form with predetermined categories of choices, are used. (7)

subculture   Smaller social groups within a culture based on age, race, ethnicity, gender, religion, geographic region, language, and lifestyles; distinguished from a larger culture of which it is a part by having beliefs, values, and customs that are unique to it. (6)

subheading   An organizational heading used to break up the body copy into more digestible bites for the reader and to emphasize important points in the copy; usually indicated in bold type or type slightly larger than the body copy. (14)

subsidiary   A foreign-owned office in another country, staffed primarily by its own personnel. (4)

sweeps   Four, four-week measurement periods (February, May, July, and November) during which Nielsen viewing diary and TV set meter measurements are taken. (10)

sweepstakes A type of consumer sales promotion that is completely random, offering prizes based solely on chance. (12)

syndicated programming A show produced by a company and then sold by that company directly to individual stations in each market. (10)

syndicated supplier A company that collects competitive expenditure and audience information and then sells it to advertisers, agencies, and media. (2)

tagline A memorable line or phrase that is repeated in all ads in a campaign to provide continuity from one ad to the next, it also summarizes the major selling premise of the ad and campaign; also known as a *slogan*. (14)

target audience The group of individuals for whom an advertising campaign or media plan is specifically devised, as defined by demographic, lifestyle, and psychographic characteristics. (9, 13)

target audience analysis Advertising research that attempts to identify the target audience, describe its characteristics, and examine the audience's consumption and media habits. (7)

target definition The definition of the target audience as perceived by the advertiser and syndicated research sources. (9)

telemarketing The sale of products or services through direct communication with the customer over the telephone. (12)

telepromotions Automatic calls made in quick succession in order to make a sale. (12)

television director The person who is responsible for the direction of talent and technical staff as they convert a storyboard into film or videotape, and who oversees the editing process until the final commercial is produced. (16)

television producer The person who is responsible for overseeing scheduling for people and studio time, budgeting, and monitoring the costs of production. (16)

testimonial Advertising in which a celebrity or product user endorses a given brand. (3)

time spent listening (TSL) The number of minutes people spend listening to a particular station; (number of quarter-hours in daypart × average quarter-hour audience)/total audience size. (10)

third person effect The name given to the claim some people make that they themselves are unaffected by advertising. (3)

thumbnail sketch The first step in the process of designing print advertisements; a small rough sketch that allows designers to create and experiment with many design ideas before committing to a particular design approach. (15)

trade ad Advertising used by firms to promote themselves to others in the advertising industry. (2)

trade allowance A special deal or price that the manufacturer offers in order to persuade the retailer to purchase larger quantities of the product; also used to entice the trade to feature a given brand in the retailer's own marketing efforts, whether advertising or promotion. (12)

trade promotions Sales promotions that work by offering incentives to retailers and distributors, such as additional discounts or deals, so that they will buy more from the manufacturer than they usually do to take advantage of the incentive. (5, 12)

trademark Any word, symbol, or device that is adopted and used by a manufacturer or merchant to identify his or her goods and distinguish them from those manufactured by others. (3)

trade regulation rules Issued by the Federal Trade Commission, these rules encompass the Commission's conclusions concerning unlawful trade practices, typically for an entire industry. (3)

transit advertising Advertising placed on buses and trains or at transit stations, platforms, or terminals. (11)

trim size   The actual size of an advertisement or brochure. (16)

turnover   A measure of how frequently a station's audience changes; the ratio of the cume audience to the average quarter-hour audience. (10)

typeface   A complete set of letters in one size and face; also known as a *font*. (15)

underdeveloped market   A country with a lack of industrialized development due to unstable or unsuitable internal conditions or its small size and lack of attention from foreign marketers. (4)

underline   A type of subheading that appears after or just under a headline as a transition into the body copy. (14)

unstructured observational method   A data collection instrument in which the researcher describes human behavior as it occurs. (7)

validity   A characteristic of research design that describes how consistent a research design or data collection technique is with known facts, or how logically consistent the research design or data collection technique is; three types are face validity, external validity, and internal validity. (7)

Values and Life-Styles (VALS)   A popular lifestyle and psychographic tool developed as a combination of Maslow's hierarchy of needs and the inner- and outer-directed categorization of people developed by sociologist David Reisman. (6)

viewing share   The proportion of all TV sets that are on at a given time and are tuned to a particular show; also known as *audience share*. (10)

visualization   The formation of a mental image of an ad. (14)

web-fed paper   A continuous sheet of paper on a roll that is cut after it has been printed. (16)

Web site   A series of screens or pages with an Internet address, organized to allow the Internet user to move through them in an easy and organized manner. (14)

white space   The blank areas in a print advertisement layout; large areas of white space can convey richness, openness, exclusivity, or simplicity in a message, while little use of white space can create excitement and curiosity. (15)

zone   A different geographic version of a newspaper. (11)

Endnotes

Chapter 1

1. David Woodruff, James B. Treece, Sunita Wadekar Bhargava, and Karen Lowry, "Saturn, GM Finally Has a Real Winner, but Success is Bringing a Fresh Batch of Problems," *Business Week*, 17 August 1992, 85–91.
2. David A. Aaker, "Building a Brand: The Saturn Story," *California Management Review* 36, no. 2 (Winter 1994): 114–133.
3. *Saturn Mission and Philosophy Card* (Spring Hill, TN: Saturn Corporation, 1990).
4. Aaker, "Building a Brand."
5. Raymond Serafin, "The Saturn Story," *Advertising Age*, 16 November 1992, 1, 13, 16.
6. Serafin, "The Saturn Story."
7. Serafin, "The Saturn Story."
8. Aaker, "Building a Brand."
9. Aaker, "Building a Brand."
10. *Saturn Communications Strategy* (Spring Hill, TN: Saturn Corporation, 1992).
11. David A. Aaker, *Building Strong Brands* (New York: The Free Press, 1996), 52.
12. Valerie Reitman, "Setting Sights on Saturn," *Asian Wall Street Journal Weekly*, 10 March 1997, 16.
13. Raymond Serafin, "Saturn Looks East with DIK," *Advertising Age*, 11 December 1995, 1, 41.
14. Aaker, *Building Strong Brands*, 60.
15. Jean Halliday, "Saturn's New Ads Aim at Younger Buyers, Men," *Advertising Age*, 1 September 1997, 4, 35.

Chapter 2

1. U.S. Bureau of Labor Statistics, "Monthly Labor Review, November 1995," in Bureau of the Census, *Statistical Abstract of the United States, 1996* (Washington, DC: U.S. Government Printing Office, 1996), 411.
2. U.S. Bureau of Labor Statistics, "Monthly Labor Review, November 1995," 411.
3. "Why Advertise: The Value of Advertising," supplement to *The Wall Street Journal*, June 1991.
4. Peter D. Bennett, ed., *Dictionary of Marketing Terms*, 2nd ed. (Lincolnwood, IL: NTC Publishing, 1995), 6.
5. Adrienne Ward Fawcett, ed., "The Marketing 100," *Advertising Age*, 4 July 1994, S1–S29.
6. American Association of Advertising Agencies, "What Every Account Executive Should Know about Account Planning," *Agency*, Fall 1994, 43.
7. "See What Develops," Special Planning Section, *Adweek*, 5 August 1996, 10.
8. John Wolfe, "Account Planning Moves Up Its Forces," *Agency*, Fall 1994, 39–43.
9. "The Affordable Luxury Car," Special Planning Section, *Adweek*, 5 August 1996, 15.
10. Jeanne Whalen, Gary Levin, and Melanie Weeks, "Ammirati's Big Win: It's a $180M Whopper," *Advertising Age*, 28 March 1994, I40–I41.
11. Fara Warner, "High Cost of Vying for Kmart Job is Creating Some Risk for Agencies," *The Wall Street Journal*, 10 February 1995, B7.
12. Veronica Byrd and Wendy Zellnar, "The Avon Lady of the Amazon," *Business Week*, 24 October 1994, 93–96; and

Alessandra Stanley, "The New Face of Russian Capitalism," *New York Times*, 14 August 1996, C1, C16.
13. Bradley Johnson, "For Computer Giants It Really Is a Small World," *Advertising Age*, 14 November 1994, S2.
14. Anne-Marie Crawford, "Master Craftsmen," *Media International*, January 1995, 32.
15. Dierdre Carmody, "U.S. Business Magazines Thriving on Foreign Ads," *New York Times*, 16 January 1995, C6.

Chapter 3

1. James W. Carey, "Advertising: An Institutional Approach," in *The Role of Advertising*, eds. Charles H. Sandage and Vernon Fryburger (Homewood, IL: Richard D. Irwin, 1960), 3–17.
2. Vincent P. Norris, "Advertising History—According to the Textbooks," *Journal of Advertising* 9, no. 3 (1980): 3–11.
3. David Potter, *People of Plenty* (Chicago: University of Chicago Press, 1954).
4. Carey, "Advertising: An Institutional Approach."
5. David Potter, *People of Plenty*.
6. Charles H. Sandage, "Some Institutional Aspects of Advertising," *Journal of Advertising* 1, no. 1 (1972): 6–9.
7. Glenn Collins, "Jordan Again Leads Athlete-Endorsers," *New York Times*, 30 August 1996, D6.
8. Mark Rechtin, "Lexus Remains Customer Satisfaction Leader; Domestics Gain in Power Survey," *Automotive News*, 12 July 1993, 16.
9. Michael Wilke, "Subaru Adds Lesbians to Niche Marketing Drive," *Advertising*

Age, 4 March 1996, 8.

10. Laura Heller, "Target Your Market," *Grocery Marketing,* June 1996, 24–27.

11. Sir Michael Perry, "Perry's Case for Advertising," speech reproduced in *Campaign,* 7 June 1996, 34–35.

12. *Children's Television Act of 1990,* P.L. 101-437, 104 Stat. 996 (18 October 1990).

13. Nielsen Media Research, *National Audience Demographic Report,* February 1995.

14. Barry Temkin and V. Dion Haynes, "Schools Open Door to Business," *Chicago Tribune,* 24 September 1995, 1,18.

15. Lawrence Bowen and Jill Schmid, "Minority Presence and Portrayal in Mainstream Magazine Advertising: An Update," in *Proceedings of the American Academy of Advertising Conference: 1995* (Norfolk, VA: American Academy of Advertising, 1995), 12.

16. U.S. Bureau of the Census, *Statistical Abstract of the United States,* 13th ed. (Washington, DC: U.S. Government Printing Office, 1995).

17. George M. Zinkhan, William J. Qualls, and Abhijit Biswas, "Use of Blacks in Magazine and Television Advertising: 1946 to 1986," *Journalism Quarterly* 67, no. 3 (Autumn 1990): 547–553; and Robert E. Wilkes and Humberto Valencia, "Hispanics and Blacks in Television Commercials," *Journal of Advertising* 18, no. 1 (1989): 19–25.

18. Tommy E. Whittler and Joan DiMeo, "Viewers' Reactions to Racial Cues in Advertising Stimuli," *Journal of Advertising* Research, December 1991, 37–46.

19. Eric Clark, The Want Makers (New York, Viking Press, 1988), 119.

20. Anthony G. Greenwald, Sean C. Draine, and Richard L. Abrams, "Three Cognitive Markers of Unconscious Semantic Activation," Science 273 (September 1996): 1699–1702.

21. Martin P. Block and Bruce G. Vanden Bergh, "Can You Sell Subliminal Messages to Consumers?" *Journal of Advertising* 14, no. 3 (1985): 59–62; Sharon E. Beatty and Del I. Hawkins, "Subliminal Stimulation: Some New Data and Interpretation," *Journal of Advertising* 18,

no. 1 (1989): 4–8; and Timothy E. Moore, "Subliminal Advertising: What You See Is What You Get," *Journal of Marketing* 46 (Spring 1982): 38–57.

22. Lee Benham, "The Effect of Advertising on the Price of Consumer Goods," *Journal of Marketing* 44 (Summer 1980): 17–35.

23. James B. Twitchell, *ADCULT USA: The Triumph of Advertising in American Culture* (New York: Columbia University Press, 1996), 117–118.

24. *Competitive Media Reporting,* 1994.

25. *Competitive Media Reporting,* 1994.

26. From the Web site of the Advertising Council (http://www.adcouncil.org), 1996.

27. Florence Fabricant, "The Geography of Taste," *New York Times Magazine,* 10 March 1996, 40–41.

28. Judann Pollack, "Rally's Big Buford Ads Stir Small Controversy," *Advertising Age,* 4 March 1996, 12.

29. John Darton, "Skeletal Models Create Furor over British *Vogue,*" *New York Times,* 3 June 1996, C2.

30. Tony L. Henthorne, Michael S. LaTour, and Rajan Nataraajan, "Fear Appeals in Print Advertising: An Analysis of Arousal and Ad Response," *Journal of Advertising* 22, no. 2 (June 1993): 59–68; Ronald Paul Hill, "An Exploration of the Relationship between AIDS-Related Anxiety and the Evaluation of Condom Advertisements," *Journal of Advertising* 17, no. 4 (1988): 35–42; and Valerie Quinn, Tony Meenaghan, and Teresa Brannick, "Fear Appeals: Segmentation Is the Way to Go," *International Journal of Advertising* 11 (1992): 355–366.

31. Nathaniel C. Nash, "Benetton Touches a Nerve and Germans Protest," *New York Times,* 3 February 1995, D1.

32. Stefano Hatfield, "Should Brand Advertising Address Social Issues?" *Campaign,* 6 October 1995, **11.**

33. "Vatican Stresses Need for Moral Advertising," *Advertising Age,* 10 March 1997, 26.

34. Stuart Elliott, "Liquor Industry Ends Its Ad Ban in Broadcasting," *New York Times,* 8 November 1996, A1, C5.

35. Robin Pogrebin, "By Design or Not,

an Ad Becomes a Fad," *New York Times,* 24 December 1995, 3.

36. Seth Schiesel, "On Web, New Threats Seen to the Young," *New York Times,* 7 March 1997, A1, C2.

37. Pogrebin, "By Design or Not."

38. Matthew L. Wald, "Group Says Alcohol-Related Traffic Deaths Are Rising," *New York Times,* 27 November 1996, A11.

39. Stephen Chapman, "Who Will Lose from the New Legal Attacks on Cigarette-Makers?" *Chicago Tribune,* 9 April 1995, sec. 4, 2.

40. Mike France, "The World War on Tobacco," *Business Week,* 11 November 1996, 99–100.

41. Alan T. Shao and John S. Hill, "Global Television Advertising Restrictions: The Case of Socially Sensitive Products," *International Journal of Advertising* 13 (1994): 347–366.

42. "Canada Lights Up with Tobacco Ads," *Promo,* January 1996, 52.

43. Stephanie Bentley, "Stubbing Out Advertising," *Marketing Week,* 5 January 1996, 18–21.

44. Wally Snyder, "Why We Must Defend Tobacco Ads," letter to the editor in *Advertising Age,* 13 November 1995, 12.

45. Paul W. Farris and Mark S. Albion, "The Impact of Advertising on the Price of Consumer Products," *Journal of Marketing* 44 (Summer 1980): 17–35.

46. 316 U.S. 52, 62 S. Ct. 920, 86 L. Ed. 1262 (1942).

47. *New York Times* v Sullivan, 376 U.S. 254, 84 S. Ct. (1964).

48. *Pittsburgh Press v Pittsburgh Commission on Human Relations,* 413 U.S. 376 (1973).

49. *Pittsburgh Press v Pittsburgh Commission on Human Relations.*

50. *Bigelow v Virginia,* 421 U.S. 809 (1975).

51. 425 U.S. 748, 96 S. Ct. 1817, 48, L. Ed. 2d 346 (1976).

52. 447 U.S. 557, 100 S. Ct. 2343, 65 L. Ed. 2d 341 (1980).

53. *City of Cincinnati v Discovery Network, Inc.,* 1993 U.S. 113 S. Ct. (1993).

54. *44 Liquormart et al. v Rhode Island,* 116 S. Ct. 1495 (1996).

55. Howard Rheingold, *The Virtual*

Community: Homesteading on the Electronic Frontier (Reading, MA: Addison-Wesley Publishing, 1996).

56. Judann Pollack, "Prego Prevails in Battle over Comparative Ad," *Advertising Age*, 16 September 1996, 12.

57. In regards to *Cooga Mooga, Inc.*, 92 F.T.C. 310 (1978), as cited in Dean K. Fueroghne, *Law & Advertising* (Chicago: The Copy Workshop, 1995).

58. Andrea Sachs, "High Court's Ruling May Color Ad Plans," *Advertising Age*, 10 April 1995, 30.

59. From the Web site of The Better Business Bureau (http://www.bbb.org).

60. Sally D. Goll, "Chinese Officials Attempt to Ban False Ad Claims," *The Wall Street Journal*, 28 February 1995, B1, B9.

61. As of 1 January 1995, three new members joined the European Union: Sweden, Finland, and Austria.

Chapter 4

1. Tom Post and Steven Strasser, "No Free Lunches Here," *Newsweek*, 20 February 1995, 39–40.

2. Amy Barrett, "It's a Small Business World," *Business Week*, 17 April 1995, 96–101.

3. Andrew Geddes, "Mind Your Language," *Media International*, September 1994, 14–16.

4. Theodore Levitt, "The Globalization of Markets," *Harvard Business Review* 61 (May–June 1983): 92–102.

5. Stefano Hatfield, "Ads Cut from the Same Cloth," *Campaign*, 25 September 1992, 37–38.

6. Alex Benady, "A Tribute to the Old Campaigner," *The Times* (London), 30 October 1996, 23.

7. Jeff Jensen, "Marketer of the Year," *Advertising Age*, 16 December 1996, 1, 16.

8. Alecia Swazy, *Soap Opera: The Inside Story of Procter & Gamble* (New York: Times Books, 1994), 289.

9. Lenore Skenazy, "How Does Slogan Translate?" *Advertising Age*, 12 October 1987, 84.

10. Charles R. Wiles, Judith A. Wiles, and Anders Tjernlund, "The Ideology of Advertising: The United States and Sweden," *Journal of Advertising Research* 36, no. 3 (May–June 1996): 57–66.

11. Jyotika Ramaprasad and Kazumi Hasegawa, "An Analysis of Japanese Television Commercials," *Journalism Quarterly* 69, no. 2 (Spring 1992): 612–622; Barbara Mueller, "Reflections on Culture: An Analysis of Japanese and American Advertising Appeals," *Journal of Advertising Research*, June–July 1987, 51–59; and Carolyn A. Lin, "Cultural Differences in Message Strategies: A Comparison between American and Japanese Television Commercials," *Journal of Advertising Research* 33, no. 3 (May–June 1993): 40–48.

12. Marc G. Weinberger and Harlan E. Spotts, "Humor in U.S. versus U.K. TV Commercials: A Comparison," *Journal of Advertising* 18, no. 2 (1989): 39–44.

13. Belinda Archer, "Does Humour Cross Borders?" *Campaign*, 17 June 1994, 32–33.

14. Ullrich Appelbaum and Chris Halliburton, "How to Develop International Advertising Campaigns That Work: The Example of the European Food and Beverage Sector," *International Journal of Advertising* 12 (1993): 223–241.

15. Penelope Rowlands, "Global Approach Doesn't Always Make Scents," *Advertising Age*, 17 January 1994, I1, I38.

16. Joji Sakurai, "Fashioning a Success," *Marketing and Media Europe*, April 1996, 48–49.

17. Thomas L. Friedman, "Big Mac I," *New York Times*, 8 November 1996, A15; and Thomas L. Friedman, "Big Mac II," *New York Times*, 11 November 1996, A21.

18. Alasdair Reid, "Where to Draw the Line?" *Media International*, May 1995, 36.

19. Stuart Elliott, "The Media Business," *New York Times*, 5 January 1995, C4.

20. *Reader's Digest* Eurodata Study, 1989.

21. Laurel Wentz, "Major Global Study Finds Consumers Support Ads," *Advertising Age*, 11 October 1993, I1, I21.

22. Internal sources, DDB Needham Worldwide, 1995.

23. Internal sources, DDB Needham Worldwide, 1995.

24. Alessandra Stanley, "On Russian TV, Sincerest Form of Frivolity," *New York Times*, 12 January 1997, 1, 4.

25. Wayne Walley, "'Sesame Street' Characters Known Worldwide," *Electronic Media*, 24 April 1995, 23.

26. Wayne Walley, "Europeans Put Local Spin on Formats," *Electronic Media*, 14 February 1994, 24.

27. Stephen Armstrong, "Battle Stations," *Marketing and Media Europe*, February 1995, 29.

28. Charles Haddad, "Turner's Epic Expansion Overseas," *International Cable*, April 1995, 30–40.

29. John A. Quelch and Lisa R. Klein, "The Internet and International Marketing," *Sloan Management Review*, Spring 1996, 60–75.

30. Ingrid Lyon, "Trouble with Eric," *Media International*, November 1995, 55.

31. Andrew Geddes, "Confusion over China's Ad Laws," *Media International*, April 1995, 5.

32. Laurel Wentz, "Spanning the World, without a Net," *Advertising Age*, 12 June 1995, 12.

Chapter 5

1. Thomas R. Duncan and Stephen E. Everett, "Client Perceptions of Integrated Marketing Communications," *Journal of Advertising Research*, May/June 1993, 31.

2. DDB Needham Worldwide, *Media Trends 1997*, 9.

3. Rick Fizdale, "Paid Media in the Age of Information," unpublished Speech, Leo Burnett USA, 13 September 1993.

4. Jeff Jensen, "ESPN Adding B3 Games for Extreme Sports," *Advertising Age*, 2 June 1997, 22.

5. David A. Aaker, *Managing Brand Equity* (New York: The Free Press, 1991), 7–16.

6. Aaker, *Managing Brand Equity*, 39.

7. Aaker, *Managing Brand Equity*, 21.

8. Peter D. Bennett, ed., *American Marketing Association Dictionary of Marketing Terms*, 2nd ed. (Lincolnwood, IL: NTC Business Books, 1995), 166.

9. Michelle Conlin, "Keep It Simple. Keep It Cheap," *Forbes*, 16 June 1997, 81–82.

10. James S. Norris, *Public Relations* (Englewood Cliffs, NJ: Prentice-Hall, 1984).

11. Georg Kacher, "The Beetle is Back," *Automobile Magazine*, June 1997, 57–61.

12. Kerry Smith, "Introduction and Overview," in *Sales Promotion Handbook*, 8th ed., eds. Tamara Brezen Block and William A. Robinson (Chicago: Dartnell Press, 1994), 5.

13. Kenneth Roman and Jane Maas, *The New How to Advertise* (New York: St. Martin's Press, 1992), 59.

14. Bob Stone, *Successful Direct Marketing Methods*, 5th ed. (Lincolnwood, IL: NTC Business Books, 1994), 79–81.

15. Don E. Schultz, "Four Basic Rules Lay Groundwork for Integration," *Marketing News*, 16 August 1993, 13.

16. Tom Duncan, "Integrated Marketing? It's Synergy," *Advertising Age*, 8 March 1993, 22.

17. This section is adapted from Don E. Schultz, Stanley I. Tannenbaum, and Robert F. Lauterborn, *Integrated Marketing Communications* (Lincolnwood, IL: NTC Business Books, 1993), 70–86.

18. Michael E. Porter, *Competitive Advantage: Creating and Sustaining Superior Performance* (New York: The Free Press, 1985), 12.

19. Theodore Levitt, *The Marketing Imagination* (New York: The Free Press, 1986), 141–172.

Chapter 6

1. Abraham Maslow, *Motivation and Personality*, 2nd ed. (New York: Harper & Row Publishers, 1970), 35–58.

2. Robert B. Settle and Pamela L. Alreck, *Why They Buy: American Consumers Inside and Out* (New York: John Wiley & Sons, 1989), 24–27.

3. Arthur S. Reeber, *The Penguin Dictionary of Psychology*, 2nd ed. (London: Penguin Group, 1995), 411–412.

4. Leon G. Schiffman and Leslie Lazar Kanuk, *Consumer Behavior*, 5th ed. (Englewood Cliffs, NJ: Prentice-Hall, 1994), 205.

5. Schiffman and Kanuk, *Consumer Behavior*, 205.

6. J. Paul Peter and Jerry C. Olson, *Consumer Behavior and Marketing Strategy*, 3rd ed. (Homewood, IL: Richard D. Irwin, 1993), 59.

7. James F. Engel, Roger D. Blackwell, and Paul W. Miniard, *Consumer Behavior*, 7th ed. (Fort Worth, TX: The Dryden Press, 1993), 275–277.

8. Alice E. Eagly and Shelly Chaiken, *The Psychology of Attitudes* (Fort Worth, TX: Harcourt Brace Jovanovich, 1993), 103.

9. Judith E. Nichols, *By the Numbers* (Chicago: Bonus Books Inc., 1990), 3.

10. J. Walker Smith and Ann Clurman, *Rocking the Ages* (New York: Harper Business, 1997).

11. Smith and Clurman, *Rocking the Ages*, 8.

12. Smith and Clurman, *Rocking the Ages*, 9–11.

13. Smith and Clurman, *Rocking the Ages*, 9–11.

14. Brad Edmondson, "The Big Picture," *American Demographics Desk Reference Series*, June 1991, 4–5.

15. Brad Edmondson, "The Minority Majority in 2001," *American Demographics*, October 1996, 16–17.

16. "Tabbing the Tube," *Minority Markets Alert*, September 1992.

17. Brad Edmondson, "Black America in 2001," *American Demographics*, November 1996, 14–15.

18. Kathy Bodovitz, "Black America," *American Demographics Desk References Series*, June 1991, 8–10.

19. "The Gray Matter," *SportStyle*, 11 May 1992, 15.

20. Dina Long, "Adventure Products More in Demand among Seniors," *Tour & Travel News*, 7 September 1992, 14.

21. Frank F. Furstenberg, Jr., "The Future of Marriage," *American Demographics*, June 1996, 37.

22. Engel, Blackwell, and Miniard, *Consumer Behavior*, 677.

23. Engel, Blackwell, and Miniard, *Consumer Behavior*, 369.

24. Martha Farnsworth Riche, "VALS2," *American Demographics*, July 1989, 25.

25. "The Changing American Household," *American Demographics Desk Reference Series*, July 1992, 2–3.

26. Ronald D. Michman, "The Male Queue at the Checkout Counter," *Business Horizons* 29, no. 3 (May/June 1986): 51–55.

27. "Children's Meals: Pathway to Profits," *Restaurant Management* 1, no. 5 (May 1987): 69–70.

28. Michael R. Solomon, *Consumer Behavior*, 3rd ed. (Englewood Cliffs, NJ: Prentice-Hall, 1996), 368.

29. Reeber, *The Penguin Dictionary of Psychology*, 646–647.

30. William O. Bearden and Michael J. Etzel, "Reference Group Influence on Product and Brand Purchase Decisions," *Journal of Consumer Research* 9 (September 1982): 185.

31. Solomon, *Consumer Behavior*, 660.

32. Donald Parente, Bruce Vanden Bergh, Arnold Barban, and James Marra, *Advertising Campaign Strategy* (Fort Worth, TX: The Dryden Press, 1996), 64.

33. Schiffman and Kanuk, *Consumer Behavior*, 409.

34. E. Jerome McCarthy and William D. Perreault, Jr., *Basic Marketing*, 10th ed. (Homewood, IL: Richard D. Irwin, 1990), 184.

Chapter 7

1. Bruce Horowitz, "Fake Fat's Big Test: OLESTRA," *USA Today*, 19 June 1997, 1B–2B.

2. "50 Years of Insights," *Information Interpretation: The Rise of Market Research* (London: Market Research Society in association with *Campaign*, October 1996), 8–9.

3. David A. Aaker, V. Kumar, and George S. Day, *Marketing Research*, 5th ed. (New York: John Wiley & Sons, 1995), 42–55.

4. Aaker, Kumar, and Day, *Marketing Research*, 277.

5. Aaker, Kumar, and Day, *Marketing Research*, 345–347.

6. Dave Kruegel, "Television Advertising Effectiveness and Research Innovation," *Journal of Consumer Marketing* 5, no. 3 (Summer 1988): 43–51.

7. Alan D. Fletcher and Thomas A. Bowers, *Fundamentals of Advertising Research*, 4th ed. (Belmont, CA: Wadsworth Publishing, 1991), 126–128.

8. Lynn G. Coleman, "Researchers Say Nonresponse Is Single Biggest Problem," *Marketing News*, 7 January 1991, 32–33; and Robin Cobb, "Researching for an Answer," *Marketing News*, 27 February 1992, 25, 27.

9. Gilbert A. Churchill, *Marketing Research: Methodological Foundations*, 6th ed. (Fort Worth, TX: The Dryden Press, 1995), 381–382.

10. Aaker, Kumar, and Day, *Marketing Research*, 190.

11. John L. Palshaw, "Using Marketing Research Effectively for Launching New Products," *Medical Marketing & Media*, 1 September 1991, 60–64.

12. David Schwartz, *Concept Testing* (New York: AMACOM, 1987), 4–9.

13. Russell I. Haley and Allan L. Baldinger, "The ARF Copy Research Validity Project," *Journal of Advertising Research*, April/May 1991, 11–32.

14. The PACT Agencies, "PACT: Positioning Advertising Copy Testing," *Journal of Advertising* 11, no. 4 (1982): 3–29.

15. "A Moment-to-Moment Method of Finding One Magic Moment," *Marketing: Canada's Weekly Newspaper of Marketing Communications*, 12 December 1988, 46–48; and "Response Analyzer Designed to Enhance Focus Groups," *Marketing News*, 2 January 1987, 38.

16. Ian Fenwick and Marshall D. Rice, "Reliability of Continuous Measurement Copy-Testing Methods," *Journal of Advertising Research* 31, no. 1 (February/ March 1991): 23–29.

17. Erwin Ephron, "How to Curb TV's Sweeps Ratings Game," *Advertising Age*, 3 February 1997, 30.

18. "Arbitron to Discontinue ScanAmerica Network Rating Service," *PR Newswire*, 2 September 1992, 1.

Chapter 8

1. Peter D. Bennett, ed., *American Marketing Association Dictionary of Marketing Terms*, 2nd ed. (Lincolnwood, IL: NTC Business Books, 1995), 276.

2. Bennett, *Dictionary of Marketing Terms*, 276.

3. John R. Rossiter and Larry Percy, *Advertising Communications Management*, 2nd ed. (New York: McGraw-Hill, 1997), 26.

4. Rossiter and Percy, *Advertising Communications Management*, 26.

5. James F. Engel, Martin R. Warshaw, and Thomas C. Kinnear, *Promotional Strategy: Managing the Marketing Communications Process*, 8th ed. (Burr Ridge, IL: Richard D. Irwin, 1994), 146.

6. Ronald B. Lieber, "Out of the Box," *Fortune*, 23 June 1997, 76.

7. Michael E. Porter, "What Is Strategy?" *Harvard Business Review*, November– December 1996, 61–78.

8. Engel, Warshaw, and Kinnear, *Promotional Strategy*, 162.

9. Engel, Warshaw, and Kinnear, *Promotional Strategy*, 162.

10. Russell H. Colley, *Defining Advertising Goals for Measured Advertising Results* (New York: Association of National Advertisers, 1961). A revised version of Colley's book has been published: Solomon Dutka, *Defining Advertising Goals for Measured Advertising Results* (Lincolnwood, IL: NTC Business Books, 1995).

11. This section is based in part on Donald Parente, Bruce Vanden Bergh, Arnold Barban, and James Marra, *Advertising Campaign Strategy: A Guide to Marketing Communication Plans* (Fort Worth: The Dryden Press, 1996), 98–102.

12. Porter, "What Is Strategy?" 64.

13. Porter, "What Is Strategy?" 64; and Al Ries, *Focus: The Future of Your Company Depends on It* (New York: Harper-Business, 1996), 120–123.

14. Al Ries and Jack Trout, *Positioning: The Battle for Your Mind* (New York: McGraw-Hill, 1986).

15. Rajeev Batra, John G. Myers, and David A. Aaker, *Advertising Management*, 5th ed. (Upper Saddle River, NJ: Prentice-Hall, 1996), 191.

16. Emory Thomas Jr., "Crush of Olympic Sponsors Inspires Efforts to Break out from the Pack," *The Wall Street Journal*, 15 July 1996, B1, B3.

17. Adapted from David W. Nylen, *Advertising*, 4th ed. (Cincinnati, OH: South-Western, 1993), 279–282.

Chapter 9

1. Tracey Taylor, "Space Invaders," *Marketing & Media Europe*, March 1995, 22–23.

2. Judann Pollack, "Magazines Reap Thanksgiving Harvest of Ads," *Advertising Age*, 4 November 1996, 28.

3. Barney H. McClure, "The Vanishing Off-Season," *Supermarket Business*, January 1995, 102–103.

4. From the DDB Needham Life Style Study, which is discussed in more detail in Chapter 6.

5. Taylor, "Space Invaders."

6. Sue Haggerty, "The Four Ps of Planning," *Inside Media*, 17 July 1996, 30.

7. Taylor, "Space Invaders."

8. Mark Hudis, "It's in the Bag," *MediaWeek*, 27 June 1994, S12–S13.

9. John Philip Jones, *When Ads Work* (New York: Lexington Books, 1996).

Chapter 10

1. Anthony Ramirez, "TV–Phone Link: Long Way to Go," *New York Times*, 2 November 1991, 37.
2. Debra Aho Williamson and Scott Donaton, "Time Warner's Orlando Fire Sale," *Advertising Age*, 26 September 1994, 13–15.
3. Joel Brinkley, "Building Your Next TV: Two Industries Fight for a $150 Billion Prize," *New York Times*, 28 March 1997, C1.
4. Michael Lindsay, "Home Shopping Operators Go for Worldwide Growth," in *Making Sense of the Digital Planet*, supplement to *Media International*, September 1995.
5. Jon Hilsenrath, "In China, a Taste of Buy-Me TV," *New York Times*, 17 November 1996, sec. 3, 1, 11.
6. For more information on the technicalities of radio broadcasting, see Bob Schulberg, *Radio Advertising* (Lincolnwood, IL: NTC Business Books, 1989).
7. Geraldine Fabrikant, "The Young and Restless Audience," *New York Times*, 8 April 1996, C1, C8.

Chapter 11

1. Robin Pogrebin, "Extending the Brand Name," *New York Times*, 18 November 1996, C1, C8.
2. Magazine Publishers of America, *The Magazine Handbook 1996/97* (New York: Magazine Publishers of America, 1997), 50.
3. Ernest Lupinacci and Bob Moore, "Marathon Runners and Couch Potatoes," in *The Power of Print*, supplement to *Adweek*, 20 May 1996, 29.
4. *The Family Circle Study of Print Advertising Effectiveness* (New York: New York Times Company Magazine Group, 1991).
5. "Raising the Roof on Route 40," *Inside Out of Home*, July 1996, 3.

Chapter 12

1. Carol Wright Survey of Promotional Practices, 1996.
2. Point of Purchase Advertising Institute (POPAI), *POPAI Consumer Buying Habits Study* (Englewood, NJ: POPAI, 1996).
3. "Spotlight: 1995 APMA Awards," *PROMO's Annual Sourcebook '97*, 196.
4. Marcia Mogelonsky, *Everybody Eats* (Ithaca, NY: American Demographics Books, 1994), 30; and Dan Hanover, "Going Places," *Promo*, 27 April 1997, 20–34.
5. "Coupon Watch," *Promo*, May 1995, 105.
6. Don E. Schultz and William A. Robinson, *Sales Promotions Essentials* (Lincolnwood, IL: NTC Business Books, 1992), 28.
7. Pete Burgess, "The Buddy System," *Direct*, April 1997, 83–84.
8. "The New Electronic Warfare," *Supermarket Business*, May 1995, 27.
9. Stephen Downer, "Coupon FSIs Dropped," *Advertising Age*, 11 October 1993, I8.
10. "Spotlight: 1995 APMA Awards," *Promo's Annual Sourcebook '97*, 196–200.
11. Kenneth Roman and Jane Maas, *The New How to Advertise* (New York: St. Martin's Press, 1992), 59.
12. Len Egol, "Online's Better Than in Line," *Direct*, October 1995, 71.
13. "Mail of the Month Club," *American Demographics*, December 1995, 17.
14. Laurie Petersen, "Coke, NBC Make Friends," *Direct*, February 1996, 87.
15. Ray Schulz, "Everything's Coming up Roses for 1-800-FLOWERS," *Interactive Monitor*, supplement to *Direct*, Fall 1996, 1, 4.
16. James S. Norris, *Public Relations* (Englewood Cliffs, NJ: Prentice-Hall, 1984), 1.
17. Norris, *Public Relations*, 50.
18. Delwyn Swingewood, "Pepsi Turns Electric Blue," *Media International*, May 1996, 13.

19. Alex Stanton, "Pentium Brouhaha a Marketing Lesson," *Advertising Age*, 25 February 1995, 18.
20. Carolyn Shea, "Taking License," *Promo*, June 1995, 33–36.
21. T. L. Stanley, "The Kingmakers," *Brandweek*, 19 June 1995, 26–27.
22. James Sterngold, "The Return of the Merchandiser," *New York Times*, 30 January 1997, C1, C6.
23. Shea, "Taking License."
24. International Events Group (IEG), "Big Deals," *IEG Sponsorship Report*, 1 July 1996.
25. Alan Mitchell, "How the Olympics Won the Big Prize," *The Times*, 24 January 1996.
26. Richard S. Dunham, "The Spirit of St. Louis, Brought to You by Ford," *Business Week*, 8 May 1995, 38.
27. International Events Group (IEG), "Centerfold," *IEG Sponsorship Report*, 5 February 1996.
28. Blair R. Fischer, "Making Your Product the Star Attraction," *Promo*, January 1996, 42–47, 88.

Chapter 13

1. James Webb Young, *A Technique for Producing Ideas* (Lincolnwood, IL: NTC Business Books, 1988), 1.
2. Leo Burnett, "Keep Listening to That Wee, Small Voice," in Arnold M. Barban and C. H. Sandage, eds., *Readings in Advertising and Promotion Strategy* (Homewood, IL: Richard D. Irwin, Inc., 1968), 153–162.
3. Graham Wallas, "Stages in the Creative Process," in Albert Rothenberg and Carl R. Hausman, eds., *The Creativity Quest* (Durham, NC: Duke University Press, 1976), 69–73; and Young, *A Technique for Producing Ideas*.
4. Young, *A Technique for Producing Ideas*, 30–41.
5. This section based on: Sandra E. Moriarty, *Creative Advertising: Theory and Practice*, 2nd ed. (Englewood Cliffs, NJ: Prentice-Hall, 1991), 104–108.
6. Moriarty, *Creative Advertising*,

104–106; J. P. Guilford, "Traits of Personality," in H. H. Anderson, ed., *Creativity and Its Cultivation* (New York: Harper & Brothers, 1959); *The Nature of Human Intelligence* (New York: McGraw-Hill, 1967); and "Creativity—Retrospect and Prospect," *Journal of Creative Behavior* 7, no. 4 (1973): 247–252.

7. Hanley Norins, *The Compleat Copywriter* (New York: McGraw-Hill, 1966), 89–109.

8. Edward de Bono, *Lateral Thinking: Creativity Step by Step* (New York: Harper & Row Publishers, 1970), 39–45.

9. de Bono, Lateral Thinking.

10. William J. Gordon, *Synectics: The Development of Creative Capacity* (London: Collier Books, 1961).

11. Daniel Goleman, Paul Kaufman, and Michael Ray, *The Creative Spirit* (New York: Dutton, 1992), 121.

12. Goleman, Kaufman, and Ray, *The Creative Spirit*, 121.

13. Goleman, Kaufman, and Ray, *The Creative Spirit*, 121.

14. Gordon, *Synectics*, 34–56.

15. Alex F. Osborn, *Applied Imagination*, 3rd ed. (New York: Charles Scribner's Sons, 1963).

16. Goleman, Kaufman, and Ray, *The Creative Spirit*, 38.

17. Don Fabun, *You and Creativity* (Beverly Hills, CA: Glencoe Press, 1971), 23.

18. Kenneth Roman and Jane Maas, *The New How to Advertise* (New York: St. Martin's Press, 1992), 5.

19. Magazine Publishers of America, "Marketing Success Stories," MPA advertisement, *Midweek*, 15 April 1991, 13.

20. Stuart Elliott, "Loneliness in a Long-Lasting Pitch," *New York Times*, 15 May 1992, C1, C17.

21. Bonnie J. Knutson, "Breaking through the Clutter: The Absolut View of the Absolut Genius," *The Greater Lansing Business Monthly*, June 1991, 44–47; and Fara Warner, "Absolut Competition," *BrandWeek*, 15 March 1993, 24, 26.

22. American Association of Advertising Agencies, *A Conversation about Advertising with William Bernbach*, videotape (New York: American Association of Advertising Agencies, 1977).

23. Roman and Maas, *The New How to Advertise*, 1–3.

24. The term "big idea" is used to describe an outrageously unusual solution to a creative problem. George Lois is the advertising person who has been associated with the phrase. See George Lois, *What's the Big Idea* (New York: Doubleday Currency, 1991). See also W. Keith Hafer and Gordon E. White, *Advertising Writing: Putting Creative Strategy to Work*, 3rd ed. (St. Paul, MN: West Publishing Company, 1989), 119–120.

25. William Marsteller, *Creative Management* (Chicago, IL: Crain Books, 1981), 38.

26. Marsteller, *Creative Management*, 38.

Chapter 14

1. Terry Kattleman, "Walkin' Small," *Creativity*, April 1995, 12.

2. W. Keith Hafer and Gordon E. White, *Advertising Writing: Putting Creative Strategy to Work* (St. Paul, MN: West Publishing Company, 1989), 321.

3. David Ogilvy, *Confessions of an Advertising Man* (New York: Dell Publishing Company, Inc., 1964), 130.

4. David Ogilvy, *Ogilvy on Advertising* (New York: Vintage Books, 1985), 71–76.

5. Ogilvy, *Ogilvy on Advertising*, 139, 162.

6. Carol Nelson, *The New Road to Successful Advertising* (Chicago: Bonus Books, Inc., 1991), 151.

7. Nelson Metcalf, Jr., "Writer Recalls Famed World War II Ad," *Advertising Age*, 3 June 1991, 24.

8. Ogilvy, *Ogilvy on Advertising*, 143.

9. Bruce Bendinger, *The Copy Workshop* (Chicago: The Copy Workshop, 1988), 218.

10. "Perspective: George Moore," *The Burnettwork* 9, no. 3 (July–August 1991): 18–19.

11. "Perspective: George Moore," 18–19.

12. Bendinger, The Copy Workshop, 218–219.

13. Kenneth Roman and Jane Maas, *The New How to Advertise* (New York: St. Martin's Press, 1992), 16; and Kenneth Roman and Jane Maas, *How to Advertise* (New York: St. Martin's Press, 1976), 15.

14. Ogilvy, *Ogilvy on Advertising*, 103–113; and Roman and Maas, *How to Advertise*, 19–28.

15. Ogilvy, *Ogilvy on Advertising*, 103.

16. Neal Yonover, "Getting a Custom Fit," *Backstage/Shoot*, 5 March 1993, 39, 42–45.

17. William Strunk Jr. and E. B. White, *Elements of Style*, 3rd ed. (New York: Macmillan Publishing Co., Inc., 1979), xvi.

Chapter 15

1. David A. Aaker, *Managing Brand Equity* (New York: The Free Press, 1991), 109–110.

2. David A. Aaker, *Building Strong Brands* (New York: The Free Press, 1996), 242–243.

3. Clive Chajet and Tom Shachtman, *Image by Design* (Reading, MA: Addison-Wesley, 1991), 69, 157, 196, 201.

4. Bob Garfield, "Coke Ads Great, but Not Always," *Advertising Age* 64, no. 7 (15 February 1993): 1, 60; and Patricia Winters, "CAA's Coke Ads Set New Ground Rules," *Advertising Age* 64, no. 7 (15 February 1993): 60.

5. Peter D. Bennett, *American Marketing Association Dictionary of Marketing Terms* (Chicago: American Marketing Association, 1988), 108.

6. Roy Paul Nelson, *The Design of Advertising*, 6th ed. (Dubuque, IA: William C. Brown, 1989), 369.

7. "Notebook: The Long Box Payoff," *Adweek's Marketing Week*, 16 March 1992, 37.

8. "Take Five," *Food & Beverage Marketing*, December 1991, 34–35.

9. Seymour Merrin, "Channel Marker: Don't Turn Your Package into a Pandora's Box," *Computer Retail Week*, 9 December 1991, 9.

10. Merrin, "Channel Marker," 9.

11. A. Jerome Jewler, *Creative Strategy in Advertising*, 5th ed. (Belmont, CA: Wadsworth, 1995), 141.

12. Doug Green and Denise Green, "DiVA VideoShop: A Complete Video Production Center," *InfoWorld* 14, no. 33 (17 August 1992): 111–112; and Cathy Madison, "Tickling the Sound Barrier," *Advertising Age* 63, no. 45 (2 November 1992): 8C, 24C.

13. Kenneth Roman and Jane Maas, The New *How to Advertise* (New York: St. Martin's Press, 1992), 14–15.

14. Roman and Maas, *The New How to Advertise*, 50–53.

Chapter 16

1. Kathy DeSalvo, "Special Report: Costs, Clients & Creativity. On the Money," *Backstage/Shoot* 34, no. 8 (19 February 1993): 25.

2. "Transamerica's 3-D Calling Card—Not Just Business as Usual," *San Francisco Examiner*, 2 April 1987, C11.

3. "TI Breaks the Sound Barrier," *Adweek Southwest Edition* 43 (23 October 1989): 1, 4; and "Talking Advertisement Argues Advantages of New Speech Synthesis," *New Scientist*, 4 November 1989, 39.

4. "Black and White and Read All Over," *Starch Tested Copy* 4, no. 3 (April 1992): 1–4.

5. *Pocket Pal*, 13th ed. (Memphis, TN: International Paper Company, 1988), 72–73.

6. *Pocket Pal*, 76.

7. *Pocket Pal*, 128.

8. Steve Chagollan, "No Static At All," *Hollywood Reporter*, 2 June 1992, S17.

9. *TV Production Costs Survey* (New York: American Association of Advertising Agencies, 1995).

10. Kenneth Roman and Jane Maas, *The New How to Advertise* (New York: St. Martin's Press, 1992), 26.

11. Joe Mandese, "Y&R Shutters Division for TV Production," *Advertising Age*, 11 March 1991, 3.

12. Julia Miller, "No-Frills Phil," *Advertising Age's Creativity*, June 1996, 26–28.

13. Huntley Baldwin, *How to Create Effective TV Commercials*, 2nd ed. (Chicago: NTC Business Books, 1989), 213–215.

14. "Computer & Digital Imaging: New Developments in the '90s," *Backstage/Shoot* 34, no. 7 (12 February 1993): 8, 13.

15. The Chevys "Fresh TV" campaign has won a Gold Lion at Cannes, an Andy, a Best of Show Andy, three Clios, a One Show Gold Pencil, an Effie, and an award from the British Design and Art Director's Association.

16. "The Winning Americans: Steve Simpson, Tracy Wong," *Adweek Easter Edition*, 6 July 1992, 20.

17. "The Winning Americans," 20.

Photo Credits

5–5   Reprinted with permission of
       NIKE, Inc.
5–7   Courtesy Intel Corporation.
5–8   © Levi Strauss de Espana, S.A.
5–10   Courtesy State Farm Insurance
       Companies.
5–11   Courtesy Mercedes-Benz of
       North America.
5–12   © M&M/Mars.
5–13   Courtesy Bill Brokaw
       Advertising, Inc.
5–14   Courtesy Mary Kay, Inc.
5–16   © 1996 General Motors Corp.
       Used with permission, GM Media
       Archives.
5–18   © Volkswagen of America, Inc.
5–19   Reprinted with permission of
       NIKE, Inc.
5–20   © Saturn Corporation, used with
       permission.

Chapter 6

6–OP   Courtesy Starbucks Coffee Company.
6–1   Courtesy The Coca-Cola Company.
6–3   Copyright, Nissan (1994). Nissan
       and the Nissan logo are registered
       trademarks of Nissan.
6–5   © 1997 The Sherwin-Williams
       Company. All rights reserved.
6–6   © 1996 General Motors Corp.
       Used with permission, GM
       Media Archives.
6–7   Courtesy State Farm Insurance
       Companies.
6–9   (left) Courtesy AM General Corp.
6–9   (right) Courtesy H. J. Heinz
       Company. The Heinz trademark is
       owned by H. J. Heinz Company and
       is used with permission.
6–10   © Children's Defense Fund. All
       rights reserved.
6–11   © Volkswagen of America, Inc.
6–14   Reprinted with the permission of
       Hilton Hotels Corporation.
6–15   Courtesy Nestlé Canada, Inc.
6–18   Courtesy Radisson Hotels Worldwide.
6–19   Courtesy Teva Sandals.
6–A   Courtesy Miller Brewing Company.
6–21   Courtesy New Balance Athletic
       Shoe, Inc.
6–22   Courtesy COSMETIQUE, INC.

Chapter 7

7–OP   Courtesy Harley-Davidson Motor
       Company.
7–3   Reprinted with the permission of
       LEXIS-NEXIS, a division of Reed
       Elsevier Inc. LEXIS and NEXIS are
       registered trademarks, and the
       INFORMATION ARRAY logo
       is a trademark of Reed Elsevier
       Properties Inc.
7–A   Courtesy of Maritz Marketing
       Research Inc., St. Louis, MO.
7–B   Courtesy of Perich + Partners, Ltd.
       for Borders, Inc.
7–11   Reprinted with permission from
       Business Marketing, Crain
       Communications, Inc.
7–12   Courtesy Mongoose Bicycles.
7–13   Courtesy Partnership for a Drug-Free
       America.
7–17   Copyright 1997, USA TODAY.
       Reprinted with permission.

Chapter 8

8–OP   (both) Copyright Elizabeth Heyert
       Studios, Inc. 1996.
8–1   Courtesy Intel Corporation.
8–A   Sharon Hoogstraten.
8–4   Courtesy Southwest Airlines.
8–5   Courtesy Black & Decker Inc.
8–6   Courtesy Polaroid.
8–7   © American Express Travel Related
       Services Company, Inc.
8–8   © Kellogg Company.

Chapter 9

9–OP   Courtesy Fluid Milk Processor Board.
9–A   © Amtrak.
9–3   (both) Courtesy American Airlines.
9–B   Courtesy Jantzen Inc.
9–C   © Garden Railways.
9–D   © Chicago Tribune.

Chapter 10

10–OP Pizza Hut is a registered trademark
       of Pizza Hut, Inc., and is used with
       permission.
10–A   Courtesy International Family
       Entertainment, Inc.
10–B   Courtesy EchoStar Communications
       Corporation.

10–C © Toshiba America Information Systems.

10–D Courtesy of ABC Radio Networks.

10–E © Nabisco.

Chapter 11

11–OP © Philadelphia Online.

11–2 © Hearst Magazines Enterprises.

11–A © *Business Week*.

11–8 Courtesy JCPenney. Photography by Robb Debenport.

11–B © HotWired.

11–9 © Ace Hardware.

11–10 © Edwardo's Natural Pizza Restaurant.

11–11 © Puerto Rico Tourism Co.

11–C © *Chicago Tribune*.

11–13 © *Chicago Tribune*.

11–14 *(both)* Courtesy Atomic Props & Effects, St. Paul, MN.

11–15 *(both)* Courtesy Gutman Advertising and Scott Lumber Co.

11–D Courtesy Leo Burnett U.S.A.

11–17 Monica Almeida/NYT Pictures.

11–18 © Doyle Dane Bernbach.

Chapter 12

12–OP Kaku Kurita/Gamma Liaison

12–2 *(left)* Courtesy of Waccamaw Home Superstores.

12–2 *(right)* Courtesy Anheuser-Busch Companies, Inc.

12–5 © Checkout Coupon.

12–6 © Culligan.

12–7 © Cornnuts, Inc.

12–10 © 1997 United States Postal Service.

12–A Courtesy Chrysler Corporation.

12–B © 1-800-FLOWERS.

12–C Ben Margot: AP/Wide World Photos.

12–D © The Procter & Gamble Company. Used by permission.

12–15 Sharon Hoogstraten.

12–E © Philip Morris Companies Inc.

12–F Courtesy Schieffelin & Somerset Co.

Chapter 13

13–OP © M&M/Mars.

13–A Andrew Toos.

13–B Courtesy Bell Atlantic.

13–2 Reproduced with permission of PepsiCo, Inc. 1997, Purchase, New York.

13–4 © Florsheim.

13–5 © W. B. Doner and Company.

13–6 Courtesy Colgate-Palmolive Company.

13–7 *(both)* © TBWA Chiat/Day for The Absolut Company.

13–C © Consumer Care Division, Bayer Corporation.

13–D Courtesy Cathay Pacific Airlines.

13–10 Courtesy CNS, Inc.

13–11 Courtesy of Procter & Gamble. Photography by Katvan.

Chapter 14

14–OP Courtesy California Milk Processor Board.

14–1 *(both)* Courtesy Simple.

14–2 © W. B. Doner and Company.

14–5 Courtesy Ford Motor Company.

14–6 © Neutrogena Corp.

14–7 Courtesy Leo Burnett U.S.A. for Jenn-Air.

14–8 © GOJO Industries, Inc.

14–9A Courtesy Pharmacia & Upjohn.

14–9B Courtesy of American Isuzu Motors Inc.

14–9C Courtesy The Clorox Company.

14–10 Courtesy Northern Star Co., Michael Foods, Inc.

14–12 Courtesy of The Brita Products Company.

14–13 © 1996 General Motors Corp. Used with permission, GM Media Archives.

14–14 James Leynse/Saba.

14–16 Courtesy Polaroid.

14–A Courtesy Chrysler Corporation.

14–B Courtesy Amazon.com.

Chapter 15

15–OP Reprinted with permission from the Spring 1995 issue of *Advertising Age*. Copyright, Crain Communications Inc., 1995.

15–2 Courtesy The Coca-Cola Company. Photography by Sharon Hoogstraten.

15–3 © Kraft Foods.

15–4 © Wyndham Music; © Comfort Coil Company; and © Hexagraph Fly Rods.

15–5 Courtesy Deere & Company.

15–6 Courtesy The Coca-Cola Company.

15–7 Courtesy VCU Adcenter.

15–A	© *Placar*; © Foto Cine Club en Chile.
15–8	Courtesy Hallmark Cards.
15–9	© K2 Inc.
15–10	Courtesy The Aveda Corporation.
15–11	Courtesy of The National Federation of Coffee Growers of Colombia.
15–12	Courtesy Pepperidge Farm, Inc.
15–13	Courtesy, The Gillette Company.
15–14	Courtesy Neiman Marcus. Photography by Chuck Shotwell.
15–18	© Volkswagen of America, Inc.
15–19	© Lee Jeans.

Chapter 16

16–OP	Courtesy R/Greenberg Associates.
16–4	Courtesy Transamerica.
16–A	Reproduced with permission of PepsiCo, Inc. 1997, Purchase, New York.
16–9	PANTONE® and other Pantone, Inc., trademarks are the property of Pantone, Inc.

Name Index

Product Index

Subject Index

Informal groups, 202
Information, advertising as, 86–87
Information center, 34
Information economy, transition of, 149–50
Information highway, selling on, 48–49
Information processing perspective, 185
In-house advertising agencies, 41–42
Inkjetting, 342
Inserts, 341
Institution, advertising as, 62–63
In-store advertising media, 360
Instrumental theory, 184–85
Integrated marketing agencies, 36
Integrated marketing communications (IMC),
　　366, 408
　　advertising in, 158–59
　　brands in, 151–62
　　consumer relationship with, 171
　　definition of, 146
　　direct marketing in, 375–82
　　focus of, 162–65
　　licensing in, 387–88
　　and promotion mix, 157–62
　　public relations in, 158, 382–87
　　road to, 146–50
　　sales promotion in, 159–60, 366–75
　　sponsorship in, 388–92
Integrated marketing communications plan
　　measuring impact of, 392
　　scheduling, 392
Intensity, 472
Intentional learning, 186
Interactive media, copywriting for, 451–52
Interactive television, 312–13
Interior body copy, 439
Internal data, 222
Internal validity, 228
International advertising versus international
　　brands, 125
International brands versus international
　　advertising, 125
International Herald-Tribune, The, 129
International regulation of advertising, 102–3
International unit, 113–14
Internet, 129–30, 323–24
Internet World, 282
Interpublic, 38
Interviewer bias, 232
Intramedia, 291
Involvement, 188

J

Jacksonville Times Union, 344

Jet, 341
Jingle, 445
Joint venture, 113
Junior copywriters, 426
Justified alignment, 477

K

Key consumer benefit, 421–22
Key visual symbol, 446

L

Ladies' Home Journal, 140, 334, 340, 341
Ladies' Professional Golf Association, 144–45
Language, culture, and lifestyle, problems of,
　　118–19
Lanham Act (1946), 90, 92, 97
Lateral thinking, 413
Latina, 196
Latin Style, 335
Layout artists, 426
Lead-in, 439
Leading, 477
Lead paragraph, 439
Learning
　　behavioral theories, 183–85
　　cognitive theories, 185–88
　　directed, 186
　　incidental, 186
　　intentional, 186
　　stimulus-response theories, 183–85
Legal considerations, global, 133–35
Legal framework, advertising in, 87–103
Letterpress printing, 502
Library of Congress, 97
Licensing, 387–88
Life, 284, 334
Lifestyle, 196–98
Lifestyle commercials, 449
Likability, 239
Line art photography, 500
Line responsibility, 25
Localized advertising, 116
Local partner, 113
Local regulation of advertising, 97–98
Local resistance and lower-common-denomi-
　　nator marketing, 120–21
Local station affiliates, 302
Logotypes, creating, 465–66
London Times, 364
Look, 284, 334
Los Angeles Times, 344, 347
Louis L'Amour Western Magazine, 335
Lower Americans, 203

M

Macworld, 71
*MacWrite(*4,22), 495
*MacWrite Pro(*4,22), 495
Magazine advertising
    benefits of, 336–37
    drawbacks for, 337–39
Magazine Publishers of America (MPA), 336, 337
Magazines, 334–36
    achieving in, 140–41
    business, 334
    consumer, 334
    farm, 334
    and technology, 342–43
Magnuson-Moss Warranty-Federal Trade Commission Improvement Act (1975), 90
Make-good, 295, 311
Mall intercept interviews, 231
Marie-Claire, 129
Marketing
    advertising within context of, 155–57
    definition of, 155–56
Marketing mix, 156
Marketing objectives, media implications of, 276–81
Marketing public, 158
Marketing public relations, 158, 383
Marketing research, 218–20
    definition of, 218
Market research, 216–17, 219–20
Markets
    advertising as power, 86
    assessing overall, 276–81, 277
    differences in characteristics, 119–20
Market segmentation, 252
    concentrated, 253–54
    differentiated, 253
    undifferentiated, 252–53
Mark-up compensation method, 43
Marque ad, 451
Maslow's hierarchy of needs, 178–80
Mass audiences, 307
Materialism, advertising in promoting, 66
McCall's, 335, 341
Mechanicals, 469, 479
Media, 45–46
    availability, 281–87, 288
    buying, 296
    career in, 519
    evaluating, 281–91, 294
    global, 53–55
    nontraditional possibilities, 281–88, 290

    scheduling, 281–90, 291
    selecting right, 281–86, 294
Media audience research, 220, 240–42
Media business services, 36
Media buyers, 35, 36, 519
Media buying services, 41
Media choices, advertising in dictating, 70–71
Media commission, 42–43
Media department, 35–36
    key functions of, 35
Media effectiveness, 220
Media environment, global, 126–32
Media measurement, 48
Media objectives, 276
Media plan, 276
    analyzing competitive situation in, 277–79
    assessing market and audience in, 276–81, 283
    brand dynamics in, 279–81
    budgetary concerns in, 279
    evaluating, 281–94, 297
    examining preferences in, 281–83, 286
    executing, 294
    finding right audience, 281–83
    message consideration in, 287
    sample, 297
    selecting right, 281–86, 294
Media planners, 35, 519
Media planning, computers in, 293
Media preferences, examining in media plan, 281–83, 286
Media representatives, 46–47
Media research, 36, 519
    global, 130–32
Media researchers, 35
Media sales, 46–48
Media self-regulation, 101–2
Media strategy, 276
Media suppliers, 46
Media type, 283
Media vehicle, 283
Mental digestive stage of creativity, 409–10
Merge and purge, 378
Message creation task, production as, 491–93
Message delivery
    effect of selective exposure on, 182
    influence of advertising production on, 490–91
Message effectiveness, 220
Message posttesting, 220, 243
Message research, 220, 238–40
Middle class, 203
Migration to South and West, 195–96

Miller's Barbie Collector, 335
Milling and Baking, 334
Milwaukee Sentinel, 282
Misredemption, 371
Moment-to-moment testing, 239–40
Money magazine, 335
Morphing, 508, 509
Mothers Against Drunk Drivers (MADD), 82
Motivation of consumers, 178–81
MS magazine, 71
Murphy's law and production, 494–95
Music in television commercial, 449

N

Narrative copy, 442
National advertising, 346
National Advertising Division (NAD), 98, 100
National Advertising Review Board (NARB), 98
National Advertising Review Council, 98–100, 105
National Association of Attorneys General (NAAG), 98
National Basketball Association (NBA), 357
National Committee for the Prevention of Child Abuse, 73
National Council for Minorities in Engineering, 73
National Crime Prevention Council, 73
National Fluid Milk Processor Promotion Board, 274–75, 278
National Football League (NFL), 388
National Geographic, 335
National Hockey League (NHL), 300, 357
National Infomercial Marketing Association (NIMA), 100
National Institute on Drug Abuse, 73
National network radio, 316–17
National Newspaper Network, 346
National Parks and Conservation Association, 391
National Public Radio, 46, 322
National Resources Defense Council, 73
Needs
    hedonic, 180
    Maslow's hierarchy of, 178
    Settle and Alreck's list of horizontal, 180, 181
    utilitarian, 180
NetGuide, 335
New products, role of advertising in introducing, 271
News headlines, 436, 438
Newspaper advertising
    benefits of, 347–48

drawbacks of, 348–49
    types of, 344, 346–47
Newspaper fax services, 351
Newspaper magazine supplements, 347
Newspaper planning, 349
Newspapers, 343
    buying space, 349–51
    and technology, 351–52
    types of, 343–44
    and the Web, 332–33
Newsweek, 118, 334, 337
New York Times, 324, 333, 344
New York Times v. *Sullivan*, 87
Niche marketing, advantage of, 253–54
Niche units, 38
Nonpersonal communication situations, 209
Nonprobability sample, 227–28
Nonresponse bias, 232
Novelty, 181
Nurturance, 181

O

Objective-and-task budgeting method, 265
Objectives
    advertising, 250, 418, 420
    criteria for setting, 257–59
    definition of, 250
    establishing time frame for, 258
    identifying unit responsibility in, 257
    including results, 258
    linking, 257
    making specific and measurable, 258–59
    setting, 254–55
    setting realistic, 258
    stating output in, 257–58
Observation, value of keen, 182
Observational methods, 232–34
Offset lithography printing, 502
Omni magazine, 343
Online services, 136–37, 323–24
Open contract rate, 28–29
Open-response question, 231
Operant conditioning, 184–85
Opportunistic purchase, 311
Ordinary person testimonial, 449
Ornamental type, 476
Ornate type, 476
Outbound telemarketing, 379
Outdoor advertising, 403
    copywriting for, 443
Outdoor Advertising Association of America, 238
Outdoor billboard advertising, 352

benefits of, 352–55
  drawbacks of, 355
  planning and buying for, 355–56
Out-of-home advertising, 352–59
Out-of-home television, 325–27
Outside, 292, 335
Outside variables, 229
Overdelivered, 339
Overline, 439

P

Package design, influencing, 466–68
Packaging, 466
Page equivalent discounts, 342
Painted bulletins, 352
Pan, 483
Paper, recycled, 499
Parenting, 282, 334, 335
Parent's Magazine, 282, 335, 340, 341
Partnership for a Drug-Free America, 237
Passalong audience, 336
Passive participation, 310
Pasteup, 479
Paste-up, 479
Patent and Trademark Office, 97
Patent medicines, advertising for, 140–41
PC Magazine, 334
PC Week, 71, 282
Peacefulness, 472
Pedestal, 483
Pennsylvania Evening Post, 343
People magazine, 274, 337, 341
People meter, 308
Perceived quality, 154
Percentage-of-sales budgeting method, 265
Perception of consumers, 181–83
Personal analogy, 414
Personal communication situations, 209
Personal profile, 421
Personal selling, 161–62
Persons using radio (PUR), 320
Persons using television (PUT), 295, 308
Persuasion, 239
Persuasion factor, 466
Pharmaceuticals, advertising of, 84
Philadelphia Daily News, 332
Philadelphia Inquirer, 332
Photoboard, 446
Photo sorts, 230
Picture interpretation tests, 230
Pitch, 44
Pitch format, 444–45
Placar soccer magazine, 475

Plan, definition of, 250
Planned simplicity, 466
Plan on spec, 44
Pocket Pal, 500
Point of diminishing returns, 264
Point-of-Purchase Advertising Institute
  (POPAI), 208
Points, 477
Popular culture, reflection in advertising,
  63–65
Population, 227
Population diversity, 192–94
Position, 341
  of ad, 351
Positioning, 260
  as concept, 238–39
  product, 154
Positioning Advertising Copy Testing (PACT),
  239
Poster panels, 352
Posting, 295
Postproduction stage, 504, 509–10
Precise positioning, 466
Preemptive claim, 423
Preemptive spots, 311
Preparation stage of advertising, 409
Prepress stage, 493–94, 500–502
Preproduction stage, 504
  decisions in, 509
Prescription drug advertising, 95–96
Presenters, 449
Press proofs, 502–3
Press releases, 383
Presswork operations and cost decisions, 502–3
Presswork production decisions, 502–3
Presswork stage, 494
Pretesting, 238
Price cut, 375
Primary data, 222
Primary information sector, 150
Primary readers, 337
Primary reference groups, 202
Primary research, 222
Print advertisements, 476–79
  advertising design in, 460
  body copy in, 439, 442
  captions in, 439, 441
  copywriting for, 435–42
  design in, 460
  designing, 468–74, 476–79
  headlines in, 436–39
  subheadings in, 439, 440
Print audience measurement, 242

Printed Advertising Rating Methods (PARM), 336
Printing flat, 502
Print media, 334. *See also* Magazines; Newspapers
    global, 129
Print production
    computer-aided, 494–96
    stages and cost decisions, 496–98, 500–503
    traditional, 493–94
PRIZM, 203
Probability sampling, 227–28
Pro bono advertising, 72–73
Product, analysis of, 165–66
Production and Murphy's law, 494–95
Production notes, 509
Production stage, 504
Production team, 509
Product positioning, 154, 423
    strategies in branding, 183
Product research, 219
Products
    advertising in selling bad, 69–70
    placement of, 391–92
Professional associations, 100–101
Program Evaluation Analysis Computer (PEAC), 240
Program rating, 308
Progressive Grocer, 372
Projective research techniques, 230
Promotional mix, 157
Proof, 495
Proportion, 472
Proprietary assets, 154–55
Proprietary study, 222
Prospect, 375
Psychographics, 196
Public presentation, 384
Public relations, 382–85
    benefits of, 385–86
    drawbacks of, 386–87
    in integrated marketing communications, 158
Puffery, 77
Pull strategy, 366
Pulsing, 290
Purchase cycle in brand dynamics, 281
Purchase situations, 207–8
Pure Food and Drug Act (1906), 95, 141
Push strategy, 366–67

Q

Quality, perceived, 154
Question bias, 232

Question headline, 439
Questionnaires, 229, 231–32

R

Radio, 315–17
    digital, 322
    frequencies, formats, and geographies, 316
    measuring audience, 319–20, 321
    national network, 316–17
    planning and buying, 320–22
    spot, 317
    and technology, 322
Radio Advertising Bureau, 504
Radio All-Dimension Audience Research (RADAR), 241, 320
Radio commercials
    benefits of, 317–18
    copywriting for, 443–45
    directing, 480–84
    drawbacks of, 318–19
    elements of, 444
    formats, 444–45
    production of, 504–5
    scripts for, 484
Ragged left, 477
Ragged right, 477
Random probability sample, 227
Rating, 295
Rating point, 291
Reach, 292, 295
Readers per copy, 295, 340
Rebates, 373
Recall, 239
Recognition, 181
Recognition test, 243
Recycled paper, 499
Reference group influences on consumers, 200–202
Refunds, 373
Release prints, 510
Reliability, 232
Rep firms, 303
Research. *See also* Advertising research; Marketing research
    and advertising planning process, 218–20
    analysis of data, 234–36
    career in, 519
    causal, 224–25, 226–27, 235–36
    descriptive, 223, 226, 229, 235
    exploratory, 223, 226, 228–29, 234–35
    important questions on, 220–29, 231–36
    reality of virtual, 224
    reasons for doing, 221–22

broadcast network, 302–3
broadcast syndication, 305
cable, 303–4
dayparts and genres, 305
interactive, 312–13
measuring audience, 308–9
out-of-home, 325–27
planning and buying for, 309–11
spot, 303
and technology, 311–14
types of, 302–5
Television commercials
benefits of, 306–7
changes in, 314–15
copywriting for, 445–47, 449–50
directing, 480–84
drawbacks of, 307–8
production of, 505–7, 509–11
stages of, 506–7
scripts and storyboards for, 483–84
types of, 449–50
Television director, 506
Television producer, 506
Testimonial ads, 92–93, 449
Theater-of-the-mind, 443
Thinking
analogical, 413–14
associative, 413
convergent, 410, 411
divergent, 410, 411, 413
lateral, 413
vertical, 413
Third person effect, 68–69
Thumbnail sketches, 468–74
Tilt, 483
Time in making purchase decisions, 208
Time magazine, 69, 118, 288, 326, 333, 334, 492
Time spent listening (TSL), 320–21
Tobacco, advertising of, 82–83
Tone, 472
Tongue, 483
Track, 483
Tracking studies, 243
Trade ads, 47
Trade allowances, 374, 375
Trade associations, 100–101
Trademark, 97
Trade promotions, 160, 366, 374–75
Trade regulation rules, 90
Trade shows, 114–15
Transit advertising, 358
advantages of, 358

copywriting for, 443
disadvantages to, 358
planning and buying of, 358–59
Transportation, U.S. Department of, 73
Travel, 289
Tree-free paper, 499
Trim size, 497
Tropical Fish, 284
Truck, 483
Turnover, 321
TV Guide, 341
Typeface, 476
Typestyle as key design element, 474, 476–78

U

Underdelivered, 339
Underdeveloped markets, 112–13
Underline, 439
Understanding, 181
Undifferentiated market segmentation strategy, 252–53
Unfairness, 90
Unified brand image, 116–17
Unified image, 163
Unique selling proposition (USP), 423
United Negro College Fund, 63, 73
United States Armed Forces, 439
United States Census, 222, 227
U.S. Postal Service (USPS), 92, 160, 378
Universal Product Codes (UPCs), 229, 233
Universe estimate, 295
Unplanned purchases, 368–69
Unstructured observational method, 232
Upper Americans, 203
USA Today, 129, 134, 239, 289, 344, 349, 351
USA Weekend, 347
Utilitarian needs, 180
Utility directories, 359

V

Valentine v. *Chrestensen*, 87
Validity, 228
external, 228
face, 228
internal, 228
Value-expressive mechanism, 201
Values, 472
advertising as reflection of, 65
Values and Life-Styles (VALS) measurement system, 196–98, 252
Vanity Fair, 336, 338–41
Vertical thinking, 413
Videocassettes, 147, 324–25

Videoconferencing, 136
Video news releases, 383
Video switcher, 510
Videotapes, producing, 503–7, 509–11
Viewing diaries, 309
Viewing share, 308
Virginia State Board of Pharmacy v. *Virginia Citizens Consumer Council*, 87
Virtual research, reality of, 224
Visual consistency, role of art direction in creating, 463–64
Visualization, 425, 432–33
Vogue, 334
Volume discounts, 342

W

Walking strategy statements, 422
Wall Street Journal, 333, 344, 351
War Advertising Council, 72, 270–71
Web-fed paper, 502
Wheat Life, 334
Wheeler-Lea Act (1938), 89, 90, 270
White space, 470
Wholly owned office, 51–52
Wired magazine, 151, 256, 283, 343, 345
Women
    depiction of, in advertising, 76
    and sexual objectification ads, 75–76
    working, 194–95
Women's College Coalition, 73
Working class, 203
Working women, 194–95
World Health Organization (WHO), 132
World Wide Web (WWW), 308, 322, 323, 324, 329, 360, 361, 376, 382, 386, 462. *See also* Internet
    designing sites on, 462

Y

Yachting, 287
Yankee, 287
Yankelovich Monitor, 125, 190–91
Yellow pages advertising, 359–60
Yolk, 335
You approach, 439
Young Miss (YM), 287, 335
Yuppies, 63

Z

Zones, 349
Zoom, 483